CompTIA® A+

220-801 and 220-802

Sixth Edition

David L. Prowse

CompTIA A+® 220-801 and 220-802 Exam Cram, Sixth Edition

ISBN-13: 978-0-7897-4971-0

ISBN-10: 0-7897-4971-8

Library of Congress Cataloging-in-Publication data is on file.

Eighth Printing: April 2015

Trademarks

All terms mentioned in this book that are known to be trademarks or service marks have been appropriately capitalized. Que Publishing cannot attest to the accuracy of this information. Use of a term in this book should not be regarded as affecting the validity of any trademark or service mark.

Warning and Disclaimer

Every effort has been made to make this book as complete and as accurate as possible, but no warranty or fitness is implied. The information provided is on an "as is" basis. The author and the publisher shall have neither liability nor responsibility to any person or entity with respect to any loss or damages arising from the information contained in this book or from the use of the CD or programs accompanying it.

Bulk Sales

Que Publishing offers excellent discounts on this book when ordered in quantity for bulk purchases or special sales. For more information, please contact

U.S. Corporate and Government Sales
1-800-382-3419
corpsales@pearsontechgroup.com

For sales outside of the U.S., please contact

International Sales
international@pearson.com

Associate Publisher
David Dusthimer

Acquisitions Editor
Betsy Brown

Development Editor
Eleanor C. Bru

Managing Editor
Sandra Schroeder

Project Editor
Seth Kerney

Copy Editor
Apostrophe Editing Services

Indexer
Lisa Stumpf

Proofreader
Leslie Joseph

Technical Editor
Aubrey Adams

Publishing Coordinator
Vanessa Evans

Multimedia Developer
Tim Warner

Designer
Gary Adair

Composition
Trina Wurst

Contents at a Glance

Table of Contents

About the Author

David L. Prowse is an author, a computer network specialist, and a technical trainer. Over the past several years he has authored several titles for Pearson Education, including the well-received *CompTIA A+ Exam Cram* and *CompTIA Security+ Cert Guide*. As a consultant, he installs and secures the latest in computer and networking technology. Over the past decade he has also taught CompTIA A+, Network+, and Security+ certification courses, both in the classroom and via the Internet. He runs the website www.davidlprowse.com, where he gladly answers questions from students and readers.

About the Tech Editor

Aubrey Adams (CCNA, Security+) is an electronic and computer system engineering lecturer and Cisco Networking Academy instructor at Central Institute of Technology in Perth, Western Australia. Coming from a background in telecommunications design, with qualifications in electronic engineering and management and graduate diplomas in computing and education, he teaches across a range of computer systems and networking vocational education and training areas. Aubrey also authors Networking Academy curriculum and assessments and is a Cisco Press author and Pearson Education technical editor.

Dedication

To my wife Georgia, for dealing with my absurd deadlines...again.

Acknowledgments

First, I'd like to thank David Dusthimer and Betsy Brown who put their faith in me for yet another A+ Exam Cram project.

Special thanks to Aubrey Adams. Your wisdom during this project has kept me on track and is a key component in the flow and technical accuracy of this book.

Thanks to Eleanor Bru, Andrew Cupp, Seth Kerney, and everyone else at Pearson that was involved in this project.

I'd also like to acknowledge my previous and current readers, students, and visitors to my website. Thank you very much for all your kind words, input, and feedback.

We Want to Hear from You!

As the reader of this book, you are our most important critic and commentator. We value your opinion and want to know what we're doing right, what we could do better, what areas you'd like to see us publish in, and any other words of wisdom you're willing to pass our way.

As an associate publisher for Pearson IT Certification, I welcome your comments. You can email or write me directly to let me know what you did or didn't like about this book—as well as what we can do to make our books better.

Please note that I cannot help you with technical problems related to the topic of this book. We do have a User Services group, however, where I will forward specific technical questions related to the book.

When you write, please be sure to include this book's title and author as well as your name, email address, and phone number. I will carefully review your comments and share them with the author and editors who worked on the book.

Email: feedback@pearsonitcertification.com

Mail: David Dusthimer
        Associate Publisher
        Pearson IT Certification
        800 East 96th Street
        Indianapolis, IN 46240 USA

Reader Services

Visit our website and register this book at http://www.pearsonitcertification.com/store/product.aspx?isbn=9780789749710 for convenient access to any updates, downloads, or errata that might be available for this book.

CompTIA.

It Pays to Get Certified

In a digital world, digital literacy is an essential survival skill.

Certification proves you have the knowledge and skill to solve business problems in virtually any business environment. Certifications are highly-valued credentials that qualify you for jobs, increased compensation and promotion.

LEARN		CERTIFY		WORK
IT is Everywhere	**IT Knowledge and Skills Get Jobs**	**Job Retention**	**New Opportunities**	**High Pay-High Growth Jobs**
IT is mission critical to almost all organizations and its importance is increasing.	Certifications verify your knowledge and skills that qualifies you for:	Competence is noticed and valued in organizations.	Certifications qualify you for new opportunities in your current job or when you want to change careers.	Hiring managers demand the strongest skill set.
• 79% of U.S. businesses report IT is either important or very important to the success of their company	• Jobs in the high growth IT career field • Increased compensation • Challenging assignments and promotions • 60% report that being certified is an employer or job requirement	• Increased knowledge of new or complex technologies • Enhanced productivity • More insightful problem solving • Better project management and communication skills • 47% report being certified helped improve their problem solving skills	• 31% report certification improved their career advancement opportunities	• There is a widening IT skills gap with over 300,000 jobs open • 88% report being certified enhanced their resume

Certification Advances Your Career

▶ The CompTIA A+ credential—provides foundation-level knowledge and skills necessary for a career in PC repair and support.

▶ Starting Salary—CompTIA A+ Certified individuals can earn as much as $65,000 per year.

▶ Career Pathway—CompTIA A+ is a building block for other CompTIA certifications such as Network+, Security+ and vendor specific technologies.

▶ More than 850,000—Individuals worldwide are CompTIA A+ certified.

▶ Mandated/Recommended by organizations worldwide—Such as Cisco and HP and Ricoh, the U.S. State Department, and U.S. government contractors such as EDS, General Dynamics, and Northrop Grumman.

Some of the primary benefits individuals report from becoming A+ certified are:

▶ More efficient troubleshooting

▶ Improved career advancement

▶ More insightful problem solving

CompTIA Career Pathway

CompTIA offers a number of credentials that form a foundation for your career in technology and allows you to pursue specific areas of concentration. Depending on the path you choose to take, CompTIA certifications help you build upon your skills and knowledge, supporting learning throughout your entire career.

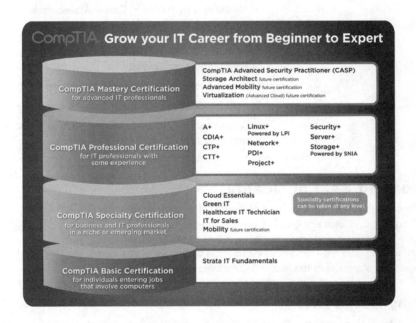

Steps to Certification

Steps to Getting Certified and Staying Certified	
Review Exam Objectives	Review the certification objectives to make sure you know what is covered in the exam. http://www.comptia.org/certifications/testprep/examobjectives.aspx
Practice for the Exam	After you have studied for the certification, take a free assessment and sample test to get an idea what type of questions might be on the exam. http://www.comptia.org/certifications/testprep/practicetests.aspx
Purchase an Exam Voucher	Purchase your exam voucher on the CompTIA Marketplace, which is located at: www.comptiastore.com.
Take the Test!	Select a certification exam provider and schedule a time to take your exam. You can find exam providers at the following link: http://www.comptia.org/certifications/testprep/testingcenters.aspx

Join the Professional Community

Join IT Pro Community
http://itpro.comptia.org

The free IT Pro online community provides valuable content to students and professionals.

Career IT Job Resources

- Where to start in IT
- Career Assessments
- Salary Trends
- US Job Board

Forums on Networking, Security, Computing and Cutting Edge Technologies

Access to blogs written by Industry Experts

Current information on Cutting Edge Technologies

Access to various industry resource links and articles related to IT and IT careers

Content Seal of Quality

This courseware bears the seal of **CompTIA Approved Quality Content**. This seal signifies this content covers 100% of the exam objectives and implements important instructional design principles. CompTIA recommends multiple learning tools to help increase coverage of the learning objectives.

Why CompTIA?

▶ **Global Recognition**—CompTIA is recognized globally as the leading IT non-profit trade association and has enormous credibility. Plus, CompTIA's certifications are vendor-neutral and offer proof of foundational knowledge that translates across technologies.

▶ **Valued by Hiring Managers**—Hiring managers value CompTIA certification because it is vendor- and technology-independent validation of your technical skills.

▶ **Recommended or Required by Government and Businesses**—Many government organizations and corporations either recommend or require technical staff to be CompTIA certified. (For example, Dell, Sharp, Ricoh, the U.S. Department of Defense, and many more.)

▶ **Three CompTIA Certifications ranked in the top 10**—In a study by DICE of 17,000 technology professionals, certifications helped command higher salaries at all experience levels.

How to obtain more information

Visit CompTIA online: www.comptia.org to learn more about getting CompTIA certified.

Contact CompTIA: Call 866-835-8020 ext. 5 or email questions@comptia.org

Connect with us :

Introduction

Welcome to the *CompTIA A+ Exam Cram*, Sixth Edition, my name is David L. Prowse. This book prepares you for the CompTIA A+ 220-801 and 220-802 Certification Exams. Imagine that you are at a testing center and have just been handed the passing scores for these exams. The goal of this book is to make that scenario a reality. I am happy to have the opportunity to serve you in this endeavor. Together, we can accomplish your goal to attain the CompTIA A+ certification.

Target Audience

The CompTIA A+ exams measure the necessary competencies for an entry-level IT professional with the equivalent knowledge of at least 12 months of hands-on experience in the lab or field.

This book is for persons who have experience working with desktop PCs and mobile devices and want to cram for the A+ certification exam—*cram* being the key word. This book does not cover everything in the PC world; how could you in such a concise package? However, this guide is fairly thorough and should offer you a lot of insight…and a whole lot of test preparation.

If you do not feel that you have the required experience, have never attempted to troubleshoot a computer, or are new to the field, then I recommend the *CompTIA A+ Cert Guide*, which goes into much more depth than this text. On a side note, another great reference book that should be on every PC technician's shelf is the latest edition of *Upgrading and Repairing PCs* by Scott Mueller.

Essentially two types of people will read this book: those who want a job in the IT field, and those who want to keep their job. For those of you in the first group, the new CompTIA A+ certification can have a powerful career impact, increasing the chances of securing a position in the IT world. For those in the second group, preparing for the exams serves to keep your skills sharp, and your knowledge up-to-date, making you a well-versed and well-sought-after technician.

Of course, I know that some of you are picking up this book solely for the practice exams, which are by the way located directly after Chapter 19, "Taking the Real Exams." But I recommend against solely studying the practice questions. This book was designed from the ground up to build your knowledge in such a way that when you get to the practice exams, they can act as the final key to passing the real exams. The knowledge in the chapters is the cornerstone, whereas the practice exam questions are the battlements. Complete the entire book, and you will have built yourself an impenetrable castle of knowledge.

About the CompTIA A+ 220-801 and 220-802 Exams

The 2012 version of the A+ exams are known as the CompTIA A+ 220-801 and 220-802 exams. There are quite a few changes and additions to these versions of the A+ exams including the following:

▶ Increased Windows 7 content.

▶ Windows 2000 operating system has been removed.

▶ Newer multicore processor technologies such as Core i7 have been added.

▶ Custom PC configurations have been included.

▶ Mobile devices such as tablets and smartphones have been added.

▶ Increased amount of networking and security topics, with increased difficulty.

▶ Additional operational procedures.

This book covers all these changes and more within its covers.

For more information about how the A+ certification can help your career, or to download the latest official objectives, access CompTIA's webpage at www.comptia.org.

About This Book

This book is broken down into 19 chapters, each pertaining to particular objectives on the exam. Because the official CompTIA objectives can have long names that sometimes deal with multiple subjects, the chapters are divided into more manageable (and memorable) topics. All the questions in this book refer to these topics. Chapter topics and the corresponding CompTIA objectives are listed in the beginning of each chapter.

For the most part, the exam topics in this book are structured to build on one another. Because of this, you should read this entire book in order to best prepare for the CompTIA A+ exams. In the case that you want to review a particular topic, for example if your CD practice exam identifies a topic deficiency, those topics are listed at the end of this introduction. In addition, you can use the index or the table of contents to quickly find the concept you are after.

Chapter Format and Conventions

Every Exam Cram chapter follows a standard structure and contains graphical clues about important information. The structure of each chapter includes the following:

▶ **Opening topics list:** This defines the topics to be covered in the chapter; it also lists the corresponding CompTIA A+ objective numbers.

▶ **Topical coverage:** The heart of the chapter. Explains the topics from a hands-on and a theory-based standpoint. This includes in-depth descriptions, tables, and figures geared to build your knowledge so that you can pass the exam. The chapters are broken down into between two to five topics each.

▶ **Cram Quiz questions:** At the end of each topic is a quiz. The quizzes, and ensuing explanations, are meant to gauge your knowledge of the subjects. If the answers to the questions don't come readily to you, consider reviewing individual topics or the entire chapter. In addition to being in the chapters, you can find the Cram Quiz questions on the disc. The questions are separated into their respective 220-801 and 220-802 categories for easier studying when you approach the exam.

▶ **Exam Alerts, Sidebars, and Notes:** These are interspersed throughout the book. Watch out for them!

ExamAlert

This is what an Exam Alert looks like. Normally, an alert stresses concepts, terms, hardware, software, or activities that are likely to relate to one or more certification test questions.

Additional Elements

Beyond the chapters, there are a few more elements that I've thrown in for you. They include

▸ **Practice Exams:** These are located directly after Chapter 19 within the book. There is one for each CompTIA A+ exam. These exams are also available on the disc.

▸ **Cram Sheet:** The tear-out Cram Sheet is located in the beginning of the book. This is designed to jam some of the most important facts you need to know for the exam into one small sheet, allowing for easy memorization. It is also in PDF format on the disc.

The Hands-On Approach

This book refers to two different computers as the following:

▸ **Media PC:** I built this desktop computer new for this sixth edition in January 2012. It is an Intel Core i5 system.

▸ **Tower PC:** This tower computer was built in 2009. It is an Intel Core 2 system. I refer to this computer to show older PC technologies still covered within the A+ objectives and to make comparisons with the newer *Media PC*.

I built *Media PC* using components that are a good example of what you will see in the field today, and for a while to come. These components are representative of the types of technologies that will be covered in the exams. I refer to the components in this system from Chapter 2, "Motherboards," onward. I like to put things into context whenever possible. By referencing the parts in the computer during each chapter, I hope to infuse some real-world knowledge and to solidify the concepts you need to learn for the exam. This more hands-on approach can help you to visualize concepts better. I recommend that every PC technician build their own PC at some point (if you haven't already). This can help to reinforce the ideas and concepts expressed in the book. You should also work with multiple computers while going through this book: one with Windows 7, one with Windows Vista, and one with Windows XP. Or you might attempt to create a dual-boot or three-way-boot on a single hard drive. Another option is to run one computer with one of the operating systems mentioned and virtual machines running the other operating systems. Finally, Windows 7 users might opt to include Windows XP mode, in addition to other solutions.

These pages refer to various ancillary websites, most notably

▸ **Microsoft TechNet:** http://technet.microsoft.com

▸ **Microsoft Support:** http://support.microsoft.com

As an IT technician, you will be visiting these sites often; they serve to further illustrate and explain concepts covered in this text.

Goals for This Book

I have three main goals in mind while preparing you for the CompTIA A+ exams.

My first goal is to help you understand A+ topics and concepts quickly and efficiently. To do this, I try to get right to the facts necessary for the exam. To drive these facts home, the book incorporates figures, tables, real-world scenarios, and simple to-the-point explanations. Also, in Chapter 19, you can find test-taking tips and a preparation checklist that gives you an orderly step-by-step approach to taking the exam. Be sure to complete every item on the checklist! For students of mine that truly complete every item, there is an extremely high pass rate for the exams.

My second goal for this book is to provide you with more than 500 *unique* questions to prepare you for the exam. Between the Cram Quizzes and the practice exams, that goal has been met, and I think it will benefit you greatly. Because CompTIA reserves the right to change test questions at any time, it is difficult to foresee exactly what you will be asked on the exam; however I think you will find that a good amount of the questions in this book are similar to the real questions. Regardless, to become a good technician, you must know the *concept*, not just memorize questions. To this effect each question has an explanation and maps back to the topic (and chapter) covered in the text. I've been using this method for more than a decade with my students (more than 2,000 of them) with great results.

My final goal is to provide support for this and all my titles, completing the life cycle of learning. I do this through my personal website: www.DavidLProwse.com/220-801, which has additional resources for you, an errata page (which you should check as soon as possible) and is set up to take questions from you about this book. I'll try my best to get to your questions ASAP. All personal information is kept strictly confidential.

Good luck in your certification endeavors. I hope you benefit from this book. Enjoy!

Sincerely,

David L. Prowse

Exam Topics

Table I.1 lists the exam topics covered in each chapter of the book.

TABLE I.1 **Exam Cram CompTIA A+ Exam Topics**

Exam Topic	Chapter
The Six-Step A+ Troubleshooting Process	1
Troubleshooting Examples and PC Tools	
Motherboard Components and Form Factors	2
The BIOS	
Installing and Troubleshooting Motherboards	
CPU 101	3
Installing and Troubleshooting CPUs	
RAM Basics and Types of RAM	4
Installing and Troubleshooting DRAM	
Understanding and Testing Power	5
Power Devices	
Power Supplies	
Magnetic Storage Media	6
Optical Storage Media	
Solid State Storage Media	
Installing, Configuring, and Troubleshooting Visible Laptop Components	7
Installing, Configuring, and Troubleshooting Internal Laptop Components	
Installing and Upgrading to Windows 7	8
Installing and Upgrading to Windows Vista	
Installing and Upgrading to Windows XP	
Windows User Interfaces	9
System Tools and Utilities	
Files, File Systems, and Disks	
Updating Windows	10
Maintaining Hard Disks	
Repair Environments and Boot Errors	11
Windows Tools and Errors	
Command-Line Tools	
The Video Subsystem	12
The Audio Subsystem	

TABLE I.1 **Continued**

Exam Topic	Chapter
Input/Output Devices, and Peripherals	13
Custom PC Configurations	
Printer Types and Technologies	14
Installing, Configuring, and Troubleshooting Printers	
Types of Networks and Network Devices	15
Cables, Connectors, and Tools	
TCP/IP	
SOHO Windows Networking	
Troubleshooting Networks	
Security Threats and Prevention	16
Windows Security	
SOHO Security	
Mobile Hardware and Operating Systems	17
Mobile Networking and Synchronization	
Mobile Security	
Safety	18
Procedures and Environmental Controls	
Professionalism and Communication Skills	
Getting Ready and the Exam Preparation Checklist	19
Tips for Taking the Real Exam	
Beyond the CompTIA A+ Certification	

CHAPTER 1

Introduction to Troubleshooting

This chapter covers the following A+ exam topics:

▶ The Six-Step A+ Troubleshooting Process

▶ Troubleshooting Examples and PC Tools

You can find a master list of A+ exam topics in the "Introduction."

This chapter covers CompTIA A+ 220-802 objectives 4.1 and 4.2.

Let's begin this book by talking about troubleshooting. Excellent troubleshooting ability is vital; it's probably the most important skill for a computer technician to possess. It's what we do—troubleshoot and repair problems! So it makes sense that a decent amount of questions about this subject are on the A+ exams. Every chapter of this book deals with troubleshooting to some extent; therefore, each chapter in a way is based off of this chapter. To be a good technician, and to pass the exams, you need to know how to troubleshoot hardware- *and* software-related issues. The key is to do it methodically. That's why CompTIA has incorporated a six-step troubleshooting process within the exam objectives. This chapter covers the six-step process and gives a couple basic examples of troubleshooting within this methodology. Because troubleshooting makes up a large portion of the CompTIA A+ objectives, you should apply this troubleshooting process throughout the rest of the chapters and also apply it whenever you attempt to solve a computer problem.

The Six-Step A+ Troubleshooting Process

It is necessary to approach computer problems from a logical standpoint, and to best do this, we use troubleshooting theory. Several different troubleshooting methodologies are out there; this book focuses on the CompTIA A+ six-step troubleshooting process.

This six-step process included within the 2012 A+ objectives is designed to increase the PC technician's problem-solving ability. CompTIA expects the technician to take an organized, methodical route to a solution by memorizing and implementing these steps. Incorporate this six-step process into your line of thinking as you read through this book and whenever you troubleshoot a PC, mobile device, or networking issue.

Step 1: Identify the problem.

Step 2: Establish a theory of probable cause. (Question the obvious.)

Step 3: Test the theory to determine cause.

Step 4: Establish a plan of action to resolve the problem and implement the solution.

Step 5: Verify full system functionality and if applicable implement preventative measures.

Step 6: Document findings, actions, and outcomes.

Let's talk about each of these six steps in a little more depth.

Step 1: Identify the Problem

In this first step you already know that there is a problem; now you have to identify exactly what it is. This means gathering information. You do this in a few ways:

- ▶ **Question the user.** Ask the person who reported the problem detailed questions about the issue. You want to find out about symptoms, unusual behavior, or anything that the user might have done of late that could have inadvertently or directly caused the problem. Of course, do this without accusing the user. If the user cannot properly explain a computer's problem, ask simple questions to further identify the issue.

▶ **Identify any changes made to the computer.** Look at the computer. See if any new hardware has been installed or plugged in. Look around for anything that might seem out of place. Listen to the computer—even smell it! For example, a hard drive might make a peculiar noise, or a power supply might smell like something is burning. Use all your senses to help identify what the problem is. Define if any new software has been installed or if any system settings have been changed. In some cases you might need to inspect the environment around the computer. Perhaps something has changed outside the computer that is related to the problem.

▶ **Review documentation.** Your company might have electronic or written documentation that logs past problems and solutions. Perhaps the issue at hand has happened before, or other related issues can aid you in your pursuit to find out what is wrong. Maybe another technician listed in the documentation can be of assistance if he or she has seen the problem before. Perhaps the user has documentation about a specific process or has a manual concerning the computer, individual component, software, or other device that has failed.

Keep in mind that you're not taking any direct action at this point. Instead, you are gleaning as much information as you can to help in your analysis. In this stage it is also important to back up any critical data before making any changes.

> **ExamAlert**
>
> Perform backups before making changes!

Step 2: Establish a Theory of Probable Cause (Question the Obvious)

In step 2 you theorize as to what the most likely cause of the problem is. Start with the most probable or obvious cause. For example, if a computer won't turn on, your theory of probable cause would be that the computer is not plugged in! This step differs from other troubleshooting processes in that you are not making a list of causes but instead are choosing one probable cause as a starting point. In this step you also need to define whether it is a hardware- or software-related issue.

Step 3: Test the Theory to Determine Cause

In step 3 take your theory from step 2 and test it. Back to the example, go ahead and plug in the computer. If the computer starts, you know that your theory has been confirmed. At that point move on to step 4. But what if the computer *is* plugged in? Or what if you plug in the computer and it still doesn't start? An experienced troubleshooter can often figure out the problem on the first theory but not always. If the first theory fails during testing, go back to step 2 to establish a new theory and continue until you have a theory that tests positive. If the problem escapes you and you can't figure out what the problem is from any of your theories, it's time to escalate. Bring the problem to your supervisor so that additional theories can be established.

Step 4: Establish a Plan of Action to Resolve the Problem and Implement the Solution

Step 4 might at first seem a bit redundant, but delve in a little further. When a theory has been tested and works, you can establish a plan of action. In the previous scenario, it's simple; plug in the computer. However, in other situations the plan of action will be more complicated; you might need to repair other issues that occurred due to the first issue. In other cases, an issue might affect multiple computers, and the plan of action would include repairing all those systems. Whatever the plan of action, after it is established, immediately implement it.

Step 5: Verify Full System Functionality and if Applicable Implement Preventative Measures

At this point verify that the computer works properly. This might require a restart or two, opening applications, accessing the Internet, or actually using a hardware device, thus proving it works. Also within step 5 you want to prevent the problem from happening again if possible. Yes, of course you plug in the computer, and in this case it works, but why was the computer unplugged? The computer being unplugged (or whatever the particular issue) could be the result of a bigger problem, which you would want to prevent in the future. Whatever your preventative measures, make sure that they won't affect any other systems or policies, and if they do, get permission for those measures first.

Step 6: Document Findings, Actions, and Outcomes

In this last step, document what happened. Depending on the company you work for, you might have been documenting the entire time, for example using a trouble ticketing system. In this step, finalize the documentation including the issue, cause, solution, preventative measures, and any other steps taken.

Documentation is extremely important; it helps in two ways. First, it gives closure to the problem, for you and the user; it solidifies the problem and the solution, making you a better troubleshooter in the future. Second, if you or anyone on your team encounters a similar issue in the future, the history of the issue will be right at your fingertips. Most technicians don't remember specific solutions to problems that happened several months ago or more. Plus, having a written account of what transpired can help to protect all parties involved.

> **Note**
>
> Try to incorporate this methodology into your thinking when covering the chapters in this book. In the upcoming chapters, apply it to any of the components, for example motherboards, adapter cards, and power supplies. In later chapters, apply it to mobile devices, Windows, and network computing.

Cram Quiz

Answer these questions. The answers follow the last question. If you cannot answer these questions correctly, consider reading this section again until you can. Each Cram Quiz is divided into sections for the 220-801 and 220-802 exams to better organize your studies when you are doing final review for the exams. Chapter 1 has questions pertaining to the 220-802 exam only.

1. What is the second step of the A+ troubleshooting methodology?

   ○ **A.** Identify the problem.

   ○ **B.** Establish a theory of probable cause.

   ○ **C.** Test the theory.

   ○ **D.** Document.

2. When you run out of possible theories for the cause of a problem, what should you do?

   ○ **A.** Escalate the problem.

   ○ **B.** Document your actions so far.

   ○ **C.** Establish a plan of action.

   ○ **D.** Question the user.

3. What should you do before making any changes to the computer? (Select the best answer.)

   O **A.** Identify the problem.

   O **B.** Establish a plan of action.

   O **C.** Perform a backup.

   O **D.** Escalate the problem.

4. Which of these is part of step 5 of the six-step troubleshooting process?

   O **A.** Identify the problem.

   O **B.** Document findings.

   O **C.** Establish a new theory.

   O **D.** Implement preventative measures.

5. What should you do next after testing the theory to determine cause?

   O **A.** Establish a plan of action to resolve the problem.

   O **B.** Verify full system functionality.

   O **C.** Document findings, actions, and outcomes.

   O **D.** Implement the solution.

Cram Quiz Answers

1. **B.** The second step is to establish a theory of probable cause. You need to look for the obvious or most probable cause for the problem.

2. **A.** If you can't figure out why a problem occurred, it's time to get someone else involved. Escalate the problem to your supervisor.

3. **C.** Always perform a backup of critical data before making any changes to the computer.

4. **D.** Implement preventative measures as part of step 5 to ensure that the problem will not happen again.

5. **A.** After testing the theory to determine cause (step 3) you should establish a plan of action to resolve the problem (step 4).

Troubleshooting Examples and PC Tools

The purpose of this section is to familiarize you with some introductory troubleshooting. As we progress through the book, we demonstrate more and more in-depth troubleshooting of problems that might occur. Let's go ahead and give a couple basic examples of troubleshooting utilizing the methodology we just covered.

Troubleshooting Example 1: Display Issue

In this scenario you are a PC technician working for the technical services department of a mid-sized company. During the morning you get a call from a member of the Graphics department. Apparently, he can't see anything on his screen. Troubleshoot!

Identify the Problem

While questioning the user you find out that the computer worked fine yesterday, but when the user came in today and started the computer, the display was blank.

While examining the computer, you can tell that it is turned on due to the power LED and can tell it is working due to the activity of the hard drive LED. The monitor has an amber LED lit next to the Power button. As the user mentions, restarting the computer and turning the monitor on and off have no effect.

Establish a Theory of Probable Cause (Question the Obvious)

Again, look for the obvious or most probable cause. In this case you surmise that the monitor is not connected to the PC.

> **ExamAlert**
>
> Check the connections first! They are a common culprit outside and inside the computer.

You guess the monitor is not connected to the PC because the computer appears to be working normally, and the monitor seems to get power (due to the amber LED). The theory is that the video signal is not getting to the monitor from the computer.

Test the Theory to Determine Cause

To test this theory, simply go to the back of the PC and check the video connection; then check the connection on the monitor if it has screw terminals. If either is loose or disconnected, firmly connect them to see if the monitor displays anything.

If the monitor now displays video, the theory is confirmed; however, if it does not, you need to construct a new theory. Maybe the monitor's backlight source (lamp) has burned out, or there is a problem with its inverter, or maybe the video card has some kind of issue. Perhaps the user neglected to tell you that he set the video resolution to a higher setting than the monitor could handle! Start with the next most likely cause and test it, moving down the line until the cause is discovered. If you can't find the cause, escalate the problem and get others involved.

Establish a Plan of Action to Resolve the Problem and Implement the Solution

Your plan of action should include connecting the monitor to the PC securely. Maybe the plug was never screwed in, making it an easy target to get disconnected, so make sure that the plug is firmly seated and screw it in tightly. Do the same if the other end of the cable screws into the monitor. As part of your plan of action, you might want to explain what the problem was to the user and show him how to reconnect the monitor in the future.

Verify Full System Functionality and if Applicable Implement Preventative Measures

At this point verify that the computer works properly. This might require a restart or two as proof, or opening applications that the user utilizes. Also within step 5 prevent the problem from happening again if possible. Maybe the user inadvertently kicked the connector loose, or a member of the cleaning crew ran over the cable with a vacuum, disconnecting it from the computer. Either way, rerouting or tie-wrapping the video cable, and any other cables, might be a good idea to prevent future problems with these connections. You should also inspect the cable for any type of wear. Any possible irresponsibility of the cleaning crew should be escalated to your supervisor.

Document Findings, Actions, and Outcomes

Document according to your company's policies. This might mean using an online ticketing system or just writing things down on paper. In this scenario you should document the user and computer that had the issue, the cause of the issue, how you repaired it, and any type of preventative measures and training of the user you implemented.

Troubleshooting Example 2: Power Issue

In this scenario you are a network support specialist within an IT department that supports 500 computers. First thing in the morning, you get a call from the Marketing department. From the statement it appears that several of its computers will not start. Troubleshoot!

Identify the Problem

While questioning the manager of the Marketing department, you find out that the computers worked fine yesterday, but when everyone came in this morning, four of the computers grouped in one area wouldn't start.

While examining the computers, you do indeed see that none of the four computers will turn on. Not only that, but the monitors at the employees' desks are also off. So the problem is that four computers and their monitors will not turn on.

Establish a Theory of Probable Cause (Question the Obvious)

Don't forget, you are looking for the most probable cause. In this case it would appear that there is a power issue because not just one computer, but all four computers, and their monitors, are not turning on. A possible theory is that a circuit breaker tripped causing all the electronic equipment on that circuit to fail.

Test the Theory to Determine Cause

To test this theory try plugging another device into any of the outlets that are part of the supposed problem. You can also use a receptacle tester to test the affected outlets.

If the outlets test negative for power and your electrician confirms that a circuit has tripped at the main panel, you know that your theory is correct. However, if the outlets test positive or have some other kind of erroneous reading, you need to troubleshoot further and most likely escalate the problem to a licensed electrician.

> **ExamAlert**
>
> If a problem is electrical, contact your building supervisor or manager so that they can contact a licensed electrician to fix the problem.

Establish a Plan of Action to Resolve the Problem and Implement the Solution

Say that the circuit tripped. The plan of action would simply be to reset the breaker and verify that the computers and monitors receive power.

Verify Full System Functionality and if Applicable Implement Preventative Measures

At this point verify that the computers and other equipment work properly. This might require a restart or two as proof and turning the monitors on and off. Also within step 5 you want to prevent the problem from happening again if possible. Chances are that the circuit was overloaded, and that's why it tripped. Consider taking one of the computer systems and moving it to another circuit, or possibly having the electrician add a new circuit to that area.

Document Findings, Actions, and Outcomes

Again, document according to your company's policies. In this scenario you would document this as an issue that affected several computers. Include names of the people dealt with including any of the marketing people, electricians, and perhaps building supervisors.

Power issues are fairly common with computers. For more information on power, power supplies, and the problems you might encounter, see Chapter 5, "Power."

PC Tools

Every technician needs to use tools when troubleshooting a computer. Field replaceable units (FRUs) such as power supplies, hard drives, and RAM will be difficult to remove without them. Remember, the best tools are your hands, eyes, and ears; though it could be debated whether these are actually "tools." But when it comes to tools that you hold in your hands, there are several you should definitely have in your toolkit. Table 1.1 lists some common PC tools and basic descriptions to go with them.

TABLE 1.1 **Common PC Tools**

PC Tool	Description
Antistatic strap	Protects from electro-static discharge (more on ESD in the next section).
Demagnetized Phillips head screwdriver	For assembling/disassembling PCs.
Multimeter	For testing wires in a PC and AC outlets.
Power Supply Tester	For testing a PC's power supply, also known as a PSU tester.
Torx screwdrivers	For assembling/disassembling PCs that use the less common Torx screw. Size T10 and T8 for PCs.
Hex screwdrivers	For cases and other components that do not use Phillips screws.
Plastic tweezers	For grabbing screws that fall into hard to reach areas, and removing jumper shunts.
Compressed air	To clean out the dust from a computer. (Do this outside!)
Penlight	Helps to illuminate when working inside the computer case, and when making connections on the back of a computer under a dark desk.
Magnifying glass	Helps to read small writing on components.

Exam Alert

Know the basic set of PC tools and their purpose!

Now, this is just a basic list of items that you should know for the A+ exams. As we progress through the book, we'll incorporate more tools that you should consider adding to your PC toolkit.

Some More Troubleshooting Tidbits

When working on the inside of a computer, it is imperative to protect against electro-static discharge (ESD), which occurs when two objects of different voltages come into contact with each other. For example, if you just walked across a carpet, your body gathered a lot of static electricity, more than enough to damage a computer component. If you were to touch the component, the static electricity would discharge from you to the component, the ending result being a wasted computer component. There are several ways to protect against this including wearing an antistatic wrist strap and connecting it to the chassis of the computer, touching the chassis of the computer before handling any components, and using an antistatic mat.

Other more indirect ways to prevent this are to keep your feet stationary when working on a computer, work in a noncarpeted area, keep the humidity raised to approximately 50 percent (if possible), and use antistatic sprays. You can find more information about protecting against ESD in Chapter 18, "Safety, Professionalism, and Procedures."

ExamAlert

To prevent ESD use an antistatic wrist strap.

If a computer won't start, you should check the power cable. But what if the computer and monitor are getting power and the display is still blank? You can narrow this down to four components: video, RAM, processor, and motherboard. From a hardware standpoint, the first thing to check is whether the monitor is securely connected to the computer's video card. Next, you want to make sure that all the other components connect properly. It's not unheard of for a connector, an adapter card, or even a processor to get jarred loose. If the video card, processor, or RAM is not connected properly, they can stop the computer from booting, and nothing shows up on the screen. Also, if the motherboard has a loose main power connector, the computer will not boot. So, when troubleshooting a no-display issue, and you know that the computer and monitor are receiving power, remember the *big 4*: video, RAM, processor, and motherboard.

Another key concept that you need to remember is that a large percentage of the issues you troubleshoot are due to user error. From a customer service standpoint, this is not something you want the user to pick up from your demeanor. You don't want to accuse or blame a user; but it is something to keep in mind when questioning the user.

On a final note, when troubleshooting, try to keep a level head. Think logically about a solution to the problem. I like to tell my students to think like Mr. Spock; try not to let emotion cloud your judgment. It is understandable that at times the amount of trouble tickets might be a bit overwhelming. Just remember that you can only do what you can do. By clearing everything from your mind except for a methodical troubleshooting approach, you can obtain solutions much more efficiently, live long, and prosper.

Cram Quiz

Answer these questions. The answers follow the last question. If you cannot answer these questions correctly, consider reading this section again until you can. Chapter 1 has questions pertaining to the 220-802 exam only.

1. There is a problem with the power supplied to a group of computers, and you do not know how to fix the problem. What should you do first?

   ○ **A.** Establish a theory of why you can't figure out the problem.

   ○ **B.** Contact the building supervisor or your manager.

   ○ **C.** Test the theory to determine cause.

   ○ **D.** Document findings, actions, and outcomes.

2. You have confirmed the theory that a video card is bad and needs to be replaced. What should you do next?

- ○ **A.** Escalate the problem.
- ○ **B.** Document your actions so far.
- ○ **C.** Establish a plan of action.
- ○ **D.** Question the user.

3. A computer won't turn on when you press the Power button. What should you check first?

- ○ **A.** If an operating system is installed.
- ○ **B.** Documentation.
- ○ **C.** If the monitor is plugged in.
- ○ **D.** If the computer is plugged in.

4. Which of these is contained within step 1 of the six-step troubleshooting process?

- ○ **A.** Question the user.
- ○ **B.** Document findings.
- ○ **C.** Establish a new theory.
- ○ **D.** Escalate the problem.

5. Which of the following are possible faulty components when there is nothing on the display? (Select all that apply.)

- ○ **A.** Sound card
- ○ **B.** Video card
- ○ **C.** Processor
- ○ **D.** Network card

6. You dropped a screw in the case of a PC. What is the best tool to use to retrieve the screw?

- ○ **A.** Compressed air
- ○ **B.** Computer vacuum
- ○ **C.** Plastic tweezers
- ○ **D.** Screwdriver with magnetized tip

7. What is the last step of the six-step troubleshooting process?

- ○ **A.** Question the user.
- ○ **B.** Verify full system functionality.
- ○ **C.** Establish a plan of action.
- ○ **D.** Document findings.

Cram Quiz Answers

1. **B.** If you can't figure out a cause to a problem and have exhausted all possible theories, escalate the problem to the appropriate persons.

2. **C.** After you confirm a theory, move to step 4 to establish a plan of action, and implement the solution.

3. **D.** Connections are quite often the culprit outside and inside the computer. If a computer won't turn on, make sure it is plugged securely into an AC outlet.

4. **A.** Questioning the user is important when gathering information to identify the problem.

5. **B** and **C.** The big four (as I like to call them) are the video card, RAM, processor, and motherboard. If your computer is definitely getting power and there is still nothing on the display, you want to check these, most likely in order.

6. **C.** Plastic tweezers is the best answer. You don't want to damage any internal components with a metal tool, or a magnetized tool. If plastic tweezers are not available, most basic PC toolkits come with a three-pronged grabber tool. If that is not available, small pliers with the tips wrapped in electrical tape will do. In some cases you can turn the computer upside down to loosen the screw. At the last, a magnetized screwdriver or extension magnet is your final resort. Just remember to try if at all possible to keep metal away from components—only touch the screw. Using your hands to grab the screw in this scenario is *not* an option, even if you think you are protected from ESD.

7. **D.** Document findings, actions, and outcomes is the sixth and last step of the CompTIA A+ troubleshooting process. Remember the process for the exam!

CHAPTER 2

Motherboards

This chapter covers the following A+ exam topics:

▶ Motherboard Components and Form Factors

▶ The BIOS

▶ Installing and Troubleshooting Motherboards

You can find a master list of A+ exam topics in the "Introduction."

This chapter covers CompTIA A+ 220-801 objectives 1.1 and 1.2 and CompTIA A+ 220-802 objective 4.2.

Without a doubt, the motherboard is the foundation of the computer. Everything connects to the motherboard, and all data is transferred through this matrix of circuitry.

In this chapter we delve into the components that make up the motherboard, the various types of motherboard form factors, the ports and interfaces you find on the face and the side of the motherboard, the Basic Input Output System (BIOS) and show proper methods for installing and troubleshooting motherboards.

Motherboard Components and Form Factors

Over the years I have found that if a student is going to lack knowledge in one area, it's quite often going to be the motherboard. Unfortunately, this is one of the key elements in a computer system. It's the starting point for a quick and efficient computer. Because it connects to everything in the computer system, you need to know many concepts concerning it. Let's begin with the parts that make up the motherboard.

Motherboard Components

You don't need to know every single chip and circuit that resides on the motherboard. Generally, if a motherboard fails, which is uncommon, the entire board needs to be replaced. However, you do need to know the main components, interfaces, and ports of a motherboard and have some knowledge of how it transmits data. This ensures compatibility of components when you design your own system, and when you add or replace devices to a motherboard. It also enhances your troubleshooting skills—when the time comes…muhahahah!

Main Components

As mentioned in the "Introduction," I decided to build a new computer for this book (and for me I suppose) and wanted to use fairly new components. Not the latest or most expensive mind you but still current, decent parts that reflect the type of components you see in the field now and for a year or two to come. Within this book I refer to this computer as *Media PC*. For the motherboard, I chose the Intel DP67DE. It is part of the Desktop Media series of motherboards and works well as part of a multimedia PC or home theater PC. (It wasn't because it has my initials, I swear!) Figure 2.1 shows this motherboard with callouts to the main components you need to know for the exam.

You might have noticed that this motherboard meets many of the characteristics of the ATX form factor; it is actually a micro-ATX motherboard; a smaller version of ATX is discussed later in this chapter. And don't worry if you are confused about one or two of the components; each of these are covered as you progress through this book. Processors are covered in more depth in Chapter 3, "The CPU," RAM is covered in Chapter 4, "RAM," power connections are covered in more depth in Chapter 5, "Power," and SATA is covered in Chapter 6, "Storage Devices." The remainder of the listed components are discussed within this chapter.

Expansion Bus slots   Port Cluster

4-pin CPU power

Processor Socket
LGA1155

RAM slots

SATA   CR2032   24-pin ATX
Connectors   Lithium   Power Connector
              Battery
P67 Express
Chipset (PCH)

FIGURE 2.1   Intel DP67DE motherboard components

ExamAlert

Identify motherboard components for the exam.

Product documentation usually accompanies a device. But if you didn't receive any, or you want more information about the components of this or any motherboard, consider grabbing a technical document from the manufacturer's website. "Go to the source!"—that's what I always tell my students. For example, for this motherboard you would go to the Intel website, locate the DP67DE board through the products menu or the search tool, and then look for "technical documentation." From there you can locate and download a PDF of the product guide, and more important, the technical product specification. The technical specification has all the information you can possibly want about a motherboard. It includes diagrams, descriptions, installation procedures...the whole nine yards. Now I know you have seen a lot of acronyms (and there are a slew more coming), but here's a vital one for you: RTM,

"Read the Manual!" It helps when installing, configuring, and troubleshooting a device. As far as Intel goes, trust in these folks; they are some of the greatest technical documentation specialists on the planet.

> **ExamAlert**
>
> Go to the manufacturer's website for technical documentation.

Chipsets and Buses

In a general sense, the chipset *is* the motherboard, incorporating all the controllers on the motherboard; many technicians refer to it in this way. But in the more specific sense, the chipset is one or two specific chips. How many will depend on the design and the manufacturer of the board. If you refer to Figure 2.1, on the Intel DP67DE motherboard, you see the chipset is the P67 Express Chipset (PCH). PCH stands for Platform Controller Hub, a name Intel uses. This chipset is composed of a single chip.

The Technical Product Specification PDF for this motherboard is in depth, even bordering on the hypertechnical! It includes schematics of the motherboard that show the chipset, buses, circuitry, and chips of the motherboard and how they interconnect. Figure 2.2 illustrates the connections between the P67 chipset and the rest of the motherboard.

The chipset connects to just about everything directly. Starting clockwise from about 2 o'clock, you can see the Ethernet controller, Serial Peripheral Interface, Serial ATA interface, HD audio controller, IEEE 1394 controller, USB controllers, PCI controller, and PCI Express x1 connectors. You've probably heard of most of these, but each one will be covered in depth as you continue through this book. The point for now is that the chipset is the central meeting point for many devices. It also has a high-speed point-to-point interconnection to the processor called the Direct Media Interface (DMI) link, also known as the DMI bus.

> **Note**
>
> A quick word on buses and lanes: A bus can be one wire (serial) or a group of wires working in unison (parallel) that carry data from one place to another. DMI makes use of *lanes*. A lane is two serial wires that enable the sending and receiving of data simultaneously. Parallel buses on the other hand are normally designed in multiples of eight wires that can send 1 byte of data (8 bits) at a time in one direction.

The DMI carries all the traffic from the previous list of controllers to the processor. You can imagine that the DMI needs to be powerful. The original DMI provided a data transfer rate of 10 gigabits per second (10 Gb/s) in each direction.

(Note the lowercase 'b' indicating bits.) This chipset makes use of a DMI 2.0 connection and can handle 20 Gb/s in each direction. This is equal to approximately 2.5 gigabytes per second (2.5 GB/s; note the uppercase 'B' for bytes.) The only things the chipset does not connect to directly are the PCI Express x16 slot and the RAM. These are controlled directly by the processor.

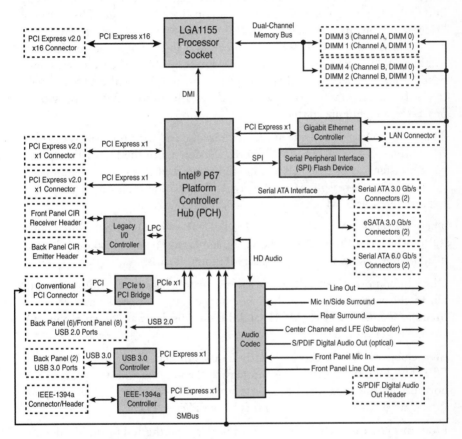

FIGURE 2.2   Intel P67 chipset connections

This Intel design differs from previous Intel designs and some AMD designs in that there is only one chip in the chipset instead of two. Historically, the motherboard chipset consisted of two chips: the northbridge and the southbridge.

▶ **Northbridge:** In charge of the connection to high data transfer devices such as PCI Express video cards and the RAM.

▶ **Southbridge:** In charge of the connection to all the secondary controllers: USB, SATA, FireWire, and so on.

ExamAlert

Know the concept of the northbridge and southbridge for the exam!

On our DP67DE motherboard, the northbridge functionality is built directly into the processor; some refer to this as an on-die northbridge. The southbridge functionality is all within the P67 chipset. However, newer AMD designs such as the AMD 990 FX chipset still make use of a northbridge and southbridge. In this scenario the northbridge controls the PCI Express connections and connects directly to the processor, and the southbridge connects to just about everything else. But the RAM is still controlled directly by the processor, a technique started by AMD.

The AMD connection between the northbridge and the processor is called HyperTransport, similar to Intel's DMI. Version 3.1 of the HyperTransport has a transfer rate of 25.6 GB/s. You might note that this is a lot more than Intel's DMI. The reason is that the HyperTransport also moves all the PCI Express video data, which accounts for a large chunk.

There is a more powerful version of Intel's DMI called Quick Path Interconnect (QPI), which can also transfer 25.6 GB/s, similar to HyperTransport. It is used by more powerful workstation and server motherboards.

Older Intel motherboard designs used the northbridge/southbridge concept, but Intel gave names to each chip. The northbridge was known as the Memory Controller Hub (MCH) and the southbridge was known as the I/O Controller Hub (ICH).

An example of an Intel motherboard that uses this configuration is the model DP35DP; Figure 2.3 shows this motherboard and points out the processor, northbridge, and southbridge. This motherboard is part of an older computer I built in 2009 which I refer to in this book as *Tower PC*.

From this you can see the MCH (northbridge) and the ICH (southbridge). These make up the P35 chipset. Specifically, for this motherboard, these are the Intel 82P35 MCH and the Intel 82801R ICH. Figure 2.4 gives a rough idea of the connections between these and the rest of the motherboard.

In Figure 2.4 you can see that there are three major buses (you can think of them as highways) that lead to and from the MCH:

▶ **Front-side-bus (FSB):** This connects the MCH to the processor (CPU) socket. On the DP35DP motherboard it is rated for 1,333, 1,066, or 800 MHz, which depends on what type of processor used. When deciding on a processor, make sure that it can run at one of the FSB speeds prescribed by the motherboard. It also needs to be compatible with, and adhere to the wattage maximum, of the motherboard's socket.

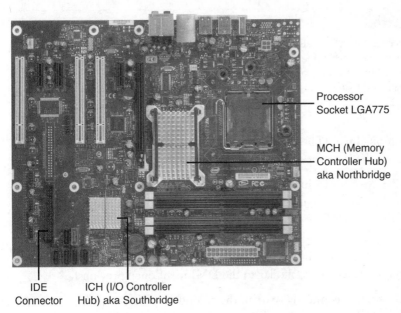

FIGURE 2.3   **Intel DP35DP Processor and Chipset Components**

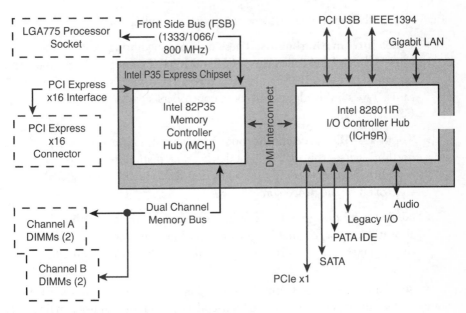

FIGURE 2.4   **Intel P35 chipset connections**

> **Note**
>
> The speed of the FSB is rated in Hertz (Hz), a unit of frequency defined as a number of cycles per second. In the DP35DP motherboard, the FSB can go as high as 1,333 MHz or 1.33 billion cycles per second (if it is not overclocked!). For a video primer on Hertz, bits, and bytes, access my website: http://www.davidlprowse.com/220-801.

- ▶ **Memory bus:** This set of wires connects the MCH to the RAM slots. It has also been referred to as the address bus.

- ▶ **PCI Express x16 interface:** This connects the MCH to the x16 PCIe slot used for video; usually there is only one of these slots on a motherboard.

The FSB and memory bus are parallel; however, PCI Express works in groups of serial buses called lanes, similar to the DMI mentioned previously.

The ICH provides connectivity to all the secondary buses, some of which are parallel buses (IDE and Audio) and some of which are serial buses (USB, SATA, IEEE 1394, and lesser PCIe slots).

Let's sum up the types of chipsets starting with the oldest.

- ▶ **Older Intel motherboards:** These utilize a northbridge and southbridge, which Intel called the MCH and ICH. The northbridge controls the connections to RAM and PCI Express x16 devices such as video cards. The southbridge connects to controllers such as SATA, IDE, USB, and PCI.

- ▶ **Today's AMD-based motherboards:** These also have a northbridge/southbridge chipset design. The main difference is that the northbridge controls only the connection to PCIe x16 devices; RAM is controlled by the processor.

- ▶ **Newer Intel designs:** These basically do away with the northbridge altogether, incorporating its functionality into the processor. The main chipset takes care of all secondary functions such as SATA and USB.

A last word about chipsets: Certain applications prefer or even require specific chipsets, usually applications on the high-end side. Graphics, music, engineering, and even gaming applications recommend specific chipsets. So before designing your computer, think about which applications you will use and whether they prefer certain chipsets.

Drive Technologies

The two types of drive technologies that have ports on your motherboards are SATA and IDE. These always connect to the southbridge, or simply the chipset if there is only one chip. SATA and IDE support the connection of hard drives, CD-ROMs, DVD-ROMs, and Blu-ray drives.

▶ **SATA:** Serial ATA has eclipsed IDE. As you can see in Figure 2.3, there is only one IDE port, but there are six 7-pin SATA ports (one of which is for external connections). And the newer motherboard in Figure 2.1 has no IDE ports whatsoever. The reason for this is speed. Even though SATA sends data in a serial fashion, or one bit at a time, it is faster than IDE. The first generation of SATA is rated at 1.5 Gb/s (once again, note the lowercase b indicating bits), equal to roughly 150 MB/s. Second-generation SATA offers a 3.0 Gb/s data rate. Third-generation SATA runs at 6 Gb/s. Most of today's motherboards are compatible with second- and third-generation SATA. Again, hard drives, CD-ROMs, DVDs, and Blu-ray drives can be connected to an SATA port.

▶ **IDE:** Integrated Drive Electronics interfaces (refer to Figure 2.3) have 40 pins. They utilize the Parallel ATA (PATA) standard that currently specifies a maximum data transfer rate of 133 MB/s. These bytes of information are transferred in parallel, for example 8 bits at a time. Hard drives, CD-ROM drives, and DVD drives can connect to IDE ports. The IDE connector is 40 pins, but depending on the version, the cables used can have 40 or 80 conductors.

> **Note**
>
> For more information on SATA and IDE, see Chapter 6.

Expansion Buses

There are six expansion buses and their corresponding adapter card slots that you need to know for the exam. They include the following:

▶ **PCI:** The Peripheral Component Interconnect bus was developed in the '90s by Intel as a faster, more compatible alternative to the deprecated ISA bus. It allows for connections to modems and to video, sound, and network adapters; however, PCI connects exclusively to the southbridge, or main chipset. Because of this, other high-speed video alternatives were developed that could connect directly to the northbridge, or directly to the processor. The PCI bus is used not only by devices that fit into the PCI slot, but also by devices that take the form of an integrated circuit on the motherboard. PCI version 2.1 cards are rated at 66 MHz, and their corresponding PCI bus is 32-bits wide, allowing for a maximum data transfer rate of 266 MB/s. Derivates of PCI include PCI-X, which was designed for servers, using a 64-bit bus and rated for 133 MHz/266 MHz; and Mini-PCI used by laptops. PCI slots are still found on today's motherboards (as shown in Figure 2.5) but are quickly being overtaken by PCIe technology. A comparison of PCI, AGP, and AMR is shown in Figure 2.6. A comparison of PCI and other expansion buses is shown in Table 2.1 at the end of this list of expansion buses.

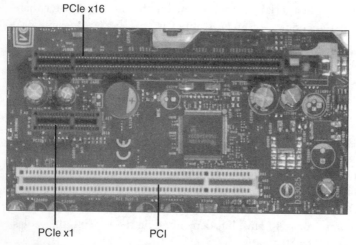

FIGURE 2.5   **PCIe x16, PCIe x1, and PCI expansion buses**

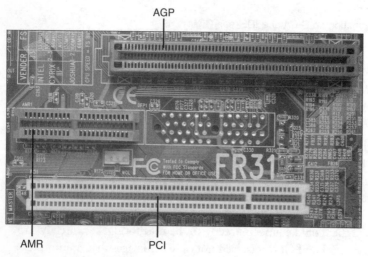

FIGURE 2.6   **AGP, AMR, and PCI expansion buses**

▶ **AGP:** Accelerated Graphics Port was developed for the use of 3D accelerated video cards and alleviated the disadvantages of PCI for video. Originally designed as a 32-bit 66 MHz bus (known as 1x), it had a maximum data transfer rate of 266 MB/s. Additional versions were delivered, for example, 2x, with a data rate of 533 MB/s, effectively doubling the fastest PCI output. (To do this the 66 MHz bus was double-pumped to an effective 133 MHz.) Two more versions included 4x (quad-pumped) offering 1 GB/s, and 8x with a maximum data rate of 2 GB/s. The AGP bus connects directly to the northbridge, addressing one of the limitations of PCI. Although there is some compatibility between cards, different slots (1x, 4x, and 8x) use different voltages. You should verify that the AGP card is compatible with the stated voltage in the motherboard documentation. An example of an AGP slot is shown in Figure 2.6. AGP has been virtually eliminated in new computers by PCI Express.

▶ **PCIe:** Currently the king of expansion buses, PCI Express is the high-speed serial replacement of the older parallel PCI standard. The most powerful PCIe slots with the highest data transfer rates connect directly to the northbridge, or directly to the processor; the lesser PCIe slots connect to the southbridge, or, for newer Intel boards, the main chipset. This expansion bus sends and receives data within *lanes*. These lanes are considered full-duplex, meaning they can send and receive data simultaneously. PCIe version 1 has a data rate of 250 MB/s per lane, version 2 is 500 MB/s, and version 3 is 1 GB/s. Remember, those numbers are for each direction, so PCIe version 3 can send 1 GB/s and receive 1 GB/s at the same time. The amount of lanes a PCIe bus uses is indicated with an x and a number, for example, x1 (pronounced "by one") or one lane. Commonly, PCIe video cards are x16 (16 lanes). They have taken the place of AGP video cards due to their improved data transfer rate. For example, a Version 2 PCIe x16 video card can transfer 8 GB of data per second (500 MB × 16 = 8 GB), which is far greater than AGP could hope to accomplish. And Version 3 PCIe x16 video cards take it even further, doubling that to 16 GB/s. Most other PCIe adapter cards are x1; although you might find some x4 cards as well. Of course, compatibility is key. A x1 card can go in a x1 slot or larger, but a x16 card currently fits only in a x16 slot. So for example, a PCIe x4 card won't fit in a x1 slot, but it will fit in a x4 slot. It also fits in a x16 slot but with no increase in performance. Figure 2.5 displays a x16 and x1 slot. Keep in mind that x4 and x16 slots are controlled by the northbridge, or by the processor, whereas x1 slots are controlled by the southbridge (refer to Figures 2.2 and 2.4). Table 2.1 shows a comparison of PCIe and other expansion buses.

> **Note**
>
> As of the publishing of this book, a x32 slot is also defined in the PCIe specification, but x16 slots are the most common in motherboards. Also, it was announced in late 2011 that PCIe version 4 would be developed at 2 GB/s per lane. (PCIe x16 slots would transfer 32 GB/s.) It is slated for release in 2014.

> **ExamAlert**
>
> Identify the PCI, AGP, and especially PCIe expansion buses for the exam.

▶ **AMR and CNR**: Intel's audio/modem riser expansion slot was designed to offer a slot with a small footprint that had the capability to accept sound cards or modems. The idea behind this was to attain Federal Communications Commission (FCC) certification (which is a time-consuming and detailed endeavor) for the adapter card once, instead of having to attain FCC certifications for integrated components on motherboards over and over again with each new motherboard released. This way, the card could be transferred from system to system. The idea was flawed from the start, because adapter cards so quickly progress. This technology, and its successor CNR, are not used in today's motherboards, but you still could see them in use in the field. Figure 2.6 shows an example of AMR. Quite often, expansion buses are labeled on the motherboard just above the slot. You can see the letters "AMR1" just above the AMR slot toward the left in Figure 2.6.

The Communications and Networking Riser (CNR) was Intel's adaptation of AMR and was meant for specialized networking, audio, and modem technologies. It was superior to AMR because it could be software or hardware controlled but had the same result as AMR and has been obsolete since about 2007.

▶ **PCMCIA**: The Personal Computer Memory Card International Association is actually an organization that develops the PC Card technology used in laptops; it is not an expansion bus, although you might see it referred to that way. PC Cards (originally called PCMCIA cards) were first designed for additional storage and later for modems, network cards, combo cards, and hard drives. You have probably seen these credit card-sized devices in the past; however, they are superseded by another technology known as ExpressCard. You can find more information on PCMCIA, PC Card, and ExpressCard in Chapter 7, "Laptops."

TABLE 2.1   **Comparison of PCI, AGP, and PCIe**

Expansion Bus	Bus Width	Frequency	Max. Data Rate
PCI	32-bit	33 MHz 66 MHz	133 MB/s 266 MB/s
AGP	32-bit	1x = 66 MHz	266 MB/s
		2x = 66 MHz (double pumped to 133 MHz)	533 MB/s
		4x = 66 MHz (quad pumped to 266 MHz)	1 GB/s
		8x = 66 MHz (octo-pumped to 533 MHz)	2 GB/s
PCIe	Serial, consists of between 1 and 16 full-duplex lanes	Version 1 = 2.5 GHz* Version 2 = 5 GHz Version 3 = 8 GHz	250 MB/s per lane 500 MB/s per lane 1 GB/s per lane

* This is also measured in transfers per second referring to the number of operations that send and receive data per second. It is often closely related to frequency. For example, PCI v1 is 2.5 gigatransfers per second (2.5 GT/s).

> **Note**
>
> Maximum data transfer rates are never attained, even in a lab environment. You can expect actual throughput to be substantially lower, but professionals use the maximum data rate as a point of reference and as a way of comparison.

I/O Ports and Front Panel Connectors

Without input and output ports, you could not communicate with the computer, unless it was through telepathy, and I don't think that technology has developed yet ☺. These ports also take care of displaying information, printing it, and communicating with other computers. Figure 2.7 shows some typical ports as found on our motherboard.

Starting at the left and continuing counter-clockwise, you see the following in the figure:

► **IEEE 1394a:** Also known as a FireWire or i.Link, this port is used for devices that demand the low-latency transfer of data, usually concerning music or video. This port has a maximum data rate of 400 Mbps; though IEEE 1394 has faster versions that Chapter 13, "Peripherals and Custom Computing," discusses.

▶ **USB:** Universal Serial Bus ports are used by many devices including keyboards, mice, printers, cameras, and much more. Most of today's motherboards come with a couple USB 3.0 ports that have a maximum data transfer rate of 5 Gbps but will also come with several USB 2.0 ports that have a maximum data rate of 480 Mbps.

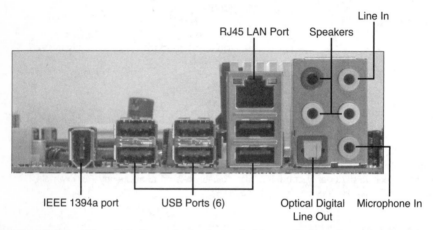

FIGURE 2.7   I/O port cluster on the back panel of the motherboard

▶ **Audio cluster:** There are six ports in this audio cluster including an optical digital output, microphone in, line in, and speaker outs.

▶ **RJ45 LAN port:** This is the wired network connection. On this particular motherboard, it is a Gigabit Ethernet LAN controller and is rated for 10/100/1000 Mbps. This means that it can connect to any of those speed networks and function properly.

ExamAlert

Identify back panel connectors (I/O ports) for the exam.

Quite often, cases come with front panel ports that might be wired to the motherboard or to an adapter card. These include USB ports, audio ports, memory card readers, external SATA ports, and more. The front panel also has connections for the Power button, reset button, power LED light, and hard drive activity LED light.

Form Factors

A computer form factor specifies the physical dimensions of some of the components of a computer system. It pertains mainly to the motherboard but also specifies compatibility with the computer case and power supply. The form factor defines the size and layout of components on the motherboard. It also specifies the power outputs from the power supply to the motherboard. The most common form factors, and the ones you need to know for the exam, are ATX, microATX, ITX, and BTX. Let's discuss these a little further now.

ATX

Advanced Technology Extended (ATX) was originally designed by Intel in the mid-'90s to overcome the limitations of the now deprecated AT form factor. It has been the standard ever since. The motherboard in Figure 2.3 is ATX. Full-size ATX motherboards measure 12 inches × 9.6 inches (305 mm × 244 mm). ATX motherboards have an integrated port cluster on the back and normally ship with an I/O plate that snaps into the back of the case, which fills the gaps between ports and keeps airflow to a minimum. One identifying characteristic of ATX is that the RAM slots and expansion bus slots are perpendicular to each other. Generally, ATX has seven expansion slots. For example, the DP35DP motherboard has four PCIe slots and three PCI slots. The ATX specification calls for the power supply to produce +3.3 V, +5 V, +12 V, and –12 V outputs and a 5 V standby output. The original ATX specification calls for a 20-pin power connector (often referred to as P1), and the newer ATX12 Version 2.x specification calls for a 24-pin power connector. The additional four pins are rated at +12 V, +3.3 V, +5 V, and ground, as shown in Table 2.2. Those pins are numbered 11, 12, 23, and 24.

TABLE 2.2 **ATX Pin Specification of the Main Power Connector**

Pin	Color	Signal	Pin	Color	Signal
1	Orange	+3.3 V	13	Orange Brown	+3.3 V +3.3 V sense
2	Orange	+3.3 V	14	Blue	–12 V
3	Black	Ground	15	Black	Ground
4	Red	+5 V	16	Green	Power on
5	Black	Ground	17	Black	Ground
6	Red	+5 V	18	Black	Ground
7	Black	Ground	19	Black	Ground
8	Grey	Power good	20	White	–5 V (optional)
9	Purple	+5 V standby	21	Red	+5 V
10	Yellow	+12 V	22	Red	+5 V
11	Yellow	+12 V	23	Red	+5 V
12	Orange	+3.3 V	24	Black	Ground

> **ExamAlert**
>
> Know the voltages supplied to an ATX motherboard by a power supply: +3.3 V, +5 V, +12 V, −12 V outputs, and +5 V standby output.

microATX

microATX (or mATX) was introduced as a smaller version of ATX; these motherboards can be a maximum size of 9.6 inches × 9.6 inches (244 mm × 244 mm) but can be as small as 6.75 inches by 6.75 inches (171.45 mm × 171.45 mm). In comparison, microATX boards are usually square, whereas full-size ATX boards are rectangular. microATX is backward compatible with ATX meaning that most microATX boards can be installed within an ATX form factor case, and they use the same power connectors as ATX. Often, they have the same chipsets as ATX as well. The DP67DE motherboard shown in Figure 2.1 is microATX. One of the reasons I selected it is because this smaller form factor is common for multimedia PCs and HTPCs.

ITX

ITX is a group of form factors developed by VIA Technologies, Inc. between 2001 and now for use in small, low-power motherboards. The ITX group includes the following:

> ▶ **Mini-ITX:** Designed in 2001, this 6.7 × 6.7 in (17 × 17 cm) motherboard is a bit smaller than microATX and is screw-compatible with it enabling it to be used in microATX and ATX cases if so desired. It uses passive cooling to keep it quiet and conserve power, making it ideal for HTPCs. The first version of these boards came with one expansion slot: PCI. The second version comes with a single PCIe x16 slot.
>
> ▶ **Nano-ITX:** Released in 2005, this measures 4.7 × 4.7 in (120 × 120 mm). It boasts low power consumption and is used in media centers, automotive PCs, set-top boxes (STB), and personal video recorders (PVR).
>
> ▶ **Pico-ITX:** Designed and released in 2007, this is half the area of Nano-ITX, measuring 3.9 × 2.8 in (10 × 7.2 cm). It uses powerful processors and RAM, and thus requires active cooling. It is used in extremely small PCs and ultra-mobile PCs (UMPCs).
>
> ▶ **Mobile-ITX:** Released in 2010, this is the smallest of the four ITX form factors, measuring 60 mm × 60 mm. There are no ports, and it requires a secondary I/O board. It is intended for military, surveying, transportation, and medical markets and is used in UMPCs and smartphones.

BTX

Balanced Technology Extended (BTX) was designed by Intel in 2004 to combat some of the issues common to ATX. More powerful processors require more power and therefore release more heat. BTX was designed with a more efficient thermal layout. There is a lower profile, and the graphics card is oriented differently than ATX, so heat is generally directed out of the case in a more efficient manner. BTX's future is dim because Intel and AMD processors, and most video cards' processors, are designed to use less power (and therefore generate less heat). BTX devices are not compatible with ATX devices. One of the ways to identify a BTX motherboard is that the RAM slots and expansion buses are parallel to each other. Also, the port cluster is situated differently on a BTX board. In addition, BTX boards are slightly wider than ATX boards; they measure 12.8 inches × 10.5 inches (325mm × 267mm). BTX is not specifically listed on the CompTIA A+ objectives, but you will probably still see these motherboards in existence in the field. You should at least know the basic differences between the ATX and BTX form factors.

Table 2.3 compares the ATX, microATX, ITX, and BTX form factors supplying the sizes of these motherboards and some of the characteristics that set them apart.

TABLE 2.3 **Comparison of Motherboard Form Factors**

Form Factor	Width	Depth	Identifying Characteristic
ATX	12 inches	9.6 inches	RAM slots and expansion slots are perpendicular to each other (90 degree angle).
microATX	9.6 inches	9.6 inches	Smaller than ATX but backward compatible to it.
ITX	From 60 mm to 6.7 inches depending on the type	From 60 mm to 6.7 inches depending on type	Designed for HTPCs, UMPCs, and smartphones.
BTX	12.8 inches	10.5 inches	RAM slots and expansion slots are parallel to each other.

ExamAlert

Know the basics of ATX, microATX, ITX, and BTX for the exam.

Cram Quiz

Answer these questions. The answers follow the last question. If you cannot answer
these questions correctly, consider reading this section again until you can.

220-801 Questions

1. What voltage does an orange pin indicate?

   O **A.** +12 V

   O **B.** +5 V

   O **C.** –5 V

   O **D.** +3.3 V

2. Which motherboard form factor measures 12 inches × 9.6 inches?

   O **A.** microATX

   O **B.** BTX

   O **C.** ATX

   O **D.** ITX

3. Which expansion bus uses lanes to transfer data?

   O **A.** PCI

   O **B.** PCI-X

   O **C.** PCIe

   O **D.** AGP

4. Which does a PCIe x16 slot connect to? (Select the two best answers.)

   O **A.** RAM

   O **B.** Southbridge

   O **C.** USB 3.0 controller

   O **D.** Northbridge

   O **E.** Processor

5. Which of these are serial technologies? (Select all that apply.)

   O **A.** USB

   O **B.** IEEE 1394

   O **C.** PCIe

   O **D.** PCI

Cram Quiz Answers

220-801 Answers

1. **D.** Orange signifies +3.3 volts. Red indicates +5 volts, and yellow is +12 volts; –5 volts would be the white optional wire.

2. **C.** ATX boards measure 12 inches × 9.6 inches.

3. **C.** PCIe (PCI Express) uses serial lanes to send and receive data.

4. **D** and **E.** PCIe x16 connects to the northbridge on AMD systems and older Intel systems. On newer Intel systems it connects to the processor.

5. **A, B,** and **C.** The only one listed that is not a serial technology is PCI, which is a 32-bit parallel technology.

The BIOS

BIOS, CMOS, and the Lithium Battery

The BIOS, CMOS, and lithium battery have a nice little relationship with each other. In a way, the BIOS relies on the CMOS, and the CMOS relies on the lithium battery, as shown in Figure 2.8.

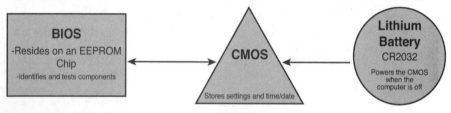

FIGURE 2.8   The BIOS, CMOS, and lithium battery

The Basic Input Output System (BIOS) is the first thing that runs when you boot the PC. The BIOS's job is to identify, test, and initialize components of the system. It then points the way to the operating system so that the OS can load up and take over. Collectively, this process is known as *bootstrapping*. Originally, the BIOS was stored on a Read-Only Memory (ROM) chip. It later progressed to a Programmable ROM (PROM) enabling the user to modify settings in the BIOS. Finally, today's system BIOS resides on an EEPROM chip on the motherboard. EEPROM stands for Electrically Erasable Programmable ROM and means that not only can you modify settings, but also fully update the BIOS by erasing it and rewriting it in a process known as *flashing*.

The complementary metal-oxide semiconductor (CMOS) stores the contents of the BIOS's findings. For example, the type and speed of the processor, capacity of the hard drive, and current time and date. It uses little power, which makes it a good choice for storing these settings. When the computer is on, the CMOS chip is powered by the power supply. However, CMOS by nature is volatile, so if it is not receiving power, it loses its stored contents.

Lithium battery to the rescue! The lithium battery powers the CMOS when the computer is shut off. The most-common battery used on today's motherboards is the CR2032, a nickel-sized battery that snaps into the motherboard and has a shelf life of anywhere from 2 years to 10 years depending on usage. The more you leave the computer on, the longer the battery lasts. The lithium battery is sometimes referred to simply as the CMOS battery. It is most commonly found in desktop and tower computers.

The POST

The power-on self-test (POST) is the first step in bootstrapping. The POST is essentially a piece of code that the BIOS runs to find out what type of processor is on the motherboard and verifies the amount of RAM. It also identifies buses on the motherboard, and other devices, and identifies what devices are available for booting.

The BIOS indicates any system problems that the POST finds by either on-screen display codes or beep codes. For example, a displayed 301 Error would most likely be a keyboard issue. Or one beep might indicate a memory error. This all depends on the type of BIOS used. The most common vendors of BIOS are American Megatrends (AMI) and Phoenix Technologies. Your motherboard should come with documentation about any possible BIOS error codes. If not, the documentation can usually be downloaded from the manufacturer's website; you just need to know the model number of the board. In the case of a proprietary computer (Dell, HP, and such), you need the model number of the computer to download any necessary documentation from its website.

But what happens if the display is blank? You might see repetitive flashing lights on the keyboard that indicate a hardware error, or there might be other more subtle indications of a problem. But to really analyze an issue when there is a blank display, use a POST adapter card. Insert one of these into an adapter card slot, and it can read the system while it is booting. It usually has a two-digit hexadecimal display. If the display shows 00 or FF after the system finishes booting, everything is probably okay. However any other number would indicate a problem that can be cross-referenced in the accompanying booklet, disc, or online documentation.

Accessing and Configuring the BIOS

Accessing the BIOS must be done before the operating system boots. This can be accomplished by pressing a key on the keyboard. It can be F1, F2, F10, DEL, and so on depending on the manufacturer and type of system. Usually, the correct key displays on the bottom of the screen when you first start the computer. If there is only a splash screen, you can press Esc to remove it, and hopefully the BIOS key displays. When you press the appropriate key, the system enters the BIOS Setup Utility, sometimes also referred to as CMOS, or just Setup, and displays a screen, as shown in Figure 2.9.

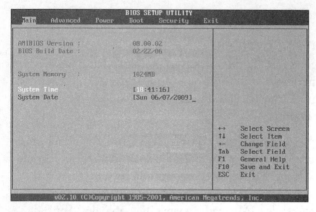

FIGURE 2.9   The BIOS Setup Utility

From here you can modify many things, several of which are important for
the exam:

▶ **Time and Date:** These are normally set on the main screen. By default,
operating systems retain their time and date from this, unless they synchronize to a time server.

▶ **Boot Device Priority:** Also known as BIOS boot order, this setting
enables you to select which media will be booted: hard drive, CD-ROM,
floppy, USB, and such. Usually, this should be set to hard drive first. But
if you install an operating system (OS) from a disc, you would want to
configure this as CD-ROM or DVD-ROM first. For a secure and trou-
ble-free system, it is recommended that you set this to hard drive first,
as shown in Figure 2.10. If the system is set to CD-ROM first, and there
is a disc in the drive, it could cause Windows to fail to load properly.

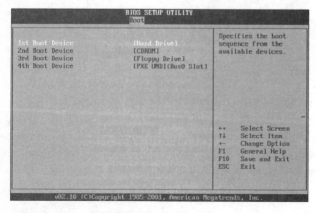

FIGURE 2.10   BIOS Boot Order

ExamAlert

If you boot a PC and see a black screen with a white blinking underscore on the top left, the issue could be the boot order.

▶ **Passwords:** Two passwords are available on most BIOS: User and Supervisor. The User password (also known as a power-on password) authenticates a user before it enables the operating system to boot. The Supervisor password authenticates a user to the BIOS Setup Utility itself. For a secure system, enter a strong Supervisor password.

▶ **Power Management:** This enables you to select if power management is running and which type is used. The older Advanced Power Management (APM) enables the OS to work with the BIOS to achieve power management. This has been supplanted by the Advanced Configuration and Power Interface (ACPI) enabling the OS to take over full control of power management.

▶ **Wake-On-LAN (WOL):** This is a tool that enables you to wake up the computer remotely by sending data to it through the network adapter.

▶ **Monitoring:** Several items can be monitored in the BIOS, for example, processor temperature. An acceptable operating range is between 60 and 75 degrees Celsius (140 to 167 degrees Fahrenheit). Thresholds can be set to increase or decrease the maximum operating temperature of the processor before automatic system shutdown. Processor fan and case fan speeds can also be monitored and changed if need be. For example, if the processor keeps tripping the temperature threshold, you should consider increasing the fan speed. Voltage can also be monitored; though this shouldn't cause a problem (unless possibly if the computer has been overclocked.) Finally, some motherboards can detect if the computer case has been opened; this is known as intrusion detection. The BIOS can notify you of this and log it for future reference.

You can also enable or disable USB ports and legacy floppy devices. Plus, you can load BIOS defaults if you configure something in the BIOS that stops the system from booting.

Did you ever know someone who forgot a password? Technicians remember their password like the back of their hand, but many users don't fare quite as well. And for some reason users love to set supervisory passwords in the BIOS—and then forget them. To fix this you need to turn off the computer, disconnect it, open it, and remove the lithium battery. By doing so, the CMOS forgets what it stored. The time and date probably revert to Jan. 1, 2000, or some other date in the past, and all passwords will be erased. In some cases you may also need to modify the BIOS Configuration Jumper Block solely, or in addition to removing the battery. Sometimes referred to as the CMOS jumper, this is a 3-pin jumper, usually near the lithium battery, that has three possibilities: Normal, Configuration, and Recovery. If necessary, move the jumper shunt from pins 1 and 2 (Normal) to pins 2 and 3 (Configuration); at that point you can access the BIOS without a password. Recovery mode is normally accomplished by removing the jumper altogether. A word to the wise; be ready for improperly labeled motherboards for this jumper configuration block. So you know, motherboards are usually shipped in the Normal state.

Flashing the BIOS

Flashing the BIOS is the term given to the process of erasing the BIOS firmware and rewriting it with a new version of the BIOS. It is sometimes referred to as *updating* the BIOS. It is important to check for updates to the BIOS, just like you would update an OS. However, only flash the BIOS if your system *needs* it; for example, if your motherboard "sees" the processor but doesn't know specifically what type it is or at what speed it runs. Motherboard manufacturers release these updates quite often, and their description can tell you exactly what they fix. If you build a new computer, you should check for a BIOS update before you even install an OS. BIOS updates close up security holes, identify new devices or identify them better, and are sometimes released simply to fix some incorrect code. There are several ways to update the BIOS, but generally you would either do it from within Windows or by using some kind of bootable media (CD-ROM, USB flash drive, floppy) to boot the system and rewrite the BIOS. Because the process varies from motherboard to motherboard, the following lists a few of the most common steps:

1. **Identify what BIOS you are running:** To do this, access the BIOS and check the main menu. There is usually some kind of code that you can check against the latest BIOS download on the manufacturer's website. If it is the same code, there is no need to update the BIOS. BIOS updates are cumulative, so you need to download and install only the newest version.

2. **Download the BIOS from the web:** This is usually downloaded in .EXE format. There is normally an instruction file you can download as well, explaining exactly how to flash the BIOS step by step.

3. **Select your method of BIOS updating:** For example, an Express BIOS Update would be done within Windows; simply download the file and double-click it to begin the process. Or a flash update could be done from a bootable USB device or bootable floppy disk. In this case there is usually a .EXE file that needs to be extracted to the bootable media and a .BAT file that will make it bootable. You could also create your own bootable media if you have the wherewithal and a lot of time on your hands. With some manufacturers you can download an ISO image to be burned to a CD-ROM. After this is done, boot the computer with the CD and continue to the BIOS update. If a BIOS update were interrupted for some reason or did not complete properly, it might be necessary to recover the BIOS. To do this you need the recovery file and might need to remove the BIOS configuration jumper from the motherboard.

4. **Flash the BIOS:** Run the BIOS flash update from the appropriate media. If the media is a floppy disk or CD-ROM, restart the computer and boot to that media. Otherwise, run the BIOS update from within Windows. Some BIOS programs are nonresponsive but be careful; they are probably updating the BIOS even though it might look like nothing is happening. Let the system do it's "thing" for several minutes. *Do not* run a BIOS update during a lightning storm. Never turn off the computer during a BIOS update, and if you use a laptop, make sure that it is plugged in before starting the update.

ExamAlert

Know how to flash the BIOS for the exam!

Cram Quiz

Answer these questions. The answers follow the last question. If you cannot answer these questions correctly, consider reading this section again until you can.

220-801 Questions

1. Which component supplies power to the CMOS when the computer is off?

   ○ **A.** Lithium battery

   ○ **B.** POST

   ○ **C.** Power supply

   ○ **D.** BIOS

2. To implement a secure boot process, which device should be listed first in the Boot Device Priority screen?

   ○ **A.** Floppy drive

   ○ **B.** CD-ROM

   ○ **C.** USB

   ○ **D.** Hard drive

3. What is the term for how the BIOS readies the computer for and initiates the booting of the operating system?

   ○ **A.** Bootlegging

   ○ **B.** Booting

   ○ **C.** Bootstrapping

   ○ **D.** POST

4. Which of the following is used by the CPU to communicate with system memory?

   ○ **A.** Southbridge

   ○ **B.** BIOS

   ○ **C.** Northbridge

   ○ **D.** PCIe

220-802 Questions

5. How can you reset a forgotten BIOS supervisory password?

   ○ **A.** Access the BIOS by pressing F2.

   ○ **B.** Remove the battery.

   ○ **C.** Extract the .EXE contents to a floppy.

   ○ **D.** Remove the P1 connector.

6. You just rebooted a PC and it displays a black screen with a white blinking underscore on the top left. What is the most likely problem?

   ○ **A.** BIOS needs to be flashed.

   ○ **B.** Recovery Console is running.

   ○ **C.** PC is in Safe Mode.

   ○ **D.** Incorrect boot order.

CramQuiz

Cram Quiz Answers

220-801 Answers

1. **A.** The lithium battery supplies power to the CMOS when the computer is off. This is because the CMOS is volatile and would otherwise lose the stored settings when the computer is turned off.

2. **D.** To ensure that other users cannot boot the computer from removable media, set the first device in the Boot Device Priority screen to hard drive.

3. **C.** Bootstrapping is accomplished by the BIOS. It is defined as one system readying the computer and leading to another larger system.

4. **C.** The northbridge is used by the CPU to communicate with system memory (RAM). Remember that on newer Intel motherboards, the northbridge functionality is built into the CPU.

220-802 Answers

5. **B.** Removing the battery (and possibly moving the BIOS configuration jumper) resets the BIOS passwords. You might also need to configure the BIOS configuration jumper.

6. **D.** If you see a black screen with a white blinking underscore, there is a good chance that the BIOS boot order is incorrect.

Installing and Troubleshooting Motherboards

Installing Motherboards

You might ask, "Haven't we talked enough about motherboards?" Not quite. But installing them is easy when you know how, so this section shouldn't take too long. We'll break it down into some simple steps:

1. **Select a motherboard**: If you build a new computer, it should be designed with a compatible case and processor in mind. Also, make sure that it has the expansion ports that you need for audio, video, and so on, and verify that it has the necessary I/O ports. Also, give a thought to the applications you will use and if they require or prefer a specific chipset. If you replace a motherboard, make sure that it is compatible with the system you put it in and that all the components can connect to it. If it is a proprietary computer (HP, Dell, and such), you won't have many choices on motherboards; see the computer manufacturer's website for details.

2. **Employ ESD prevention methods:** Use an antistatic strap and mat. And before touching the motherboard, place both hands on an unpainted portion of the case chassis. For more information on ESD preventative measures, see Chapter 18, "Safety, Professionalism, and Procedures."

3. **Ready the case:** Most cases come with brass standoffs that are already screwed directly into the case. Additional standoffs usually accompany the motherboard. Line up the motherboard's predrilled holes with the standoffs and eye it out. Add more standoffs as necessary so that the motherboard is supported properly. Some motherboards come with additional rubber standoffs that provide additional support and protection from ESD.

4. **Install the motherboard:** Carefully place the motherboard into the case so that the holes meet and line up with the brass standoffs. Secure the motherboard by screwing it in wherever there is a standoff. You might prefer to install the processor and RAM first before installing the motherboard. This has advantages and disadvantages. One advantage is that you wouldn't have to install them while the motherboard is within the case, decreasing the chances of bending the motherboard. One disadvantage is that the processor and RAM are expensive components that can be easily damaged when installing other components. Of course, in some cases (pun intended), you have no choice in the matter, but in general, if you worry about damaging the processor and RAM, install them last.

5. **Connect cables:** Now it's time to connect the 24-pin power cable from the power supply to the motherboard. This connector is tabbed; make sure that the tabs match up. When connected it should lock into place. Case connectors can be fitted to the motherboard as well. These wires start at the inside front of the case and have thin 2, 3, or 4-pin plugs on the other end. They are labeled POWER LED, POWER SW (for power switch), HDD LED, and so on. These plugs connect to items such as the power button, reset button, and LED lights. Connect them to the corresponding ports on the edge of the motherboard closest to the front of the case. There might also be front panel ports (USB, audio), external SATA connectors, and more that need to be connected from the case to the motherboard. You can usually find documentation for all these connections with the motherboard. If not, download the technical PDF from the motherboard manufacturer's website.

6. **Install or re-install components:** Now it's time to install the rest of the components such as the hard drives, optical drives, and any other components. Installation of these additional components is covered in their corresponding chapters.

7. **Test the installation:** Finally, after you install anything, test it! Make sure it works. Boot the computer and access the BIOS. Tool around awhile until you are satisfied the motherboard is functional. If there is an issue, troubleshoot the problem using the techniques discussed in the next section.

Troubleshooting Motherboards

That time has come. Remember the "big four" mentioned in Chapter 1, "Introduction to Troubleshooting." The motherboard is one of them. Here's a common issue: If you boot the computer and don't get anything on the display, and you are sure that power is not an issue and that the computer is actually booting, you should check all connections. Chances are, it isn't the motherboard. A loose video card can cause these types of issues; make sure it is firmly pressed into its slot. Check the processor, RAM, and any connectors and other adapter cards in an attempt to rule out the motherboard as the culprit. You see, it is rare that the motherboard fails, and checking these connections doesn't take long; however, removing the motherboard can be time-consuming. If you suspect a particular component has failed, for example the video card, attempt to swap out the video card with a known good device. Do the same with the RAM, even the processor. Finally, if you rule out the rest of the devices, continue troubleshooting the motherboard. Use a POST card if necessary, and if worst comes to worst, swap the motherboard with a known good one.

Let's run through a quick troubleshooting scenario using the CompTIA six-step troubleshooting methodology outlined in Chapter 1.

Motherboard Issue

In this scenario you are a PC technician working for the PC repair department of an electronics store. You are given a PC that supposedly reverts back to 12:00 AM, January 1, 2000, every time it starts. Troubleshoot!

1. **Identify the problem:** While viewing the work order, you see some of the customer comments: "PC worked fine until a few days ago. Now, every time it starts, it shows the date as Jan. 1, 2000. After changing the time and date in Windows, it reverts back to Jan 1, 2000 when restarted. Service pack 2 must have messed the computer up; I had updated to service pack 2 and that is when the problem started. Now my Outlook calendar and meetings are not synchronized to my employees' Outlook! Please fix right away!"

   A co-worker tells you the motherboard should be replaced, and your manager just wants the job done as quickly as possible.

   Remember to respect the user/customer, but don't always take the user's word for it. Test the computer yourself; you might find something entirely different is causing the problem, and you can save yourself a lot of time. Also, don't rush, regardless of how fast the manager wants the work done. When you rush, you risk the chance of overlooking the obvious, simple solution.

   So, while examining the computer you notice it runs Windows and that Windows does indeed revert to Jan 1, 2000, even after you reconfigured the Date and Time Properties window. Otherwise, the computer seems to work fine, aside from Outlook synchronization issues, which is understandable. It doesn't display anything peculiar or make any strange sounds. And service pack 2 seems to have been installed correctly and is operating properly without any errors in the Event Viewer.

2. **Establish a theory of probable cause (question the obvious):** Again, look for the obvious or most probable cause. Remembering your training you surmise that the lithium battery in the motherboard has discharged causing the CMOS to lose its contents. If this happens, the BIOS has no recourse but to revert back to its earliest known time, in this case January 1, 2000. It sounds logical, so you move onto the next step.

3. **Test the theory to determine cause:** To test this theory, you decide to restart the computer and access the BIOS. When in the BIOS, you change the time to the current time and date, and then you save the settings and shut down the computer. After turning it back on, you access the BIOS again and note that the time has once again reverted back to

Jan. 1, 2000. You never accessed Windows in this procedure, so it would seem that the theory is correct. Now, if the time and date you had configured remained in the BIOS without reverting, your theory would probably be incorrect, and you would need to go back to step 2 to formulate a new theory. Although you try to establish and test theories without opening the PC, you can also test the lithium battery with a multimeter. The CR2032 lithium battery has a nominal voltage of 3.0 V. If it measures below 2.0 volts, you know the battery has discharged to such a state that it cannot power the CMOS any longer.

4. **Establish a plan of action to resolve the problem and implement the solution:** Your plan of action should be to replace the CR2032 lithium battery with a new one. Implementing this requires you to shut down the PC and unplug it, open the PC, employ ESD prevention methods, and remove the CR2032 battery. This battery is easy to spot; it is shiny and is about the size of a nickel. They are usually labeled as a CR2032 as well. Removing it entails pushing on a tab and gently prying the battery out. Use something nonmetallic to do this. Then, find or requisition a new lithium battery. Next, test the new battery with your trusty multimeter to make sure it is within proper voltage range (the closer to 3.0 volts the better). Remember that batteries slowly discharge, even when they sit on the shelf. Finally, install the battery into the motherboard.

5. **Verify full system functionality and if applicable implement preventative measures:** Now you need to make sure it works, so you boot the PC and access the BIOS. From there you update the time and date, save the settings to the BIOS, and shut down the computer. Next, boot the system again, and again access the BIOS. At this point you verify that the time and date have not reverted back to Jan. 1, 2000. If the time is correct, boot to Windows. Check the time in Windows after several "full cycles" (shutting the computer off and turning it back on) and warm boots to ensure that it works properly. As a preventative measure, you might want to recommend that the user synchronize Windows to a time server. This can be done by opening the Date and Time Properties window, selecting the Internet Time tab, and configuring the system to automatically synchronize with an Internet time server. (Newer versions of Windows are set this way by default.) This way, even if the lithium battery fails, Windows resynchronizes to the time server every time it boots. This also creates a more consistent meeting time for the user and other employees when meetings are set in Outlook.

6. **Document findings, actions, and outcomes:** Document according to your company's policies. Complete the work order and any other paperwork necessary. Additional documentation might be required in a trouble-ticketing software program—and make a mental note of who the person was that said to replace the motherboard; be careful of that person's suggestions in the future!

Again, it is uncommon to see a motherboard fail, but if it does, it can be because of a few different things. Let's discuss several of these now.

First and probably the most common of these rarities are BIOS issues. Remember that you might need to flash the BIOS to the latest version. One example is when I built a PC for a friend several years back. He had picked up an AMD 1.8 GHz processor and compatible motherboard. The motherboard specifically stated that it could run 1.0 GHz to 1.8 GHz processors. But when I booted the system, the BIOS recognized an AMD processor but no specific speed. After running some diagnostic software, I found that the computer was rated at 100 MHz processing speed. Not what my friend wanted! However, there were no BIOS updates on the manufacturer's website concerning this problem. And updating to the latest BIOS did not fix the problem. E-mailing the motherboard manufacturer was the only way to fix this issue, which it was not aware of at the time because the AMD processor was so new. After a few days, a new BIOS update was released, and after flashing the system, the BIOS quickly identified the processor as 1.8 GHz. On a separate note, you might encounter a PC that instead of booting normally, accesses the BIOS instead. A faulty CMOS battery is the most common culprit of this. Change out the battery, and the system should boot normally.

Second are ESD and other electrical issues. These might present themselves intermittently. If you find some intermittent issues, for example the computer reboots out of nowhere, or you receive random Blue Screens of Death, ESD could be the culprit. Or a surge could cause the problem. A particular wire, circuit, or capacitor on the motherboard could have been damaged. Document when failures occur. Swap out the motherboard with a known good one to see if the issue happens again when running through the same processes. If the issue doesn't recur, chances are the original motherboard is headed for the bit bucket. To give an example of this, let me bring you back in time, 4 years ago, to a customer of mine. In my first visit, I recommended that all computers connect to surge protectors—many were connected directly to AC outlets with no protection. During my second visit, I was presented with a computer (still not surge-protected) that crashed every time a user attempted to log on to the domain. BAM! Blue screen of death. However, he could log on locally with no problems! The Event Viewer in Windows was trying to

blame the hardware, and after remembering the bad lightning storms we had the weekend before, I decided to use a POST tester on the motherboard. Sure enough, one of the circuits on the motherboard that led to the integrated network adapter had failed. However, in this case, I changed the I/O and memory address settings for the network adapter, and the problem was fixed. Other computers don't fare so well, and electrical damage can go right through the power supply to the motherboard, disabling it permanently.

Third are component failures. It is possible that a single component of the motherboard, say the SATA controller, can fail, but the rest of the motherboard works fine. This can also be verified with a POST card tester. To fix this, a separate PCI or PCIe SATA controller card can be purchased. Then, you connect the hard drives to the new controller and disable the original SATA controller in the BIOS. Be wary though; sometimes these add-on cards can be pricey—perhaps more pricey than a new motherboard.

And last are manufacturing defects. Printed circuit boards (PCBs) are mass produced at high speed. Defects are uncommon but can occur due to mechanical problems in the machinery or due to engineering error. If you suspect a manufacturing defect, you need to replace the motherboard.

Cram Quiz

Answer these questions. The answers follow the last question. If you cannot answer these questions correctly, consider reading this section again until you can.

220-801 Questions

1. Before installing a motherboard, what should you do? (Select the best answer.)

   - ○ **A.** Install the processor.
   - ○ **B.** Verify that it is compatible with the case.
   - ○ **C.** Employ ESD prevention methods.
   - ○ **D.** Test the motherboard with a multimeter.

220-802 Questions

2. Which of the following are possible reasons for motherboard failure? (Select all that apply.)

   - ○ **A.** Power surge
   - ○ **B.** Manufacturer defect
   - ○ **C.** CD-ROM failure
   - ○ **D.** Incorrect USB device

3. How can you tell if a lithium battery has been discharged? (Select the best answer.)

   ○ **A.** Use a power supply tester.

   ○ **B.** Check within Windows.

   ○ **C.** Use a multimeter.

   ○ **D.** Plug it into another motherboard.

4. A PC reboots without any warning. You ruled out any chance of viruses. When you look at the motherboard, you see that some of the capacitors appear distended and out of shape. What should you do?

   ○ **A.** Replace the motherboard.

   ○ **B.** Replace the hard drive.

   ○ **C.** Remove and replace the capacitors.

   ○ **D.** Reconfigure the BIOS.

5. A computer you are troubleshooting won't boot properly. When you power on the computer, the video display is blank, and you hear a series of beeps. What should you do?

   ○ **A.** Check power supply connections.

   ○ **B.** Consult the vendor documentation for the motherboard.

   ○ **C.** Remove all memory and replace it.

   ○ **D.** Unplug the speakers because they are causing a conflict.

Cram Quiz Answers

220-801 Answers

1. **C.** Always employ ESD prevention methods before working with any components inside the computer. Although A and B are correct, they are not the best answers.

220-802 Answers

2. **A and B.** Power surges and manufacturing defects are possible reasons for motherboard failure. If a CD-ROM fails, it should not affect the motherboard, and any USB device can connect to a USB port (if it has the right connector). There isn't actually an "incorrect" USB device.

3. **C.** Although there might be a Windows application that monitors the battery, the surefire way is to test the voltage of the lithium battery with a multimeter.

4. **A.** You should replace the motherboard if it is damaged. It would be much too time-consuming to even attempt replacing the capacitors, and probably not cost-effective for your company.

5. **B.** You should check the BIOS version and consult the documentation that accompanies the motherboard. You might need to go online for this information. You can also try using a POST card tester to discern the problem.

CHAPTER 3

The CPU

This chapter covers the following A+ exam topics:

▶ CPU 101

▶ Installing and Troubleshooting CPUs

You can find a master list of A+ exam topics in the "Introduction."

This chapter covers CompTIA A+ 220-801 objective 1.6, and CompTIA A+ 220-802 objective 4.2.

The central processing unit, or CPU, is quite often referred to as the "brain" of the computer. Today's CPUs are like superbrains! A typical CPU today runs at 2 to 3 GHz or higher, uses two or more cores, and some can easily process 100 billion operations per second. That's a good deal more than you would have seen just 5 years ago. Some mornings I have trouble processing the thought: *Need coffee!* Of course we know that the human brain is much more sophisticated and functional than a CPU, but the CPU wins out when it comes to sheer calculating power.

You might hear the CPU referred to as a microprocessor, which technically it is. It's a much smaller version of the processors that were used 50 years ago. And although microprocessor might be a more accurate term, it has become more acceptable to refer to it as CPU, which this chapter does. However, you also see CPU manufacturers such as Intel refer to them as processors, so for all intents and purposes, the three terms mean the same thing. A computer has other processors used by video cards and elsewhere, but know that the CPU is the main processor.

To start, this chapter discusses some CPU technologies and cooling methods. Afterward, the chapter demonstrates how to install and troubleshoot the CPU.

CPU 101

The CPU is often the most-expensive component in the computer; it's also one of the, if not *the*, most important. The CPU's main function is to execute instructions or programs. Its speed, or *clock rate*, is measured in Hertz. For example, at 3.1 GHz, a CPU operates at 3.1 billion cycles per second; we speak more to this concept in a moment. But although the speed of the CPU might be important, other factors should also play into your decision when choosing a CPU, including the chipset on the motherboard, *CPU technology*, and cooling. Chapter 2, "Motherboards," covers chipsets, but let's go ahead and talk about' the various CPU technologies and brands of CPUs now.

CPU Technology

CPU technology is a key factor when considering a CPU. It all comes back to the motherboard; the CPU must be compatible with the motherboard in a number of ways. It is important to think about the speed (clock rate) of the CPU you want to use and whether that speed can be supported by the motherboard, and if the CPU fits in the motherboard's socket. Also, a decision must be made as to whether to use a 64-bit or 32-bit CPU, and choose either a multicore or single-core CPU; this will be based off the motherboard and the type of operating system you plan to install, as well as whether this is a new install or an upgrade of an older computer. Getting deeper into the technical side of the CPU, you might want to know the amount of cache included with the CPU, and the amount of power it requires.

Clock Rate

The *clock rate* is the frequency (or speed) of a component. It is rated in cycles per second and measured in hertz (Hz). For all practical purposes, the term clock rate is the same as the more commonly used term: *clock speed*.

Components are sold to consumers with a *maximum* clock rate, but they don't always run at that maximum number. To explain, let me use a car analogy. The CPU is often called the "engine" of the computer, like a car engine. Well, your car's speedometer might go up to 120 MPH, but you'll probably never drive at that maximum—for a variety of reasons! When it comes to CPUs, the stated clock rate is the *maximum* clock rate, and the CPU usually runs at a speed less than that. In fact, it can run at any speed below the maximum; though there are only several plateaus that it will usually hover around.

Now, we're all familiar with speeds such as 2.4 GHz, 3.0 GHz, or 3.2 GHz. But what is the basis of these speeds? Speed can be broken down into three categories that are interrelated:

▶ **Motherboard bus speed:** The base clock of the motherboard, often referred to simply as "*bus speed*". This is generated by a quartz oscillating crystal soldered directly to the motherboard. For example, the base clock on the DP67DE motherboard used in *Media PC* in Chapter 2 is 100 MHz. The base clock of the DP35DP motherboard from *Tower PC*, though an older motherboard, is 333 MHz.

▶ **External clock speed:** Newer Intel and AMD-based motherboards don't use this measurement anymore. But for older boards such as the DP35DP, this is the frequency of the front side bus (FSB), which connects the CPU to the northbridge on the motherboard. This is usually a variable and depends on the CPU you install. In addition, it is determined from the base clock of the motherboard. For example, the DP35DP's maximum external clock (or FSB) is 1333 MHz. Simply put, this means that it can transfer four times the amount of data per cycle as compared to the original base clock speed. 333 MHz × 4 = 1,333 MHz. Newer motherboards are less concerned with frequency and more concerned with data transfer rate. For example, the Intel Direct Media Interconnection (DMI) version 2, which replaced the FSB, runs at 20 Gb/s. But you should still understand FSB speeds for the exam, and you will see systems in the field for a while that use this technology.

▶ **Internal clock speed:** This is the internal frequency of the CPU and is the well-known number that CPUs are associated with. For the DP67DE motherboard I purchased the Intel Core i5-2400, which is rated at 3.1 GHz maximum. The CPU uses an internal multiplier based off the motherboard base clock. The multiplier for this particular CPU is 31. The math is as follows: base clock × multiplier = internal clock speed. In our example, that would be 100 MHz × 31 = 3.1 GHz. This motherboard can support faster and slower CPUs from a variety of groups, all the way from 1.6 GHz Celerons to 3.5 GHz Core I7-2700K CPUs. At 3.5 GHz, the default multiplier would be 35. My *Tower PC* motherboard, the DP35DP, uses the Intel Q8400 CPU that is rated at 2.66 GHz. The multiplier for this CPU is 8. So, 333 MHz × 8 = 2.66 GHz. This motherboard has a higher base clock in comparison to the DP67DE, but the multiplier is much less. Effectively, this means that the newer DP67DE motherboard runs more efficiently and at its core runs at a lower voltage. Some motherboards allow for overclocking, which enables the user to increase the multiplier within the BIOS, thereby increasing the internal clock speed of the CPU. The DP67DE has a basic example of this that Intel calls "Turbo Boost" technology; it increases the multiplier from 31 to as high as 34, thereby increasing the CPU speed from 3.1 GHz to 3.4 GHz maximum. It is also possible on many motherboards to increase the base clock, for example from 100 MHz to as much as 300 MHz. This not only increases the speed of the CPU, but also increases the speed of RAM, which Chapter 4, "RAM," discusses. Either one of these methods of overclocking increases the voltage, creates more heat, and could possibly cause damage to the system, analogous to blowing the engine of a car when attempting to run a 10-second 1/4 mile. So approach overclocking with extreme caution!

> **ExamAlert**
>
> For today's CPUs, two of the most commonly used terms are *bus speed*, the base clock of the motherboard; and *clock speed*, the frequency of the CPU. They might not be completely accurate technically, but you will see and hear them often and could see them on the exam as well.

32-Bit Versus 64-Bit

The bulk of today's CPUs are 64-bit; it's a type of CPU architecture that incorporates registers that are 64 bits wide. These registers, or temporary storage areas, allow the CPU to work with and process 64-bit data types and provide support for address space in the terabytes. 64-bit CPUs have been available for PCs since 2003. Examples of 64-bit CPUs include the AMD FX and Intel Core CPUs.

The predecessor to the 64-bit CPU was the 32-bit CPU. Intel started developing well-known 32-bit CPUs as early as 1985 with the 386DX CPU (which ran at a whopping 33 MHz!), and AMD did likewise in 1991 with the Am386. A 32-bit CPU can't support nearly as much address space as a 64-bit CPU; 32-bit is limited to 4 GB. Most editions of Windows are available in both 32-bit and 64-bit versions.

You still see 32-bit CPU technologies in the field; however, due to applications' ever-increasing need for resources, these older CPUs continue to diminish, whereas 64-bit technologies (such as the Core i5) will become more prevalent.

You might hear of the terms x86 and x64. x86 refers to older CPU names that ended in an 86—for example, the 80386 (shortened to just 386), 486, or 586 CPU and so on. Generally, when people use the term x86, they refer to 32-bit CPUs that enable 4 GB of address space. x64 (or x86-64) refers to newer 64-bit CPUs that are a superset of the x86 architecture. This technology has a wider data path to handle program execution; it can run 64-bit software *and* 32-bit software, and can address a default maximum of 256 terabytes (TB) of RAM. This can optionally be extended to 4 petabytes (PB), but that extension isn't currently used. As of the writing of this book, only a true supercomputer would need more than 256 TB of RAM. The real limitation right now is the operating system. For example, Windows XP 64-bit and Vista 64-bit are "limited" to 128 GB max pending on the version. Some Windows 7 64-bit versions can go as high as 192 GB. To put this all in perspective, the DP67DE motherboard supports only a maximum of 32 GB of RAM. This is far less than Windows 7 can handle, which in itself is just a tiny slice of what a 64-bit CPU can address.

Windows 7, Vista, and XP come in 64-bit and 32-bit versions so that users from both generations of computers can run the software efficiently.

Sockets

The *socket* is the electrical interface between the CPU and the motherboard. It attaches directly to the motherboard and houses the CPU. It also physically supports the CPU and heat sink and enables for easy replacement of the CPU.

The socket is either made of plastic or metal, with metal contacts for connectivity to each of the pins/lands of the CPU. A metal lever (retaining arm) locks the CPU in place. Figure 3.1 shows an example of an unlocked LGA1155 socket on the DP67DE motherboard. Figure 3.2 shows an older LGA775 socket on the DP35DP motherboard.

FIGURE 3.1 **An unlocked LGA1155 socket**

FIGURE 3.2   **An unlocked LGA775 socket**

Historically the socket has been considered a ZIF, short for zero insertion force. This means that the CPU should connect easily into the socket, with no pressure or force involved during the installation. Installing the CPU into these ZIF sockets is kind of like moving a planchette over a Ouija board until the CPU falls into place! Today's newer Land Grid Array (LGA) sockets require you to place the CPU into the socket housing, but it still doesn't require much force at all. The socket will have many pin inserts, or lands (on newer sockets), for the CPU to connect to. Pin 1 can be found in one of the corners and can be identified by either: a white corner drawn on the mother-board (refer to Figure 3.1), or one or more missing pins or pinholes (refer to Figure 3.2.) This helps you to orient the CPU, which also has the missing pin(s), or an arrow, in the corresponding corner. Here are two types of sockets you should know for the exam:

▶ **PGA:** Pin Grid Array sockets accept CPUs that have pins covering the majority of their underside. The pins on the CPU are placed in the pin-holes of the socket, and the CPU is locked into place by a retaining arm. PGA has been in use since the late '80s and is still in use on some moth-erboards today. Many AMD CPUs use PGA sockets. Examples of AMD sockets include the 940, AM2, AM2+, AM3, AM3+, and FM1.

▶ **LGA:** Land Grid Array sockets use lands that protrude out and touch the CPU's contact points. This newer type of socket (also known as Socket T) offers better power distribution and less chance to damage the CPU compared to PGA. LGA has been used since the later versions of Pentium 4 and is commonly used today on Intel motherboards. Examples of Intel sockets include the aforementioned 775 and 1155, as well as the 1156, and 1366. Although one numeral less, the 1155 was designed to replace the 1156.

The CPU and socket must be compatible. For example, the DP67DE motherboard used has an LGA1155 socket, which is common but not the only socket that Intel uses on its motherboards. The Core i5-2400 CPU used is designed to fit into the LGA1155 socket, and many other CPUs can fit into this socket as well, but not all. For example, The Intel Core i7 900 series needs to be installed into an LGA1366 socket, which means purchasing a completely different motherboard. Table 3.1 shows various Intel and AMD sockets and the CPUs that can be installed to them.

TABLE 3.1 **Common Sockets and Corresponding CPUs**

Intel Socket	Intel CPUs	AMD Socket	AMD CPUs
LGA775	Core 2 Duo Core 2 Quad Xeon Pentium, Celeron	940	Opteron Athlon 64 FX
LGA1155	Core i7, i5, i3 Xeon Pentium, Celeron	AM2	Athlon 64 X2 Athlon 64
LGA1156	Core i7, i5, i3 Xeon Pentium, Celeron	AM2+	Phenom II Phenom Athlon X2 Athlon 64
LGA1366	Core i7 Xeon	AM3 AM3+ FM1 F (replaced by Socket C32 and G34)	Phenom II Sempron Athlon II FX Llano Opteron

ExamAlert

Know the sockets used with common Intel and AMD CPUs.

CPU Cache

Several types of cache are used in computers, but CPU cache is a special high-speed memory that reduces the time the CPU takes to access data. By using high-speed static RAM (SRAM) and because the cache is often located directly on, or even in the CPU, CPU cache can be faster than accessing information from dynamic RAM (DRAM) sticks. However, it will be limited in storage capacity when compared to DRAM. Cache is divided into levels:

▶ **Level 1:** L1 cache is built into the CPU and gives fast access to *the most frequently* used data. This level cache is the first one accessed by the CPU and is usually found in small amounts. However, it is the fastest cache to be found, offering the lowest latency of any of the types of cache. One of the reasons for this is that it resides within the CPU core. The Core i5-2400 CPU has 4×32 KB of L1 cache; 32 KB for each of its four cores. You can find more information about multicore technology later in this chapter.

▶ **Level 2:** L2 cache is usually built on to the CPU (on-die). It is accessed after L1 cache, and it serves the CPU with less frequently used data in comparison to L1 but still more frequently used than DRAM data. L2 cache feeds the L1 cache, which in turn feeds the CPU. L2 is not as fast as L1 cache but is superior to DRAM sticks. This and L3 take up the majority of the CPU's real estate. The Core i5-2400 CPU used for the build has 256 KB per core, for a total of 1 MB L2 cache.

▶ **Level 3:** L3 cache comes in the largest capacities of the three types of cache and has the most latency; therefore, it is the slowest. If the CPU can't find what it needs in L1, it moves to L2 and finally to L3. Or you could think of it this way: L3 cache feeds L2 cache, which feeds L1 cache, which in turn feeds the CPU with data. If the CPU can't find the data it is seeking, it moves on to the DRAM sticks. L3 cache could be on-die or on-board, but most of today's CPUs have it on-die; however it is shared among the cores of the CPU. The Core i5-2400 has 6 MB of L3 cache.

ExamAlert

Know the difference between L1, L2, and L3 cache for the exam.

Generally, the more cache the better. The less the CPU needs to access DRAM, the faster it can calculate data.

Note

You might hear of L4 cache. This is rare in PCs but is used on more powerful workstation and server computers. Although not accurate, some people may refer to main memory as L4 cache.

Hyper-Threading

Intel's Hyper-Threading (HT) enables a single CPU to accept and calculate two independent sets of instructions simultaneously, simulating two CPUs. The technology was designed so that single CPUs can compete better with true multi-CPU systems but without the cost involved. In an HT environment, only one CPU is present, but the operating system sees two virtual CPUs and divides the workload, or threads, between the two.

Hyperthreading began during the Pentium 4 days but is not used in Intel's Core 2 CPUs. However, in 2009 it made a return with the Core i3, i5, and i7 CPUs.

> **Note**
>
> Don't confuse Hyper-Threading with HyperTransport used by AMD. HyperTransport is a high-speed, low latency, point-to-point link that increases communication speeds between various devices; such as the CPU and the northbridge.

Multicore Technologies

Whereas HT technology simulates multiple CPUs, *multicore* CPUs physically contain two or more actual processor cores, in one CPU package. These newer CPUs can have 2, 4, 6, or even 8 cores, each acting as a single entity, but in some cases sharing the CPU cache. This enables for more-efficient processing of data. Not only is less heat generated, but also a 1.8 GHz dual-core CPU can process more data per second than a 3.6 GHz single-core CPU.

Current examples of multicore CPUs include Intel's Core 2 Duo, Core 2 Quad, Core 2 Extreme, and Core i3, i5, i7; as well as AMD's X2, Phenom, Phenom II, A-Series, and FX CPUs. Today's CPUs combine multicore technology with Hyper-Threading enabling for as many as 12 or 16 simultaneous threads in a single CPU package. It just goes on and on!

> **ExamAlert**
>
> Know the differences between Hyper-Threading and multicore technologies for the exam. Hyper-Threading enables a single core CPU to calculate two instruction sets simultaneously, whereas multicore CPUs calculate two or more instruction sets simultaneously, one instruction set per core.

Power Consumption

Power consumption of CPUs is normally rated in watts. For example, the Core i5-2400 is rated as a 95 watt-hour CPU. This rating is known as *thermal design power (TDP)*, and it signifies the maximum power that the computer's cooling system needs to dissipate heat generated by the CPU. This doesn't mean that it always uses that much power, but it should play into your decision when planning what power supply to use and what kind of cooling system. For more information on power supplies, see Chapter 5, "Power." One hundred watts, or thereabouts, is a common amount for multi-core CPUs. They are more efficient than their predecessor single-core CPUs, that could use as much as 215 watts.

Because we are talking electricity, another important factor is voltage. CPUs are associated with a voltage range; for example, the Core i5-2400 runs at about 1 V by default but can go higher (to about 1.3 V max). It is important to monitor the voltage that is received by the CPU; you can do this in the BIOS, or better yet with applications within Windows. If the CPU goes beyond the specified voltage range for any extended length of time, it *will* damage the CPU. This becomes especially important for overclockers.

Brands of CPUs

For the average user, it doesn't matter too much which CPU you go with. However, for the developer, gamer, video editor, or musician, it can make or break your computer's performance. Although the CompTIA A+ objectives cover only Intel and AMD (Advanced Micro Devices), you should be aware that there are others in the market. Intel and AMD dominate the PC and laptop arena, but other companies such as VIA have made great inroads into niche markets and are moving deeper into the laptop/mobile markets as well.

CPU manufacturers use the make/model system. For example, the CPU used in *Media PC* is the Intel (make) Core i5-2400 (model). An example of an AMD CPU is the AMD (make) FX 8-Core Processor Black Edition (model).

Intel and AMD are both good companies that make quality products, which leads to great competition. Which is better? In all honestly, it varies and depends on how you use the CPU. You can find advocates for both (albeit subjective advocates), and the scales are constantly tipping back and forth. On any given day, a specific Intel CPU might outperform AMD, and 3 months later, a different AMD CPU can outperform an Intel. It's been that way for many years now. Whatever CPU you choose, make sure that you get a compatible motherboard. A few things to watch for are compatibility with the chipset, socket type, and voltage. However, Intel and AMD have tools on their websites that make it easy for you to find compatible motherboards. Again, the most important compatibility concern is that the CPU is the right one for the user.

Note

Periodically visit the Intel and AMD websites for the latest and greatest CPUs.

Cooling

Now that you know a CPU can effectively use as much electricity as a light bulb, you can understand why it gets so hot. Hundreds of millions of transistors are hammering away in these powerhouses, so you need to keep it and other devices in the computer cool. This is done in a few ways as outlined in this section.

Heat Sinks

The *heat sink* is a block of metal made to sit right on top of the CPU, with metal fins stretching away from the CPU. It uses conduction to direct heat away from the CPU and out through the fins. With passive heat sinks, that's all there is to it; it dissipates heat and requires no moving parts. But with active heat sinks, a fan is attached to the top of the heat sink. The fan plugs into the motherboard for power and usually blows air into the heat sink and toward the CPU helping to dissipate heat through the heat sink fins. More powerful aftermarket CPU fans can be installed as well; just make sure that your power supply can handle the increased power requirements. In today's motherboards the chipset's northbridge and southbridge usually have passive heat sinks, but all new CPUs come with active heat sinks. Traditionally, heat sinks have been made of aluminum, but now you also see copper heat sinks used due to their superior conductivity. An important point about heat sinks: If they come loose, they could adversely affect the performance of the CPU, or cause overheating, which could lead to random reboots. Make double sure that the heat sink is attached securely.

Thermal Compound

The CPU cap and the bottom of the heat sink have slight imperfections in the metal. Surface area is key; the best heat dissipation from CPU to heat sink would occur if the metal faces on each were completely and perfectly straight and flat, but...we live in the real world. So, to fill the tiny gaps and imperfections, thermal compound is used. (This is also known as thermal paste or thermal interface material.) One example of thermal compound is Arctic Silver, available online and at various electronics stores. Now, if this is a new installation, thermal compound is probably not needed. Most new CPUs' heat sinks have factory applied thermal compound that spreads and fills the gaps automatically after you install the heat sink and boot the computer. However, if you need to remove the heat sink for any reason, for example to clean it, or when upgrading, thermal compound should be applied to the CPU cap before re-installing the heat sink, or installing a new heat sink. To do this, first clean any old thermal compound off of the CPU cap and the heat sink with TIM remover such as Akasa TIM-Clean. Then, clean a small, thin plastic card (such as a credit card) with isopropyl alcohol or denatured alcohol. Next, apply a *small* amount of thermal compound to the center of the CPU cap. (This is the top of the installed CPU. You don't want to get any thermal compound on the actual CPU or motherboard.) With the plastic card, spread the thermal compound carefully so that that you end up with a thin layer. Finally, install the heat sink. Try to do so in one shot without jostling the heat sink excessively.

> **ExamAlert**
>
> Reapply thermal compound whenever removing and re-installing a heat sink.

Fans

Case fans are also needed to get the heat out of the case. The power supply has a built-in fan that is adequate for lesser systems. However, multicore systems should have at least one extra exhaust fan mounted to the back of the case, and many cases today come with one for this purpose. An additional fan on the front of the case can be used as an intake of cool air. If you aren't sure which way the fan blows, connect its power cable to the computer but don't mount it; then hold a piece of paper against the fan. The side that pulls the paper toward it should be the side facing the front of the computer when it is mounted. Some cases come with fans that are mounted to the top, which is also ingenious because heat rises. Another thing to consider is where the heat goes after it leaves the case. If the computer is in an enclosed area, the heat has a hard time escaping and might end up back in the computer. Make sure there is air flow around the computer case. I have seen some people point the front of their computer toward an AC vent in the summer and even use special exhaust fans (such as bathroom fans) that butt up against the power supply or secondary exhaust fan on the case and lead hot air directly out of the house, but I digress.

Another possibility is a solution Intel developed called the Chassis Air Guide system, which is essentially a hollow tube that leads from the side of the case to the CPU, guiding cool room ambient air toward the CPU. For more information on the Intel Chassis Air Guide and Intel's Thermally Advantaged Tested Chassis list, see the following link: http://www.intel.com/support/processors/pentium4/sb/cs-008537.htm. Of course, three or four fans can make a decent amount of noise, and they still might not be enough for the most powerful computers, especially the overclocked ones, which leads us to our next option.

Liquid Cooling Systems

Although this method is not as common as the typical CPU/heat sink/fan combination, liquid cooled systems are looked at as more of a viable option than they would have been 5 or 10 years ago. And newer water cooling kits can be used to not only cool the CPU, but also the chipset, hard drives, video cards, and more. A kit usually comes with a CPU water block, pump, radiator/fan, PVC tubing, and of course, coolant. The advantages are improved heat dissipation (if installed properly), higher overclocking rates, and support for the latest, hottest CPUs. Some of the disadvantages include the risk of a leak that can damage components; water pumps becoming faulty over time, air being trapped in the lines, which can cause the system to overheat; and maintenance in the form of inspecting the lines and replacing the coolant every few years. Due to the complexity of the installation, and that most computers do not need this level of heat dissipation, liquid cooling is usually employed by enthusiasts such as gamers. But you might see it in other CPU-intensive systems such as virtualization computers, CAD/CAM systems, and audio/video editing systems. Regardless of cost, installation complexity, and maintenance, liquid cooling systems dissipate heat the most efficiently.

> **ExamAlert**
>
> Of all PC cooling methods, liquid cooling systems dissipate heat the most efficiently.

Cram Quiz

Answer these questions. The answers follow the last question. If you cannot answer these questions correctly, consider reading this section again until you can.

220-801 Questions

1. Which of these is the speed of the CPU?

   ○ **A.** External clock speed

   ○ **B.** DMI transfer rate

   ○ **C.** Internal clock speed

   ○ **D.** Bus speed

2. Which of the following sockets work with an i7 processor?

- ○ **A.** AM2
- ○ **B.** 1366
- ○ **C.** 940
- ○ **D.** 775

3. Which is the fastest cache memory?

- ○ **A.** L2
- ○ **B.** L3
- ○ **C.** HTTP
- ○ **D.** L1

4. What does Hyper-Threading do?

- ○ **A.** It gives you multiple cores within the CPU.
- ○ **B.** It enables for four simultaneous threads to be processed by one CPU core.
- ○ **C.** It enables for two simultaneous threads to be processed by one CPU core.
- ○ **D.** It is a high-speed connection from the CPU to RAM.

5. What seals the tiny gaps between the CPU cap and the heat sink?

- ○ **A.** Thermal jelly
- ○ **B.** Peanut butter and jelly
- ○ **C.** 3-in-1 house oil
- ○ **D.** Thermal compound

6. What is the amount of power required to cool the computer?

- ○ **A.** FSB
- ○ **B.** TDP
- ○ **C.** MMX
- ○ **D.** TDK

7. Which kind of socket incorporates "lands" to ensure connectivity to a CPU?

- ○ **A.** PGA
- ○ **B.** Chipset
- ○ **C.** LGA
- ○ **D.** Copper

8. Which of these is a difference between clock speed and bus speed?

   ○ A. The clock speed is the external speed of the CPU; it is the same as the bus speed.

   ○ B. The clock speed matches the RAM speed.

   ○ C. The clock speed is the internal speed of the CPU.

   ○ D. The bus speed is the speed of the CPU.

220-802 Questions

9. A customer's liquid cooled system is intermittently overheating. What are possible reasons for this? (Select the two best answers.)

   ○ A. Memory is overheating.

   ○ B. Air is trapped in the lines.

   ○ C. Power supply has failed.

   ○ D. Water pump is becoming faulty.

   ○ E. Hard drive is getting too much voltage.

Cram Quiz Answers

220-801 Answers

1. **C.** The internal clock speed is the speed of the CPU, for example 2.4 GHz. The external clock speed is the speed of the FSB (not used in newer motherboards). The DMI data transfer rate is the amount of data transmitted between the CPU and chipset, for example 20 Gbps. The bus speed (base clock) is what the internal clock speed is based off. An example of a base clock system bus speed would be 100 MHz.

2. **B.** Intel's LGA 1366 socket can house a Core i7 CPU. (The 1155 and 1156 could as well.) LGA 775 is an older Intel socket. AM2 and 940 are AMD sockets.

3. **D.** L1 is the fastest cache memory and is located within the CPU's core.

4. **C.** Hyper-Threading allows for an operating system to send *two* simultaneous threads to be processed by a single CPU core. The OS views the CPU core as two virtual processors. Multiple cores would infer multicore technology that means that there are two physical processing cores within the CPU package. The high-speed connection used by AMD from the CPU to RAM is HyperTransport.

5. **D.** Thermal compound is used to seal the small gaps between the CPU and heat sink. Did I ever tell you about the time I found grape jelly inside a customer's computer?

6. **B.** TDP (Thermal design point) is the amount of power required to cool a computer and is linked directly to the amount of heat a CPU creates.

7. **C**. LGA (Land Grid Array) is the type of socket that uses "lands" to connect the socket to the CPU. PGA sockets have pinholes that make for connectivity to the CPU's copper pins.

8. **C**. The clock speed (also known as clock rate) is the internal speed of the CPU, for example the Core i5-2400 runs at 3.1 GHz by default.

220-802 Answers

9. **B** and **D**. The water cooled system could be caused to overheat due to a faulty water pump and air being trapped in the coolant lines. If the memory or hard drive receive too much voltage and over heat they should stop working, but probably won't overheat the entire system. If the power supply fails, the system will shut off.

Installing and Troubleshooting CPUs

This section delves into the hands-on steps involved when installing or troubleshooting a CPU. Installation of CPUs has actually become easier over time, especially with the advent of LGA sockets. However, troubleshooting a CPU can be just as much of a challenge as ever. It's important to note that proper installation of a CPU can reduce the amount of CPU failures and the ensuing amount of CPU troubleshooting.

Installing CPUs

As with most computer components, installing a CPU is easy. But you must be careful, it can be easily damaged. Take it slow, and employ proper safety measures. Let's break it down into some simple steps:

1. **Select a CPU:** If you build a new computer, the CPU needs to be compatible with the motherboard for the type of CPU, speed, socket type, and voltage. If you upgrade a CPU, be sure that it is on the manufacturer's compatible list (which can be found on its website). This might be the motherboard manufacturer, or it could be a proprietary computer manufacturer (such as HP or Dell).

   Power down the PC, disconnect the power cable (or turn off the kill switch), open the PC, and get your boxes of components ready!

2. **Employ ESD prevention methods:** Use an antistatic strap and mat. Remove the CPU and heat sink from the package and place them on an antistatic bag. (One usually comes with the motherboard, but you should have extra ones handy.) Make sure that the CPU's lands (or pins) are facing up to avoid damage. Never touch the lands or pins of a CPU. Before touching any components, place both hands on an unpainted portion of the case chassis. For more information on ESD preventative measures, see Chapter 18, "Safety, Professionalism, and Procedures."

3. **Ready the motherboard:** Some technicians prefer to install the CPU into the motherboard and then install the motherboard into the case. If so, place the motherboard on the antistatic mat. (The mat should be on a hard flat surface.) If you install the CPU directly into an already installed motherboard, clear away any cables or other equipment that might get in the way or could possibly damage the CPU, heat sink, or fan.

4. **Install the CPU:** Be careful with the CPU! It is extremely delicate! Always touch the case chassis before picking up the CPU. Hold it by the edges (the way you would properly hold a CD) and do not touch any pins, lands, or other circuitry on the CPU. If you need to put it down, put it down on an antistatic mat with the pins/lands facing up. Most of the time a CPU will be installed to either an LGA socket or a PGA socket. The following two bullets show how to install a CPU into each type of socket.

> ▶ If you install to an LGA socket, unlock the socket by releasing the retaining arm and swinging it open as far as it can go. Open the socket hatch, unhook it if necessary, and remove any plastic cover. Next, place the CPU into the socket. One corner of the CPU has an arrow that should be oriented with either a white corner or other similar marking on the motherboard, or the socket's missing pin(s); both of these corresponding corners indicate pin 1, as shown in Figures 3.3 and 3.4. Carefully place the CPU into the socket. The lands on the CPU match up with the lands on the socket if it is oriented correctly. Make sure it is flush and flat within the socket. Close the cap, and secure the retaining arm underneath the tab that is connected to the socket, thus securing the CPU. Next, install the heat sink/fan assembly. On LGA sockets these usually have four plastic snap-in anchors. Carefully press each of these into and through the corresponding motherboard holes. Don't use too much force! Then turn each of them one quarter turn to lock the heat sink in place. Make sure that the heat sink is installed flush with the CPU by inspecting the assembly from the side. You want to be positive of this before turning on the computer because the thermal compound will begin to expand and fill the imperfections right away. Plug the fan into the appropriate motherboard power connector, as shown in Figure 3.5. (These are usually labeled directly on the motherboard, or see your motherboard documentation for details on where to plug in the fan.) Install the entire motherboard assembly into the case if that is your method of choice.

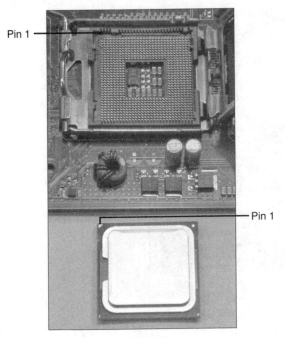

FIGURE 3.3   Orientation markings on a CPU and LGA 775 socket

FIGURE 3.4   Orientation markings on a LGA 1155 socket

Fan Power Connector   Plastic Anchor

FIGURE 3.5   **An installed multi-core CPU with connected fan**

> ▶ If you install to a PGA socket, unlock the socket by moving the
>   retaining arm out and upward until it is at a 90-degree angle to the
>   motherboard. Then gently place the CPU into the ZIF socket.
>   There will be an arrow on one corner of the CPU that should cor-
>   respond to a missing pin (or arrow) on the socket. Don't use force;
>   slide the CPU around until it slips into the socket. Look at the
>   CPU from the side and make sure it is flush with the socket. Lock
>   down the retaining arm to keep the CPU in place. Then attach the
>   heat sink/fan assembly to the metal clips that are on the sides of
>   the socket. Make sure that the heat sink is installed flush with the
>   CPU by inspecting the assembly from the side. You want to be
>   positive of this before turning on the computer because the ther-
>   mal compound will begin to expand and fill the imperfections right
>   away. Attach the power cable for the fan to the motherboard. (See
>   your motherboard documentation for details on where to plug the
>   fan in.) Install the entire motherboard assembly into the case if
>   that is your method of choice.

Note

With some CPUs you might need to lock down the retaining arm *after* the heat sink/
fan is installed. This depends on the CPU. Remember to RTM...read the manual!

5. **Test the installation:** With the case still open, boot the computer to make sure that the BIOS POST recognizes the CPU as the right type and speed. Halt the POST if necessary to read the details, and when done, enter the BIOS and view the CPU information there as well. If the BIOS doesn't recognize the CPU properly, check if a BIOS upgrade is necessary for the motherboard. Also make sure that the CPU fan is functional. Then view the details of the CPU within the BIOS. Be sure that the voltage reported by the BIOS is within tolerance. Then access the operating system (after it is installed) and make sure it boots correctly. Complete several full cycles and warm boots. Finally, view the CPU(s) within Windows and with CPU-Z:

> ▶ **Within Windows:** Check in the Device Manager to make sure that the CPU is identified correctly. Navigate to Start and right-click on Computer (My Computer in XP); then select Manage from the drop-down menu. This brings up the Computer Management window. From here locate the Device Manager in the left window pane and click it. Now, from the list in the right window pane, there should be a category named Processors; click the plus sign to expand it, and the CPU you installed should be listed. In Figure 3.6 you can see the system I am running that has the Core i5-2400; the CPU shows up as four separate CPUs running at 3.1 GHz. You can view similar information in Windows at the System Information window, which can be accessed by pressing Windows+R to open the Run prompt and typing msinfo32 (in Windows 7/Vista) or winmsd (in Windows XP).

FIGURE 3.6   A Core i5-2400 CPU as shown in the Device Manager

▸ **With CPU-Z:** The CPU-Z program can be downloaded from http://www.cpuid.com/softwares/cpu-z.html; it is freeware that gathers all the information you just saw in the Device Manager and also identifies the voltage, clock speeds, cache memory, and much more. This is a great program to use when analyzing and monitoring your CPU. When installed (which is easy), simply run it to analyze your CPU. You can see the CPU in Figure 3.7; this program ties in everything talked about in this chapter in a more real-world way. It shows the socket, cache, TDP, voltage, and so on, and it does it in real-time. For example, on the bottom left you see the core speed is 1596.6 MHz (1.6 GHz). Remember that the CPU can run at any clock rate below the maximum. With Windows 7 running, this CPU sits at 1.6 GHz, multiplying the bus speed by 16 times. However, if you open additional CPU-intensive programs, this number can go up as shown in Figure 3.8. Notice the core speed has risen to 3.2 GHz, now a multiplier of 32. You are actually into Intel Turbo Boost range here, which allows this CPU to be overclocked slightly from 3.1 GHz to as high as 3.4 GHz. Also notice the voltage has gone up from 1.048 V to 1.216 V. This means that heat increases as a result.

FIGURE 3.7   **CPU-Z showing the same Core i5-2400 CPU**

FIGURE 3.8   CPU-Z showing the same Core i5-2400 CPU at a higher clock rate

6. **Close the case and monitor the system:** Finally, if everything looks okay, close up the case, and consider monitoring the clock rate, voltage, and heat during the first few hours of operation. Voltage and heat can usually be monitored within the BIOS. All three can be monitored within Windows using third-party applications (such as CPU-Z), or with monitoring utilities that accompany the motherboard. If all went well, congratulate yourself on a job well done!

Troubleshooting CPUs

The most common issue with a CPU is when it isn't installed properly or securely. This could possibly cause a complete failure when trying to turn the system on. This failure could be accompanied by a series of beeps from the POST. If this happens, always check the power first, just in case. Another possibility is that the system will turn on, and power will be supplied to the system, but nothing else will happen: no POST, no display, no hard drive activity. In either of these situations, after checking power, make sure of the following:

▶ **Check the big four:** Remember that the CPU is part of the big four including the video card, RAM, and motherboard. Be sure to check these other components for simple connectivity problems, which could be the real culprit and not the CPU at all. Always check connections first before taking the CPU assembly apart.

▶ **Fan is connected and functional:** Some motherboards have a safe-guard that disables booting if the fan is defective or not plugged in. Or you might get a message on the screen or other type warning depending on the motherboard. Be sure that the fan is plugged into the correct power connector on the motherboard (or elsewhere), and verify that it turns when the computer is on. If the fan has failed, replacement fans can be purchased; just make sure that the new fan is compatible with the heat sink and motherboard.

▶ **Heat sink is connected properly:** Make sure that the heat sink is flush with the CPU cap and that it is securely fastened to the motherboard (or socket housing).

▶ **CPU is installed properly:** Make sure it was installed flush into the socket and that it was oriented correctly. Of course, this means removing the heat sink. If you do so, you should clean off excess thermal compound and reapply thermal compound to the CPU cap before reinstalling the heat sink.

ExamAlert

When troubleshooting the CPU, be sure to first check all connections, and then make sure the fan, heat sink, and CPU are secure and installed properly.

Note

As always, turn off the computer, unplug it, and employ ESD measures before working on the inside of the computer.

Following are a few more possible symptoms of a failing CPU:

▶ Unexplained crashes during boot up or during use.

▶ The computer locks after only a short time of use.

▶ Voltage is near, at, or above the top end of the allowable range.

Sometimes, the CPU is just plain defective. It could have been received this way, or maybe it overheated. Perhaps there was a surge that damaged it, or maybe someone overclocked it too far, and it was the victim of overvoltage (and subsequent overheating). Regardless of these reasons, the CPU needs to be replaced. Now, by default CPUs come with a heat sink and fan, and if that is the case, install the CPU as you normally would. But in some cases, you can save money by purchasing the CPU only and use the existing heat sink. In this case, remember to clean excess thermal compound and then reapply thermal compound; but reapply to the CPU cap, not to the heat sink. If the CPU were installed properly, users don't usually have many problems with it (aside from the overclockers). Keep this in mind when troubleshooting the CPU, or when troubleshooting an issue that might *appear* to be a CPU issue but is actually something else altogether.

On a lighter note, sometimes you might get reports from customers about strange noises coming from inside a PC, almost a buzzing of sorts. The noise could be caused by a wire or cable that is brushing up against the CPU fan (or other case fan). Be sure to reroute cables inside the computer so that they are clear of the CPU and any other devices. This will also aid with airflow within the PC, keeping the PC cooler. The CPU fan might also make noise due to it being clogged with dust, especially in dirtier environmental conditions. If the fan is still functional, you can take the computer outside and use compressed air to clean it out. Keep a computer vacuum handy to clean up the mess if necessary; I've seen computers that had so much dust and dirt inside, it could fill a garden.

Cram Quiz

Answer these questions. The answers follow the last question. If you cannot answer these questions correctly, consider reading this section again until you can.

220-801 Questions

1. When deciding on a CPU for use with a specific motherboard, what does it need to be compatible with?

   ○ A. Case

   ○ B. Socket

   ○ C. Wattage range

   ○ D. PCI slots

220-802 Questions

2. You are troubleshooting a CPU and have already cut power, disconnected the power cable, opened the case, and put on your antistatic strap. What should you do next?

   ○ A. Check the BIOS.

   ○ B. Check connections.

   ○ C. Remove the CPU.

   ○ D. Test the motherboard with a multimeter.

3. You have installed the CPU and heat sink/fan assembly. What should you do next?

   ○ **A.** Apply thermal compound.

   ○ **B.** Boot the computer.

   ○ **C.** Plug in the fan.

   ○ **D.** Replace the BIOS jumper shunt.

4. What is a possible symptom of a failing CPU?

   ○ **A.** CPU is beyond the recommended voltage range.

   ○ **B.** Computer won't boot.

   ○ **C.** BIOS reports low temperatures within the case.

   ○ **D.** Spyware is installed into the browser.

5. You just completed a CPU installation. However, when you turn on the computer, the POST sounds a series of beeps, and the system won't boot. What is the most likely cause?

   ○ **A.** The mouse is not plugged in.

   ○ **B.** The operating system is corrupted.

   ○ **C.** The CPU is not properly seated.

   ○ **D.** The fan is running to fast.

Cram Quiz Answers

220-801 Answers

1. **B.** The CPU needs to be compatible with the socket of the motherboard. The case doesn't actually make much of a difference when it comes to the CPU. (Just make sure it's large enough!) There is no wattage range, but you should be concerned with the voltage range of the CPU, and PCI slots don't actually play into this at all because there is no direct connectivity between the two.

220-802 Answers

2. **B.** Check connections first; it is quick, easy, and a common culprit.

3. **C.** After installing the heat sink/fan assembly, plug in the fan to the appropriate connector on the motherboard.

4. **A.** If the CPU is running beyond the recommended voltage range for extended periods of time, it can be a sign of a failing CPU. If the computer won't boot at all, another problem might have occurred, or the CPU might have already failed. Low case temperatures are a good thing (if they aren't below freezing!) and spyware is unrelated, but we talk about it plenty in Chapter 16, "Security."

5. **C.** The most likely cause is that the CPU needs to be reseated, or there is a RAM problem. None of the other answers would cause the POST to issue a series of beeps. Also, the POST doesn't look for operating system corruption, it is relegated to hardware only.

CHAPTER 4

RAM

This chapter covers the following A+ exam topics:

▶ RAM Basics and Types of RAM

▶ Installing and Troubleshooting DRAM

You can find a master list of A+ exam topics in the "Introduction."

This chapter covers CompTIA A+ 220-801 objective 1.3 and CompTIA A+ 220-802 objective 4.2.

When people talk about the RAM in their computer, they are almost always referring to the "sticks" of memory that are installed into the motherboard. This is known as DRAM, or main memory, and often comes in capacities of 1 GB, 2 GB, or 4 GB. This type of RAM has its own clock speed and must be compatible with the motherboard's RAM slots. It's not the only type of RAM, but it's the one you should be most concerned with for the exam. For all practical purposes the terms *stick*, *DIMM*, and *memory module* mean the same thing; they refer to the RAM installed into a motherboard's RAM slots.

The most important concept in this chapter is compatibility. There are a lot of RAM technologies to know, but the bottom line is, "Will it be compatible with my motherboard?" The best way to find out is to go to the RAM manufacturer's website and search for your motherboard. They usually list the matching RAM.

This chapter concentrates on SRAM and DRAM; however, there are other types, for example NVRAM that is covered in Chapter 6, "Storage Devices." This chapter discusses SRAM, DRAM, and DRAM types and demonstrates how to install and troubleshoot DRAM memory modules.

RAM Basics and Types of RAM

RAM Basics

Memory is the workspace for the CPU. Random-access memory (RAM) is the main memory that the CPU uses to store or retrieve data, which can be done in any order, regardless of what the CPU last accessed. The beauty of RAM is that the CPU can access any piece of memory it needs from anywhere in RAM, and any of these accesses take an equal amount of time. You often hear people associate RAM with a person's memory. But a person might take longer to recall certain memories in comparison to others. The CPU has equal access to all contents of RAM. It's fast and efficient, but the drawback is that RAM is typically cleared when the computer is shut off. To store data permanently, it would need to be written to a hard drive or other device, which is slower and less uniform in its storage and delivery of data. An example of this is when you work on a Word document; as you work, the contents of that file are stored in RAM, but when you save the file, the contents are then stored on a hard drive, or other media of your choice, which is done at a substantially slower rate.

The CPU though, is sort of closed off from memory, and the rest of the computer for that matter. It's kind of like the wizard behind the curtain. But someone does indeed pay attention to it—the memory controller chip. The memory controller is the go-between; basically, information is stored in and retrieved from RAM with the help of the memory controller. When the CPU wants to store or retrieve data to and from RAM, the memory controller is the chip responsible for getting the job done. It does this by moving the data along the address bus, which connects the memory controller to RAM. Figure 4.1 shows the two possible locations for the memory controller.

As you can see in the figure, the memory controller can be in one of two places:

- ▶ **Within the chipset:** In older systems the memory controller is within the northbridge, which Intel calls the Memory Controller Hub (MCH). Refer to the left side of Figure 4.1 to see this deprecated design.

- ▶ **Integrated to the CPU:** In most of today's systems, the memory controller is part of the CPU (known as "on-die") (refer to the right side of Figure 4.1). It does the same job regardless, but it's going to be faster than a northbridge memory controller.

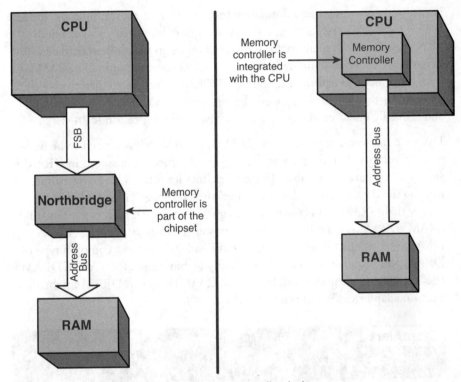

FIGURE 4.1 **Comparison of the two memory controller designs**

RAM discussed in this chapter is considered *volatile* (unless otherwise noted). This means that it loses any stored contents if it stops receiving power; for example, if you shut the computer off. However, not all RAM is volatile. Chapter 6 talks about *non-volatile* types of RAM (for example NVRAM).

Today's RAM is a set of integrated circuits (ICs) that works at high speed. These ICs could be on the motherboard, on adapter cards, within or on the processor, and of course, on those RAM sticks installed into the motherboard.

Types of RAM

Let's start by discussing the two main categories of RAM. Afterward, you move on to the types of RAM sticks you might install in a computer.

SRAM Versus DRAM

Static random-access memory (SRAM) is RAM that does not need to be periodically refreshed. Memory refreshing is common to other types of RAM and is basically the act of reading information from a specific area of memory and immediately rewriting that information back to the same area without modifying it. Due to SRAM's architecture, it does not require this refresh. You can find SRAM used as cache memory for CPUs, as buffers on the motherboard or within hard drives, and as temporary storage for LCD screens. Normally, SRAM is soldered directly to a printed circuit board (PCB) or integrated directly to a chip. This means that you probably won't be replacing SRAM. SRAM is faster than, and is usually found in smaller quantities, than its distant cousin DRAM.

Dynamic random-access memory (DRAM) is RAM that *does* need to be periodically refreshed. This is because every bit of information stored in DRAM is stored in a separate capacitor. These capacitors lose their charge over time, causing the data to fade unless the capacitor is recharged or *refreshed*. It is slower than SRAM but is of simple design and can reach high capacities. Like SRAM, DRAM is volatile and requires power to retain its data. Sticks of DRAM are installed into the motherboard and are the most common type of DRAM you install and troubleshoot. Many technicians refer to these DRAM sticks simply as memory modules, or just RAM. However, DRAM might also exist on adapter cards and other devices as well.

Exam**Alert**

Know the differences between SRAM and DRAM for the exam.

Note

Another type of memory you should know for the exam is ROM or read-only memory. Unlike the RAM types discussed in this chapter, ROM is nonvolatile, meaning that it retains its contents, even if it is not supplied with power. Historically, ROM chips could be read from but not written to. But now you have ROM chips that can do both, for example EEPROM implemented as a BIOS chip. For more information on EEPROM and the BIOS see Chapter 2, "Motherboards."

Let's talk about the different types of DRAM sticks you see in computers and how fast they can go!

SDRAM

Synchronous DRAM (SDRAM) is DRAM that is synchronized to the base clock of the motherboard (also referred to as the system bus speed). If your system bus (and corresponding memory bus) were 100 MHz, you would want to install compatible 100 MHz SDRAM because that SDRAM receives its clock signal from the system bus on the motherboard.

Typical SDRAM clock rates are 66 MHz, 100 MHz, and 133 MHz; the physical RAM sticks are referred to as PC66, PC100, and PC133, respectively. Although you rarely see this type of RAM anymore, you can still purchase PC100 and PC133 versions. It is designed as a 168-pin DIMM. Dual in-line memory modules (DIMMs) have been in use for more than a decade. They are the successor to the single in-line memory module (SIMM). The main difference between the two is that DIMMs have *separate* electrical contacts on each side of the module (or stick), whereas SIMMs might have contacts on both sides, but they are redundant. SDRAM voltage is 3.3 volts.

Data transfer rates vary depending on the speed of the RAM, but SDRAM in general has a bus width of 64 bits (8 bytes). A 100 MHz SDRAM bus can, therefore, transfer 8 bytes of data, 100 million times per second, equaling 800 MB/s. Keep in mind that this data rate is a theoretical maximum, and actual data throughputs are less.

Figure 4.2 shows an example of the "stick" or DIMM version of SDRAM.

Notch Used by Locking Tab

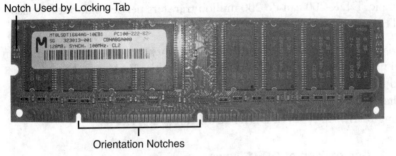

Orientation Notches

FIGURE 4.2 **A 168-Pin PC100 SDRAM 128 MB stick**

The stick has two notches located at the bottom, which help to orient the stick during installation. The sticker shows this RAM has a capacity of 128 MB, which gives you an idea of the age of this technology; however it is still covered on the A+ exam. There is also a notch on each side of the stick of RAM. These lock it into place when inserting it into the RAM slot of a motherboard. Basically, you press the stick straight down into the slot until the slot's tabs lock around the side notches.

DDR

Let's talk about today's RAM—Double Data Rate (DDR) is by far the most commonly used RAM on the planet. DDR is synchronized to the memory clock just like SDRAM; it's also called DDR SDRAM. The original DDR (aka DDR1) is actually SDRAM that has been double-pumped, meaning that twice the data is transferred but at the same clock speed. It does this by transferring data on the rising *and* falling edges of each clock signal (every cycle). So let's use DDR-200 as an example. Our original 100 MHz system bus's transfers are doubled, so instead of 100 million transfers, it can now do 200 million transfers per second. (That's where the 200 comes from in DDR-200.) DDR also has a 64-bit wide bus allowing for 8 bytes of data per cycle. A 100 MHz DDR bus can, therefore, transfer 8 bytes of data, 100 million times per second, *times* 2, equaling 1600 MB/s. The equation for this data transfer rate (also known as bandwidth) is

Clock speed × bytes × 2 = Data Transfer Rate

Example: 100 MHz × 8 × 2 = 1,600 MB/s

Whenever you do these types of equations, be interested in solving for bytes because that is what these data rates measure.

People, and even manufacturers, sometimes refer to transfers per second as MHz. Although this is not completely accurate, it is common terminology. For example, DDR-200 can do 200 million transfers per second, but it is also referred to as 200 MHz.

Table 4.1 gives the low-down about DDR1 memory modules including the standard names, clock speeds, how many transfers the RAM can do per second, and the total data transfer rate, also referred to as bandwidth. Finally, it shows the module name that is the name you would go by when ordering or purchasing RAM. All types of DDR1 RAM run at 2.5 V.

TABLE 4.1 **Comparison of DDR1 Types**

DDR Standard	I/O Clock Speed	Transfers per Second	Transfer Rate	Module Name
DDR-200	100 MHz	200 Million	1,600 MB/s	PC1600
DDR-266	133 MHz	266 Million	2,133 MB/s	PC2100
DDR-333	166 MHz	333 Million	2,667 MB/s	PC2700
DDR-400	200 MHz	400 Million	3,200 MB/s	PC3200

Now, an easier way to solve the data transfer rate equation for *all* types of DDR is to simply multiply the megatransfers per second (MT/s) by 8. Why 8? Because DDR sends 8 bytes per transfer. Now solve for DDR-400.

Equation: 400 MT/s × 8 = 3,200 MB/s.

Boom, simple. Just remember that you are solving for bytes. If you know you are using DDR-400 RAM, then you know it is capable of 400 MT/s. (The numbers match up.) And because you know that DDR sends 8 bytes of data per transfer, you can easily find the total data transfer rate per second.

ExamAlert

Know how to calculate the data transfer rate of DDR RAM for the exam.

The DDR DIMM has 184 pins and is not compatible with 168-pin SDRAM DIMMs. DDR DIMMs have one notch instead of two; this notch prevents using the wrong memory module in a RAM slot.

Note

Laptops use smaller configurations of DDR with different pin configurations. These are known as SODIMMs. You can find more information about laptops and SODIMMs in Chapter 7, "Laptops."

DDR2

DDR2 builds on the original DDR specification by decreasing voltage (to 1.8 V) and by increasing speed. It increases speed through faster signaling, which requires additional pins. Standard DDR2 DIMMs have 240 pins and cannot be used in DDR1 memory slots. Table 4.2 gives a comparison of the various types of DDR2, their speeds, and transfer rates.

TABLE 4.2 **Comparison of DDR2 Types**

DDR2 Standard	I/O Clock Speed	Transfers per Second	Transfer Rate	Module Name
DDR2-400	200 MHz	400 Million	3,200 MB/s	PC2-3200
DDR2-533	266 MHz	533 Million	4,266 MB/s	PC2-4200
DDR2-667	333 MHz	667 Million	5,333 MB/s	PC2-5300
DDR2-800	400 MHz	800 Million	6,400 MB/s	PC2-6400
DDR2-1066	533 MHz	1.066 Billion	8,533 MB/s	PC2-8500

ExamAlert

Know the DDR2 standards for the exam.

Now calculate the data transfer rate of a stick of DDR2 RAM. Remember that it is MT/s × 8. Solve for DDR2-800.

Equation: 800 MT/s × 8 = 6,400 MB/s.

Remember to solve for bytes.

Figure 4.3 shows an example of a DDR2-800 DIMM. There is a difference in the orientation notch location compared with DDR, again preventing mismatching of memory and RAM slot.

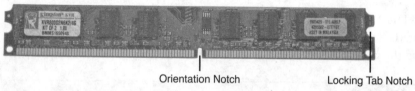

Orientation Notch   Locking Tab Notch

FIGURE 4.3   A 240-pin PC2-6400 2 GB DIMM (DDR2-800)

ExamAlert

Know the amount of pins in the various DDR memory modules.

DDR3

When is enough, enough? Never! Actually, DDR3 was designed for lower power consumption, and higher reliability, while enabling higher levels of performance. 240-pin DDR3 DIMMs are similar to DDR2 DIMMs but are *not* backward compatible. As of 2012, DDR3 is the most common DIMM installed in new PCs, due to its capability to transfer twice as much data, using less voltage (1.2 to 1.5 V), and basically working faster and more efficiently. Table 4.3 gives a comparison of the various types of DDR3, their speeds, and transfer rates. Figure 4.4 shows a DDR3-1333 memory module.

TABLE 4.3 **Comparison of DDR3 Types**

DDR3 Standard	I/O Clock Speed	Transfers per Second	Transfer Rate	Module Name
DDR3-800	400 MHz	800 Million	6,400 MB/s	PC3-6400
DDR3-1066	533 MHz	1.066 Billion	8,533 MB/s	PC3-8500
DDR3-1333	667 MHz	1.333 Billion	10,667 MB/s	PC3-10600
DDR3-1600	800 MHz	1.600 Billion	12,800 MB/s	PC3-12800
DDR3-1866	933 MHz	1.866 Billion	14,933 MB/s	PC3-14900
DDR3-2133	1066 MHz	2.133 Billion	17,066 MB/s	PC3-17000

> **Note**
>
> The standards listed in Table 4.3 are based on the JEDEC standards (www.jedec.org). You might also see RAM for sale called DDR-1800 or DDR-2000. These are near equivalents to DDR3-1866 and DDR3-2133.

> **ExamAlert**
>
> Know the various DDR3 standards for the exam.

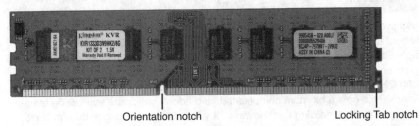

                Orientation notch   Locking Tab notch

FIGURE 4.4   **A 240-pin PC3-10600 4 GB DIMM (DDR3-1333)**

The DDR3 module in Figure 4.4 has a sticker on the left that shows an identification code. You might not be able to read it, but it says KVR1333D3N9HK2/8G and Kit of 2, 1.5 V. The 1333 and D3 in the code tells you that this is DDR3-1333 RAM. The 8G tells you the capacity: 8 GB, but only when installed as a kit of 2 memory modules as the label goes on to say. Finally, it tells you that the memory runs at 1.5 volts. Leave the sticker on the memory module so that the warranty is not voided, and so you can find out important characteristics of the RAM later on. Often, you come across sticks of RAM just laying about, and you might not remember what they are—the code on the sticker tells you everything you need to know.

Now calculate the data transfer for DDR3-800. Remember that you can solve this by multiplying the MT/s × 8.

Equation: 800 MT/s × 8 = 6,400 MB/s

Does this look familiar? It should; you used the same equation for DDR2. Although the end result is the same as far as transfer rate, remember that DDR3 is more efficient, uses less voltage, and gives off less heat. Because of this, you can ultimately attain higher levels of transfer, such as DDR3-2133 that wouldn't be possible with DDR2.

Now, you should be able to figure out the data transfer rate of DDR3 given any one of the following pieces of information:

▸ **DDR standard, such as DDR3-1333:** The 1333 in the name is the same number as the megatransfers per second.

▸ **I/O clock speed for DDR3, such as 667 MHz:** This is always half the megatransfers.

▸ **Module name, such as PC3-10600:** The data transfer rate is in the name itself! PC3-10600 can transfer 10,600 MB/s.

> **Note**
>
> If you have heard of the term *base memory clock*, or just *memory clock*, and wonder about it, well, it is simply the initial frequency of a given type of DDR before being multiplied to get the I/O clock speed. For DDR3 it is one-quarter of the I/O clock speed. So for example, DDR3-1600 has a 200-MHz base memory clock and an 800 MHz I/O clock. However, for DDR2 the base memory clock is only half of the I/O clock. This gets a bit more complicated, and I don't anticipate you seeing questions on the exam regarding this. However, if you have an inquiring mind and want to learn more, feel free to contact me at my website.

DDR4

Make way for DDR4. As of January 2011, DDR4 modules have been introduced but are not mainstream. They have a lower voltage range, from 1.05 to 1.2 V than does DDR3 and are expected to go as high as 4,266 MT/s. DDR4 has been delayed and may continue to be delayed for a while due to compatibility issues with other hardware. DDR4 is not currently listed within the A+ objectives, but I recommend you keep an eye on the development of this technology.

RDRAM (Rambus)

Rambus DRAM is another type of synchronous dynamic RAM designed by the Rambus Corporation and used primarily at the turn of the millennium. Because RDRAM was proprietary and not part of the JEDEC standard, many manufacturers would not support or license it. This and other factors led to the general demise of RDRAM; for PCs it's difficult to find it today, but a few components and gaming consoles use it. The chances of you working with it in a PC or seeing questions on the exam about it are unlikely A few examples of RDRAM (also known as RIMMs) are PC800 (single channel, 16-bits wide, 1600 MB/s bandwidth), the more advanced RIMM 3200 (dual channel, 32-bits wide, 3200 MB/s), and RIMM 6400 (dual channel, 32-bits wide, 6400 MB/s.)

> **Note**
>
> You can find a newer, different type of memory from Rambus in the Sony
> PlayStation 3 video game console, which uses 256 MB of extreme data rate (XDR)
> DRAM, providing 25.6 GB/s bandwidth. XDR version 2 can provide 80 GB/s.
> Rambus also released a Mobile XDR version for mobile devices that has a maxi-
> mum of 17 GB/s of bandwidth. Rambus also makes its own version of DDR3 that
> can do either 800 or 1600 MT/s.

RAM Technologies

When you decide on the type of RAM to use, you must decide on more technical details; for example, whether to use single or dual-channel RAM that
will be dictated for the most part by the motherboard. Your particular environment might need RAM that doesn't lag, so memory latency should be
another consideration. There are several other lesser considerations such as
whether to use single-sided or double-sided RAM, parity, or ECC RAM. For
the most part, these additional factors don't play into the decision much: Your
motherboard dictates whether the RAM is single-sided or double-sided, and
parity and ECC RAM is more rare nowadays.

Single Channel Versus Dual Channel Versus Triple Channel

Single channel is the original RAM architecture. In modern computers, there
is a 64-bit bus (or data channel) between the memory and the memory controller. One or more sticks of RAM can be installed into the motherboard, but
they share the same channel.

Dual channel is a common technology that essentially doubles the data
throughput. Two separate 64-bit channels are employed together resulting in
a 128-bit bus. To incorporate this, the proper motherboard will have color-
coded matching banks. See Figure 4.5 for an example of this.

In Figure 4.5 you can see four RAM slots. The topmost slot, labeled DIMM
3, is black, and underneath that you see a blue slot, labeled DIMM 1.
Collectively they are known as Channel A. Then you see another black and
blue slot, labeled DIMM 4 and DIMM 2. These are known as Channel B. To
use dual-channel architecture, a kit of two RAM sticks would be installed to
the matching color (matching bank), for example both blue slots: one in
Channel A and one in Channel B, collectively forming the first bank of RAM.
Both DIMMs should be identical for best performance. This means the capacity, speed, and number of chips must be the same on both DIMMs. However,

if you access a website such as www.kingston.com, you can find a user-friendly memory database that tells you exactly which kits of RAM will be compatible with your motherboard. This is the easiest way to ensure a harmonious system. As a final note, it is recommended to install to banks sequentially, meaning install two memory sticks to the blue bank, and then (optionally) install two memory sticks to the black bank. These colors may vary depending on the motherboard; Intel uses blue and black. Another simple method is to look at the motherboard (or documentation) and identify DIMM 1 and DIMM 2. Use those first!

Channel A, DIMM 3 (Black)

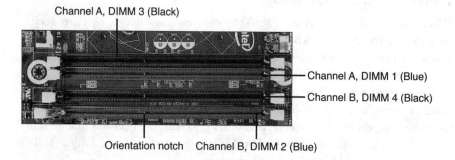

Channel A, DIMM 1 (Blue)

Channel B, DIMM 4 (Black)

Orientation notch   Channel B, DIMM 2 (Blue)

FIGURE 4.5 **A motherboard's dual-channel memory slots**

> **Note**
>
> Older systems might do this a bit differently. For example, both blue slots might be referred to as DIMM 0. The key is to install in pairs of the same color.

Triple-channel architecture accesses three memory modules at the same time, in effect a 192-bit bus. In this less common setup; a motherboard would have one of two configurations. The first would be three channels of two different color memory slots each. A bank of RAM would include Channel A DIMM 0, Channel B DIMM 0, and Channel C DIMM 0. The first bank is usually blue, and the second bank is black. The other configuration would have three blue slots, each its own channel, and a separate black slot that can be used for single channel mode, if the triple-channel option is not used. Normally the black slot would be left unused. Triple channel is limited to Intel Core i7-900 series processors and the LGA 1366 socket.

> **ExamAlert**
>
> Know the difference between single, dual, and triple channel for the exam.

Quadruple channel architecture takes this idea to the next level. It works only when four identical memory modules are placed in the correct slots. If only two are used, the motherboard scales back to dual-channel architecture. Intel LGA 2011 and AMD G34 platforms are compatible with quad-channel. This architecture is the most rare of the four and is not covered in the A+ objectives.

> **Note**
>
> DDR4 is expected to move away from the single/dual/triple/quad channel technology and instead incorporate a point-to-point technology in which each channel from the memory controller connects to just one memory module.

Memory Latency

Memory latency or Column Address Strobe (CAS) latency happens when a memory controller tries to access data from a memory module. It is a slight delay (usually measured in nanoseconds) while the memory module responds to the memory controller. It is given a rating of CAS, or more commonly CL. The higher the CL number, the longer the delay. For example, the DDR3 RAM I purchased from Kingston is CL-9. The general range of DDR3 memory is between CL5 and CL10, so I'm near the slowest end of the spectrum. However, the difference between the ratings is small, so it usually has an effect only on users that run powerful memory-intensive applications, for instance graphics rendering. Video editors, graphic designers, and gamers beware! Otherwise CL9 is fine for the purpose of this computer.

Single-Sided Versus Double-Sided

The terms single-sided and double-sided are not quite literal. Use your motherboard's documentation or a memory manufacturer's database to verify whether your motherboard accepts single-sided or double-sided memory modules, and acquire the compatible RAM from a reputable vendor. Single-sided refers to a memory module with a single "bank" of chips. The computer's memory controller can access all the chips at once. The memory module might have chips on both physical sides, or only on one side, but it is known as single-sided because the computer can address all the chips at once.

Double-sided memory modules have their chips divided into two "sides" known as banks. Only one "side" can be seen by the computer at any time. To use the second half of the storage available, the computer must switch to the second bank and can no longer read or write to the first half until it switches back again.

> **Note**
>
> Don't confuse double-sided memory and dual-channel memory when it comes to banks. An individual stick of RAM that is double-sided is broken down into two banks, but this has no bearing on the installation of the RAM. A bank of dual-channel RAM is two sticks of RAM that must be installed as a pair to matching color-coded slots. More often you will be concerned with dual-channel banks.

Parity Versus Nonparity

There are several types of parity in computing; RAM parity is when memory stores an extra bit (known as a parity bit) used for error *detection*. This means that the memory module can store 9 bits instead of 8 bits for every byte of data. So, parity RAM includes this extra bit, and the more common nonparity RAM does not. Parity RAM might be required when data integrity is a necessity.

ECC Versus Non-ECC

Error Correction Code (ECC) in RAM can detect *and* correct errors. Real-time applications might use ECC RAM. Like parity RAM, additional information needs to be stored, and more resources are used in general. This RAM is the slowest and most expensive of RAM types. DDR3 ECC modules are identified with either the letter E, or ECC, for example PC3-10600E.

> **Note**
>
> Most new PCs do not need or support parity or ECC RAM due to the low possibility of data corruption. If it is supported, but not necessary, these options can be disabled in the BIOS.

Registered and Fully Buffered

Registered memory (also known as buffered memory) improves the integrity of the signal between RAM and the memory controller by electrically buffering the signals using an extra register. This is done for stability, especially when using multiple memory modules; however, this could cause additional latency. An example of DDR3 registered memory would be PC3-10600R.

Fully buffered memory goes beyond this and introduces an advanced memory buffer between the memory controller and the memory module. For this to work, a completely different memory module must be used, with the notch in a different location, making it incompatible with motherboards that support regular DDR or registered DDR. This kind of memory module is known as a FB-DIMM; an example would be PC3-10600F or PC3-10600FB.

The terms registered and fully buffered are not listed in the A+ objectives, but you never know if you will see mention of these terms on the exam, and you might see them in the field, especially in systems that require a lot of RAM while keeping signal integrity.

One Final Note About RAM

The main thing to "remember" when working with RAM is that it needs to be compatible with the motherboard. Check your motherboard's documentation regarding capacity per slot (or channel), maximum capacity, speed, and whether it accepts single- or dual-channel RAM. The best thing to do is to run a search on your particular motherboard at the RAM manufacturer's website to attain a complete list of a compatible RAM.

Cram Quiz

Answer these questions. The answers follow the last question. If you cannot answer these questions correctly, consider reading this section again until you can.

220-801 Questions

1. Which technology divides the RAM slots into colors?

   ○ **A.** ECC

   ○ **B.** Parity

   ○ **C.** Double-sided

   ○ **D.** Dual channel

2. Which of these is the delay it takes for a memory module to start sending data to the memory controller?

   ○ **A.** DDR

   ○ **B.** Propagation

   ○ **C.** Latency

   ○ **D.** FSB

3. What is the transfer rate of DDR2-800?

   ○ **A.** 6,400 MB/s

   ○ **B.** 8,533 MB/s

   ○ **C.** 5,333 MB/s

   ○ **D.** 800 MHz

4. Which of these would you find internal to the CPU?

   ○ **A.** DRAM

   ○ **B.** DIMM

   ○ **C.** SDRAM

   ○ **D.** SRAM

5. What is the transfer rate of DDR3-1600?

   ○ **A.** 6,400 MB/s

   ○ **B.** 12,800 MB/s

   ○ **C.** 14,933 MB/s

   ○ **D.** 17,066 MB/s

6. Which chip designates where data will be stored in RAM?

   ○ **A.** Southbridge

   ○ **B.** Northbridge

   ○ **C.** CPU

   ○ **D.** DRAM

7. How many pins are on a DDR3 memory module?

   ○ **A.** 168

   ○ **B.** 184

   ○ **C.** 240

   ○ **D.** 200

Cram Quiz Answers

220-801 Answers

1. **D.** Dual-channel memory configurations have two RAM slots of a particular color, each one of which is placed in a different channel; these are collectively known as banks.

2. **C.** Latency is the delay between the memory module and the memory controller, usually rated as CL and a number.

3. **A.** DDR2-800 can transfer 6,400 MB/s; DDR2-1066 transfers 8,533 MB/s. DDR2-667 transfers 5,333 MB/s. MHz is sometimes used to refer to the amount of megatransfers per second; in this case, the RAM can do 800 MT/s.

4. **D.** One function of SRAM is to act as CPU cache. L1 cache would be internal to the CPU or in the core. L2 would be on-die.

5. **B.** The transfer rate of DDR3-1600 is 12,800 MB/s. DDR3-800 is 6,400 MB/s. DDR3-1866 is 14,933 MB/s. DDR3-2133 is 17,066 MB/s.

6. **B.** The northbridge, specifically the memory controller chip, is in charge of storing and retrieving data to and from RAM. Even though new systems use a memory controller that is part of the CPU, it is not the CPU that is in charge of this. The CPU knows what bytes it wants but not the location of those bytes.

7. **C.** DDR3 is a 240-pin architecture. 168-pin is the original SDRAM, 184-pin is the first version of DDR (DDR1), and you can find 200-pin architectures in laptops; they are known as SODIMMs.

Installing and Troubleshooting DRAM

Installing DRAM

Installing DRAM is fun and easy. Simply stated, it can be broken down into this: Orient the RAM properly, insert the RAM into the slot, and press down with both thumbs until the ears lock. Then, test. Easy! But let's take it a little further. Remember that some people refer to memory modules as DIMMs, DRAM, RAM sticks, or just plain RAM, and you could get any of these terms on the exam as well. The following describes the steps involved when installing RAM:

1. **Select the correct memory module:** The memory module must be compatible with the motherboard. Again, this means it must be of the right size and pin configuration, the right type or standard, the correct speed, the correct size, and within voltage parameters. Don't forget to use the memory manufacturer's website. It has a search engine that enables you to input the motherboard you have, by make and model, and then the search displays all the different RAM configurations compatible with the motherboard. If you have a proprietary computer such as an HP or Dell, the website asks for the make and model of the computer instead of the motherboard. How much simpler could it be? Be wary of websites that don't have searchable databases like these.

   For our computer I used Kingston RAM. I went to its website, plugged in the make (Intel) and the model (DP67DE) of the motherboard, and it came up with a whole slew of different DDR3 RAM stick configurations; from 2 GB configs all the way up to 8 GB. As you might have guessed, I chose the 8 GB configuration, which is actually a kit of two 4 GB sticks, running at 1,333 MHz, which work in a dual-channel configuration, as we display in a minute. To be sure, I checked Intel's website to verify how much RAM I could use per slot and what speeds would run. The documentation shows that I could use up to 32 GB maximum of DDR3 RAM, a maximum of 8 GB per slot, at a top speed of 1,333 MHz. Well, for now I don't need more than 8 GB, but I can always upgrade, or add an identical kit later if I want; otherwise, everything sounds compatible. When the RAM is added, the BIOS should find it automatically; however, it is wise to check if any BIOS upgrades are available on the motherboard's website that deal with the latest types of RAM.

When the RAM arrives, you are ready to install. Power down the PC, disconnect the power cable (or turn off the kill switch), open the PC, and get ready!

2. **Employ ESD prevention methods:** Use an antistatic strap and mat. Before touching any components, place both hands on an unpainted portion of the case chassis. For more information on ESD preventative measures, see Chapter 18, "Safety, Professionalism, and Procedures." Never touch any of the pins or chips on the memory module; instead grab the module from the side edges. Remove the memory modules (could be one or more) from the package and place them on an antistatic bag.

3. **Ready the motherboard:** Some technicians prefer to install the RAM into the motherboard and then install the motherboard into the case; this can also depend on whether you are building a new computer or upgrading one. If you do choose to install the RAM to the motherboard separately, place the motherboard on the antistatic mat. (The mat should be on a hard, flat surface.) If you install the RAM directly into an already installed motherboard, clear away any cables or other equipment that might get in the way or could possibly damage the RAM during installation.

You see a plastic tab (ear) on each side of the RAM slot in the motherboard; they are usually white. Swing them out from the slot carefully so that they end up at an angle from the slot; this enables room for the memory module to be inserted.

4. **Install the RAM:** Be careful with the RAM and the RAM slot! They are delicate! Always touch the case chassis before picking up the RAM. Hold it by the edges and do not touch any pins or other circuitry on the memory module. If you need to put it down, put it down on an antistatic mat.

Take a look at the slot, there should be a break in the slot somewhere near the middle (but not the exact middle); this is where the notch in the memory module will go. Gently place the memory module in the slot, pins down. If the notch does not line up with the break in the slot, you might need to turn the module around. When it appears that the RAM is oriented correctly, press down with both thumbs on the top of the memory module. Keep your thumbs as close to the edge as you can so that you can distribute even pressure to the memory module. Press down with both thumbs at the same time until the "ears" on the edge of the RAM slot close and lock on to the memory module. You might hear a click or two when it is done. You might also have to push both of the ears toward the RAM to completely lock them into place. Take a look at the memory module from the side, or compare them to other ears in unused slots; the plastic ears should be standing straight up now. You may need a bit of force to fully insert the RAM, but don't go overboard! If the motherboard is bending excessively, you are using too much force. If this is the case, make sure that the RAM is oriented correctly; the notches should match up, and the RAM should be straight within the slot. Figure 4.6 shows a bank of DDR3 memory modules installed into the blue DIMM slots.

Channel A, DIMM 1 (Blue)

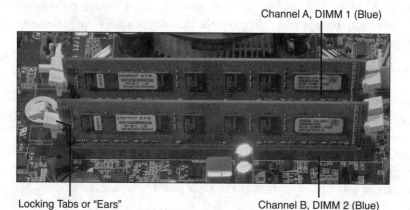

Locking Tabs or "Ears"   Channel B, DIMM 2 (Blue)

FIGURE 4.6 **Installed bank of DDR3 memory modules**

Install the entire motherboard assembly into the case if that were your method of choice.

5. **Test the installation:** With the case still open, boot the computer and make sure that the BIOS POST recognizes the new RAM as the right type and speed. Halt the POST, if necessary to read the details, and when done, enter the BIOS. Next, view the details of the RAM within the BIOS. The amount is often on the main page, but you might need to look deeper for the exact configuration, depending on the motherboard. Next, access the operating system (after it is installed) and make sure it boots correctly. Complete several full cycles and warm boots. Also, at some point, you should view the RAM with CPU-Z or in Windows to verify that the operating system sees the correct capacity of RAM. Following are a couple ways to do this in Windows and with CPU-Z:

   ▶ **System Properties:** Click Start; right-click Computer (My Computer in Windows XP) and select Properties. The total RAM should be listed within this window.

   ▶ **Task Manager:** As mentioned before you can view the Task Manager by right-clicking the taskbar and selecting Task Manager.

There are several other ways to open this; I like this one: Press Windows+R to bring up the Run prompt and type **taskmgr**. When it is open, go to the Performance tab and view the Physical Memory box. It should show the total physical memory. Keep in mind that this shows the amount of RAM in megabytes and that 1024 MB is roughly 1 GB. Figure 4.7 shows *Media PC* running Windows 7, displaying 8 GB of RAM in the Task Manager.

▶ **CPU-Z:** Simply open CPU-Z, and click the Memory tab, as shown in Figure 4.8. This shows the type and total amount of RAM, (8192 MB or 8 GB of Dual-Channel DDR3), the DRAM Frequency (666 MHz approximately), and the latency (CL 9).

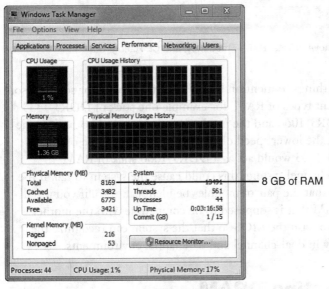

FIGURE 4.7 **Windows 7 Task Manager displaying 8 GB of RAM**

Consider testing the RAM by seeing if you can open several applications at once without any issues or delays.

ExamAlert

Know how to select, install, and verify RAM for the exam.

Finally, if everything looks okay, close up the case, and if all went well, congratulate yourself on another job well done!

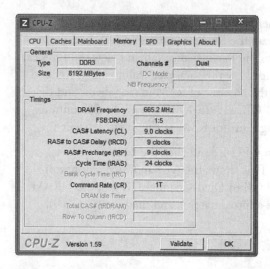

FIGURE 4.8 **CPU-Z showing Total RAM, Frequency, and CL Rating**

A couple important things to mention here: First, if you were for some reason to install two different types of RAM, for example one stick of DDR3-1333 and one stick of DDR3-1066 and the motherboard supported both; then the system would run at the lower speed of 1066. This is an example of under-clocking; the DDR3-1333 would act as a DDR3-1066 stick of RAM. However, in a dual-channel system, this could cause the system to fail, if the motherboard insists that the pair of modules be identical. Also, if you install the latest type of RAM that is supposed to be compatible with the mother-board, be prepared to flash the BIOS so that the system can recognize the new RAM, especially in dual-channel and tri-channel environments.

Troubleshooting DRAM

It's not common, but RAM memory modules can cause intermittent issues, or they can fail altogether. Always make sure that the RAM is fully seated within the RAM slot and that the plastic ears are locking the RAM into place. An unstable system can be caused by several components including RAM. Remember to check the "big four": video card, CPU, RAM, and motherboard.

A lot of the issues you see are because a user has purchased and installed a memory stick that is not compatible, or is semi-compatible, with the mother-board: wrong speed, incorrect capacity, improper configuration, and so on. Be ready for this; check the RAM compatibility against the motherboard, even if the user swears he checked it already. A good technician has documentation available and has access to the Internet. This can help to ensure that the correct RAM has been installed originally and that it is configured properly. Some RAM manufacturers (www.kingston.com, www.crucial.com) have tools to check compatibility issues.

Perhaps there was some kind of surge inside the computer; maybe the computer is not protected by a surge protector or UPS. Another possibility is that the RAM was damaged by ESD, and this damage manifests itself as intermittent problems. There are expensive hardware-based RAM testers that can tell you if the RAM is electrically sound and if it can process data correctly. If your company owns one, or if you can get your hands on one for a short time, you might narrow the problem down further. However, from personal experience, I have rarely needed to use these.

Here are some possible symptoms of a RAM issue and corresponding troubleshooting techniques:

> ▸ **Computer will not boot/intermittently shuts down:** If there is no RAM in the computer, or the RAM is damaged, or not installed securely, it can prevent the computer from doing anything at all, aside from draining electricity from your AC outlet. For example, the power supply fan turns but nothing else—no beeps and no displays. First, if the RAM were just installed, make sure that the RAM is compatible. Next, and in general, try reseating the RAM before you attempt to troubleshoot a CPU or motherboard. Add RAM if none exists. (Sounds silly but I've seen it!) If you suspect faulty RAM, corroded contacts, or a faulty RAM slot, you can try taking the RAM out, cleaning the RAM and RAM slot if necessary (with compressed air or with Stabilant 22a or like cleaner), and putting the RAM back in, being sure to seat the memory module properly. Next, if the computer has two memory modules, try booting it with just one (if the motherboard allows it), or try moving memory modules to different slots. As mentioned in previous chapters, a POST card tester can be helpful in these situations as well. If necessary, replace the memory module with an identical one (if you have an extra one handy), or at worst, purchase a new one if you have identified the memory module as the source of the problem. In some cases, RAM can overheat and cause intermittent shutdowns. Heat sinks can be purchased for RAM. These are made of aluminum or copper just like CPU heat sinks

and are sometimes referred to as heatspreaders. RAM can also be purchased with heat sinks pre-installed. This type of RAM might be necessary for high-end systems such as virtualization systems, computer-aided design workstations, and gaming systems.

▶ **BIOS indicates a memory error:** The BIOS can indicate a memory error through a gray message on the screen and a flashing cursor, or by beeping. If it beeps, you need to reference your motherboard documentation for the specific beep codes. Sometimes a BIOS setting can be incorrect. For example, maybe the RAM's latency setting or some other setting needs to be modified. If the computer has a saved version of the BIOS settings, you can try reverting to them, or you can try loading the BIOS defaults; I can't tell you how many times this has worked for me! Sometimes the BIOS indicates the wrong amount of RAM. If this is the case, check the RAM as explained in the first bullet. Finally, a BIOS update can be the cure; perhaps the BIOS just doesn't have the programming necessary to identify the latest type of RAM that was installed.

▶ **Memory errors occur:** Several types of memory errors are initiated by the operating system:

   ▶ **Stop error, aka BSOD or Blue Screen of Death:** This is a critical system error that causes the operating system to shut down. Most of the time, these are due to device driver errors (poor code), but they can be associated with a physical fault in memory. One example of this would be an nonmaskable interrupt (NMI). An NMI can interrupt the processor to gain its attention regarding nonrecoverable hardware errors, resulting in a BSOD. The BSOD usually dumps the contents of memory to a file (for later analysis) and restarts the computer. If you don't encounter another BSOD, it's probably not much to worry about. But if the BSOD happens repeatedly, you want to write down the information you see on the screen and cross-reference it to the Microsoft Support website at http://support. microsoft.com. Again, if you suspect faulty RAM, try the troubleshooting methods in the first bullet "Computer will not boot."

   ▶ **Page faults (hard faults), out-of-memory or low-on-virtual memory errors:** These are usually issues with the operating system or application that was running. However, you see less and less of these with each new Windows version. If a particular application keeps failing, or if you get a particular message listing a specific memory location over and over again, it can indicate a physical problem with RAM. Be sure to document error messages and any error codes or memory locations that display on the screen.

▶ **General protection fault (GPF):** This can cause a program to fail, and in older versions of Windows, it would cause the entire OS to shut down and display a black screen. Today, these errors are uncommon and are usually related to the OS, running applications, and CPU. It is also possible that memory errors can cause a GPF, for example writing to a read-only portion of memory, or a conflict in a particular part of memory, but again, these are rare.

Chapter 11, "Troubleshooting Windows," troubleshoots these BSODs, page faults, and other Windows issues.

Chances are you won't need them often, but a few memory testing programs are available online; a few examples follow:

▶ GoldMemory: http://www.goldmemory.cz/

▶ MemTest86: http://www.memtest86.com/

▶ PC-Diagnosys: http://www.windsortech.com/pcdiags.html

▶ Windows Memory Diagnostic: http://oca.microsoft.com/en/windiag.asp

These can help diagnose whether a memory module needs to be replaced. But in general, trust in your senses; look at and listen to the computer to help diagnose any RAM issues that might occur.

Cram Quiz

Answer these questions. The answers follow the last question. If you cannot answer these questions correctly, consider reading this section again until you can.

220-801 Questions

1. Where can you view how much RAM you have in the computer? (Select all that apply.)

   ○ **A.** Task Manager

   ○ **B.** My Computer

   ○ **C.** System Properties

   ○ **D.** BIOS

2. How should you hold RAM when installing it?

   ○ **A.** By the edges

   ○ **B.** By the front and back

   ○ **C.** With tweezers

   ○ **D.** With an Integrated Circuit (IC) puller

220-802 Questions

3. You suspect a problem with a memory module; what should you do first?

    ○ **A.** Replace the module with a new one.

    ○ **B.** Install more RAM.

    ○ **C.** Clean the RAM slot.

    ○ **D.** Test the RAM with MemTest86.

4. If a BSOD occurs, what should you do?

    ○ **A.** Replace all the RAM.

    ○ **B.** Re-install the operating system.

    ○ **C.** Check the RAM settings in the BIOS.

    ○ **D.** Wait for it to happen again.

5. You just upgraded a PC's motherboard and CPU. However, when you turn the computer on, it will not POST. What should you do first?

    ○ **A.** Check that the system hasn't overheated.

    ○ **B.** Check if the RAM is properly seated.

    ○ **C.** Check that the OS was installed properly.

    ○ **D.** Check if the mouse and keyboard are connected properly.

6. You just investigated a computer that is suffering from intermittent shutdowns. You note that the RAM modules are overheating. What is the best solution?

    ○ **A.** Install a heat sink on the memory controller.

    ○ **B.** Install more CPU fans.

    ○ **C.** Install heat sinks on the RAM modules.

    ○ **D.** Install a heat sink on the chipset.

7. You just installed new, compatible RAM into a motherboard, but when you boot the computer it does not recognize the memory. What should you do?

    ○ **A.** Flash the BIOS.

    ○ **B.** Replace the RAM.

    ○ **C.** Upgrade the CPU.

    ○ **D.** Add more RAM.

Cram Quiz Answers

220-801 Answers

1. **A, C**, and **D**. The BIOS displays what type of RAM you have and the amount. Windows has several locations in which you can discern how much RAM there is, including the Task Manager, System Properties, and System Information.

2. **A**. Hold RAM by the edges to avoid contact with the pins, chips, and circuitry.

220-802 Answers

3. **C**. Clean the RAM slot and memory module. Consider using compressed air or the proper spray (such as Stabilant 22a).

4. **D**. A singular BSOD doesn't necessarily mean that the RAM or any other components have gone bad. Often, a single BSOD occurs, but you never see it again. You want to see two or more of the same error before starting into a lengthy troubleshooting session!

5. **B**. The first thing you should do is check if the RAM is seated properly. This is easier than troubleshooting the CPU or motherboard and is a more common culprit due to the amount of force it takes to install DIMMs. A system will not have enough time to overheat before it gets to the POST. The OS hasn't even started yet, so you can rule that out. Mice and keyboards don't play a part in a system not posting.

6. **C**. The best thing to do in this situation is to install heat sinks on the RAM modules. On older computers the memory controller in a northbridge doesn't usually overheat because it already has a heat sink; on newer computers it is within the CPU. A CPU can have only one fan. You can't install more; although an additional case fan might help. The chipset also usually has a heat sink.

7. **A**. If you are sure that the RAM is compatible and the system doesn't recognize it during POST, try flashing the BIOS. It could be that the RAM is so new that the motherboard doesn't have the required firmware to identify the new RAM.

CHAPTER 5

Power

This chapter covers the following A+ exam topics:

▶ Understanding and Testing Power

▶ Power Devices

▶ Power Supplies

You can find a master list of A+ exam topics in the "Introduction."

This chapter covers CompTIA A+ 220-801 objectives 1.8 and 5.2, and CompTIA A+ 220-802 objective 4.2.

Everything relies on power. Clean, well-planned power is imperative in a computer system. It's so important that I almost made this the first chapter of the book. I can't tell you how many power-related issues I have troubleshot in the past. Many of the issues that you see concerning power are due to lack of protection and improper planning, and as such you will see several questions (if not more) on the A+ exams regarding this subject.

Imagine a scenario in which you work for a technical services division of a company. You are required to install a new, more powerful power supply in a computer that contains many devices and requires a lot of electricity. You need to install the computer in a new area of the company's building. This requires you to plug the computer into an AC receptacle that has never been used or tested.

What kind of power supply should you select? How can you verify that the AC outlet is properly wired? And how can you protect the computer? This chapter answers all those questions and furnishes you with the knowledge you need to install, test, and troubleshoot power supplies and test power that comes from the wall outlet.

Understanding and Testing Power

The power for your computer is derived from electricity, which is basically the flow of electric charge. Electricity is defined and measured in several ways, most commonly:

▶ **Voltage:** A representation of potential energy; sometimes it's more simply referred to as pressure; its unit of measurement is volts (V).

▶ **Wattage or electric power:** The rate of electric energy in a circuit, measured in watts (W).

▶ **Amperage or electric current:** The movement of electric charge, measured in amperes or amps (A).

▶ **Impedance:** The amount of resistance to electricity, measured in ohms (Ω).

This chapter covers each of these, but by far the most common of these that you will be testing is voltage. Following are two examples of voltages you are probably familiar with:

▶ 120 Volts AC (the voltage associated with many U.S. homes)

▶ 5 Volts DC (the voltage associated with some of the internal power connections in your PC)

The difference in these two examples (aside from the amount of volts) is that a house's outlets use alternating current (AC), in which the flow of electrons alternate, and your computer, again internally, uses direct current (DC), in which the flow of electrons is one way.

ExamAlert

In AC, electrons flow alternates.

In DC, electrons flow one way.

Back to our scenario; because you can't control who wired the AC outlet that you will be connecting the computer to, or how clean the power is that comes from your municipality, you should test the outlet prior to plugging the computer in. Two good tools to use when testing are a receptacle tester and a multimeter.

ExamAlert

Warning: Read through these sections carefully before attempting to test a live AC outlet. If you still feel unsure, contact a qualified electrician to test and make repairs to an AC outlet.

Testing an AC Outlet with a Receptacle Tester

Type B AC outlets are the most common and might also be referred to as wall sockets, electric receptacles, or power points. It is type B that you need to be concerned with for the A+ exam. If any of the hot, neutral, or ground wires are connected improperly, the computer connected to the outlet is a sitting duck, just waiting for irreparable damage. To ensure that the AC outlet is wired properly, you can use a receptacle tester, like the one shown in Figure 5.1. These are inexpensive and are available at most home improvement stores and electrical supply shops. When you plug in the receptacle tester, it tells you if the receptacle is wired properly or indicates which wires are incorrect.

FIGURE 5.1   **A common receptacle tester and labeled receptacle**

In Figure 5.1 the test has passed. With this particular tester, two yellow lights tell you that the outlet is wired correctly. Any other combination of lights tells you that there is a wiring error. The different combinations are usually labeled on the tester itself; for example, an open ground error is displayed by one single, yellow light on this tester. Important: If you receive any erroneous readings or if there are no lights at all, *do not use the outlet* and contact your supervisor and/or building management so that they can bring in a licensed electrician to fix the problem.

> **ExamAlert**
>
> If you find an AC outlet is improperly wired, contact your supervisor and/or building management to resolve the problem.

Testing an AC Outlet with a Multimeter

Every PC technician should own a multimeter, and we use one throughout this chapter. A multimeter is a hand-held device that, among other things, can be used to measure amps and impedance, and to test voltage inside a computer and from AC outlets. It has two leads, a black and a red. Whenever using the multimeter, try to hold both of the multimeter leads with one hand, and hold them by the plastic handles; don't touch the metal ends. It will be like holding chopsticks but is a safer method, reducing the severity of electric shock in the uncommon chance that one occurs. To test an AC outlet with a multimeter, run through the following steps:

1. Place the multimeter's black lead in the outlet's ground. (The parts of the outlet are labeled in Figure 5.1.)

2. Place the red lead in the hot opening.

3. Turn on the multimeter to test for volts AC (sometimes labeled as VAC). Hold the leads steady and check for readings. Optimally, the reading will hover around 115 volts or 120 volts depending on where you are in the United States. Watch the readings for a minute or so. Remember the reading or range of readings that display. A common reading is shown in Figure 5.2.

4. Turn off the multimeter.

5. Remove the red lead.

6. Remove the black lead.

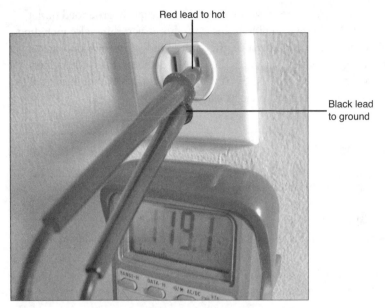

Red lead to hot

Black lead to ground

FIGURE 5.2 **A receptacle tested with a multimeter**

What was your reading? A steady reading closest to 120 volts is desirable. It might be less in some areas, but the key is that it's steady at one voltage; this is also known as *clean power*. If the reading fluctuates a lot, say between 113 volts and 121 volts, for example, you have one of the varieties of *dirty power*. This could be because too many devices use the same circuit or because power coming from the electrical panel or from the municipal grid fluctuates, maybe because the panel or the entire grid is under/overloaded. A quick call to your company's electrician can result in an answer and possibly a long-term fix. However, you are concerned with an immediate solution, which in this case is to install an uninterruptible power supply (UPS) or other line-conditioning device between the computer and the AC outlet. This can regulate the output of AC to the computer.

ExamAlert

To keep an AC outlet's voltage steady, use a UPS or line conditioner.

You can also test the neutral and ground wires in this manner. You should be especially concerned with whether the ground wire is connected properly. Previously you saw how to test this with the receptacle tester, but to test this with the multimeter, connect the black lead to ground and the red lead to neutral. This should result in a reading of 0 volts. Any other reading means that the outlet is not grounded properly, which can result in damage to a computer that connects to it. You can also use a voltage detector, which is a pen-shaped device that beeps when it comes into contact with voltage. On a properly grounded outlet, the only part that should give audible beeps is the hot. Everything else including the screw and outlet plate should not register any sounds. If sounds do register by simply touching the outlet plate with the voltage detector, the outlet is not grounded properly. If this is the case, or if you got any other reading besides 0 volts on the multimeter, contact an electrician right away.

Cram Quiz

Answer these questions. The answers follow the last question. If you cannot answer these questions correctly, consider reading this section again until you can.

220-801 Questions

1. What tool would you use to test the amount of voltage that comes from an AC outlet?

   - O **A.** Multimeter
   - O **B.** Voltage detector
   - O **C.** Receptacle tester
   - O **D.** Impedance tester

2. Which of the following is a representation of potential energy?

   - O **A.** Wattage
   - O **B.** Voltage
   - O **C.** Impedance
   - O **D.** Amperage

3. Which wire when tested should display zero volts on a multimeter?

   - O **A.** Neutral
   - O **B.** Hot
   - O **C.** Ground
   - O **D.** Red

Cram Quiz Answers

220-801 Answers

1. **A.** The multimeter is the only testing tool that can display voltage numerically.

2. **B.** Voltage is a representation of potential energy; an analogy for voltage would be water pressure in a pipe.

3. **C.** When testing the ground wire with a multimeter, it should display a reading of zero volts.

Power Devices

Utilizing proper power devices is part of a good preventative maintenance plan and helps to protect a computer. You need to protect against several things:

▶ Surges

▶ Spikes

▶ Sags

▶ Brownouts

▶ Blackouts

A *surge* in electrical power means that there is an unexpected increase in the amount of voltage provided. This can be a small increase or a larger increase known as a spike. A *spike* is a short transient in voltage that can be due to a short circuit, tripped circuit breaker, power outage, or lightning strike.

A *sag* is an unexpected decrease in the amount of voltage provided. Typically, sags are limited in time and in the decrease in voltage. However, when voltage reduces further, a brownout could ensue. During a *brownout* the voltage drops to such an extent that it typically causes the lights to dim and causes computers to shut off.

A *blackout* is when a total loss of power for a prolonged period occurs. Another problem associated with blackouts is the spike that can occur when power is restored. In the New York area, it is common to have an increased amount of tech support calls during July; this is attributed to lightning storms! Quite often this is due to improper protection.

Some devices have specific purposes, and others can protect against more than one of these electrical issues. Let's describe a few of these devices.

Power Strips

A *power strip* is a group of sockets, usually in-line, with a flexible cable that plugs into an AC outlet. It allows multiple devices to share a single receptacle in that outlet. Due to this, a maximum wattage rating can be applied to the power strip; for example, 3,000 watts is a decent amount. A computer might have a 300-watt power supply, but on the average, it might use less than that while running. A monitor might use between 35 watts and 100 watts depending on the type of monitor. You can check the wattage rating on the back or side of most devices. Add the total for all devices connected to the power strip, and remember not to exceed the maximum rating. This concept applies to other devices in this section including surge protectors and UPSs.

Power strips might not have surge protection functionality. If they don't have surge protection capabilities, they cannot protect from any of the electrical issues (surges and spikes) listed in the previous section.

A power strip has a master on/off switch and usually has a 15-amp circuit breaker to prevent overloading. If an overload occurs, the circuit breaker trips, cutting power, and the device can usually be reset by pressing a black button normally located somewhere near the power button. Overloads occur because the power strip tries to pull too much current (amps) from the wall outlet, or when too much current is supplied *to* the power strip. As a rule of thumb, no more than three or four computers (and monitors) should use the same power strip and, therefore, the same circuit. This calls into question whether any other AC outlets connect to the same circuit. To find this out, a qualified electrician can use a circuit testing tool and locate all the outlets on the circuit in question, or this information might be included in your building's electrical diagram. By the way, you can also calculate the amount of computers and monitors that can connect to a circuit by their amperage rating. For example, at AC (wall-outlet level) a typical computer would draw 2 to 3 amps and perhaps another 2 amps for the monitor maximum. (Keep in mind that these are estimates.) So on a standard 15-amp circuit, it would be wise to have no more than three computers and three monitors running simultaneously.

Surge Protectors

A *surge protector* or surge suppressor is a power strip that also incorporates a metal-oxide varistor (MOV) to protect against surges and spikes. Most power strips that you find in an office supply store or home improvement store have surge protection capability. The word *varistor* (sometimes spelled varsistor) is a blend of the two terms *variable resistor*.

ExamAlert

To protect against surges and spikes, use a surge protector!

Surge protectors are usually rated in joules, which are a way to measure energy, and in essence, the more joules the better. For computer systems, 1,000 joules or more is recommended. This joule rating gives you a sense of how long the device can protect against surges and spikes. Surges happen more often than you might think, and every time a surge happens, part of the varistor is burned out. The higher the joule rating, the longer the varistor (and therefore the device) should last. Most of today's surge protectors have an indicator light that informs you if the varistor has failed.

Because surges can occur over telephone lines, RG-6 cable lines, and network lines, it is common to see input and output ports for any or all these on a decent surge protector. Higher-quality surge protectors have multiple MOVs not only for the different connections such as AC and phone, but also have multiple MOVs for the individual wires in an AC connection.

Uninterruptible Power Supplies

An *uninterruptible power supply (UPS)* takes the functionality of a surge suppressor and combines that with a battery backup. So now, our computer is protected not only from surges and spikes, but also from sags, brownouts, and blackouts.

> **Exam Alert**
>
> Use a UPS to protect your computer from power outages!

But the battery backup can't last indefinitely! It is considered emergency power and typically keeps your computer system running for 5 to 30 minutes depending on the model you purchase. Figure 5.3 shows an example of a typical inexpensive UPS. Notice that some of the outlets on the device are marked for battery backup *and* surge protection, whereas others are for surge protection only.

Most UPS devices also act as line conditioners, protecting from over- and under-voltage; they condition (or regulate) the voltage sent to the computer. If you happen to see a customer's lights flickering, this could be dirty power, and you should consider recommending a UPS for the customer's computers and networking equipment. The device shown in the figure, and most UPS devices today, has a USB connection so that your computer can communicate with the UPS. When there is a power outage, the UPS sends a signal to the computer telling it to shut down, suspend, or stand-by before the battery discharges completely. Most UPSs come with software that you can install that enables you to configure the computer with these options.

Battery backup and surge protection

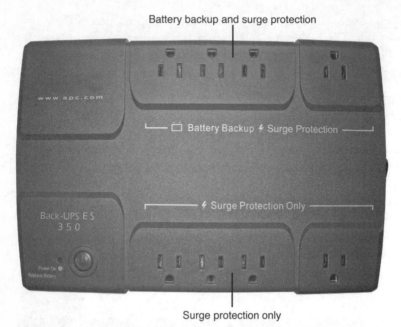

FIGURE 5.3   A common UPS

UPS devices' output power capacity is rated in volt-amps (VA) and watts. Although you might have heard that volt-amps and watts are essentially the same, this is one of those times that they are somewhat different. The volt-amp rating is slightly higher due to the difference between apparent power (when in battery backup mode) and real power (when pulling regular power from the AC outlet). For example, the device in Figure 5.3 has a volt-amp rating of 350 VA but a wattage rating of 200 watts. Generally, this is enough for a computer, monitor, and a few other devices, but a second computer might be pushing it given the wattage rating. The more devices that connect to the UPS, the less time the battery can last if a power outage occurs; if too many devices are connected, there may be inconsistencies when the battery needs to take over. Thus many UPS manufacturers limit the amount of battery backup-protected receptacles. Connecting a laser printer to the UPS is *not* recommended due to the high current draw of the laser printer; and *never* connect a surge protector or power strip to one of the receptacles in the UPS, to protect the UPS from being overloaded.

ExamAlert

Do *not* connect laser printers to UPS devices.

The UPS normally has a lead-acid battery that, when discharged, requires 10 to 20 hours to recharge. This battery is usually shipped in a disconnected state. Before charging the device for use, you must first make sure that the battery leads connect to the UPS. If the battery ever needs to be replaced, a red light usually appears accompanied by a beeping sound. Beeping can also occur if power is no longer supplied to the UPS by the AC outlet.

There are varying levels of UPS devices, which incorporate different technologies. For example, the cheaper standby UPS (known as an SPS) might have a slight delay when switching from AC to battery power, possibly causing errors in the computer operating system. Although it isn't important to know these different technologies for the exam, you should realize that some care should be taken when planning the type of UPS to be used. When data is crucial, you had better plan for a quality UPS!

Cram Quiz

Answer these questions. The answers follow the last question. If you cannot answer these questions correctly, consider reading this section again until you can.

220-801 Questions

1. Which device should you use to protect against power outages?
   - ○ **A.** Multimeter
   - ○ **B.** UPS
   - ○ **C.** FedEx
   - ○ **D.** Surge protector

2. You want a *cost-effective* solution to the common surges that can affect your computer. Which device would be the best solution?
   - ○ **A.** UPS
   - ○ **B.** Surge protector
   - ○ **C.** Power strip
   - ○ **D.** Line conditioner

3. Which of these is an unexpected increase in voltage?
   - ○ **A.** Sag
   - ○ **B.** Blackout
   - ○ **C.** Spike
   - ○ **D.** Whiteout

220-802 Questions

4. You are fixing a computer for a customer when you notice a few of the fluorescent lights flickering every now and then. What should you recommend to the customer to protect their equipment?

- ○ **A.** To get an electrician
- ○ **B.** To install a UPS
- ○ **C.** To get an extra power supply
- ○ **D.** To buy a generator

Cram Quiz Answers

220-801 Answers

1. **B**. The UPS is the only item listed that protects the computer from power outages like blackouts and brownouts.

2. **B**. A surge protector is the right solution at the right price. A UPS is a possible solution but costs more than a surge protector. A line conditioner also would be a viable solution but, again, is overkill. And a power strip doesn't necessarily have surge protection functionality.

3. **C**. A spike (or a surge) is an unexpected increase in voltage. A sag is a decrease in voltage, a blackout is a power outage, and a whiteout is actually a blizzard, which could result in a blackout!

220-802 Answers

4. **B**. You should recommend the customer installs a UPS for computer equipment. Flickering lights could be a sign of voltage fluctuations (dirty power) which could also affect the computers. The UPS can combat dirty power by conditioning it.

Power Supplies

Okay, now that you've tested your AC outlet and put some protective power devices into play, let's go ahead and talk power supplies. The power supply acts as an inverter; it is in charge of converting the alternating current (AC) drawn from the wall outlet into direct current (DC) to be used internally by the computer. But the PC power supply actually makes use of a transformer (which essentially steps down power), a rectifier, and an inverter, working together to convert AC over to DC. The power supply feeds the motherboard, hard drives, optical drives, and any other devices inside of the computer. Talk about a single point of failure! That is why many higher-end workstations and servers have redundant power supplies.

Planning Which Power Supply to Use

It is important to use a reliable brand of power supply that is certified; for example, in the USA power supplies can be certified by the Underwriter Laboratories (known as UL listed.)

There are a few other things to take into account when planning which power supply to use in your computer:

- ▶ Type of power supply and compatibility
- ▶ Wattage and capacity requirements
- ▶ Amount and type of connectors

Now, in the scenario mentioned in the beginning of the chapter, you need a power supply that can support many devices in your workstation; one that can output a lot of power. In this scenario the computer has two SATA hard drives, a Blu-ray drive, a DVD-ROM, an older IDE drive, and a PCIe video card. And just say that you use an ATX 12V 2.0 motherboard. So you need to look for a high–capacity, compatible ATX power supply with a decent amount of connectors for your devices. Let's discuss planning now.

Types of Power Supplies and Compatibility

The most common form factor today is Advanced Technology Extended (ATX). Depending on the type of ATX, the main power connector to the motherboard will have 20 pins or, more commonly, 24 pins. Table 5.1 shows a few different form factors and their characteristics. The key is compatibility. In this scenario you have a previously built computer, which means that the case and motherboard are already compatible. If this computer were *propri-etary*, you could go to the computer manufacturer's website to find out the exact form factor, and possibly a replacement power supply for that model computer. Some third-party power supply manufacturers also offer replacement power supplies for proprietary systems. However, if this computer were custom built, you would need to find out the form factor used by the motherboard and/or case, and should open the computer to take a look at all the necessary power connections. Then you need to find a compatible power supply according to those specifications from a third-party power supply manufacturer. Table 5.1 displays the form factors you need to know for the exam.

TABLE 5.1 **Common Power Supply Form Factors**

Form Factor	Main Power Connector	Other Characteristic
ATX	P1 20-pin connector	An older standard but you will probably still support it!
ATX 12V 1.0 – 1.3	P1 20-pin connector & P4 4-pin 12V connector	Supplemental 6-pin AUX Connector provides additional 3.3V and 5V supplies to the motherboard.
ATX 12V 2.0	P1 24-pin connector (backward compatible)	6-pin AUX was removed. SATA power cable is required.
ATX 12V 2.1	P1 24-pin connector	Added a separate 6-pin power connector for PCIe video cards; delivers 75 watts.
ATX 12V 2.2	P1 24-pin connector	Added 8-pin power connector for PCIe video cards; delivers 150 watts.
ATX 12V 2.3	P1 24-pin connector	Recommended efficiency is now 80% due to Energy Star 4.0 regulations.

Figure 5.4 gives examples of a P1 20-pin (the white connector) and P1 24-pin connector (the black connector). Toward the left of the black connector, it has an additional four pins beyond the initial group of 20 pins. Both have locking tabs to keep the P1 connector fastened to the motherboard. (In the figure this is shown only on the 20-pin connector.)

> **ExamAlert**
>
> Original ATX power supplies connect to the motherboard with a 20-pin connector. Newer ATX 12V 2.x power supplies connect with a 24-pin connector.

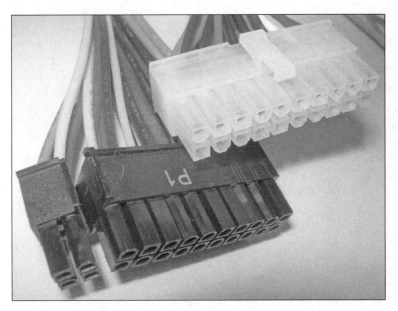

FIGURE 5.4   **24-pin and 20-pin power connectors**

Most of today's motherboards have an additional 4-pin or 8-pin 12 V power connector for the CPU. A typical power supply offers one or two 4-pin connectors, or one 8-pin connector. If the motherboard and power supply don't match up, there are 4 to 8-pin adapters available. Figure 5.5 shows the DP67DE motherboard's main 24-pin and additional 4-pin CPU power connections. Also, remember about case fans. Some case fans must connect directly to the power supply feeds. However, if they have 4-pin connectors, then they can connect directly to the motherboard, as shown in the figure. Finally, case connectors for the power on and reset buttons are usually located toward the front of the motherboard. When connecting these, the colored wire normally goes to positive (+) if necessary. Some of the case connectors can be connected either way, and it won't make a difference. But connectors like the power LED and the hard drive activity LED need to be connected properly for the LEDs to display. Quite often the motherboard will be color-coded, and the fold out instruction sheet will show exactly where to plug in each case connector, and the case connectors themselves are normally labeled.

There are many other types of form factors such as microATX, ITX, and BTX (covered in Chapter 2, "Motherboards") and older form factors such as AT; however, the form factors listed in Table 5.1 are the important ones to know regarding power supplies for the A+ exam. For any other form factors, just remember that the power supply, case, and motherboard all need to be compatible.

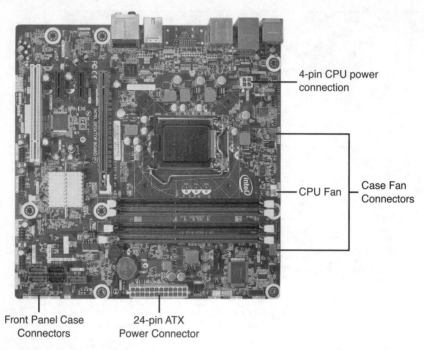

FIGURE 5.5   Main power, 4-pin CPU power, case fan, CPU fan, and case connections

Another important piece to consider is the type of case used. Larger cases require longer power cables to reach the devices. You can find the measurements for the cables on the power supply manufacturer's website. There are several different types of cases that you need to be familiar with:

▶ **Desktop:** Lies horizontally, usually has one or two 5 1/4-inch drive bays.

▶ **Mini-tower**: Stands vertically, usually has two or three drive bays.

▶ **Mid-tower**: Usually has three or four bays.

▶ **Full tower**: Usually has six bays.

▶ **Slim line**: Compaq and the Playstation III and other third-party case manufacturers use this case design.

Many power supply manufacturers also make computer cases and often sell them as a package or to be purchased separately.

Wattage and Capacity Requirements

Power supplies are usually rated in watts. They are rated at a maximum amount that they can draw from the wall outlet and pass on to the computer's devices. Remember that the computer will not always use all that power the way in which a light bulb does. And the amount depends on how many devices work and how much number crunching your processor does! In addition, when computers sleep or suspend, they use less electricity. What you need to be concerned with is the maximum amount of power all the devices need collectively. Most power-supply manufacturers today offer models that range from 300 watts all the way up to 1,000 watts. Although 300 watts is a decent amount of power for many computers, it might not suffice in our scenario. Devices use a certain amount of power defined in amps and/or watts. By adding all the devices' power consumption together, you can get a clearer picture of how powerful a power supply you need. Consult the manufacturer's web page of the device for exact requirements. In this scenario the computer has two SATA hard drives, a Blu-ray drive, a DVD-ROM, an older IDE drive, and a PCIe video card. It also has a quad-core processor and 8 GB of RAM (in two sticks).

After doing the math, it appears that the computer in the scenario needs approximately 400 watts or so to run smoothly. The power supply you purchase should be rated slightly higher just in case; so in this scenario you would obtain a 450-watt or 500-watt power supply. Most power supplies are rated for 15 amps, so it is important to connect the computer to a 15-amp circuit or higher.

Amount and Type of Power Connectors

It is important to know how many of each type of power connector you need when planning which power supply to use. In the scenario you need four SATA power connectors (for the two hard drives, Blu-ray drive, and DVD-ROM), and one IDE power connector for the older hard drive. You also need a 6-pin power connection for your video card and have two case fans that require power. You need to be familiar with each of these types of power connectors for the A+ exams. Be prepared to identify them by name and by sight. Table 5.2 defines the usage and voltages for the most common power connectors: Molex, mini (Berg), SATA, and PCIe, which display in Figures 5.6 through 5.9.

TABLE 5.2 **Power Connectors**

Power Connector	Usage	Pins and Voltages
Molex	Case fans, IDE hard drives, and optical drives	Red (5V), black (G), black (G), and yellow (12V)
Mini (Berg)	Floppy drives	Red (5V), black (G), black (G), and yellow (12V)
SATA	Serial ATA hard drives and optical drives	15-pin, 3.3V, 5V, and 12V
PCIe	PCI Express video cards	6-pin (ATX version 2.1) 12 V 8-pin (ATX version 2.2 and higher) 12 V

Note

Many power supplies come with 6-pin PCIe power. Before purchasing a power supply, be sure that it has the proper video power you require (6-pin or 8-pin).

FIGURE 5.6   **Molex power connector**

FIGURE 5.7   **Mini power connector**

FIGURE 5.8   **SATA 15-pin power connector**

FIGURE 5.9   **PCIe 6-pin power connector**

Installing the Power Supply

When the power supply arrives, you can install it. But first, take a look at the back of the power supply to identify the components you see, as shown in Figure 5.10.

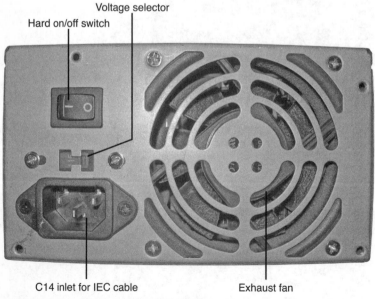

FIGURE 5.10   **Rear view of power supply**

On the top-left portion of Figure 5.10, you see a hard on/off switch some-times referred to as a kill switch. This is a nice feature when troubleshooting PCs. Instead of disconnecting the power cable, you can shut off this switch. It works nicely in emergencies as well. Below that you see a red voltage selector switch. This should be set to 115V in the United States. It also has a 230V option to be used in other countries. (An additional adapter might be neces-sary for the different wall outlets you might encounter.) Never change the voltage selector switch while the computer is running. Be sure to check this setting before using the power supply. Many newer power supplies are now equipped with a universal input enabling you to connect the power supply to any AC outlet between 100V to 240V, without having to set a voltage switch. Below that you see the power cable inlet; this is known as a C14 inlet and is where you attach your power cord to the power supply. These inlets and cables that connect to them are defined by the IEC 60320 specification (previ-ously the IEC 320 spec) and because of this many techs refer to the power cord as an IEC cable (which by the way stands for International Electrotechnical Commission). This cord actually has a standard three-prong connector suitable for an AC outlet on one end and a C13 line socket on the other to connect to the power supply. To the right you see the power supply fan that is of great importance when troubleshooting power supplies.

If there is a power supply connected to the computer, turn off the computer and unplug the power supply. ATX motherboards are always receiving 5 volts even when they are off, if the computer is plugged in. Be sure that you use antistatic methods. Remove the old power supply and prepare to install the new one.

You might want to test the new power supply before installing it. This can be done by connecting a power supply tester (described in the next section), plugging in the power supply to the AC outlet, and turning on the hard on/off switch. Or you can test the power supply after it is installed by simply turning the computer on.

The power supply is placed inside the case and mounted with four standard screws that are screwed in from the back of the case. In some instances, a plas-tic housing inside the case might need to be removed. In addition, the power supply might not fit without the removal of other devices, such as the proces-sor and such, but in most cases (pun intended) you should install the power supply without too much trouble. Next, connect the P1 connector to the motherboard and attach the Molex, mini, SATA, and PCIe as necessary to their corresponding devices. The main 24-pin connector can be plugged in only in one way: a locking tab. Also, most other connectors are molded in such a way as to make it difficult to connect them backward. If you need a lot of strength to plug in the connector, check and make sure that it is oriented correctly. Don't force the connection. Afterward, remove any antistatic protection, and finally, plug the power supply into the AC outlet, turn on the hard on/off switch (if the power supply has one), and turn on the computer. Check to see if the fan in the power supply is working and if the computer boots correctly.

In some instances, you might notice an odor coming from the power supply while it is on. This is normal. The power supply requires a burn-in period of approximately 48 hours, in which oils are burned off of the device's internal components. Whenever installing new computers or power supplies for a customer, instruct them about the burn-in period.

Troubleshooting Power Supply Issues

Installation of the power supply was easy, and there aren't usually many issues when doing so, but power supplies don't last forever. Moreover, many issues that occur with power supplies are intermittent making the troubleshooting process a little tougher. Your best friends when troubleshooting power supplies are going to be a multimeter, power supply tester, and your eyes and ears. Of course, always make sure that the power supply connects to the AC outlet properly before troubleshooting further. Here are a couple of the issues you may encounter with power supplies:

▶ Fan failure

▶ Fuse failure

▶ Quick death

▶ Slow death

Fan failure can be due to the fact that the power supply is old, extremely clogged with dirt, or the fan was of a cheaper design (without ball bearings). However, for the A+ exam it doesn't make a difference. As far as A+ is concerned, if the fan fails, the power supply needs to be replaced, and it makes sense. Chances are, if the fan has failed, other components of the power supply are on their way out also. It is more cost-effective to a company to simply replace the power supply than to have a technician spend the time opening it and trying to repair it. More important, although it is possible to remove and replace the fan by opening the power supply, this can be a dangerous venture because the power supply holds an electric charge, so the A+ rule is to never open the power supply.

ExamAlert

Do not open a power supply! If it has failed, replace it with a working unit.

Fan failure can sometimes cause a loud noise to emanate from the power supply; it might even sound like it is coming from inside the computer. Any fan in the computer (power supply fan, case fan, and CPU fan) can make some strange noises over time. If a customer reports a loud noise coming from the inside of a PC, consider the power supply fan.

Fuse failure can occur due to an overload or due to the power supply malfunctioning. Either way, the proper course of action is to replace the power supply. Do not attempt to replace the fuse. Chances are that the power supply is faulty if the fuse is blown.

Note

If you need to test a fuse used for other purposes, then use your multimeter to test its continuity. Make sure that your red lead is connected to the ohms (Ω) input, and set the meter to Ohm (Ω). (When performing continuity and resistance tests, you don't want any electrical flow, so make sure the fuse is not connected to anything!) Touch the probes to both ends of the fuse. A good fuse should show zero ohm or display continuity. A bad or "blown" fuse will not show any reading. This is an example of testing impedance.

If the power supply dies a quick death, it might be because of several reasons, from an electrical spike to hardware malfunction. First, make sure that the IEC cable is connected properly to the power supply and to the AC outlet. Sometimes, it can be difficult to tell whether the power supply has failed or if it's something else inside or outside the computer system. You should check the AC outlet with your trusty receptacle tester and make sure that a circuit hasn't tripped, and verify that any surge protectors and/or UPS devices work properly. Depending on what you sense about the problem, you might decide to just swap out the power supply with a known good one. Otherwise, move to the following numbered steps.

If the power supply is dying a slow death and is causing intermittent errors, or frequent failure of hard drives and other devices, it could be tough to troubleshoot. If you suspect intermittent issues, first make sure that the power cord is connected securely and then try swapping out the power supply with a known good one. Boot the computer and watch it for a while to see if the same errors occur.

> **Note**
>
> If a system were recently upgraded, the power supply could cause the system to reboot intermittently because the new components are causing too much of a power drain. When upgrading components, be sure to check if you need to upgrade the power supply as well!

Whether the power supply has apparently failed completely or is possibly causing intermittent errors, and you can't figure out the cause to this point, continue through the following steps:

1. Remove the computer case.

2. Connect a power supply unit tester (PSU tester), as shown in Figure 5.11, to the P1 connector and look at the results. (Make sure you have the correct power supply tester; this depends on whether you have a 20-pin or 24-pin power connector.) These power supply testers normally test for +12 V, –12 V, +5 V, –5 V, and 3.3 V, but they might not test every individual pin. If there are error lights, no lights, or missing lights for specific voltages on the tester, replace the power supply. If all the lights are green, move to the next step.

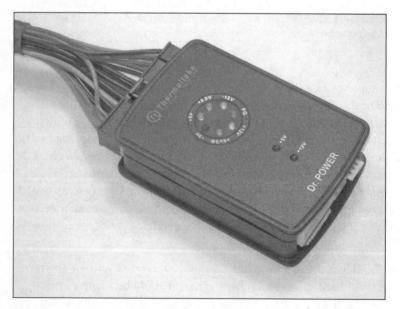

FIGURE 5.11 **Testing a 24-pin P1 connector with a power supply tester**

3. Use a multimeter to test the power supply. Use the same methodology for testing with a multimeter as in the beginning of this chapter.

   a. Turn off the hard on/off switch. (If there is one; if not, unplug the IEC cord.)

   b. With the main motherboard connector (P1) inserted into the motherboard, connect the black lead to a ground wire (or other source of ground) and insert the red lead to a colored voltage wire in the main power connector, as shown in Figure 5.12. You need to dig a little bit to get the lead in there, but don't press too hard. When the leads are stationary, move to the next step.

FIGURE 5.12 **Testing the 3.3 volt wire with a multimeter set to volts DC**

   c. Turn on the hard on/off switch (or plug the IEC cord back in) and turn on the computer.

    d. Turn on the multimeter to volts DC and view the results. In Figure 5.12 you notice that we test an orange wire (which is rated for +3.3 volts). Generally, supply voltages should be within +/– 5 percent of the nominal value. The result was +3.43 volts, which is within tolerance.

> **Note**
>
> If you have an analog multimeter, you would usually set this to 20 or higher. Just remember to move the decimal point in the reading for every increment higher than 20!

    e. Shut off the multimeter and computer every time before moving to another wire. Check each of the wires for proper voltages. A chart of all the voltages for 20-pin and 24-pin connectors is available in Chapter 2.

    f. If one of the wires fails or gives intermittent results, first verify you have a decent connection with the multimeter leads; then see if the wire just needs to be inserted into the main motherboard connector better, and if it continues, replace the power supply. If all the wires are fine (which is doubtful), move to the next step.

  4. Swap the power supply with a known good power supply. Boot the computer and watch it for several minutes or longer to see if there are any strange and intermittent occurrences.

Remember that sometimes connections can be jarred loose inside and outside the computer. Check the IEC cord on both ends and all power connections inside the computer. This includes the main motherboard connector, Molex, mini, SATA, and PCIe connectors. Any one loose connector can have interesting results on your computer!

Heating and Cooling

Another thing to watch for is system overheating. This can happen for several reasons:

- ▶ Power supply fan failure
- ▶ Auxiliary case fan failure
- ▶ Inadequate amount of fans
- ▶ Missing or open slot covers

▶ Case isn't tightly closed and screwed in

▶ Location of computer

Air flow is important on today's computers because processors can typically operate at 50 billion operations per second (GFLOPS) or more. That creates a lot of heat! Add to that the video card and other cards have their own on-board processors, it can get hot inside the computer case. Plus, environmental factors and higher temperature areas such as kitchens and warehouses can cause heat to be trapped in the case producing intermittent shutdowns. Circulation is the key word here. Air should flow in the case from the front and be exhausted out the back. Any openings in the case or missing slot covers can cause circulation to diminish. If you have a computer that has a lot of devices, or does a lot of processing, or runs hot for any other reason, your best bet is to install a case fan in the front of the case, which pulls air into the case, and a second case fan in the back of the case, which with the power supply fan helps to exhaust hot air out the back. Standard sizes for case fans are 80 and 120 mm. Also, try to keep the computer in a relatively cool area and leave space for the computer to expel its hot air! Of course there are other special considerations and options, such as liquid cooling, and special processor cooling methods, such as the Intel Chassis Air Guide. For more on these, see Chapter 2.

Cram Quiz

Answer these questions. The answers follow the last question. If you cannot answer these questions correctly, consider reading this section again until you can.

220-801 Questions

1. Which device tests multiple wires of a power supply at the same time?
   - ○ **A.** Multimeter
   - ○ **B.** Power supply tester
   - ○ **C.** Line conditioner
   - ○ **D.** Surge protector

2. Which power connector would be used to power an IDE hard drive?
   - ○ **A.** Molex
   - ○ **B.** Mini
   - ○ **C.** P1
   - ○ **D.** P8/P9

3. Which of the following uses a 24-pin main motherboard power connector?

   ○ **A.** ATX

   ○ **B.** ATX 12V 1.3

   ○ **C.** ATX 12V 2.0

   ○ **D.** ATX 5V 2.0

4. What voltages are supplied by a Molex power connector?

   ○ **A.** 12 V and 5 V

   ○ **B.** 5 V and 3.3 V

   ○ **C.** 3.3 V and 1.5 V

   ○ **D.** 24 V and 12 V

220-802 Questions

5. A company salesperson just returned to the United States after 3 months in Europe. Now the salesperson tells you that the PC, which worked fine in Europe, won't turn on. What is the best solution?

   ○ **A.** Install a new power supply.

   ○ **B.** The computer will not work in the United States due to European licensing.

   ○ **C.** Install a power inverter to the power supply.

   ○ **D.** Change the voltage from 230 to 115.

6. You are troubleshooting a computer that won't power on. You have already checked the AC outlet and the power cord, which appear to be functioning properly. What should you do next?

   ○ **A.** Test the computer with a PSU tester.

   ○ **B.** Plug the computer into a different outlet.

   ○ **C.** Check that the RAM is seated correctly.

   ○ **D.** Install a UPS.

7. You suspect that incorrect voltage is provided to a power supply. What tool should you use to test this?

   ○ **A.** PSU tester

   ○ **B.** Loopback adapter

   ○ **C.** Multimeter

   ○ **D.** Voltage detector

8. You just upgraded a motherboard in a computer, and put the system back together. It boots, but the power LED on the front of the computer case doesn't light when the system is on. The rest of the computer seems to work fine. What should you do first?

   ○ **A.** Check the power supply.

   ○ **B.** Check the power LED pinout.

   ○ **C.** Replace the LED.

   ○ **D.** Replace the power button.

9. A computer you are troubleshooting shuts down without warning. After a few minutes it boots back up fine, but after running for a short time, it shuts down again. What components could be the cause? (Select the two best answers.)

   ○ **A.** Power supply

   ○ **B.** SATA hard drive

   ○ **C.** RAM

   ○ **D.** CPU fan

   ○ **E.** Video card

Cram Quiz Answers

220-801 Answers

1. **B.** The power supply tester tests 3.3 V, 5 V, –5 V, 12 V, and –12 V simultaneously. A multimeter tests only one wire at a time. Line conditioners and surge protectors are preventative devices, not testing devices.

2. **A**. Molex connectors power IDE devices. Mini connectors are for floppy drives, P1 is a name used for the main motherboard connector, and P8/P9 are legacy main power connectors for AT systems.

3. **C**. ATX 12V 2.0 combined the 20-pin and 4-pin connectors used in ATX 12V 1.3 into one 24-pin connector.

4. **A**. Molex connectors provide 12 volts and 5 volts. There are four wires: Yellow is 12 V, red is 5 V, and two blacks which are grounds.

220-802 Answers

5. **D**. Most likely, the voltage selector was set to 230 V so that it could function properly in Europe (for example, in the UK.) It needs to be changed to 115 V so that the power supply can work properly in the United States. Make sure to do this while the computer is off and unplugged.

6. **A.** You should test the computer with a PSU tester. This can tell you whether the power supply functions properly. You already know that the AC outlet is functional, so there is no reason to use another outlet. The computer would still turn on if the RAM wasn't seated properly. A UPS won't help the situation because it is part of the power flow before the power supply.

7. **C.** In this scenario, you should test the AC outlet with a multimeter because you suspected incorrect voltage. The multimeter can tell you exactly what voltage is supplied. A voltage detector and PSU tester tell you only if voltage is present on a given wire, not the exact amount; plus, you don't want to test the power supply. However, the multimeter is the right tool to use if you wanted to find exactly what voltages were supplied to the motherboard. Loopback adapters are used to test network cards and serial ports.

8. **B**. You should check the power LED pinout. The case connector that goes to the motherboard is probably installed backward. Motherboards are usually labeled. If not, check your documentation for the computer. If the power button works, there is no reason to replace it. The rest of the computer works fine, and other case connectors are getting power, so the power supply can be ruled out. Replacing the LED can be difficult and time-consuming, plus LEDs almost never need to be replaced.

9. **A** and **D**. The two components that could cause the system to shut down are the power supply and the CPU fan. Check the CPU fan settings and temperature in the BIOS first before opening the computer. If those are fine, then you most likely need to replace the power supply. The RAM, video card, and hard drive should not cause the system to suddenly shut down.

CHAPTER 6

Storage Devices

This chapter covers the following A+ exam topics:

▶ Magnetic Storage Media

▶ Optical Storage Media

▶ Solid-State Storage Media

You can find a master list of A+ exam topics in the "Introduction."

This chapter covers CompTIA A+ 220-801 objectives 1.5, 1.7, and 1.11 and CompTIA A+ 220-802 objective 4.3.

Everyone needs a place to store data. Whether it's business documents, audio/video files, or data backups, users must decide on the right storage medium. This can be magnetic media such as a hard drive, optical media such as a DVD, or solid-state media such as a USB flash drive. It all depends on what is stored, and how often and where it is needed. This chapter concentrates on those three categories of media and how to identify, install, and troubleshoot them.

Magnetic Storage Media

The three main types of magnetic storage are hard disk drives, floppy disk drives, and tape drives. By far the most common is the hard disk drive; this is where the operating system is normally stored. Users also store frequently accessed data on the hard drive as well, such as Word documents, music, pictures, and so on. Floppy drives are not part of the bulk of today's computers, due to their small capacity. However, in special cases they might be needed by the user, perhaps to access older data and programs. The technician, however, uses the floppy drive to boot systems with special startup and analysis disks. Tape drives are used for archival, the long-term backup of data that is not accessed often. Because floppy drives and tape drives are far less common, let's begin with hard drives.

Hard Disk Drives

Hard disk drives (HDDs) are the most common of magnetic media. They are nonvolatile, which means that any information stored on them cannot be lost when the computer is turned off. They are not as fast as RAM but are faster than most other storage mediums available; this makes them a good choice to store permanent data that is accessed frequently.

Hard Drive 101

The hard disk drive (often shortened to hard drive or hard disk) contains one or more platters with a magnetic surface. Data is recorded to the disk by magnetizing ferromagnetic material directionally, basically, as 0s and 1s. The disk is usually made of a cobalt-based alloy. As the platters rotate at high speed, read/write heads store and read information to and from the disk. The heads are located on an actuator arm that arcs across the disk. Together, the arm and read/write heads are similar to the arm and needle combination of a record player. Figure 6.1 shows some of the components inside and outside of the drive.

The hard drive depicted in Figure 6.1 is a typical Serial ATA 3.5-inch wide drive. This hard drive, like all internal hard drives, has a data connector and power connector. On this particular drive, the data connector attaches to the motherboard (or expansion card) by way of a 7-pin cable. The power connector attaches to the power supply by way of a 15-pin power cable. Regardless of the type of hard drive, always make sure that the data and power cables are firmly connected to it. Let's talk about the two main types of hard drives: PATA and SATA.

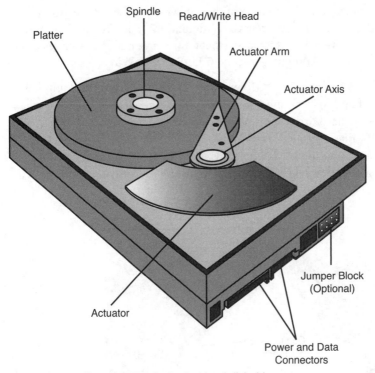

FIGURE 6.1   **Components of a typical hard disk drive**

PATA

In this corner, coming in at a maximum data throughput of 133 MB/s is PATA (Parallel ATA). This was the traditional hard drive and the standard for many years but has been all but phased out by SATA hard drives on most new computers; however, it is still on the CompTIA A+ objectives. PATA hard drives are often referred to as Ultra ATA drives and sometimes as IDE drives. They transfer data in parallel, for example 16 bits (2 bytes) at a time.

Internal PATA hard drives use the Integrated Drive Electronics (IDE) interface to transmit data to and from the motherboard. Every IDE port on a motherboard can have up to two drives connected to it. For a long time, motherboards would be equipped with two IDE ports, enabling for a maximum of four IDE devices. However newer motherboards often come with only one, limiting you to two IDE devices. The IDE ports on the motherboard and the hard drive manifest themselves as 40-pin connectors to which you can connect either a 40 or 80-wire ribbon cable. Newer IDE cables are all 80-wire; however, they look identical to the older 40-wire versions, except for the blue connector on one end that you find on many 80-wire cables. The cable has three connectors, one for the controller (often blue), one for the master drive (often black), and a connector in the middle of the cable for the slave drive (often gray). We talk more about master/slave configurations in a little bit. The IDE port on the hard drive is keyed for easy orientation. External PATA drives usually transfer data to the computer by way of USB or FireWire.

PATA hard drives accept a 4-pin Molex power connector from the computer's power supply. The Molex connector is keyed so that it is easier to orient when connecting to the hard drive. This power cable has four wires: Red (5 V), Black (ground), Black (ground), and Yellow (12 V). For more information about Molex and other power connections, see Chapter 5, "Power." Figure 6.2 shows an actual Ultra ATA hard drive's data and power connectors.

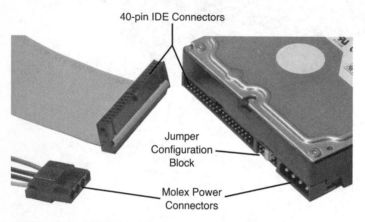

FIGURE 6.2   **PATA Ultra-ATA data and power connectors**

There is a jumper block in between the power and data connectors. This enables you to select the configuration of the hard drive. There are usually four options, which are often labeled on the drive:

▶ **Single:** In a single drive configuration, no jumper shunt is needed. If you want, you can connect the jumper horizontally across two pins. Although this does not configure the drive in any way, it keeps the jumper handy for future use.

▶ **Master:** Each of the motherboard's IDE connections enables for two drives. In a two-drive configuration on a single IDE cable, one must be set to drive 0 (master), and one must be set to drive 1 (slave). To set a drive to master, connect the jumper vertically to the correct pair of pins (for example, Western Digital drives use the center location; refer to Figure 6.2), and connect the black end connector of the IDE ribbon cable to the hard drive. The master hard drive is normally where the operating system would go.

▶ **Slave:** To set a drive to slave, connect the jumper vertically to the correct pair of pins (for example, Western Digital drives use the second position from the right), and connect the gray, middle connector of the IDE cable to the hard drive. The slave hard drive is where the bulk of the data would usually be stored.

▶ **Cable Select:** This drive mode automatically configures the drive as master or slave according to where you connect it to the IDE cable. This might be marked on the drive as CS.

> **Note**
>
> You might still see a PATA drive in the field. The two newest standards are ATA-6, known as Ultra ATA/100 because it can transfer 100 MB/s; and ATA-7, known as Ultra ATA/133, which can transfer 133 MB/s. ATA-6 introduced 48-bit addressing, which allows for a maximum hard drive capacity of 144 petabytes (PB.) Previous versions had a maximum drive size of only 137 GB.

SATA

And in this corner, coming in at a whopping maximum data rate of 600 MB/s is SATA (Serial ATA). These drives are the most-common hard drives in use today. If you remember, the older DP35DP motherboard used in Chapter 2, "Motherboards," had six SATA ports but only one PATA IDE port, most likely for use with optical drives. And the newer DP67DE motherboard had no PATA IDE ports. So as you can surmise, hard drives, like expansion buses, and several other technologies, have gone serial. A Serial ATA drive transmits serial streams of data (one bit at a time) at high-speed over two pairs of conductors and can do so in full duplex, meaning it can send and receive simultaneously. Because SATA and PATA do not interfere with each other, you can run both simultaneously; however, by default one will not mate to the other; they are not compatible without a converter board or adapter.

To transmit data the SATA drive uses a 7-pin flat (or right-angle) cable, as shown in Figure 6.3. Obviously, the motherboard should be equipped with one or more SATA connectors to use SATA hard drives. The other option would be to install an SATA PCIe or PCI expansion card. Most motherboards come with one or more SATA data cables. These cables are easily connected to the drive but to remove them, press down on the top of the connector at the end of the cable before pulling the cable out. Only one drive can connect to the SATA cable.

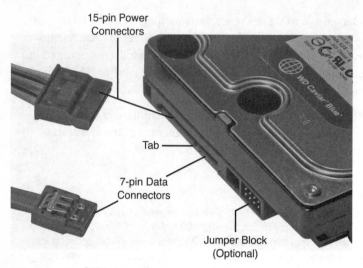

FIGURE 6.3 **SATA data and power connectors**

For power, the SATA drive utilizes a 15-pin power connector, as shown in Figure 6.3. The hard drive's power connector has a vertical tab at the right side, making for easier orientation when connecting the power cable. Power supplies send 3.3 V, 5 V, and 12 V to the SATA drive via orange, red, and yellow cables respectively. Your power supply must be equipped with this power cable to support SATA drives; otherwise, you need an IDE 4-pin to SATA 15-pin power adapter. Because IDE doesn't use the orange 3.3 V wire, this is omitted in IDE-SATA power adapters.

SATA revision 1.0 (1.5 Gb/s) was the first generation of SATA devices. Currently, the latest SATA revision is 3.0 (6 Gb/s). Table 6.1 shows the different SATA versions you need to know for the exam.

TABLE 6.1 **Comparison of SATA Standards**

Standard	Maximum Data Transfer Rate
SATA Revision 1.0	1.5 Gb/s
SATA Revision 2.0	3 Gb/s
SATA Revision 3.0	6 Gb/s

> **Note**
>
> Actual data transfer rates are less when you take encoding into account. SATA revision 1.0 goes from 1.5 Gb/s to 1.2 Gb/s (which comes to about 150 MB/s). Rev 2 goes from 3.0 to 2.4 Gb/s (about 300 MB/s.) Rev 3 goes from 6.0 to 4.8 Gb/s (about 600 MB/s.)
>
> You may also see some organizations refer to SATA measurements as Gbit/s instead of Gb/s, but they mean the same thing.
>
> As of the writing of this book, external SATA (eSATA) connections can produce a maximum of 3 Gb/s.

> **ExamAlert**
>
> Know the maximum data transfer rates for SATA Revisions 1, 2, and 3.

Older SATA drives can run on a newer SATA controller; however, data transfer will be limited to the speed of the drive, not the controller. For example, *Media PC's* DP67DE motherboard has two SATA 6 Gb/s interfaces and four 3 Gb/s interfaces (including one internal and one external eSATA port). Drives can be installed to any of the ports, but to take full advantage of an SATA revision 3.0 (6 Gb/s) controller, you need a 6 Gb/s drive.

> **ExamAlert**
>
> Remember that older SATA drives installed to newer SATA controllers can run only at the speed of the drive.

The *Tower PC* I built uses a SATA revision 2.0 hard drive (3 Gb/s); specifically the Western Digital Caviar Blue WD5000AAKS. This model is an average hard drive when it comes to speed and other major specifications. The specifications that you should be interested in when purchasing a hard drive (PATA or SATA), and should know for the A+ exams, include the following:

- ▶ **Capacity:** The example drive is marketed as a 500 GB drive, but accessible capacity can vary depending on the environment the hard drive is used in. For example, after being formatted, this drive can normally hold 500,107 MB. But in a RAID 1 mirrored environment, it can hold 490,402 MB.

▶ **Data transfer rate:** Because it is an SATA revision 2.0 drive, it has a theoretical maximum of 300 MB/s; but the theoretical numbers are never actually achieved. This particular drive can sustain in the neighborhood of 120 MB/s. This is sometimes also referred to as *data throughput*.

▶ **Rotational speed:** The platters in the example hard drive can rotate at a maximum of 7,200 RPM, which is common; other typical speeds for hard drives include 5,400 RPM (slower access time) and 10,000 RPM (faster access time).

▶ **Cache:** This drive has 16 MB of cache, which is also known as a buffer. The cache on most hard drives is on-board DRAM. Compare this with CPUs that use SRAM cache that is significantly faster. Like CPUs, the hard drive's cache helps to access frequently used information faster than if it were to get the information from the disk.

▶ **Latency:** After a track has been reached by the read head, latency is the delay in time before a particular sector on the platter can be read. It is directly related to rotational speed and is usually half the time it takes for the disk to rotate once. For example, our 7,200 RPM drive has an average latency of 4.2 ms (milliseconds), but a 10,000 RPM drive has an average latency of 3.0 ms.

ExamAlert

Understand a hard drive's specifications including capacity, data transfer rate, rotational speed, cache, and latency.

SCSI

Small Computer System Interface (SCSI) hard drives are often used in servers and power workstations that need high data throughput. You can identify a SCSI drive by the different (and usually louder) sound it makes compared to ATA drives; it's kind of like the difference between a diesel engine and a standard car engine. SCSI standards describe the devices, controllers, cables, and protocols used to send data. Part of the beauty of SCSI is that you can have up to 16 devices including the controller. They can be internal, external, or both. For the longest time SCSI was a parallel technology, but of late serial versions such as Serial Attached SCSI (SAS) have emerged. When installing SCSI devices, it is important to remember that each end of the SCSI chain must be terminated and that each device gets its own ID, between 0 and 15 (0–7 on older SCSI chains). The controller normally gets ID 7 and has its own BIOS, known as Option ROM, in which you can configure the controller, drives, and drive arrays. This SCSI BIOS often loads up and appears on the display *before* the PC BIOS. Because the card has a BIOS, its firmware might need to be updated from time to time, just like a motherboard's BIOS. Also, a software driver might need to be installed to the operating system for the SCSI controller. This is done during the Windows installation process. Table 6.2 shows a few of the current SCSI technologies you might see in the field.

TABLE 6.2 **Comparison of SCSI Standards**

SCSI Standard	Maximum Data Transfer Rate	Connector Type	Transmission Type
Ultra3 SCSI	160 MB/s	68-pin; 80-pin	Parallel
Ultra-320 SCSI	320 MB/s	68-pin; 80-pin	Parallel
Ultra-640 SCSI	640 MB/s	68-pin; 80-pin	Parallel
SAS (Serial Attached SCSI)	300 MB/s	SFF 8482, 8484, and 8470	Serial

Note: Older, deprecated SCSI connections use 50 pins. An example of a 50-pin SCSI connection is Ultra2 SCSI (Fast-40) which can transmit 40 MB/s. It only allows for a maximum of 8 devices.

ExamAlert

For the exam, know that the SCSI controller normally uses ID 7, and memorize the data transfer rates for the various SCSI Ultra versions.

Installing Hard Disk Drives

Installing hard drives is quite easy. First, make sure you employ antistatic measures and verify that the computer is off and unplugged.

Next, if it is an Ultra ATA drive (IDE), be sure to configure the jumper setting correctly. SATA drives do not need to be jumpered, unless they are coexisting with Ultra ATA drives on an IDE bus. Most SATA drives do not even come with jumpers. Most internal drives are 3.5 inches, and most cases have several 3.5-inch internal bays. The drive bay might need to be removed before attaching the drive, or you might screw it directly into the chassis. Some cases have a latching screwless system. However, if you need to screw in the drive, make sure you use all four screws, and turn the screws with a screwdriver until they are tight; but don't go any further. Try to stay away from motorized screwdrivers or other tools that might have too much torque and can possibly damage the hard drive.

After the drive is screwed in or attached to the case chassis, connect the data and power connectors. For Ultra ATA drives, the data connector is keyed. There is a tab on each end of the cable (in the middle), which corresponds to a notch on the hard drive's port and on the motherboard's port. In addition, these types of cables indicate the first pin (known as Pin 1) with a colored stripe on one side of the cable. Pin 1 is normally on the upper-right corner of the hard drive's IDE port, so just match the colored stripe up to it. Or remember that the colored stripe of the IDE cable should be oriented next to the power connector. The power connector (Molex) is also keyed; it has two diagonal corners that should be oriented at the top of the connector when plugging it into the drive. Try not to force these connections; it can damage an individual pin. It should take a bit of pressure, but if it doesn't seem right, pull the connector away, and make sure it is oriented correctly. For SATA drives, attach the data connector with the exposed metal or Serial ATA label facing up. Orient the power connector according to the tab on the right side of the hard drive's port. Verify that both the data and power connectors are firmly secured to the drive and to the motherboard. A loose connector can cause a boot failure in the operating system. However, don't force the connection, especially the data connection. If SATA data cable is upside down and forced into the port, it could cause damage to the port.

Finally, test the drive and make sure it is recognized by the BIOS at the correct capacity. If for some reason, the BIOS doesn't see the full capacity, check for any possible BIOS updates. Then, either install an operating system to the drive, or verify that a current operating system (on another pre-existing disk) can see the new drive at its correct capacity. Remember that a drive might show up as slightly less than its marketed amount within the operating system, depending on the environment the drive is used in.

Preventative Maintenance and Troubleshooting Hard Drives

Hard drives will fail. It's not a matter of *if*; it's a matter of *when*, especially when it comes to mechanical drives. The moving parts are bound to fail at some point. Hard drives have an average warranty of 3 years, as is the case with the SATA drives used in this book. It is interesting to note that most drives last around 3 years before failing. Of course, by implementing good practices, you can extend the lifespan of any hard drive, for example:

> ▶ **Turn the computer off when not in use:** By doing this, the hard drive is told by the operating system to spin down and enter a "parked" state. It's kind of like parking a car or placing a record player's arm on its holder. Turning the computer off when not in use increases the lifespan of just about all its devices (except for the lithium battery). You can also set the computer to hibernate, standby, or simply set your operating system's power scheme to turn off hard disks after a certain amount of inactivity,

such as 5 minutes. The less the drive is in motion, the longer lifespan it will have. Of course, if you want to take the moving parts out of the equation, you could opt for a solid-state drive, as discussed later in this chapter.

▶ **Clean up the disk:** Use a hard drive cleanup program to remove temporary files, clean out the recycle bin, and so on. Microsoft includes the Disk Cleanup program in Windows. Another free program is CleanUp! that you can download from the Internet after a quick Google search. By removing the "junk" from the hard drive, there is less data that the drive must sift through, which makes it easier on the drive when it is time to defragment.

▶ **Defragment the disk:** Defragmenting, also known as defragging, rearranges the data on a partition or volume so that it is laid out in a contiguous, orderly fashion. You should attempt to defragment the disk every month, maybe more if you are a power user. Don't worry; the operating system tells you if defragging is not necessary during the analysis stage. Over time, data is written to the drive, and subsequently erased, over and over again, leaving gaps in the drivespace. New data will sometimes be written to multiple areas of the drive, in a broken or fragmented fashion, filling in any blank areas it can find. When this happens, the hard drive has to work much harder to find the data it needs. Logically, data access time is increased. Physically, the drive will be spinning more, starting and stopping more, in general, more mechanical movement. It's kind of like changing gears excessively with the automatic transmission in your car. The more the drive has to access this fragmented data, the shorter its lifespan becomes due to mechanical wear and tear. Defragmenting the drive can be done with Microsoft's Disk Defragmenter, with the command-line **defrag**, or with other third-party programs. If using the Disk Defragmenter program, you need 15 percent free space on the volume you want to defrag. If you have less than that, you need to use the command-line option **defrag -f**. To sum it up, the more contiguous the data, the less the hard drive has to work to access that data, thus decreasing the data access time and increasing the lifespan of the drive.

ExamAlert

Know the tools available to defragment a hard drive.

▶ **Scan the drive with antimalware:** Make sure the computer has an antimalware program installed, which includes antivirus and antispyware. Verify that the software is scheduled to scan the drive at least twice a week. (Manufacturers' default is usually every day.) The quicker the software finds and quarantines threats, the less chance of physical damage to the hard drive.

You might find several issues when troubleshooting hard drives:

▶ **BIOS does not "see" the drive:** If the BIOS doesn't recognize the drive you have installed, you can check a few things. First, make sure the power cable is firmly connected and oriented properly. Second, verify that the correct end of the data cable is securely connected and oriented; for example on Ultra-ATA drives, the black connector on the ribbon cable should connect to the drive. The other end of the data cable should be firmly connected to the motherboard. Make sure SATA data cables weren't accidentally installed upside down; and if you find one that was, consider replacing it because it might be damaged due to incorrect installation. An OS Not Found error message could also be caused by improperly connected drives. Next, make sure that the drive is jumpered correctly. (Or not jumpered at all, if that is the scenario.) Finally, check if there is a motherboard BIOS update to see the drive; sometimes newer drives require new BIOS code to access the drive. If the drive is SCSI, check for a SCSI BIOS update.

▶ **Windows does not "see" a second drive:** There are several reasons why Windows might not see a second drive. Maybe a driver needs to be installed for the drive or for its controller (for example a PCI SATA card or SCSI card). Perhaps the secondary drive needs to be initialized within Disk Management. Or it can be that the drive was not partitioned or formatted. Also try the methods listed in the first bullet.

▶ **Slow reaction time:** If the system runs slow, it can be because the drive has become fragmented or has been infected with a virus or spyware. Analyze and defragment the drive. If it is heavily fragmented, the drive can take longer to access the data needed resulting in slow reaction time. You might be amazed at the difference in performance! If you think the drive might be infected, scan the disk with your antivirus/antispyware software to quarantine any possible threats. It's wise to schedule deep scans of the drive at least twice a week. More on viruses and spyware in Chapter 16, "Security." In extreme cases, you might want to move all the data from the affected drive to another drive, being sure to verify the data that was moved. Then format the affected drive, and finally move the data back. This is common in audio/video environments, and when dealing with data drives, but should not be done to a system drive, meaning a drive that contains the operating system.

▶ **Missing files at startup:** If you get a message such as NTLDR Is Missing or BOOTMGR Is Missing, these files need to be written back to the hard drive. For more on how to do this, see Chapter 11, "Troubleshooting Windows." In severe cases, this can mean that the drive is physically damaged and needs to be replaced. If this happens, the drive needs to be removed from the computer and slaved off to another drive on another system. Then the data needs to be copied from the damaged drive to a known good drive (which might require a third-party program), and a new drive needs to be installed to the affected computer. Afterward, the recovered data can be copied on the new drive.

▶ **Noisy drive/lockups:** If your Ultra ATA or SATA drive starts getting noisy, it's a sure sign of impending drive failure. You might also hear a scratching or grating sound, akin to scratching a record with the record player's needle. Or the drive might intermittently just stop or lockup with one or more audible clicks. You can't wait in these situations; you need to slave off the drive in another computer immediately and copy the data to a good drive. Even then, it might be too late. However, there are some third-party programs that might help recover the data.

Network Attached Storage (NAS)

Another type of hard drive storage is network attached storage (NAS). This is when one or more hard drives are installed into a device known as a NAS box that connects directly to the network. The device can then be accessed as a mapped network drive from any computer on the network. A basic example of this that I use on my network is the D-Link DNS-323. It can hold two SATA drives to be used together as one large capacity or in a RAID 1 mirrored configuration for fault tolerance. RAID 1 Mirroring means that two drives are used in unison, and all data is written to both drives, giving you a mirror or extra copy of the data, in the case that one drive fails. RAID levels 0, 1, and 5 are covered in Chapter 9, "Configuring Windows." It connects to the network by way of an RJ45 port that is rated at 10/100/1000 Mbps. Of course, there are much more advanced versions of NAS boxes that would be used by larger companies. These often have *hot-swappable* drives that can be removed and replaced while the device is on. Usually, they are mounted to a plastic enclosure or tray that is slid into the NAS device. But watch out, not every hard drive in a plastic hard drive enclosure is hot-swappable. There are cheaper versions of this for PCs that can be swapped in and out but not while the computer is on.

Floppy Disk Drives

As mentioned before, floppy disk drives (FDD) are not nearly as common as they were 10 years ago; in fact, most computers don't come with a floppy drive. However, some businesses might need them to access older data or programs, and technicians use them to start up a computer with special boot disks. Due to this, there is a chance you might see a question on them on the exam.

Floppy Drive Basics

The standard floppy drive is a 3.5-inch 1.44 MB floppy drive. Historically, this has been the A: drive and possibly the B: drive in a computer. These drive letters are reserved for floppy drives and other devices; now you know why operating systems use C: by default! The floppy drive uses a "mini" floppy power connector (shown in Chapter 5), also known as Berg, and a 34-pin keyed data cable that connects to the motherboard, *if* your motherboard supports it.

The floppy drive is known as removable media because the floppy disks are inserted into the drive. The most common of these disks has a 1.44 MB capacity. You can store only 1.38 MB of data to these disks due to formatting and because the boot sector takes up a small amount of space on the disk. Floppy disks are normally formatted using the FAT12 file system.

Floppy drives are installed much the same way as hard drives: They are screwed into the chassis of the case, and data and power cables connect to the floppy ports; these ports are shown in Figure 6.4. The mini power cable has a linear plastic tab that needs to face up when you connect the cable to the drive.

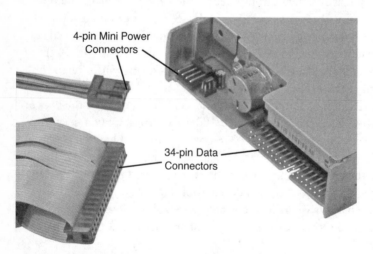

FIGURE 6.4   **Floppy data and power connectors**

Floppy Drive Troubleshooting and Boot Disks

As always, make sure that the data and power cables firmly connect to the floppy drive and to the motherboard. A floppy drive fails if the data connector is connected upside down, which is possible because many floppy drive's data ports are not keyed. You will know if the data cable is upside down because the floppy drive's activity light will remain on. If a disk is placed in the drive in this state, it will be erased and/or damaged. By the way, if there is a nonbootable disk in the floppy drive, and the floppy drive is set to first in the BIOS boot order, the system will probably give a Nonsystem Disk error when booted. If the floppy drive doesn't work, ensure that the BIOS has the floppy drive enabled. Otherwise, floppy drives are quite resilient and last a long time.

Examples of boot disks that a technician might use include Windows startup disks, to boot/repair or install a Windows computer; antivirus boot disks, to scan the boot sector of a hard drive; BIOS Flash boot disks, to update the BIOS on a computer; and specialized third-party boot disks, to repair a computer, recover data, and so on. If you plan to boot from a floppy disk, verify that the floppy drive is first in the BIOS boot order. If your computer doesn't have internal connectivity for a floppy drive, go external! USB floppy drives are available, and the BIOS boot order on some motherboards can be changed to allow USB devices to boot first, allowing you to start the computer from that bootable floppy disk.

Tape Drives

Tape drives are devices primarily used for archival or backup of data. These devices use removable media in the form of magnetic tape cartridges, which are inserted into the tape drive. Usage of tape drives has declined greatly in recent years due to the advent of writable optical media; however, you might still see some devices in use.

The tape drive is rated in one of two ways: native capacity, for example 100 GB; and compressed capacity, for example 200 GB. As you can see, compressed capacity will normally be at a 2:1 ratio compared to native capacity. A common example of a tape drive is Quantum's Digital Linear Tape (DLT) and the higher capacity Super DLT, which can go as high as 800 GB.

The tape drive can be internal or external. If it is internal, it might connect to a SCSI controller card or to an IDE port. If external, you might see it connect to a SCSI port, USB, IEEE 1394, or the older parallel port.

The driver for the tape drive must be installed, and a tape drive must be used with backup software. Some drives come with their own third-party software, or you can use Windows backup programs. Be careful with these programs.

Quite often, they backup all the data into one big compressed file, for example one file with the .bkf extension. Be sure to use the verify option when backing up data, and consider running a test backup and restore when you first start using a tape drive to verify it works properly.

Other deprecated backup technologies related to tape drives include products from Iomega such as the ZIP or JAZ disk technology, or the SuperDisk technology. Again, these and tape drives have been all but phased out due to the popular usage of optical storage and flash media.

Cram Quiz

Answer these questions. The answers follow the last question. If you cannot answer these questions correctly, consider reading this section again until you can.

220-801 Questions

1. What is the maximum data transfer rate of SATA revision 1.0?
   - A. 1.5 Mbps
   - B. 300 MB/s
   - C. 150 MB/s
   - D. 1.5 GB/s

2. Which of these is the delay it takes for the hard drive to access a particular sector on the disk?
   - A. Actuator
   - B. Latency
   - C. Lag
   - D. Propagation

3. What should you do first to repair a drive that is acting sluggish?
   - A. Remove the drive and recover the data.
   - B. Run Disk Cleanup.
   - C. Run Disk Defragmenter.
   - D. Scan for viruses.

4. How much data can a SATA revision 3.0 drive transfer per second?
   - A. 1.5 Gb/s
   - B. 3.0 Gb/s
   - C. 4.5 Gb/s
   - D. 6.0 Gb/s

5. How many pins are there in a SATA drive's data and power connectors?

   ○ **A.** 40 and 4

   ○ **B.** 8 and 16

   ○ **C.** 7 and 15

   ○ **D.** 80 and 4

6. What kind of cable does a floppy drive use?

   ○ **A.** 40-pin IDE

   ○ **B.** 80-pin IDE

   ○ **C.** 34-pin IDE

   ○ **D.** 168-pin IDE

7. What is the maximum data transfer rate of an Ultra3 SCSI device?

   ○ **A.** 320 MB/s

   ○ **B.** 160 MB/s

   ○ **C.** 640 MB/s

   ○ **D.** 300 MB/s

8. In a two drive IDE configuration, drive 0 would be the _____, and drive 1 would be the _____.

   ○ **A.** Slave, master

   ○ **B.** Cable select, slave

   ○ **C.** Slave, single

   ○ **D.** Master, slave

9. What is a standard connector for an external SCSI device?

   ○ **A.** 240 pin

   ○ **B.** 68 pin

   ○ **C.** 40 pin

   ○ **D.** 7 pin

10. Which of the following is hot-swappable?

    ○ **A.** Floppy drive

    ○ **B.** Tape drive

    ○ **C.** Hard drive

    ○ **D.** DVD drive

11. What devices would use a SCSI cable? (Select the two best answers.)

- ○ **A.** SSD
- ○ **B.** Tape drive
- ○ **C.** Floppy drive
- ○ **D.** IDE drive
- ○ **E.** Hard drive

220-802 Questions

12. You upgrade a computer's older SCSI drive with a new and much larger SCSI drive and upgrade the driver for the controller. However, when you reboot, the computer's SCSI controller still doesn't recognize the new drive. What should you do?

- ○ **A.** Format the SCSI drive as NTFS.
- ○ **B.** Check that the SCSI controller is receiving power.
- ○ **C.** Change jumper settings on the SCSI controller.
- ○ **D.** Check for a firmware update for the SCSI controller.

13. Which of the following are possible symptoms of hard drive failure? (Select the two best answers.)

- ○ **A.** System lock-up
- ○ **B.** Antivirus alerts
- ○ **C.** Failing bootup files
- ○ **D.** Network drive errors
- ○ **E.** BIOS doesn't recognize the drive

14. You just replaced a SATA hard drive that you suspected had failed. You also replaced the data cable between the hard drive and the motherboard. When you reboot the computer, you notice that the SATA drive is not recognized by the BIOS. What most likely happened to cause this?

- ○ **A.** The drive has not been formatted yet.
- ○ **B.** The BIOS does not support SATA.
- ○ **C.** The SATA port is faulty.
- ○ **D.** The drive is not jumpered properly.

CramQuiz

15. You are troubleshooting a SATA hard drive that doesn't function on a PC. When you try it on another computer it works fine. You suspect a power issue and decide to take voltage readings from the SATA power connector coming from the power supply. What readings should you find?

   ○ **A.** 5 V and 12 V

   ○ **B.** 5 V, 12 V, and 24 V

   ○ **C.** 3.3 V, 5 V, and 12 V

   ○ **D.** 3.3 V and 12 V

Cram Quiz Answers

220-801 Answers

1. **C.** SATA Revision 1.0 can transfer a maximum of 150 MB/s; though most devices won't ever attain that maximum. The standard specifies the transmission of 1.5 Gbps (notice the lowercase 'b' for bits); 300 MB/s is the data transfer rate of SATA Revision 2.0.

2. **B.** Latency is the delay it takes for the hard drive to access the data; it is directly related to the rotational speed (RPM) of the disk.

3. **C.** Attempt to defragment the disk. If it is not necessary, Windows lets you know. Then you can move to other options such as scanning the drive for viruses.

4. **D.** SATA Revision 3.0 drives can transfer 6.0 Gb/s. Revision 1.0 does 1.5 Gb/s. Revision 2.0 does 3.0 Gb/s.

5. **C.** The SATA drive uses a 7-pin data connector and a 15-pin power connector. Ultra ATA IDE hard drives have a 40-pin data connector and 4-pin power connector. The IDE drive's cable might have 80 *conductors* or wires, but it still physically connects through 40 pins.

6. **C.** The floppy drive uses a 34-pin ribbon cable to transfer data. IDE hard drives use a 40-pin ribbon cable; 168-pin refers to the amount of pins in SDRAM.

7. **B.** Ultra3 SCSI can transfer a maximum of 160 MB/s. Ultra-320 SCSI can transfer 320 MB/s, Ultra-640 can transfer 640 MB/s, and SAS (Serial Attached SCSI) and SATA Revision 2.0 can transfer 300 MB/s.

8. **D.** In PATA IDE two-drive configurations, drive 0 would be the master and drive 1 would be the slave. Cable select is a drive mode that autoconfigures drives as master or slave depending on their cable position. Single means a single drive configuration with no configuration necessary.

9. **B.** External SCSI connections often have 68 pins. DDR2 and DDR3 have 240 pins. IDE data cables have 40 pins. SATA data cables have 7 pins.

10. **C.** Hard drives can be hot-swappable. This is common in NAS devices and advanced servers. It is not common in PCs. Tape drives, floppy drives, and DVD drives are not hot-swappable. However, they use media that can be inserted and removed while the computer is on. Tricky, eh? Be ready for these types of questions.

11. **B** and **E**. The best answers are tape drives and hard drives. Not IDE or SATA drives, but SCSI drives themselves.

220-802 Answers

12. **D**. Because the drive is new, you should try updating the BIOS (firmware) of the SCSI controller. After that, it should see the newer, larger capacity SCSI drive. It won't be possible to format the drive until it is recognized. Most SCSI controllers come in the form of adapter cards (or are embedded directly into the motherboard) so if you can boot the system, then the controller should be getting power. Most SCSI controllers today do not use jumpers.

13. **A** and **C**. System lockups and failed boot files or other failing file operations are possible symptoms of hard drive failure. Antivirus alerts tell you that the operating system has been compromised and viruses should be quarantined and a full scan should be initiated. Sometimes hard drives can fail due to heavy virus activity, but usually, if the malware is caught quick enough, the hard drive should survive. Network drives are separate from the local hard drive; inability to connect to a network drive suggests a network configuration issue. If the BIOS doesn't recognize the drive, consider a BIOS update.

14. **C**. Most likely, the SATA port is faulty. It might have been damaged during the upgrade. To test the theory, you would plug the SATA data cable into another port on the motherboard. We can't format the drive until it has been recognized by the BIOS, which by the way should recognize SATA drives if the motherboard has SATA ports! SATA drives don't use jumpers unless they need to coexist with older IDE drives.

15. **C**. If you test a SATA power cable you should find 3.3 V (orange wire), 5 V (red wire), and 12 V (yellow wire). If any of these don't test properly, try another SATA power connector.

Optical Storage Media

The three main types of optical media in use today are Compact Discs (CD), Digital Versatile Discs (DVD), and Blu-ray discs. These discs have a variety of functions, including audio, video, application, data, and so on. Some discs can be read from, and some can also be written to. Finally, some discs can be *re*written to as well. It all depends on which media you use. Now there are a lot of different versions of optical media; let's try to organize them so that they will be easier to remember. Start with the most familiar, the compact disc.

> **ExamAlert**
>
> You've probably noticed by now that most magnetic media is known as "disk" and optical media is known as "disc." Keep this in mind for the exam.

Compact Disc (CD)

A Compact Disc (CD) is a flat, round, optical disc used to store music, sounds, or other data. It can be read from a compact disc player. For example, audio CDs can be played on a compact disc player that is part of a stereo or a computer. However, data CDs can be read only from CD-ROM drives that are part of, or externally connected to, a computer. The A+ exam focuses on data CDs, so let's talk about some of the different data CD technologies.

Data CD Technologies

The most common acronym that comes to mind is the CD-ROM, compact disc-read-only memory. Data is written to a CD-ROM in a similar way that audio is written to a music CD; a laser shines on the reflective surface of the CD and stores data as a plethora of microscopic indentations known as lands and pits. These are the types of CDs you get when you purchase a computer program or game. They can be read from but not written to, and can be read only from a compatible CD-ROM drive. CD-ROM drives are rated in read speeds, for example 48x. The x equals 150 KB/s. So to calculate a CD-ROM drive's maximum read speed, you multiply the number preceding the x by 150 KB. In this example, this would be 48 x 150 KB = 7.2 MB/s. CD-ROM drives connect via SATA or IDE. Both provide plenty of throughput for a CD-ROM running at 48x (IDE at 133 MB/s, SATA at a minimum of 150 MB/s).

Over time, the technology to write to CDs was developed, enabling users to store information to CD that they would previously store on floppy disks or

Zip drives. A typical CD can hold up to 700 MB of data; although there are 650 MB, 800 MB, and other versions available. Table 6.3 describes the two most common recordable technologies.

TABLE 6.3 **Comparison of CD Recording Technologies**

Technology	Full Name	Typical Maximum Recording Speed
CD-R	Compact Disc-Recordable	48x (7.2 MB/s) or 52x (7.8 MB/s)
CD-RW	Compact Disc-ReWritable	24x (3.6 MB/s) or 32x (4.8 MB/s)

Most optical drives that you can purchase for a computer today have all three compact disc functions. They can read from CD-ROMs, write to CD-Rs, and write/rewrite to CD-RWs. Usually, the read speed and CD-R speed are the same. Because CD-Rs are extremely inexpensive, this technology took off as an archival method; it was a massive nail in the coffin for technologies such as tape backup, Zip/Jaz drives, and of course floppy disks.

Exam Alert

Know the difference between CD-ROM, CD-R, and CD-RW.

SATA CD-ROM drives connect the same way as their hard drive counterparts: a 7-pin data cable and a 15-pin power cable. IDE CD-ROM drives have the same types of connectors as an Ultra ATA IDE hard drive: 40-pin data connector, 4-pin power connector (Molex), and a jumper block to set the CD-ROM drive to either master or slave. They also have a stereo audio out that connects to a sound card or to the motherboard if the sound card is integrated. This enables you to play and hear audio CDs on the CD-ROM drive. However, SATA CD-ROMs send stereo music information through the SATA data cable.

CD-ROM discs are known as removable media; however the drive is normally fixed in the computer. It installs much like an SATA or IDE hard drive. One notable exception is that most CD-ROM drives are 5.25-inches wide. So they need to be installed to one of the larger bays in a case that has an opening on the front; this way the drive tray is accessible. Most CD-ROM drives can also play audio CDs and have a volume knob on the front. In addition, many drives have a pinhole near the volume knob. This small hole is for when a CD (or the tray) gets jammed. Use a paper clip and insert it into the hole in an attempt to free the tray and CD.

ExamAlert

The paper clip should be added to your toolkit; it dislodges jammed CD trays.

Digital Versatile Disc (DVD)

For data, Digital Versatile Discs, also known as Digital Video Discs, are the successor to CDs for a variety of reasons. First, they can be used to play and record video. Second, they have a much greater capacity than CDs. This is because the pits etched into the surface of the DVD are smaller than CD pits (.74 micrometers compared to 1.6 micrometers). Also, DVDs can be written to faster than CDs. So, there are read-only DVDs and writable DVDs; however, there are a lot more variations of DVDs than there are CDs. Table 6.4 describes some of the DVD-ROM (Digital Versatile Disc-Read-Only Memory) versions, specifications, and differences starting with the common DVD-5 version.

TABLE 6.4 **Comparison of DVD Technologies**

DVD-ROM Technology	Sides	Total Layers	Capacity
DVD-5	1	1	4.7 GB
DVD-9	1	2	8.5 GB
DVD-10	2	2	9.4 GB
DVD-14	2	3	13.2 GB
DVD-18	2	4	17 GB

The most common DVD is currently the single-sided, single-layer (SS, SL) DVD-5 technology that can store 4.7 GB of data. But some DVDs can be written to two sides (known as dual-sided or DS); simply flip the DVD to access the information on the other side. Layers however work differently. A DVD with two layers (known as dual layer or DL) incorporates both layers onto a single side of the disc. The second layer is actually underneath the first one; the DVD laser reads this second layer by shining through the first semi-transparent layer. By combining dual-sided and dual-layer technologies together, you end up with a DVD that can store up to 17 GB of data (known as DVD-18) at 8.5 GB per side.

ExamAlert

Know the capacity of DVD-5 and DVD-18 for the exam.

Once again, for DVD-ROMs, and recordable DVDs, the most common by far is DVD-5. Typically, a DVD drive reads these discs at 16x. However, the x in DVD speeds is different than the x in CD-ROM speeds. For DVDs, the x means approximately 1.32 MB/s or about nine times the core CD speed. So, a typical 16x DVD is equal to 21 MB/s. Typically, a DVD drive reads at 16x, records once at 22x or 24x, and rewrites at 6x or 8x. Table 6.5 gives a description of the different types of recordable DVDs.

TABLE 6.5 **Comparison of DVD Recordable Technologies**

DVD Recordable Technology	Capacity	Typical Write Speed*
DVD–R SL	4.707 GB	22x or 24x
DVD+R SL	4.700 GB	22x or 24x
DVD–R DL	8.544 GB	12x
DVD+R DL	8.548 GB	16x
DVD–RW SL or DL	4.707 or 8.544 GB	6x
DVD+RW SL or DL	4.700 or 8.548 GB	8x

*The write speeds vary from drive to drive. The stated typical speeds are the write speeds of a Samsung combo drive (DVD/CD) used for this book.

There is a slight difference in capacity between DVD– and DVD+ as you can see in Table 6.5. DVD– was developed by Pioneer and approved by the DVD Forum, whereas DVD+ was developed by a group of corporations headed up by Sony. Likewise, DVD–RW was developed by Pioneer and approved by the DVD Forum, and DVD+RW was developed by the same group of corporations that developed DVD+R; this group is now known as the DVD+RW Alliance. It's probably not important to know all this for the exam, because most DVD drives support all these formats. However, always check your drive to be sure before purchasing recordable DVDs.

Like most CD-ROM drives, the bulk of DVD drives connect via SATA or IDE. Most DVD drives are known as combo drives, meaning they can read and write to CDs and read DVDs (DVD-ROM drive), write DVDs (DVDR), and rewrite DVDs (DVDRW). The Samsung drive mentioned earlier does all these things, plus it includes the LightScribe technology that can create labels by etching text and graphics onto specially coated CDs and DVDs.

Because they are relatively cheap, DVD drives, like CD-ROM drives, are usually replaced if they fail. It could easily cost a company more money to try to repair a DVD drive, instead of simply purchasing one for between $10 to $20. However, if a problem does occur, remember to check the obvious; it takes only a few minutes. For example, if a DVD (or CD) drive tray won't open, press the eject button one time and wait. It can take a few moments for the DVD to spin down before opening. Then press it a few more times waiting a couple of moments after each time. You can also try to eject the disc from within the operating system. To do this, go to Windows Explorer, and right-click the drive in question; then select Eject. If this doesn't work, you can try to restart the computer and try the eject options again. Don't forget the pinhole near the open button. You can slide a paperclip in there to get the tray to open. Sometimes, DVD drives have been installed with incorrect screws that are too long. This can cause damage to the drive tray. Finally, make sure that the drive is getting power! A loose Molex or SATA power connector results in the tray not opening or closing.

DVD and CD Usage

DVDs are used as much or more than CDs in computers nowadays. The only place where DVDs haven't taken off is in the music arena. Although DVD-Audio (DVD-A) discs arguably have superior audio quality compared to audio CDs (DVD-A boasts a 24-bit rate, and up to 192 kHz sampling compared to CDs 16-bit/44 kHz), not many people have DVD-Audio players, so the audio CD is still by far the most common of the two.

Blu-ray

In 2008 the Blu-ray Disc Association won the high-definition battle against Toshiba's HD DVD. Currently Blu-ray is *the* standard for high-definition video. It is used by high-def movies, PlayStation 3 games, and for storing data, up to 50 GB per disc, ten times the amount of a typical DVD-5 disc. The standard disc is 12 cm (same size as a standard DVD or CD), and the mini-disc is 8 cm. Table 6.6 shows some of the Blu-ray specs.

TABLE 6.6 **Comparison of Blu-ray Specifications**

Blu-ray Type	Layers	Capacity
Standard disc, single-layer	1	25 GB
Standard disc, dual-layer*	2	50 GB
Mini-disc, single-layer	1	7.8 GB
Mini-disc, dual-layer	2	15.6 GB

*The Blu-ray specification leaves room for the future addition of layers beyond two.

Drive speeds range from 1x to 12x (with more undoubtedly on the way). 1x is equal to 36 Mb/s or 4.5 MB/s. 12x would be twelve times that core amount, which is 432 Mb/s or 54 MB/s, which is superior to DVD write speeds. The reason you see read speeds in bits is because Blu-ray players normally transfer data serially via Serial ATA connections. Single-layer discs, though their capacity is half, can be written to in half the time of dual-layer discs.

To play movies, games, or read the data from a Blu-ray disc, the computer must have a compatible Blu-ray drive. Currently, there are combo drives on the market that can read Blu-ray discs (but not write to them, these are known as BD-ROMs), read/write DVDs, and read/write CDs.

Like CD and DVD drives, Blu-ray drives for the PC are installed into a 5.25-inch bay in the computer case. However, Blu-ray drives almost always have SATA connections. If you upgrade a computer; the power supply needs an extra 15-pin SATA power connector, and the motherboard (or SATA card) needs to have one free SATA data port.

I had to install a Blu-ray drive to *Media PC*. It wouldn't be complete without the ability to watch Blu-ray movies! I chose a Samsung 12x model with Lightscribe. It reads Blu-ray discs as well as DVD and CD, and can write to DVD-ROMs and CD-ROMs, plus it can etch labels onto the disc. However, if I wanted to burn a lot of data to a single disc (say 20 GB or more), I would have to upgrade to a Blu-ray burner, which often comes with disc encryption methods as well. (Refer to Chapter 16 for more about encryption.) There are two methods of burning Blu-ray discs: Blu-ray Disc Recordable (BD-R), which can write to a disc once; and Blu-ray Disc Recordable Erasable (BD-RE), which can be erased and rerecorded multiple times. Burning speed depends on the drive, but as of the writing of this book, there are some that can go as high as 12x. To burn discs in Blu-ray format, you must either install the drivers and software that came with the drive or utilize a third-party program such as Nero.

Cram Quiz

Answer these questions. The answers follow the last question. If you cannot answer these questions correctly, consider reading this section again until you can.

220-801 Questions

1. What does the x refer to in Compact Disc technology?

   - ○ **A.** 150 KB/s
   - ○ **B.** 1.32 MB/s
   - ○ **C.** 133 MB/s
   - ○ **D.** 4.5 MB/s

2. Which of the following has the largest potential for storage capacity?

   - ○ **A.** CD-R
   - ○ **B.** CD-RW
   - ○ **C.** DVD-RW
   - ○ **D.** Blu-ray

3. What is the maximum capacity of a Blu-ray disc?

○ **A.** 700 MB

○ **B.** 4.7 GB

○ **C.** 17 GB

○ **D.** 50 GB

4. If a user wants to write information more than one time to a DVD, which type should you recommend? (Select all that apply.)

○ **A.** DVD-R

○ **B.** DVD–RW

○ **C.** DVD+RW

○ **D.** DVD+R

220-802 Questions

5. A customer complains that an important disc is stuck in the computer's DVD-ROM drive. What should you recommend to the customer?

○ **A.** To get a screwdriver and disassemble the drive

○ **B.** To format the disc using CDFS

○ **C.** To use a paper clip to eject the tray

○ **D.** To dispose of the drive and replace the media

6. A marketing kiosk requires a CD-ROM to be in the drive for the program to work correctly. However, the kiosk fails to boot when restarted. What should you do?

○ **A.** Change the drive letter assignments.

○ **B.** Defrag the hard drive.

○ **C.** Replace the CD-ROM with rewritable media.

○ **D.** Configure the BIOS settings.

7. One of your customers attempts to copy a DVD with a third-party application. It reads the source DVD fine, but when a blank disc is inserted, the program keeps asking the customer to insert blank media. What are some possible reasons for this? (Select the three best answers.)

○ **A.** Wrong DVD type.

○ **B.** The program cannot copy the DVD due to copyright laws.

○ **C.** There isn't enough free space on the hard drive.

○ **D.** A CD was inserted into the drive.

○ **E.** The drive is a CD-RW drive.

○ **F.** The DVD was inserted upside down.

Cram Quiz Answers

220-801 Answers

1. **A.** The x in CD technology is equal to 150 KB/s. A 1x drive can read or write 150 KB/s; a 2x drive can read or write 300 KB/s; and so on. 1.32 MB/s is the 1x speed of a DVD. 133 MB/s is the maximum data transfer rate of an Ultra ATA-7 connection, and 4.5 MB/s is the 1x speed of a Blu-ray disc.

2. **D.** Blu-ray, at a maximum of 50 GB has the largest storage capacity. CDs top out just under 1 GB. DVDs have a maximum of 17 GB.

3. **D.** Standard 12cm Blu-ray discs have a maximum capacity of 50 GB. A typical CD capacity is 700 MB; 4.7 GB is the capacity of the common DVD-5, and 17 GB is the capacity of a DVD-18 (using both sides).

4. **B** and **C**. DVD–RW and DVD+RW are the rewritable versions of DVDs. DVD-R and DVD+R are write-once formats.

220-802 Answers

5. **C.** Tell the customer to use a paper clip to eject the DVD-ROM tray. Disassembling the drive is not necessary, and the customer shouldn't be told to do this. If the disc is rewritable, formatting it would erase the contents, even if you could format as CDFS in this scenario. Never tell a customer to dispose of a DVD-ROM drive; they rarely fail.

6. **D.** You should configure the BIOS boot order so that the CD-ROM is first, and the kiosk computer will boot to that drive. Changing drive letter assignments in the operating system will have no effect on the boot order. The hard drive has nothing to do with this scenario. And if you replace the CD-ROM, you lose the program that the kiosk needs to boot to.

7. **A, D,** and **F**. If the source DVD was read fine, then there are three possible correct answers: A blank CD was inserted into the drive; an incorrect DVD type was inserted into the drive; or the DVD was inserted upside down. The hard drive doesn't play into this scenario because the program's message is simply to insert blank media. The drive can't be a CD-RW if it accepted the source DVD.

Solid-State Storage Media

There are many types of solid-state media. Solid-state media by definition is media with no moving parts, based on the semiconductor. Most of these are implemented as large amounts of nonvolatile memory, known as flash memory, and are located on a card or drive. Remember that *nonvolatile* means any data on the device is retained, even if the device is not receiving power. Examples of cards include SD cards and CompactFlash cards. Examples of drives include the solid-state drive (SSD), USB flash drives, and even PCIe drives (that are integrated into a PCIe card). This section focuses on four types of solid-state media: Solid-state drives, USB flash drives, SD cards, and CompactFlash.

Solid-State Drives

Solid-state drives (SSD) are used to store operating systems and files, similar to a magnetic hard disk drive. However, they don't use spinning disks or read/write heads, and instead write data to nonvolatile microchips or to DRAM. Because of this, they are silent, more resistant to physical shock, and have lower access time and less latency. Because there are no moving parts, you are not concerned with rotation speed.

The newer *Media PC* I built uses a Western Digital SATA 3 Gb/s solid state drive (SSD). As of the writing of this book, SSD SATA drives are not used as often as their magnetic disc counterparts, generally because of increased price and decreased capacity. For example, the SSD drive I purchased has only a capacity of 128 GB. However, if you are looking for a small, quiet drive with no moving parts for your media PC or HTPC, this is the way to go.

Standard SATA SSD drive form factor is 2.5 inches in width. Installation requires either special screw holes drilled directly into the computer case or an adapter kit to install it to a 3.5-inch internal bay. Usually, SSD drives connect via the SATA interface, the same 7-pin data and 15-pin power connectors that other SATA drives use.

Most SSD manufacturers such as Western Digital use nonvolatile NAND flash memory, though you can purchase DRAM-based versions, but know that the DRAM type is going to be volatile. These versions often use memory modules that are added to a PCIe card. This type of SSD has much faster data access and less latency than flash-based SSDs. The drawback is that they need either external power or battery backup, due to the volatility of the memory.

USB Flash Drives

The USB flash drive is probably the most familiar of all flash media. Also known as USB thumb drives, they are often retractable and can be carried on a keychain. Figure 6.5 shows an example of a USB flash drive connected to a laptop's USB port.

FIGURE 6.5   A typical USB flash drive in a laptop's USB port

Notice that the USB flash drive is lit, indicating that it is connected to the laptop's USB port and ready to transfer data. In this scenario, the drive shows up as a volume within Windows Explorer, usually named Removable Disk. Connecting the drive is easy; just find an open USB port. But remember that you should safely remove hardware in the operating system before disconnecting the drive physically. If you don't, it can cause electrical irregularities that can damage the data on the drive. In Windows, you can either double-click the Safely Remove Hardware icon in the System Tray, or right-click it to bring up the Safely Remove Hardware window. From there click Stop to shut down power to the selected USB device. Then it can be safely removed from the physical USB port. The icon appears as a device with a green arrow above it pointing to the left and slightly down. Sometimes, if you right-click the icon and simply click Safely Remove Hardware, the device will be turned off, and the icon disappears. If your USB device has a light, make sure that light is off before physically removing the device.

ExamAlert

Remember to *safely remove* USB flash drives in the operating system before physically disconnecting them.

Note

Sometimes, a USB or other flash-based solid-state device can't be removed with the Safely Remove Hardware option in Windows. If this happens, consider shutting down the computer before physically disconnecting the device to avoid data corruption or loss.

The advantages of a USB flash drive are obvious. For example, the drive in Figure 6.5 is an 8 GB flash drive that cost approximately $10. That is a good cost-to-MB ratio for an instantly rewritable media. It would take 2 standard DVD-RWs, 10 standard CD-RWs, or 5,000 floppy disks to match that capacity. The best part is that no special setup is necessary, and data can simply be dragged and dropped to the drive, unlike CDs and DVDs that need to be burned. In addition, USB flash drives' read/write speed is comparable to DVD technology, averaging about 30 MB/s reads and 15 MB/s writes. Finally, it's *small*: it has a little footprint. What I used to carry around in a CD case is now on one flash drive on my keychain. Plus, newer flash drives are ranging all the way up to 128 GB and beyond and have a much longer lifespan than just a few years ago. They can also be used to boot or install operating systems.

Let's talk about the type of memory used in this solid-state device: NAND flash memory is the core of a USB flash drive. This memory is broken up into blocks that are generally between 16 KB and 512 KB. Know that a USB flash drive's blocks can be written to only so many times before failures occur. With some flash drives, manufacturers estimate this at up to 1 million write/erase cycles, or 10 years of use. However, just like hard drives will never attain their maximum data transfer rate, it is doubtful that a flash drive will ever attain that maximum amount of write/erase cycles. In addition, the amount of years is subjective; it all depends on how often a user works with the flash drive. Basically, if you take the number given by the manufacturer and cut it in half, you should be in good shape, unless you are an extreme power user. Now back to NAND flash failures: Because this type of memory incurs a small amount of faults over time (as opposed to NOR flash, which should remain free of faults), a method known as Bad Block Management is implemented, which maintains a table of the faulty blocks within the USB flash device, making sure not to save data to those blocks. Blocks are broken down further into pages, which can be between 512 bytes and 4 KB. Each page has error detection and correction information associated with it. All this is done to prolong the lifespan of devices using NAND memory.

Normally, USB flash drives are shipped in a formatted state, usually FAT32. This enables the drive to be accessed by just about any computer on the market and makes for easy repair of corrupted files with Windows utilities. These drives can also be formatted as NTFS if the user wants. Sometimes NAND flash devices such as USB flash drives act up intermittently. Unless the device has failed completely, a quick reformat usually cures the flash drive of its woes. Just be sure to backup your data first! This method applies to other forms of solid-state NAND-based media.

Troubleshooting of these devices is not usually necessary, but you might see a couple of issues:

▶ Sometimes USB flash drives and other solid-state media can conflict with each other, prompting you to change the drive letter of one or more devices within Disk Management.

▶ USB flash drives might intermittently fail when writing or reading data. As this occurs more often, consider reformatting the drive. After reformatting, test the drive by moving files to it and opening them. Of course, after a certain point, the drive will fail and will need to be replaced.

▶ In some cases, Windows XP SP2 will not "see" your device no matter what you do. Microsoft has released a hotfix for these types of USB controller issues. See article 892050 at http://support.microsoft.com for the download. And consider updating to XP SP3. Microsoft also has a USB Flash Drive Manager for Windows XP to aid in backing up and restoring information to and from USB flash drives.

In general, make sure that your operating system has the latest service pack and updates installed. For more information on USB, see Chapter 13, "Peripherals and Custom Computing."

Some USB flash drives are preloaded with software that can restore data and possibly secure transferred data. The only problem with USB flash drives is that although they are small, they can't fit inside most digital cameras, cell phones, PDAs, and other hand-held devices. For that, you need something even smaller: Enter the SD card.

Secure Digital Cards

Secure Digital cards (SD cards), for the most part, are technically the same type of device as a USB flash drive. They are solid-state, use NAND memory, and have most of the same pros and cons as a USB flash drive. The difference is the form factor of the device and because of this, the usages. Instead of connecting an SD card to a USB port of a computer, it slides into a memory card reader. There are specialized memory card readers for SD cards only, and other readers that can read multiple formats of cards. Like USB flash drives, be sure to use the Safely Remove icon in Windows before physically removing the SD card. There are three sizes of SD cards, each smaller than the last: standard (32 mm × 24 mm), miniSD (21.5 mm × 20 mm), and microSD (15 mm × 11 mm). You can still find many standard size SD cards used in cameras and some other devices but note that most cell phones and smartphones use microSD cards for additional memory. Figure 6.6 shows a full-size SD card and a microSD card. Figure 6.7 shows the standard SD card inserted into a laptop's memory card reader slot. Note that this slot can accommodate SD cards or smaller but nothing bigger than an SD card.

FIGURE 6.6   A typical microSD card (left) and a standard SD card (right)

FIGURE 6.7   A standard SD card inserted in a laptop's Memory Card Reader.

Standard SD cards have capacities up to 4 GB. High-capacity (SDHC) cards range up to 32 GB. An upcoming specification, eXtended Capacity (SDXC), will supposedly have a maximum capacity of 2 TB, but as of the writing of this book, the maximum capacity is 128 GB. When it comes to data transfer rate, SD cards are divided into three different classes: SD Class 2, 4, and 6, each with a different range of speeds. Class 6 is the fastest and ranges between 6 and 45 MB/s. Some SD cards, like the one in Figure 6.6, have a write-protect tab within the notch on the left side of the card. Sliding the tab down "locks" the card so that it can be read from but not written to.

You might encounter an issue where a new SDHC or SDXC card will not work in a PC or laptop card reader, however older standard SD cards work fine. This suggests that the card reader needs the latest firmware and drivers.

> **Note**
>
> Another flash-based card similar to SD is the Extreme Digital-Picture Card (xD-Picture Card). It was used in older Olympus and Fujifilm cameras, and obtained a maximum capacity of 2 GB, but is for the most part now obsolete.

A derivative of SD is the Secure Digital Input Output (SDIO) card. This takes the capabilities of an SD card and merges them with the functionality of an I/O device. Some smartphones use this technology to integrate GPS, WLAN,

Bluetooth, and many other types of radio technologies. SDIO cards do not work in standard SD card slots, but standard SD cards can be read in SDIO slots.

> **Note**
>
> Don't confuse an SDIO card with a SIM (Subscriber Identity Module) card. A SIM card identifies the user/subscriber of a phone or PDA and allows the telecommunications company to lock the phone to that SIM card. The SIM is a slightly different size than the SD and SDIO cards.

CompactFlash Cards

CompactFlash (CF) is another kind of solid-state memory that can be used in a variety of formats, the most common of which is the CompactFlash card. These are categorized as either Type I cards that are 3.3 mm thick and Type II cards that are 5 mm thick. These cards are larger than SD cards and are often used in hand-held computers, high-end cameras (Type I) and for Microdrives (Type II).

Common capacities for CF cards max out at about 32 GB; however, the technology can go as high as 137 GB. The cards are formatted by the manufacturer as either FAT32 or FAT, in the same manner as USB flash drives and SD cards. Like USB flash drives and SD cards, CF cards have a built-in ATA controller that makes them appear as a hard drive to the operating system; they show up as a volume within Windows Explorer. In the past CompactFlash cards used NOR memory but are typically NAND-based nowadays, again like USB flash drives and SD cards. The data transfer rate ranges from 6 to 133 MB/s. CF speeds have increased with each new version, starting with the original CF and moving on to CF High Speed, CF 3.0, though the speed increases stopped with CF 4.0. Newer versions allow for larger block transfers of data, up to 32 MB.

CompactFlash cards have taken on a new meaning as well; you can find various CF cards that have built-in Ethernet, WLAN, Bluetooth, GPS, and other technologies. The CF card is identical to a PC card from an electrical standpoint, so you see the same types of technologies in a CF card as you would in a PC card. You can use a CF card directly within a PCMCIA slot with the right adapter. For more information on PC cards and PCMCIA, see Chapter 7, "Laptops."

Cram Quiz

Answer these questions. The answers follow the last question. If you cannot answer these questions correctly, consider reading this section again until you can.

220-801 Questions

1. What should you do before physically removing a USB flash drive? (Select the best answer.)

   ○ **A.** Turn it off.

   ○ **B.** Shut down Windows.

   ○ **C.** Format the drive.

   ○ **D.** Use the Safely Remove icon.

2. How are most solid-state media formatted by the manufacturer?

   ○ **A.** As FAT32

   ○ **B.** As NTFS

   ○ **C.** As FAT16

   ○ **D.** As FAT12

3. What is the main difference between SD and SDIO?

   ○ **A.** SD cards are faster.

   ○ **B.** SDIO cards incorporate input/output functionality.

   ○ **C.** SD cards incorporate input/output functionality.

   ○ **D.** SDIO cards can identify a user's cell phone.

4. What kind of controller is built into a CF card?

   ○ **A.** SATA

   ○ **B.** IDE

   ○ **C.** ATA

   ○ **D.** SCSI

220-802 Questions

5. You discover that a new SDXC card won't work in the card reader of a user's
    PC. It works fine in another computer's card reader, and standard SD cards work
    fine in the user's PC. What should you do to fix the problem?

    ○ **A.** Format the card.

    ○ **B.** Install the latest firmware and drivers.

    ○ **C.** Purchase a new external USB card reader.

    ○ **D.** Use a CF card instead.

Cram Quiz Answers

220-801 Answers

1. **D.** In Windows you can either double-click the Safely Remove Hardware icon in
    the System Tray (Notification Area) or right-click it to bring up the Safely Remove
    Hardware window. From there click Stop to shut down power to the device.
    Shutting off Windows is another possibility but not the best answer because it
    is time-consuming.

2. **A.** FAT32 is the most common file system used on solid-state media such as
    USB flash drives, SD cards, and CF cards. FAT16 is another possibility but less
    common. Users have the option to reformat most of these devices as NTFS if
    they want.

3. **B**. SDIO cards integrate I/O functionality into a standard SD card. They are basi-
    cally the same speed as SD cards. Answer D is referring to SIM cards, not SDIO
    cards.

4. **C.** An ATA controller is built into the CF card and many other solid-state tech-
    nologies.

220-802 Answers

5. **B.** If older SD cards work, but new ones don't, install the latest firmware and/or
    drivers for the card reader. Do this before trying other technologies or making pur-
    chases. No reason to try formatting the card if it works fine on another computer.

CHAPTER 7

Laptops

This chapter covers the following A+ exam topics:

▶ Installing, Configuring, and Troubleshooting Visible Laptop Components

▶ Installing, Configuring, and Troubleshooting Internal Laptop Components

You can find a master list of A+ exam topics in the "Introduction."

This chapter covers CompTIA A+ 220-801 objectives 3.1, 3.2, and 3.3 and CompTIA A+ 220-802 objective 4.8.

Ah, the laptop. The beauty of laptops is that they are portable, and all the connections are right at your fingertips. However, quite often there is a trade-off in performance and in price. This chapter assumes a basic knowledge of laptops and jumps straight into how to install, configure, and troubleshoot laptop devices.

Laptops were originally designed for niche markets but today are used in businesses almost as much as desktop PCs are. Laptops (also known as notebooks or portable computers) have integrated displays, keyboards, and pointing devices making them easy to transport and easy to use in confined spaces. There are plenty of other portable devices on the market today including smartphones, tablets, Ultra-Mobile PCs, and more, which are covered in Chapter 17, "Mobile Devices." However, I wanted to keep laptops separate from those because laptops usually run Windows (like a PC), and are more similar to PCs in most hardware respects. This ordering of the chapters allows us to cover all the PC and laptop hardware *before* jumping into Windows operating systems.

For the exams, it is important to identify the components of a laptop and the ports that surround the machine, how to install and configure hardware, and how to take care of and troubleshoot the laptop. In many respects, laptops work the same way as desktop computers. This chapter focuses on the differences that make a laptop stand out from the desktop PC.

Installing, Configuring, and Troubleshooting Visible Laptop Components

In this section, we discuss the visible components of the laptop such as the keyboard and the display. These two devices are probably the most prone to failure, so we discuss some methods and step by steps on how to repair them. In addition, we talk about a laptop's audio, power, expansion buses, and optical disc drives.

Laptop 101

For the exam, it is important to identify the main components of a laptop and its ports. Figure 7.1 shows some of the main components of the laptop.

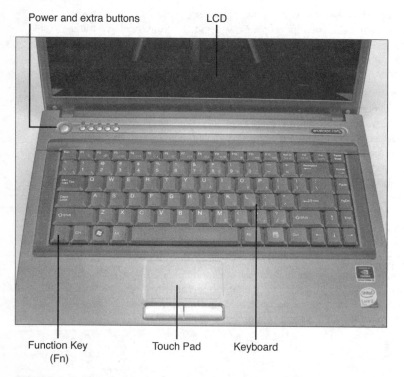

FIGURE 7.1 **A typical laptop's main components**

The main components of the laptop include the liquid crystal display (LCD), keyboard (with special Fn key), touch pad, the power button, and extra buttons.

The extra buttons offer additional functionality, for example; enabling and disabling wireless, turning the sound on or off, and opening applications such as Internet Explorer and Outlook.

A laptop manufacturer needs to squeeze in ports wherever it can find space, so quite often you find ports on three of the sides of the laptop. Figures 7.2 through 7.4 identify the various ports around the sides of the laptop.

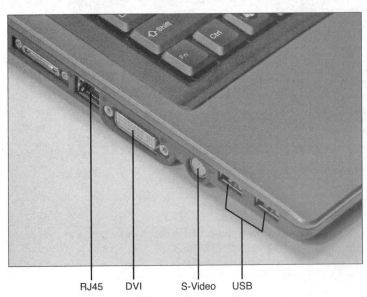

RJ45   DVI   S-Video   USB

FIGURE 7.2   **A typical laptop's ports part A**

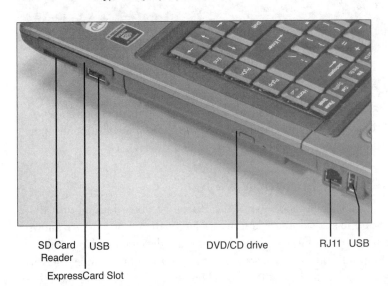

SD Card   USB   DVD/CD drive   RJ11 USB
Reader

ExpressCard Slot

FIGURE 7.3   **A typical laptop's ports part B**

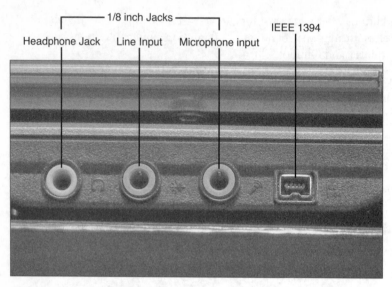

FIGURE 7.4 **A typical laptop's ports part C**

> **Note**
>
> The ports in Figures 7.2 through 7.4 are described in detail as we progress through this chapter, Chapter 12, "Video and Audio," Chapter 13, "Peripherals and Custom Computing," and Chapter 15, "Networking."

> **ExamAlert**
>
> Be able to identify the main components and ports of a laptop for the exam.

Input Devices

Inputting information to a laptop is just like inputting information to a PC, except all of the devices are miniaturized. Laptops have a few different input devices including keyboards, pointing devices, and the stylus.

Keyboards and Function Keys

Some laptops have keyboards similar to the 101-key keyboard found on a PC including a numeric keypad; these laptops are larger than most and are known as desktop replacements. However, most laptops are designed with a small form factor in mind, and this means a smaller keyboard. For example, the keyboard in Figure 7.5 has 86 keys. But as you note in the figure, a user has the option of using the Fn key. The Fn key (Function key) is a modifier key used on most laptops. This is designed to activate secondary functions of other keys (usually marked in blue). For example, in Figure 7.5 the F8 key has the secondary function "volume up" but only if you press the Fn key at the same time.

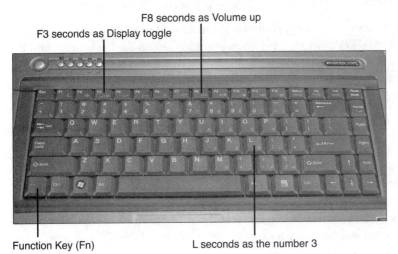

FIGURE 7.5   **A typical laptop keyboard**

Using this method, much more functionality can be incorporated into the keyboard without the need for additional keys. This idea has since grown to include all kinds of controls; for instance, using media player controls, putting the computer to sleep, and a variety of other functions including enabling an external monitor (refer to Figure 7.5); on this laptop the F3 key seconds as a display toggle between the built-in LCD and an external monitor. In addition, the entire numeric keypad is added to the keyboard as secondary keys. For example, in Figure 7.5 the L key seconds as the number 3, but this works only if the Number Lock (Num Lk) key has been enabled. (The Fn key is not necessary for the numeric keypad to work.) Quite often, users forget about the Num Lk key, and when they try to type, strange garbled code comes out! Simply press the Num Lk key once to fix the problem. This is also common if the user works with an external keyboard at the office and disconnects it when leaving the office.

ExamAlert

Press the Num Lk key to enable/disable the numeric keypad on a laptop.

I have had a dozen people I know approach me telling me that their laptop's keyboard wasn't working properly. Over time I've noticed several culprits: overuse, loose ribbon cables, spilled coffee, or users simply pounding the tar out of the keyboard! Here are a couple of problems you might encounter:

▶ **Stuck keys:** Stuck keys could occur because of overuse, damage to the individual key's switch, or if liquid were spilled on the keyboard. (And if a stuck key is the worst that happens due to a liquid spill, consider yourself lucky!) A stuck key can be identified because the key fails to work in Windows, or if the BIOS reports a 3xx error. (It might say something similar to Keyboard Stuck Key Failure.) If there is a BIOS error, look for a two-digit hexadecimal code just before the 3xx error. This code identifies which key(s) is stuck. Of course, you have to access your BIOS documentation to find out which key a particular hexadecimal code refers to. (In some cases this will be based off of the standard ASCII printable character code.) By removing the keycap and cleaning the keyswitch underneath, you can usually fix the problem. If not, the entire keyboard will probably have to be replaced. See Table 7.1 for more information.

▶ **Loose connection:** If the laptop is moved around and jostled a lot, as many laptops are, it could possibly cause loose connections. One of these is the ribbon cable that connects the keyboard to the motherboard. To fix this, the keyboard must be lifted away from the laptop and the ribbon cable attached securely. Follow the steps listed in Table 7.1 to accomplish this.

▶ **Damaged keyboard:** Users who inadvertently drop heavy items onto the keyboard or operate the keyboard with a heavy hand might cause a warped or bent keyboard. Some brands of laptops suffer from this more than others. This is usually impossible to repair, and the keyboard needs to be replaced, as shown in Table 7.1.

TABLE 7.1 **Steps Involved in Replacing a Laptop Keyboard**

Step	Procedure
1. Prepare the laptop for surgery!	Shut down the laptop, unplug it, and disconnect the battery. Then employ ESD prevention measures. Because there is nowhere on a laptop to connect an antistatic wrist strap or mat, you need to connect these to the chassis of a nearby unplugged desktop computer, or a proper earth bonding point of some sort.

TABLE 7.1   **Continued**

Step	Procedure
2. Remove the trim.	Usually the keyboard is held in place by a piece of trim or an entire plastic housing (also known as a bezel). The trim might be in-between the keyboard and the monitor, or it might surround the keyboard. The plastic housing might have to be pried out with a thin flat tool, which can be a little tricky. You can use wooden trim sticks, which are thin, cylindrical pieces of wood that have an angled edge to get underneath plastic housings (available at drug stores, and some hardware stores), or use a fine flathead screwdriver. In addition, some laptops come with a special tool to remove trim, bezels, and hinge covers. Go slow and be gentle with these plastic parts that snap in and out of the laptop case.
3. Remove the screws.	When the trim is removed, you should see two screws. You might need a small Phillips head screwdriver or a small Torx screwdriver. (Most laptops require smaller Torx screwdrivers than PCs do, as low as T8 or even T6, something to add to your PC toolkit!)
4. Disconnect the keyboard.	When the keyboard can be lifted up, you can see it is connected to the system board by a ribbon cable, also known as a flex cable. Figure 7.6 shows the keyboard lifted up and back displaying the flex cable connector. Be gentle with this cable and its connection. The connector usually has two locking tabs, one on each end of the flex cable connector. Unlocking this is a delicate procedure; the locks need to be pulled out only a little bit to unlock the flex cable. Some technicians use an extremely small screwdriver or a toothpick to move these tabs into the unlocked position. On many systems, this also enables you access to the hinges that can remove the display.
5. Replace the keyboard.	A new keyboard can sometimes be purchased from the manufacturer, but you might not find out the part # you need from the manufacturer by giving them the model # of the laptop. If you can't find the part #, or the manufacturer will not supply the component you need, look for the part number on the bottom of the keyboard and search for that part on the Internet. After you acquire the correct part (always check the part # of the new keyboard against the old one), connect the flex ribbon cable, lock it on both sides with those tiny locking tabs, screw in the keyboard, and replace the plastic trim.
6. Test the keyboard.	Verify that the new keyboard works by testing every key within a word processor like WordPad, and test Fn enabled keys as well.

Note

Step 1 should be employed whenever you replace parts in the laptop.

ExamAlert

Understand the steps involved when replacing keyboards for the exam.

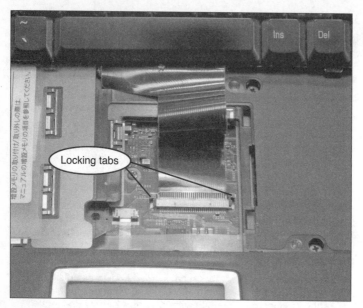

FIGURE 7.6   **Keyboard flex cable connector**

If a user needs access to a laptop right away before it can be repaired, a temporary solution would be to connect a USB or PS/2 external keyboard. This should be recognized automatically by Windows. There are USB to PS/2 adapters available if the laptop has only USB ports, and the only keyboard accessible is PS/2. Examples of sites where these types of adapters can be acquired include www.cablestogo.com, and www.cyberguys.com.

> **Note**
>
> When repairing a laptop, try to document the process as you go. Write down what you see and how and where cables and screws were attached. Also make note of how devices were oriented before they were removed. Label any parts that you remove for easier identification later on. If available, refer to the manufacturer's documentation that came with the laptop.

Pointing Devices

Whereas a PC uses a mouse, the laptop uses a pointing device. The bulk of laptops come with a pointing device known as a touch pad. By gliding a finger across the touch pad surface, a user can move the cursor on the screen. Touch pads also come with two buttons that take the place of a mouse's buttons. In portable computing lingo, the word "click" is replaced with the word "tap." In addition to using the buttons, most touch pad surfaces can also be tapped or double-tapped upon, just by tapping with the finger. The buttons are oriented in such a way as to be used with the thumb. Touch pads can be replaced though it is uncommon to do so; they are connected by two cables similar to the flex cable that connects the keyboard. However, you might have to remove other devices first to get at the touch pad. You might also have to work from the bottom and from the top of the laptop; this depends on the brand of laptop. Some touch pad buttons can be replaced the way keys on the keypads are. Touch pads are sometimes referred to as track pads as well.

Now and again you will encounter users reporting that when they type on the keyboard, the mouse pointer scrolls across the screen. This is sometimes referred to as a "ghost cursor." It could be because the user's sleeve is brushing up against the touchpad. To remedy this, pointing devices can be turned off within Windows, usually through the laptop manufacturer's software. Watch out for situations in which the entire device was disabled or perhaps just the pad portion of the touch pad was disabled. It's also possible to disable tapping ability of the touch pad, while still allowing movement of the cursor. . In rarer cases, a ghost cursor occurring while working in the operating system or in a word processor can be caused by a bad driver or the OS itself. If this happens, reinstall or update the mouse/touchpad driver, the video driver, and update the OS as well.

Another common type of pointing device is the pointing stick, known within IBM/Lenovo laptops as the TrackPoint. This device manifests itself as a smaller rubber cap (that looks like an eraser head) just above the B key, and two buttons that work essentially the same as a touch pad's buttons. External keyboards are also sold with integrated TrackPoint devices.

Of course, external mice can be connected to the laptop or its docking station as well. These would be connected to USB ports or could be wireless devices that connect via Bluetooth.

Stylus/Digitizer

A stylus is a writing tool, usually a thin plastic "pen" looking device used to take the place of a mouse by tapping and "writing" on a touch screen (also known as a digitizer screen). This method is widely used in tablet PCs, PDAs, and hand-held computers. Whenever you sign for a package from a package company, you sign with a stylus on a touch screen. This takes the place of pencil and paper.

Video

A laptop's video subsystem is composed of a liquid crystal display (LCD) and a graphics processor unit (GPU):

- **LCD:** A flat panel display that consists of two sheets of polarizing material surrounding a layer of liquid crystal solution. It connects to the motherboard by way of a flex ribbon cable and gets its power from an inverter board. Some laptops now use LED displays, more information can be found on the different types of displays in Chapter 12.

▶ **GPU:** The GPU is the processor for video. On a laptop it is usually integrated with the motherboard. In some cases it is part of the chipset and utilizes RAM as shared video memory. In others scenarios, namely more powerful laptops, it is a separate processor that has its own memory and possibly is situated upon its own circuit board.

Most of today's LCD screens are thin-film transistor (TFT) active-matrix displays, meaning they have three transistors for each pixel, which are contained within a flexible material. These are located directly behind the liquid crystal material. In general, LCDs use low amounts of power, generate a small amount of heat, and cause little in the way of interference and emissions.

Display Controls

Brightness can be adjusted from the keyboard on most laptops. On the laptop keyboard shown previously in Figure 7.5, pressing the Fn and F4 key decreases brightness, and pressing the Fn and F5 key increases brightness. There usually aren't contrast controls on a laptop's LCD.

Resolution is the amount of pixels, measured horizontal by vertical, on the display, and is user selectable. The higher the resolution, the more that can be fit on the screen, which is beneficial to a certain point, especially if the laptop's screen isn't big. Table 7.2 shows some of the common resolutions that laptops use currently.

TABLE 7.2 **Common Laptop Resolutions**

Resolution Standard	Full Name	Pixels (HxV)	Aspect Ratio
WXGA	Widescreen Extended Graphics Array	1280x800	16:10 (1.6:1)
HD	High-Definition display similar to WXGA	1366x768	16:9 (1.78:1)
WSXGA+	Widescreen Super Extended Graphics Array Plus	1680x1050	16:10 (1.6:1)
HD	High-Definition display similar to WSXGA+	1680x945	16:9 (1.78:1)

Laptops' active-matrix screens are usually set to run at one specific resolution. The laptop used during the writing of this book uses a default resolution of 1280x800 pixels. If the resolution is changed to something else, the laptop usually scales the resolution, making the picture unclear and perhaps not even fit on the screen correctly. Because of this you're stuck with the default resolution. Sometimes this default resolution can be a bit tough on the eyes, for example if the laptop's display runs at WXGA 1280x800 but the screen size is only 13.3 inches. If a user plans on using the laptop for long periods of time, they should consider a laptop with a larger display or an external display.

That brings us to the capability to send video signal to an external monitor. Some people refer to this technology as *screen switching*. Most laptops come with an external connection (either VGA or DVI or both) for a second monitor. When this monitor is plugged in, it can be enabled by pressing the display toggle key, otherwise known as the secondary monitor button. On the laptop used in this chapter, this can be done by pressing the Fn key and the F3 key simultaneously; however, it can be a different key than F3 on other brands of laptops. The icon on the key usually looks like an open laptop viewed from the side with a monitor to its right. Normally, you have the option to display the desktop to the laptop, to the external display, or a copy of the desktop to both. Many laptops offer a greater resolution to external displays than they can provide internally, but only when the external display is being used exclusively. For example, the laptop used in this chapter can run a resolution of 1280x800 on the integrated display but can run at 1920x1200 on the external monitor (again, exclusively). If the external monitor won't display anything, make sure that the cable is firmly connected to the external port, verify that the external monitor is plugged in and on, and then try cycling through the various video options by pressing the button several times, waiting a few seconds each time. Make sure you are holding down the Fn key while doing so. Finally, restart the computer if necessary. This can get a little trickier if using a projector as the second display. Sometimes, the projector might need time to warm up or might need to be configured via its on-screen display (OSD). Locate the projector's documentation for more details.

Well, displaying the same desktop on two monitors is great, but what if you want to take it to the next level and *stretch out* the Windows desktop across two monitors? That would be known as DualView on laptops and Multiple Monitor on desktops. More on that in Chapter 12.

Troubleshooting Video Issues

The video display in laptops is integrated, which while being a main feature of the portability of laptops can be a point of failure as well. Minor issues such as intermittent lines on the screen suggest that the display cable needs to be reconnected or replaced. However, complete display failures suggest a worse problem that will take longer to repair. Display failures can be broken down into a few categories:

▶ **Damaged inverter:** The LCD is lit by a Cold Cathode Fluorescent Lamp (basically a bulb); it is the LCD backlight. The backlight is driven by a high-voltage inverter circuit. Because the inverter runs at high voltage, and possibly at high temperatures, it is prone to failure. If the inverter fails, the display will go dark; however, an external monitor should work properly. Another possibility is that the backlight has failed. You can verify if it is an inverter/backlight issue by shining a flashlight directly at the screen. When you do this you should be able to make out Windows! This means that the display is getting the video signal from the motherboard, and the problem, most likely, is indeed the inverter or the backlight. If the display's flex cable that connects the LCD to the motherboard was loose or disconnected, nothing would show up on the screen at all. The inverter circuit is usually situated on its own circuit board. To replace this circuit board follow the steps in Table 7.3.

▶ **Damaged LCD screen:** An LCD could be damaged in a variety of ways. Sometimes, the damage could be minor, perhaps caused by the keyboard scratching against the display due to worn down or missing rubber bumpers, or rubber screw cover inserts. Simply attach new ones with adhesive or by snapping them into place. But the damage could be more extensive. For example, you might see a crack in the screen, or a portion of the screen doesn't display properly. Or you might notice dark, irregular lines that run the width of the display in all video modes. If any of these are the case, the LCD will have to be replaced, follow steps 1–3 in Table 7.3 to open the display assembly.

▶ **Worn out backlight:** A laptop's backlight usually lasts a long time. However, at some point the lamp starts to wear out. You might notice a dimmer screen than before, or a reddish/pinkish hue to the screen, or maybe a loss of color. All these things indicate the possibility of a worn-out lamp. To replace the backlight, follow the steps in Table 7.3 but during steps 4 and 5, instead of replacing the inverter, replace the backlight.

TABLE 7.3 **Steps to Replace a Damaged Inverter Board**

Step	Procedure
1. Prepare the laptop for surgery!	Shut down the laptop, unplug it, and disconnect the battery. Then employ ESD prevention measures.
2. Remove the display.	To remove the display, the keyboard must be removed first. (Depending on the brand of laptop, there might be a few other items to unscrew and remove.) Then, remove the screws holding the hinges down to the base of the laptop. Finally, disconnect the flex cable and any other connectors from the display to the system board.

TABLE 7.3 **Continued**

Step	Procedure
3. Open the display.	Several screws hold the display together located on the plastic bezel that surrounds the LCD. These screws are covered with either tape or plastic domes. Remove the tape/domes and then remove the screws. Pry the plastic bezel open (carefully!) and remove the LCD. Note: Sometimes the display case needs to be opened with a plastic shim or similar tool. Insert the shim between the two pieces of plastic and slowly pry around the case until it is opened.
4. Remove the inverter.	The inverter often has two connectors: one for the high-voltage connection that leads to the power source and a flex cable that connects to the LCD. Disconnect these, and remove the inverter. As always, hold circuit boards by the edges, and try not to touch any actual circuits or chips. Note: At this stage, the bulb could be replaced (if it failed) on some laptops. It is usually located on the back of the LCD at the bottom. However, some LCDs have nonremovable bulbs. If this is the case, the entire LCD must be replaced.
5. Install the new inverter.	LCD inverters can be purchased from a variety of places online including the manufacturer of the laptop, or of the display. Verify that you are getting the correct part#. Connect the flex cable and the other connector to the inverter board.
6. Rebuild the display.	Now the tough part. The LCD must be put back into the bezel. Then the bezel needs to be snapped together and screwed in. Replace the tape or domes that covered the screws. Then reconnect the display assembly to the rest of the laptop; the hinges normally connect with a few screws. Next, reconnect the flex cable and any other connectors from the display to the system board. Finally, reconnect and screw in other components like the keyboard.

ExamAlert

Warning! The inverter should not be handled if the laptop is on! Be sure to turn off and unplug the laptop and remove the battery before removing an inverter.

Audio

Almost all laptops have an integrated sound card (often a Mini-PCI card) and speakers. These work in the same manner as a PC's sound card and speakers, just on a smaller scale. Quite often, a laptop comes equipped with a speaker out/headphone out connector, line in connector, microphone connector, and perhaps an IEEE 1394 (FireWire) connector. For more information on audio, see the section titled "The Audio Subsystem" in Chapter 12.

A laptop's volume can be adjusted in one of two ways:

▸ **Volume knob/button:** Older laptops have a knob, which can sometimes be a little hard to find. This can be the culprit when a user informs you that they cannot hear anything from their speakers. Newer laptops use a button, usually one that is activated with the Fn key (refer to Figure 7.5). Most new laptops have an on-screen display that shows the volume level as you adjust it.

▸ **Software adjustment:** Volume can be adjusted within Windows 7/Vista by navigating to Start > Control Panel > Sound and then accessing the Speakers Properties window and adjusting the volume slider. Volume can be adjusted in Windows XP by navigating to Start > Control Panel > Sounds and Audio Devices, and then adjusting the volume slider. From here you can also place a volume icon on the taskbar (within the Notification Area/System Tray) for easy access to the volume control and to the Sounds and Audio Devices window. Windows 7 and Vista place an icon within the Notification Area automatically. Most sound cards come with their own software as well in which a user can adjust volume, the equalizer, and more. This software might place an icon within the Notification Area as well.

Optical Discs

Due to the amount of abuse a typical laptop receives, it is not uncommon to see a DVD or CD drive fail. However, optical disc drives are usually easy to replace on a laptop, easier than on a desktop PC in fact. Most of the time there will be two screws on the bottom of the laptop that hold the DVD or CD drive in place. When removed, the drive can be slid out of the side of the laptop. Drives that can be installed simply by sliding them into a slot are becoming more and more commonplace; most laptops incorporate them. Check your laptop's documentation for a compatible replacement (or upgrade), or check the bottom of the drive for part numbers that you can use to find a replacement drive online.

Fans

Laptops need to exhaust hot air just like PCs do. To accomplish this, a laptop might have fans on the side or bottom. These can get clogged easily; more easily than PC fans, given the abuse that laptops receive. Indicators of a clogged fan include a clicking sound or worse, an unusually high-pitched noise. The first thing to do in this case is to blow compressed air through the fan slot and out of the computer. Be sure not to blow the air into the system, and I recommend doing this outside, you never know what will come out. If this doesn't work, consider checking if something is obstructing the fan. Use a penlight to look through the fan and inside the system if possible. If not, you'll have to open the system to see what is causing the problem. The worst case scenario is that you would have to replace the fan.

> **ExamAlert**
>
> If the fan makes a high-pitched noise, try blowing compressed air through the fan slots and out of the laptop.

Power

Laptops are designed to run on battery power, but laptops can run only between 2 and 5 hours on these batteries. So, the laptop comes with an AC power adapter to plug into an AC outlet; these adapters should always be carried with the laptop. How many times have I heard from a user that they forgot their power brick! Recommend to users that they always put the AC adapter back in the laptop case.

The worst is when a laptop won't turn on! Without power a user can't do anything. When troubleshooting power problems, envision the entire chain of power in your mind (or write it on paper); from the AC outlet, to the AC adapter, all the way to the power button on the laptop. There are a few things you can check if it appears that the laptop is not getting any power.

▶ **Check the power LED:** Check the power light on the AC adapter. If this is off, not only will the laptop not get power, but the battery won't charge as well. Most laptops also have a power LED just above the keyboard. If this lights up, then maybe it isn't a power problem at all. For example, the user might start the laptop, see nothing on the display, and determine that the laptop has no power, when in reality, it is a display issue. Many laptops also have hard drive and wireless LEDs, which can tell you more about the status of the laptop, without seeing anything on the screen.

▶ **Check connections:** Verify that the laptop is firmly connected to the AC adapter and that the AC Adapter is firmly connected to the AC outlet. Sometimes a user presses the power button expecting the laptop to start but not realizing that the battery is discharged and that the AC adapter is not connected. Also, check for damage. Inspect the DC jack that is soldered onto the motherboard of the laptop. Make sure it isn't loose or damaged. Sometimes the battery only charges if the output cord of the AC adapter is held at an angle; probably because the laptop was transported while the output cord was plugged into the laptop, causing damage to the DC jack.

▶ **Make sure the user uses the right power adapter:** Swapping power adapters between two different laptops is not recommended, but users try to do it all the time. Two different laptop models made by the same manufacturer might use what appear to be similar power adapters, with only one or two volts separating them; however, the laptop usually won't power on with that "slightly" different power adapter. Laptop AC adapters are known as fixed input power supplies, meaning they work at a specific voltage. The adapter is not meant to be used on another model laptop. Unfortunately, a user might have plugged in the incorrect power adapter, and the laptop worked fine for 4 or 5 hours because it was actually running on battery power, but the user might not have noticed, even though the system should have notified the user when the battery was low (and critical). If you do suspect that an AC power adapter is faulty, consider testing your theory by swapping it out with an *identical* power adapter. Chances are a company will have extra power adapters or will have several laptops of the same make and model. Another power adapter-related issue could be that the user is trying to work in another country. To do this, the user needs an auto-switching AC adapter, meaning that it can switch from 120 to 240 VAC automatically. Some laptops do not come with auto-switching AC adapters, but after-market versions can be purchased for many models of laptops. Remember that an additional adapter might be necessary to make the actual connection to the AC outlet in foreign countries.

▶ **Check the battery and voltage:** It might sound silly, but check if the battery hasn't been removed for some odd reason. Also, check if the battery is fully inserted into the battery compartment. There is usually a locking mechanism that should hold the battery in place. Finally, test the battery's voltage. Batteries last a finite amount of time. They can be recharged (known as cycles) by the laptop just so many times before failure. After a few to several years, the battery won't hold a charge any longer or will lose charge quickly. In some cases you can try discharging and recharging the battery a few times to "stimulate" it, but in most scenarios the battery must to be replaced. In general, lithium-ion batteries last longer if the laptop is operated and stored at the right temperature ranges. Acceptable operating range for laptops is from 50–95°F (10–35°C), and acceptable storage ranges are from –4 to 140°F (– 20 to 60°C).

> **Note**
>
> For more information on how to prolong lithium-ion batteries (the most common laptop battery), see the following link: http://batteryuniversity.com/learn/article/how_to_prolong_lithium_based_batteries.

- ▶ **Check whether standby or hibernate mode has failed:** If the user regularly puts the laptop into standby or hibernate mode, they could encounter issues once in a while. In some cases, the power button needs to be held down for several seconds to reboot the machine out of a failed power down state. This might have to be done with the battery removed. If either of these modes failed, check the Event Viewer for any relative information, and possibly turn off hibernation and or standby mode until the situation has been rectified. (On a slightly different note, sometimes laptops take a long time to come out of standby mode, but it is not an issue with standby but a case of the lid switch being stuck. It looks like a power issue, but it's a simple hardware fix.)

- ▶ **Reconnect the power button:** In rare cases the power button might have been disconnected from the system board. To fix this the laptop must be opened; usually removing the keyboard and laptop housing gives access to the buttons.

- ▶ **Check the AC outlet:** Make sure the AC outlet that the user has plugged the laptop into is supplying power. A simple test would be to plug a lamp, clock, or other device into the outlet, but a more discerning and safe test would be to use a receptacle tester. For more information on testing AC outlets see Chapter 5, "Power."

There are a few different types of batteries that a laptop might use including Lithium-ion (Li-ion), Nickel-metal hydride (NiMH), and Nickel-cadmium (NiCd), but Li-ion is by far the most common. They have the best energy to weight ratio and don't suffer from "memory effect" like NiCd batteries. They also discharge slowly when they are not used.

However, you can't run on batteries forever! So Windows includes alarms that can be set to notify the user when the battery is getting low, and *real* low, known as critical. These alarms are set in Power Options.

To modify battery alarms in Windows XP, click Start > Control Panel, and in Classic mode double-click the Power Options icon. Select the Alarms tab; from here the low battery and critical battery alarm thresholds can be modified. Additional settings like the power scheme used, what to do when the lid of the laptop is closed, and enabling hibernation can also be modified in the Power Options Properties dialog box. To conserve battery power, consider setting the display and hard disk to turn off after the computer has been idle for 5 minutes; this can be done from the Power Schemes tab.

Power options on portable systems running Windows 7/Vista can be modified by going to the Control Panel, and double-clicking the Power Options applet. By default, there are three Preferred plans: Balanced, Power saver, and High performance; however, users can create their own power plans as well. Each of these plans can be modified by clicking the Change plan settings link. There are a lot of settings in this window; following is one example. In Balanced, click Change plan settings. The Display is set to turn off in 20 minutes by default; it can be set from 1 minute to 5 hours, or set to never. If you click the Change advanced power settings link, the Power Options button appears. From here you can specify how long before the hard disk turns off, and set power savings for devices such as the processor, wireless, USB, and PCI Express. To configure alarms in 7/Vista, go to the Battery Area and Low Battery Notification. Take a few minutes looking through these options, and the options for the other power plans. Almost all of today's laptops use the Advanced Configuration and Power Interface (ACPI), which enables Windows to control the device power management instead of the BIOS.

> **ExamAlert**
>
> Know where to modify battery alarms in Windows 7, Vista, and XP.

Expansion Devices

There are several ways to expand upon your laptop, including external and internal expansion slots and docking stations. Let's talk about each of these briefly.

▶ **External expansion buses:** The most common types of external expansion buses are called PC Card (also known as PCMCIA), CardBus, and ExpressCard; I'm talking about those 2-inch-wide slots on the side of the laptop. These expansion buses accept credit card-size devices that can be added to a laptop to increase memory, or add functionality in the form of networking, hard disks, and more. They are hot-swappable, meaning they support hot plugging into the expansion slot while the computer is powered on.

▶ **PC Cards must be supported by the computer on two levels:** The card level (Card Services) and the socket level (Socket Services). Card

Services deal with the installation of compatible drivers to the operating system and enable the allocation of system resources automatically. Socket Services is the BIOS-level software interface that provides access to the sockets (slots) in the computer.

PC Cards have a 16-bit bus width and can be used in PC Card slots and CardBus slots. However, CardBus cards have a 32-bit bus width (essentially they are PCI); they look similar to PC Cards but cannot be used in a PC Card slot. ExpressCard (also known as PCI ExpressCard) is a separate technology altogether and not compatible with either of the other two (without an adapter). There are two form factors of ExpressCard: /34, which is 34 mm wide, and /54, which is 54 mm wide and can be identified by a cutout in one corner of the card. Also, PC Cards and CardBus cards have a 68-pin connector, whereas ExpressCard has a 26-pin connector. PC Card and CardBus were the most-used expansion cards in laptops for many years but since 2006 have been losing ground to ExpressCard, especially in higher-end laptops. This is yet another example of a technology that is moving from parallel to serial data transfer. A manufacturer of ExpressCard devices can select to design them using the PCI Express technology or USB 2.0 technology depending on what type of card they make. For example, an ExpressCard soundcard wouldn't need the speed of PCI Express, so it would probably be designed from a USB 2.0 standpoint. Table 7.4 breaks down the characteristics of PC Card, CardBus, and ExpressCard expansion buses.

TABLE 7.4   **PC Card, CardBus, and ExpressCard Details**

Technology	Type	Data Transfer Rate	Typical Usage
PC Card	Type I (3.3 mm thick)	20 MB/s	RAM, Flash memory
PC Card/ CardBus	Type II (5 mm thick)	PC Card = 20 MB/s CardBus = 133 MB/s	Network adapters, modems
PC Card/ CardBus	Type III (10.5 mm thick)	PC Card = 20 MB/s CardBus = 133 MB/s	Hard drives
ExpressCard	PCI Express mode USB mode	2.5 Gbps (250 MB/s) 480 Mbps (60 MB/s)	External SATA drives, soundcards, Ethernet devices, and so on

ExamAlert

Memorize the differences between the PC Card, CardBus, and ExpressCard /34 and /54 expansion buses for the exam.

> **Note**
>
> Many owners of high-end laptops complain about the quality of the integrated soundcards and look for alternatives. To meet this need, some manufacturers such as Creative Labs make high-quality ExpressCard soundcards that rival the latest soundcard technology in desktop computers.

▶ **Internal expansion buses:** As far as internal expansion buses go, laptops use Mini-PCI and Mini-PCI Express. These are about a quarter the size of their desktop computer counterparts and work essentially the same, although there might be less performance in the laptop versions. For example, Mini-PCI has a maximum data transfer rate of 133 MB/s, which is one-half of some PCI cards in desktops. However, Mini-PCIe (also known as PCI Express x1 Mini Card) can double this speed; it is commonly used in laptops for solid state drives. These types of cards might be used as video cards or as wireless cards. If you find that a laptop will not display video through the laptop screen or an external monitor, you'll probably have to replace the mini video adapter. Replacing them can be a bit of a chore on some laptops. You need to remove the keyboard first, then either disconnect a cable or two from the card, or remove the card from a slot, and possibly remove two screws that hold the card in place. (The card is often flat against the system board.) By the way, when replacing components like this, be sure to put the keyboard upside down on an antistatic bag, and put the cards in an antistatic bag as well until you are ready for them.

▶ **Docking Stations:** The docking station expands the laptop so that it can behave more like a desktop computer. By connecting the laptop to the docking station, and adding a full-size keyboard, mouse, and monitor, the user doesn't actually touch the laptop anymore except perhaps to turn it on. Most laptops can *hot dock*, meaning they can connect to the docking station while powered on. The docking station recharges the laptop's battery, and possibly a second battery, and has connections for video, audio, networking, and expansion cards. Docking stations might even have an optical disk drive or additional hard disk; it all depends on the brand and model. If all these extras aren't necessary, a user might require only a *port replicator*, which is a similar device but it has only ports; for example, video, sound, network, and so on.

> **Note**
>
> Of course, you can also expand your laptop by using integrated USB and IEEE 1394 ports and built-in memory card readers. For more information on USB and IEEE 1394, see Chapter 13, "Peripherals and Custom Computing." For more information on memory cards, see Chapter 6, "Storage Devices."

Communications

Communicating quickly and efficiently is key in business environments. To do so, laptops use a variety of different devices including the following:

> ▶ **Ethernet:** Most laptops today come equipped with wired and wireless Ethernet adapters to connect to a local area network (LAN) or a wireless local area network (WLAN). The wired connection presents itself as an RJ45 port and can typically transfer data at 1000, 100, and 10 Mbps, auto-negotiating its speed to the network it is connected to. Wireless connections are made with an internal Mini-PCI card that can connect to 802.11n, g, and b networks (a maximum of 600, 54, and 11 Mbps, respectively). It is also possible to connect wired or wireless network adapters to USB ports or to ExpressCard or PC Card slots. Otherwise, these technologies work the same on a laptop as they do on a desktop computer. For more information on wired and wireless LAN technologies, see Chapter 15. There is usually a WLAN button (located near the power button) that can enable/disable the wireless adapter. Keep this in mind when troubleshooting. If this is disabled, the laptop cannot connect wirelessly, even if the device is enabled in the Device Manager. If a wireless adapter is enabled but is detecting a weak signal even though it is in close proximity to the wireless access point, check the antenna and make sure it is connected and/or screwed in properly. Many laptops use proprietary software for the configuration of wireless network connections, instead of using the built-in Windows Wireless Zero Configuration program. In some cases, it might be easier to disable the proprietary application and use Wireless Zero Configuration instead.

> **ExamAlert**
>
> If the laptop can't connect to the wireless network, try pressing the WLAN button near the power button.

▶ **Bluetooth:** Bluetooth adapters enable a laptop to connect to other Bluetooth devices over short distances, thus joining or creating a personal area network (PAN). A Bluetooth adapter might be included inside the laptop as an individual Mini-PCI card or as a combo Bluetooth/WLAN Mini-PCI card. External USB and ExpressCard Bluetooth adapters and remote controls are also available. For more information on Bluetooth, see Chapter 13. Many laptops come with WLAN and Bluetooth capabilities; however, the two technologies compete over frequencies. It is recommended that a user make use of only one at a time if possible. Buttons are usually available on the laptop (near the power button) for enabling/disabling WLAN and Bluetooth.

▶ **Infrared:** Infrared or IrDA wireless ports can be used to transfer data between the laptop and another computer, smartphone, or other mobile device over a short distance. Unlike Bluetooth, IrDA connections must be line-of-sight. Built-in IrDA ports are not seen as often on laptops as Bluetooth but can be purchased in USB format if necessary.

▶ **Cellular WAN:** Connecting to the Internet through 3G cellular WAN cards has become more popular over the past few years. Telecommunications providers like Verizon, Sprint, and AT&T offer cellular WAN ExpressCards (also known as wireless WAN cards) and USB-based travel routers. Some laptops are designed with built-in Mini-PCI cellular devices (sometimes called modems).

▶ **Modem:** The standard traditional dial-up modem can still be found on many laptops. This circuitry is often built into the motherboard but can also be a Mini-PCI card or a separate card altogether. If the modem fails and it is integrated into the motherboard, the entire motherboard would have to be replaced (which would be costly) or a PC Card, ExpressCard, or USB version could be purchased.

Exam Alert

Know the various ways that a laptop could communicate with other computers for the exam including wired and wireless Ethernet, Bluetooth, IrDA, Cellular WAN, and dial-up modems.

Cram Quiz

Answer these questions. The answers follow the last question. If you cannot answer
these questions correctly, consider reading this section again until you can.

220-801 Questions

1. Which kinds of ports can typically be found on a laptop? (Select all that apply.)

   ○ **A.** RJ45

   ○ **B.** USB

   ○ **C.** IEEE 1284

   ○ **D.** DVI

2. What kind of video technology do most laptops incorporate currently?

   ○ **A.** TFT Active Matrix

   ○ **B.** Passive Matrix

   ○ **C.** CRT

   ○ **D.** TFT Passive Matrix

3. What is a common resolution on today's laptops?

   ○ **A.** 640x480

   ○ **B.** 800x600

   ○ **C.** 1280x800

   ○ **D.** 2048x1536

4. If a user wanted to stretch their desktop across two monitors, what Windows
   technology would they look for?

   ○ **A.** Multiple monitor

   ○ **B.** Video replication

   ○ **C.** SideCar

   ○ **D.** DualView

5. What is the most common battery used by today's laptops?

   ○ **A.** Double AA batteries

   ○ **B.** Lithium-ion (Li-ion)

   ○ **C.** Nickel-metal hydride (NiMH)

   ○ **D.** Nickel-cadmium (NiCd)

6. Where would a user go to modify the battery alarms in Windows?

   ○ **A.** Display Properties window

   ○ **B.** Power Properties window

   ○ **C.** BIOS

   ○ **D.** Power Options window

7. Which of the following has the fastest data transfer rate?

   ○ **A.** CardBus

   ○ **B.** ExpressCard PCIe

   ○ **C.** PC Card

   ○ **D.** ExpressCard USB

8. Which of the following are ways that a laptop can communicate with other computers? (Select all that apply)

   ○ **A.** Bluetooth

   ○ **B.** WLAN

   ○ **C.** Ultraviolet

   ○ **D.** Cellular WAN

220-802 Questions

9. When a user types, a laptop's screen displays letters and numbers instead of only letters. What should you check first?

   ○ **A.** Fn key

   ○ **B.** LCD cutoff switch

   ○ **C.** Num Lk key

   ○ **D.** Scroll Lock key

10. Which of the following are possible reasons that a laptop's keyboard might fail completely? (Select the best two answers.)

   ○ **A.** A stuck key.

   ○ **B.** A disconnected ribbon cable.

   ○ **C.** The user spilled coffee on the laptop.

   ○ **D.** The keyboard was disabled in the Device Manager.

11. What are two possible reasons why a laptop's display suddenly went blank?

   ○ **A.** Damaged inverter

   ○ **B.** Damaged LCD

   ○ **C.** Burned out backlight

   ○ **D.** Incorrect resolution setting

12. A user doesn't see anything on his laptop's screen. He tries to use AC power and thinks that the laptop is not receiving any. What are two possible reasons for this?

- ○ **A.** Incorrect AC adapter.
- ○ **B.** The AC adapter is not connected to the laptop.
- ○ **C.** Windows won't boot.
- ○ **D.** The battery is dead.

13. One of your customers reports that she walked away from her laptop for 30 minutes. When she returned, the display was very dim. The user increased the brightness setting and moved the mouse but to no effect. What should you do first?

- ○ **A.** Replace the LCD screen.
- ○ **B.** Check the operating system for corruption.
- ○ **C.** Connect an external monitor to verify that the video card works.
- ○ **D.** Check if the laptop is now on battery power.

Cram Quiz Answers

220-801 Answers

1. **A, B,** and **D.** RJ45, USB, and DVI ports are all common on a laptop. However, IEEE 1284 printer ports are not common.

2. **A.** TFT active matrix LCDs are the most common in laptops today. Passive matrix screens have been discontinued; although you might see an older laptop that utilizes this technology. There is no TFT passive matrix, and cathode ray tubes (CRTs) were used only on the first laptops many years ago. Due to a CRT's weight and heavy power usage, it is not a good solution for laptops.

3. **C.** 1280x800 (WXGA) is a common resolution used by today's laptops. 640x480 and 800x600 are older VGA modes that can't fit much on the screen. 2048x1536 (QXGA) is a higher resolution than most laptops' video adapters can display. For more information on resolutions see Chapter 12.

4. **D.** DualView enables a laptop running Windows to stretch the desktop across two monitors. It is a basic version of Multiple Monitor that is only available on desktop PCs. SideCar is a third-party hardware/software solution that enables a desktop PC or laptop to stretch the desktop over multiple monitors but is not included in Windows.

5. **B.** There are a few different types of batteries that a laptop might use including Lithium-ion (Li-ion), Nickel-metal hydride (NiMH), and Nickel-cadmium (NiCd), but Lithium-ion is by far the most common. Believe it or not, some laptops (namely children's) can run on 4 AA batteries, but it is not common or feasible in today's business environments.

6. **D.** To change the thresholds for battery alarms, a user would access the Power Options window.

7. **B.** ExpressCard in PCI Express mode (PCIe) has the highest data transfer rate at 250 MB/s. The next fastest would be CardBus, followed by ExpressCard in USB mode, with PC Card bringing up the rear.

8. **A, B,** and **D.** Laptops can communicate with other computers through Bluetooth, WLAN, IrDA, and Cellular WAN wireless connections, plus wired connections like Ethernet (RJ45) and dial-up (RJ11).

220-802 Answers

9. **C.** The number lock key (Num Lk) can enable or disable the numeric keypad. This might be necessary if the user inadvertently turned it on or disconnected an external keyboard from the laptop. Some laptops require you to press CTRL+Num Lk to enable or disable the numeric keypad. Laptops are usually color-coded: White options require the CTRL key and blue options require the Fn key. In this scenario, pressing the Function (Fn) key is not necessary when pressing the Num Lk key. The LCD cutoff switch is used to turn off the bulb that lights the LCD. The scroll lock key is used little but is meant to lock any scrolling done with the arrow keys.

10. **B** and **C.** A laptop's keyboard could fail due to a disconnected or loose keyboard ribbon cable. It could also fail if a user spilled coffee on the laptop, or through general abuse, or by being dropped on the ground, and so on. One stuck key will not cause the entire keyboard to fail, and on most laptops, the keyboard cannot be disabled in the Device Manager.

11. **A** and **C.** A damaged inverter or burned out bulb could cause a laptop's display to go blank. You can verify if the LCD is still getting a signal by shining a flashlight at the screen. A damaged LCD usually works to a certain extent and will either be cracked, have areas of Windows missing, or show other signs of damage. An incorrect resolution setting usually makes Windows look garbled on the screen.

12. **A** and **B.** An incorrect adapter will usually not power a laptop. The adapter used must be exact. And of course, if the laptop is not plugged in properly to the adapter, it won't get power. Windows doesn't play into this scenario. And if the battery was dead, it could cause the laptop to not power up, but only if the AC adapter was also disconnected; the scenario states that the user is trying to use AC power.

13. **D.** It could be that the laptop is now on battery power, which is usually set to a dimmer display and shorter sleep configuration. This indicates that the laptop is not getting AC power from the AC outlet anymore for some reason. The battery power setting is the first thing you should check; afterward, start troubleshooting the AC adapter, cable, AC outlet and so on. It's too early to try replacing the display; try not to replace something until you have ruled out all other possibilities. A dim screen is not caused by OS corruption. No need to plug in an external monitor; you know the video adapter is working, it's just dim.

Installing, Configuring, and Troubleshooting Internal Laptop Components

Now that you know how to troubleshoot the visible components of a laptop, let's discuss the internal components a little bit. Because they are not exposed, these devices won't fail as often as components such as the keyboard and the display, but sometimes failures still occur. At times you might need to replace a hard drive (and possibly recover the drive's data) and add or swap out memory. Hard drives and memory are known as field replaceable units (FRUs). This means that the part can be quickly removed from the system, and that you can do it at the customer location. On a laptop it requires that the component be accessible by opening a hatch or unlatching and sliding it out. Other items such as the CPU and motherboard are not usually field replaceable. If one of these fails, the repair process will be longer and will usually require bringing the laptop back to the shop. Dealing with hard drive trouble and working with RAM is more common, so let's begin with those.

Hard Drives

So far, we mentioned a few times that hard drives will fail; it's just a matter of when. And laptop hard drives are more susceptible to failure than desktop computers due to their mobility and the bumps and bruises that laptops regularly sustain. The majority of new laptops are available with SATA hard disks, but you will probably still see laptops with IDE drives in the field. The bulk of the hard drives in laptops are 2.5-inches wide, as opposed to a desktop computer's 3.5-inch hard drive. Obviously, the smaller form factor is necessary in today's laptops. Ultra-small laptops and other small portable devices might use a hard disk as small as 1.8 inches.

2.5-inch SATA hard drives use the same connectors as their 3.5-inch counterparts, another benefit of using SATA. Because of this, no adapters are needed when transferring information from a laptop drive to a desktop drive (which is common when attempting to recover data). However, 2.5-inch PATA drives use a different connector than their 3.5-inch counterparts. Remember from Chapter 6 that a 3.5-inch PATA desktop hard drive has a 40-pin IDE connector for data and a 4-pin Molex connector for power. The problem is that a 2.5-inch PATA hard drive just doesn't have the space for these types of connectors. So a different 44-pin IDE connector was developed, which is much smaller and contains both the data *and* the power pins in one 44-pin package.

However, this means that an adapter is necessary if you want to transfer data from the 2.5-inch PATA drive to a 3.5-inch PATA drive. An example of this adapter is shown in Figure 7.7.

This end connects
to the 2.5" hard drive

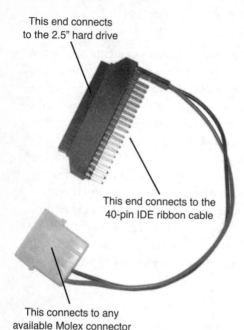

This end connects to the
40-pin IDE ribbon cable

This connects to any
available Molex connector

FIGURE 7.7   **44-pin to 40-pin IDE adapter**

> **Note**
>
> If you are serious about PC repair, this item should be added to your PC toolkit. I also recommend an all-in-one SATA/IDE to USB adapter from vendors such as Vantec. This type of device enables you to plug in just about any hard drive (SATA, IDE 40-pin, and IDE 44-pin) and transfer the information from that drive via USB to another computer. Nice.

44-pin 2.5-inch PATA hard drives have four additional pins to the right of the IDE connector; these are used for master/slave configurations, which might be necessary to configure when rescuing data from a laptop drive. Of course, to rescue data from a hard drive, you first must remove it. Laptop hard drives can be accessed from one of three places. The first, and maybe the most common, is from an access panel on the bottom of the laptop. The second is from underneath the keyboard. And the third would be from the side of the laptop. In this last scenario, the hard drive is inside of a caddy that has a handle for easy removal; it should slide right out of the side of the laptop. In the third scenario, the hard drive would have to be removed from the caddy, and in any scenario there will usually be some kind of bracket that has to be unscrewed from the drive when replacing it. Hold on to this bracket for the new hard drive.

Memory

Most of today's laptops use DDR SDRAM like desktop computers do. But again, you are dealing with a much smaller device, so the memory is also smaller; it is known as a SO-DIMM or small outline dual in-line memory module. Table 7.5 shows the four types of SO-DIMMs and their pin formats. As with desktop RAM, different versions of memory in laptops are not compatible; for example, you can't put a DDR2 SO-DIMM into a DDR SO-DIMM slot.

TABLE 7.5 **SO-DIMM Versions**

Memory Type	Module Format	Version
SDRAM	144 pin	PC66—PC133
DDR	200 pin	DDR-200—DDR-400
DDR2	200 pin	DDR2-400—DDR2-1066
DDR3	204 pin	DDR3-800—DDR3-2133

ExamAlert

Memorize the types of SODIMMs, and understand the pin format differences between them and DIMMs.

Note

For more information on RAM types, see Chapter 4, "RAM."

RAM has a center notch that helps to orient the RAM during installation. This notch will usually be in a different location for DDR, DDR2, and DDR3.

Before installing any new RAM, check compatibility. Remember to consult the laptop's documentation to find out exactly how much RAM and what type the laptop will accept. When you have purchased compatible RAM, installing it to a laptop is usually quite simple. Often RAM is located on the bottom of the laptop underneath an access cover. In other laptops it might be underneath the keyboard, or there could be one stick of RAM under the keyboard and a second (usually for add-ons) under an access cover underneath the laptop. Consult your laptop's documentation for the exact location of the RAM compartment. Sometimes the compartment has a small icon identifying it as the location for memory. Table 7.6 shows the steps involved in adding RAM to a laptop. Keep in mind that SO-DIMMs, and their corresponding memory board, are much more delicate than their counterparts in a desktop computer.

TABLE 7.6 **Installing a SO-DIMM to a Laptop**

Step	Procedure
1. Prepare the laptop for surgery!	Shut down the laptop, unplug it, and disconnect the battery. Then employ ESD prevention measures.
2. Review your documentation.	Review your documentation to find out where RAM is located. For this step assume that the RAM can be added to a compartment underneath the laptop.
3. Open the memory compartment.	Usually there will be two screws that you need to remove to open the memory compartment door. Often, these are captive screws and will stay in the door. But if they are not, store them in a safe place and label them.
4. Insert the RAM.	There could be one or two slots for RAM. One of them might already be in use. Some laptops support dual-channel memory. If this is the case and you install a second memory module, make sure it is identical to the first. Insert the memory module at a 45-degree angle into the memory slot, aligning the notch with the keyed area of the memory slot. Press the module into the slot; then press the module down toward the circuit board until it snaps into place (GENTLY!). Two clips, one on either side, lock into the notches in the side of the memory module. Press down again to make sure it is in place. See Figure 7.8 for an example of an installed SO-DIMM. There are actually two SODIMMs on top of each other, the one on top is farther to the left. Note the locking clips holding the memory module into place.
5. Close the compartment and test.	Screw the compartment door back on to the laptop. Then boot the computer into the BIOS and make sure it sees the new memory module. Finally, boot into Windows and make sure that the operating system sees the new total amount of RAM, and verify that applications work properly.

Sometimes, upgraded memory fails to be identified by the BIOS. This usually means that the memory was not installed properly. Turn off the computer and reseat the RAM modules, reboot, and this usually fixes the problem.

Occasionally, a laptop fails to boot and emits a series of continuous beeps. This could be due to faulty memory. However, it could simply be that the memory contacts are dirty. As mentioned before, laptops are not often treated well and are used in a variety of environments. Pop the memory hatch and inspect the RAM modules. If they require cleaning, use compressed air or try Stabilant 22a or a similar cleaner. Plug the modules back in and verify functionality by rebooting the system several times. If they still don't work, try swapping out the RAM with known good modules.

Memory slot   Locking clip

Notch   Locking clip

FIGURE 7.8   **Installed SO-DIMM**

System Board and CPU

As mentioned before the worst thing that could happen to a laptop is if it doesn't start. Let me rephrase; that would be the worst thing that could happen to a *user*. The worst thing for a tech would be if the system board failed. This is because it would require almost a complete disassembly of the unit to repair, which is time-consuming and requires heavy documentation to get all the parts back together properly when done. However, CPU replacement (and upgrading) is not quite as difficult but still requires removing at least the keyboard, and more than likely, a few other components that will be in the way; documentation is still important when replacing a CPU.

Sometimes a system board's lithium battery needs replacement. This is done in the same manner as it is within a desktop computer; however, you need to remove the keyboard, and perhaps other devices and connections, to get access to the battery. Most laptops come with the same CR2032 battery that desktop models use; however, a few laptops (and other handheld devices) come with a rechargeable system board lithium battery that has a shelf life of up to 10 years, but this is a fairly new technology.

Before you do decide to take this type of plunge into a laptop, one thing to keep in mind is that a lot of companies will purchase 1- to 3-year warranties for the laptops they use. Even though there is a cost involved in doing this, it is usually the wise choice. If the laptop did fail, the alternative would be to have a technician spend several hours (at least) disassembling, testing, replacing, and reassembling the laptop; all of which could cost the company more money in man hours than it would have to just get the warranty. Warranties are a type of insurance, and this type is usually acceptable to a company. So check your company's policies and procedures first before doing these types of repairs.

Before removing a CPU or other internal components, employ ESD prevention measures. If the CPU is surface-mounted, you cannot remove it; if it has failed the entire system board would need to be removed. But if it is socketed (which is more likely on newer laptops), with either a pin grid array (PGA) or ball grid array (BGA), it can be removed. Usually there is some kind of locking arm mechanism that must be unlocked to remove the CPU from the socket. Common sockets for mobile Intel CPUs include the Socket M (for several CPUs including the Core 2 Duo), Socket P (the replacement for Socket M), and the newer Socket G1 and G2 for Core i3, i5, and i7 CPUs. Upgrade ranges for laptop CPUs are usually quite narrow. If a CPU fails, it is usually best to install an identical CPU. If you do plan to upgrade a CPU, check the documentation carefully to make sure that the exact model laptop (and its motherboard) can support the faster CPU. After removing the CPU, be sure to place it on top of an antistatic bag with the pins facing up. When installing CPUs, employ the same delicate procedure as you would with a desktop PC. These CPUs require no force to insert them into the socket.

> **Note**
>
> For more information on installing motherboards and CPUs into desktops, see Chapter 2, "Motherboards," and Chapter 3, "The CPU."

Cram Quiz

Answer these questions. The answers follow the last question. If you cannot answer these questions correctly, consider reading this section again until you can.

220-801 Questions

1. What is the pinout for a stick of SO-DIMM DDR RAM?

   ○ **A.** 200

   ○ **B.** 168

   ○ **C.** 144

   ○ **D.** 204

2. How many pins are in a laptop's PATA hard drive?

   ○ **A.** 40

   ○ **B.** 200

   ○ **C.** 68

   ○ **D.** 44

3. How are SODIMMs installed to a laptop?

   ○ **A.** By pressing straight down

   ○ **B.** Into a ZIF socket

   ○ **C.** On a 45-degree angle

   ○ **D.** On a 90-degree angle

4. What should you do when upgrading a CPU in a laptop? (Select all that apply.)

   ○ **A.** Check documentation to see if the CPU is supported.

   ○ **B.** Install more RAM.

   ○ **C.** Employ antistatic measures.

   ○ **D.** Remove the system board.

220-802 Questions

5. You need to replace the CMOS battery in a laptop. Which of the following is a common location for the battery?

   ○ **A.** Under the DVD-ROM

   ○ **B.** Behind the laptop battery

   ○ **C.** Under the keyboard

   ○ **D.** Behind the hard drive

6. You just added a second memory module to a laptop. However, after rebooting the system the OS reports the same amount of memory as before. What should you do next?

   - ○ **A.** Replace both memory modules.
   - ○ **B.** Run Windows Update.
   - ○ **C.** Replace the motherboard.
   - ○ **D.** Reseat the laptop memory.

7. You are required to add a second memory module to a laptop. You open the hatch on the bottom of the laptop only to find a single memory module installed to the only slot. Where should you look for a second memory slot?

   - ○ **A.** Behind the removable hard drive
   - ○ **B.** Underneath the keyboard
   - ○ **C.** Under the battery
   - ○ **D.** Behind the DVD-ROM drive

Cram Exam Answers

220-801 Answers

1. **A.** DDR SODIMM modules have 200 pins. Desktop SDRAM has 168 pins. SODIMM SDRAM has 144 pins, and DDR3 SODIMMs have 204 pins.

2. **D**. A laptop's PATA hard drive has a 44-pin IDE connection that includes the four power pins.

3. **C.** SODIMMs are installed to a laptop at a 45-degree angle unlike a desktop's DDR memory that is installed by pressing straight down. ZIF sockets refer to CPUs.

4. **A** and **C.** When upgrading a CPU in a laptop, check for laptop documentation to see if the faster CPU is supported; then employ ESD prevention measures. More RAM is not necessary when upgrading a CPU, but it could help the laptop get the best out of the CPU if an open memory slot is available. Usually the system board does not have to be removed to replace or upgrade a CPU.

220-802 Answers

5. **C.** The CMOS battery is usually underneath the keyboard. Once you locate it, it is usually removed and replaced in the same manner as in a PC.

6. **D.** The next step you should take is to reseat the memory. SODIMM can be a bit tricky to install. They must be firmly installed, but you don't want to press too hard and damage any components. If the laptop worked fine before the upgrade, then you shouldn't have to replace the modules or the motherboard. Windows Update will not find additional RAM.

7. **B.** Memory modules are either located inside a hatch on the bottom of the laptop (optimally), or underneath the keyboard (not quite so optimal). Sometimes, one is accessed via the hatch, and for add-ons or upgrades, the second goes underneath the keyboard.

CHAPTER 8

Installing and Upgrading Windows

This chapter covers the following A+ exam topics:

▶ Installing and Upgrading to Windows 7

▶ Installing and Upgrading to Windows Vista

▶ Installing and Upgrading to Windows XP

You can find a master list of A+ exam topics in the "Introduction."

This chapter covers CompTIA A+ 220-802 objectives 1.1 and 1.2.

Now that we have discussed the "guts" of desktop and laptop computers, it's time to talk about installing operating systems. Over the next four chapters the focus will be on Windows 7 and Windows Vista, but Windows XP is also briefly discussed.

For the CompTIA A+ 220-802 exam, you need to know how to:

▶ Install Windows 7, Vista, and XP

▶ Upgrade to Windows 7 and Vista

▶ Troubleshoot Windows 7/Vista/XP installations and upgrades

Note

I recommend that you attempt to get your hands on a full-version copy of Windows 7 and Vista (Ultimate is preferred for both of them) and Windows XP (Professional is preferred), and a test computer to run clean installations and upgrades of the operating systems. If you have been building a computer as you progress through this book, install to that one. This hands-on approach can help you to better visualize how operating system installs and upgrades perform.

I've broken this chapter into three main sections so that we can first focus on everything to do with Win7, then Vista, and finally XP. Let's start by talking about how to install and upgrade Windows 7.

Installing and Upgrading to Windows 7

Before you can install Windows 7 or upgrade to it, you first need to decide which version of it you will use. Then, you should check the computer's hardware to make sure it is compatible with Windows 7. Next, you need to decide on an installation method: from DVD, from USB, as an image, or over the network. Finally, start the installation. New installations are known as "clean" installs; the other option is to upgrade. Upgrades to Windows 7 can be done directly from Windows Vista (depending on hardware and the current version of Vista), but they require more effort from Windows XP; we will cover more about upgrades to Windows 7 later in this chapter.

Windows 7 Versions

Windows 7 is an entire line of Microsoft operating systems designed for desktop PCs and laptops. Within the Windows 7 group are the versions Starter, Home Premium, Professional, Ultimate, and Enterprise. Starter is only available through original equipment manufacturers (OEMs) and is common among laptops. In addition, Starter is only available in a 32-bit version. However, the other versions are all available in 64-bit and 32-bit versions. In Table 8.1, the check marks indicate the components that are included in these various versions of Win7. Chapter 9, "Configuring Windows," talks more about these components.

TABLE 8.1 **Comparison of Windows 7 Versions**

Component	Starter	Home Premium	Professional	Ultimate	Enterprise*
Internet Explorer 8	✓	✓	✓	✓	✓
Create Home Group	—	✓	✓	✓	✓
Domain Join	—	—	✓	✓	✓
Windows XP Mode	—	—	✓	✓	✓
Backup to home or business network	—	—	✓	✓	✓
BitLocker Encryption	—	—	—	✓	✓

*Windows 7 Enterprise is not sold through retail or OEM channels.

ExamAlert

Know the differences between the various versions of Windows 7.

Windows 7 Minimum Requirements and Compatibility

When you decide on the version of Win7 you want to use, and before installing that operating system, you should learn as much as you can about the computer you plan to install to. Components in a computer should meet Windows 7 minimum requirements and should be listed on Microsoft's website as compatible with Windows 7. Table 8.2 shows the minimum hardware requirements for Windows 7.

TABLE 8.2   **Windows 7 Minimum Requirements**

Component	Requirement
Processor	1 GHz
RAM	1 GB (32-bit) or 2 GB (64-bit)
Free disk space	16 GB (32-bit) or 20 GB (64-bit)
Video	DirectX 9 with WDDM 1.0 or higher driver
Other	DVD-ROM drive

ExamAlert

Memorize the *minimum* requirements for Windows 7.

An important consideration is the CPU. Not only must it be fast enough, but it must also be the right type: 32-bit or 64-bit.

You can use several websites and system analysis tools to check whether a system's hardware is compatible with Windows 7. If you check a computer that already has an operating system installed, use the following tools:

▶ **Windows Compatibility Center:** Go to http://www.microsoft.com/windows/compatibility/ and access the hardware section. This was previously known as the hardware compatibility list (HCL).

▶ **System Information:** The Windows System Information tool can be accessed by opening the Run prompt and typing `msinfo32.exe`.

▶ **Belarc Advisor:** Currently a free download, you can find this program at http://www.belarc.com/free_download.html. To run the program subsequently after installation, just access Start > All Programs > Belarc Advisor.

For computers without an installed operating system, consider using self-booting diagnostic programs from organizations such as

▶ **PC Diagnostic tools:** http://www.pc-diagnostics.com

▶ **#1-TuffTEST:** http://www.tufftest.com/

▶ **PC Check:** http://www.eurosoft-uk.com

You might also opt to make use of the Microsoft Assessment and Planning (MAP) toolkit, one of Microsoft's Solution Accelerators. This kit takes inventory of most currently deployed Microsoft operating systems and server software, analyzes the inventory, and gives in-depth reports on the assessment and analysis of those operating systems and software. It is designed to simplify the planning process for IT infrastructures with multiple platform scenarios. The kit can be downloaded from the following link: http://technet.microsoft.com/en-us/library/bb977556.aspx.

Windows 7 Installation Methods

There are several types of installation methods for Windows operating systems:

▶ **Local installation from DVD-ROM:** Installation by DVD-ROM is the most common. A "local" installation is the default type. It means that you insert the DVD-ROM into the DVD-ROM drive of the computer you are sitting at, known as the local computer. When you sit at the computer and answer all the questions it asks you, it is known as an Attended Installation; you are attending to the computer as the install progresses. The steps for this type of installation are listed later in the next section titled "Installing Windows 7."

▶ **Local installation from USB:** Installation by USB is much easier than it used to be. Images of Windows operating systems can be purchased and downloaded from the Microsoft website in .ISO format and then copied to a USB flash drive. After this, the image can be made bootable by downloading, installing, and running the Windows 7 USB/DVD download tool. This can be obtained from http://www.microsoftstore.com/store/msstore/html/pbPage.Help_Win7 _usbdvd_dwnTool. To run this program and install from USB, the user must be an administrator, and the computer must have the .NET Framework 2.0 or higher installed. This process makes things a lot easier for users with netbooks or other small form factor devices that might not have optical drives.

▶ **Network installation:** You can install Windows over the network in a variety of ways. To automate the process, Windows 7 can be installed from a server automatically, using either Windows Deployment Services, which can be installed on Windows Server 2008/2003, or the Remote Installation Services (RIS) program, which can be installed on Windows Server 2003. These two server-based programs work with the Windows System Image Manager program in Win7. This program can be used to create an answer file that is used during an *Unattended Installation*. The answer file provides the responses needed for the installation, with no user intervention. In Windows 7, there is a single XML-based answer file called Unattend.xml.

> **Note**
>
> The Windows System Image Manager (SIM) for Win7 is part of the Windows Automated Installation Kit (AIK), which can be downloaded from www.microsoft.com; just search for Windows Automated Installation Kit (AIK). For detailed instructions on how to use SIM, see the following link:
>
> http://technet.microsoft.com/en-us/library/dd744394(WS.10).aspx.
>
> The Windows Preinstallation Environment, known as Windows PE, or simply WinPE is also available as part of the Windows AIK. It can be booted from optical disc, USB flash drive, over the network via PXE or from the hard drive. Windows 7 uses WinPE version 3.0 and 3.1. It can be used to run recovery tools such as the Windows Recovery Environment (WinRE), and Winternals and for running disk cloning utilities.
>
> For general information about Windows 7 deployment, see the following link:
>
> http://technet.microsoft.com/en-us/library/dd744519(WS.10).aspx.

▶ **Disk image:** Windows can also be installed from a previously made System Restore image (more on System Restore in Chapter 11, "Troubleshooting Windows"), or by cloning the entire disk image of another installation. This can be done by using programs such as Acronis True Image or Norton Ghost. When cloning a disk image, both computers need to be identical, or as close to identical as possible. The hard disk of the target for a cloned installation must be at least as large as the original system. To avoid Security Identifier (SID) conflicts, use the Sysprep utility. The Sysprep utility for Windows 7 is installed with the operating system and can be found by navigating to: C:\Windows\System32\ Sysprep. Sysprep uses an answer file created with the System Image Manager (SIM). It creates a unique SID and makes other changes as needed to the network configuration of the system.

> **Note**
>
> If installing an OS over the network from a disk image or through deployment, your network adapter needs to be Preboot Execution Environment (PXE)-compliant. PXE needs to be enabled in the BIOS.

▸ **Installing from a recovery disc:** Computers with Windows preinstalled use a recovery disc, hidden partition, or both. This disc and/or partition contains a factory image of Windows. The purpose of this is to give users the ability to return their computer back to the state when it was first received. This means that the system partition (usually the C: drive) will be formatted, and re-imaged with Windows. This works well in a two partition system, in which the operating system is on C: and data is stored on D: or another drive letter. In this scenario, if the operating system fails and cannot be repaired, the computer can be returned to its original "factory" state, but the data won't be compromised. Whenever buying a computer from a company such as HP, Dell, and so on, make sure that they offer some kind of factory recovery partition, recovery disc, or other recovery option.

ExamAlert

Know the difference between a local, network, disk image, and recovery disc installation.

▸ **Multiboots:** Since the 1990s technicians have been setting up two or more operating systems on the same hard drive; this is known as dual-booting, tri-booting, and so on. This is easier than it used to be back in the 1990s; nowadays you can usually get away with using built-in tools in Windows. For example, if you have Windows Vista installed, you could modify the partition structure with Disk Management, create a second partition, and install Windows 7 to that partition. If successful, both operating systems display in a menu when the computer is booted. The information pertaining to these operating systems is stored in the Boot Configuration Data (BCD) store in Windows 7/Vista. In Windows XP this data is stored in the boot.ini file. You might also want to dual-boot different types of operating systems such as Windows and Linux. This is easier done with third-party tools such as Partition Magic or GParted.

ExamAlert

Understand that multiboots allow two or more operating systems to inhabit one hard drive.

Installing Windows 7

Now that you have decided on the version of Win7 to use and have verified compatibility of hardware, it's time to install. The Windows 7 installation is more simplified than earlier versions of Windows. This section covers the steps involved in a "clean" local installation of Win7. This type of installation can remove any data currently stored on the computer's hard drive. The following steps detail an installation of Windows 7 Ultimate.

Step 1. Begin the installation from the DVD-ROM. There are two methods to perform a clean install of Windows 7 from DVD:

> ▶ Install Windows 7 by running the Setup program from within the current version of Windows. (This is the recommended method.) Insert the Windows 7 DVD. The disc most likely autoruns and you see a setup screen. Otherwise, just go to the DVD drive in Windows Explorer, and double-click the setup.exe file to start the installation.

> ▶ Boot the computer from the Windows 7 DVD. This is necessary if no operating system exists on the computer. If you choose this option, do the following:

> ○ Make sure the DVD drive is configured as the first boot device in the system BIOS.

> ○ Insert the Windows 7 DVD into the system's DVD drive. (If the drive won't open while in the BIOS, insert the disc immediately after saving the BIOS during the next step.)

> ○ Save the BIOS and restart the system.

> ○ The DVD should boot automatically and start the installation, but if you are prompted to boot from the DVD, press any key. There is only a small window of time for this, approximately 5 seconds. This prompt is a protective measure; if you get the prompt, it means that there is data of some sort on the drive. Startup of the installation might take a minute or two; then you see a GUI-based window asking for information. (There is no text portion.) Setup loads Windows files for several minutes and starts the installation within the Windows GUI.

Step 2. Input the Language to install, Time and currency format, and Keyboard or input method. At this time there is also an option to learn more about the installation by clicking the What to Know Before Installing Windows link. After you input your settings for step 2, you must click Next, and then on the next screen click Install Now. A few minutes or so will pass as files are copied and the installation is prepared.

Step 3. Accept the license terms.

Step 4. Select whether you are doing a custom install, which includes a clean installation or an upgrade. (These steps here do a clean installation.) If you install to a computer with no operating system, the Upgrade option will be disabled. For this exercise do a clean installation, so select Custom (advanced).

Step 5. Select where to install Windows 7. From here you can select the drive and administer partitions as you see fit. The proper disk preparation order when installing Windows 7 is to optionally load third-party drivers (SATA, SCSI, or RAID); then partition the drive, format the partition (or partitions), and start the installation (copy files). If you do click the option Load Driver and cannot supply a proper driver for Windows 7, or the computer cannot read the media in which the driver is stored, you need to exit the installation program. If a RAID array is not detected during installation, you must exit, check all hard drive and RAID adapter connections, and make sure that there are no other conflicting RAID devices that need to be disabled (for example, integrated into the motherboard.) If there are no problems, click Next, and the system automatically copies files from the DVD, expands those files, installs features and updates, and completes the installation. The system might need to restart several times during this installation process (for example, after it installs updates and when it completes the installation), but you can let the Windows 7 installation work its magic until you get to the next step.

Step 6. Type a username and a computer name.

Step 7. Type a password, confirm it, and type a password hint.

Step 8. Enter the Product key, and decide whether to automatically activate Windows (can be delayed up to 30 days).

Step 9. Configure Windows Update to Use Recommended Settings, Install important Updates Only, or Ask Me Later. For more information on Windows Update see Chapter 10, "Maintaining Windows."

Step 10. Set the time zone, time, and date.

Step 11. Set the computer's location: home, work, or public network. (This step may not be visible if the computer is not connected to a network.)

Now it's time to start Windows. Windows 7 checks the computer's performance (which might take a while), prepares the desktop, and then logs you in. Afterward, you can continue with initial tasks such as connecting to the Internet or transferring files and settings.

Upgrading to Windows 7

Upgrades are done in essentially the same manner as clean installs. The difference is that all the settings, applications, and user files will ultimately be kept in place *if* the upgrade is successful (and if it is the right type of upgrade). However, it is recommended that those files and settings are backed up previous to the upgrade—just in case. Before starting the upgrade, you should first check to see if your computer (and operating system) is compatible and if it will survive the process. Refer to Table 8.2 for the Windows 7 minimum requirements. You can also use the following utilities and websites to do this:

▶ **Windows Upgrade Advisor:** This is a website that is accessed by clicking on the Check compatibility online button when you first insert the Windows 7 DVD. Of course, the computer that you want to upgrade needs to have Internet access. You can also download the Windows 7 Upgrade Advisor from Microsoft's website.

▶ **Windows Compatibility Center:** http://www.microsoft.com/ windows/compatibility/.

> **ExamAlert**
>
> Remember that the Upgrade Advisor and Compatibility Center can be used to check if a system meets Windows 7 requirements.

Only Windows Vista can be upgraded directly to Windows 7. To upgrade Windows Vista to Windows 7, make sure that service pack 1 or 2 is installed to Vista prior to the upgrade, insert the DVD, and select the Upgrade option. The steps to complete the upgrade are similar to the clean installation steps. Table 8.3 shows which versions of Windows 7 can be upgraded from the various versions of Windows Vista.

TABLE 8.3 **Windows Vista to 7 Upgrade Paths**

From Windows Vista (SP1, SP2)	To Windows 7
Business	Professional, Enterprise, Ultimate
Enterprise	Enterprise
Home Basic	Home Basic, Home Premium, Ultimate
Home Premium	Home Premium, Ultimate
Ultimate	Ultimate

Any *other* combinations of upgrades from Vista to Win7, or upgrading from XP to Win7, would require

- ▸ Backing up all data prior to the upgrade
- ▸ A Custom/advance installation (basically wipes the hard drive)
- ▸ The reinstallation of any applications post-upgrade
- ▸ The restoration of all data files

Microsoft recommends the program Windows Easy Transfer for the backup and restoration of files.

Here are a couple of important points concerning 32-bit and 64-bit versions of Windows.

- ▸ 32-bit versions of Windows *cannot* be directly upgraded to 64-bit versions.
- ▸ 32-bit or 64-bit versions of Windows 7 can be installed to a computer with a 64-bit processor.
- ▸ However, 32-bit processors accept only 32-bit versions of Windows 7.

Okay, let's all take a deep breath!

Moving on! Let's talk about Anytime Upgrades and Repair-In-Place Upgrades.

An *Anytime Upgrade* is when a person upgrades one version of Windows 7 to a more advanced edition of Windows 7. For example, say that a user working with Home Premium needs access to the BitLocker functionality. That user would have to upgrade to Ultimate. Anytime Upgrades do not require a physical disc or a download because all the Windows 7 software is preloaded to the disc. All a user needs to do is purchase an upgrade key online. Table 8.4 shows what the various versions of Windows 7 can be upgraded to.

TABLE 8.4 **Windows 7 Anytime Upgrades**

From Windows 7	Anytime Upgrade to Windows 7
Home Basic	Home Premium, Professional, Ultimate
Home Premium	Professional, Ultimate
Professional	Ultimate
Starter	Home Premium, Professional, Ultimate

When troubleshooting a system, a *Repair-In-Place Upgrade* is your last resort before doing a complete reinstall of the OS. It's also known as a repair installation. Say there was an issue with Windows 7 Ultimate and you tried your best to fix it, but no dice. You could close all applications, insert the Windows 7 Ultimate DVD and start the upgrade, being sure to select Upgrade when the time comes. This type of repair installation is not supposed to damage files and applications that are currently installed to the computer. However, it can copy original system files and reset certain settings. A lot can go wrong with these repair installations, so again, try to solve any issues in another way, and use this as your last hope. You learn more about this in Chapter 11.

Verifying and Troubleshooting Windows 7 Installations

When you complete the clean installation or upgrade, verify that your installation has gone smoothly by testing it. For example, attempt to navigate through Windows, access administrative functions, connect to the Internet, and so on.

If you have confirmed that Windows is working normally, update the system. Install the latest service pack and additional updates as necessary. It is possible that the service pack was included on your installation media, but if not, download it and install it before going any further. Then, download any other updates that are necessary utilizing the Windows Update feature. More information about service packs and updates can be found in Chapter 9.

Installations usually go smoothly, but not always. If an installation fails for any reason, or if the installation completed but Windows doesn't seem to be behaving properly, consider reviewing the log files to find out more about the problem and why it occurred. Table 8.5 describes the important log files you should know and their locations.

TABLE 8.5 **Windows 7 Setup Log Files and Locations**

Log File Location	Description
$windows.~bt\Sources\Panther	Log location before Setup can access the drive.
$windows.~bt\Sources\Rollback	Log location when Setup rolls back in the event of a fatal error.
%WINDIR%\Panther	Log location of Setup actions after disk configuration.
%WINDIR%\Panther\setuperr.log	Contains information about setup errors during the installation. Start with this log file when troubleshooting. A file size of 0 bytes indicates no errors during installation.
%WINDIR%\Panther\setupact.log	Contains information about setup actions during the installation.
%WINDIR%\Inf\Setupapi*.log	Used to log Plug and Play device installations. setupapi*.log can refer to multiple files (the asterisk is wild) including setupapi.offline.log (as on a Win7 computer), and Online configuration phase files: setupapi.dev.log and setupapi.app.log. This applies to any other references in the book to setupapi*.log. See the following links for more information on Windows setup log files: http://technet.microsoft.com/en-us/library/dd744583(v=ws.10) http://support.microsoft.com/kb/927521
%WINDIR%\Panther\Setup.etl	Location of Windows Setup performance events.
%WINDIR%\Memory.dmp	Location of memory dump to use for bug checks.
%WINDIR%\Minidump*.dmp	Location of mini-memory dumps to use for bug checks.
%WINDIR%\System32\Sysprep\	Location of logs generated by Sysprep Panther.

> **ExamAlert**
>
> Know the difference between setuperr.log and setupact.log for the exam.

In Table 8.5 you can see the variable directory called %WINDIR%. By default, the name of this folder in Windows 7 will be Windows. %WINDIR% is the new name of the variable previously called %systemroot%. Also, $windows.~bt is a temporary boot folder created during setup. It remains if the installation were not successful, allowing you to analyze the log files, but should be automatically deleted when the installation completes properly.

Windows 7, Vista, as well as Server 2008, include the capability to review Setup events within the Event Viewer, or by way of a script. See the following link for details:

http://technet.microsoft.com/en-us/library/dd744583(WS.10).aspx

If the system won't start, you can still view these files. However, this depends on the type of installation and how far the installation got. If it was a clean installation, you should boot to the Windows 7 DVD; select Repair your computer, then access the System Recovery Options menu, and select the Command Prompt. If it was an upgrade that didn't get far, and if Windows Vista/XP was previously installed on an NTFS drive, you can boot to the System Recovery Options in Vista, or the Recovery Console from a Windows XP CD and view the log files from there. For more information about System Recovery Options (Win7/Vista), and the Recovery Console (XP), see Chapter 11.

If you cannot start the clean installation or upgrade, check the following:

- **Processor speed and memory size:** Verify that your computer meets the minimum requirements for Windows 7. Refer to Table 8.2 for more information.

- **Windows type and version:** Make sure you are installing the correct type (32-bit or 64-bit) and version of Windows 7 (Starter, Home Premium, and so on).

- **Free disk space:** You need 16 GB/20 GB free for Windows 7 (for 32-bit and 64-bit editions respectively); the more space available, the better.

- **Hardware conflicts or hardware issues:** Use the Device Manager to ensure that all hardware works correctly before you start an upgrade.

- **Installation media:** Make sure that your DVD-ROM media is not scratched or damaged in any way. Verify that it is genuine Microsoft software and that you have the right type of media for your installation, for example, Windows 7 Full Version License or Upgrade DVD.

ExamAlert

Know your Windows 7 installation troubleshooting methodology for the exam.

Cram Quiz

Answer these questions. The answers follow the last question. If you cannot answer these questions correctly, consider reading this section again until you can.

220-802 Questions

1. What is the minimum RAM requirement for Windows 7?
   - ○ **A.** 1 GB
   - ○ **B.** 256 MB
   - ○ **C.** 1536 MB
   - ○ **D.** 768 MB

2. Which log file contains information regarding Windows 7 Setup performance events?
   - ○ **A.** Setupapi*.log
   - ○ **B.** Setupact.log
   - ○ **C.** Setup.etl
   - ○ **D.** Event Viewer

3. Where can you go to find out if your current operating system can be upgraded to Windows 7?
   - ○ **A.** MSKB
   - ○ **B.** Windows Upgrade Advisor
   - ○ **C.** HAL
   - ○ **D.** Belarc Advisor

4. Which versions of Windows 7 have the capability to back up to a home or business network? (Select the best two answers.)
   - ○ **A.** Starter
   - ○ **B.** Home Premium
   - ○ **C.** Professional
   - ○ **D.** Ultimate

5. What is the minimum hard drive requirement for Windows 7?
   - ○ **A.** 16 GB free space
   - ○ **B.** 15 GB partition
   - ○ **C.** 25 GB free space
   - ○ **D.** 16 GB partition

6. To avoid SID conflicts when disk imaging, which program should you use in Windows 7?
   - ○ **A.** Sysprep
   - ○ **B.** Setup Manager

○ **C.** SIM

○ **D.** Windows Deployment Services

7. Which of the following are possible ways to install Windows 7? (Select all that apply.)

   ○ **A.** From DVD

   ○ **B.** From CD

   ○ **C.** Over the network

   ○ **D.** Using Norton Ghost

8. What would you do first when installing Windows 7?

   ○ **A.** Partition the hard disk.

   ○ **B.** Format the partition.

   ○ **C.** Load any necessary RAID or SATA drivers.

   ○ **D.** Configure the username/password.

9. You want to perform a network installation of Windows. What must the client computer support?

   ○ **A.** PCIe

   ○ **B.** PXE

   ○ **C.** HCL

   ○ **D.** Multiboot

10. Which of the following is available in Windows 7 Professional but not in Windows 7 Home Premium?

   ○ **A.** Windows XP Mode

   ○ **B.** IE 8

   ○ **C.** Aero

   ○ **D.** Home Group

11. Which of the following can be used to install a manufacturer's image on a computer? (Select the two best answers.)

   ○ **A.** Data backup

   ○ **B.** Recovery CD

   ○ **C.** Recovery Agent

   ○ **D.** System Restore utility

Cram Quiz Answers

220-802 Answers

1. **A.** The minimum RAM requirement for Windows 7 is 1 GB for 32-bit versions and 2 GB for 64-bit versions.

2. **C.** Setup.etl contains information regarding Windows 7 Setup performance events. Setupapi*.log is used for events about Windows 7 Plug and Play device installations. Setupact.log is a log file that contains information regarding actions during installation. The Event Viewer is an application, not a file.

3. **B.** The Windows Upgrade Advisor can tell you if your current operating system can be upgraded to Win7. This, and other tools like it, are located at www.microsoft.com, not at the MSKB (http://support.microsoft.com). The HAL is a file in Windows; it stands for hardware abstraction layer. Belarc Advisor is a third-party offering that analyzes your computer but does not determine whether it can be upgraded.

4. **C** and **D**. Windows 7 Professional and Ultimate include the capability to back up to a home or business network easily.

5. **A.** Windows 7 (32-bit) requires a minimum 16 GB of free space. 64-bit versions require 20 GB.

6. **A.** Sysprep can modify unattended installations so that every computer gets a unique SID (and other unique information). Windows SIM (System Image Manager) creates the answer files for unattended installations. Setup Manager (setupmgr.exe) is the program that Windows XP/2000 uses to create answer files. Windows Deployment Services is run on Windows Server 2008/2003 and is used to deploy operating systems across the network.

7. **A, C,** and **D**. Windows 7 can be installed from DVD, USB, over the network, and by using programs such as Norton Ghost.

8. **C.** The first thing listed is to load any necessary RAID, SCSI or SATA drivers. Then you would partition the hard disk. The OS would then format the partition unless you manually do it. Finally, after a few reboots, you would configure Windows settings such as username/password.

9. **B.** To perform a network installation, a network adapter in a computer must be PXE-compliant. PCIe is an expansion bus. HCL is the hardware compatibility list. Multiboot technology means that the computer can boot to two or more operating systems.

10. **A.** Windows XP Mode is available in Windows 7 Professional, Ultimate, and Enterprise. It is not included in Home Premium or Starter. Internet Explorer 8, Aero, and Home Group are all components included in both Windows 7 Professional and Home Premium.

11. **B** and **D**. A recovery CD and an image previously made with System Restore can be used to install an image to a computer. Data backups are the files that must be recovered after the OS is installed or recovered. The Recovery Agent is used in Windows to recover encryption keys from deleted or unavailable user accounts to gain access to lost data.

Installing and Upgrading to Windows Vista

Before you can install Windows Vista or upgrade to it, you first need to decide which version of Vista to use. Then, you should check the computer's hardware to make sure it is compatible with Windows Vista. Next, you need to decide on an installation method: from DVD, CD, as an image, or over the network. Finally, start the installation. New installations are known as "clean" installs; the other option is to upgrade from Windows XP or earlier.

Windows Vista Versions

Windows Vista is an entire line of Microsoft operating systems designed for desktop PCs and laptops. Within the Windows Vista group are the versions Home Basic, Home Premium, Business, and Ultimate, available in 64-bit and 32-bit versions. In Table 8.6, the check marks indicate the components that are included in these various versions of Vista. We talk more about these components in Chapter 9.

TABLE 8.6 **Comparison of Windows Vista Versions**

Component	Home Basic	Home Premium	Business	Ultimate	Enterprise*
Windows Aero	—	✓	✓	✓	✓
Share Documents	—	✓	✓	✓	✓
Media Center Functionality	—	✓	—	✓	✓
Windows Complete PC Backup	—	—	✓	✓	✓
Remote Desktop Connection	—	—	✓	✓	✓
BitLocker Encryption	—	—	—	✓	✓

> **Note**
>
> There is an additional version of Vista called Vista Starter (sold in underdeveloped technology markets).
>
> *Vista Enterprise is not sold through retail or OEM channels.

ExamAlert

Know the main differences between the Vista editions Home Premium, Business, and Ultimate for the exam.

Windows Vista Minimum Requirements and Compatibility

When you decide on the version of Vista you want to use, and before installing that operating system, you should learn as much as you can about the computer you plan to install to. Components in a computer should meet Windows Vista's minimum requirements and should be listed on Microsoft's website as compatible with Vista. Table 8.7 shows the minimum hardware requirements for Windows Vista.

TABLE 8.7 **Windows Vista Minimum Requirements**

Component	Requirement
Processor	800 MHz
RAM	512 MB
Free disk space	15 GB (20 GB partition)
Other	DVD-ROM or CD-ROM drive

ExamAlert

Memorize the *minimum* requirements for Windows Vista.

You can use several websites and system analysis tools to check whether a system's hardware will be compatible with Windows Vista including the System Information tool, Belarc Advisor, and PC Diagnostic tools, as mentioned in the Windows 7 portion of this chapter. However, nowadays it will be uncommon for you to find a computer that can't run Windows Vista.

Note

The Windows Vista DVD has a Check compatibility online option, but this is meant more for upgrades, as opposed to clean installations.

Windows Vista Installation Methods

Windows Vista can be installed in the same ways as Windows 7 with the addition of a local installation from CD-ROM: Microsoft recommends that the DVD-ROM be used for installations of Windows Vista; however, you can order a CD-ROM version, if you can provide proof of purchase.

The installation of Vista is similar to Windows 7. For a written step-by-step and video of the process, access my website at www.davidlprowse.com/220-801, and go to the "Videos" section.

Upgrading to Windows Vista

Upgrades are done in essentially the same manner as clean installs. The difference is that all the settings, applications, and data remain in the system partition if the upgrade is successful. However, before starting the upgrade, you should first check to see if your computer (and operating system) is compatible and if it will survive the process. Refer to Table 8.7 for the Vista minimum requirements. You can also use the Windows Vista Upgrade Advisor: This is a website that is accessed by clicking the Check compatibility online button when you first insert the Windows Vista DVD. Of course, the computer that you want to upgrade needs to have Internet access.

You should know the upgrade paths available from Windows XP to Windows Vista. Table 8.8 describes these.

TABLE 8.8 **Windows XP to Vista Upgrade Paths**

From Windows XP	To Windows Vista
Home Edition	Home Basic, Home Premium, Business, Ultimate
Professional (32-bit)	Business, Ultimate
Tablet PC Edition	Business, Ultimate
Media Center 2004 Edition	Home Premium, Ultimate
Media Center 2005 Edition	Home Premium, Ultimate

Windows XP Professional x64 edition (the 64-bit version) and Media Center 2002 edition cannot be upgraded to Windows Vista.

Verifying and Troubleshooting Windows Vista Installations

When you complete the clean installation or upgrade, *test it*. If you have confirmed that Windows is working normally, update the system. As of the publishing of this book, the latest service pack (SP) for Windows Vista is SP2. It is possible that the service pack was included on your installation media, but if not, download it and install it before going any further. Then, download any other updates that are necessary utilizing the Windows Update feature. More information about service packs and updates can be found in Chapter 10.

Installations usually go smoothly, but not always. If an installation fails for any reason, or if the installation completed but Windows doesn't seem to be behaving properly, consider reviewing the log files to find out more about the problem and why it occurred. Windows Vista is a bit more complicated than older Windows systems when it comes to log files. Vista's log files might vary slightly and have different locations depending on the phase of the installation when they were logged. The Vista installation process is broken into four phases:

▶ **Downlevel phase:** This is the phase that is run from within the previous operating system, meaning when you start the installation from the DVD in Windows XP, for example.

▶ **Windows Preinstallation Environment phase:** Also known as Windows PE, this phase occurs after the restart at the end of the downlevel phase. If installing to a new hard drive, this phase occurs when you first boot the computer to the Windows Vista DVD.

▶ **Online configuration phase:** The online configuration phase starts when a user receives the following message: Please wait a moment while Windows prepares to start for the first time. Hardware support is installed during this phase.

▶ **Windows Welcome phase:** During this phase, a computer name is selected for the computer, and the Windows System Assessment Tool (Winsat.exe) checks the performance of the computer. This is the final phase before the user first logs on.

There are log files for each phase; they are pretty much the same log files but in different locations. However, you are most concerned with the last two phases. For the most part in these two phases, the log files are in the same location. Table 8.9 covers the important log files during these two phases.

TABLE 8.9 **Windows Vista Installation Log Files**

Log file	Description	Location
setuperr.log	Contains information about setup errors during the installation. Start with this log file when troubleshooting. A file size of 0 bytes indicates no errors during installation.	C:\Windows\Panther
setupact.log	Contains information about setup actions during the installation.	C:\Windows\Panther
miglog.xml	Contains information about the user directory structure. This information includes security identifiers (SIDs).	C:\Windows\Panther
setupapi.dev.log	Contains information about Plug-and-Play devices and driver installation.	C:\Windows\inf
setupapi.app.log	Contains information about application installation.	C:\Windows\inf
PostGatherPnPList.log	Contains information about the capture of devices that are on the system after the online configuration phase.	C:\Windows\Panther
PreGatherPnPList.log	Contains information about the initial capture of devices that are on the system during the downlevel phase.	C:\Windows\Panther
Winsat.log (Windows Welcome phase only)	Contains information about the Windows System Assessment Tool performance testing results.	C:\Windows\Performance\Winsat

Note

For a list of all log files within all phases of the Windows Vista installation, see the following link: http://support.microsoft.com/kb/927521.

If you cannot start the clean installation or upgrade, check the following:

▶ **Processor speed and memory size**: Verify that your computer meets the minimum requirements for Windows Vista. Refer to Table 8.7 for more information.

▶ **Free disk space:** You need 15 GB free for Windows Vista; the more space available, the better.

▶ **Hardware conflicts or hardware issues:** Use the Device Manager to ensure that all hardware works correctly before you start an upgrade.

▶ **Installation media:** Make sure that your DVD-ROM (or CD-ROM) media is not scratched or damaged in any way. Verify that it is genuine Microsoft software and that you have the right type of media for your installation, for example, Vista Full Version License or Upgrade DVD.

Upgrades to Windows Vista can be especially troublesome. You might experience problems connecting to a LAN or the Internet, or some hardware might not work properly. Be sure to access the Microsoft Knowledge Base (MSKB) at http://support.microsoft.com for clues as to why these errors occur.

> **Note**
>
> For a list of specific errors concerning a Windows Vista upgrade, see the following link: http://support.microsoft.com/kb/930743.

Cram Quiz

Answer these questions. The answers follow the last question. If you cannot answer these questions correctly, consider reading this section again until you can.

220-802 Questions

1. What is the minimum RAM requirement for Windows Vista?

   ○ **A.** 2 GB

   ○ **B.** 256 MB

   ○ **C.** 512 MB

   ○ **D.** 768 MB

2. Which file contains information regarding errors during a Windows Vista installation?

   ○ **A.** Setuperr.log

   ○ **B.** Setupact.log

   ○ **C.** Event Viewer

   ○ **D.** Unattend.xml

3. Where can you go to find out if your current operating system can be upgraded to Windows Vista?

   ○ **A.** MSKB

   ○ **B.** Windows Vista Upgrade Advisor

   ○ **C.** HAL

   ○ **D.** Belarc Advisor

4. Which versions of Vista have media center functionality? (Select the best two answers.)

   ○ **A.** Home Basic

   ○ **B.** Home Premium

   ○ **C.** Business

   ○ **D.** Ultimate

5. What is the hard drive requirement for Windows Vista?

   ○ **A.** 15 GB free space

   ○ **B.** 15 GB partition

   ○ **C.** 20 GB free space

   ○ **D.** 25 GB partition

Cram Quiz Answers

220-802 Answers

1. **C**. The minimum RAM requirement for Windows Vista is 512 MB. Microsoft recommends 1 GB of RAM for Home Premium, Business, and Ultimate.

2. **A**. Setuperr.log contains information regarding errors during installation. Setupact.log contains information regarding *actions* during installation. The Event Viewer is an application, not a file, and might not contain installation details. Unattend.xml is the answer file generated by Windows SIM for unattended installations.

3. **B**. The Windows Vista Upgrade Advisor can tell you if your current operating system can be upgraded to Vista. This, and other tools like it, are located at www.microsoft.com, not at the MSKB (http://support.microsoft.com). The HAL is a file in Windows; it stands for hardware abstraction layer. Belarc Advisor is a third-party offering that analyzes your computer but does not determine whether it can be upgraded.

4. **B** and **D**. Home Premium and Ultimate include media center functionality; the others do not.

5. **A**. Vista requires 15 GB of free space within a 20 GB partition.

Installing and Upgrading to Windows XP

Although Windows XP was released many years ago, you will still see it in the field and might need to install it as well, or upgrade older Windows computers to XP. Before you can install or upgrade to Windows XP, you first need to decide which edition of XP you'll be using. Then, you should check the computer to make sure it is compatible with Windows XP. Next, you need to decide on an installation method: from CD, floppy to CD, as an image, or over the network.

Windows XP Versions

There are several editions of Windows XP:

▶ **Windows XP Home:** Designed for home users, this edition has limited networking and security capabilities.

▶ **Windows XP Professional:** This is the most common version of XP that you will see in the field. The A+ exams focus mostly on this edition. The XP Pro edition expands on the Home edition by offering the capability to connect to domains, make Remote Desktop connections, utilize the Encrypting File System (EFS), and support two physical CPUs. It is designed for power users, business people, and developers. There is a 64-bit version of this as well.

▶ **Windows XP Media Center:** This edition was developed for people concerned with audio and video. The Windows Media Center is part of the GUI that displays well on a TV and can be controlled remotely. It is also designed to playback videos and music. Normally, the Media Center edition is found preinstalled on computers that have been purchased from an original equipment manufacturer (OEM).

> **ExamAlert**
>
> Know the differences between the Windows XP Home, Professional, and Media Center.

Windows XP Minimum Requirements and Compatibility

When you have decided which version of XP you want to use, and before installing that operating system, you should learn as much as you can about the computer you plan to install to. Components in a computer should meet Windows XP's minimum requirements and should be listed on Microsoft's website as compatible with XP. Table 8.10 shows the minimum hardware requirements for Windows XP Professional.

TABLE 8.10 **Windows XP Minimum Requirements**

Component	XP Home/Professional Requirement	Windows XP Media Center
Processor	233 MHz	1.6 GHz
RAM	64 MB	256 MB
Free disk space	1.5 GB (2 GB partition)	2 GB partition
Other	CD-ROM or DVD-ROM	Hardware accelerated graphics card that can use DirectX 9.0 or higher

Various websites and system analysis tools can verify that a system's hardware will be compatible with Windows XP. Chances are that the computer will be, but you can use tools mentioned previously in this chapter including the System Information tool and Belarc Advisor.

If upgrading to Windows XP, You can run the Upgrade Advisor from the Windows XP CD. Click Check System Compatibility from the Welcome to Windows XP menu; then click Check My System Automatically. (Note that this upgrade advisor is no longer available for download from the Microsoft website). After the analysis is complete, the Upgrade Analyzer displays any incompatible hardware or software it finds.

Windows XP is normally installed by CD-ROM but can also be done via image or over the network. Unlike Windows 7/Vista installs, the XP installation is a mixture of text screens and graphic screens. Also, if third-party SCSI or RAID hard disk drivers are needed, you must press F6 to install them.

The network installation also differs from Windows 7/Vista. To automate the process, Windows XP can be installed from a server, for example by using the Remote Installation Services (RIS) program, which can be installed on Windows Server 2003. This program works along with Windows XP's Setup Manager program that creates the automated answer files like unattend.txt. These files are text-based, unlike the Windows 7/Vista unattend.xml. For more information on how this works, the differences between Vista and XP, and how to combine XP and Vista deployment technologies, see the following link: http://technet.microsoft.com/en-us/library/cc765993.aspx.

Windows XP uses the Sysprep utility to prepare unique systems for installation over the network. It is provided on the CD-ROM at \SUPPORT\TOOLS\ in a cabinet file called DEPLOY.CAB. The most recent version of Sysprep for Windows XP can also be downloaded from the Microsoft website as part of the Windows XP Service Pack 2 Deployment Tools. See the following link for more information: http://support.microsoft.com/kb/838080.

For a video and written step-by-step of the Windows XP installation access my website at: www.davidlprowse.com/220-801 and go to the "Videos" section.

Verifying and Troubleshooting Windows XP Installations

When you complete the clean installation or upgrade, *test it*. For example, attempt to navigate through Windows, access administrative functions, connect to the Internet, and so on. After you confirm that Windows is working normally, update the system. As of the publishing of this book, the latest service pack (SP) for Windows XP is SP3; however, some companies might still use SP2, so check your documentation, policies, and procedures to confirm. It is possible that the service pack was included on your installation media, but if not, download it and install it before going any further. Then, download any other updates that are necessary utilizing the Windows Update feature. More information about service packs and updates can be found in Chapter 10.

As mentioned previously, installations don't always go as planned. If an installation fails, first verify that your computer has met the minimum hardware requirements and that it doesn't have any hardware that will conflict with Windows XP. Also make sure that you have enough free disk space and that the installation media isn't damaged.

Now, let's talk about Windows XP log files. These files can be used to review what went wrong with an installation. In Windows XP, most of these files are plain text and are stored in the %systemroot% folder of the operating system. The %systemroot% folder is a variable that indicates the folder where the operating system was installed. In most cases this will be C:\Windows. Table 8.11 describes the most important log files you need to know for the exam and their location within the operating system.

Cram**Quiz**

TABLE 8.11 **Windows XP Installation Log Files**

Log file	Description	Location
setuperr.log	Records errors (if any) during installation. This is the most important and descriptive log file for troubleshooting installation errors.	C:\Windows
setuplog.txt	Records events during the text-mode portion of installation.	C:\Windows
setupact.log	Logs all events created by the GUI-mode setup program.	C:\Windows
setupapi.log	Records events triggered by an .inf file.	C:\Windows
setup.log	The Recovery Console utilizes this to acquire information about the Windows installation during repair.	C:\Windows\ Repair
NetSetup.log	Information about membership to workgroups and domains.	C:\Windows\ Debug

ExamAlert

Know the differences between setuperr.log, setuplog.txt, and setupact.log for the exam.

If the system won't start, you can still view these files. However, this depends on the type of installation and how far the installation got. Attempt to boot to the Recovery Console from a Windows XP or 2000 CD and view the log files from there. For more information about the Recovery Console, see Chapter 11, "Troubleshooting Windows."

Cram Quiz

Answer these questions. The answers follow the last question. If you cannot answer these questions correctly, consider reading this section again until you can.

220-802 Questions

1. What is the minimum CPU requirement for Windows XP?
   - O **A.** 133 MHz
   - O **B.** 233 MHz
   - O **C.** 800 MHz
   - O **D.** 1 GHz

2. Which log file records errors during the installation of Windows XP?
   - O **A.** setuperr.log
   - O **B.** setuplog.txt
   - O **C.** setup.log
   - O **D.** setupact.log

3. Which key should be pressed if you want to install a driver for a mass storage device during the Windows XP installation?

   ○ **A.** F2

   ○ **B.** F3

   ○ **C.** F6

   ○ **D.** F8

4. What program creates answer files in Windows XP?

   ○ **A.** Windows SIM

   ○ **B.** Sysprep

   ○ **C.** RIS

   ○ **D.** Setup Manager

5. How much free disk space do you need to install Windows XP?

   ○ **A.** 2 GB

   ○ **B.** 1.5 GB

   ○ **C.** 650 MB

   ○ **D.** 1 GB

Cram Quiz Answers

220-802 Answers

1. **B.** Windows XP requires a minimum 233 MHz CPU. 133 MHz is the requirement for the now unsupported Windows 2000 Professional. For Windows Vista, 800 MHz is the minimum requirement. 1 GHz is the minimum requirement for Windows 7.

2. **A.** Setuperr.log records errors that occurred during installation. Setuplog.txt records events during the text portion of the installation. Setupact.log records events during the GUI portion of the installation. Setup.log is used by the Recovery Console during repair.

3. **C.** There is a short time period during the beginning of the XP installation in which you can press F6 to install mass storage drivers. F2 invokes the Automatic System Recovery (ASR), F3 quits the installation, and F8 agrees to the EULA (license).

4. **D.** Setup Manager (setupmgr.exe) is the tool that creates answer files such as unattend.txt in Windows XP. Windows SIM (System Image Manager) is used in Win7/Vista. Sysprep helps create unique installations over the network and works with the answer file. RIS or Remote Installation Services is the server component that initiates over the network installs.

5. **B.** Windows XP requires 1.5 GB of free space within a 2 GB partition and 650 MB is the required space by the now deprecated Windows 2000 Professional.

CHAPTER 9

Configuring Windows

This chapter covers the following A+ exam topics:

▶ Windows User Interfaces

▶ System Tools and Utilities

▶ Files, File Systems, and Disks

You can find a master list of A+ exam topics in the "Introduction."

This chapter covers CompTIA A+ 220-802 objectives 1.1 through 1.5.

So, the computer is built, and Windows is installed; now it's time to configure the operating system! This chapter covers Windows user interfaces, system tools, utilities, and describes how to manage files and disks. Our focus is on Windows 7, but we also discuss Windows Vista and Windows XP. However, this time, instead of breaking the sections up by the operating system, this chapter merges Windows 7, Vista, and XP together by topic. Because these operating systems are similar, you will find that many of the configurations work the same way. By default, the chapter refers to Windows 7, but if something is different in Windows Vista, or XP, it is specifically stated. You will find that navigation might be slightly different from 7 to Vista to XP, when trying to access the same feature in both operating systems. The learning curve is small though. Also, there are differences in application names between 7/Vista and XP. For example, what used to be My Computer in XP is now simply Computer in 7 and Vista, and what was My Network Places in XP is just Network in 7/Vista. By default, this chapter refers to the Windows 7/Vista titles because they are the newer operating systems. Keep this in mind as we progress through the chapter. Also, make note that a particular setting in Windows might be arrived at from several different routes. This chapter tries to show alternative routes but doesn't cover all of them. Use the route that is the fastest and easiest for you, but try to remember as many routes as possible for the exam.

> **Note**
>
> I recommend that you run through all the configurations in this chapter on your computer(s). If you don't have extra physical computers for Windows 7, Vista, and XP available, consider running virtual machines to act as the additional computers. Microsoft offers Virtual PC for free; it can be downloaded from Microsoft's website. And don't forget that Windows 7 Professional and Ultimate can use Windows XP Mode. This hands-on approach can help you to better visualize how operating systems are configured.

Windows User Interfaces

The essence of Windows is the graphical user interface (GUI), which is what Windows employs to interact with the user. Normally, a keyboard and pointing device such as a mouse are used to input information to the operating system's GUI, and whatever is inputted is shown on the screen. Basically everything you see on the display including windows, icons, menus, and other visual indicators is part of the GUI, but remember that the GUI also governs how the user interacts with the OS.

The Windows GUI has many parts including the desktop with all its pieces, applications such as Windows Explorer and the Control Panel, and Administrative Tools such as Computer Management and the Device Manager. To master Windows, you need to learn how to navigate quickly through the GUI to the application or tool that you need. The GUI can be customized for a particular user, or it can be customized to optimize the system. Let's begin this section by talking about the various components of Windows.

Windows Components

What do you see when you start Windows? Some of the components that make up Windows include

- ▶ **Desktop:** The desktop environment is basically what you see on the screen, essentially it *is* Windows, from a cosmetic standpoint. An example is shown in Figure 9.1, which displays the Start menu in the open position. The desktop is a key component of the GUI; it includes icons, wallpapers, windows, toolbars, and so on. It is meant to take the place of a person's physical desktop, at least to a certain extent, replacing calculators, calendars, and so on. The desktop is designed to be a user-friendly environment in which the user can easily save and retrieve files, make changes to the OS, and modify features. However, for more control of the OS, a user might still need advanced programs such as the command line or the registry.

> **Note**
>
> Some users refer to the desktop as just the area where the icons and shortcuts reside (the background or wallpaper) to differentiate that area from the rest of the screen.

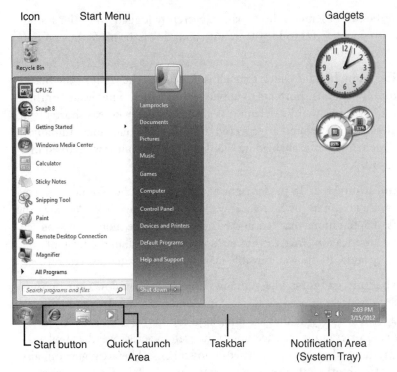

FIGURE 9.1   **Windows 7 Desktop**

▶ **Icons:** Icons are the little, clickable pictures you see on the desktop.
They can be entire programs that run directly from the desktop, files
that are stored directly on the desktop, or *shortcuts* that redirect to a program or file that is stored elsewhere in Windows. You can often tell if it's
a shortcut by the little arrow in the lower-left corner of the icon.
Shortcuts are small, usually around 1 KB to 4 KB in size, which store
well on the desktop. However, storing actual files and programs on the
desktop is not recommended because it can adversely affect the performance of the computer—and can quickly get really unorganized!

▶ **Taskbar:** This is the bar that spans the bottom of the desktop. It houses
the Start button, Quick Launch, any open applications, and the
Notification Area. It can be moved to the top or either of the sides of
the desktop and can be resized to fill up to 40 percent of the screen.

▶ **Start menu:** This is the main menu that is launched from the Start button. It contains a listing of all the tools within Windows and any
Microsoft and third-party applications. From here you can search for
files and access the Control Panel—you can get anywhere in Windows

from the Start menu. It shows who is currently logged on to the system and also enables you to log off, restart, shut down, or place the computer in sleep mode.

▶ **Quick Launch:** The Quick Launch is directly to the right of the Start button. It contains shortcuts to applications or files. The beauty of the Quick Launch is that by default it is always visible, whereas shortcuts on the desktop background are covered up by open applications. Initially, the Quick Launch is enabled in Windows 7/Vista, but it is disabled in Windows XP.

▶ **Notification Area:** To the far right of the taskbar is the Notification Area, otherwise known as the System Tray. This houses the clock and shows the icons of applications that run in the background. The more icons you see in the Notification Area, the more resources are used, in the form of memory and CPU power, possibly making the computer less responsive.

▶ **Sidebar and gadgets:** The Windows Sidebar is a window pane on the side of the desktop used exclusively in Windows Vista. It is primarily used to house gadgets that are mini-applications offering a variety of services, for example, connecting to the web to access weather updates and traffic, and accessing Internet radio streams. These gadgets can also interact with other applications to streamline the Windows experience. Additional gadgets can be downloaded from Microsoft. Windows 7 does away with the Sidebar but you can still add gadgets to the desktop by right-clicking the open desktop and selecting Gadgets, by right-clicking any gadget and selecting Add Gadgets, or by accessing the Gadget Gallery by navigating to Control Panel > Desktop Gadgets. Figure 9.1 displays two gadgets: a clock and a CPU meter.

▶ **Application windows and dialog boxes:** Application windows are the windows that are opened by programs such as Microsoft WordPad, as shown in Figure 9.2. The window consists primarily of a title bar (which says Document — WordPad), a menu bar (with the File, Edit, and other menus), a toolbar (with icons for opening, saving, and printing documents), and a work area. This program runs as an actual process known as wordpad.exe. Dialog boxes are windows that open from within another window, usually an application window. For example, Figure 9.2 shows the Computer Name/Domain Changes dialog box, which was opened from the System Properties window. System Properties (not shown) runs as a process, but the Computer Name dialog box is just part of that overall process. The dialog box prompts a user for information, in this case, for the name of the computer, and the name of the network the computer is a member of.

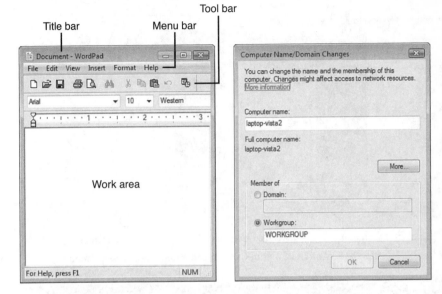

FIGURE 9.2 **An application window and a dialog box**

> ## ExamAlert
>
> Be able to identify the various Windows components by name.

Configuring the Taskbar and Start Menu

The taskbar and Start menu can be customized to just about any user's liking. To make modifications to these, right-click the taskbar and select Properties. This brings up the Taskbar and Start Menu Properties window. The default tab is called Taskbar; from here you can unlock/lock the taskbar, auto-hide it, and so on. The next tab is Start Menu; from here you can customize the menu by adding or removing items, selecting secondary menus, or selecting to show items as a link. Figure 9.3 shows a default Windows 7 Start menu, a customized Start menu, and the Classic menu.

As you can see, the customized menu has smaller program icons, and I added the Run command (which is *always* accessible by pressing Windows+R on the keyboard, even if you can't see it). The Classic menu is a more basic graphic representation of the menu that uses less computer resources. This is a smart option to select if your computer needs every ounce of power it can muster. Also, people that are used to older versions of Windows might be more comfortable working with this. It can be initiated in Windows 7 by right-clicking the Desktop, selecting Personalization, and selecting the Windows Classic theme. In Windows Vista you would configure the Classic Start menu from the Taskbar and Start Menu Properties Window.

Original Start menu   Customized menu   Classic menu

FIGURE 9.3   **Standard Win7 Start menu, Customized menu, and Classic menu**

ExamAlert

Know how to switch to the Classic Start menu for the exam.

Windows 7/Vista can also modify the Notification Area. For example, in Windows 7, if you were to access the Taskbar and Start Menu Properties window, and click the Customize button, a window would display with the option to hide the icons, or hide the icons and their notifications. This can also be accessed by right-clicking the clock and selecting Customize notification icons.

ExamAlert

Know how to modify notification icons for the exam.

Windows Aero

Windows Aero is Windows' visual experience featuring translucent windows, window animations, three-dimensional viewing of windows, and a modified taskbar. You can make modifications to the look of Aero by right-clicking the desktop and selecting Personalize; from here you can select different themes, desktop background colors, and Windows colors. However, Windows Aero uses a lot of resources and can be taxing on the computer. To improve system performance (especially on older systems), you have the option to disable Aero. To do so, go back to the Personalize window and select Theme. At the Theme drop-down menu, select Windows 7 Basic; or even better, select Windows Classic, and watch the transformation!

To make more specific changes to the look of Aero, go to Start, right-click Computer, and select Properties; this opens the System window. Then click the Advanced system settings link; this opens the System Properties dialog box. Click the Advanced tab; then click Settings in the Performance box. This displays the Performance Options dialog box where you can change various visual effects, for example enabling/disabling sliding menus, or removing drop shadows from icon labels. You might have to restart the system for these visual effects changes to take effect. A quicker way to get to the Performance Options dialog box is to click Start and in the Search area type `Adjust the` and press Enter. And the hyper-technical way would be to open the Run prompt and type `SystemPropertiesPerformance.exe`. (Capital letters are not necessary.)

> **Note**
>
> Windows XP and Windows 7/Vista Starter are not configured to run Aero.

Windows Applications

There are lots of built-in applications within Windows. The following is a description of some of the programs you will use frequently:

▶ **Computer:** The Computer window can be accessed by clicking Start and selecting Computer. If you use the classic Start menu in Windows Vista, Computer shows up as an icon on the desktop; just double-click to open it. Windows XP refers to this as My Computer. Unlike older versions of Windows, the Computer window shows up as a complete two-pane window by default (known in Windows XP as Folders view). Computer is tightly integrated with Windows Explorer; Microsoft just refers to it as a folder now. From this folder you can browse through your computer to access data on the hard disk, DVD and CD-ROM, and other removable media, such as USB flash drives. By right-clicking Computer on the Start menu, you can also access things such as System Properties and Computer Management. Figure 9.4 compares the newer Windows 7 Computer window with Windows XP's default My Computer window.

The Computer window has some additional functionality compared to Windows XP; you notice an additional toolbar in Figure 9.4 with options such as Organize and Uninstall or Change a Program.

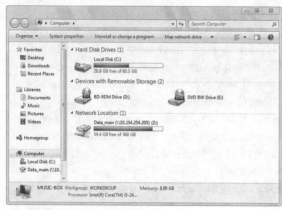

Windows 7
Computer Window

Windows XP
My Computer Window

FIGURE 9.4   Windows 7 Computer window and XP's My Computer window

> **Windows Explorer:** This works much like Computer. It can be
> accessed by clicking Start > All Programs > Accessories and clicking
> Windows Explorer. By default in Windows 7, it brings the user to
> the Libraries view. In Windows Vista, this brings you to the
> \%username%\Documents folder.

Note

%username% is a variable. It refers to any real username of a particular user, for
example Administrator, or DavidP. This variable enables you to refer to usernames
as a collective whole. They might be different from one computer to another and
from one user to the next. Whenever you see something enclosed by percentage
signs (%), it is a variable name.

Actually, any folder that you access will open up within the Windows Explorer interface; the difference will be the amount of functionality given to you in the toolbar. These folders show up as different applications in the Task Manager, but they are all controlled by one process: explorer.exe. To see for yourself, open up Computer and Windows Explorer. Then open the Task Manager by right-clicking the taskbar and selecting Task Manager. Click the Applications tab. From there you should see the various windows that are running. Next, view the process called explorer.exe within the Processes tab. Try an experiment: Watch explorer.exe's memory size go down as you close the Windows Explorer window and the Computer window. This should drive the point home.

Windows 7's version of Windows Explorer incorporates Libraries. *Libraries* are user-defined collections of folders that act as logical representations of the user's content. This has been incorporated into Windows to enable faster indexing and searching of important and commonly used documents, even if they are spread out among the entire computer. This is done by analyzing file properties and *metadata* of files and folders; this is why Windows 7 Libraries are commonly known as *metafolders*. Metadata is information that describes a file's definition and structure, as well as how it is administered. Building on that idea, metafolders such as libraries have information that describes the definition and structure of the contents within. The Libraries portion of Windows Explorer is the default view in Windows 7. Normally, you see the Documents, Music, Pictures, and Videos libraries when opening Windows Explorer. Double-clicking a library shows all the folders and documents that are part of it, regardless of the location of the folder they are stored in. For example, The Documents library includes two locations by default: My Documents, and Public Documents. This can be discerned by clicking the two locations' link. (The number of actual locations may vary from computer to computer.) You can add locations if you want, by clicking the link, and clicking the Add button. This allows users to organize their documents and media by category, even if the files are scattered throughout the computer and beyond to locations on the network. You can also add new libraries within the main Libraries window by right-clicking Libraries (or right-clicking the work area) and selecting New > Libraries. After a library has been created, you can add folders to it by right-clicking it and selecting Properties. From there you can also specify the default folder location to save files in a library and optimize the library. The concept of libraries has been in use for some time, especially in media players, but Windows 7 is the first Microsoft operating system to incorporate it for use with any and all files. Some third-party applications might not integrate properly with Windows libraries due to programming inadequacies. If this is the case, a user must store the files created in that application by navigating to the actual folder where they are to be stored, bypassing the library. Always check for updates to third-party applications that might make them library-compatible.

▶ **Control Panel:** The Control Panel (CP) is where a user would go to make system configuration changes, for example, changing the color scheme, making connections to networks, installing or modifying new hardware, and so on. The Control Panel can be opened by going to Start > Control Panel. By default, the Control Panel shows up in Category view. For example, in Windows 7, System and Security is a category. To see all the individual Control Panel icons, click the drop-down arrow next to View by: Category, and select either Large icons or Small icons. (In Vista, click the Classic View link on the left side.) Within the Taskbar and Start Menu Properties window, the Control Panel option in the Start menu can be configured to show up as a sub-menu, composed of the individual icons.

> **ExamAlert**
>
> The CompTIA A+ exams expect you to know the individual icons in the Control Panel. In Windows this is also referred to as All Control Panel Items. Study them!

▶ **Network:** The Network window shows computers and other devices on the network. It can be opened by clicking Start > Network. It opens in an Explorer-type window and might take a few moments to register the devices on the network. The address bar at the top of the window shows the status of the registration of devices as a bar that extends from left to right. The Network window should automatically find other computers, routers, wireless access points, and network attached devices if you are configured as a member of the network. You can add printers and wireless devices from here. You can also open the Network and Sharing Center, in which you can add networking connections and share resources. The Windows 7/Vista Network window takes the place of My Network Places in Windows XP.

▶ **Command Prompt:** Microsoft's Command Prompt is its command-line interface (CLI). This is the text-based interface in which you can issue commands concerning files and folders, networking, services, and so on. You can open it in several ways including

▶ Navigating to Start > All Programs > Accessories > Command
  Prompt.

▶ Press Windows+R to open the Run prompt and type **CMD** (my personal favorite). In Windows XP, Run is available directly from the
  Start menu. You can also get to the Run prompt in 7/Vista by clicking Start and typing **Run** in the search field. In Windows 7/Vista,
  some commands need to be run as an administrator; to open the
  Command Prompt as an administrator, do one of the following:

  1. Click Start > All Programs > Accessories; then right-click
     Command Prompt, and select Run as Administrator.

  2. Click Start and type **CMD** in the search field, and instead of
     pressing Enter, press Ctrl+Shift+Enter.

Running the Command Prompt as an Administrator is also known as
running it in *elevated mode*.

An additional command line called the PowerShell is integrated into
Windows 7 and can be downloaded for use with other versions of
Windows. The PowerShell is a combination of the Command Prompt
and a scripting language. (It is the successor to the Windows Script Host.)
It enables administrators to perform administrative tasks that integrate
scripts and executables. This can be started by navigating to Start > All
Programs > Accessories > Windows PowerShell. It should be noted that if
you decide to use the PowerShell in place of the Command Prompt, that
you should remember to always use a space after a command; otherwise
the shell will not recognize the command. For example, typing **ipconfig**
/all would be correct, whereas **ipconfig/all** would not function. For
administrators that run scripts often, there is also the Windows
PowerShell ISE (Integrated Scripting Environment); this color codes the
syntax and is generally a friendlier environment to work in.

ExamAlert

Know how to open programs from the Start menu and from the Run prompt.

This is just the tip of the iceberg when it comes to programs you will be
working with. There are many more in Windows, and that doesn't even get
into third-party programs. An operating system such as Windows 7 can run
32-bit and 64-bit applications as long as the CPU is 64 bit, which is typical.
64-bit programs are installed to C:\Program Files by default. However, 32-bit
programs are installed to C:\Program Files (x86) by default. There will come

a time when you need to uninstall programs, change programs, and repair them. In Windows 7 and Vista this can be done by going to the Control Panel and selecting Programs and Features. In Windows XP this is done within Control Panel > Add/Remove Programs. As your hard drive gets filled up with applications, you might realize that you don't need all of them. Uninstalling unused applications can save hard drive space and make the system more secure. However, if you remove a lot of programs that took up a lot of space, you might consider defragmenting the hard drive. More on that in Chapter 10, "Maintaining Windows."

Administrative Tools and the MMC

The administrator (that's you) of a computer or network can access Administrative Tools by going to Start > All Programs > Administrative Tools. There are several tools here used to configure advanced options for the computer. We cover each of them as we go through this chapter and Chapters 10 and 11. One example is Computer Management that you will use quite often. It has many utilities loaded into one nice, little *console* window. An example of Computer Management is shown in Figure 9.5.

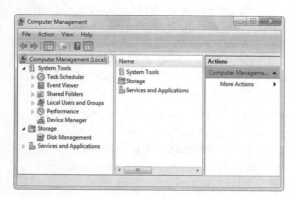

FIGURE 9.5   Windows 7 Computer Management window

Note, this is a three-pane window. The left pane has all the modules that you might work on such as the Event Viewer, Device Manager, and Disk Management. The middle pane shows the details of whatever you click in the left pane. The right pane gives additional actions, which are also available on the menu bar. This right pane does not show up in Windows XP. There are a few other ways to open this window including

▶ Click Start; then right-click Computer and select Manage.

▶ Access the Run prompt and type `compmgmt.msc`. The extension .msc defines the file type as a Microsoft Management Console Snap-in Control file, also known as a Microsoft Console.

Computer Management and other console windows can be grouped together into one master console window known as the Microsoft Management Console (MMC). The MMC acts as a shell for these other console windows. You can also use it to control remote computers in addition to the local computer. And you can control what particular users see by changing the Console Mode. Finally, part of the beauty of the MMC is that it saves everything you added and remembers the last place you worked. Windows 7 and Vista use MMC version 3.0, and Windows XP uses Version 2.0, but version 3.0 can also be downloaded for XP. To create an MMC, open the Run prompt and type MMC. By default, the MMC is empty.

> **Note**
>
> You will learn quickly that administrative functions should be carried out only by those users who have administrative privileges. Even if you have administrative privileges, a pop-up User Account Control (UAC) window displays every time you try to access tools such as the MMC. Simply click Yes or Continue to open the program. If a user does not have administrative capabilities, they will either be blocked altogether, or when the UAC window pops up, they cannot continue. For more information on UAC, see Chapter 16, "Security."

To add consoles (known as snap-ins) do the following:

1. Click File on the menu bar; then click Add/Remove Snap-in. The Add/Remove Snap-ins window should appear.

2. Select the components you want from the left by highlighting them one at a time and clicking the Add button. You need to select the local computer or a remote computer. Click OK when finished. These snap-ins should now be shown inside of the Console Root. An example MMC is shown in Figure 9.6.

3. Save the MMC. By default this window prompts you to save to the Administrative Tools folder of the user who is currently logged on.

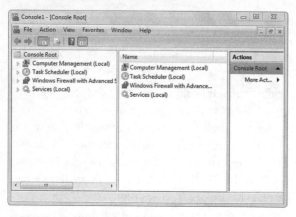

FIGURE 9.6   **Windows 7 MMC**

Exam**Alert**

Know how to add snap-ins to an MMC.

Cram Quiz

Answer these questions. The answers follow the last question. If you cannot answer these questions correctly, consider reading this section again until you can.

220-802 Questions

1. A small arrow at the lower-left corner of an icon identifies it as what?

    ○ **A.** A super icon

    ○ **B.** An icon headed for the Recycle Bin

    ○ **C.** A shortcut

    ○ **D.** A large file

2. What could be described as mini-applications offering a variety of services?

    ○ **A.** Gadgets

    ○ **B.** Widgets

    ○ **C.** Bracelets

    ○ **D.** Icons

3. What can a user do to cut back on the amount of resources that Windows 7 uses? (Select the two best answers.)

   ○ **A.** Increase RAM.

   ○ **B.** Use the Classic Theme.

   ○ **C.** Disable some of the Performance Options.

   ○ **D.** Use the computer less.

4. Which utility groups snap-ins into one window?

   ○ **A.** Computer Management

   ○ **B.** MSC

   ○ **C.** MCC

   ○ **D.** MMC

5. When you open Windows Explorer in Windows Vista, what folder does it bring you to by default?

   ○ **A.** Computer

   ○ **B.** Network

   ○ **C.** Documents

   ○ **D.** Recycle Bin

6. How can the Run prompt be opened? (Select the two best answers.)

   ○ **A.** Pressing Windows+R

   ○ **B.** Pressing Windows+Run

   ○ **C.** Clicking Start and typing Run

   ○ **D.** Pressing Ctrl+Shift+Esc

Cram Quiz Answers

220-802 Answers

1. **C.** An icon with an arrow is a shortcut, redirecting to a file or program in another location in Windows. They are actually very small, from 1 KB to 4 KB.

2. **A.** Gadgets are applications on the desktop that offer specialized information such as weather and traffic; these gadgets come from Microsoft. Widgets are the same types of small applications, but they come from various vendors, can be downloaded from the Internet, and usually work outside of the sidebar. Icons are files or programs on the desktop.

3. **B** and **C**. By using the Classic Theme, or by disabling some or all the Performance Options, the operating system will not need as much graphics computing power. Increasing RAM increases the amount of resources your computer has, but it won't decrease the amount of resources that Windows uses.

4. **D.** The MMC or Microsoft Management Console can have one or more snap-ins such as Computer Management and so on. MSC is the extension that the MMC and individual console windows use. MCC stands for memory controller chip.

5. **C.** When opening Windows Explorer in Windows Vista, the folder that is displayed is Documents, which is within the folder of the currently logged on user Windows 7 displays Libraries.

6. **A** and **C**. By pressing Windows+R on the keyboard, you can open the Run prompt, or you can click Start, and type run in the Search field. There is no Run key, so there is no Windows+Run shortcut, and pressing Ctrl+Shift+Esc would usually bring up the Task Manager. In Windows XP, the Run Prompt can be accessed directly from the Start menu.

System Tools and Utilities

Windows 7, Vista, and XP have a cornucopia of system tools and utilities. There are tools that help you to analyze and manage devices such as the Device Manager and System Information. There are also tools that can aid in optimizing the operating system and customizing the user environment. And there are advanced utilities that enable you to edit the registry and connect remotely to other computers. Knowledge of these types of tools and utilities separates the good technician from the "okay" technician. Let's discuss how to manage devices first.

Managing Devices

A computer probably has a dozen or more devices that all need love and attention. Taking care of a computer means managing these devices. The primary tool with which a technician does this is the Device Manager.

Device Manager

There are a few ways to open the Device Manager, for example:

▶ Open Computer Management, expand System Tools, and select Device Manager. (This and an MMC with a Computer Management snap-in are the preferred methods.)

▶ Open the System Properties window, click the Hardware tab, and select the Device Manager button. To get to the System Properties window in 7/Vista, click Start, right-click Computer, and select Properties; then click Advanced system settings. (Note that Device Manager is also listed.) You can also open the Run prompt and type **systempropertieshardware.exe** to directly access the Hardware tab of the System Properties window in 7/Vista. To get to the System Properties window in Windows XP, click Start, right-click My Computer, and select Properties.

▶ Open the Run prompt and type **devmgmt.msc**.

When you have the Device Manager open, you notice that there are categories for each type of device. By expanding any one of these categories, you see the specific devices that reside in your computer. Figure 9.7 shows the Device Manager.

FIGURE 9.7   Device Manager in Windows 7

By right-clicking a specific device, you can update its driver, enable or disable it, uninstall it altogether, check for any hardware changes, and access additional properties such as the driver details and resources used by the device. Figure 9.7 shows the resulting menu when right-clicking The Intel network adapter. These are the standard options, but your options might be more or less depending on the device right-clicked.

ExamAlert

Know how to access the properties of a device, install drivers, and enable/disable devices in the Device Manager.

Some drivers are installed/updated through .exe files that are downloaded from the manufacturer's website. Others are installed from within the Device Manager. The Device Manager can search for drivers automatically, or you can manually install the driver by browsing for the correct file (quite often a file with an .inf extension). Windows attempts to install drivers automatically when it recognizes that a device has been added to the system. But usually, it is recommended that you use the driver disk that came with the device, or download the latest version of the driver from the manufacturer's website, especially when dealing with video, audio, and hard disk controller drivers.

Driver Signing

Windows device driver files are digitally signed by Microsoft to ensure quality. The digital signature ensures that the file has met a certain level of testing, and that the file has not been altered. In Windows 7 and Vista, driver signing is configured automatically, and in Windows 7, Vista, and XP, only administrators can install unsigned drivers. In Windows XP, driver signing can be configured to either ignore device drivers that are not digitally signed, display a warning when Windows detects device drivers that are not digitally signed (the default behavior), or prevent installing device drivers without digital signatures. To configure driver signing in Windows XP, open the System Properties window, click the Hardware tab, and select Driver Signing.

System Information Tool

Another tool that Windows offers for device analysis is the System Information tool. This can be accessed by navigating to Start > All Programs > Accessories > System Tools and clicking System Information, or by opening the Run prompt and typing `msinfo32.exe`. (The .exe actually isn't necessary.) From here you can view and analyze information about the hardware components, the software environment, and the hardware resources used, for example: hardware conflicts, IRQ settings, and Input/Output (I/O) settings, as shown in Figure 9.8. An Interrupt ReQuest (IRQ) is the circuit that a device uses to "interrupt" the CPU and get its attention in an attempt to send data to it. In previous CompTIA A+ exams, a person would need to memorize each of the IRQ numbers between 0 and 15 and their corresponding device. However, it is rare that IRQ conflicts occur anymore; therefore, you won't be making changes to IRQ settings often (if ever), and so the chance of a question about this on the new exams is unlikely. It is also uncommon, but you might have to configure an I/O setting at some point. The I/O setting is the range of memory that is used by a particular device to transmit the data to the CPU. In the figure you can see that the VIA 1394 OHCI Compliant Host Controller's I/O setting is highlighted. This is the controller for the IEEE 1394 port on the back of the computer. If you needed to modify this setting, you would do it in the Device Manager.

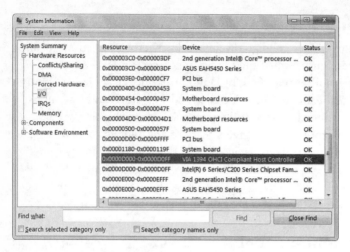

FIGURE 9.8 System Information Tool—I/O Setting

DxDiag

When it comes to making sure your devices work properly, one of the most important is the video card, and a utility you can use to analyze and diagnose the video card is DxDiag. To run the DxDiag program, open the Run prompt and type dxdiag. First, the utility asks if you want it to check whether the corresponding drivers are digitally signed. A digitally signed driver means it is one that has been verified by Microsoft as compatible with the operating system. After the utility opens, you can find out what version of DirectX you are running. DirectX is a group of multimedia programs that enhance video and audio, including Direct3D, DirectDraw, DirectSound, and so on. With the DxDiag tool, you can view all the DirectX files that have been loaded, check their date, and discern whether any problems were found with the files. You can also find out information about your video and sound card, what level of acceleration they are set to, and test DirectX components such as DirectDraw and Direct3D. Windows 7 ships with DirectX version 11, as shown in Figure 9.9. Windows Vista ships with DirectX version 10, whereas Windows XP currently can use up to DirectX 9.0c. The DirectX feature is important to video gamers and other multimedia professionals.

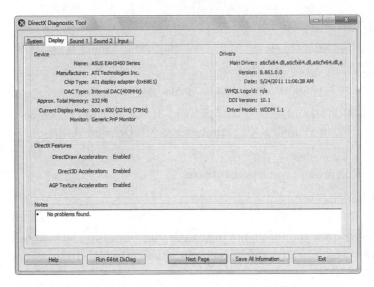

FIGURE 9.9   Windows 7 DxDiag window showing the Display tab

Removing Hot Swappable Devices

When it comes to removing devices, most devices can be physically removed only if the computer has first been shut down. However, some devices can be *hot-swapped*, meaning they can be removed while the power to the computer is on; no reboot is necessary. USB flash drives are an example of this; however, you should "Safely Remove" them within the operating system first. This can be done by right-clicking or double-clicking the Safely Remove icon in the Notification Area and stopping the device. Other devices that can be hot-swapped include printers, digital cameras, scanners, webcams, microphones, and so on.

Operating System Optimization

A fresh installation of Windows will probably not work exactly the way you want it to right from the start. It might take some tweaking and some optimization to get it just right. You will also find that systems running Windows for a while have of late suffered performance setbacks. These systems also need to be optimized. But to optimize you first need to do some analysis of the system.

Task Manager

One simple, yet effective, tool to use when analyzing the computer is the Task Manager. There are several ways to open the Task Manager including

▶ Right-click on the taskbar and select Task Manager.

▶ Press Ctrl+Alt+Del and select Task Manager. (If you have the Welcome Screen enabled in Windows XP, pressing Ctrl+Alt+Del alone brings up the Task Manager.)

▶ Open the Run prompt and type `taskmgr`.

▶ Press Ctrl+Shift+Esc.

The Task Manager gives you the ability to analyze your processor and memory performance in real time; this can be done from the Performance tab, as shown in Figure 9.10.

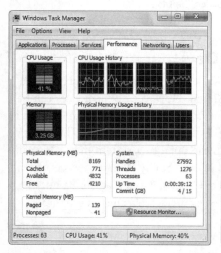 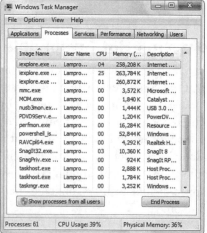

FIGURE 9.10 Windows 7 Task Manager showing the Performance tab and the Processes tab

As you can see, the processor in Figure 9.10 hovers at 41 percent usage. Something is gobbling up a big portion of the processing power! You also note that nearly 3.25 GB of memory is used; that's quite a bit for a Windows 7 computer. If this system were simply browsing the web, the CPU would be hovering at approximately 2 to 5 percent, and the memory would be at only 1 GB or so. What could be the reason for this jump in resource usage? Was the processor not recognized by the BIOS properly? Is there a powerful application that is using all those resources? Maybe the computer, unbeknown to the user, is used as a zombie to send attacks out to various organizations? Or has the user turned the computer into an MP3 file server for friends? These are the types of things you would want to investigate. In reality, the reason for the 41 percent processor and 3.25 GB memory usage is because I am receiving multiple video feeds in Internet Explorer and am running a Windows Vista virtual machine at full power (among other things.) Audio, video, and virtual machines can be quite a drain on the system. Now we are crossing over into the realm of troubleshooting, but then again, sometimes the lines between configuration, optimization, and troubleshooting can be blurred.

Optimizing the system can be as simple as shutting down programs. Programs can be shut down in the Applications tab. But sometimes you need to shut down the underlying process. For example, in Figure 9.10, the Processes tab shows all the processes that are running and the amount of CPU and RAM resources they are using individually. A process that is hording resources can be stopped by highlighting it and clicking End Process. Keep in mind that this shuts down only the process or application temporarily. If it is designated to do so, it will turn back on when the computer is rebooted. Later in this section, we discuss the programs that can be used to permanently disable programs, processes, and services. Note that the Windows 7 Task Manager has six tabs: Applications, Processes, Services, Performance, Networking, and Users.

ExamAlert

Understand how to open the Task Manager, how to read its Performance tab, and how to end processes and applications.

Optimizing the system can also mean temporarily boosting the power to a particular process. For example, if you were working within an important application that was crunching some heavy duty numbers, and you needed to increase that one process's performance, you could do so by right-clicking the process, highlighting Set Priority, and selecting an option higher than Normal. The higher the option on the list, the more processing power that process gets. Be wary though, changing a process's priority can have undesired effects such as system lockups or other errors. Be sure to save your work before attempting this, and consider testing it on an application before running it on something important.

Note

Other tools that can analyze the performance of a computer include Windows Performance Monitor, which is covered in Chapter 11 and CPU-Z, which was covered briefly in Chapter 3, "The CPU."

Msconfig

Msconfig.exe (Microsoft System Configuration Utility) is one of the programs mentioned in the previous section that can permanently disable programs and services that are designed to run when the computer starts up, thus optimizing the system. To open this program, first open the Run prompt and then type **msconfig**. To disable programs from starting, click the Startup tab, and deselect the desired entries. Msconfig also lets you select different boot options and can *enable/disable* services. The Windows XP version enables you to modify the wini.ini and boot.ini files, but the Windows 7 and Vista versions do away with this because they don't utilize those files. We will revisit Msconfig in Chapter 11.

ExamAlert

If you need to disable programs from starting at bootup, use Msconfig.

Virtual Memory

Virtual memory makes a program think that it has contiguous address space, when in reality the address space can be fragmented and often spills over to a hard disk. RAM is a limited resource, whereas virtual memory is, for most practical purposes, unlimited.

There can be a large number of processes, each with its own virtual address space. When the memory in use by all the existing processes exceeds the amount of RAM available, the operating system moves pages of information to the computer's hard disk, freeing RAM for other uses. In Windows, virtual memory is known as the paging file, specifically pagefile.sys that exists in the root of C:. To view this file you need to unhide it. This can be done in Windows Explorer by clicking Tools on the menu bar and then selecting Folder Options. In the resulting Folder Options window, click the View tab and select the radio button called Show Hidden Files, Folders, and Drives. Then, a few lines below, deselect the check mark where it says Hide Protected Operating System Files. While you're at it, deselect the option that says Hide extensions for known file types. This allows you to not only see the filename, but the three letter extension as well. Finally, Pagefile.sys should now show up in the root of C: where Pagefile is the filename and .sys is the extension.

Note

If you cannot see the Windows Explorer menu bar in Windows, press Alt+T to bring it up temporarily. Alternatively, click the Organize button; then Layout, and select Menu Bar to display it permanently. Layout also allows you to enable or disable any of the window panes in Windows Explorer.

Take a look at the size of your page file and jot down what you find. To modify the size and location of the page file, open the System Properties dialog box, and click the Advanced tab. Next, click the Settings button within the Performance box; this brings up the Performance Options window. Now, click the Advanced tab, and click Change in the Virtual memory box. From here you can let Windows manage the virtual memory for you, or select a custom size for the page file. The paging file has the capability to increase in size as needed. Historically in Windows computers, the rule was that the page file would have an initial size of $1.5 \times$ RAM, and a maximum size of $3 \times$ RAM, but the page file can be increased beyond that if necessary. This rule might not be used on today's computers for a variety of reasons; however, if a user runs a lot of programs simultaneously, then increasing the page file size might be the answer for performance issues. Another option would be to move the page file to another volume on the hard drive, or to another hard drive altogether. It is also possible to create multiple paging files, or stripe a paging file across multiple disks to increase performance. Of course, nothing beats adding physical RAM to the computer, but when this is not an option, possibly because the motherboard has reached its capacity for RAM, optimizing the page file might be the solution. For more information about configuring virtual memory in Windows 7, see the following link: http://technet.microsoft.com/en-us/magazine/ff382717.aspx. For more information on Windows XP virtual memory, see this link: http://support.microsoft.com/kb/314482.

> ## ExamAlert
> Know where to configure virtual memory, and know the location of pagefile.sys.

Working with Services

Services control particular functions in Windows such as printing, wireless networking, and so on. If a service is stopped or disabled, its corresponding program or utility will not run. You can start or stop services in the GUI or in the command line. As mentioned previously, services can also be started or stopped from Msconfig or the Task Manager. You should also know how to do this within the Services console and in the Command Prompt.

> ▸ **Start and stop services in the Services console window:** You can open the Services console from Administrative Tools, by typing **services.msc** in the Run or Search fields, or within the Computer Management console window. Now, in the right window pane, scroll until you find the service you want. To start a stopped service, right-click it and click Start, as shown in Figure 9.11. Alternatively, you can click the Start button on the toolbar,

or double-click the service and click the Start button from the Properties window. The Properties window of the service also enables you to change the startup type (refer to Figure 9.11). There are four startup types. At times you might need to set a service to Automatic so that the service starts automatically every time the computer boots; many services are set this way by default. (There is also a delayed start option if needed.) Or you might want to set a service to Manual so that you have control over it. In other cases, you might want to set it to Disabled, if it is not necessary, or if it is a security concern.

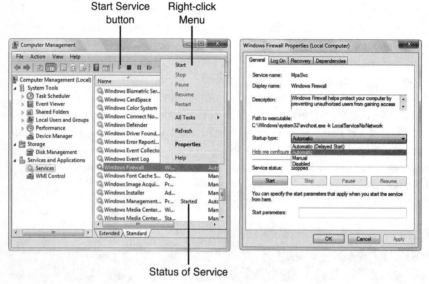

FIGURE 9.11 **The Firewall Service in the Computer Management window and its Properties window**

▶ **Start and stop services in the Command Prompt:** In Windows 7/Vista you need to run these commands as an administrator; now review the two ways to do this.

    1. Click Start > All Programs > Accessories; then right-click Command Prompt and select Run as Administrator.

    2. Click Start and type **cmd** in the search field, and instead of pressing Enter, press Ctrl+Shift+Enter.

Windows XP does not require opening the Command Prompt as an administrator. When the Command Prompt is open, you can start a service by typing **net start** [service]; for example, **net start spooler** starts the Print Spooler service. net stop spooler stops the service.

ExamAlert

Know how to start and stop services within the Services console and in the Command Prompt.

Power Management

Part of optimizing an operating system is to manage power wisely. You can manage power for hard disks, the display, and other devices; you can even manage power for the entire operating system.

To turn off devices in Windows 7/Vista after a specified amount of time, navigate to Start > Control Panel. Then select Large icons for Windows 7, or Classic view for Windows Vista. (From now on, I will assume you know to use the individual icons in the Control Panel.) Next, open the Power Options icon. From here you can select a power plan from Balanced, Power Saver, and High Performance. There are a lot of settings in this window; here's one example. In Balanced, click Change plan settings. By default in Windows 7 the Display is set to turn off after 10 minutes; it can be set from 1 minute to 5 hours, or set to never. If you click the Change Advanced Power Settings link, the Power Options dialog box appears. From here you can specify how long before the hard disk turns off and set power savings for devices such as the processor, wireless, USB, PCI Express, and so on. Take a few minutes looking through these options and the options for the other power plans.

To turn off devices in Windows XP after a specified amount of time, navigate to Start > Control Panel. Then select Classic view in the left window pane. Next, double-click the Power Options icon. This opens the Power Options Properties window. From here you can tell the system when to shut off the display and the hard disks. You can also specify when the system will standby or hibernate.

Some users confuse the terms standby and hibernate; let's try to eliminate that confusion now. *Standby* means that the computer goes into a low power mode, shutting off the display and hard disks. Information that you were working on and the state of the computer is stored in RAM. The processor still functions but has been throttled down and uses less power. Taking the computer out of standby mode is a quick process; it usually requires the user to press the power button or a key on the keyboard. It takes only a few seconds for the CPU to process the standby information in RAM and return the computer to the previous working state. Hard drives and other peripherals might take a few more seconds to get up to speed. Keep in mind that if there is a loss of power, the computer will turn off and the contents of RAM will be erased, unless it is a laptop (which has a built-in battery), or if the computer is connected to a UPS; but either way, uptime will be limited. Note that some laptops still use a fair amount of power when in standby mode. *Hibernate* is different than standby in that it effectively shuts down the computer. Hibernation consumes the least amount of power of any power state except for when the computer is turned off. All data that was worked on is stored to the hard drive in a file called hiberfil.sys in the root of C:. This will usually be a large file. Because RAM is volatile, and the hard drive is not, hibernate is a safer option when it comes to protecting the data and the session that you were working on, especially if you plan on leaving the computer for an extended period of time. However, because the hard drive is so much slower than RAM, coming out of hibernation will take longer than coming out of standby mode. Hibernation has also been known to fail in some cases and cause various issues in Windows.

Standby is known as "Sleep" in Windows 7/Vista and is accessible by clicking Start, clicking the arrow, and selecting Sleep. In Windows XP, Standby can be accessed by clicking Start > Shut Down and selecting Standby from the drop-down menu.

Hibernation however needs to be turned on first before it can be used. To enable hibernation in Windows 7/Vista, open the Command Prompt as an administrator. Then type **powercfg.exe/hibernate on**. Next, you need to turn off Hybrid sleep in the Power Options dialog box. To do this, navigate to Start > Control Panel > Power Options; then select Change Plan Settings, and click Change advanced power settings. This brings up the Power Options dialog box. Next, expand Sleep, and expand Allow Hybrid Sleep; then set it to off. Finally, set the Hibernate After option to the amount of minutes you desire. Now check the Start menu again, the Hibernate option should be there just below Sleep.

If the Hibernate option still does not show up in the Shut Down area of the Start menu, verify that you have typed the command properly within the Command Prompt (and that you are running the Command Prompt as an administrator). Restart the computer if necessary. To turn hibernation off, type **powercfg.exe/hibernate off**. To enable hibernation in Windows XP, go to the Power Options Properties window that you were in previously, but this time click the Hibernate tab, and check mark Enable hibernation. If you use the Welcome Screen in Windows XP, you might not see the Hibernate option. Press the Shift key and the Standby option should change to Hibernate. Otherwise, if you are not using the Welcome Screen, it should show up in the Shut Down Windows drop-down menu.

ExamAlert

Know the differences between Standby, Sleep, and Hibernate for the exam.

User Migrations and Customizations

Users often customize their own computer to a certain extent; modify colors, auto-hide the taskbar, add shortcuts, and so on. But some customizations, modifications, and migrations can be done only by the administrator.

Migrating User Data

If a user will be using a new operating system, either on the same computer or on a new computer, you might need to move his files and settings to the new system. When doing so, make sure that the destination computer has the latest service packs and updates and the same programs that are currently running on the original computer. There are a few options for migrating data:

▶ **Windows Easy Transfer:** This program enables you to copy files, photos, music, email, and settings to a Windows 7/Vista computer; all this information is collectively referred to as *user state*. It is installed with Windows 7/Vista and can be downloaded for Windows XP from www.microsoft.com; just search for Windows Easy Transfer for Windows XP. Either way, the program will be located in Start > All Programs > Accessories > System Tools. Files and settings can be migrated over the network or by USB cable. The data can also be stored on media like a CD, DVD, or USB flash drive until the destination computer is ready. Normally you would start with the computer that has the files and settings that you want to transfer (the source computer). You can transfer the files and settings for one user account or all the accounts on the computer. All the files and settings will be saved as a single .MIG file (Migration Store). Then, you would move to the computer in which you want to transfer the files to (destination computer), and either load the .MIG file from CD, DVD, USB flash drive, or locate the file on the source computer through the use of a USB cable or network connection. For more information on how to migrate files with Windows Easy Transfer, see the following MSKB article: http://support.microsoft.com/kb/928634.

▶ **User State Migration Tool (USMT):** This is a command-line tool that can be used to migrate user files and settings for one *or more* computers. The program can be downloaded from www.microsoft.com. When installed, two different tools are used: Scanstate.exe saves all the files and settings of the user (or users) on a computer, known as the user state; and loadstate.exe transfers that data to the destination computer(s). There are many options when using the scanstate and loadstate commands, including the ability to select which users are migrated and whether the store of data is uncompressed, compressed, or compressed and encrypted. By utilizing scripting programs, the transfer of files to multiple computers can be automated over the network. For more information on how to transfer files and settings with USMT in Windows 7, see the following TechNet link: http://technet.microsoft.com/en-us/library/dd560801(v=ws.10).aspx. For Vista, see the link: http://technet.microsoft.com/en-us/library/cc722032(WS.10).aspx. Windows 7 employs features such as AES encryption support and shadow copying of volumes. For more information on Windows 7 USMT differences, see the link: http://technet.microsoft.com/en-us/magazine/dd443646.aspx.

▶ **Files and Settings Transfer (FAST) Wizard:** This is the older version of Windows Easy Transfer and is installed by default on Windows XP. It is meant for transferring files and settings from a Windows XP, 2000, or 9x computer to a Windows XP computer but otherwise works in a similar fashion to Windows Easy Transfer. To transfer files from XP to 7/Vista, download the Windows Easy Transfer program for XP.

> ## Exam**Alert**
>
> Understand the various tools that can be used to migrate user data.

Customizing the User Environment

A user might not be completely comfortable using Windows 7 or Vista, or perhaps the user's computer is not the newest or most powerful system, and 7/Vista is making it crawl due to the resources required to run it. To create a more enjoyable user experience, and to make the best use of the resources a computer has, you might need to customize the user's environment. There are a couple ways to do this:

▶ **Revert to Classic mode:** By reverting to the original Windows look, the user might feel more comfortable, and you can free up additional resources on the computer. There are two ways to accomplish this. First, turn off Windows Aero: Right-click the desktop wallpaper and select Personalize, and select the Windows Classic theme; this removes the glassy translucent windows and lets the video card and processor in a lesser computer breathe a sigh of relief. Second, in Windows Vista, revert to the classic Start menu: Right-click the Taskbar and select

Properties, click the Start Menu tab, and select the Classic Start menu radio button. (This is not necessary in Windows 7.) Even if you are a power user that runs intensive applications, this might be a smart solution, effectively trading style for performance. Although Windows Aero is not used in Windows XP, similar techniques can be used to revert the XP desktop and Start menu to Classic mode.

▶ **Disable visual effects:** Any special graphic effects will put a strain on the computer's performance. Open the System Properties window to the Advanced tab, click the Settings button within the Performance box; this brings up the Performance Options dialog box. (Don't forget, you can quickly get here by typing `SystemPropertiesPerformance.exe` in the Run prompt.) Select the Adjust for Best Performance radio button. This can be done on Windows XP as well.

A few other tools you can use to customize a user's experience are the Task Scheduler, and Region and Language Options.

The Task Scheduler (known as Scheduled Tasks in Windows XP) can run particular programs, send emails, or display messages at a scheduled time (or times) designated by the user. This program can be accessed from Start > All Programs > Accessories > System Tools (and from the Control Panel in Windows XP). Aside from basic scheduling, you can specify certain conditions and triggers that cause a task to run, and you can tell the scheduler what actions to take when the task starts. Plus, there is a slew of built-in preprogrammed tasks in the Task Scheduler Library from memory diagnostics to registry backups. Instead of re-creating the wheel, consider using one of these tasks to help automate the process. Some of these built-in tasks are enabled by default. For example, if two computers mistakenly get the same IP address, an IP conflict occurs and the IpAddressConflict1 task (located in Tcpip) logs the event and places a notification on the screen and in the System log of the Event Viewer. You can run any task in the library at any time. To see the IpAddressConflict1 task in action, go to Task Scheduler Library > Microsoft > Windows > and click Tcpip. Then go to Action on the Menu bar and click Run. This should display the IP conflict notification. Try creating some tasks yourself such as memory diagnostic, registry backup, and time synchronization.

Region and Language Options is available in the Control Panel. This enables the user to modify the format of numbers, currency, time and date. The user can also change how programs service the computer based on its location, and different keyboards, keyboard layouts, and languages can be installed in the case that the user spends most of their time in another country or needs to work with documents in different languages.

Advanced System Tools

Several tools can affect advanced configuration changes in Windows. This section describes a few of those: the Registry Editor, Remote Desktop, and Windows Compatibility.

The Windows Registry

The Windows Registry is a database that stores the settings for Windows 7/Vista/XP. It contains hardware and software information, and user settings. If you cannot make the modifications that you want in the Windows GUI, the registry is the place to go. To modify settings in the registry, use the Registry Editor; open the Run prompt and type **regedit.exe**. This displays a window like the one shown in Figure 9.12.

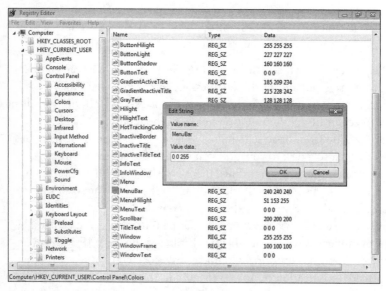

FIGURE 9.12 The Registry Editor in Windows

The registry is divided into several sections known as hives that begin with the letters HKEY. Table 9.1 describes the five visible hives in the Registry Editor.

TABLE 9.1   **Description of Registry Hives in Windows**

Registry Hive	Description
HKEY_CLASSES_ROOT	Stores information about applications' file associations and Object Linking and Embedding (OLE).
HKEY_CURRENT_USER	Stores settings that concern the currently logged on user. It is common to make changes in this hive.
HKEY_LOCAL_MACHINE	Stores hardware and software settings that are specific to the computer. This is where the bulk of a PC technician's registry edits are made. One example of data stored here are the programs that run when the OS starts.
HKEY_USERS	Stores data corresponding to all users who have ever logged on to the computer.
HKEY_CURRENT_CONFIG	Contains information that is gathered every time the computer starts up.

Hives are also known as keys that contain other keys and subkeys. This forms the organizational system for the registry; it is similar to folders and subfolders within Windows Explorer; however, the registry does not store actual data files; instead it stores settings. Inside the keys and subkeys are registration entries that contain the actual settings. These can be edited, or new entries can be created. The types of entries include: String values, used for decimal numbers; Binary values, used for binary entries; DWORD and QWORD entries, used for binary and hexadecimal entries; and multistring values that can have a variety of information. Registry hives are stored in: \%systemroot%\System32\Config.

Many users fear the registry, but the technician need not. Just follow a couple simple rules: 1) Back up the registry before making changes and 2) Don't make modifications or additions until you have a thorough understanding of the entry you are trying to modify or add. Figure 9.12 shows a registry entry called MenuBar within HKEY_CURRENT_USER\Control Panel\Colors. By double-clicking the MenuBar entry, an Edit String window appears as shown. Again, the beauty of the registry is that you can make modifications to things that normally can't be modified in the Windows GUI. MenuBar is one of these examples. In the figure the entry's string value has been changed to 0 0 255, which means the color blue. To effect this change, close the Registry Editor (no saving necessary) and log off and log back on. Some Registry changes require a reboot of the system.

As mentioned, you need to know how to back up the registry. You can back up any individual key or the entire registry. Say a user wanted to back up the Colors subkey before making changes to the MenuBar entry. The proper procedure would be to highlight the Colors subkey, click File on the Menu bar, and select Export. Then, it's as simple as selecting a location to save the registry entry and naming it. It exports as a .reg file. A typical subkey like this is about 2 KB in size. Backing up the entire registry can be done in two ways. First, by highlighting Computer (My Computer in XP), selecting Export, and saving the file. The other option is to select any registry key; then select Export and in the Export Registry File window, select the All radio button in the Export range box. The entire Windows Registry for Windows 7/Vista can be upward of 300 MB and 50 MB for Windows XP. Later, individual keys or the entire registry can be imported with the Import option on the File menu, in case a modification was not successful. For example, certain changes to the registry could cause the graphical interface (GUI) to fail to load. Or audio could become disabled. Again, be sure to make a backup before playing around with the registry. To repair a missing graphical interface or audio issue that is registry-related, attempt a System Repair from the Windows DVD, or if possible restore an older version of a backed up registry. (More about System Repair in Chapter 11 "Troubleshooting Windows.")

Lastly, you can connect to remote computers to gain partial access to their respective registries. To do this, select File, Connect Network Registry. You can then browse for computers that are members of the same network your computer is a member of, connect to them, and make modifications to those remote registries. Of course, you need to have administrative privileges on the remote computer.

> **ExamAlert**
>
> Know how to open the Registry Editor, modify entries, export the registry, and connect to remote registries for the exam.

Remote Desktop

Ever want to control a computer remotely? Remote Desktop software, included with Windows, enables a user to see, and control, the GUI of a remote computer. This enables users to control other computers on the network or over the Internet without leaving their seat, and aids technicians in their attempt to repair computers, without having to go to the system that needs repair. But first, to have a remote desktop session, you need to configure the software. To do so, open the System Properties window, and select the Remote tab. From here there are two boxes of information:

▸ **Remote Assistance:** This is check marked by default. This means that connections can be made by sending Remote Assistance invitations, by email (Outlook) or via instant messaging (Windows Messenger). These invitations can be to ask for help or to offer help. This is often implemented in help desk scenarios in which a user invites a technician to take control of her computer so that it can be repaired. Invitations are made by clicking Start > Help and Support, clicking More support options, and selecting the Windows Remote Assistance link (in 7/Vista) or Invite Someone to Help You link (in XP). If the user has access to only web-based email such as Yahoo or AOL, the user can select Save invitation as a file that enables the user to attach the invitation to the web-based email message. Of course for all this to function, the Remote Assistance option must be selected in the System Properties Remote tab; plus Remote Control must be check marked, which can be enabled by clicking the Advanced button. When the proper settings are enabled, Remote Assistance calls flow right through the Windows Firewall.

▶ **Remote Desktop:** This is where you can select whether other users can connect to, and control, your computer at any time without an invitation from you. In Windows 7/Vista, there are options to disable remote connections, enable connections with any version of remote desktop, and enable connections running Remote Desktop with Network-level Authentication for security. This is disabled by default, but if enabled, the remote users can make connections to your computer by computer name or by IP address. Finally, you can select the users that are allowed to connect to your computer. If your network is a workgroup, then the local user account(s) you select, is just that, local. For the remote user to connect, the remote computer must have an identical account (same username and password) as the one you selected on your computer, and the remote user must know the username/password. If the network is a domain, this is not an issue due to centralized administration of accounts.

ExamAlert

Be able to explain the difference between Remote Assistance and Remote Desktop for the exam.

To make a Remote Desktop connection to a remote computer, first make sure that the remote computer has Remote Desktop enabled. Next, click Start > All Programs > Accessories and Remote Desktop Connection. (In Windows XP the path is Start > All Programs > Accessories > Communications.) This opens the remote Desktop Connection window. Click Options for more logon settings, as shown in Figure 9.13. To make the connection, you need to supply a computer name or the IP address of the remote computer and a username and password of an account on the remote computer.

FIGURE 9.13 **Remote Desktop Connection window**

Click Connect and the screen of the other computer should show up on your local display. At this point, you can control the remote computer as if you were sitting locally at it. By default, the remote computer's screen locks and can be unlocked only with a username/password.

> **Note**
>
> Remote Desktop is based off the Remote Desktop Protocol (RDP). When Remote Desktop is enabled, this protocol is allowed through the Windows Firewall. Give strong consideration to using Network Level Authentication in Windows 7/Vista when allowing Remote Desktop connections.

You can also use the mstsc command to make Remote Desktop connections, edit existing Remote Desktop configuration files, and migrate old connection files to newer systems. This command can be used in the Command Prompt or in the Run prompt. For example, if you wanted to remotely control another system with the mstsc command in full-screen mode, you would type

```
Mstsc.exe /v:computername /f
```

For more information on the mstsc command, see the following link:

http://technet.microsoft.com/en-us/library/cc753907(v=ws.10).aspx

Program Compatibility Wizard

Most applications run properly on Windows 7/Vista/XP. However, some applications that were designed for older versions of Windows might not run properly on Windows 7, Vista, or XP. To make applications written for older versions of Windows compatible with Windows 7/Vista/XP, use the Program Compatibility Wizard, or the Compatibility tab of a file's Properties window.

▶ To start the wizard in Windows 7/Vista, click Start > Control Panel and then click the Programs icon (this time in category mode). Then, under Programs and Features, click the link called Run Programs Made for Previous Versions of Windows (in Win7), or Use an Older Program with This Version of Windows (in Vista). This program asks you which programs you want to make compatible, which OS it should be compatible with, and inquires as to the resolution and colors that the program should run in.

▶ To start the wizard in Windows XP, click Start > All Programs > Accessories > Program Compatibility Wizard. This works essentially the same in XP as it does in Vista.

▶ To use the Compatibility tab, right-click the program you want to make compatible from within Windows Explorer, and click Properties. From there, click the Compatibility tab. From there you can select which OS compatibility mode you want to run the program in (Windows 95/98/ME/2000/XP and so forth) and define settings such as resolution, colors, and so on.

> ### ExamAlert
>
> Know how to use the Compatibility Wizard and the Compatibility tab in a program's Properties window.

Windows XP Mode

Windows 7 can emulate the entire Windows XP OS if you so desire. This is done to help with program compatibility—meaning older programs that run or perform better with Windows XP, or perhaps will *only* run with Windows XP. To do this, you must first have Windows 7 Professional or Ultimate installed. Then, additional components must be installed to emulate Windows XP. First, install Windows XP Mode, then Virtual PC, and finally the Windows XP Mode update. These additional components can be downloaded for free (as long as you have a valid copy of Windows 7) starting at the following link: http://www.microsoft.com/windows/virtual-pc/download.aspx.

ExamAlert

Understand what XP Mode does for the exam.

Component Services

Component Services is a snap-in you can add to the MMC. It allows you to configure and administer three types of components: the Component Object Model (COM), COM+ Applications, and the Distributed Transaction Coordinator (DTC).

Component Object Model (COM) is a software interface used to allow inter-process communications and dynamic object creation using different programming languages. The term COM includes the following technologies: ActiveX controls (such as the real-time charts found in Task Manager), Object Linking and Embedding (OLE databases), COM+ (an extension to COM with better memory and processor management), and DCOM (programming as it relates to networked computers).

The Microsoft Distributed Transaction Coordinator (MSDTC) is a relatively newer component of Windows that uses a transaction manager to coordinate information between databases, file systems, and other resources. It works in conjunction with COM and .NET architectures.

For more information on Component Services administration, see the following link: http://technet.microsoft.com/en-us/library/cc731901.aspx.

If certain Dynamic-Link Libraries (DLLs) or ActiveX controls need to be troubleshot (for example ones that work with Internet Explorer), they can be manipulated with the REGSVR32 command. Controls can be registered or unregistered in the Command Prompt. For example, to register a sample ActiveX control, you would type **regsvr32 sample.ocx**. Unregistering requires the /u parameter. To register a .DLL file you would type **regsvr32 msi.dll**, replacing "msi" with whatever DLL you wish to register or unregister. To use the REGSVR32 command, you must run the Command Prompt as an administrator. More information on REGSVR32 can be found at the following link: http://support.microsoft.com/kb/249873.

Data Sources (ODBC)

Open Database Connectivity (ODBC) is an interface used within the C programming language to access database management systems. It is primarily used by Microsoft for their SQL database systems but can also be utilized by Microsoft Access Databases, dBASE, and Excel files. Different applications within Windows and from third-party vendors might make use of one of these technologies, and therefore will need ODBC. If you want to make configuration changes to ODBC, you can access it by going to Start > All Programs > Administrative Tools > Data Sources (ODBC). That opens the ODBC Data Source Administrator. From here you can add or remove Database Source Names (DSNs) which are data structures that describe a connection to a data source. DSNs include the name of the data source, the folder it is located in, the driver used to access the data source, and so on. For example, if you wanted to run a program in Windows 7 that was reliant on a SQL Server database, or just make a connection to a SQL DB, you would need to add the Microsoft SQL Server data source to the User DSN list. The name of the SQL Server would be required to complete the connection. For more information on ODBC in Windows see the following links: http://windows.microsoft.com/en-US/windows-vista/Using-the-ODBC-Data-Source-Administrator and http://msdn.microsoft.com/en-us/library/ms188691.aspx.

> **Note**
>
> The last two sections (COM and ODBC) and REGSVR32 deal with in-depth system configuration and application developing within Windows, going a bit beyond what a PC technician will usually be required to perform. However, they are listed on the CompTIA A+ objectives, so you should at least know what they are and how to access them in Windows.

Cram Quiz

Answer these questions. The answers follow the last question. If you cannot answer these questions correctly, consider reading this section again until you can.

220-802 Questions

1. What would you type to open the Device Manager in the Run prompt?

   ○ **A.** MMC

   ○ **B.** secpol.msc

   ○ **C.** CMD

   ○ **D.** devmgmt.msc

2. Where is the best place to get a driver for a video card?

   ○ **A.** CD-ROM

   ○ **B.** USB flash drive

   ○ **C.** Manufacturer's website

   ○ **D.** Microsoft's website

3. Which command opens the System Information tool?

   ○ **A.** `devmgmt.msc`

   ○ **B.** `compmgmt.msc`

   ○ **C.** `winmsd.msc`

   ○ **D.** `msinfo32.exe`

4. Which tab of the Task Manager tells you about the total usage of the CPU?

   ○ **A.** Performance

   ○ **B.** Processes

   ○ **C.** Networking

   ○ **D.** Processing

5. Where can a user go to start and stop services in Windows 7? (Select all that apply.)

   ○ **A.** msconfig

   ○ **B.** Task Manager

   ○ **C.** Computer Management

   ○ **D.** Command Prompt

6. Which file is used by the operating system for virtual memory?

   ○ **A.** swapfile.sys

   ○ **B.** pagefile.sys

   ○ **C.** pagingfile.sys

   ○ **D.** virtualfile.sys

7. Which command should you use to stop a service in the Command Prompt?

   ○ **A.** `spooler stop`

   ○ **B.** `network stop`

   ○ **C.** `net stop`

   ○ **D.** `stop`

8. Which power management mode stores data on the hard drive?

   ○ **A.** Sleep

   ○ **B.** Hibernate

   ○ **C.** Standby

   ○ **D.** Pillow.exe

9. Which tool enables a technician to move user state data from within the command line?

   ○ **A.** Windows Easy Transfer

   ○ **B.** Elevated mode

   ○ **C.** USMT

   ○ **D.** FAST

10. What is HKEY_LOCAL_MACHINE considered to be?

    ○ **A.** A registry entry

    ○ **B.** A subkey

    ○ **C.** A string value

    ○ **D.** A hive

11. When users invite a technician to help repair their computer, what is this called?

    ○ **A.** Remote Desktop

    ○ **B.** Remote Assistance

    ○ **C.** RDP

    ○ **D.** Remote connectivity

12. You see a yellow exclamation mark next to a device in the Device Manager. What does this indicate?

    ○ **A.** The device driver is corrupt.

    ○ **B.** The device driver is outdated.

    ○ **C.** The device driver is missing.

    ○ **D.** The device is disabled.

Cram Quiz Answers

220-802 Answers

1. **D.** Devmgmt.msc is the Microsoft console window known as Device Manager. Typing **MMC** opens up a new blank Microsoft Management Console. **Secpol.msc** opens the Local Security Policy window. And **CMD** opens the Command Prompt.

2. **C.** The manufacturer's website is the best place to get the latest driver for your device; next on the list would be the CD-ROM that came with the device, and last, attempt to have Microsoft automatically install its version of the driver.

3. **D.** **Msinfo32.exe** opens the System Information tool. **Devmgmt.msc** opens the Device Manager, **compmgmt.msc** opens Computer Management, and **winmsd.msc** doesn't exist; however, **winmsd.exe** opens the System Information tool in Windows XP, but **winmsd.exe** does not function in 7/Vista.

4. **A.** The Performance tab shows the percentage of processing power used in real time. The Processes tab shows the individual processes that are running, the amount of processing power each of them is using, and the amount of memory they are utilizing. The Networking tab shows the percentage of network utilization for each network adapter. There is no Processing tab.

5. **B, C,** and **D.** Task Manager, Computer Management, and the Command Prompt. Msconfig is not a correct answer as it lets you *enable/disable* services, but not *start/stop* them.

6. **B.** Pagefile.sys is the virtual memory file that is located by default in the root of C:.

7. **C. Net stop** (and the service name) stops the service in the Command Prompt. For example, **net stop spooler**.

8. **B.** When a computer hibernates, all the information in RAM is written to a file called hiberfil.sys in the root of C: within the hard drive.

9. **C.** USMT (User State Migration Tool) is the command-line version that can move any or all the user states to and from multiple computers. Window Easy Transfer is the successor to FAST (Files and Settings Transfer Wizard). Elevated mode is what you need to be in when running administrative-level functions from within the Command Prompt.

10. **D.** HKEY_LOCAL_MACHINE is one of the five visible hives that can be modified from within the Registry Editor.

11. **B.** Remote Assistance calls can be made from users to invite other users to help fix a problem for them. Remote Desktop connections are the connections that a computer makes to a remote computer to control it.

12. **C.** A yellow exclamation point in the Device Manager indicates that the device driver is missing. You should download the latest driver from the manufacturer's website. If the device were disabled, it would have a down arrow (Windows 7/Vista) or a red X (Windows XP).

Files, File Systems, and Disks

This section covers file structures, file locations, ways of manipulating files, and file systems. It also delves into how to manage disks, including how to partition and format drives, create mount points, and identify drive status. Finally, the various levels of RAID are discussed. Let's start by talking about files and file systems.

Working with Files and File Systems

Files are what makes the world go round it seems. But because there are so many of them, you need to organize them efficiently. To do so, operating systems use a directory structure. It all starts with the root of the operating system and moves on from there, as detailed in Table 9.2.

TABLE 9.2 **Directory Structure in Windows 7/Vista**

Directory	Usage
C:\	This is the root of the C: drive, which is the drive in which the OS is usually installed. Boot files such as bootmgr and NTLDR are stored here.
C:\Windows	This folder is the %systemroot%, in which the operating system is actually installed to, folder by folder, and file by file. This is also known as %WINDIR% in Windows 7.
C:\Windows\System32	Contains the critical Windows system files (for instance NTOSKRNL.EXE) and many applications such as cmd.exe and dxdiag.exe.
C:\Boot	This contains the Boot Configuration Data Store in Windows 7/Vista.
Note: This folder might be in a different partition depending on which one is the system partition. In Windows 7, this will default to a hidden 100MB system partition. See my video to remove this partition: www.davidlprowse.com/220-801.	
C:\Program Files	This is where the bulk of applications are installed to, for example Microsoft Office or Adobe Acrobat Reader.
C:\Documents and Settings	This is where all user account information is stored in Windows XP. In Windows 7/Vista, this protected folder redirects to the Users folder. (This is also known as a *junction*.)
C:\Windows\Temp	This is where temporary files are stored.
C:\Windows\CSC	This is where offline files are stored. Offline files are files that you have previously selected from the network to be available to you even if the network is not available.
C:\Windows\Fonts	This is the default location for fonts used by Windows and installed applications. If additional fonts are downloaded from the Internet, they should be placed in this folder.

> **Note**
>
> If the operating system were installed to another volume, for example D:, all the paths above would be modified to reflect this. If the operating system were installed in a different folder than the %systemroot%, that would affect all subfolders of the systemroot as well.

Windows 7/Vista and XP Boot Files

After the BIOS is done bootstrapping, and the MBR and boot sector of the hard drive have been located and accessed, a loader file is accessed on the hard drive. In Windows 7/Vista, this is the Windows Boot Manager; in Windows XP, it is NTLDR. The following files are required to start Windows 7/Vista:

▶ **Bootmgr (Windows Boot Manager):** Bootmgr is the first file to load on the hard drive and is initiated by the BIOS. It takes care of reading the BCD and displaying the OS menu (if you have one). So it is responsible for starting a particular OS. It is outside of the OS (as it would have to be) so it can call on one of multiple versions of Windows. It can be shared among various versions of Windows and even other operating systems if configured properly (with the use of the Extensible Firmware Interface or EFI). Bootmgr switches CPU operation from real mode to protected mode, which could be 32-bit or 64-bit, depending on what version of the OS you installed. Among other things, this allows the Bootmgr to access all memory (not just limited to 1 MB).

▶ **BCD (Boot Configuration Data):** This is located in \boot\bcd; it furnishes the Windows Boot Manager with information about the operating system(s) to be booted. It is the successor to boot.ini and can be modified with MSCONFIG or with the bcdedit.exe program. BCD was developed to provide an improved mechanism for describing boot configuration data and to work better with newer firmware models such as the Extensible Firmware Interface (EFI). If you want to modify your dual-boot menu configuration manually, this is what you would go to.

▶ **Winload.exe:** Winload.exe is the Windows Boot Loader program and is within the OS. This program loads the kernel file (ntoskrnl.exe) of the particular OS that was selected from the Bootmgr program. Bootmgr invokes winload.exe for the OS that was selected. Bootmgr and Winload.exe collectively take the place of the older NTLDR.

> **Note**
>
> If a system is in hibernate mode, Winresume.exe is initiated by the Bootmgr/BCD instead of Winload.exe being initiated by Bootmgr.
>
> More about the boot process can be found at the following links: http://technet.microsoft.com/en-us/library/ee221031(WS.10).aspx and http://msdn.microsoft.com/en-us/windows/hardware/gg463059.aspx.

The following files are required to start Windows XP:

- ▶ **NTLDR:** The Windows loader program determines which operating system to start (if there is more than one).

- ▶ **Boot.ini:** Contains the menu of operating systems that can be selected and options for booting Windows.

- ▶ **Ntdetect.com:** Detects the hardware installed on your system.

The following files are optional when starting Windows XP:

- ▶ **Ntbootdd.sys:** This device driver is used only if Windows is started from a SCSI drive whose host adapter does not have an onboard SCSI BIOS enabled.

- ▶ **Bootsect.dos:** This contains the boot sectors for another operating system if you multiboot.

> **ExamAlert**
>
> Memorize the required Windows 7/Vista and XP boot files and their function.

File Associations

File associations are the relationships between files and the applications that are used to open them. The extension of the file is what determines this. Take for instance the file sales-report.doc. The filename is sales-report, but the important part, the extension is .doc. This tells you it is a Microsoft Word document, and that the relationship is such that Microsoft Word will be opened automatically when the file is double-clicked.

In Windows 7/Vista these associations are stored in Start > Default Programs and can be modified by clicking the Set your default programs link. For example, if you wanted Windows Media Player to open additional files by default, you would highlight it, and then select Choose Defaults for This Program.

From there you can check the various audio and video file formats you want associated with Windows Media Player.

ExamAlert

It is common for multimedia applications to attempt to become the default program of audio and video file formats. Be prepared to add or remove file associations for these types of applications.

Indexing

Because there are so many files, Windows 7, Vista, and XP offer the Indexing service to help find the files you want faster. However, indexing too much content can lead to poor operating system performance.

To adjust the indexing settings in Windows 7, go to Start > Control Panel > Indexing Options (show individual icons in the Control Panel). From here you can modify whether folders are indexed by clicking the Modify button and selecting or deselecting the folders you want. It is not recommended to select an entire volume (like C:) because it can cause poor performance. Use indexing for specific folders in which you store important data that you search for on a regular basis. If you don't want indexing at all, you can either deselect all folders that are check marked or disable the indexing in general. To disable indexing altogether:

1. Click Start, right-click Computer, and select Manage. This brings up the Computer Management window.

2. From here, expand Services and Applications in the left window pane, and click Services.

3. In the right window pane, scroll down to Windows Search, right-click it, and select Stop. You can restart the service at any time by right-clicking and selecting Start. Check the startup type by right-clicking the service and selecting Properties. If the startup type is set to Automatic, you should change it to manual or disabled; otherwise, the service starts back up again when you restart the computer.

You can also turn off indexing for individual drives. To do so:

1. Open Windows Explorer.

2. Right-click the volume you want to stop indexing on; for example C:, and select Properties.

3. At the bottom of the window, deselect the indexing option.

To turn off indexing in Windows XP:

1. Click Start, right-click My Computer, and select Manage. This brings up the Computer Management window.

2. From here expand Services and Applications in the left window pane, and click Services.

3. In the right window pane, scroll down to Indexing Service, right-click it, and select Stop. You can restart the service at any time by right-clicking and selecting Start. Check the startup type by right-clicking the service and selecting Properties. If the startup type is set to Automatic, you should change it to manual or disabled; otherwise the service starts back up again when you restart the computer.

Working with Directories and Files in the Command Prompt

Have I mentioned yet that just about anything you can do in Windows can also be done in the Command Prompt? It's true. And sometimes the Command Prompt is faster (if you can type quickly) than the GUI. There are three commands used to work with directories in the Command Prompt, and by the way, "directory" is the original name for "folder."

▶ **CD:** Change Directory. This command enables you to move from one directory to another. Actually, you can go from any one directory to any other using just one **CD** command.

▶ **MD:** Make Directory. This command creates directories.

▶ **RD:** Remove Directory. This command enables you to remove directories. It can also remove directories that contain files by utilizing the /S switch.

All these commands can be used in such a way in which their function affects any folder you choose within the directory structure (which used to be known as the DOS tree, but I digress). Figure 9.14 gives a sample directory structure.

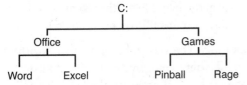

FIGURE 9.14 **Sample directory structure**

Say that your current position was C:\Office. From here or any other location, you can do anything to any folder in the entire directory tree. Let's give a couple examples:

▶ Change the current position to the Pinball folder. To do this, the command would be either **cd c:\games\pinball** or just **cd \games\ pinball**.

▶ Make a directory called "documents" within Word. To do this the command syntax would be **md c:\office\word\documents**.

▶ Delete the directory Excel. To do this the command would be **rd c:\office\excel**.

> **Note**
>
> Making directories can be quick in the command line. If you need to create several subdirectories, using the **MD** command can be quicker than clicking with the mouse in Windows Explorer. For example, to make four folders with one command, you could type: **md folder1; folder2; folder3; folder4**.

> **ExamAlert**
>
> Know the difference between **CD**, **MD**, and **RD** for the exam.

Some other commands you might use when working with directories and files include DIR, TREE, COPY, and DEL.

▶ **DIR:** This is the directory command. When used alone, it displays the contents of the current directory. But can be configured to show information in any other directory, for example; DIR \office\excel will show the contents of the excel director regardless of what directory you are currently in. You can also customize how content is listed with the DIR command. For example, /p will show information by the page, /w is wide list format, and so on. To find out more about the DIR command (or any other command for that matter) type **DIR /?**. The /? is the switch that tells the Command Prompt to display the help file for that command. It can be placed on the end of any valid Command Prompt command.

▶ **TREE:** This command shows all the directories and subdirectories within your current position. Be careful where you run this as it could list information for quite a while and cause some stress on the hard drive. For example, stay away from big directories such as the root, which is C:\, \Windows, and \Windows\System32.

▶ **COPY:** This command allows you to copy one or more files to another location. If I wanted to copy a file named test.txt from the office directory to the excel directory, I would type **copy \office\test.txt \office\excel**. Now the original is in \office, and the copy is in \excel. There are more powerful versions of this command known as xcopy and robocopy that we will talk about in Chapter 11.

▶ **DEL:** When you are done with a file and are ready to delete it, use DEL. For example, if you wanted to delete the test.txt file that you just copied to the excel folder, type **del \office\excel\test.txt**.

Note

By the way, I created the test.txt text file within Notepad available at Start > All Programs > Accessories. That is Windows default graphical text editor that you should use for editing text and batch files. However, some versions of Windows also allow you to use the command-line-based MS-DOS Text Editor. This is accessed in the Command Prompt by simply typing **edit**. It can be useful when dealing with text files from other operating systems.

These are some of the basic commands you can make use of in the Command Prompt. We'll get into some more advanced commands in Chapter 11.

ExamAlert

Understand how to use DIR, TREE, COPY, and DEL for the exam.

Managing Disks

So you have three 1 TB SATA 3.0 hard disks. Now what do you do with them? You manage them. The main tool with which to do this is called Disk Management. It can be accessed by opening Computer Management and expanding Storage.

Partitioning, Formatting, and Drive Status

The proper order for disk preparation is to partition the disk, format it, and then copy files to your heart's delight. However, sometimes you might also need to initialize additional disks within Windows; this would be done before partitioning. All these things can be done within the Disk Management program. The Disk Management tool within Computer Management is the GUI-based application for analyzing and configuring hard drives. You can do a lot from here including:

▶ **Initialize a new disk:** A secondary hard disk installed in a computer might not be seen by Windows Explorer immediately. To make it accessible, locate the disk (for example Disk 1), right-click where it says Disk 1, Disk 2, and such, and select Initialize Disk. When you install an OS to the only disk in the system, it is initialized automatically.

▶ **Create volumes, partitions, and logical drives:** When creating these Windows 7 refers to them simply as volumes. Windows Vista and earlier use the terms *partition* and *logical drive*. Regardless, you must right-click the area with the black header named unallocated. Figure 9.15 shows an example of creating a new simple volume by right-clicking that area.

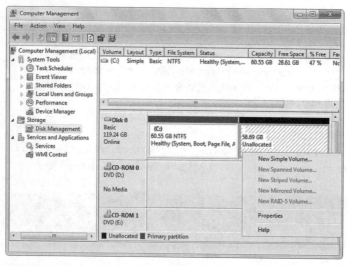

FIGURE 9.15 **Creating a volume within unallocated disk space**

▶ **Format volumes:** When formatting, select the file system (NTFS usually) and whether to do a quick format. If it is a new drive, quick formats are okay, but if the drive were used previously, you might want to leave this option unchecked. ALL DATA WILL BE ERASED during the format procedure.

▶ **Make partitions active:** Partitions need to be set to active if you want to install an operating system to them.

▶ **Convert basic discs to dynamic:** Basic discs can have only simple volumes, or regular partitions/logical drives. If you want to create a spanned, striped, mirrored, or RAID-5 volume, you need to convert the disc to dynamic. This is done by right-clicking the disk where it says Disk 0 or Disk 1, for example, and selecting Convert to Dynamic Disk. It's highly recommended that you back up your data before attempting this configuration.

▶ **Extend and shrink volumes:** A volume can also be extended or shrunk. Any volume can be shrunk, but to extend a volume you need available unallocated space on the disk. By shrinking a volume that takes up the entire hard drive, you can also ultimately split that partition into two pieces, allowing you to better organize where the OS and where the data files are stored.

You might ask: What is the difference between a partition and a volume? The partitions are physical (and logical) divisions of the drive. A volume is actually any space among one or more drives that receives a drive letter.

Disk 0 has a C: drive that is a primary partition. The first partition you create on a disk must be a primary partition. This primary partition gets a letter, for example C:. Afterward, you can create more primary partitions or an extended partition. The extended partition starts as free space but can be divided into logical drives. Logical drives are also given letter assignments. You can have up to four primary partitions, or three primary partitions and an extended partition. The purpose of the extended partition is to allow you to logically divide up the hard drive into more than just four parts. For example, Figure 9.16 shows a disk divided into three primary partitions and an extended partition with two logical drives.

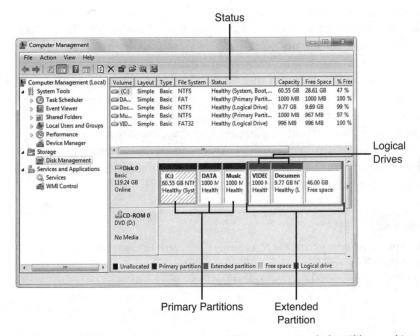

FIGURE 9.16 A Disk with three primary partitions, one extended partition, and two logical drives

Though you might not make out the colors, the color key in Figure 9.16 shows that you have three primary partitions. These are named C: (where your OS is installed), Data (the F: drive), and Music (the G: drive). Dark blue headers equate to primary partitions. The letters D: and E: were skipped because those letters are used by the DVD-ROM and Blu-ray drives. Furthermore, there is a dark green boxed area that contains three other items. Dark green means it is an extended partition. The extended partition does not get a drive letter. But the two medium blue logical drives inside, named Video and Documents, do get drive letters, H: and I:.

> **ExamAlert**
>
> Understand the differences between primary partitions, extended partitions, logical drives, and volumes.

These volumes were given a variety of files system types: NTFS (the most common), FAT, and FAT32. We'll talk more about these in a little bit.

You can also see the disks at the top of the window and their status. For example, the C: partition is healthy. You see it is a System partition, which tells you that the OS is housed there. Plus, it is a Boot partition; this is the partition that is booted to when the computer starts up. It also shows the capacity of the disk, free space, and percentage of the disk used. What's more, this section tells you if the disk is basic or dynamic, or if it has failed. In some cases, you might see "foreign" status. This means that a dynamic disk has been moved from another computer (with another Windows operating system) to the local computer, and it cannot be accessed properly. To fix this and access the disk, add the disk to your computer's system configuration. This is done by right-clicking the disk and then clicking Import Foreign Disks. Any existing volumes on the foreign disk become visible and accessible when you import the disk. For more information on the plethora of disk statuses, see the following link: http://technet.microsoft.com/en-us/library/cc738101(WS.10).aspx.

> **Note**
>
> The command-line version of Disk Management is called diskpart. With this tool you can accomplish most of what we discussed in this section.

File System Basics

When formatting a hard drive, you have the option to format it as either the NTFS (recommended), FAT32, or FAT file system. NTFS is a more secure and stable platform and can support larger volume sizes. It also supports encryption with the Encrypting File System (EFS) and works better with backups. FAT32 and FAT should be used only to interact with older versions of Windows and to format devices such as USB flash drives. Depending on the cluster size used, NTFS can support up to either 16 TB (4 KB clusters), or 256 TB (64 KB cluster) partitions, but some systems will be limited to 2 TB due to the limitations of partition tables on MBR-based disks. This hardware limitation applies to maximum FAT32 partition sizes of 2 TB as well (aside from the installation maximum of 32 GB). To go beyond this, a set of striped or spanned dynamic disks would have to be employed, creating a multidisk volume. FAT (specifically known as FAT16) was the predecessor to FAT32. Windows XP can be installed to a FAT partition up to 4 GB in size; some older flash devices also use FAT, but it is recommended to stay away from FAT16 in general because it is deprecated. One other file system of note is FAT12, which is used mostly by floppy disks. Another file system introduced by Microsoft is called the Extended File Allocation Table (exFAT), which is suited specifically for USB flash drives but addresses the needs of many other mobile storage solutions. The successor to FAT32, it can handle large file sizes and can format media that is larger than 32 GB with a single partition. In fact, exFAT (also known as FAT64) has a recommended maximum of 512 TB for partitions, with a theoretical maximum of 64 ZB (zettabytes). The file size limit when using exFAT is 16 EB (exabytes). This file system can be used in Windows 7, Server 2008, Vista with SP1, XP/Server 2003 with SP2, and Windows CE 6.0. If NTFS is not a plausible solution, and the partition size needed is larger than 32 GB, exFAT might be the best option. As of the writing of this book, exFAT is not used for internal SATA or IDE hard drives; instead it is used for flash memory storage and other external storage devices. exFAT is considered to be a more efficient file system than NTFS when it comes to flash memory storage, with less fragmentation, leading to more possible read/write cycles over the life of the flash memory device.

Another file system you should be concerned with is the Compact Disc File System (CDFS). This is the ISO 9660 standard, which defines how information is written to optical discs and is used by Windows and Mac OS. A CD-ROM consists of frames, which can each hold 24 bytes. Ninety-eight frames put together creates a sector. Those bytes are divided up; the majority of them are used for data, others are used for error detection and correction. How they are divided is determined by the Mode used. CD-ROM Mode 1 and Mode 2 Form 1 are usually used for computer data. CD-ROM Mode 2 Form 2 is more tolerant of errors and is used by audio and video data.

ExamAlert

Know the differences between NTFS, FAT, FAT32, and CDFS for the exam.

Mount Points and Mounting A Drive

You can also "mount" drives in Disk Management. A mounted drive is a drive that is mapped to an empty folder within a volume that has been formatted as NTFS. Instead of using drive letters, mounted drives use drive paths. This is a good solution for when you need more than 26 drives in your computer because you are not limited to the letters in the alphabet. Mounted drives can also provide more space for temporary files and can allow you to move folders to different drives if space runs low on the current drive. To mount a drive:

1. Right-click the partition or volume you want to mount, and select Change Drive Letters and Paths.

2. In the displayed window, click Add.

3. Then browse to the *empty* folder you want to mount the volume to, and click OK for both windows.

As shown in Figure 9.17, the DVD-ROM drive has been mounted within the Data folder on the F: volume on the hard drive. It shows that it is a mounted volume and shows the location of the folder (which is the mount point) and the target of the mount point, which is the DVD drive containing a Windows 7 DVD. To remove the mount point, just go back to Disk Management, right-click the mounted volume, and select Change Drive Letters and Paths; then select Remove. Remember that the folder you want to use as a mount point must be empty, and it must be within an NTFS volume.

RAID

RAID stands for Redundant Array of Inexpensive Disks. RAID technologies are designed to either increase the speed of reading and writing data or to create one of several types of fault tolerant volumes, or both. Fault tolerance is the capability of the hard drive system to continue working after there is a problem with one of the drives. The test requires you to know RAID levels 0, 1, 5, and 10. Table 9.3 describes each of these.

FIGURE 9.17 **Empty NTFS folder acting as a mount point**

TABLE 9.3 **RAID 0, 1, 5, and 10 Descriptions**

RAID Level	Description	Fault Tolerant?	Minimum Number of Disks
RAID 0	Striping. Data is striped across multiple disks in an effort to increase performance.	No	2
RAID 1	Mirroring. Data is copied to two identical disks. If one disk fails, the other continues to operate. When each disk is connected to a separate controller, this is known as Disk Duplexing. See Figure 9.18 for an illustration. RAID 1 is not available in Windows XP/Vista but is available in Windows 7 Professional and Ultimate.	Yes	2 (and 2 only)
RAID 5	Striping with Parity. Data is striped across multiple disks; fault tolerant parity data is also written to each disk. If one disk fails, the array can reconstruct the data from the parity information. See Figure 9.19 for an illustration. RAID 5 is not available in Windows XP/Vista but is available in Windows 7 Professional and Ultimate.	Yes	3
RAID 10	Combines the advantages of RAID 1 and RAID 0. Requires a minimum of two disks, but will usually have four or more. The system contains at least two mirrored disks that are then striped.	Yes	2 (usually 4)

Even though Windows Vista/XP cannot support RAID 1 and 5 from within the operating system, they *can* support hardware controllers that can create RAID 1 and 5 arrays. Of course, Windows 7 also supports hardware-based RAID controllers. Some motherboards have built in RAID functionality as well. Figure 9.18 shows an illustration of RAID 1; you can see that data is written to both disks and that both disks collectively are known as the M: drive or M: volume. Figure 9.19 displays an illustration of RAID 5. In a RAID 5 array, blocks of data are distributed to the disks (A1 and A2 are a block, B1 and B2 are a block, and so on), and parity information is written for each block of data. This is written to each disk in an alternating fashion (Ap, Bp, and such) so that the parity is also distributed. If one disk fails, the parity information from the other disks will reconstruct the data. It is important to make the distinction between fault tolerance and backup. Fault tolerance means that the hard drives can continue to function (with little or no down-time) even if there is a problem with one of the drives. Backup means that you are taking the data and copying it (and possibly compressing it) to another location for archival in the event of a disaster. An example of a disaster would be if *two* drives in a RAID 5 array were to fail.

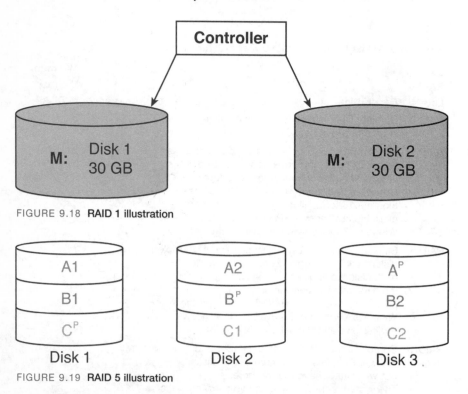

FIGURE 9.18 **RAID 1 illustration**

FIGURE 9.19 **RAID 5 illustration**

Sometimes, hardware RAID arrays will fail. They might stop working or the OS could have trouble finding them. If you see an issue like this, check if the hard drives are securely connected to the controller, and that the controller (if an adapter card) is securely connected to the motherboard. Also, if you use a RAID adapter card or external enclosure, and the motherboard also has built-in RAID functionality of its own, make sure you disable the motherboard RAID within the BIOS—it could cause a conflict. Verify that the driver for the RAID device is installed and updated. Finally, check if any of the hard drives or the RAID controller has failed. If a RAID controller built into a motherboard fails, you will have to purchase a RAID adapter card.

Cram Quiz

Answer these questions. The answers follow the last question. If you cannot answer these questions correctly, consider reading this section again until you can.

220-801 Questions

1. Which level of RAID uses two disks only?

   ○ **A.** RAID 0

   ○ **B.** RAID 1

   ○ **C.** RAID 5

   ○ **D.** Striping

2. Which level of RAID stripes data and parity across three or more disks?

   ○ **A.** RAID 0

   ○ **B.** RAID 1

   ○ **C.** RAID 5

   ○ **D.** Striping

3. Which level of RAID contains two sets of mirrored disks that are then striped?

   ○ **A.** RAID 0

   ○ **B.** RAID 1

   ○ **C.** RAID 5

   ○ **D.** RAID 10

220-802 Questions

4. Where is NTOSKRNL.EXE located?

   ○ **A.** C:\Window

   ○ **B.** C:\Boot

   ○ **C.** C:\Windows\System

   ○ **D.** C:\Windows\System32

5. Which of these is the boot loader for Windows 7?

    ○ **A.** BCD

    ○ **B.** Winload.exe

    ○ **C.** NTLDR

    ○ **D.** Boot.ini

6. Which command creates a directory?

    ○ **A.** CD

    ○ **B.** MD

    ○ **C.** RD

    ○ **D.** Chdir

7. Which operating system enables you to extend volumes?

    ○ **A.** Windows XP

    ○ **B.** Windows 2000

    ○ **C.** Windows Aero

    ○ **D.** Windows 7

Cram Quiz Answers

220-801 Answers

1. B. RAID 1 (mirroring) uses two disks only. RAID 0 (striping) can use two disks or more, and RAID 5 (striping with parity) can use three disks or more.

2. C. RAID 5 stripes data *and* parity across three or more disks. RAID 0 does not stripe parity, it stripes data only and can use two disks or more. RAID 1 uses two disks only. Striping is another name for RAID 0.

3. D. RAID 10 contains two sets of mirrored disks that are then striped. RAID 0 is a set of two or more disks that stripe data. RAID 1 is a mirror. RAID 5 is striping with parity.

220-802 Answers

4. D. NTOSKRNL.EXE is located in C:\Windows\System32, otherwise referred to as \%systemroot%\System32.

5. B. Winload.exe (Windows Boot Manager) is the boot loader for Windows 7. BCD is the Boot Configuration Data store, NTLDR is the boot loader for Windows XP, and Boot.ini contains the menu of OSs and boot options in Windows XP.

6. B. MD (Make Directory) creates directories. CD is change directory, RD is remove directory, and chdir is the older version of CD.

7. D. Windows 7 is the only listed operating system that can extend volumes. Windows Aero is not an OS; it's the look of the 7/Vista GUI.

CHAPTER 10

Maintaining Windows

This chapter covers the following A+ exam topics:

▶ Updating Windows

▶ Maintaining Hard Disks

You can find a master list of A+ exam topics in the "Introduction."

This chapter covers CompTIA A+ 220-802 objectives 1.1, and 1.7.

Windows maintenance is important as a security precaution and as a way to prevent any strange and unforeseen issues that might occur. Bad guys are always finding ways to exploit Windows code, and as these exploits are discovered, Microsoft releases updates (also known as patches) to fix those issues.

Keeping up maintenance on the hard disk drives is one of the best things you can do for your computer. By maintaining the hard drive, you increase its lifespan and reduce the chance of corrupted files.

This chapter shows how to update Windows and how to configure the Windows Update program. It also shows how to maintain the hard disk with cleanup and defragmenting programs. This chapter is a little less intense than the last one, but it still contains some important information for the exams and for the IT field in general.

Updating Windows

Updating Windows can be done in two ways: first, by updating to the latest service pack, and second by using the Windows Update program. Let's begin by discussing service packs.

Service Packs

A service pack (SP) is a group of updates, bug fixes, updated drivers, and security fixes that are installed from one downloadable package or from one disc. Service packs are numbered, for example SP1, SP2, and so on. Installing the SP is relatively easy and asks only a few basic questions. When those questions are answered, it takes several minutes or more to complete the update; then a restart will be required. While the service pack is installed, it rewrites many files and copies new ones to the hard drive as well.

Historically, many service packs have been cumulative, meaning that they also contain previous service packs. An example of an incremental SP is Windows Vista SP2; SP1 must be installed first before updating to SP2 in Windows Vista.

To find out which service pack is installed to the operating system, do the following:

▶ **In Windows 7/Vista**: Click Start; then right-click Computer and select Properties. This opens the System window. In the Windows Edition section, you should see system information including the operating system version and the SP that is installed. If the words "service pack" do not appear, there is no SP installed. This is informally known as SP0. You can also find out your SP level by going to the Run prompt and typing Winver. Plus, you can discern SP levels directly in the Command Prompt. For example, if you open the Command Prompt in Windows 7 and see on the top line Microsoft Windows [Version 6.1.7600] then no SP is installed. But if you do this on Windows 7 with SP1, you will see Microsoft Windows [Version 6.1.7601]. Note the difference in the last number. Typing Ver in the Command Prompt also gives this information. Finally, you can also open the System Information tool. (Open the Run prompt and type **msinfo32.exe.**) It will be listed directly in the system summary.

▶ **In Windows XP**: Click Start; then right-click My Computer and select Properties. This opens the System Properties window. Toward the top of the General tab, you should see system information including the operating system version and the service pack that is installed. If the words "service pack" do not appear, there is no SP installed.

ExamAlert

Know where to check the SP level of Windows.

Note

You can also find out the OS name, version, and SP level by using the following syntax in the Command Prompt:

```
systeminfo|findstr /B /C:"OS Name" /C:"OS Version"
```

Note the pipe symbol between systeminfo and findstr. Also, the text within the quotes is case-sensitive.

In this example, the resulting output on a Windows 7 Ultimate OS with SP1 installed would be

```
OS Name: Microsoft Windows 7 Ultimate
OS Version: 6.1.7601 Service Pack 1 Build 7601
```

For the Version/SP level only, omit the following: `/C:"OS Name"`

As of the writing of this book, the latest service packs are Windows 7, SP1; Windows Vista, SP2; and Windows XP, SP3. But new service packs are always being released.

For the individual user, the SP can be automatically downloaded and installed if you have configured Automatic Updates (which we'll discuss in the next section); this is the easiest way for the average user.

You can also download the SP in .exe, .msi, or .iso format. For example, Windows 7 SP1 can be downloaded from the following link: http://www.microsoft.com/download/en/details.aspx?id=5842.

These various packages can be helpful if you need to deploy SP1 to multiple computers. Your particular environment will dictate which file you should download. Before downloading, I recommend reading the article at the following link: http://support.microsoft.com/kb/2505743.

Service packs can also be acquired through a Microsoft Developer Network (MSDN) subscription. A SP might have been incorporated into the original operating system distribution DVD/CD. This is known as *slipstreaming*. This method enables the user to install the OS and the SP at the same time in a seamless manner. It is also possible for system administrators to create slip-streamed images of the OS and SP by using the Windows Automated Installation Kit (AIK). The Win7 version of this is available at this link: http://www.microsoft.com/download/en/details.aspx?displaylang=en&id=5753.

The latest and greatest is exciting, but if something works, why replace it, right? For example, a Windows Server 2003 might be happily churning out the data necessary to users. That's okay; just make sure that it uses the latest SP and updates so that it can interact properly with other computers on the network. Keep in mind that older operating systems are no longer supported by Microsoft. As of 2012, this includes Windows 2000 and anything earlier.

Windows Update

As with any OS, Windows 7, Vista, and XP should be updated regularly. Microsoft recognizes deficiencies in the OS—and possible exploits that could occur—and releases patches to increase OS performance and protect the system. After the latest SP has been installed, the next step is to see if any additional updates are available for download.

To install additional updates for Windows through Windows Update

1. Click Start > All Programs > Windows Update.

2. Windows 7 and Vista open the Windows Update window in which you can turn on updates, or click the Install Updates button. Windows XP opens a web page in which you can select Express or Custom installation of updates. Follow the prompts to install the latest version of the Windows Update software if necessary.

Note

Do not select Express or let Microsoft automatically install *all* updates if you do not want to use newer applications, for example the latest version of Internet Explorer.

---

3. The system (or web page) automatically scans for updates. Updates are divided into the following categories:

   ▶ **Critical Updates and Service Packs:** These include the latest service pack and other security and stability updates. Some updates must be installed individually; others can be installed as a group.

   ▶ **Windows Updates:** Recommended updates to fix noncritical problems certain users might encounter; also adds features and updates to features bundled into Windows.

   ▶ **Driver Updates:** Updated device drivers for installed hardware.

If your system is in need of updates, a shield (for the Windows Security Center) appears in the system tray. Double-clicking this brings up the Security Center window in which you can turn on automatic updates. To modify how you are alerted to updates, and how they are downloaded and installed, do the following:

- ▶ **Windows 7/Vista:** Click Start > Windows Update; then click the Change Settings link.

- ▶ **Windows XP:** Click Start > Control Panel; then select Classic view, and double-click Automatic Updates.

From here there will be four options:

- ▶ **Install Updates Automatically:** This is the recommended option by Microsoft. You can schedule when and how often the updates should be downloaded and installed.

- ▶ **Download Updates but Let Me Choose Whether to Install Them:** This automatically downloads updates when they become available, but Windows prompts you to install them instead of installing them automatically. Each update has a check box, so you can select individual updates to install.

- ▶ **Check for Updates but Let Me Choose Whether to Download and Install Them:** This lets you know when updates are available, but you are in control as to when they are downloaded and installed.

- ▶ **Never Check for Updates:** This is not recommended by Microsoft because it can be a security risk but might be necessary in some environments in which updates could cause conflicts over the network. In some networks, the administrator takes care of updates from a server and sets the local computers to this option.

> **ExamAlert**
>
> Know how to install Windows updates and how to modify how they are downloaded and installed.

Larger organizations with a lot of computers will be concerned with *patch management*, the patching of many systems from a central location. Microsoft updates can be pushed out to multiple clients from a server system such as System Center Configuration Manager (SCCM) 2012 and 2007, or Systems Management Server (SMS) 2003, or less commonly, with the Windows Server Update Services (WSUS) program. Third-party tools can be used as well. The patch management process should be considered thoughtfully. Typically a patch management strategy will consist of four steps: planning, testing, implementing, and auditing. So before actually pushing the updates out, you should carefully consider what you will be updating, and test it thoroughly on a couple of systems on a separate test network. After you implement the patch across the network, you should analyze whether the patch took to the systems. By using this four step process, you can minimize errors in Windows updating.

Cram Quiz

Answer these questions. The answers follow the last question. If you cannot answer these questions correctly, consider reading this section again until you can.

220-802 Questions

1. Which Windows Update option is not recommended?

   ○ **A.** Download Updates but Let Me Choose Whether to Install Them

   ○ **B.** Install Updates Automatically

   ○ **C.** Never Check for Updates

   ○ **D.** Check for Updates but Let Me Choose Whether to Download and Install Them

2. Where can you find out the latest service pack that is used by Windows Vista? (Select all that apply.)

   ○ **A.** System window

   ○ **B.** System Properties window

   ○ **C.** System Information

   ○ **D.** System Tools

3. In Windows 7, where would you go to modify how you are alerted to updates?

   ○ **A.** Click Start > Windows Update; then click the Change settings link.

   ○ **B.** Click Start > Control Panel; then select Classic view, and double-click Automatic Updates.

   ○ **C.** Click Start; then right-click My Computer and select Properties.

   ○ **D.** Click Start > Windows Update; then click the Check for updates link.

Cram Quiz Answers

220-802 Answers

1. **C.** It is not recommended that you set Windows Update to Never Check for Updates because it is a security risk.

2. **A** and **C**. You can find out the latest SP in use by Windows Vista within the System window and the System Information tool. The SP for Windows XP can be found in the System Properties window.

3. **A.** To modify how you are alerted to updates and how they are downloaded and installed in Window 7, click Start > Windows Update; then click the Change settings link.

Maintaining Hard Disks

In Chapter 6, "Storage Devices," I made a bold statement: "Hard disks *will* fail." But it's all too true; it's not a matter of *if*; it's a matter of *when*. By maintaining the hard disk with various hard disk utilities, you attempt to stave off that dark day as long as possible. To further protect data, you can back it up with programs that Windows provides to you or third-party programs. And to protect operating system files, Windows offers the System Restore utility. Let's start with some of the hard disk utilities that you will use in the field.

Hard Disk Utilities

To keep that hard drive running clean, I recommend that you remove temporary files, check the disk periodically, and defragment the disk when necessary. Let's talk about these three now.

Removing Temporary Files

Temporary files and older files can clog up a hard disk and cause a decrease in performance. You can view and delete a user's temporary files by going to Run and typing %temp%. However, you might want to use a program that deletes information from multiple locations in one shot. One program used to remove these files is called Disk Cleanup. Within this program users can select which volume they want to cleanup; it then scans the volume and calculates how much space you can save. It can clean away temporary files and downloaded program files, offline web pages, Office setup files, older files, and empty the Recycle Bin. This program can be accessed from Start > All Programs > Accessories > System Tools > Disk Cleanup. It is recommended that all programs are closed prior to running Disk Cleanup.

> **Note**
>
> Another good disk cleanup program available freely on the web is called simply "CleanUp!"

You can also delete temporary files and Internet files manually. To remove temporary files manually, navigate to C:\Windows\Temp and remove any temp files and Internet files necessary. (You will need administrator access to do this.) There are also various folders within the user profile folder (for example the Recent folder) that have temporary files. However, it is easier to remove these files with one of the programs mentioned previously. Temporary Internet files and cookies can be removed by accessing the Internet Properties window by going to Start > Control Panel > Internet Options. Within the Internet Properties window's General tab, locate the Browsing History section and click Delete. This offers you the option to remove a variety of information including temporary Internet files, cookies, history, form data, and passwords.

> **Note**
>
> The preceding information about deleting information in Internet Explorer is based on Internet Explorer version 8. Other versions will be similar.

> **ExamAlert**
>
> Be able to remove temporary files from the OS and from IE for the exam.

Checking the Disk

Windows provides a program that checks for basic errors on the hard drive. You can check any volume in this manner. Simply right-click the volume in Windows Explorer and select Properties; then click the Tools tab. From here you can click the Check now button. This can check for and fix basic errors on the drive. You can also run a thorough check of the drive by selecting Scan for and attempt recovery of bad sectors. You cannot check a disk while it is in use, so remember to close all files before checking a volume. If you need to check the C: then you should schedule the check. You can schedule one, or recurring Check Disks to occur by opening the Task Scheduler, creating a basic task, and telling it to run chkdsk.exe with whatever parameters you wish. We'll talk more about this command in Chapter 11, "Troubleshooting Windows."

Defragmenting the Disk

Over time, data is written to the drive, and subsequently erased, over and over again, leaving gaps in the drivespace. New data will sometimes be written to multiple areas of the drive in a broken or fragmented fashion filling in any blank areas it can find. When this happens, the hard drive must work much harder to find the data it needs, spinning more, starting and stopping more; in general, more mechanical movement. The more the drive has to access this fragmented data, the shorter its lifespan becomes due to mechanical wear and tear. Also, the computer will run slower and continually get worse until the problem is fixed. A common indicator of this is if the hard drive LED light constantly shows activity. When this happens you need to rearrange the file sectors so that they are contiguous—you need to defragment!

Defragmenting the drive can be done with Microsoft's Disk Defragmenter, with the command-line `defrag`, or with other third-party programs. The Disk Defragmenter is located in different places depending on whether 7/Vista or XP is used:

▶ **Windows 7/Vista Disk Defragmenter:** Click Start > All Programs > Accessories > System Tools > Disk Defragmenter. The program automatically analyzes volumes and lets you know if a volume needs to be defragmented. (You can also access this by right-clicking the volume in Windows Explorer, selecting Properties, and clicking the Tools tab.)

▶ **Windows XP Disk Defragmenter:** Open Computer Management > Storage and click Disk Defragmenter. From here you have the option to analyze or defragment volumes.

If using the Disk Defragmenter program, you need 15 percent free space on the volume you want to defrag. If you have less than that, you need to use the command-line option **defrag -f**.

ExamAlert

Know how to access the disk defragmenter in Windows 7, Vista, and XP, and the defrag command in the Command Prompt.

Figure 10.1 shows the Windows 7 Disk Defragmenter. Figure 10.2 displays Windows XP's Disk Defragmenter after it has completed defragmenting the D: drive.

Before clicking the Defragment button, it's recommended that the Analyze button be clicked first to find out if the drive needs to be defragmented. If the drive requires defragmentation, Windows will tell you so. Otherwise, the program simply shows the amount that is currently fragmented. As you can see in Figure 10.1, the C: is 1% fragmented. Although this doesn't need a defrag just yet, I'll keep an eye on it and re-check it every week or so. Or better yet, I could turn on the Task Scheduler directly within the window in Figure 10.1 and schedule when I want analysis and possible defragmentation to occur.

If you do initiate a defrag it could take a while, so it's best to do this off-hours. After it completes, a restart is recommended.

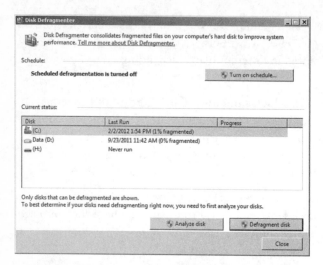

FIGURE 10.1 Windows 7 Disk Defragmenter

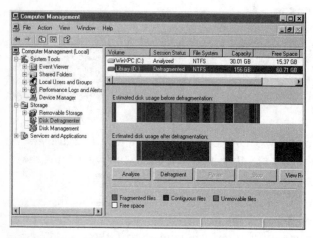

FIGURE 10.2 Windows XP Disk Defragmenter

Backups

Backing up data is critical for a company. It is not enough to rely on a fault tolerant array. Individual files or the entire system can be backed up to another set of hard disks, or to optical discs, or to tape. Windows 7, Vista, and Windows XP use three separate programs for backing up data. They are each accessed in different ways, but work in similar ways.

Using Windows 7's Backup and Restore

Backup and Restore can back up individual files, create an image of the system, and create a system repair disc. You might have to set up the backup program prior to use, depending on your configuration. To create a backup with Windows 7's Backup and Restore:

1. Start Backup and Restore by accessing Start > Control Panel > Backup and Restore. (If in category mode, add the step System and Security after Control Panel.)

2. Click the Set Up Backup link (if necessary) or the Back Up Now button if a backup device has already been set up. You need to have an external storage device, second hard drive, or second partition to backup to. If no device or media can be found, the only other option is to back up to the network.

3. Select the media or partition you want to back up to, and click Next.

4. Select whether Windows will automatically back up data or choose your own files to be backed up, and click Next.

5. Select the folders and files you want to backup and whether to include a system image of each drive; then click Next.

6. Review the settings, and click the Save Settings and Backup button. This initiates the backup. Backups can be restored using this program as well.

After you have set up what you want to backup, scheduled backups are automatically configured to run every week. You can disable this by clicking the Turn Off Schedule link. You can modify when the automatic backups occur by clicking the Change Settings link. Go through the backup questions again until you get to the Review your backup settings page. From there click the Change Schedule link to tell the system when to automatically backup.

> **Note**
>
> You can also initiate backups of volumes by right-clicking the volume in Windows Explorer, clicking Properties, and clicking the Tools tab.

Using Windows Vista's Backup Status and Configuration

Backup Status and Configuration is the successor to Windows XP's NTBackup. It can back up individual files or an entire image of your system (using Complete PC Backup) to the removable media of your choice, for example DVD. To create a complete backup of your PC with Vista's Complete PC Backup:

1. Start the Complete PC Backup by going to Start > All Programs > Accessories > System Tools > Backup Status and Configuration.

2. Click the Complete PC Backup button.

3. Select Create a backup now and follow the directions. Have media ready that can hold an image of your operating system, for example DVD-R. Be ready; this will be a sizeable image!

Using Windows XP's NTBackup

Windows XP Professional offers the built-in program called NTBackup. This is accessible by opening the Run prompt and typing **ntbackup**. From here you can backup individual files and back up the System State, which includes everything that makes one installation of Windows XP different from another. Unfortunately, Windows XP does not include a Complete PC Backup option; however, the Automated System Recovery (ASR) option in NTBackup does enable you to back up and restore the system state (user accounts, settings, boot files, and so on).

To create an ASR backup with NTBackup:

1. Switch to Advanced Mode (if NTBackup starts in Wizard mode) and click the Automated System Recovery Wizard button. When the wizard's opening dialog appears, click Next to continue.

2. Specify where to store the backup, and click Next.

3. Click Finish to complete the wizard. You will be asked to provide a floppy disk to store configuration files.

> **ExamAlert**
>
> Be able to demonstrate how to back up data in 7, Vista, and XP.

Creating Restore Points

System Restore can fix issues caused by defective hardware or software by reverting back to an earlier time. Registry changes made by hardware or software are reversed in an attempt to force the computer to work the way it did previously. Restore points can be created manually and are also created automatically by the operating system before new applications, or hardware is installed.

To create a restore point in Windows 7/Vista:

1. Right-click Computer and select Properties. This opens the System Properties window. Then click the System Protection link. This displays the System Protection tab of the System Properties dialog box, as shown in Figure 10.3.

2. Click the Create button. This opens the System Protection dialog box.

3. Enter a name for the restore point, and click Create.

Alternatively, you can go to Start > All Programs > Accessories > System Tools > System Restore to create a restore point.

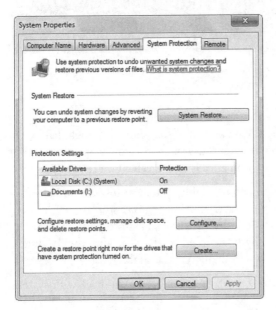

FIGURE 10.3 **The System Protection Tab of the System Properties Dialog Box in Windows 7**

To create a restore point in Windows XP:

1. Navigate to Start > All Programs > Accessories > System Tools > System Restore. This opens the System Restore window.

2. Click Create a Restore Point and then click Next.

3. Enter a name for the restore point and click Create.

If System Restore is not available, it might be turned off. There are several reasons why a person might turn it off, for example if the system were scanned for viruses recently.

To enable or disable system restore in Windows 7, click the Configure button within the System Protection tab of the System Properties dialog box. In Windows Vista you can enable or disable System Restore on any volume by simply checking or unchecking the volume that you want to enable or disable. Within Windows XP, the state of System Restore affects all drives; you can turn the utility on and off only. This is done from the System Restore tab of the System Properties dialog box. You can also change the amount of disk space it uses here.

ExamAlert

Understand how to enable and disable System Restore, and how to create restore points.

Shadow Copy

Shadow Copy, or the Volume Snapshot Service, is a Windows technology that allows you to make backup copies of data known as snapshots. It is included in Windows 7 and Vista, and is dependent on the Volume Shadow Copy service. The data can be backed up manually or automatically and is reliant on restore points.

To use this service you would first need to enable system restore on one or more volumes as mentioned in the previous section. After that is complete, Windows creates shadow copies of files automatically whenever a restore point is created. You can find out if a file has been shadow copied by right-clicking the file and selecting Properties, and clicking the Previous Versions tab.

Figure 10.4 shows an example of a text file that is stored on a drive with system restore enabled.

System Restore was configured for the I: drive of the computer. This means that any files within that drive will be shadow copied. As you can see in the figure, a restore point was created on 3/16/2012. When that happened, the file Shadow Copy Test1.txt was shadow copied. If the file were somehow modified and the user wanted an older version, you could open or restore that older version from here.

There are a few caveats to all this. First, Shadow Copy does not take the place of an actual file backup. Second, restored files that were Shadow Copied can at times have missing data or other errors. Lastly, System Restore and Shadow Copy work decently on the system partition where the OS is stored. But they can seriously slow down a system when used on data volumes, especially seeing as how additional Shadow Copies of the files will be made each time they are modified.

FIGURE 10.4 **Previous Versions tab of a text file**

Users should be encouraged to backup data with one of the programs mentioned in the "Backups" section previously. Shadow Copy does not take the place of a backup; it should be treated as a supplement to a regular file backup and only used as a last resort. A final word on this, due to the drawbacks of Shadow Copy, Microsoft is developing new technology to replace this service in future generations of Windows.

ExamAlert

Know what Shadow Copy is and where to find Shadow Copies of files.

Cram Quiz

220-802 Questions

Answer these questions. The answers follow the last question. If you cannot answer these questions correctly, consider reading this section again until you can.

    1. Which program removes temporary files?

        ○ **A.** Disk Backup

        ○ **B.** Disk Cleanup

        ○ **C.** System Restore

        ○ **D.** Disk Defragmenter

2. If there is less than 15 percent free space within a volume, how would a user defragment it in Windows?

- ○ **A.** With Disk Defragmenter
- ○ **B.** With the command `defragment -f`
- ○ **C.** With the command `defrag -f`
- ○ **D.** With a third-party tool

3. Which program in Windows Vista creates a Complete PC Backup?

- ○ **A.** Backup Status and Configuration
- ○ **B.** NTBackup
- ○ **C.** ASR
- ○ **D.** System Restore

4. Where would you go in Windows 7 to enable System Restore? (Select the best answer.)

- ○ **A.** System Properties window
- ○ **B.** Advanced Protection tab of the System Properties window
- ○ **C.** Task Manager
- ○ **D.** System Protection tab of the System Properties window

5. Which program in Windows 7 allows you to backup files?

- ○ **A.** Backup Status and Configuration
- ○ **B.** Backup and Restore
- ○ **C.** NTBackup
- ○ **D.** System Restore

6. Which program in Windows 7 should not be used to backup data?

- ○ **A.** Backup Status and Configuration
- ○ **B.** Backup and Restore
- ○ **C.** Shadow Copy
- ○ **D.** NTBackup

7. One of your customers complains that applications take a long time to load and that the LED light on the front of the computer is constantly blinking. What is the most likely cause?

- ○ **A.** The power supply is faulty.
- ○ **B.** The processor is faulty.
- ○ **C.** The motherboard is sending faulty signals to the LED.
- ○ **D.** The file system is fragmented.

8. Which of the following is accomplished by defragging a disk?

○ **A.** File sectors are made contiguous.

○ **B.** The disk is checked for errors.

○ **C.** The MBR is rewritten.

○ **D.** The pagefile size is increased.

Cram Quiz Answers

220-802 Answers

1. **B.** Disk Cleanup removes temporary files and other types of files and clears the recycle bin.

2. **C.** `defrag` **-f** defragments the drive even if free space is low. However, be prepared to use a lot of system resources to complete the defrag. Close any open windows before starting the process.

3. **A.** Backup Status and Configuration has an option called Complete PC Backup within Windows Vista. NTBackup is a Windows XP program that can back up individual files and the System State but not the entire PC. ASR is the Automated System Recovery option in Windows XP that backs up the System State and other data. System Restore creates restore points that deals more with settings than it does data.

4. **D.** To enable (or disable) System Restore in Windows 7/Vista, go to the System Protection tab of the System Properties window.

5. **B.** The Backup and Restore program allows you to back up files in Windows 7. Backup Status and Configuration is used in Windows Vista. NTBackup is used in Windows XP. System Restore is available on all three operating systems.

6. **C.** Shadow Copy should not be used to *back up* data. It should be used to restore data only in the chance that a real backup is not available. It is a last resort. Real backup programs should be used depending on the operating system you are working with. The Backup and Restore program allows you to back up files in Windows 7. Backup Status and Configuration is used in Windows Vista. NTBackup is used in Windows XP to back up files.

7. **D.** If applications are loading slowly, and the hard drive LED light is constantly active, then the hard drive is most likely fragmented. A defrag is in order. The other answers are hardware-based and should not be the cause of those symptoms.

8. **A.** When you defrag the disk, all the file sectors are straightened out and made contiguous. This makes the disk more efficient. CHKDSK or SFC checks a drive for errors. The pagefile can be increased by the user in the System Properties dialog box. The master boor record would be updated if the FIXMBR command were issued.

CHAPTER 11

Troubleshooting Windows

This chapter covers the following A+ exam topics:

▶ Repair Environments and Boot Errors

▶ Windows Tools and Errors

▶ Command-Line Tools

You can find a master list of A+ exam topics in the "Introduction."

This chapter covers CompTIA A+ 220-802 objectives 1.2, 1.3, 1.4, 1.7, and 4.6.

Now for the toughest part of working with Windows: troubleshooting. Before beginning this chapter, I recommend that you review the six-step troubleshooting process in Chapter 1, "Introduction to Troubleshooting." As I mentioned in Chapter 1, troubleshooting is the most important skill for a computer technician to possess. There are many different things that can go wrong in a computer; the majority of them are software-related. This chapter endeavors to give you the tools, utilities, and skills necessary to troubleshoot the various boot errors, stop errors, and other Windows errors that you might encounter.

Repair Environments and Boot Errors

Windows startup errors prevent you from accessing the operating system. Because of this, Windows 7, Vista, and XP have various startup tools, menus, and repair environments that you can use to troubleshoot these startup and boot errors.

Windows Repair Tools

There are many tools included with Windows 7, Vista, and XP designed to help you troubleshoot and repair just about any issue that might come up. Before getting into the exact issues you might face, let's discuss some of these advanced repair and pre-installation environment repair tools, what they do, and where you can access them. Let's start with the Advanced Boot Options menu.

Advanced Boot Options Menu

If Windows 7/Vista/XP won't start and you don't see an error message, the culprit might be a video driver, new configuration, or other system issues. There are several startup options that can aid in fixing the problem. To access these startup options, press the F8 key immediately after the computer starts up; this brings up the Windows Advanced Boot Options menu, as shown in Figure 11.1.

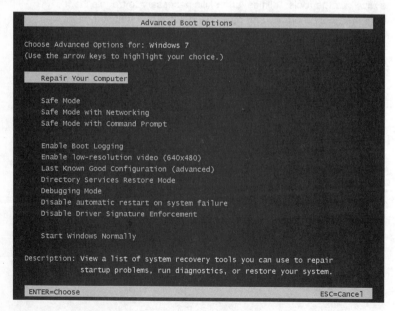

FIGURE 11.1   Windows 7 Advanced Boot Options menu

The following options are included in the Advanced Boot Options menu (also known as ABOM):

- ▶ **Safe Mode:** Starts system with a minimal set of drivers; used in case one of the drivers fails. Safe Mode is a good option when attempting to use System Restore and when scanning systems for viruses.

- ▶ **Safe Mode with Networking:** Starts system with a minimal set of drivers and enables network support.

- ▶ **Safe Mode with Command Prompt:** Starts system with a minimal set of drivers but loads command prompt instead of Windows GUI.

- ▶ **Enable Boot Logging:** Creates a ntbtlog.txt file.

- ▶ **Enable low-resolution video (640x480):** Uses a standard VGA driver in place of a GPU-specific display driver but uses all other drivers as normal. (This is called Enable VGA Mode in Windows XP.)

- ▶ **Last Known Good Configuration:** Starts the system with the last configuration known to work; useful for solving problems caused by newly installed hardware or software. The last known good (LKG) configuration is derived from the most recent successful login.

- ▶ **Directory Services Restore Mode:** This is used to restore a domain controller's active directory (Windows Server). Even though it is listed, it is not used in Windows 7/Vista/XP.

- ▶ **Debugging Mode:** Enables the use of a debug program to examine the system kernel for troubleshooting.

- ▶ **Disable automatic restart on system failure (7 and Vista only):** Prevents Windows from automatically restarting, if an error causes Windows to fail. Choose this option only if Windows is stuck in a loop in which Windows fails, attempts to restart, and fails again repeatedly.

- ▶ **Disable driver signature enforcement (7 and Vista only):** Enables drivers containing improper signatures to be installed.

- ▶ **Start Windows Normally:** This can be used to boot to regular Windows. This option is listed in case a person inadvertently pressed F8 but did not want to use any of the Advanced Boot Options.

ExamAlert

Know the Advanced Boot Options for the exam.

If Windows 7/Vista fails to start properly, and then restarts automatically, it normally displays the Windows Error Recovery screen and gives you the following options: Safe Mode, Safe Mode with Networking, Safe Mode with Command Prompt, Last Known Good Configuration, and Start Windows Normally. This means that Windows has acknowledged some sort of error or improper shut down and offers a truncated version of the Advanced Options Boot menu.

> **Note**
>
> There is a small window of time available to press F8; it's right between the BIOS and when the normal operating system boots. Press F8 repeatedly right after the BIOS POST begins.
>
> It is recommended that you attempt to repair a computer with the Advanced Boot Options *before* using the Windows 7/Vista System Recovery Options or Windows XP's Recovery Console.

Windows Recovery Environment (WinRE)

WinRE is a set of tools included in Windows 7, Windows Vista, Windows Server 2008, and other upcoming Windows operating systems. It takes the place of the Recovery Console used in Windows XP. Also known as System Recovery Options, WinRE's purpose is to recover Windows from errors that prevent it from booting; it can also be instrumental in fixing issues that cause a computer to "freeze" up. There are two possible ways to access WinRE:

> ▶ **Booting to the Windows 7/Vista DVD:** This option is more common with an individual computer that had Windows installed; for example, if you performed a clean installation with the standard Windows DVD and made no modifications to it. To start WinRE, make sure that the DVD drive is first in the boot order of the BIOS, boot to the Windows DVD (as if you were starting the installation), choose your language settings and click next, and then select Repair Your Computer, which you can find at the lower-left corner of the screen. Select the Use Recovery Tools radio button and click Next.

> **Note**
>
> Important! Do not select Install Now because that would begin the process of reinstalling Windows on your hard drive.

> ▶ **Booting to a special partition on the hard drive that has WinRE installed:** This option is used by OEMs (original equipment manufacturers) so that users can access WinRE without having to search for and

boot off of a Windows DVD. These OEMs (computer builders and system integrators) will preinstall WinRE into a special partition on the hard drive, separate from the operating system, so the user can boot into it at any time. Compare this to the older Recovery Console that was installed into the same partition as the operating system. To access WinRE that has been preinstalled, press F8 to bring up the Advanced Boot Options menu, highlight Repair Your Computer, and press Enter. If you don't see Repair Your Computer in the Advanced Boot Options menu, then it wasn't installed to the hard drive, and you have to use option 1, booting from the DVD. Note that you can still use option 1, even if WinRE was installed to the hard drive; for example, in a scenario where the hard drive installation of WinRE has failed.

> **Note**
>
> The process to install WinRE to the hard drive is a rather complicated one and is not covered on the A+ exam. However, if you are interested, here is a link that gives the basics of installing WinRE: http://blogs.msdn.com/winre/archive/2007/01/12/how-to-install-winre-on-the-hard-disk.aspx.

Regardless of which option you selected, at this point a window named System Recovery Options should appear. There are two options: one prompting you to select an operating system to repair and the other option is to restore from a previously made image. To access the System Recovery Option, leave the first option selected. Most users will have only one OS listed. Regardless, highlight the appropriate operating system in need of repair and click Next. This displays the options at your disposal, as shown in Figure 11.2. Table 11.1 describes these options in more depth.

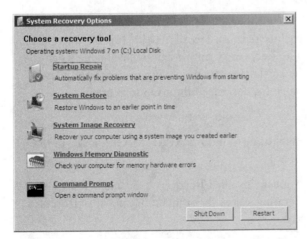

FIGURE 11.2   Windows 7 System Recovery Options window

TABLE 11.1   **Description of the Windows 7/Vista System Recovery Options**

System Recovery Option	Description
Startup Repair	When clicked, this automatically fixes certain problems, such as missing or damaged system files that might prevent Windows from starting correctly. When you run Startup Repair, it scans your computer for the problem and then tries to fix it so your computer can start correctly.
System Restore	Restores the computer's system files to an earlier point in time. It's a way to undo system changes to your computer without affecting your personal files, such as email, documents, or photos. Note: If you use System Restore when the computer is in safe mode, you cannot undo the restore operation. However, you can run System Restore again and choose a different restore point, if one exists.
System Image Recovery (Win7) Windows Complete PC Restore (Vista)	This restores the contents of a hard disk from a backup. System Image Recovery is included only in Windows 7 Professional and Ultimate. Windows Complete PC Backup and Restore is included only with Vista Business and Vista Ultimate.
Windows Memory Diagnostic Tool	Scans the computer's memory for errors.
Command Prompt (Replaces the Recovery Console in XP)	Advanced users can use the Command Prompt to perform recovery-related operations and also run other command-line tools for diagnosing and troubleshooting problems. Puts the user into a directory called X:\Sources. Works much like the previous Recovery Console in Windows XP, with the addition of a few new commands.

Recovery Console

The Windows XP Recovery Console is the command-line interface used for repairs such as rebuilding the master boot record (MBR). It is included on the Windows XP CD-ROM. The Recovery Console can be invaluable when the system cannot start from the hard drive due to missing or corrupted files. These missing files could block the Advanced Boot Options menu.

To start Windows XP's Recovery Console, you have two options:

Option 1:   Boot the computer to the Windows XP CD-ROM, and run the Recovery Console.

Option 2:   Boot from a previously installed Recovery Console. This appears as part of the operating system boot menu but not if startup files have been affected.

To run the Recovery Console from CD-ROM:

1. Boot the system from the Windows XP CD.

2. When prompted, press R to start the Recovery Console.

3. Log into Recovery Console by selecting the installation to log into and providing the Administrator password for the operating system.

To install the Recovery Console to hard disk:

1. While in Windows, insert the Windows CD-ROM into the drive. (Close any pop-up install windows.)

2. Open the Run prompt and type `x:\i386\winnt32.exe /cmdcons`. (For this scenario, x is the drive letter for the CD-ROM drive, this is usually D: but can vary from system to system.)

3. Confirm the installation by clicking Yes and restart the computer. Now, Microsoft Windows Recovery Console should appear on the boot menu. Select it to start Recovery Console.

ExamAlert

Memorize the different WinRE options in 7/Vista, and know how to use the Recovery Console in XP.

Repair Installations

If all the previous methods don't fix the problems you are experiencing, there is one more thing you can try before wiping the drive and doing a clean installation, and that's a repair installation. There are a couple ways to do this with Windows 7.

First, you could try advanced recovery. Go to Control Panel > Recovery. When in the Recovery window, click the Advanced recovery methods link. From here you have two options. First is the use a system image that you created earlier to recover the computer (similar to some of the image restore options mentioned earlier), and second is to reinstall windows. The second option requires you to back up your files and then reinstall applications and restore the files when the reinstall of the OS is complete. Existing files *might* remain in a folder named Windows.old. This method can also be done by simply inserting the OS DVD and starting setup, making sure to select Upgrade when the time comes. This is known as a Repair/In-Place Upgrade.

The other way is to boot to the DVD and access the disc in Windows Explorer. Locate the setup.exe file, right-click it, and select Properties. Click the Compatibility tab, and check the Run This Program in Compatibility Mode For check box. In the drop-down menu select Windows Vista (Service Pack 2). Run the setup as usual and select the Upgrade option. Again, if user settings are missing, they can be found in the Windows.old folder.

These can be tricky, time-consuming solutions, plus they might not work correctly; therefore they should be your last resort for repairing Windows.

Boot Errors

There are various reasons why a computer will fail to boot. If it is operating system-related, you usually get some type of message that can help you to troubleshoot the problem. Windows 7/Vista and Windows XP have different boot files, so it stands to reason that they have different boot error messages.

Windows 7/Vista Boot Errors

Windows 7/Vista uses the bootmgr and BCD files during the startup process. If these files are corrupted or missing, you see corresponding error messages:

▸ **BOOTMGR is missing:** This message displays if the bootmgr file is missing or corrupt. This black screen probably also says Press Ctrl+Alt+ Del to Restart; however doing so will probably have the same results.

There are two methods to repair this error. The first is to boot to the System Recovery Options and select the Startup Repair option. This should automatically repair the system and require you to reboot. If this doesn't work, try the second method, which is to boot to the System Recovery Options and select the Command Prompt option. Type the command **bootrec /fixboot**, as shown in Figure 11.3.

FIGURE 11.3   Repairing BOOTMGR.exe with Windows 7's WinRE Command Prompt

▶ **The Windows Boot Configuration Data file is missing required information:** This message means that either the Windows Boot Manager (Bootmgr) entry is not present in the Boot Configuration Data (BCD) store; or the Boot\BCD file on the active partition is damaged or missing. Additional information you might see on the screen includes File: \Boot\BCD, and Status: 0xc0000034. Unfortunately, this means that the BCD store needs to be repaired or rebuilt. Hold on to your hat; there are three methods of repair for this error:

The first method of repair is to boot to the System Recovery Options and select the Startup Repair option. This should automatically repair the system and require you to reboot. If not, move on to method 2.

The second method of repair is to boot to the System Recovery Options and select the Command Prompt option. Type **bootrec /rebuildbcd**. At this point the bootrec.exe tool either succeeds or fails. If the Bootrec.exe tool runs successfully, it displays an installation path to a Windows directory. To add this entry to the BCD store, type **Yes**. A confirmation message appears that indicates the entry was added successfully.

If the Bootrec.exe tool can't locate any missing Windows installations, you have to remove the BCD store and then re-create it. To do this, type the following commands:

```
Bcdedit /export C:\BCD_Backup
ren c:\boot\bcd bcd.old
Bootrec /rebuildbcd
```

Methods one and two usually work, but if not, there is a third method which is more in depth and requires rebuilding the BCD store manually. For more information you can find this step-by-step process at the following link: http://support.microsoft.com/kb/927391.

Windows XP Boot Errors

Windows XP uses the NTLDR (boot loader), Boot.ini, NTDETECT.COM, and Ntoskrnl.exe files during startup. If any of these files are corrupted or missing, you see one of the following error messages:

▶ **NTDETECT failed:** This displays if the NTDETECT.COM file is missing or corrupt.

▶ **NTLDR is missing:** This displays if the NTLDR file is missing or corrupt.

▶ **Invalid boot.ini:** This displays if the boot.ini file is missing or corrupt. In some cases, the operating system boots anyway because there is usually only one disk partition on the hard disk. If not, the file needs to be recopied to the hard disk.

▶ It should be noted that commands, such as fixboot and fixmbr, can be used in the Windows XP Recovery Console to fix issues such as "NTLDR is Missing" or other issues where a virus has infected the Master Boot Record.

To repair these issues, you can

▶ Reboot to the Windows CD and access the Recovery Console; then recopy the file from the Windows CD-ROM or from backup media.

▶ Repair the installation or restore Windows. (More on restoring Windows later in this chapter).

(Exam**Alert**)

Know how to recover from Windows 7, Vista, and XP boot errors.

Cram Quiz

Answer these questions. The answers follow the last question. If you cannot answer these questions correctly, consider reading this section again until you can.

220-802 Questions

1. Which option starts the system with a minimal set of drivers?
   - ○ **A.** Last Known Good Configuration
   - ○ **B.** System Restore
   - ○ **C.** Safe Mode
   - ○ **D.** Debugging Mode

2. Which tool should be used if a person wanted to do Startup Repair in Windows 7?
   - ○ **A.** Recovery Console
   - ○ **B.** WinRE
   - ○ **C.** System Restore
   - ○ **D.** Safe Mode

3. What switch should be used to install the Recovery Console to a hard drive?
   - ○ **A.** /recovery
   - ○ **B.** /winnt32
   - ○ **C.** /console
   - ○ **D.** /cmdcons

4. What command repairs the bootmgr.exe file in Windows 7/Vista?
   - ○ **A.** bootrec /fixboot
   - ○ **B.** bootrec /fixmbr

○ **C.** bootrec /rebuildbcd

○ **D.** boot\bcd

5. Which tool should be used to fix the NTLDR if it is missing or corrupt?

    ○ **A.** Safe Mode

    ○ **B.** bootrec /fixmbr

    ○ **C.** Recovery Console

    ○ **D.** WinRE

6. One of your customers went ahead and updated the software for a wireless adapter on a PC. After rebooting the user logs in and the computer displays a blue screen. What should you do?

    ○ **A.** Install the device on a known good computer.

    ○ **B.** Reboot the computer and use the Last Known Good Configuration.

    ○ **C.** Purchase a new wireless adapter.

    ○ **D.** Roll back the device drivers in Safe Mode.

Cram Quiz Answers

220-802 Answers

1. **C.** Safe Mode starts the operating system with a minimal set of drivers.

2. **B.** WinRE (System Recovery Options) includes Startup Repair. The Recovery Console is used by Windows XP. Safe Mode is part of the Advanced Boot Options menu, and System Restore is a different tool that is also available in WinRE and can be used in Windows XP as well.

3. **D.** /cmdcons is the switch (or option) that is added to the winnt32.exe command.

4. **A.** bootrec /fixboot is one of the methods you can try to repair bootmgr.exe in Windows 7/Vista. Bootrec /fixmbr rewrites the master boot record in 7/Vista. Bootrec /rebuildbcd attempts to rebuild the boot configuration store, and boot\bcd is where the boot configuration store is located.

5. **C.** The Recovery Console can be used to repair NTLDR if it is missing or corrupt. Safe Mode enables a user to boot into Windows with a minimal set of drivers, but this would be impossible if NTLDR is malfunctioning or nonexistent. Bootrec /fixmbr rewrites the master boot record in Windows 7/Vista. WinRE is the Windows Recovery Environment in Windows 7/Vista.

6. **D.** You should boot into Safe Mode and roll back the drivers of the device in the Device Manager. The drivers that the customer installed were probably corrupt and caused the Stop error. No need to remove the device and install it anywhere just yet. Last Known Good Configuration won't work because the user has already logged in. Never purchase new equipment until you have exhausted all other ideas!

Windows Tools and Errors

Windows could fail while you work within the operating system. Quite often, error messages accompany these failures. There are various Windows repair tools you can use to troubleshoot these issues. The worst possible scenario is when Windows fails and cannot be repaired. In these cases, a restoration is necessary. There are several types of restoration techniques available to you in Windows as well. But before restoring the system, because it can be time-consuming and possibly unnecessary, you should attempt to troubleshoot with Windows repair tools first.

Troubleshooting Within Windows

If there are not any boot errors, then Windows should start and operate properly. However, errors (recoverable ones) can occur while Windows runs. Devices can fail, applications can terminate for various reasons, and hardware could suffer performance issues.

Troubleshooting Tool

The Windows 7 Troubleshooting tool (within the Control Panel) is your first step to troubleshoot errors that happen while Windows is running. It is an automated program that tries to figure out what has gone wrong and fix it while you sit there sipping Earl Grey tea, or whatever it is you kids do these days. From this tool you can have Windows troubleshoot program issues, hardware problems, network and Internet connectivity difficulties, and security glitches. If for some reason you do not want Windows to automatically troubleshoot errors that occur, click the Change settings link; then click the Off radio button in Computer Maintenance.

If you are lucky, Windows will fix the problem for you. However, the majority of problems you face need to be fixed manually...by you. Let's get into the tools you will be troubleshooting within Windows.

Device Manager

The Device Manager can detect if a device is malfunctioning, if it has the wrong driver installed, if it has a conflicting resource (like an IRQ or I/O setting), or if it has been disabled. Figure 11.4 shows a malfunctioning PCI Simple Communications Controller (highlighted). You know it's malfunctioning because of the exclamation mark (!) within a yellow triangle. If a device is disabled, this will be displayed as a down arrow in Windows 7/Vista, as shown in the AMD device in the figure. (In Windows XP a disabled item is shown by a red X.) These devices won't work properly until they are fixed.

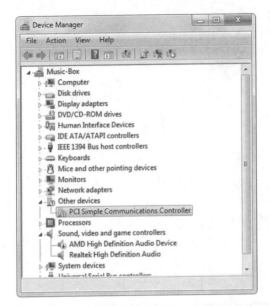

FIGURE 11.4 **Device Manager window in Windows 7 showing a malfunctioning device and a disabled device**

ExamAlert

Know what the exclamation point, down arrow, and red X indicate in the Device Manager.

Of course, we can't just leave these devices this way! A clean Device Manager is a good sign of a healthy computer. When a user opens this program, they should see nothing but collapsed categories; none of them should be open. Conflicting resources like IRQs and I/O settings are for the most part a thing of the past and are controlled automatically. But it is certainly possible for a device driver issue. Perhaps the driver failed, or the wrong one was installed initially, or a device was updated with the wrong type of driver. Either way, you would need to repair it by opening Control Panel > Device Manager, right-clicking on the device with the exclamation point, and selecting Properties. Look at Figure 11.5. Notice in the Device status area that it says The drivers for this Device Are Not Installed (Code 28). Well, the solution is obvious; you need to install the driver! In reality, I neglected to install this driver for demonstration purposes. The PCI Simple Communications Controller is part of the Intel DP67DE motherboard in *Media PC*. These controllers are sometimes used for HD audio or for internal modems or similar devices.

FIGURE 11.5   **PCI Simple Communications Controller Properties window**

To repair this, you have a few options. Your first instinct might tell you to click the Update Driver button. In some cases this might locate and install the correct driver automatically. But you might remember me saying previously: "Get the driver from the manufacturer's disc or website"; in fact I probably sound like a broken record. But that is the right course for this situation.

In this case, what I neglected to install was the Intel Management Engine driver. It is located on the disc, but I could and probably would search for the latest version on the Intel website.

Internet installs are usually quite easy; download the .exe (or .zip) file and double-click it to install. But if the driver is already on the computer, it might be a bit more detailed. For example, you might need to find a specific .inf file, or you might need to search for the driver within Windows' driver database (a manual install). If you install the driver within the Device Manager do the following:

1. In the Properties window of the device, click the Driver tab.

2. Click Update Driver. (You could also click the Update Driver button in the General tab.)

3. Select whether you would like Windows to search for the driver, or whether you will manually do it.

If Windows fails in its search, you have to manually find the driver. You need to specify the manufacturer and model of the device and either find the driver file on the hard disk or supply your own media. If this fails, then you are back to square one and must locate the correct driver on the Internet. But I'll let you in on a secret: *Every* driver is on the Internet...somewhere. And if you download the driver from the manufacturer, you don't have to risk a Microsoft version of the driver being installed.

As mentioned, a down arrow or a red X on a device means that it has been disabled. To enable it, simply right-click it and select Enable. You can also enable it on the Driver tab of its Properties sheet. Enabling some devices require a restart.

It is possible in older Windows operating systems to create a hardware profile that disables certain devices. To find out if a hardware profile is used, restart the computer and watch for a hardware profile menu when the computer first boots.

Codes can be helpful when troubleshooting issues with devices. If a device is malfunctioning or is configured incorrectly, it should show a code number within its Properties sheet on the General tab. Table 11.2 gives a few examples of these codes.

TABLE 11.2 **Description of Codes in the Device Manager**

Device Manager Code Number	Problem	Recommended Solution
Code 1	This device is not configured correctly.	Update the driver.
Code 3	The driver for this device might be corrupted, or your system might be running low on memory or other resources.	Close some open applications. Uninstall and reinstall the driver. Install additional RAM.
Code 10	Device cannot start.	Update the driver. View Microsoft Support article 943104 for more information.
Code 12	This device cannot find enough free resources that it can use. If you want to use this device, you need to disable one of the other devices on this system.	You can use the Troubleshooting Wizard in Device Manager to determine where the conflict is, and then disable the conflicting device.

Note

These are just a few examples of the codes you might see in the Device Manager. For more information, see the following links: http://support.microsoft.com/kb/310123 and http://support.microsoft.com/kb/943104.

Event Viewer

Applications are a boon and a bane to mankind. They serve a purpose, but sometimes they are prone to failure. The operating system itself can cause you grief as well by underperforming, locking up, or causing other intermittent issues. One good tool for analyzing applications and the system is the Event Viewer.

The Event Viewer tells a technician a lot about the status of the operating system and programs. It notifies of any informational events or audits, warns about possible issues, and displays errors as they occur. It can be accessed from Start > All Programs > Administrative Tools, or through the System Tools node in the Computer Management console window (or by typing eventvwr.msc in the RUN or Search prompts). Information, auditing entries, warnings, and errors are stored in log files. In 7/Vista they are inside a folder called Windows Logs; in XP they are directly within the Event Viewer. There are three main log files located inside the Event Viewer that you should know for the exam:

▶ **System:** The System log contains information, warnings, and errors about hardware, device drivers, system files, and so on. This log deals primarily with the operating system.

▶ **Application:** The Application log contains events about programs that are built into Windows, such as the Command Prompt or Windows Explorer, and might contain information about applications that have been loaded after the operating system was installed.

▶ **Security:** The Security log holds information that was gathered for auditing and security purposes; for example, it might log who logged on to the computer, or who tried to gain access to a particular file.

An event can be viewed by double-clicking it. Events are broken into four categories:

▶ **Information**—Indicated by an "i" in a circle. This tells you basic information about a service starting or an application that ran successfully. The log files are usually chock-full of these as part of the normal operation of the system.

▶ **Warning**—Indicated by an exclamation point "!" within a yellow triangle. This might be messages telling you an installation did not complete or a service timed out. You should check for these now and again and investigate them if nothing else is pressing.

▶ **Error**—Indicated by an exclamation point "!" in a red circle. (An "X" in Windows XP.) This means that something failed or has been corrupted, a service failed to start, and so on. Errors should be investigated right away.

▶ **Audit Success**—Indicated by a gold colored key; these entries are located within the Security log file. They track what a user attempts to accomplish within the operating system. For example, if auditing was turned on for a specific folder, and a person attempted to access that folder, a security event would be written to the log, especially if the person was denied access. Auditing entries are maintained by organizations so that they can trace what happened to deleted or modified data.

You can find more information about a specific error code by either typing in the code number for the event or typing the description into Microsoft Help and Support: http://support.microsoft.com. Sometimes you can find out information about these types of services just by running a search, but it is best to go to the source: Microsoft. You never know when an error can occur, so the Event Viewer logs should be reviewed regularly. Entire logs can be erased by right-clicking the log file (for example, System) and selecting Clear Log. The system asks if you want to save the log for future viewing. By right-clicking a log and selecting Properties, you can modify the maximum size of the log and disable logging altogether.

> **ExamAlert**
>
> Be able to describe the System, Application, and Security log files, and the information, warning, error, and audit success events for the exam.

Problem Reports and Solutions, the Action Center, and Dr. Watson

Problem Reports and Solutions is a program in Windows Vista that can be accessed directly within the Classic view of the Control Panel. Problem Reports and Solutions enables you to check for solutions to hardware and software problems. Windows can be set to report problems and check for solutions automatically, or solutions can be checked for manually when a problem occurs. To modify how problems will be reported, click the Change settings link. Problem descriptions and solutions are saved, for later viewing.

In Windows 7 this functionality is built into the Action Center, which can be accessed by clicking its icon in the Notification Area of the taskbar or by navigating to Start > Control Panel > System and Security > Action Center. Chapter 16, "Security," talks more about the Action Center.

This program took the place of Dr. Watson in Windows XP that was used as a system and application failure analysis tool. Dr. Watson can be accessed in XP by opening the Run prompt and typing `drwtsn32`. Application failures that are listed in Dr. Watson are rare and are often listed in the Application log of the Event Viewer as well.

Performance

There are several tools you can use to track the performance of a PC or laptop. Windows 7 uses the Performance Monitor and Resource Monitor. Windows Vista uses the Reliability and Performance Monitor. Windows XP makes use of Performance. These programs track how much your devices are utilized; for example, what percentage of the processor is used, or how much RAM is currently being accessed.

Most of these utilities, including the Performance Monitor, are accessed from Administrative Tools. However, you can find the Resource Monitor in Start > All Programs > Accessories > System Tools. The Resource Monitor tracks the usage of the CPU, disks, network, and memory; these are ActiveX graphs like the ones used in the Performance tab of the Task Manager. They are done in real-time but are not stored. To customize what you want to track, and save the information, use the Performance Monitor, as shown in Figure 11.6.

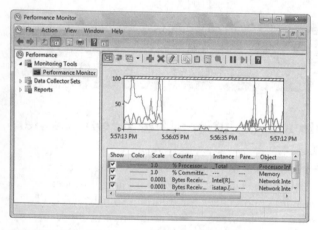

FIGURE 11.6   **Performance Monitor in Windows 7**

By clicking Performance Monitor, you can track the usage of any device in the computer (known as objects), in a variety of measurements (known as counters). By default this screen tracks only the CPU. By clicking the + sign toward the top of the window, you can add devices to track, and in a myriad of ways. In Figure 11.6 I added the default counters for memory and the network adapter card. The highest spikes are from the network adapter; at the time of this monitor, it is sending and receiving a lot of data over the Internet. The second highest levels are from the processor, which is running about seven real-time applications simultaneously.

Information can be viewed in different formats such as line charts and histograms and can also be viewed and saved in Report view. They can be exported as well. However, any objects that are added in this program are not saved when you close the window. But you can configure the program so that it saves your additions; enter the MMC. From an MMC a user in Windows 7 can add the Performance Monitor. Other versions of Windows can use the ActiveX Control called System Monitor which *is* the Performance Monitor. You can also add Performance Logs and Alerts to log your findings and alert you to any changes or tripped thresholds. The MMC saves its contents and remembers the last place you were working in, which works great if you are going to be analyzing the same things day in and day out.

The Performance Monitor (and similar Windows applications) can tell you a lot about the functionality of your computer. When troubleshooting why a certain piece of hardware isn't living up to its reputation, it can be invaluable.

Windows Memory Diagnostics

Chapter 4, "RAM," talked about several ways to troubleshoot RAM. One way is to use Windows Memory Diagnostics. Now you might need to check your memory while within Windows, or perhaps Windows won't boot and you want to check the memory from bootup. Because of this, there are a few ways to open this tool: within Administrative Tools, by booting to the System Recovery Options, and by booting to the Advanced Boot Options menu (ABOM). When in the ABOM press the tab key, and then select Windows Memory Diagnostics.

If you do this from within Windows (from Administrative Tools, or by going to Run/Search and typing **mdsched**) a pop-up window asks you if you want to restart the computer immediately and run the check, or wait until the next time the computer is restarted. The System Recovery and ABOM methods start the check immediately. The test checks if there are any physical issues with the RAM and attempts to identify which memory module is causing the problem. When done it restarts the computer automatically. If an error is found, it displays after you log back on. You can also view errors in the System log of the Event Viewer. To find results quickly, right-click the System log, click Find, and enter MemoryDiagnostics-Results. If there are errors with a particular stick of memory, try removing it, cleaning it and the RAM slot, and reseating it. Run the test again; if you get the same results, replace the RAM.

Msconfig

Msconfig is the System Configuration tool. It can help troubleshoot various things, from operating system startup issues to application and service problems. To open Msconfig open the Run prompt and type **msconfig.exe**. A program similar to Figure 11.7 should display.

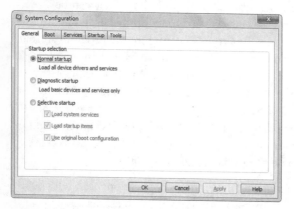

FIGURE 11.7   **Msconfig Application**

This is an excellent troubleshooting tool that has multiple tabs that do the following:

▶ **General**—At this tab you can configure the system for diagnostic or selective startup. This helps to troubleshoot devices or services that are failing.

▶ **Boot**—From here you can modify OS bootup settings such as using safe boot, logging the boot process, and booting without video. If you have multiple operating systems, you can change the order and choose which to set as default (instead of configuring the BCD or boot.ini file). Also, the advanced options lets you choose such things as how much memory you want to use, and what port to use if you need to output debugging information.

▶ **Services**—This lists the services and their current status. You can enable or disable them from here (requires a computer restart). However, you can't start or stop them. To do that you would need to go to the Services section of Computer Management or do it from within the Command Prompt. The beauty of this tab is the speed at which you can enable/disable services compared to other options in Windows.

▶ **Startup**—This tab lists the various applications that start when the computer boots up. You can disable and enable these here to aid you in troubleshooting slow applications, failures, and lock ups.

▶ **Tools**—This lists a lot of the common utilities you might use in Windows and allows you to launch them from there. As a launching point for programs we have used a lot (Computer Management, System Properties, Task Manager, Command Prompt, and so on), this section of Msconfig can be a real time-saver.

Consider Msconfig as a time-saver when running applications, changing boot settings, working with services and apps, and troubleshooting the system. One word of caution: Be sure to reset Msconfig to the regular settings when you finish using it. If a user complains about a system booting to Safe Mode every time, or other similar problems in which the user doesn't have full access to the system, Msconfig might need to be reconfigured to Normal Startup.

ExamAlert

Know the reasons to use Msconfig for the exam.

Stop Errors

A stop error (also known as a Blue Screen of Death or BSOD) is the worst type of error that can happen while Windows is operating. It completely halts the operating system and displays a blue screen with various text and code. Anything you were working on is for the most part lost. In some cases, it reboots the computer after a memory dump has been initiated. (This is also known as auto-restart.) If not, you need to physically turn the computer off at the power button and turn it back on. Some BSODs happen only once, and if that is the case, then you need not worry too much. But if they happen two or three times or more, you should investigate why. Quite often they are due to a hardware issue such as improperly seated memory or a corrupt driver file. If you see two columns of information with a list of drivers and other files, a driver issue could be the culprit. Look at the bottom of the second (or last) column and identify the driver that has failed, for example cdrom.sys. These drivers can become corrupt for a variety of reasons and would need to be replaced when you boot into Windows. Or if you can't boot into Windows, replace them from within WinRE's Command Prompt (7/Vista) or the Recovery Console (XP). Less commonly a BSOD might be caused by a memory error that will have additional code that you can research on Microsoft's websites (Microsoft Support and TechNet).

By default, three things happen when a Stop error occurs:

1. An event will usually be written to the System Log within the Event Viewer, if that option has been selected in the Startup and Recovery

window, as shown in Figure 11.8. When a STOP error is written to the System Log, it is listed as an Information entry, not as an Error entry. The STOP error will be listed as The System Has Rebooted from a Bugcheck. The Bugcheck was (Error Number). Use the error number to look up the problem, and hopefully find a solution, on Microsoft Support and/or TechNet.

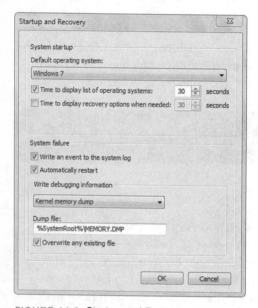

FIGURE 11.8 **Startup and Recovery window**

The settings shown in Figure 11.8 can be accessed in the following ways:

▶ **In Windows 7/Vista:** Click Start, right-click Computer, select Properties, and click the link for Advanced system settings; this brings up the System Properties Advanced tab. (You could also open the Run prompt and type SystemPropertiesAdvanced.exe). Click the Settings button in the Startup and Recovery box.

▶ **In Windows XP:** Click Start, right-click My Computer, select Properties, select the Advanced tab, and click the Settings button in the Startup and Recovery box.

2. Windows will write debugging information to the hard drive for later analysis with memory dump debugging programs; this debugging information is essentially the contents of RAM. The default setting in Windows 7 is to only write a portion of the contents of RAM, known as a Kernel memory dump. The Kernel memory dump is saved as the file

%systemroot\MEMORY.DMP. You can also select a Small Memory Dump; this is written to %systemroot%\Minidump. Windows 7, Vista, and XP operating systems all support the option for a Complete Memory Dump, which dumps the entire contents of RAM to a file again named MEMORY.DMP. To support the complete memory dump, the paging file must be large enough to hold all the physical RAM plus 1 megabyte. For more information on how to analyze the debugging information resulting from these stop errors, and about various dump files, see the following links: http://support.microsoft.com/kb/315263 http://support.microsoft.com/kb/254649 http://msdn.microsoft.com/en-us/windows/hardware/gg463009.aspx.

3. The computer automatically restarts, if that option is selected, which is the default in Windows 7 and Vista.

ExamAlert

Know how Stop errors occur and how memory dumps function.

Improper and Spontaneous Shutdowns

You've probably seen a Windows computer fail and reboot with the message Windows Was Shut Down Improperly. Improper shutdowns and spontaneous shutdowns could happen for a variety of reasons: brownouts or blackouts, a power surge, hardware failure, a user inadvertently unplugging the computer, or perhaps a virus or other malware. It can be a disturbing phenomenon to users, and one that could be going on for a while, so be patient with the user (and the computer) when troubleshooting this problem.

Some of the methods you can use to troubleshoot these issues include:

▶ **Check the Event Viewer:** Look in the System log to see if there are any alerts about hardware failures, service failures, and so on. If there are, consider upgrading the driver for the affecting hardware, or upgrading the software that the service is dependent on. Check if the computer is running the latest SP and patches.

▶ **Use Msconfig:** On the General tab click the Selective Startup and Load startup items check boxes. To weed out third-party program issues, click the Services tab, click the Hide All Microsoft Services check box, and then click Disable All. Restart the system and see if the same issues return or if events are still written to the Event Viewer. Remember to restore Normal startup in Msconfig when finished troubleshooting.

- ▶ **Boot into Safe Mode:** Use Safe Mode to further investigate the problem. Safe Mode uses only the most basic drivers, so if it is a driver issue, this could help you find out about it.

- ▶ **Run a virus scan:** Run a scan for malware and quarantine anything unusual. Update the AV software when you are finished.

- ▶ **Check power:** Make sure the AC outlet is wired properly and is supplying clean power. Verify that the power plug is firmly secured to the computer. If necessary, you might have to check the power supply. Intermittent and unexplainable shutdowns can sometimes be linked to power supply or other hardware failures.

Additional Windows Errors and Error Reporting

Windows errors less serious than STOP errors might display a pop-up window, like the one shown in Figure 11.9, after the application has closed. You might get similar pop-up windows if a device or service fails to start, or if there is a missing Dynamic-Link Library (DLL). DLLs provide much of the functionality of a Windows operating system. They can be used by more than one program at a time, which could lead to conflicts. A missing DLL can cause a program or a device to fail. However, the OS usually continues to function if any of these errors occur.

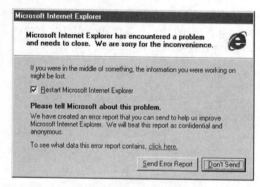

FIGURE 11.9 **An Internet Explorer error**

Figure 11.10 shows a critical error (runaway loop) that caused an application to close. However, the OS and other applications still function. Figure 11.11 displays a critical application error known as a general protection fault (GPF) that also caused the application to fail, but again, without crashing the operating system.

FIGURE 11.10 **A critical error**

FIGURE 11.11 **A General Protection Fault (GPF)**

As you can see, Windows 7/Vista/XP can recover from these types of errors and continue to function. You can find more information about the error in the Event Viewer, and in the case of Figure 11.9, you can view the error report information just by clicking the link Click Here within the error window. You also have the option to send an error report to Microsoft, in the hopes of acquiring a solution or fix. To have Windows 7 automatically check for solutions to problems, go to the Action Center, click the Change Action Center settings link, and then click the Problem reporting settings link. You can also select programs to exclude from error reporting here. To enable/disable error reporting in Windows Vista, navigate to Control Panel > System and Maintenance > Problem Reports and Solutions > Change settings > Advanced settings. To find out if any new solutions are available, click the Check for New Solutions link within Problem Reports and Solutions. To enable/disable error reporting in Windows XP, navigate to the System Properties window, Advanced tab, and click the Error Reporting button.

If you have a program compatibility issue and a particular program (perhaps an older one) won't run, or won't install properly in your version of Windows do the following. First, try installing or running the program as an administrator. Also, check out events in the Reliability Monitor. (Go to the Search and type the name to open it.) Then, check the Windows 7 Compatibility Center (http://www.microsoft.com/windows/compatibility/windows-7/en-us/default.aspx) to make sure it is actually compatible with the OS. Finally, attempt to run the program in compatibility mode. To do this, locate and right-click the program; then select Properties. Click the Compatibility tab and select what OS the program should be compatible with. Also, modify any settings such as colors or resolution if necessary. This is common for older games and applications written for previous versions of Windows. Finally, check with the manufacturer to see if there is an update to the program that can make it compatible with your version of Windows.

If a file fails to open every time you double-click it, you might be the victim of a virus. Scan the system with antivirus software and consider downloading the Microsoft Safety Scanner to scan the system as well at http://www.microsoft.com/security/scanner/en-us/default.aspx.

Restoring Windows

Beyond even Stop errors, a complete system failure is when a system cannot be repaired. When this happens, the only options are to reinstall or to restore Windows. There are several methods for restoring Windows including

▶ **Windows 7:** Boot to the DVD , click the repair option, and at the first System Recovery Options window (with the possible list of operating systems) select the Restore Your Computer Using a System Image That You Created Earlier. (You will be required to provide the backup media.)

▶ **Windows 7/Vista:** Boot to the DVD, click the repair option; at the main System Recovery Options window, select System Image Recovery (Win7) or Windows Complete PC Restore (Vista). Provide backup media.

▶ **Windows XP:** Boot to the Windows XP Professional CD, press F2, insert the automated system recovery (ASR) disk (made previously) and provide backup media. In some cases you might need to supply an Emergency Repair Disk. This floppy disk loads the drivers necessary to access the CD-ROM. This disk can be made in the NTBackup utility.

▶ **All Windows:** Use third-party tools such as Norton Ghost or Acronis. Remember, the image needs to be created before the disaster!

Cram Quiz

220-802 Questions

Answer these questions. The answers follow the last question. If you cannot answer these questions correctly, consider reading this section again until you can.

1. What could a yellow exclamation point in the Device Manager indicate?

    ○ **A.** Disabled device

    ○ **B.** Event Viewer error

    ○ **C.** Incorrect driver

    ○ **D.** Device is not installed

2. Which log file in the Event Viewer contains information concerning auditing?

- O **A.** System
- O **B.** Application
- O **C.** Internet Explorer
- O **D.** Security

3. A Stop error could manifest itself as what?

- O **A.** A BSOD
- O **B.** An Event Viewer error
- O **C.** A Dr. Watson error
- O **D.** Internet Explorer error

4. Which tools can be used to restore a computer? (Select all that apply.)

- O **A.** Windows Complete PC Restore
- O **B.** ASR
- O **C.** System Image Recovery
- O **D.** Dr. Watson

5. What can you *not* perform in Msconfig?

- O **A.** Enable services
- O **B.** Disable applications
- O **C.** Stop services
- O **D.** Enable applications

6. You try to install a program on a Windows 7 laptop but the installation fails. What should you do next?

- O **A.** Run the installer as an administrator.
- O **B.** Reinstall Windows 7.
- O **C.** Contact the manufacturer of the program.
- O **D.** Restore from an earlier restore point.

7. Which tool should you first use when troubleshooting software installation issues and application failures in Windows 7?

- O **A.** Task Manager
- O **B.** System Information
- O **C.** System Restore
- O **D.** Reliability Monitor

8. Which of the following might cause a blue screen?

- ○ **A.** Faulty DVD-ROM
- ○ **B.** CPU without a fan
- ○ **C.** Bad drivers
- ○ **D.** Program compatibility issue

Cram Quiz Answers

220-802 Answers

1. **C.** A yellow exclamation point could indicate an incorrect device driver or other malfunction of a device. A disabled device would be indicated by a down arrow or a red x. If the device is not installed, it will either not show up on the list at all, or it will show up in a category named Unknown devices.

2. **D.** The Security log contains information about auditing and other security events.

3. **A.** A BSOD (Blue Screen of Death) is what results from a Stop error in Windows.

4. **A, B,** and **C.** Windows Complete PC Restore is the Windows Vista solution for restoring an image. Automatic System Recovery (ASR) restores the system state of the Windows XP computer. System Image Recovery is the Windows 7 solution for restoring an image. Dr. Watson is a Windows XP tool that reports errors.

5. **C.** Msconfig cannot start or stop services. However, it can enable/disable them and report on the status of those services. It can also enable/disable applications.

6. **A.** If a program won't install on Windows 7/Vista, try installing it as an administrator. Administrative privileges are usually needed to install programs to Windows. Afterward, you can check the compatibility center at the Microsoft website and attempt to install the program in compatibility mode. If all else fails, contact the manufacturer of the program for help. Restoring the computer and reinstalling should not be necessary in this scenario.

7. **D.** The Reliability Monitor is the first of the listed tools you should use when troubleshooting software installs and application failures. You should also try running the install or program as an administrator, check compatibility, and use the Event Viewer to find out more about errors.

8. **C.** Bad drivers could cause a blue screen error (Stop error). Blue screens could also be caused by improperly seated RAM among other hardware issues. A faulty DVD-ROM drive would not cause a blue screen. A CPU installed without a fan would overheat causing the system to shut down. Incompatible programs simply don't run.

Command-Line Tools

Let's face it; the command-line interface, or CLI, is where the extreme techs live. Some things are just easier to do in the command-line, or the functionality needed might be accessible only in the command-line. This section covers two groups of commands: First, ones that run from within Windows and second, ones that should be run within the Command Prompt option in WinRE's System Recovery Options (7/Vista), or the Recovery Console (XP). Commands use switches. For example, if you typed **DIR /?**, the switch would be **/?**. Switches are also referred to as options.

Windows Command Prompt

Microsoft's name for the command line is the Command Prompt. The Command Prompt can be found in Start > All Programs > Accessories. However, if you troubleshoot Windows 7/Vista, you probably need to run the Command Prompt in elevated mode (as an administrator), which can be done in one of two ways:

1. Click Start > All Programs > Accessories; then right-click Command Prompt and select Run as Administrator.

2. Click Start and type **cmd** in the search field, and instead of pressing Enter, press Ctrl+Shift+Enter.

Chkdsk

By running the command **chkdsk**, this tool checks a disk, fixes basic issues like lost files, and displays a status report; it can also fix some errors on the disk by using the **/F** switch. Here's an example of the three stages of results when running the chkdsk command:

```
The type of the file system is NTFS.
Volume label is WinXPC.
WARNING!  F parameter not specified.
Running CHKDSK in read-only mode.
CHKDSK is verifying files (stage 1 of 3)...
File verification completed.
CHKDSK is verifying indexes (stage 2 of 3)...
Index verification completed.
CHKDSK is recovering lost files.
Recovering orphaned file ~WRL3090.tmp (59880) into directory
file 28570.
Recovering orphaned file ~DFA188.tmp (59881) into directory file
28138.
```

```
CHKDSK is verifying security descriptors (stage 3 of 3)...
Security descriptor verification completed.
Correcting errors in the master file table's (MFT) BITMAP
attribute.
Correcting errors in the Volume Bitmap.
Windows found problems with the file system.
Run CHKDSK with the /F (fix) option to correct these.
   31471300 KB total disk space.
   13053492 KB in 56091 files.
      16340 KB in 4576 indexes.
          0 KB in bad sectors.
     133116 KB in use by the system.
      65536 KB occupied by the log file.
   18268352 KB available on disk.
       4096 bytes in each allocation unit.
    7867825 total allocation units on disk.
 4567088 allocation units available on disk.
```

Notice that the utility warned that the /F switch was not specified, and because of this it ran in read-only mode. Also notice that the orphaned files were recovered, although they are just .tmp files and most likely not necessary for the functionality of Windows. Finally, the program found issues with the file system; if you want to repair these, you would have to use the /F option. Be sure that you actually need to run chkdsk with the /F parameter before doing so. For example, if the system seems to function properly, but the standard chkdsk command gave an error, it might not be absolutely necessary to run chkdsk with the /F parameter.

One issue that plagues users is the infamous Missing Operating System message. If you get this it usually means that either the disk has a few small errors or the master boot record has been damaged. But even though the system won't boot, you can still run a chkdsk to find and fix problems on the disk. Boot to the Windows DVD, select Repair Your Computer, and from the System Recovery Options, select Command Prompt. From there run a chkdsk with either the /F switch (which fixes errors on the disk), or the /R switch (which locates bad sectors and recovers data) or both. This procedure can also help with Invalid Boot Disk errors. (Of course, first check that the BIOS is booting to the correct drive in the boot priority menu.)

SFC

System File Checker (SFC) is a Windows 7/Vista/XP utility that checks protected system files. It replaces incorrect versions or missing files with the correct files. SFC can be used to fix problems with Internet Explorer or other Windows applications. To run SFC, open the command prompt, and type **SFC** with the appropriate switch. A typical option is **SFC /scannow**, which scans all protected files immediately. Another is **SFC /scanonce**, which scans all protected files at the next boot. If SFC finds that some files are missing, you are prompted to reinsert the original operating system disc, so the files can be copied to the DLL cache.

Convert

The convert command enables you to convert a volume that was previously formatted as FAT32 over to NTFS, without losing any data. An example of the convert command would be **convert d: /FS:NTFS**, which would convert the hard disk volume D: to NTFS. Sometimes you might encounter older computers' hard drives (or flash media) that require being formatted as NTFS for compatibility with other devices and networked computers.

Format

Format is a command used to format magnetic media such as hard drives and solid-state media such as USB flash drives to the FAT, FAT32, or NTFS file systems. An example of formatting a USB flash drive in the command-line would be **format F:**. The type of file system that the media will be formatted to can be specified with the switch **/FS:filesystem**, where file system will equal either FAT, FAT32, or NTFS. For more information on the various switches available with format, type **format /?**.

Diskpart

The Diskpart utility is the command-line counterpart of Windows' Disk Management program. This program needs to be run by typing **diskpart** before any of the diskpart actions can be implemented. This brings the user into the DISKPART> prompt. From here you can create, delete, and extend volumes, assign drive letters, make a partition active, and so on. Essentially, everything that was covered in the Disk Management portion of Chapter 9 can be done with Diskpart. When you finish using Diskpart, type **exit** to return back to the standard command prompt.

This is the successor to the older FDISK program found on older versions of Windows. The FDISK program was often accessed from a bootable floppy disk to make changes to the partition table before installing an OS.

Defrag

This is the command-line version of the Disk Defragmenter. To analyze a disk, type the command **defrag -a**. If a volume needs to be defragmented, but has less than 15 percent free space, use the **-f** parameter.

Xcopy

The Xcopy command is meant to copy large amounts of data from one location to another; it even makes exact copies of entire directory trees. One example of its usage would be to copy the contents of a Windows 7 DVD-ROM over to a USB flash drive so that you can use the USB flash drive as installation media. The command for this would be **xcopy d:*.* /E/F e:**. This is assuming that D: is the DVD-ROM drive and E: is the USB flash drive. *.* means all files with all extensions within the D: drive. **/E** indicates that all folders and subfolders will be copied including empty ones. **/F** displays full source and destination files while copying. For more information about Xcopy type **xcopy /?**.

Robocopy

Robocopy (Robust File Copy) is a directory replication tool. It is meant to copy directories that contain lots of data, it can even mirror complete directory trees from one computer to another. Robocopy is the successor to Xcopy. Some of the advantages of this tool are that it can tolerate network interruptions, skip past junctions (such as the \Documents and Settings to \Users junction), and preserve data attributes and time stamps. Robocopy does not copy individual files, it copies only directories, for example; Robocopy c:\office   c:\games. This will copy all the information within the \office directory to the \games directory. It also gives in-depth results of its actions. You can also use robocopy to copy information to other computers by using the \\computername\share universal naming convention which we speak more about in Chapter 15, "Networking."

Tasklist

Tasklist (previously tlist) shows all the processes running similar to the Processes tab of the Task Manager. Each process is assigned a Process Identification number or PID. These are assigned dynamically and won't use the same number for an application twice. Tasklist also shows the memory usage of each process. An example of a process would be excel.exe (Microsoft Excel) or winword.exe (Microsoft Word).

Taskkill

Just as you can shut processes down in the Task Manager, you can also use the command-line tool Taskkill (previously kill). Perhaps you run into a situation where certain applications or processes are frozen, and you cannot open the Task Manager. If you can get to the Command Prompt, you could end these processes without restarting the computer. For example, if Microsoft Excel hung up and stopped responding, you could find out its process ID with Tasklist (say it was 4548) and close it by either typing `taskkill /IM excel.exe` or `taskkill /PID 4548`. Tasklist and Taskkill are not available in the Recovery Command Prompt.

Shutdown

The shutdown command is used to turn off the computer, restart it, send it to hibernate mode, log a person off, and so on. For example, if you want to shut down the computer after a short delay, you would type `shutdown /s`. For an immediate shutdown it would be `shutdown /p`. The command can also be used programmatically to shutdown systems at specific times while providing a pop-up window explaining the reason for the shutdown.

> **Exam Alert**
>
> Memorize as many of the commands mentioned in this section as you can! Try them on your computer, and write them down to force those little gray cells into action.

Recovery Command Prompt

The System Recovery Options Command Prompt in Windows 7 and Vista, and Windows XP's Recovery Console are used to repair issues with the operating system. For example, a system file causing the system to fail at startup can be copied from installation media. This environment can also be used to edit files and run commands that can fix the boot sector and master boot record. This section refers to both Windows 7/Vista's System Recovery Options Command Prompt and Windows XP's Recovery Console collectively as "recovery Command Prompts" for easier reading.

Edit

This command is not available in all versions of Windows. For example, Windows 7 64-bit versions do not support it, but 32-bit versions do.

The **edit** command can be used to create and modify text files within Windows or within a recovery Command Prompt. For example, maybe the boot.ini file in Windows XP needs to be modified. Within the root of C: the command to modify this would be simply **edit boot.ini**. Here is an example of a default Windows XP boot.ini file that has some incorrect information:

```
[boot loader]
timeout=30
default=multi(0)disk(0)rdisk(0)partition(1)\WINNT
[operating systems]
multi(0)disk(0)rdisk(0)partition(1)\WINDOWS="Microsoft Windows
XP Professional" /fastdetect /NoExecute=OptIn
```

Did you notice the error? The default %systemroot% folder name in Windows XP is \Windows, not \Winnt, as is incorrectly shown in line 3. Line 3 contains an Advanced RISC Computing (ARC) path. It tells you the type of disk being used, which disk and partition the operating system is installed to, and finally the installation folder. Errors within an ARC path can be easily fixed with the edit command, or you could simply delete the file, and Windows XP would re-create a default boot.ini automatically upon restart. However, the file that XP re-creates automatically would be a default file, assuming one hard drive with the operating system installed to the C: drive. Any other configurations would require the boot.ini be modified. For example, if Windows was installed to D: instead of C:, the "partition" section of the ARC path would have to be modified to partition(2). If using SATA or IDE hard drives, the default setting for rdisk is 0, which means the first hard drive; the default setting for partition is 1, which means the first partition on the drive. Note that the partition setting does *not* start with 0. For more information on ARC paths, an older but still valid article can be found at http://support.microsoft.com/kb/102873.

Copy

The copy command obviously copies files from one location to another. An example of its usage in a recovery Command Prompt would be to replace a missing NTLDR file in Windows XP. To do this, the file would have to be copied from the CD-ROM to the hard disk. Assuming that all drive letters are standard (hard disk is C: and CD-ROM drive is D:), the syntax for this would be `copy d:\i386\ntldr c:\`. This copies the NTLDR file from the I386 folder on the CD-ROM to the root of C: on the hard drive.

Expand

Sometimes you can't just copy files from a DVD/CD to the hard drive. Many of these files are compressed. If a file ends with an underscore, for example ntoskrnl.ex_ then it is a compressed file and has to be expanded. Let's just say that it was a dark day and that ntoskrnl.exe had failed. You can't do much without that core operating system file. To fix the problem in the recovery Command Prompt, you would expand the file from DVD/CD to the hard drive. In a standard environment where the hard drive is C: and the DVD/CD drive is D:, the syntax would be

`expand D:\i386\ntoskrnl.ex_ C:\Windows\System32\ntoskrnl.exe`.

This decompresses the file and places a copy of the decompressed version on the hard drive. Be sure to type the entire name of the file in the destination; otherwise, you need to rename the file.

Other Recovery Environment Commands

If Windows 7/Vista has startup issues, you can use several commands:

- ▶ **bootrec /fixboot:** Replaces the bootmgr file and writes a new Windows 7/Vista compatible boot sector to the system partition.f

- ▶ **bootrec /fixmbr:** Rewrites the Windows 7/Vista compatible master boot record to the system partition. This can also repair boot sector blocks after a virus has been removed.

- ▶ **bootrec /rebuildbcd:** Repairs the BCD store.

- ▶ **bootrec /ScanOs:** This scans all disks for installations compatible with Windows 7/Vista. This option also displays the entries that are currently not included in the BCD store. Use this command if there are Windows 7/Vista installations that the Boot Manager menu does not list.

If Windows XP has startup issues, there are a couple of commands that you can use:

- ▶ **FIXMBR:** Use this command to repair the MBR of the system partition. Use this command if a virus has damaged the MBR and Windows cannot start.

- ▶ **FIXBOOT:** Use this command to write new Windows boot sector code to the system partition.

Cram Quiz

Answer these questions. The answers follow the last question. If you cannot answer these questions correctly, consider reading this section again until you can.

1. Which command can fix lost files?
   - ○ **A.** Chkdsk
   - ○ **B.** Diskpart
   - ○ **C.** Chkdsk /R
   - ○ **D.** FIXMBR

2. Which Recovery Console command can decompress a file as it copies it to the hard drive?
   - ○ **A.** Extract
   - ○ **B.** Expand
   - ○ **C.** Compress
   - ○ **D.** Encrypt

3. Which command can copy multiple files and entire directory trees?
   - ○ **A.** Copy
   - ○ **B.** Cut
   - ○ **C.** Paste
   - ○ **D.** Xcopy

4. Which command can write a new boot sector and replace the bootmgr file in Windows 7/Vista?
   - ○ **A.** bootrec /fixboot
   - ○ **B.** bootrec /fixmbr
   - ○ **C.** bootrec /rebuildbcd
   - ○ **D.** bootrec /ScanOs

5. Which command will determine if protected system files have been overwritten and replace those files with the original version?
   - ○ **A.** CHKDSK
   - ○ **B.** MSCONFIG
   - ○ **C.** SFC
   - ○ **D.** XCOPY

6. An application is frozen and cannot be closed. However, the rest of the operating system works fine. Which tool can be used to close the application?

   ○ **A.** Tasklist

   ○ **B.** Taskkill

   ○ **C.** Shutdown

   ○ **D.** Convert

Cram Quiz Answers

1. **C.** Chkdsk /R verifies the integrity of a disk and can fix lost (or orphaned) files. Chkdsk checks the disk only.

2. **B.** The expand command decompresses files that are compressed on the CD, such as ntoskrnl.ex_.

3. **D.** Xcopy can copy an entire disc of information with just one command (including switches).

4. **A.** Bootrec /fixboot replaces the bootmgr file and writes a new Windows 7/Vista compatible boot sector to the system partition.

5. **C.** SFC determines if system files have been overwritten and replaces those files with the original versions. CHKDSK can check for errors and fix some errors but not when it concerns system files. MSCONFIG is used to boot the system in a selective way and disable services and applications. XCOPY is used to copy large amounts of data exactly to a new location.

6. **B.** Taskkill ends the underlying process of an application, closing the application. Tasklist is used to view which processes are running, their process IDs, and memory used by each. Shutdown is a command used to turn off the computer in a variety of ways. Convert is used to alter a FAT32 partition to NTFS.

CHAPTER 12

Video and Audio

This chapter covers the following A+ exam topics:

▶ The Video Subsystem

▶ The Audio Subsystem

You can find a master list of A+ exam topics in the "Introduction."

This chapter covers CompTIA A+ 220-801 objectives 1.4, 1.6, 1.10, and 1.11, and CompTIA A+ 220-802 objectives 1.5, and 4.4.

Video makes a computer sparkle, and audio makes it rock. This chapter describes the technologies and devices that transform the computer from a boring block of metal to a multimedia juggernaut. We could talk about video and audio for days, but lucky for you this chapter has a page limit! So we'll stick to what you need to know for the exam.

This chapter is broken down into two sections: first, the video subsystem, which includes the video card and display; second, the audio subsystem, which includes the sound card and speakers. However, the bulk of the information in this chapter pertains to video, so let's begin with that first.

The Video Subsystem

The computer can be broken down into several subsystems, the video subsystem being one of the most important. The video subsystem includes the video card (or integrated video), the card's expansion bus, internal connections, external connections between the video card and the display, the display itself, and the video driver. This section details those portions of the video subsystem. Of course, it's also vital to know how to install and configure video cards and how to troubleshoot any issues that might occur.

Video Cards

Today's video cards are like little self-contained computers! They have a processor, known as a graphics processing unit (GPU), and a substantial amount of RAM. When deciding on a video card to use, there are several things to take into account including the expansion bus that the card connects to, the card's GPU speed and amount of memory, the connectors it offers, if there is an expansion slot available for it on the motherboard, whether the video card can fit in the case, and whether the case has adequate power and cooling capabilities for the card.

Expansion Buses: PCI, PCIe, AGP

Before purchasing and installing a video card, make sure that the motherboard in the computer has a corresponding open expansion slot for the card. There are three expansion buses that can be used by video cards: Peripheral Component Interconnect (PCI), Accelerated Graphics Port (AGP), and PCI Express (PCIe), with PCIe easily being the most common expansion bus slot in today's motherboards. Because PCIe and AGP have high data transfer rates, those expansion slots connect directly to the northbridge of a motherboard's chipset (or directly to the CPU on newer Intel designs). PCI however, has a lesser data transfer rate; therefore, PCI slots connect to the southbridge. Because of this, you won't see many PCI video cards. Table 12.1 reviews the three expansion buses' characteristics and differences. The color listed for each expansion bus is typical but not definite because some motherboard manufacturers select their own proprietary colors. Figure 12.1 shows a comparison of these expansion bus slots.

TABLE 12.1 **Video Card Expansion Buses**

Expansion Bus	Typical Color	Distance from Edge of Motherboard	Data Transfer Rate
PCI	White	Closest to the edge	133 MB/s or 266 MB/s
AGP	Brown	Farthest from the edge	266 MB/s–2 GB/s
PCIe	Black	Slightly farther from the edge than PCI	250 MB/s–1 GB/s per lane (Ver. 1-3)

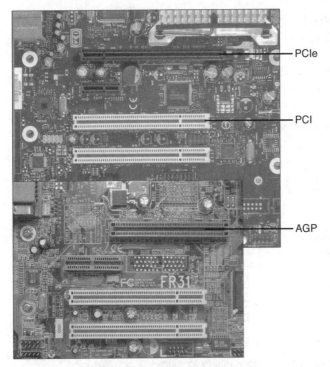

FIGURE 12.1   PCIe, PCI, and AGP expansion bus slots

Exam Alert

Know the differences between PCI, AGP, and PCIe for the exam. But know that the majority of questions will be about PCI Express.

PCI Express won the battle against AGP as soon as the PCIe x16 card was released, which could initially transfer 4 GB of data per second, double that of AGP. Since then, PCI Express has only gotten faster. (Version 2 can transfer 8 GB/s and version 3 does 16 GB/s.) PCI video cards are less common; although, an old PCI card works great in a pinch, and many motherboards still come with PCI slots. PCI also works well in some Multiple Monitor scenarios.

Installing a video card to a PCI or to an AGP slot is easy; just press the card straight down into the slot, and screw it into the chassis. However, PCI Express cards require a little bit more work, which is discussed later. For more information on expansion buses, see Chapter 2, "Motherboards."

Connector Types

After a video card is decided on, that will probably dictate the connector used. Most of today's PCIe video cards come with one or two DVI outputs, but there are several other connectors that you see in the field. Table 12.2 details these. Figure 12.2 shows a video card's two DVI ports and the other ports described in Table 12.2.

TABLE 12.2 **Video Card Connectors**

Connector Type	Full Name	Description
VGA (also known as SVGA)	Video Graphics Array	15-pin, usually blue, known as DE15F (also sold as DB15). Used for older monitors that display VGA, SVGA, and XGA resolutions.
DVI	Digital Visual Interface	High-quality connections used with LCD displays. Carries uncompressed digital video, is partially compatible with HDMI. Types include ▶ **DVI-D:** Digital-only connections ▶ **DVI-A:** Analog-only connections ▶ **DVI-I:** Digital and analog ▶ **DVI-DL:** Dual link (There are dual-link versions for DVI-I and DVI-D.) ▶ **M1-DA:** Digital, analog, and USB
HDMI	High-Definition (HD) Multimedia Interface	Used mainly for high-definition television. Can carry video and audio signals. Some video cards do not offer HDMI, but instead offer DVI: ▶ **Type A:** Supports all HD modes, compatible with DVI-D connectors ▶ **Type B:** Double-video bandwidth, supports higher resolutions ▶ **Type C:** Mini-HDMI, used in portable devices ▶ **Type D:** Micro-HDMI, smallest connector, also used in portable devices
DisplayPort	DisplayPort	▶ Royalty-free interface similar to HDMI, designed to be the replacement for HDMI and DVI ▶ Uses packet transmission similar to Ethernet ▶ Connector looks similar to USB ▶ Not as common as DVI and HDMI
S-Video	Separate Video	Used for standard-definition video, no audio signal. Uses a mini-DIN 4-, 6-, 7-, or 9-pin connector.
Component/RGB	Component Video	Used to send analog or digital signal over three wires: red, green, and blue, each wire ending with an RCA plug. Can send high-definition signals digitally. A composite video RCA connection (yellow plug) sends an analog video signal; it is sometimes used by older gaming systems and other electronic devices, possibly in combination with stereo RCA audio connections (red and white plugs.)

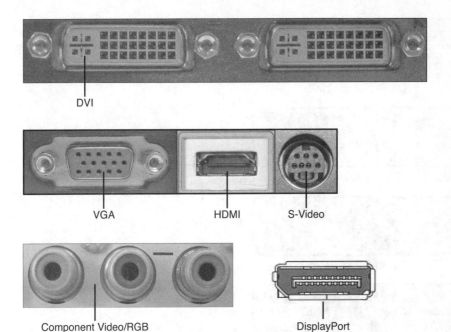

FIGURE 12.2   **DVI, VGA, HDMI, S-Video, DisplayPort, and component video ports**

ExamAlert

Be able to identify DVI, VGA, HDMI, S-Video, component video, and DisplayPort ports for the exam.

Many DVI connectors on a video card look the same; however, it is the monitor's cable and plug that define which type of DVI it can support. Figure 12.3 shows an illustration of the various DVI plugs, and their associated pins, that you might see on the end of a monitor cable.

A computer's DVI connector is usually compatible with HDMI and VGA. Adapters and adapter cables are available if a user wants to connect a VGA monitor or HDMI television to the DVI port of a computer.

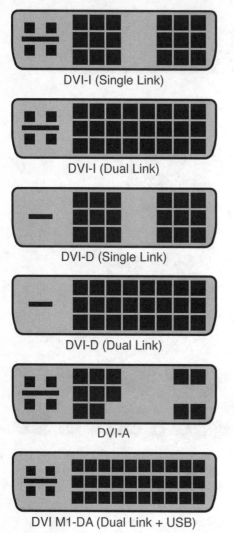

DVI-I (Single Link)

DVI-I (Dual Link)

DVI-D (Single Link)

DVI-D (Dual Link)

DVI-A

DVI M1-DA (Dual Link + USB)

FIGURE 12.3   **Various DVI plug connector pins**

Video Card Chipset, GPU, and Memory

It was mentioned before that today's video cards are like computers unto themselves. To a certain extent this is true. These cards have a chipset, similar to a motherboard's chipset but more simplified; it takes care of the connection between the graphics processing unit (GPU) and the RAM on the card. The GPU of a video card is measured quite like a CPU. For example, the GPU in a video card might run at 630 MHz; this is known as its core clock. Likewise, a video card's RAM is measured like a motherboard's RAM. Many video cards already in the field use DDR3, DDR4 or DDR5. Video card RAM is known as GDDR or Graphics Double Data Rate. A typical video card might have 1, 2, or 3 GB of DDR3 RAM, running at 1 or 2 GHz. Most video cards are PCI Express x16, meaning they use 16 lanes and can connect only to a PCIe x16 slot. Because today's video cards have powerful GPUs, the GPU may have its own heat sink and fan, or the entire card will be enclosed and will have its own exhaust fan, thus cooling the GPU, chipset, and RAM.

Installing and Troubleshooting Video Cards

Video cards, like other adapter cards, are inserted into an expansion bus slot and then screwed into the chassis of the case to keep them in place. However, PCI Express cards require the installer to do a few more things. And keep in mind that some newer PCIe cards are *big*. When deciding on a video card, make sure it fits in the computer case first! The following steps describe how to install a PCIe video card:

Step 1. **Check if the card is compatible:** Verify that there is an open, compatible slot on the motherboard. Also, make sure that the card is compatible with the operating system. For more information on OS compatibility, see Chapter 8, "Installing and Upgrading Windows."

Step 2. **Ready the computer:** Make sure that the computer is turned off and unplugged. Then implement ESD prevention measures (anti-static mat, antistatic wrist strap, and so on).

Step 3. **Ready the video card:** Remove the card from the package and place it on an antistatic bag until it is ready to be inserted. (Make sure the card is sealed when first opening it. In rare cases, used cards are repackaged and resold as new.)

Step 4. **Document:** If the computer had a video card already, document how and where it was connected. Otherwise, review documentation that came with the motherboard and video card, so a plan can be put into place as to where to install the card, and what cables need to be connected to the card (and how they should be routed through the case).

Step 5. **Prepare the slot:** Use a Phillips head screwdriver to remove the slot cover (or covers) where the card will be installed. Bigger PCIe cards inhabit the space used by two slot covers. On most PCIe slots there will be a thumb lever. Open this gently. When the card is inserted, the lever locks the card into place. In some cases, this lever isn't necessary.

Step 6. **Install the card to the slot:** Insert the card, using both thumbs, with equal pressure, straight down into the slot. Try not to wiggle the card in any direction. Press down until the card snaps into place and you can't see any of the gold edge connectors. If it doesn't seem to be going in, don't force it. There might be something in the way; for example, one of the slot covers hasn't been removed, or the thumb lever isn't in the correct position.

Step 7. **Connect cables:** PCIe cards need their own power connection (or two). These are 6- or 8-pin PCIe power connectors. Many cases come with PCIe power connectors, but if not, most PCIe video cards have a PCIe to Molex adapter (or two). Next, make any SLI connections necessary, if you have two or three video cards (less common). Then, connect optional cables, for example, an S/PDIF header cable to the motherboard, and any other ancillary cables. When complete, it should look something like Figure 12.4.

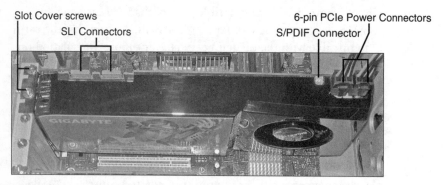

FIGURE 12.4   An installed PCIe video card

Step 8. **Test:** Testing is simple; plug the monitor into the video card's port, and boot the computer. If you don't get anything on the display, it's time to troubleshoot. Make sure that the monitor is connected securely to the correct port. Then (after shutting down the PC) make sure that the card is seated properly and that the power connections and any other connections are connected firmly. Listen for any beep codes that might be issued by the BIOS POST. Check if the computer is booting without video; this can be done by watching the LED lights on the front of the case and listening for the power supply fan and hard drive activity.

Step 9. **Install the driver:** When the system boots properly, install the driver from the manufacturer's CD. If for some reason no CD was supplied with the device, or it is missing, go to the manufacturer's website and download the latest version of the driver for the *exact* model of the video card.

Step 10. **Test again:** Now that the driver is installed, test again. Verify that the card is seen as the correct make and model in the Device Manager. Then make sure the display can output the desired resolution. Keep in mind that some video cards can output a higher resolution than a monitor can support. If the computer is used for graphics or gaming, open the appropriate application and verify that it works as expected. For example, check for fluidity, quick response, frame rate, and so on.

> **Exam Alert**
>
> Know how to install and test a video card for the exam.

When troubleshooting video issues, there are a number of things to check including

- **Connections:** If nothing is showing up on the display, first make sure that the monitor is plugged into the video card properly (and to the correct video port); then verify that the monitor is connected to the AC outlet and is powered on. If the image on the display is scrambled, check that it is connected to the correct port on the video card because some cards come with DVI and VGA ports. If necessary, try removing the video card and reseating it carefully.

- **Power cycle the computer, display, and any power protection equipment:** Power cycling the equipment can fix all kinds of problems, and is an easy solution to start. Problems such as display flickering and stuck pixels might be easily repaired by a power cycle of the display, the computer, and any surge suppressor that the equipment is plugged into.

- **Check for an onboard video setting in the BIOS:** If you install a new video card to a computer that previously used onboard video, always check that the onboard video setting is disabled in the BIOS. It can conflict with the new video card. And of course, be sure to plug the monitor into the new video card, not the old onboard connection.

- **Resolution setting:** In the case that the resolution was set too high, or to a resolution not supported by the monitor, you might get a distorted image or no image at all. Boot into low resolution VGA mode or Safe Mode. This starts the computer with a resolution of 640x480. Then modify the resolution setting in the Display Properties window. More on resolution later in this chapter.

▶ **Check the driver:** Maybe the driver failed, or perhaps the wrong driver was installed during installation, or maybe an update is necessary. If there is nothing on the display, or if the image is distorted, or if the monitor only displays a lower resolution, boot into low res mode or Safe Mode, and update the driver from within the Device Manager. Driver failures could also be the cause of BSODs.

▶ **Check the version of DirectX:** DirectX is a Windows technology that includes video, animation, and sound components. It helps a computer get more performance out of multimedia, games, and movies. The DirectX Diagnostic Tool (DxDiag) helps to troubleshoot DirectX-related issues. This tool gives information about the installed version of DirectX and whether it is operating correctly, among other things. The DirectX Diagnostic Tool can be started by opening the Run prompt and typing **dxdiag**.

▶ **Check the temperature threshold of the video card:** High-end video cards are intensely used by gamers and designers. If the temperature surpasses the safeguards in place, it might cause the card to throttle back the GPU speed, or the video card might stop working altogether, causing the current application to close, or at worst, the display could go blank. Consider additional cooling fans or a liquid cooling system if this happens more than once or twice.

▶ **Use software to check and repair stuck or dead pixels:** When a single pixel fails, it can be irritating. But there are software programs that can be used to identify stuck pixels and possible dead pixels and attempt to fix them. Software such as LCD Repair, UDPixel, and Monitor Test are examples of this software. Always try power cycling the device as well. If you can't repair the stuck or dead pixel, you might have to bring the display in for repair or for replacement.

▶ **Calibrate the monitor:** If you see artifacts (image distortions) or you notice incorrect color patterns, or the display just doesn't seem to look quite as good as it used to, try calibrating the monitor by either resetting it with the on-screen display, or adjusting the contrast, brightness, and color level. Also try adjusting the color depth in Windows, and check the screen resolution. Try to limit reflections on the screen. If using a CRT and the artifacts still appear, consider upgrading to an LCD display. Dim images could also be caused by misconfiguring the brightness and contrast.

▶ **Check for newly installed applications:** New applications could cause the display to malfunction or stop working altogether. Check the application manufacturer's website for any known hardware compatibility issues.

▶ **Check inside the computer:** I usually leave this for last because it is
time-consuming to open the system, unless I have a sneaky suspicion
that one of the connections inside the computer is loose. Check if the
card is seated properly. In areas in which the temperature and humidity
change quickly, the card could be unseated due to thermal expansion and
contraction. (Some refer to this as chip creep or card creep!) Also, if the
computer were moved recently, it could cause the card to come out of
the slot slightly. Verify that the power connections and other cables are
not loose. Check all other connections inside the PC to make sure it
isn't a video problem. For example, you never know, if the system makes
use of an onboard video controller, and you start seeing garbled images,
strange colors, cursor trails, you might have defective RAM (or maybe
have been working on computers too long). Remember that onboard
video controllers rely on the sticks of RAM in the motherboard, as
opposed to individual video cards that have their own RAM.

Again, verify that it is actually a video problem. Don't forget about the "big
four." When you can't see anything on the display and you know the computer is receiving power, you can narrow it down to video, RAM, processor, and
the motherboard. But if the system appears to boot, if you can hear the hard
drive accessing data, and can see hard drive activity from the LED light on
the front of the case, it is most likely a video problem. Go back to the basics,
and check power and connections. Try substituting a known-good monitor in
place of the current one. When it comes to video, the simple answers are the
most common.

Video Displays

Regardless of what type of video card (or cards) is in a computer, it all means
nothing if the computer doesn't have an output device. The most common
video output device in a computer system is the liquid crystal display (LCD).

LCD

A liquid crystal display (LCD) is a flat panel display that consists of two sheets
of polarizing material surrounding a layer of liquid crystal solution. Most of
today's LCD screens are thin-film transistor (TFT) active-matrix displays,
meaning they have three transistors for each pixel, which are contained within
a flexible material. The transistors store the electrical state of each pixel, while
all the other pixels are updated. These transistors are located directly behind
the liquid crystal material. LCD displays use a cold cathode fluorescent lamp
(CCFL) as the lighting source. The CCFL develops ultraviolet light by

discharging mercury into the lamp. The lamp's inner fluorescent coating then allows for the emitting of visible light, which is sent to the actual display panel. LCDs typically have DVI and VGA connections but might also be equipped with HDMI. In general, LCDs use low amounts of power, generate a small amount of heat, and cause little in the way of interference and emissions. Common LCD resolutions include WXGA, SXGA+, UXGA, WSXGA+, and WUXGA. Generally, an LCD will be designed for one resolution, known as the *native resolution*; it's the resolution that the LCD works best at. If this is the case, any other resolution selected will be scaled and will usually appear stretched or compressed. If a user complains of these symptoms, check the LCDs documentation to find its native resolution, and switch to that resolution in the Display Properties window. More on video resolution later in this chapter.

Another measure of an LCD is contrast ratio. Contrast ratio is a comparison of the brightest and darkest colors (white and black) that can be generated on a display. It can be measured statically, or dynamically (known as DC). Generally, the higher the contrast ratio, the better. Dynamic will always be a higher number than static. For example, one of the monitors used for this book has a static contrast ratio of 1000:1 and a dynamic contrast ratio of 20000:1.

When it comes to cleaning displays, be careful; liquid can possibly get between the bezel and the screen; when it infiltrates the display assembly, bad things can happen! To avoid this, conservatively spray the cleaner on to a soft, clean, lint-free cloth first; then carefully clean the display with the cloth. Many manufacturers of displays recommend using isopropyl alcohol diluted with water; basically no more than 50 percent of the solution should be alcohol; the rest should be water. Isopropyl alcohol can be found in most supermarkets and drug stores; the higher the purity level the better, for example 90 percent purity is acceptable; it will say this directly on the bottle. Again, use the solution conservatively, apply it to the cloth first, and try not to get any on the plastic bezel, apply to the screen only. It usually isn't necessary to clean the screen often; once every 3 to 6 months is fine unless you work in a dirty environment. Instead of cleaning the screen, you can also try removing the dust (which can affect visibility) with a soft lint-free cloth or a canister of compressed air. This might help as an added step before cleaning the screen to avoid streaking. There are also various spray cleaners available at electronics stores and online; some of them are simply expensive isopropyl alcohol/water solutions! But personally, for over a decade I have simply mixed my own isopropyl/water solution for use on LCDs, CRTs, laptop LCDs, handheld computers, smartphones, and cell phones and have never had a problem.

LED Monitors

LED monitors utilize light-emitting diodes to display images. LED display technology is used in computer monitors, televisions, billboards and storefront signs. LED monitors can use two different kinds of technologies: conventional discrete LEDs and surface-mounted device (SMD) technology. SMD is more common for LED monitors; it uses red, green, and blue diodes that are mounted as individual triads as opposed to discrete LED technology, which clusters these triads together into pixels.

LED monitors are essentially LCD monitors with a different backlight. Whereas LCD monitors use CCFL as the illumination source, LED monitors use light emitting diodes, which release photons; this process is known as electroluminescence. These are commonly known as LED-backlit LCD displays.

OLED

OLED stands for organic light emitting diodes. OLED displays use organic semiconductor material usually in the form of polymers. Organic colored molecules are held in place between electrodes. A conductive layer made up of plastic molecules allows the organic colored molecules to emit light. The main advantage of OLED over LED is expected to be cost; OLEDs can be printed onto just about any substrate using simple printing processes. However, as of the writing of this book, manufacturing processes have not realized this cost reduction. OLED is still an emerging technology and as such is expensive and will not be seen often in the workplace.

Plasma

Plasma displays are rarely found in computer monitors but are often found in televisions. Nowadays, computers can use many types of televisions as their display, including plasma, as long as the computer has the correct type of video port. Plasma displays use small cells that contain electrically charged ionized gases; effectively these are fluorescent lamps. Plasma screens are known for brightness and low-luminance black level in comparison to LCD screens. This makes the plasma screen a higher energy consumer than LCD. It also prompted the LCD community to release LED-backlit LCD displays that were mentioned previously.

CRT

A cathode ray tube (CRT) is an older type monitor that uses a vacuum tube display and utilizes three electron guns to display the colors red, green, and blue to a fluorescent screen. (Red, green, and blue are the three primary colors of the computer display world.) These colors are grouped into triads and are emitted by phosphors within the screen so that a user can see the image on the display. A triad consists of three "dots": red, green, and blue. One way that CRTs are measured is in dot pitch, which is the distance between two like colors of adjacent triads. The lower the dot pitch, the better the CRT's image quality because the triads are closer together. Another measurement is dots per inch (DPI.) Common DPI defaults in Windows include 96 and 120, which are also measured as PPI, or pixels per inch. CRTs are higher in emissions and interference than LCDs. Extended usage of CRTs can result in user complaints of headaches. This can usually be solved by increasing the refresh rate and implementing a glare guard.

Projectors

Video projectors can be plugged into a computer's external video port to project the computer's video display to a projection screen. An extremely bright bulb is necessary to project this image to the screen. The light output is measured in *lumens*. More lumens are necessary for locations with a higher amount of ambient light (existing light in the room). Projectors are used for presentations and for teaching and are common in conference rooms and training centers; however, some schools and companies opt to go for large flat-screen TVs instead of using projectors, even though projectors can usually project a larger image. Projectors are available in CRT, LCD, and DLP versions. The CRT and LCD technologies work in a similar fashion to the monitor technologies of the same name, whereas DLP uses light valves with rotating color wheels. Common display resolutions for projectors include SVGA (800x600), XGA (1024x768), and high-definition resolutions such as 720p and 1080p; the price of the projector increases with each type of resolution mentioned, and with other characteristics such as the brightness, contrast, and noise. A video projector can be used with a laptop, by utilizing the display toggle button, or can be used with a computer that has a video card with dual outputs.

Video Settings and Software

So, you've selected and installed a video card, and the monitor is connected to the computer. What next? Now it's time to install drivers (if not done already during the installation process) and configure settings in Windows such as the color depth, resolution, and refresh rate, plus features such as Multiple Monitor and on-screen settings.

Drivers

Device drivers (otherwise known as software drivers) are programs that enable the operating system to communicate with the actual device. For example, a video driver enables the operating system to interact with the video card. The driver simplifies the amount of work that an application needs to do by acting as a go-between for the application and the device.

Video drivers (or the lack thereof) have been known to cause headaches for technicians. However, if a couple simple rules are adhered to, many of the plaguing video driver issues can be avoided:

▶ Use the *manufacturer's* driver. When you install a video card, Windows attempts to use a Microsoft version of the driver. This is usually not the best option, especially for newer cards. Instead, use the driver that came on disc with the device, or better yet, access the manufacturer's website to download the latest driver for the device. You can check the date of the driver on the website against the date listed in the Device Manager to see if you currently have the latest.

▶ Watch out for new operating systems. Newer operating systems don't always have all the kinks worked out. Sometimes new hardware will not operate properly with a new operating system until updates have been released, or the first service pack has been issued for the operating system. Before installing a new operating system, verify that the device is listed as compatible. For example, when installing Windows, visit the Windows Compatibility Center. (For more information on compatibility, see Chapter 8.) Make sure to update the operating system after the installation is complete.

To work with video drivers in Windows, open the Device Manager and then expand the Display Adapters category. This shows the video card. Right-click the device and select Properties; then select the Driver tab. This shows a lot of information including the manufacturer of the driver. If it says Microsoft, consider downloading the latest driver from the manufacturer's website. If it says NVIDIA, ATI, or something else, then you already have a manufacturer's version of the driver, though it might not be the latest. From this window you can also see the date of the driver, update the driver to the latest version, roll back the driver if a new installation has failed, or uninstall the driver completely.

Sometimes, if a driver fails, the system will not display anything on the screen. If this happens, try pressing F8 during startup and boot into either Enable Low-Resolution Video (in 7/Vista), Enable VGA Mode (in XP), or if those don't work, attempt to boot into Safe Mode. These start the computer without the normal video driver and instead will use a basic VGA driver at 640x480 resolution. In some cases, the computer automatically asks you if you want to start in Safe Mode, recognizing that there is a video issue. Note that Enable Low-Resolution Video and Enable VGA Mode use a basic VGA driver, but all other drivers work normally. However, Safe Mode starts the system with a minimal set of drivers. If a driver does fail, Internet access might be required to download the latest driver. This is not available in Safe Mode, but it is available in either of the low resolution modes named previously.

Color Depth

Color depth (also known as bit depth or color quality) is a term used to describe the amount of bits that represent color. For example, 1-bit color is known as monochrome, those old screens with a black background and one color for the text, like in old "Six Million Dollar Man" episodes, or like Neo's computer in *The Matrix!* But what is 1 bit? 1 bit in the binary numbering system means a binary number with one digit; this can be a zero or a one, for a total of two values: usually black and white. This is defined in scientific notation as 2^1, (2 to the 1st power equals 2). Another example would be 4-bit color, used by the ancient but awesome Commodore 64 computer. In a 4-bit color system you can have 16 colors total. In this case $2^4 = 16$. Of course 16 colors aren't nearly enough for today's applications; 16 bit, 24 bit, and 32 bit are the most common color depths used by Windows.

Now that you know the basics, take a look at Table 12.3 that shows the different color depths used in Windows.

TABLE 12.3   **List of Color Depths Used in Windows**

Color Depth	Amount of Colors	Calculation
8 bit	256	2^8
16 bit	65,536	2^{16}
24 bit	16,777,216	2^{24}
32 bit	4,294,967,296	2^{32}

8-bit color is used in VGA mode, which is uncommon for normal use, but you might see it if you boot into Safe Mode, or other advanced modes that disable the normal video driver. 16-bit is usually enough for the average user who works with basic applications; however, many computers are configured by default to 24-bit or 32-bit (also known as 3 bytes and 4 bytes respectively). Most users will not have a need for 32-bit color depth; in fact, it uses up resources that might be better put to work elsewhere. If the user works only on basic applications, consider scaling them down to 24-bit or 16-bit to increase system performance. However, gamers, graphics artists, and other designers probably want 32-bit color depth. Some applications and games have the capability to work outside of Windows when it comes to color depth, and a user can select a different color depth for the application than what they use for Windows.

To modify color depth do the following:

- ► **In Windows 7:** Right-click the desktop and select Screen Resolution. Click the monitor you want to modify (if there is more than one), and click the Advanced Settings link. In the video card's Properties window, select the Adapter tab, and click the List All Modes button. From here you can select color depth, as well as resolution options and refresh frequency.

- ► **In Windows Vista:** Right-click the desktop and select Personalize. Then click the Display Settings link. A drop-down menu for color depth is located near the bottom-right part of this window.

- ► **In Windows XP:** Right-click the desktop and select Properties. Then click the Setting tab within the Display Properties window. A drop-down menu for color depth is located near the bottom right of this window.

Resolution

Display resolution is described as the amount of pixels (picture elements) on a screen. It is measured horizontally by vertically (HxV). The more pixels that can be used on the screen, the bigger the desktop becomes, and a user can fit more windows on the display. The word *resolution* is somewhat of a misnomer and will also be referred to as *pixel dimensions*. Table 12.4 shows some of the typical resolutions used in Windows.

TABLE 12.4 **List of Resolutions Used in Windows**

Resolution Type	Full Name	Pixel Dimension	Aspect Ratio
VGA*	Video Graphics Array	640x480	4:3 (1.333:1)
SVGA*	Super Video Graphics Array	800x600	4:3 (1.333:1)
XGA	eXtended Graphics Array	1024x768	4:3 (1.333:1)
WXGA min. (720p)	Widescreen eXtended Graphics Array minimum	1280x720	16:9 (1.78:1)
WXGA	Widescreen eXtended Graphics Array	1280x800	16:10 (1.6:1)
WXGA (HD)	Widescreen eXtended Graphics Array (High Definition)	1366x768	16:9 (1.78:1)
SXGA	Super eXtended Graphics Array	1280x1024	5:4 (1.25:1)

TABLE 12.4 **Continued**

Resolution Type	Full Name	Pixel Dimension	Aspect Ratio
SXGA+	Super eXtended Graphics Array Plus	1400x1050	4:3 (1.333:1)
UXGA	Ultra eXtended Graphics Array	1600x1200	4:3 (1.333:1)
WSXGA+	Widescreen Super eXtended Graphics Array Plus	1680x1050	16:10 (1.6:1)
WSXGA+ (HD)	Widescreen Super eXtended Graphics Array Plus (High-Definition)	1680x945	16:9 (1.78:1)
WUXGA	Widescreen Ultra eXtended Graphics Array	1920x1200	8:5 (1.6:1)
HD 1080P and 1080i	Full High Definition	1920x1080	16:9 (1.78:1)

*VGA and SVGA modes are usually seen only if you attempt to boot the system into Safe Mode or other advanced boot mode, or if the video driver has failed.

Aspect ratio can be defined as an image's width divided by its height; for example, XGA's resolution is 1024x768. If you divide the width (1024) by the height (768), your result would be 1.333. You also hear this referred to as a four-to-three ratio (4:3). This means that for ever 4 pixels running horizontally, there are 3 pixels running vertically. Wider resolutions have a higher first number, for example 16:9. Most current laptops and desktop LCD screens use a widescreen format by default, either 16:9 or 16:10; though you can still purchase LCD monitors that are based off the 4:3 ratio.

A common resolution for older desktop LCDs is XGA; however, even though they are older, you still see them in the field for a while. In fact, I have one running in DualView mode off my laptop right now. Today's common resolutions for desktop LCDs and laptops are WXGA, SXGA+, UXGA, and WSXGA+. Display resolutions continue to get larger; there are a dozen or so higher standards that aren't listed in Table 12.4. For example, the monitor used during the writing of this book has a maximum resolution of 2048x1152, which is known as QWXGA (Quad Wide eXtended Graphics Array). Keep in mind however that the maximum resolution of a monitor can be achieved only if the video card can support it. Video cards' maximum resolution is rated in two ways: maximum digital resolution and maximum VGA resolution. The VGA number is usually less than the digital number.

ExamAlert

Memorize the basic differences between XGA, WXGA, SXGA+, UXGA, WSXGA+, and WUXGA for the exam.

To modify screen resolution in Windows do the following:

▶ **In Windows 7:** Right-click the desktop, and select Screen Resolution. The Resolution drop-down menu is within that window.

▶ **In Windows Vista:** Right-click the desktop, and select Personalize. Then click the Display Settings link. Toward the bottom-left part of the window is a box called Resolution, which has a slider that enables you to configure the pixel dimensions. Drag the slider to the appropriate resolution.

▶ **In Windows XP:** Right-click the desktop, and select Properties. Then click the Setting tab within the Display Properties window. Toward the bottom-left part of the window is a box called Screen resolution, which has a slider that enables you to configure the pixel dimensions. Drag the slider to the appropriate resolution.

Sometimes a user might set the resolution too high, resulting in a scrambled or distorted display. This can happen when video cards support higher resolution modes than the monitor does. If this happens, reboot the computer into either Enable Low Resolution Video (Enable VGA Mode in XP) or Safe Mode and adjust the resolution setting to a level that the monitor can support.

A video card's amount of memory dictates the highest resolution and color depth settings. You can multiply the resolution by the color depth to find out how much memory will be needed. For example, if a user wanted to run a 1920×1080 resolution at 32-bit color (4 bytes of color), the equation would be $1920 \times 1080 \times 4$, which would equal approximately 8 MB, easily covered by most video cards. But keep in mind that this is the bare minimum needed to display Windows and that more will be necessary for advanced GUIs such as Windows Aero. Much more video memory is necessary to run games and graphics programs. Some desktop computers and laptops have integrated video, which use shared video memory. This means that instead of the video device having its own memory, it shares the motherboard's RAM. Motherboard RAM will usually be slower than a video card's memory, and there will probably be less available. Due to this, a PCI Express video card is recommended over integrated video for computers that run resource-intensive applications and games.

Refresh Rate

Refresh rate is generally known as the amount of times a display is "painted" per second. It is more specifically known as *vertical refresh rate*. Refresh rate works differently in LCDs and CRTs.

On a CRT, the display is painted in horizontal lines one at a time from top to bottom, at high speed. This is done by an electron beam. When the entire display has been painted, it is considered one refresh. By default on many systems, this is set to occur 60 times per second, or 60 Hz. However, to reduce eye strain when working with CRTs, it is possible to increase this number to a higher amount, for example 72 Hz or 85 Hz, which reduces *flicker*. The faster the screen is painted, the less a user's eyes have to work to register what they see. Keep in mind that the video card must support a higher refresh rate to match the monitor.

On an LCD, refresh rate works differently because LCDs use a completely different technology to paint the screen. Instead of painting the screen at x times per second, the liquid crystal material is illuminated. However, you can still modify the Windows refresh rate, which effectively configures how many times per second a new image is received from the video card. This is usually set to 60 Hz and is not configurable on most LCDs. Flicker is not as much of an issue on LCDs because the backlight (lamp) is set to its own rate, often at 200 Hz. Because refresh rate is not configurable on most LCDs, you might not see this measurement in an LCDs specifications (aside from the newer 120 and 240 Hz models).

To modify the Windows refresh rate for CRTs or LCDs:

- ▶ **In Windows 7:** Right-click the desktop and select Screen Resolution. Click the monitor you want to modify (if there is more than one), and click the Advanced Settings link. In the video card's Properties window, select the Adapter tab and click the List All Modes button. From here you can modify the refresh frequency (along with other settings).

- ▶ **In Windows Vista:** Right-click the desktop and select Personalize. Then click the Display Settings link. Click the Advanced Settings button and click the Monitor tab. Select the Screen refresh rate from the drop-down menu.

- ▶ **In Windows XP:** Right-click the desktop and select Properties. Then click the Setting tab within the Display Properties window. Click the Advanced button and then click the Monitor tab. Select the Screen refresh rate from the drop-down menu.

Don't confuse the refresh rate with frames per second (frames/s or fps). Although the two are directly related, they are not the same thing. For example, if playing a video game that is set to run at 90 frames/s, the game attempts to send those frames of video data from the video card to the monitor. However, the monitor might be limited to a 60 Hz refresh rate. If this is the case, the video card attempts to display the additional frames within the given refresh rate, causing a sort of blur, which might or might not be acceptable to the user. To many users in the gaming community, the higher the frames/s, the better. But to actually attain a higher frame rate, a higher refresh rate will also be necessary. With a CRT monitor this was historically 85 Hz or higher; with an LCD monitor, this higher refresh rate wasn't available until recently with newer 120 Hz and higher technologies.

OSD and Degaussing

The on-screen display (OSD) can help configure picture quality. It can aid in fixing problems of all types including distortion, picture size, centering, and contrast and brightness. The OSD is superimposed on top of the monitor's display and can usually be accessed by pressing a Menu button or other like button on the monitor either below the display or on one of the sides of the monitor. From there, arrow buttons enable the user to make modifications to the settings. Typical settings for LCDs and CRTs include picture size, picture centering, contrast, and brightness. Keep in mind that laptop displays usually have only a brightness setting.

CRT displays also offer the ability to *degauss* the screen. Degaussing is the process to decrease an unwanted magnetic field in the CRT. The CRT has a metal plate near the front of the monitor that picks up magnetic fields, which over time produce discoloration or other undesired effects on the screen. To degauss the screen (and remove the unwanted effects), there is usually a degauss option within the OSD menu, or there will be a degauss button directly on the monitor. If pressed, the whole screen distorts and shakes for a moment, and then should return to normal, without the discoloration or other undesired effects. Be careful with the degauss feature, it is not meant to be used often.

Multiple Monitor

Multiple Monitor (also referred to as DualView) is a Windows feature that allows you to either duplicate the display onto other monitors, or extend the desktop across to multiple displays. In the latter case it enables you to spread applications over two or more monitors that effectively work together as one. This works well for applications that are wide, or if a user needs to see multiple windows at the same time. If you extend the display, the additional screens used in Multiple Monitor do not have a taskbar; they just have the wallpaper or background that was selected. It is possible to select any of the monitors connected to the computer as the primary monitor, meaning the one with the Start button, taskbar, and so on. You need to connect an additional monitor to one of the extra video ports on the computer. Newer video cards have DVI ports and/or HDMI ports. But you can still connect older SVGA monitors; just use a DVI to VGA adapter. Then you need to open the Multiple Monitor configuration window.

▶ **In Windows 7:** Right-click the desktop and select Screen Resolution. Detect and configure multiple monitors from here.

▶ **In Windows Vista:** Right-click the desktop and select Personalize. Then select Display Settings. This opens the Display Settings window.

▶ **In Windows XP:** Right-click the desktop and select Properties. This opens the Display Properties window. Select the Settings tab.

On a PC, up to ten monitors can be used with the Multiple Monitor feature. On a laptop you are often limited to two (also known as DualView.)

It is possible to use multiple video cards, but keep in mind that Windows 7/Vista prefers identical video cards and drivers. Windows XP might work with different cards/drivers, but it is not recommended. Some applications (for example video players) might not work perfectly on a secondary screen. This depends on the type of video played, the application, and the type of monitor used.

Cram Quiz

Answer these questions. The answers follow the last question. If you cannot answer these questions correctly, consider reading this section again until you can.

220-801 Questions

1. Which expansion bus slot is typically white in color?

   ○ **A.** PCIe

   ○ **B.** AGP

   ○ **C.** PCI

   ○ **D.** LCD

2. Which of the following supports digital only connections?

   ○ **A.** DVI-A

   ○ **B.** DVI-D

   ○ **C.** DVI-I

   ○ **D.** VGA

3. When installing a video card, what should you do before inserting the card into the slot?

- ○ **A.** Connect cables.
- ○ **B.** Install drivers.
- ○ **C.** Test.
- ○ **D.** Prepare the slot.

4. Which of the following uses a TFT active-matrix display? (Select all that apply.)

- ○ **A.** LCD
- ○ **B.** CRT
- ○ **C.** Projector
- ○ **D.** Laptop

5. Where is the best place to get the latest driver for a video card?

- ○ **A.** Microsoft
- ○ **B.** CD-ROM
- ○ **C.** A friend
- ○ **D.** Manufacturer's website

6. How many colors are there if the color depth in Windows is set to 24 bit?

- ○ **A.** 16
- ○ **B.** 65,536
- ○ **C.** 16,777,216
- ○ **D.** 24

7. A computer is set to 1280x1024 resolution. Which standard is it using?

- ○ **A.** XGA
- ○ **B.** SXGA
- ○ **C.** UXGA
- ○ **D.** WXGA

8. What resolution does Windows use when started in Safe Mode?

- ○ **A.** 800x600
- ○ **B.** 1024x768
- ○ **C.** 640x480
- ○ **D.** 1280x800

9. What is a common refresh rate for an LCD?

   ○ **A.** 30 Hz

   ○ **B.** 60 Hz

   ○ **C.** 200 Hz

   ○ **D.** 60 MHz

10. What is the maximum amount of monitors Windows allows in a Multiple Monitor environment?

    ○ **A.** 10

    ○ **B.** 2

    ○ **C.** 4

    ○ **D.** 1

220-802 Questions

11. A user set the resolution in Windows too high resulting in a scrambled distorted display. What should you do?

    ○ **A.** Upgrade the video driver.

    ○ **B.** Boot into low resolution mode.

    ○ **C.** Boot into the recovery console.

    ○ **D.** Check the video connections.

12. You are troubleshooting a video issue. Which utility should you use?

    ○ **A.** Regedit

    ○ **B.** Msconfig

    ○ **C.** Dxdiag

    ○ **D.** Task Manager

13. You receive a computer that has a broken on-board DVI connector. What should you attempt first?

    ○ **A.** Replace the motherboard.

    ○ **B.** Replace the DVI connector.

    ○ **C.** Install a video card.

    ○ **D.** Use an adapter.

14. You just replaced a video card in a PC with another card from a different manufacturer. However, the driver installation does not complete. What should you do first?

    ○ **A.** Install the driver again.

    ○ **B.** Locate the latest version of the driver.

    ○ **C.** Roll back the driver.

    ○ **D.** Install the original video card.

Cram Quiz Answers

220-801 Answers

1. **C.** Peripheral Component Interconnect (PCI) slots are usually white in color. PCIe are often black or blue, AGP slots are often brown, and LCD is a type of monitor.

2. **B**. DVI-D supports digital-only connections, which are common on newer LCDs. DVI-A supports analog-only. DVI-I supports both digital and analog, and VGA is an analog connection.

3. **D.** Before inserting the card into the slot, prepare the slot by manipulating any locking mechanism and removing the appropriate slot cover(s).

4. **A** and **D**. Liquid Crystal Displays normally use the TFT active-matrix technology. Laptops have LCDs so they use the same technology.

5. **D.** The manufacturer's website is the best place to get the latest driver. The disc supplied with the card is usually satisfactory, but it will not be the latest driver.

6. **C.** 24-bit color is equal to 16,777,216 colors in total, otherwise known as 2^{24} power. Sixteen colors would be 4-bit, 65,536 colors would be 16-bit, and there is no setting that allows for 24 colors.

7. **B**. Super eXtended Graphics Array (SXGA) resolution is 1280x1024.

8. **C.** Safe Mode boots the computer with a minimal set of drivers including the video driver. Due to this, the resolution is set to 640x480 VGA mode.

9. **B.** A typical refresh rate for LCDs is 60 Hz.

10. **A**. The Multiple Monitor feature in Windows 7/Vista/XP supports up to 10 monitors. A laptop supports a lesser version of Multiple Monitor known as DualView, which supports a maximum of 2 monitors.

220-802 Answers

11. **B**. Boot into a low-resolution mode. In Windows 7/Vista this is called Enable Low Resolution Mode, and in XP it is called Enable VGA Mode. Safe Mode is another valid option, but keep in mind that Safe Mode loads Windows with a minimal set of drivers, and you can't access the Internet if necessary.

12. **C**. You should use Dxdiag to troubleshoot video issues. The other three answers are not used to troubleshoot video.

13. **C**. Try installing a video card first to see if the system will still work. Unless it is a specialized system, the video card should be less expensive than the motherboard. (Not to mention it will take a lot less time to install.) As PC techs we usually do not replace connectors, but it is a possibility, but farther down the list. An adapter cannot help if the DVI port is broken.

14. **C**. If the driver installation doesn't complete, you should roll back the driver. It could be that you have attempted to install the incorrect driver. After you roll back the faulty installation, go and find the correct latest version of the video driver from the manufacturer's website. Installing the driver again can most likely have the same result. Only re-install the original video card temporarily if you cannot find a proper solution right away.

The Audio Subsystem

In some environments, sound is not required; but more often than not, it is either wanted or is mandatory. So although troubleshooting sound is not as common as troubleshooting video (in most environments), it is still something that a technician will do fairly commonly in the field.

The audio subsystem consists of the sound card, the expansion bus used, audio ports, connectivity in the form of internal and external audio cables, speakers, sound card drivers, and any additional third-party audio software. The sound card is the basis for audio, so let's begin by discussing that device now.

Sound Cards

The sound card is responsible for generating sound from the data sent to it by either the operating system, or in older systems, by the CD-ROM drive. Audio devices can be integrated into the motherboard, installed to PCI and PCIe slots, and can be connected to USB and IEEE 1394 ports. However, the typical audio device known as the soundcard is installed to a slot on the motherboard.

One of my computers uses a Creative Labs Sound Blaster soundcard. It's a PCIe x1 card, which means that it can fit within a x1, x4, or x16 slot. It has most of the ports a user would need for outputting and inputting sound. Figure 12.5 shows the ports on the back of this card and typical integrated audio ports on the back of a motherboard.

Most sound cards are color-coded. This color scheme is defined by the PC System Design Guide, version PC 99 (which was finalized as version PC 2001). It specifies the following colors for the TRS 1/8 inch mini-jacks like the ones shown in Figure 12.5:

▶ **Light blue:** Line input. Sometimes this seconds as a microphone input.

▶ **Pink:** Microphone input.

▶ **Lime green:** Main output for stereo speakers or headphones. Can also act as a line out.

▶ **Black:** Output for surround sound speakers (rear speakers).

▶ **Silver/Brown:** Output for additional two speakers in a 7.1 system (middle surround speakers).

▶ **Orange:** Output for center speaker and subwoofer.

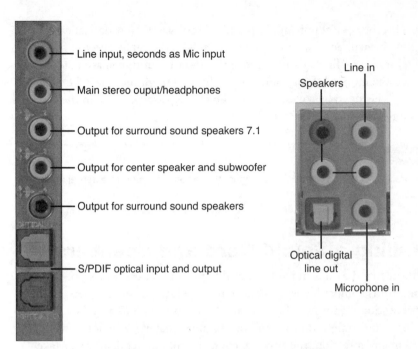

FIGURE 12.5 **A typical sound card's ports and integrated audio ports on a mother-board**

ExamAlert

Know the PC 99 audio port color codes for the exam.

On the sound card in Figure 12.5, note an optical input and output. This is known as a Sony/Phillips Digital Interconnect Format (S/PDIF) port. This particular version of S/PDIF is called TOSLINK. It delivers high-quality digital sound over fiber optic cable. It is also known as a *digital optical port*. It is considered by some to be sonically superior to the analog 1/8-inch mini-jacks described previously. The S/PDIF output can be used to connect to a home theater system or other receiver; this enables the user to play CDs, MP3s, and so on, on the system of their choice. The input can connect recording equipment, game consoles and so on, enabling a user to bring high-quality audio into the computer to be manipulated as the user sees fit. The input is usually black and the output is gray. Cables connecting TOSLINK ports can be a maximum of 10 meters, but are normally found in 5 meter lengths. The optical port (when enabled in Windows) emits a red, laser-like light. Normally, the port has a soft plastic cover that should block this when a cable is not plugged in. If this is missing, you can block it with electrical tape, or better yet, turn off the optical port in the soundcard software. New optical cables are shipped with small end caps to protect the ends of the cable, and to protect your eyes from this light. Don't remove the end caps until you are ready to plug the cable in. (And if the cable doesn't fit, you might have left the plug on, or the cable needs to be rotated.) Store the end caps somewhere in the case you need to store the cable later.

> **Note**
>
> There are also coaxial-based S/PDIF connectors, more common to external audio devices.

Installing a Sound Card and Speakers

Installing a sound card is much like installing any other card. First, be sure that the card is compatible with the installed operating system. Then employ ESD prevention measures. The card should be inserted into a PCI or PCIe slot by pressing straight down with both thumbs, making sure not to wiggle the card in any direction; this way the contacts will not get damaged. Make sure it is fully inserted; you shouldn't see any of the gold-colored edge contacts. Then screw the card in where the slot cover used to be within the case.

However, you aren't finished. Now you need to connect any front panel case connections that the card might support, hook up the CD-ROM drive if necessary, connect the speakers, and finally install the driver for the card:

▶ **Make front panel connections:** One common type of front panel connection is known as Intel High Definition Audio (HD Audio). This uses a 10-pin cable that goes from a compatible sound card (or motherboard if sound is integrated) to the front of the compatible case. It is keyed at pin 8 so that the cable cannot be connected upside down. This port enables a user to connect headphones and a microphone to the front of the case instead of having to connect them to the sound card on the back of the computer. Creative Labs and other manufacturers also offer advanced devices that can be installed to a 5.25-inch bay so that the user can have greater access to connections, volume, and so on. The predecessor to the HD Audio connection is AC'97. You might see both connectors inside your computer case, but HD Audio is usually preferred.

▶ **Connect the CD-ROM drive:** Newer computers do not need a CD audio cable. Music CDs are played directly through the data connection, be it SATA or IDE. However, to play audio CDs on an older computer with an older operating system, you need to connect a CD audio cable from the sound card to the CD-ROM drive. The two options are to connect a 4-pin analog cable or a 2-pin digital cable if your CD-ROM drive supports it. These two ports are usually located on the edge of the sound card and can be found on the back of the CD-ROM drive. Without this cable, audio CDs cannot be heard from the computer's speakers on older systems. Many newer sound cards do not even offer a CD audio cable port, and newer SATA CD-ROM drives and DVD/CD combo drives will not have the CD audio cable port.

▶ **Connect the speakers:** Back in the day a pair of speakers would be connected to the sound card, and you were done. But now, you might be using a 5.1 or 7.1 system, and if so, you need to color coordinate! 5.1 surround sound means that the system uses five regular speakers (left, right, center, back left, and back right) and one speaker for low frequencies, which is usually a subwoofer. 7.1 builds upon this by adding two additional surround speakers. Normally, the lime green output is for the first two speakers (or headphones), which gives standard stereo 2.1 output (two speakers + sub). The black output is for two rear speakers, and the orange output is for the center channel and the subwoofer; an AC outlet will be necessary to power the subwoofer. A grey, brown, or other dark port is used for two additional speakers (middle surround) in a 7.1 system. Another option is to use the digital fiber optical output or digital coaxial output. There are a lot of options, so read the manual on the sound card and the speakers when trying to hook everything together, and pay attention to the little icons that are engraved into the back of the sound card next to the ports.

▶ **Install the driver and software:** Installing a sound card driver is usually done from the Installation CD that accompanies the sound card. It's also wise to check the manufacturer's website for any critical updates to the driver files. The CD usually comes with additional software to take control of the sound card. Keep in mind that this software might conflict with other audio software, or media player software that was already installed on a PC. Consider using one or the other for things such as volume, equalization, and sound effects. Disable or uninstall any unused audio applications or media players to avoid conflicts.

ExamAlert

Know how to install sound cards, connect speakers, and connect other internal audio connections for the exam.

Audio Quality

Audio quality is measured in several ways, but it all starts with the sampling rate and the amount of bits per sample (known as bit depth). Standard audio CDs have a sampling rate of 44 kHz, sampling 16 bits at a time (known as 16-bit) per channel, using two channels (known as stereo or 2.1). This is referred to collectively as 16-bit/44 kHz and is considered CD-quality. For stereo output of music this has been the standard ever since CDs were first developed in the 1980s. Songs are recorded to the CD in an uncompressed format known as a .WAV file. Another measurement you might see or hear of is the total data rate (or bit rate). This is the amount of bits that the CD plays per second and is calculated as sampling rate × bits × channels, or 44,100 × 16 × 2 = 1,411,200 bits, or 1411 kbps. A standard audio CD is designed to play a maximum of 74 minutes of music at 1411 kbps. To find the total capacity of an audio CD, we would multiply 1,411,200 bits × 74 (minutes) × (seconds). This would come to a total of 783 million bytes, essentially a 750 MB CD.

There are technologies that use higher data rates, and technologies that use lower data rates. For example, DVD-Audio (DVD-A) can be recorded at a maximum of 24-bit/192 kHz in stereo. Given this fact, many sound cards (including the one installed during this chapter) can output at 24-bit/192 kHz. And DVD-Audio might go beyond just two speakers; it might be designed for 5.1 surround sound; however, it would be at a lesser sampling rate. On the other end of the spectrum, MP3s, which are compressed versions of audio files, generally range between 128 kbps and 320 kbps. Compare this to CD quality that is 1411 kbps. However, MP3s and other compressed audio files are done in a smart way to retain CD-quality sound. Table 12.5 compares CDs, DVDs, and a couple types of compressed music files.

TABLE 12.5 **Comparison of Audio Types**

Audio Type	Sampling Rate	Bit Depth	Data Rate
Audio CD	44 kHz	16 bit	1411 kbps
DVD-Audio	192 kHz maximum	24-bit maximum	9.6 Mbps
MP3 (MPEG Layer-3)	n/a	n/a	128−320 kbps (typically)
WMA (Windows Media Audio)	n/a	n/a	48−192 kbps (typically)

ExamAlert

Know the basic differences between Audio CDs, DVD-Audio, and compressed music files for the exam.

Media players like Windows Media Player (which is built in to Windows), iTunes, and Winamp can play audio CDs, DVD-Audio, and compressed files such as .wma, .aac, and .mp3 (which are all digital audio-only formats). Certain versions of these programs can also "rip" CDs, taking the song from the CD and creating a compressed .wma, .aac, or .mp3 from it (if the CD is not encrypted). These compressed files can be anywhere from one-tenth to one-fourth the size of the original .WAV file on CD. They can then be transferred to just about any type of device including portable music players, USB flash drives, SD cards, and so on.

Cram Quiz

Answer these questions. The answers follow the last question. If you cannot answer these questions correctly, consider reading this section again until you can.

220-801 Questions

1. What types of cables are used to connect speakers/audio devices to a sound card? (Select all that apply.)
   - ○ **A.** 1/8-inch mini-jacks
   - ○ **B.** DVI
   - ○ **C.** S/PDIF
   - ○ **D.** RCA

2. Which of the following are commonly used expansion buses for sound cards? (Select all that apply.)
   - ○ **A.** AGP
   - ○ **B.** PCI
   - ○ **C.** PCIe
   - ○ **D.** AMR

3. What standard is followed by most sound card manufacturers for the colors of the 1/8 mini-jacks?
   - ○ **A.** PCI
   - ○ **B.** PC 99
   - ○ **C.** PC 100
   - ○ **D.** PCIe

4. What is the total data rate of an audio CD?
   - ○ **A.** 320 kbps
   - ○ **B.** 160 kbps
   - ○ **C.** 1411 kbps
   - ○ **D.** 9.6 Mbps

220-802 Questions

5. A customer has a PC with a sound card that is emitting a red light out of one port. What is happening?

   - ○ **A.** The sound card is about to fail.
   - ○ **B.** The sound card is defective.
   - ○ **C.** The optical cable is not connected to the sound card.
   - ○ **D.** That is the normal sound card LED.

6. A user complains that speakers are connected to the PC but are not playing audio. What should you do first?

   - ○ **A.** Move the speaker cable to another jack on the sound card.
   - ○ **B.** Move the speaker cable to the headphone jack on the optical drive.
   - ○ **C.** Reinstall the sound drivers.
   - ○ **D.** Install a new sound card.

Cram Quiz Answers

220-801 Answers

1. **A** and **C**. The colored connectors on the back of the sound card are known as TRS 1/8-inch mini-jacks. S/PDIF is the optical output (and possibly input) found on the back of the sound card. DVI is a video port, and RCA is another port that can be used for video and audio but won't be found on the back of a sound card; however, RCA might be found on I/O drives that are loaded into the front of a computer in a 5.25-inch bay, enabling for greater connectivity on the computer's front panel.

2. **B** and **C**. PCI Express (x1) and PCI are common expansion buses for sound cards. AGP is for video-only, and AMR, although it used to be utilized for combination sound/modem cards, is rarely seen today.

3. **B**. PC 99 specifies the color scheme used by all kinds of equipment including a sound card's 1/8 mini-jacks.

4. **C**. 1411 kbps is the total data rate (or bit rate) of an audio CD. 320 kbps is the maximum data rate for MP3, 160 kbps is a common data rate for WMA files, and 9.6 Mbps is the total data rate of DVD-Audio.

220-802 Answers

5. **C**. If a red light is emitting from the sound card's port, it is because there is no cable plugged into the optical port. There is not a LED on the back of a sound card, and the card is not about to fail, nor has it failed already.

6. **A**. The first thing you should check when there is no audio is if there is volume (and if the volume is muted). Then check if the speakers have power (if they are required to be plugged in.) But after that the best answer is to move the speaker to another jack (the correct jack) on the sound card. Only try reinstalling sound drivers or a new card after you have eliminated the basic culprits.

CHAPTER 13

Peripherals and Custom Computing

This chapter covers the following A+ exam topics:

▶ Input/Output, Input Devices, and Peripherals

▶ Custom PC Configurations

You can find a master list of A+ exam topics in the "Introduction."

This chapter covers portions of CompTIA A+ 220-801 objectives 1.4, 1.6, 1.7, 1.9, 1.11 and 1.12, and CompTIA A+ 220-802 objectives 1.4, and 1.9.

The computer is built, the OS is installed, and video is configured. Now let's discuss the devices and peripherals we add on to the computer, the ports they connect to, as well as some custom PC configurations you will undoubtedly encounter in the field.

Input/Output, Input Devices, and Peripherals

To take advantage of a computer, the appropriate input/output devices and peripherals must be connected to the proper input/output (I/O) ports. Keyboards, mice, and multimedia devices can be connected to a variety of ports, most commonly, USB. This section briefly describes those devices and the ports they connect to.

I/O Ports

I/O ports enable a user to input information by way of keyboard, mouse, and microphone; plus they enable the output of information to printers, monitors, USB devices, and so on. The CompTIA A+ exams require a person to describe USB, IEEE 1394 (FireWire), Bluetooth, serial, and parallel ports. The most common of these by far is USB.

USB

Universal Serial Bus (USB) ports are used by many devices including keyboards, mice, printers, cameras, and much more. The USB port enables data transfer between the device and the computer and usually powers the device as well. The speed of a USB device's data transfer depends on the version of the USB port, as shown in Table 13.1.

TABLE 13.1 **Comparison of USB Versions**

USB Version	Name	Data Transfer Rate
USB 1.0	Low-speed	1.5 Mbps
USB 1.1	Full-speed	12 Mbps
USB 2.0	High-speed	480 Mbps
USB 3.0	Super-speed	5.0 Gbps

USB 1.0 is deprecated, and although the USB 3.0 specification was completed in 2008, many computers still have only a couple USB 3.0 ports, whereas the rest of the ports are only USB 2.0.

ExamAlert

Memorize the specifications for USB versions 1.1, 2.0, and 3.0 for the exam.

A computer can have a maximum of 127 USB devices. However, most computers have only four to eight USB ports. To add devices beyond this, a USB hub can be used, but no more than five hubs can be in a series of USB devices. All cables connecting USB devices must comply with their standard's maximum length. USB version 1.1 cables are limited to 3 meters in length (a little less than 10 feet), and USB version 2.0 cables can be a maximum length of 5 meters (a little more than 16 feet). Maximum recommended USB 3.0 length is 3 meters. The standard USB cable has four pins: a +5 V pin for power, positive and negative data pins, and a ground pin. Most USB connections are half-duplex, meaning that the device can send or receive data, but not both simultaneously.

There are various plugs used for the different types of USB connections. The most common are Type A and Type B, which are 4-pin connectors, but there are also mini- and micro-connectors, which are 5-pin. Type A connectors are the type you see on the back of a computer or on the side of a laptop. Figure 13.1 displays an illustration of these connectors.

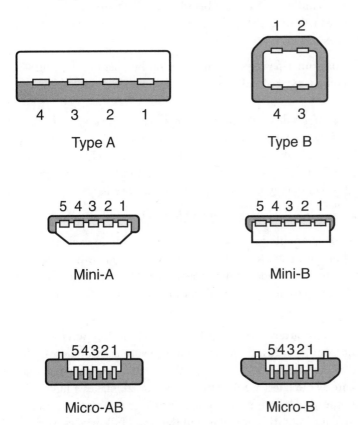

FIGURE 13.1 **USB connectors**

Type A and Type B connectors are commonly used for printers and other larger devices. Mini- and micro-connectors are often used for handheld computers, smartphones, digital cameras, portable music players, and cell phones. However, some companies create proprietary cables and connectors for their devices based off of the USB specifications. These devices will not connect properly to Type A, Type B, and mini- or micro-connectors.

By default, a USB device is designed to be a host *or* a slave. The host is in charge of initiating data transfers. However, USB version 2.0 introduced On-The-Go (OTG), which enables a device to act as both host *and* slave. This is more common in handheld computers, and smartphones; devices that connect with either mini- or micro-plugs.

USB devices connect to what is known as a root hub, regardless of whether they are USB version 1.1, 2.0, or 3.0 devices. The USB devices, root hub, and host controllers can be viewed from within Windows in a couple ways:

▶ **Device Manager:** Within Device Manager, click Universal Serial Bus Controllers to expand it. The root hub and controllers are listed within. Individual devices will be listed under such categories as Human Interface Devices.

▶ **System Information:** Open System Information by opening the Run prompt and typing `msinfo32`. Expand Components, and select USB.

Windows 7 and Vista offer a disk caching component called ReadyBoost. This uses flash-based memory such as USB flash drives and SD cards to cache information for the OS at high speeds. The cache can be as much as 32 GB in size on one device, or 256 GB in size if spread across multiple devices. For USB flash drives, this technology works best at USB 3.0 speeds.

When troubleshooting USB devices, keep a few things in mind:

▶ **Verify that USB is enabled in the BIOS:** It is possible to enable/disable USB within the BIOS. Keep this in mind when troubleshooting USB devices that are not functioning whatsoever. The user might have inadvertently set this to disabled, or perhaps the computer was shipped in that state.

▶ **Make sure the computer is running USB 3.0:** If the computer is USB 3.0-compliant from a hardware standpoint, make sure it is running USB 3.0 on the software side. Some versions of Windows need to be updated to communicate at the latest USB speeds. This update makes a huge difference in the speed of data transfer. Sometimes Windows informs the user that an update to USB is available and that the USB devices work faster if this update is completed. In other cases, a USB firmware update for the motherboard is needed.

▶ **Verify connectivity:** Make sure the device is plugged in and that it is using the correct cable. Some incompatible USB plugs might look similar to the correct plug and might even connect to a device.

When removing USB devices from a computer, remember to disable them in the Notification Area before disconnecting them. This will avoid damage to a USB device, for example corruption to the USB flash drive. If for some reason you cannot disable it in the system, power down the computer and then disconnect them.

One of the problems with USB is how it suffers from latency. Due to this fact, users who work with audio and video prefer a zero-latency connection such as IEEE 1394.

IEEE 1394

The Institute of Electrical and Electronics Engineers (IEEE) is a nonprofit organization that creates standards regarding cables and connectors and other technology related to electricity. One common standard is IEEE 1394, also known by the brand name versions FireWire, i.Link, and Lynx. It is a port used for devices that demand the low-latency transfer of data in real time, usually music or video. Up to 63 devices can be powered by a computer, with no more than 16 devices per chain. Table 13.2 describes some of the IEEE 1394/FireWire versions.

TABLE 13.2 **Comparison of IEEE 1394/FireWire Versions**

IEEE 1394 Version	Data Transfer Rate	Connector Type	Cable Length Between Devices
IEEE 1394a	400 Mbps	4-conductor and 6-conductor	4.5 meters (15 feet)
IEEE 1394b	800 Mbps[1]	9-conductor	10 meters (100 meters with Category 5e cable)
FireWire 400	400 Mbps	4-conductor and 6-conductor	4.5 meters
FireWire 800	800 Mbps	9-conductor	10 meters
FireWire S1600	1.6 Gbps	9-conductor	10 meters
FireWire S3200	3.2 Gbps	9-conductor	10 meters

[1]The full IEEE 1394b specification describes data rates of 1,600 Mbps and 3,200 Mbps in addition to 800 Mbps.

> **ExamAlert**
>
> Memorize the specifications for IEEE 1394a and b, and FireWire 400 and 800 for the exam.

Serial Versus Parallel

USB and FireWire are both serial buses that were designed to be faster than the original serial bus, which for the most part utilizes the RS-232 standard for the transmission of data. The original 9-pin serial ports are known as DE-9 connectors. (Some people incorrectly refer to them as DB-9 connectors.) These ports, also known as COM ports, are used with external modems. They are also used to communicate directly with networking equipment such as routers. It is rare to see these integrated into today's motherboards anymore, but in networking environments, you might see them on older computers/laptops or perhaps added on as a PCI card so that a network engineer can communicate with various networking equipment. These ports send data serially, meaning one bit at a time. Generally Windows limits these ports to 115.2 Kbps (115,200 bps). Dial-up connections through an external modem are limited to 56 Kbps. Serial ports can be tested with loopback plugs that are similar to the loopback plugs used to test network adapter RJ45 connections.

Parallel connections can deliver more than one bit simultaneously, usually in multiples of eight. This way, one, two, or more bytes of information can be sent at one time. An example of a parallel port is the deprecated 25-pin DB-25 port, also known as a printer port; although other devices like scanners and older SCSI devices could connect to that port. Later, additional types of parallel connectors were developed for the SCSI standard. See Chapter 6, "Storage Devices," for more information on SCSI.

PS/2

The PS/2 connector is used for connecting keyboards and mice to a desktop computer or laptop. The PS/2 port was originally introduced in the late '80s as part of IBM's Personal System/2 computer. Keyboards and mice connect via a 6-pin Mini-DIN connector. In the PC 99 color scheme, PS/2 keyboard ports are purple, and PS/2 mouse ports are green.

Though PS/2 had almost a 20-year run, these connectors are extremely rare on new computers; they were the standard until USB became popular. If they are used on an older Windows system, PS/2 keyboards are automatically configured as Interrupt ReQuest (IRQ) 1, and PS/2 mice are configured as IRQ 12.

Bluetooth

Moving on to a wireless option for peripherals: Bluetooth is a short-range, low-speed wireless network primarily designed to operate in peer-to-peer mode (known as ad-hoc) between PCs and other devices such as printers, projectors, smart phones, mice, keyboards, and so on. Bluetooth runs in virtually the same 2.4 GHz frequency used by IEEE 802.11b, g, and n wireless networks, but uses a spread-spectrum frequency-hopping signaling method to help minimize interference. Bluetooth devices connect to each other to form a personal area network (PAN).

Some systems and devices include integrated Bluetooth adapters, and others need a Bluetooth module connected to the USB port to enable Bluetooth networking. Bluetooth devices must first be paired before they can be used together.

Bluetooth version 1.2 offers a data transfer rate of 1 Mbps. Version 2 is 3 Mbps. Newer versions of Bluetooth can go faster, but they do so by combining with 802.11 WLAN technologies. Bluetooth is divided into classes, each of which has a different range. Table 13.3 shows these classes, their ranges, and the amount of power their corresponding antennae use to generate signal.

TABLE 13.3 **Bluetooth Classes**

Class	mW	Range
Class 1	100 mW	100 meters (328 ft.)
Class 2	2.5 mW	10 meters (33 ft.)
Class 3	1 mW	1 meter (3 ft.)

As you can see, Class 1 generates the most powerful signal and as such has the largest range. The most common Bluetooth devices are Class 2 devices with a range of 10 meters. Examples of this include portable printers, headsets, and computer dongles that connect to USB ports and allow the PC to communicate with other Bluetooth-enabled devices.

Input Devices and Peripherals

Let's briefly discuss the types of devices used to input information and the various peripherals a technician might see in the field.

The usual suspects include the keyboard, for typing information in Windows, and the mouse, for manipulating the GUI. These two are known as human interface devices (HID). Some other devices that you might not have seen yet include KVM switches, touch screens, digital cameras, web cameras, microphones, biometric devices, bar code readers, and MIDI devices. Table 13.4 describes these devices.

TABLE 13.4   **Description of Various Input Devices and Peripherals**

Device	Description	Types and Connections
Keyboard	Used to type text and numbers into a word processor or other application.	101-key keyboard is Standard, USB, PS/2, and wireless connections
Mouse	Used to control the GUI, works in two dimensions. Might have two or more buttons and a scroll wheel to manipulate Windows. The button tab in Mouse Properties is used to switch left and right buttons.	Ball mouse, optical mouse, USB, PS/2, and wireless connections
KVM switch	Enables a user to control two or more computers from one Keyboard, Video display, and Mouse (KVM).	Passive: works off computer's USB power Active: plugs into an AC outlet
Touch screen	A video display that detects the presence of either a finger, stylus, or light pen that enables interaction with Windows. It incorporates a digitizer that converts the tapping on the screen into digital functions.	Used in tablet PCs and smartphones
Digital cameras (digicam)	Takes still photographs and/or video using an electronic image sensor. Images are displayed on screen and can be saved to solid-state media such as SD cards and CompactFlash.	Can be a single device or integrated into PDAs and mobile phones Can connect to the PC via USB
Web cameras (webcam)	Enables a user to monitor other areas of a home or building, communicate via video telephony, and take still images.	Can connect to a PC via USB, to a LAN via RJ45, or a WLAN via 802.11n, g, or b
Scanner	Image scanners are used to optically scan images and other objects and convert them into digital images to be stored on the computer.	Can connect via USB, FireWire, SCSI, and parallel port.
Microphones	Enables the user to record his or her voice, or other sounds to the computer. Common usages are webcasts, podcasts, for voice-overs while screen capturing, and for gaming.	Can connect to a PC via 1/8-inch mini-jack (sound card) or via USB
Biometric devices	Analyzes what a person is. Used for authentication purposes, for example a fingerprint reader.	May be integrated to the PC or can be connected via USB, or connected to the network
Bar code readers	Reads bar codes, for example linear barcodes, 2D barcodes, Post Office barcodes, and such. After physical installation, they need to be programmed to understand these codes.	Connects to the PC via USB, PS/2, or might be integrated into handheld computers and smartphones

TABLE 13.4 **Continued**

Device	Description	Types and Connections
MIDI devices	Musical Instrument Digital Interface. Enables computers, music keyboards, synthesizers, digital recorders, samplers, and so on to control each other and exchange data.	Uses a 5-pin DIN Connector
Game pads and joysticks	A game pad is a game controller. Made famous by Nintendo, Playstation, and Xbox, there are also game pads for PCs. Joysticks are often used for flight simulator games.	Connect via USB Type A connections. Older versions used the 15-pin gaming port on a sound card.

Troubleshooting any of the devices in Table 13.4 is usually quite easy. Make sure that the device is connected properly to the computer (or has a working wireless connection), and verify within the Device Manager that the latest drivers are installed for the device. Then, find out if any additional software is necessary for the device to function. Portions of the software might have to be installed to the device and to Windows.

Keyboards and mice can be especially troublesome. Keyboard errors are commonly caused by jammed keys and defective cables or cable connectors. A common mouse issue is when the cursor jumps around the screen. This could be due to an incorrect mouse driver, or perhaps the mouse is on an uneven or nonreflective surface. Also, you might encounter a mouse that stops working after a computer comes out of sleep mode. Make sure that Windows is updated to the latest service pack and that the correct and latest driver is being used for the mouse.

Cram Quiz

220-801 Questions

Answer these questions. The answers follow the last question. If you cannot answer these questions correctly, consider reading this section again until you can.

1. What is the data transfer rate (speed) of USB 3.0?

    ○ **A.** 12 Mbps

    ○ **B.** 400 Mbps

    ○ **C.** 480 Mbps

    ○ **D.** 5 Gbps

2. What is the maximum amount of USB devices a computer can support?

- ○ **A.** 4
- ○ **B.** 63
- ○ **C.** 127
- ○ **D.** 255

3. Which type of USB connector is normally found on a desktop PC or laptop?

- ○ **A.** Type A
- ○ **B.** Type B
- ○ **C.** Type C
- ○ **D.** Type D

4. What is the maximum data transfer rate of IEEE 1394a?

- ○ **A.** 400 Mbps
- ○ **B.** 800 Mbps
- ○ **C.** 1,600 Mbps
- ○ **D.** 3,200 Mbps

5. You just installed a bar code reader to a laptop. What should you do next?

- ○ **A.** Adjust the light wavelength.
- ○ **B.** Test the reader by reading bar codes.
- ○ **C.** Program the reader to recognize codes.
- ○ **D.** Point the bar code reader at someone.

6. What does a KVM do?

- ○ **A.** Connects a computer to Bluetooth-enabled devices
- ○ **B.** Allows multiple users to share a single computer
- ○ **C.** Networks multiple computers together
- ○ **D.** Connects multiple computers to save resources

7. You are installing a wireless keyboard to a PC. What does the PC require?

- ○ **A.** Bluetooth dongle
- ○ **B.** Infrared connection
- ○ **C.** Ethernet connection
- ○ **D.** USB port

220-802 Questions

8. A user calls you with a complaint that *none* of his USB devices are working. What is the most probable cause?

    ○ **A.** The USB 3.0 controller has failed.

    ○ **B.** The root hub is not configured.

    ○ **C.** USB is disabled in the BIOS.

    ○ **D.** USB is disabled in Windows.

9. You had to disable the USB ports on an infected PC after a virus outbreak. However, the user needs to transfer several large files (1.2 GB each) from a home computer to a work computer. What should you use to transfer the files?

    ○ **A.** Network card

    ○ **B.** Infrared device

    ○ **C.** IEEE 1394 device

    ○ **D.** CD-ROM burner

10. You plug a USB device into the front panel port of a PC but nothing happens. What is the most likely cause?

    ○ **A.** The front panel connectors are not plugged into the motherboard.

    ○ **B.** You plugged a USB 3.0 device into a USB 2.0 port.

    ○ **C.** You need to reboot the computer.

    ○ **D.** You plugged a USB 2.0 device into a USB 3.0 port.

Cram Quiz Answers

220-801 Answers

1. **D**. 5 Gbps is the data rate for USB 3.0; 12 Mbps is the data rate for USB version 1.1; and 400 Mbps is the data rate of IEEE 1394a (FireWire 400). USB 2.0 has a maximum data transfer rate of 480 Mbps.

2. **C**. USB can support up to 127 devices on one computer. However USB hubs will be necessary to go beyond the amount of USB ports (usually 4 or 6) commonly found on a system. FireWire supports up to 63 devices.

3. **A**. Type A connectors are almost always included on desktop PCs and laptops.

4. **A**. IEEE 1394a specifies a maximum data transfer rate of 400 Mbps. IEEE 1394b specifies 800 Mbps, 1,600 Mbps, and 3,200 Mbps.

5. **C**. After physical installation and installing the driver for the device, program the reader to recognize the codes.

6. **D**. A KVM connects multiple computers to a single keyboard, mouse, and monitor. This way, fewer resources in the way of peripherals (input/output devices) are necessary to use the computers.

7. **A**. Wireless keyboards and mice often use Bluetooth to transmit to a PC or laptop. The computer must either have a built-in Bluetooth antenna or a Bluetooth dongle connected to a USB port for the keyboard to function.

220-802 Answers

8. **C**. If none of the USB devices are working, chances are that USB has been disabled in the BIOS. This might be company policy so that users can't access USB drives or boot the computer to one. If the USB 3.0 controller fails, the USB 2.0 controller should still be functioning for other ports. The USB root hub requires no configuring; it is auto-configured by Windows. Although it might be possible to disable one USB device at a time in Windows, it will be uncommon; disabling all the devices in Windows is rare.

9. **C**. You should use an IEEE 1394 (FireWire device). This can transfer large files in an efficient manner. Also, there are many portable IEEE 1394 devices that would make the job easier. The home computer should not be taken to the office, nor should it be connected to the office network, so the network card option is doubly wrong. Infrared devices are not made to transfer big files. CD-ROMs hold only approximately 750 MB max. per disc. The files are too big for this without spanning the files, which is not recommended.

10. **A**. Most likely, the front panel connectors are not plugged into the motherboard. A USB 3.0 device will work fine in a USB 2.0 port but at the lower speed. A USB 2.0 device will work at USB 2.0 speed when plugged into a USB 3.0 port. Rebooting is usually not necessary when installing USB devices.

Custom PC Configurations

There are several custom configurations that you might encounter in the IT field. You should be able to describe what each type of computer is and the hardware that is required for these custom computers to function properly.

Audio/Video Editing Workstation

Multimedia processing requires a fast computer with lots of storage and big displays. Examples of audio/video workstations include

▶ **Graphic art PCs:** These run software such as Adobe Photoshop, Corel products, GIMP, and many more.

▶ **Music recording PCs:** These run software such as Logic Pro or ProTools.

▶ **Video recording PCs:** These run software such as Sony Vegas, Pinnacle, and Camtasia.

> **Note**
>
> Look up each of the software programs and take a look at exactly what they are used for.

This just scratches the surface, but you get the idea. These computers need to be designed to easily manipulate images, video files, and music files. So from a hardware-standpoint they need a specialized video or audio card, the fastest hard drive available with a lot of storage space, and multiple monitors (to view all of the editing windows). Keep in mind that the video and sound cards are going to be expensive devices; be sure to employ all antistatic measures before working with those cards.

> **ExamAlert**
>
> Remember that audio/video workstations need specialized A/V cards, fast hard drives, and multiple monitors.

CAD/CAM Workstation

Computer-aided design (CAD) and computer-aided manufacturing (CAM) workstations are common in electrical engineering, architecture, drafting, and many other engineering arenas. They run software such as AutoCAD, TurboCAD, or CorelCAD. This software is CPU-intensive and images require a lot of space on the screen. Hardware-wise a CAD/CAM workstation needs a powerful CPU (or more than one if using advanced CAD software), a high-end video card, and as much RAM as possible. If a program has a minimum RAM requirement of 2 GB of RAM, you ought to quadruple that amount; plus, the faster the RAM, the better.

> **ExamAlert**
>
> Don't forget, CAD/CAM computers need powerful CPUs and video cards, and as much RAM as possible.

Virtualization Workstation

A virtualization workstation is a computer that runs one or more virtual operating systems (also known as virtual machines or VMs). Did you ever wish that you had another two or three extra computers lying around so that you could test Windows 7, Windows Vista, and Windows XP, and possibly a Windows Server OS all at the same time? Well, you can with virtual software by creating virtual machines for each OS. But if you run those at the same time on your main computer, you are probably going to bring that PC to a standstill. However, if you were to build one virtualization workstation, you could run whatever operating systems on it that you need. The virtualization workstation uses what is known as a hypervisor. A hypervisor allows multiple virtual operating systems (guests) to run at the same time on a single computer. It is also known as a virtual machine manager (VMM). But there are two different kinds:

▶ **Type 1: Native:** This means that the hypervisor runs directly on the host computer's hardware. Because of this it is also known as *bare metal*. Examples of this include VMware ESX Server, Citrix XenServer, and Microsoft Hyper-V. Hyper-V can be installed as a stand-alone product known as Microsoft Hyper-V Server 2008, or it can be installed as a role within a standard installation of Windows Server 2008 (R2). Either way, the hypervisor runs independently and accesses hardware directly, making both versions of Hyper-V Type 1 hypervisors.

▶ **Type 2: Hosted:** This means that the hypervisor runs within (or "on top of") the operating system. Guest operating systems run within the hypervisor. Compared to Type 1, guests are one level removed from the hardware and therefore run less efficiently. Examples of this include Microsoft Virtual PC, VMware Server, and VMware Workstation.

Generally, Type 1 is a much faster and efficient solution than Type 2. Because of this, Type 1 hypervisors are the kind used for virtual servers, by web-hosting companies, and by companies that offer cloud computing solutions. It makes sense, too. If you have ever run a powerful operating system such as Windows Server 2008 within a Type 2 hypervisor such as Virtual PC 2007, you will note that a ton of resources are being used that are taken from the hosting operating system. It is not nearly as efficient as running the hosted OS within a Type 1 environment. However, keep in mind that the hardware/software requirements for a Type 1 hypervisor will be more stringent, and more costly. For example, many older CPUs do not support virtualization such as Intel Virtualization Technology (VT). To check if your CPU can support VT, go to the following website:

http://ark.intel.com/VTList.aspx

Intel CPUs that support x86 virtualization use the VT-x virtualization extension. Intel chipsets use the VT-d and VT-c extensions for input-output memory management and network virtualization respectively. AMD CPUs that support x86 virtualization use the AMD-V extension. AMD chipsets use the AMD-Vi extension.

Any computer designed to run a hypervisor often has a powerful CPU (or multiple CPUs) and as much RAM as can fit in the system. Keep in mind that the motherboard BIOS and the CPU used should have virtualization support.

> **Exam Alert**
>
> Remember that virtualization systems depend on the CPU and RAM heavily.

In general, the security of a virtual machine operating system is the equivalent to that of a physical machine OS. The VM should be updated to the latest service pack, should have the newest AV definitions, perhaps have a personal firewall, have strong passwords, and so on. However, there are several things to watch out for that if not addressed could cause all your work compartmentalizing operating systems to go down the drain. This includes considerations for the virtual machine OS as well as the controlling virtual machine software. Keep an eye out for network shares and other connections between the virtual machine and the physical machine, or between two VMs.

Consider disabling any unnecessary hardware from within the virtual machine such as optical drives, USB ports, and so on. One last comment: A VM should be as secure as possible, but in general, because the hosting computer is in a controlling position, it is likely more easily exploited, and a compromise to the hosting computer probably means a compromise to any guest operating systems. Therefore, if possible, the host should be even more secure than the VMs it controls.

Thin and Thick Clients

A thin client (also known as a cloud client) is a computer that has few resources compared to a typical PC. It is often a small device the size of a gaming console, and might even mount to the back of a display. They are also known as diskless workstations because they have no hard drive or optical discs. They do have a CPU, RAM, and ports for the display, keyboard, mouse, and network. When a thin client is turned on it loads the OS and applications from an image stored (embedded) on flash memory, or from a server. The OS and apps are loaded into RAM; when the thin client is turned off, all memory is cleared. Either way, the thin-client is dependent on the server for a lot of resources. Examples of thin client manufacturers include Wyse, HP, and NComputing. These devices can connect to a server that runs specially configured Microsoft Terminal Services, or software by other companies such as Citrix or VMware, or can connect to a network and platform infrastructure in the cloud.

> **ExamAlert**
>
> Viruses have a hard time sticking around a thin client because the RAM is completely cleared every time it is turned off.

The whole idea behind thin-clients is to transfer a lot of the responsibilities and resources to the server. An organization would purchase more powerful and expensive servers, but save money overall by spending less on each thin-client, while benefitting from a secure design. A typical Wyse thin client can have a 1.5 GHz CPU, 4 GB of flash memory, and 2 GB of RAM. It might have one of several operating systems embedded into the flash memory depending on the model you purchase, for example Windows Embedded Standard 7. This method of centralizing resources, data, and user profiles is considered to be a more organized solution than the typical PC-based client/server network.

A thick client, or fat client, is effectively a PC. Unlike the thin client, it performs the bulk of data processing operations by itself and has a disk to store the OS, user profile, files, and so on.

Home Server PC

A real server runs software such as Windows Server 2008. But this software is expensive and requires a lot of know-how. For the average home user it is too much power and takes too much time to configure. However, a server OS such as that is not necessary in today's home networks. If a person wants to have a home server PC, they can do so with any Windows 7 OS that can start a HomeGroup (Home Premium, Professional, or Ultimate.) At that point, information can be stored centrally on the one Windows 7 computer. Files and printers can be shared to the rest of the devices on the network, and media can be streamed to the other systems as well. To configure media streaming in Windows 7 go to Control Panel > HomeGroup, and then click the Change Advanced Settings link. Open the appropriate network type (usually Home or Work), and click the Choose Media Streaming Options link. Then click Customize for any particular device. From these last two locations you can choose what is to be streamed and select parental ratings if you want.

> **Note**
>
> Linux is another great option for powerful home server PCs, but it is unlikely that you will encounter a question about that on the A+ exams.

To make this server function quickly, and recover from faults, we would equip it with a gigabit network adapter (or even a 10 Gbps adapter) and set up a RAID array. The RAID array could be RAID 0 (striping), but to incorporate fault tolerance, we would want RAID 1 (mirroring, 2 drives) or RAID 5 (striping w/parity, 3 drives or more). To do this on a Windows system, we might need a RAID controller either embedded on the motherboard or installed as a separate adapter card. Or an external RAID array could be connected to the computer or connected to the network directly (NAS box) and controlled by the computer.

> **ExamAlert**
>
> Remember that a home server PC should have a fast network adapter and a RAID array, and needs to be part of a network such as a HomeGroup.

Home Theater PC (HTPC)

A home theater PC (or HTPC for short) can take the place of a Blu-ray player, DVD player, CD player, and various audio equipment. In some cases it can also take the place of a set-top-box (STB) or Tivo. However, this depends on the area you live in. It has become more difficult to use the HTPC for television reception due to cablecards and encryption techniques.

The *Media PC* I built for this book would work well as an HTPC, a media center PC, or even an audio/video workstation. The requirements for an HTPC include a small form factor (micro-ATX or mini-ITX), a quiet desktop case with silent video card, surround sound audio, and an HDMI output for connectivity to LCD televisions. To keep the rest of the computer quiet, a liquid cooled CPU (instead of fan) and solid state hard drive would complete the equation. Finally, if you want to get TV reception, you would need a TV tuner, and possibly an antenna.

Home entertainment enthusiasts often have a computer hooked up to their home theater. If this is the case, they might install a TV tuner card. These cards can accept the signal from a cable or satellite provider or antenna and then send it back out to the TV or other devices in the home theater. Some TV tuners also act as capture cards, meaning that they can capture the signal and record TV programs. The purpose of all this is to record shows onto the computer and basically use the computer as a digital video recorder (DVR), among other things. By using Window Media Center, which is built-in to Windows 7/Vista and comes as a separate edition for Windows XP, users can control their TV experience. (If you haven't taken a look at Windows Media Center yet, and you have Windows 7 or Vista, access it at Start > All Programs > Windows Media Center, and familiarize yourself with it.) TV tuner cards are available with PCI Express, PCI, ExpressCard (for laptops), and USB interfaces. TV tuners often have RG-6 connectors for cable in, and antenna. Make sure you connect to the right one!

> **ExamAlert**
>
> Know that an HTPC needs a small form factor, quiet equipment, surround sound, HDMI output, and possibly a TV tuner.

Gaming PC

Now we get to the core of it: Custom computing is taken to extremes when it comes to gaming. Gaming PCs require almost all the resources mentioned previously: a powerful CPU, lots of RAM, liquid cooling (if you want to be serious), a high-end video card and specialized GPU, an above average sound card, plus a fast network adapter and strong Internet connection (and mad skills.) This all creates a computer that is expensive, and requires care and maintenance to keep it running in perfect form.

Games are some of the most powerful applications available. If any one of the elements is missing from a gaming system, it could easily ruin the experience. The video card is a huge component of this equation. One of the ways to better the video subsystem is to employ SLI.

Gamers are always looking to push the envelope for video performance. It's possible to take video to the next level by incorporating a technology known as Scan Line Interleave (SLI). This is when a computer has two (or more) identical video cards that work together for greater performance and higher resolution. The SLI compatible cards are bridged together to essentially work as one unit. It is important to have a compatible motherboard and ample cooling when attempting this type of configuration. Currently this is done with two or more PCI Express video cards and is most commonly found in gaming rigs, but you might find it in other PCs as well such as video editing or CAD/CAM workstations. Because the typical motherboard comes with only one PCIe x16 slot for video, a gaming system needs a more advanced motherboard: one with two PCIe x16 slots to accomplish SLI.

Cram Quiz

220-801 Questions

Answer these questions. The answers follow the last question. If you cannot answer these questions correctly, consider reading this section again until you can.

1. Which of the following is the best type of custom computer for use with ProTools?

   ○ **A.** CAD/CAM workstation

   ○ **B.** Audio/Video Workstation

   ○ **C.** Gaming PC

   ○ **D.** HTPC

2. What do CAD/CAM workstations require most?

   ○ **A.** Liquid cooling and RAM

   ○ **B.** TV tuner and silent hard drive

   ○ **C.** Surround sound card and joystick

   ○ **D.** Powerful CPU and RAM

3. Your organization needs to run Windows 7 in a virtual environment. The OS is expected to require a huge amount of resources for a powerful application it will run. What should you install Windows 7 to?

   ○ **A.** Type 2 hypervisor

   ○ **B.** Gaming PC

   ○ **C.** Type 1 hypervisor

   ○ **D.** Thin client

4. What are some of the elements of a home server PC? (Select the two best answers.)

   ○ **A.** Liquid cooling

   ○ **B.** Fast network adapter

   ○ **C.** The best CPU

   ○ **D.** RAID array

   ○ **E.** Gamepad

220-802 Questions

5. You just set up an HTPC. However, the Windows Media Center live TV option is not working. All connections are plugged in, and all the other portions of Windows Media Center work. What is the most likely cause of the problem?

   ○ **A.** The coax cable is plugged into the antenna port.

   ○ **B.** Media Center needs to be reinstalled.

   ○ **C.** Windows 7 libraries are malfunctioning.

   ○ **D.** The computer overheated.

Cram Quiz Answers

220-801 Answers

1. **B.** The audio/video workstation is the type of custom computer that would use ProTools, Logic Pro, and other music and video editing programs.

2. **D.** A CAD/CAM workstation most requires a powerful CPU and RAM. Liquid cooling, surround sound cards, and joysticks are required by gaming PCs. TV tuners and silent hard drives are needed by HTPCs.

3. **C.** If the virtual operating system needs a lot of resources, the best bet is a "bare metal" type 1 hypervisor. Type 2 hypervisors run on top of an operating system and therefore are not as efficient with resources. Gaming PCs have lots of resources but are not meant to run virtual environments. Thin clients have the least amount of resources.

4. **B** and **D.** Home server PCs require a fast network adapter for the quick transfer of files over the network and a RAID array to offer fast and reliable access to data.

220-802 Answers

5. **A.** If everything is working except for the live TV option, then the coax cable is probably plugged into the antenna port instead of the cable in port of the TV tuner card. This is also a common mistake on set-top-boxes.

CHAPTER 14

Printers

This chapter covers the following A+ exam topics:

▶ Printer Types and Technologies

▶ Installing, Configuring, and Troubleshooting Printers

You can find a master list of A+ exam topics in the "Introduction."

This chapter covers CompTIA A+ 220-801 objectives 4.1 through 4.3 and CompTIA A+ 220-802 objectives 1.4, 1.5, and 4.9.

Printers are the number two output device right behind video displays. Their main purpose is to output hard copy versions of what you see on the computer screen. Many printers connect via USB; although you also encounter printers that connect directly to the network—and on the rare occasion, printers that connect to parallel ports. Some printers also act as fax machines, copiers, and scanners; these are known as multifunction devices or multifunction printers (MFPs).

Generally, Windows 7 and Vista behave the same as Windows XP for printing. So whenever one operating system is mentioned in this chapter, the same applies to the other operating system, unless otherwise stated.

This chapter is broken into two sections: printer types and technologies, and installing, configuring, and troubleshooting printers.

Printer Types and Technologies

Businesses utilize several types of printers. The most common business-oriented printer is the laser printer. However, inkjet printers are more prevalent in the home due to their lower cost and their capability to print in color with excellent resolution. A technician might also encounter thermal and impact printers. Some printers connect directly to a computer; others connect to the network or to a print server. This section describes the four main types of printers and how they function; it also discusses the differences between local and network printers.

Types of Printers

Each type of printer has its own characteristics that affect how a technician installs, configures, and troubleshoots them. The most common type of printer that a business would use is the laser printer; this type of printer also happens to be the most complicated and difficult to troubleshoot.

Laser Printers

Laser printers can produce high-quality text and graphics on cut sheets of paper; printers that print to individual pieces of paper are known as *page printers*. The bulk of laser printers print in black, but there are also color laser printers, which of course are more expensive. They are called laser printers because inside the printer is a laser beam that projects an image of the item to be printed onto an electrically charged drum; this image is later transferred to the paper. Text and images that are shown on paper are created from electrically charged toner, which is a type of powder stored in a replaceable toner cartridge. The type of toner used can vary from one brand to the next, but they all work essentially the same way.

Known also as a photoelectric or photosensitive drum, the laser printer drum is at the center of the whole laser printing process, but there are a couple of other important components including the primary corona wire, transfer corona wire, fusing assembly, and of course, the laser itself. These components are shown in Figure 14.1.

The imaging process that a laser printer goes through is often referred to as a six-step process. However, prior to this is another step known as *processing*. The text or image to be printed is calculated at the computer, and sent to the printer where a processor recalculates it, and stores it in RAM while the printer readies itself for the ordeal of laser printing!

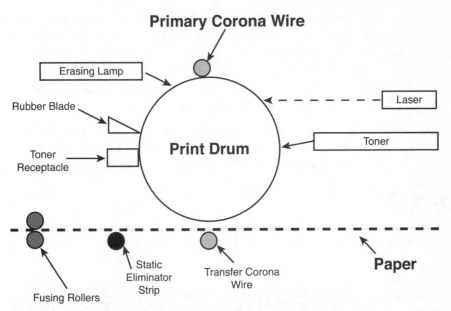

FIGURE 14.1   **Components involved in the laser printing process**

The following list describes the typical six-step laser printing process:

1. **Cleaning:** A rubber blade removes excess toner from the drum as it spins. An erasing lamp removes any leftover charge on the drum bringing it to zero volts.

2. **Conditioning:** Also known as charging. A negative charge is applied to the drum by the primary corona wire, which is powered by a high-voltage power supply within the printer.

3. **Writing:** Also known as exposing. The laser is activated and "writes" to the drum as it spins. Where the laser hits the drum, it dissipates the negative charge toward the center of the drum that is grounded. The "written" areas of the drum now have a lesser negative charge. (The drum is also known as an imaging drum.)

4. **Developing:** The surface of the drum that was previously exposed to the laser is now applied with negatively charged toner. This toner has a higher charge than the areas of the drum that were written to.

5. **Transferring:** The toner, and therefore the text or image, is transferred to paper as the drum rolls over it. The movement of the paper is assisted by transfer rollers. On many laser printers, the paper slides between the drum and a positively charged corona wire (known as the transfer corona wire). The transfer corona wire applies the positive charge to the

paper. Because the paper now has a positive charge, and the toner particles on the drum have a negative charge, the toner is attracted to the paper. (For voltages, opposites attract.) In many printers the paper passes by a static elimination device (often a strip), which removes excess charge from the paper. Some color laser printers use a transfer belt to apply the various layers of colors to the paper.

6. **Fusing:** The toner is fused to the paper. The paper passes through the fusing assembly that includes pressurized rollers and a heating element that can reach approximately 400 degrees F (or about 200 degrees C).

Note

On some laser printers, the cleaning stage occurs at the end of the fusing stage, cleaning off the photosensitive drum and reducing its voltage to zero.

Exam Alert

Know the laser printing process (also known as the electrophotographic printing process) for the exam.

In some laser printers the drum, laser, and primary corona wire are contained within the toner cartridge. Issues that are caused by these components can usually be fixed just by replacing the toner cartridge.

Note

Toner cartridges are replaceable; they are known as *consumables*. Whatever material it is that actually prints on to paper is usually considered a consumable, regardless of the type of printer.

Laser printers have some advantages over other printers:

▶ **Speed:** A laser printer can print anywhere from 10 to 100 pages per minute depending on the model and whether it is a color or black-and-white laser printer.

▶ **Print quality:** The laser printer commonly prints at 600 DPI (dots per inch), which is considered letter quality, but 1,200 DPI, and 2,400 DPI resolution printers are also available.

> **Exam Alert**
>
> Of all printer types, the laser printer is considered to have the lowest cost per page.

Inkjet Printers

Inkjet printers are common in small offices, in home offices, and for personal use. They can print documents but more commonly print photographs and graphical information in color; most of the time they connect to the computer by way of USB.

The inkjet printer works by propelling ink onto various sizes of paper. Many inkjets store ink in multiple ink cartridges that are consumable; they have to be replaced when empty. Some inkjet printers stop operating if just one of the ink cartridges is empty. Two common types of inkjet printers are the thermal inkjet and the piezoelectric inkjet:

▶ **Thermal inkjets:** These account for the bulk of consumer inkjets and are the more recognizable type. To move the ink to the paper, heat is sent through the ink cartridge, forming a bubble (known as the thermal bubble) that pushes the ink onto the paper; immediately afterward another charge of ink is readied. The reservoir of ink is within the ink cartridge; this is where the heat transfer occurs. HP and Canon develop many models of thermal inkjet printers. Don't confuse thermal inkjets with thermal printers.

▶ **Piezoelectric inkjets:** These account for the bulk of commercial inkjets. The printing processes within a piezoelectric inkjet and a thermal inkjet are similar; however, the piezo inkjet applies current to the ink material, causing it to change shape and size, forcing the ink onto the paper. The reservoir of ink is in another area outside of where the current is applied. This process enables longer print head life as compared to thermal inkjets. Epson develops many models of piezoelectric inkjet printers. Piezoelectric inkjets can also be found in manufacturing assembly lines.

The inkjet print process is fairly simple:

1. The paper or other media is pulled or moved into position by a roller mechanism, or moved into position by an assembly line's conveyor belt as with some piezoelectric inkjets.

2. The print head, located on a mechanical arm, moves across the paper, placing black and colored ink as directed by the print driver.

3. At the end of the line, the paper or media is advanced, and the print head either reverses direction and continues to print (often referred to as Hi-Speed mode) or returns to the left margin before printing continues.

4. After the page is completed, the paper or other media is ejected.

Thermal Printers

Thermal printers produce text and images by heating specially coated thermal paper. It is typical to see thermal printers used in point-of-sale systems, gas station pumps, and so on. Thermal printers consist of the following parts:

▶ **Thermal head:** This generates the heat and takes care of printing to the paper.

▶ **Platen:** This is the rubber roller that feeds the paper past the print head.

▶ **Spring:** Applies pressure to the print head, which brings the print head into contact with the paper.

▶ **Circuit board:** Controls the mechanism that moves the print head.

To print, thermal paper is inserted between the thermal head and the platen. The printer sends current to the thermal head, which in turn generates heat. The heat activates the thermo-sensitive coloring layer of the thermal paper, which becomes the image.

Impact Printers

Impact printers use force to transfer ink to paper, for example, a print head striking a ribbon with paper directly behind it, similar to a typewriter. This type of printer is somewhat deprecated although certain environments might still use it: auto repair centers, warehouses, accounting departments, and so on.

One type of impact printer, the daisy-wheel, utilizes a wheel with many petals, each of which has a letter form (an actual letter) at the tip of the petal. These strike against the ribbon that impresses ink upon the paper that is situated behind the ribbon. But by far the most common type of impact printer is the dot-matrix.

Dot-matrix printers are also known as line printers because they print text one line at a time and can keep printing over a long roll of paper, as opposed to page printers that print to cut sheets of paper. Dot-matrix printers use a matrix of pins that work together to create characters, instead of a form letter. The print head that contains these pins strikes the ribbon that in turn places the ink on the paper. Print heads either come with 9 pins or 24 pins, with the 24-pin version offering better quality, known as *near letter quality (NLQ)*. Dot-matrix printers are loud and slow but are cheap to maintain.

Local Versus Network Printers

A local printer is one that connects directly to a computer, normally by USB, or parallel connection. When a user works at a computer, that computer is considered to be the local computer. So, if a printer is connected to that computer, it is known as the local printer.

A network printer is one that connects directly to the network or to a print server device. Network printers are shared by more than one user on the computer network. Usually, network printers are given an IP address and become yet another *host* on the network. If the printer connects directly to the network, it is usually by way of a built-in RJ45 port on the printer, just as a computer's network card connects to the network. A print server could be a computer or smaller black box device. Many SOHO routers from Linksys and D-link offer print server capabilities. In this case the printer connects via USB to the print server/router, and a special piece of software is installed on any client computers that want to print to that printer.

Regardless of whether a printer is local or on the network, it can be controlled by Windows, described in the following section.

Cram Quiz

Answer these questions. The answers follow the last question. If you cannot answer these questions correctly, consider reading this section again until you can.

220-801 Questions

1. Which type of printer uses a photoelectric drum?
   - ○ **A.** Impact
   - ○ **B.** Dot-Matrix
   - ○ **C.** Laser
   - ○ **D.** Inkjet

2. During which step of the laser printing process is the transfer corona wire involved?
   - ○ **A.** Developing
   - ○ **B.** Transferring
   - ○ **C.** Fusing
   - ○ **D.** Cleaning

3. Which stage of the laser printing process involves extreme heat?

   ○ **A.** Fusing

   ○ **B.** Transferring

   ○ **C.** Exposing

   ○ **D.** Writing

4. What is the most common type of consumer-based printer?

   ○ **A.** Thermal printer

   ○ **B.** Laser printer

   ○ **C.** Thermal inkjet

   ○ **D.** Impact printer

5. What is the rubber roller that feeds the paper past the print head known as?

   ○ **A.** HVPS

   ○ **B.** Cartridge

   ○ **C.** Spring

   ○ **D.** Platen

6. What is a common amount of pins in a dot-matrix printer's print head?

   ○ **A.** 40

   ○ **B.** 24

   ○ **C.** 8

   ○ **D.** 84

Cram Quiz Answers

220-801 Answers

1. **C.** The laser printer is the only type of printer that uses a photoelectric drum.

2. **B.** The transfer corona wire gets involved in the laser printing process during the transferring step.

3. **A.** The fusing step uses heat (up to 400 degrees Fahrenheit/200 degrees Celsius) and pressure to fuse the toner permanently to the paper.

4. **C.** The thermal inkjet is the most common type of printer used in the consumer market today. Don't confuse a thermal inkjet (often simply referred to as an inkjet) with a thermal printer.

5. **D.** The platen is the rubber roller that feeds the paper past the print head in thermal printers.

6. **B.** Dot-matrix printer print heads usually have 24 pins or 9 pins.

Installing, Configuring, and Troubleshooting Printers

Physically installing printers and installing device drivers is usually straightforward, but the configuration of printers in Windows is more complex because so many configurable options exist. Troubleshooting as always should be approached from a logical standpoint. This section covers the installation, configuration, and troubleshooting of printers.

Printer Installation and Drivers

When installing printers focus on several things:

▶ **Compatibility:** Make sure that the printer is compatible with the version of Windows that runs on the computer that controls the printer. Check the Windows compatibility lists to verify this. If the printer is to connect to the network, make sure that it has the right type of compatible network adapter to do so.

▶ **Installing printer drivers:** Generally, the proper procedure is to install the printer driver to Windows before physically connecting the printer. However, if the driver already exists on the computer, the printer can simply be connected. Usually, the best bet is to use the driver that came on disc with the printer, or download the latest driver from the manufacturer's website. Verify that the driver to be installed is the correct one and that it is for the correct operating system and version of the operating system, for example 32-bit or 64-bit versions of Windows. Printer drivers are installed in a similar fashion to other drivers described in this book, but Windows includes a wizard specifically for printers called the Add Printer Wizard. This can be accessed by navigating to Start and opening the Control Panel in Classic mode; then select Devices and Printers (In Windows 7) Printers (in Vista) or Printers and Faxes (XP). Any current printers should be listed. From there, right-click anywhere in the work area and select Add a Printer.

▶ **Connecting the device:** In general, devices connecting via USB or IEEE 1394 can be connected without turning the computer off. (That is, they are hot-swappable.) However, devices that connect to a parallel, SCSI, or serial port require that the computer be shut down first. (Parallel ports are less common today, but if a user wants to connect a printer to one, they need to use a compatible IEEE 1284 cable that has a 25-pin parallel connector on one end and a centronics connector on the other.) Plug the USB or other connector cable into the computer first, and then connect the printer to an AC outlet. (It's recommended to use a surge protector for printers but it is *not* recommended to use a UPS for a laser printer.) Verify that the device turns on.

▶ **Calibrating the printer:** Color laser printers, inkjet printers, and multi-function printers might need to be calibrated before use. This involves aligning the printing mechanism to the paper and verifying color output. Usually the software that accompanies the printer guides a user through this process. In some cases, these calibration tests can be done via the small display on the printer.

▶ **Testing the printer:** First test the printer by printing a test page in Windows. This can be done by locating the printer in the Devices and Printers window (Printers window in Vista and Printers and Faxes in XP), right-clicking it, and selecting Printer Properties (or just Properties in some cases); then click the Print Test Page button on the General tab. The resulting page should show the operating system the local computer runs, and various other configuration and driver information. If the page can be read properly and the Windows logo is using the correct colors, the test passed. Some printers offer a test page option on the display of the printer as well. After a test page has been printed, it might be wise to try printing within the most used applications as well, just to make sure they work properly. Some applications might behave differently, and some configurations of printers in Windows could cause a particular application to have print failures.

Configuring Printers

Configuration of printers can be done in one of three places. The first is the small display that might be included on a printer; these are more common on laser printers. These menu-driven displays are usually user-friendly and intuitive. The second is within a printer's web interface if it is a network printer; this is often accessed through a web browser. But the third, and the one that I'd like to focus on in this section, is within Windows, specifically by double-clicking the printer icon within the Devices and Printers window (Printers in Vista or Printers and Faxes in XP) and by accessing the Properties page of the printer. To open a printer, simply double-click it. To manage its properties right-click the printer in question and select Printer Properties or simply Properties. If you work with printers often, consider placing a shortcut to the printer or printers on the desktop or within the Quick Launch. Several items can be configured by double-clicking the printer and within the Printer

Properties window including Managing print jobs, setting the priority of the printer, configuring the print spooler, and managing permissions.

Managing Printers and Print Jobs

To manage a printer or an individual print job, just double-click the printer in which the job was sent to. A window similar to Figure 14.2 should display on the monitor.

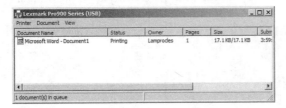

FIGURE 14.2   **A typical printer window with one print job**

In Figure 14.2 you can notice that one print job called Document1 is listed. The job went to the printer properly; you can tell because it says Printing under the Status column. Any other message would mean that the job was either spooled, queued, stopped, or has failed. These jobs can be paused, restarted, or stopped completely if they are not printing properly. This can be done by right-clicking in the job or by selecting the Document menu. Keep in mind that larger documents take longer to spool before they start printing. In addition to this, all documents can be paused or canceled, or the entire printer can be taken offline from the Printer menu. Use these tools to troubleshoot any printing misqueues.

Printer Priority

Printer priority can be configured within the Advanced tab of a printer's Properties page, as shown in Figure 14.3.

The priority of a printer can be configured from 1 to 99; 99 being the highest. This is useful in two situations:

> ▶ **Scenario 1:** Let's say that several users and their manager share a print-er. Chances are that you would want to give the manager the highest priority when it comes to print jobs. It is possible to install two software printers in Windows that point to the same physical printer. The first software printer could be given a higher priority (say 99) and a share name such as "manager," with permissions that allow access only by the manager. The second software printer would be given a lower priority

(say 50) and use a share name such as "users." After the client computers are configured properly to access the correct printers, the manager should always get precedence over other print jobs on the shared physical printer.

▶ **Scenario 2:** Imagine that there are two or more physical printers that have been combined to create a printer pool. Each printer in the pool can be given a different priority. One printer in the pool is often set aside for managers and executives with a higher priority than the others.

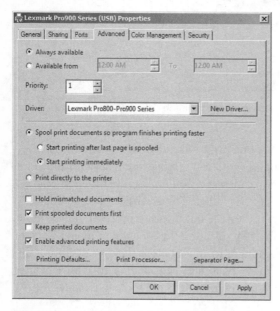

FIGURE 14.3 **Printer priority and spooling**

Print Spooling

Whenever a job goes to print, there are three possible options:

▶ **Print directly to the printer:** This means that the print job goes right to the printer without any delays. This relies solely on the amount of memory in the printer (which can be increased BTW just like in computers). Of course, if the print job is larger than the amount of RAM in the printer, the job will probably fail. Usually a better solution is to spool the document.

▶ **Start printing immediately:** This is the first of two spooling options. When this setting is selected, one page at a time of the document will be *spooled* to the hard disk drive. When an entire page has been spooled, it is sent to the printer for printing. This repeats until all the pages of the document have been spooled and ultimately printed. This is the default setting in Windows and is usually the best option, as shown in Figure 14.3.

▶ **Start printing after last page is spooled:** This means that the entire document will be spooled to the hard drive, and then pages are sent to the printer for printing. This is usually slower than Start Printing Immediately but might have fewer issues such as stalls or other printing failures.

The print spooler is controlled by the Print Spooler service. This service processes print requests and sends them to the printer. Not only can you have issues in which print jobs or printers stop working, but also the Print Spooler service can fail. This service can be started, stopped, and restarted from the GUI and from the Command Prompt:

▶ **Adjusting the Print Spooler service in Computer Management:** Open the Computer Management console window; then click the + sign to expand Services and Applications and click Services. Now, in the right window pane, scroll until you find the Print Spooler service. To start a stopped service, right-click it and click Start. Alternatively, you can click the Start or other buttons on the toolbar.

▶ **Adjusting the Print Spooler service in the Command Prompt:** In Windows 7/Vista you need to run these commands as an administrator; let's review the two ways to do this.

1. Click Start > All Programs > Accessories; then right-click Command Prompt and select Run as Administrator.

2. Click Start and type cmd in the search field, and instead of pressing Enter, press Ctrl+Shift+Enter.

Windows XP does not require opening the Command Prompt as an administrator. When the Command Prompt is open, you can start the Print Spooler service by typing net start spooler. Typing Net stop spooler stops the service.

> **ExamAlert**
>
> Know how to configure spooling and how to start and stop the Print Spooler service within Computer Management and in the Command Prompt.

XPS Feature in Windows 7/Vista

Windows 7/Vista incorporates the XML Paper Specification (XPS) print path. The XPS spooler is meant to replace the standard Enhanced Metafile print spooler that Windows has used for years. With XPS (part of the Windows Presentation Foundation) 7/Vista provides improved color and graphics support, and support for the CMYK colorspace, and reduces the need for color-space conversion.

This is implemented as the Microsoft XPS Document Writer that can be found in Start > Control Panel > Devices and Printers (Printers in Vista). A document created within any application in Windows can be saved as an .XPS file to be later viewed on any computer that supports XPS. It can also be printed from any computer that supports XPS but prints only with proper fidelity if the computer has an XPS-compliant printer. Windows 7 SP1 fixed some problems with XPS and made some improvements as well.

Printer Pooling

Printer pooling takes multiple separate printers and combines them to form a team of printers that work together to complete print jobs as quickly as possible. This can be accomplished from the Ports tab of the printer's Properties window. Normally a printer will be shown next to the port it connects to. To add a second installed printer to the pool, click Enable printer pooling; then check mark the other printer listed, as shown in Figure 14.4.

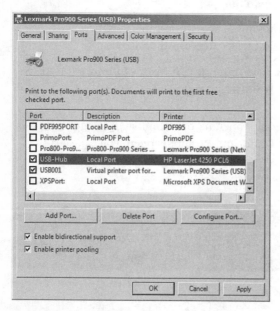

FIGURE 14.4   Enabled printer pooling option

As you can see in Figure 14.4, the Printer Pooling option has been selected, and a second printer (HP LaserJet) has been check marked that adds it to the pool along with the Lexmark Pro900 printer. At this point, any jobs sent to the first printer that can't be processed right away will be transferred to the second printer. This is a one-way printer pool; two-way printer pools are also possible but aren't done as much. Quite often, printer pools consist of all identical printers.

> **Note**
>
> Remote printers can be connected to and controlled from the Ports tab. This can be done by adding a port and then entering the IP address of the printer to be controlled, or the computer name of the computer that the remote printer connects to.

Sharing Printers and Managing Permissions

A networked printer must first be shared before other users can send print jobs to it. There are two steps involved in sharing printers in Windows. First, printer sharing in general must be enabled:

- ► To enable Printer Sharing in Windows 7, go to Start > Control Panel > Network and Sharing Center. Then click the Change Advanced Sharing Settings link. Click the down arrow for your network type (usually Home or Work) and select the radio button labeled Turn on File and Printer Sharing.

- ► To enable Printer Sharing in Windows Vista, go to Start > Control Panel > Network and Sharing Center; click the down arrow for Printer Sharing and select the radio button labeled Turn on Printer Sharing.

- ► To enable Printer Sharing in Windows XP, go to Start > Control Panel > Network Connections. Then right-click any network adapter and select Properties. Check mark File and Printer Sharing for Microsoft Networks. This is normally enabled by default.

Next, the individual printer needs to be shared. This can be done in the Sharing tab of the printer's Properties window. Click the Share This Printer radio button and give the printer a share name. Note that the share name does not need to be the same as the printer name. Click OK, and the printer should show up as shared within the Printers window.

Permissions can be set for a printer in the Security tab of the printer's Properties window. Users and groups can be added in this window, and the appropriate permission can be assigned including Print, Manage Printers, and

Manage Documents. Regular users normally are assigned the Print permission, whereas administrators get all permissions, enabling them to pause the printer or cancel all documents (Manage Printers), and pause, cancel, and restart individual documents. For more information on permissions, see Chapter 16 "Security."

Selecting a Separator Page

Separator pages help users to find the start and end points of their print job. The separator page might be printed as a blank piece of paper or with the username and title of the document to be printed. This can be added from the Advanced tab by clicking the Separator Page button. From there click the Browse button; this shows the System32 folder by default. Initially four separator pages are in this folder, the most common of which are pcl.sep and pscript.sep. However, some companies opt to use a custom separator page. Click the appropriate separator page and click open; then click OK. The separator page will be added to the appropriate documents.

> **Note**
>
> There are a lot of other settings in the printer Properties window. Spend some time looking through the various tabs and configurations to better prepare for the exam.

Troubleshooting Printers

Sometimes companies have paid consultants that take care of all printers and copying machines, and sometimes taking care of these devices is the job of the in-house IT guy. Either way, it is a good idea to know some of the basic issues that can occur with printers and how to troubleshoot them. Table 14.1 describes some of these issues and possible solutions. Some of these issues, for example paper jams and resulting error codes, might be displayed on a printer's LCD.

TABLE 14.1 **Printer Problems and Solutions**

Printer Issue	Possible Solution
Paper jams or creased paper	1. Attempt to turn the printer on and off in the hopes that the printer will clear the jam. This is known as power cycling the printer. If that doesn't work, you have to open the printer. Turn the printer off and unplug it before doing so. 2. Remove paper trays and inspect them for crumpled papers that can be removed by grabbing both ends of the paper firmly and pulling or rotating the rollers to remove it. In general, clear the paper path.

TABLE 14.1 **Continued**

Printer Issue	Possible Solution
	3. Verify that the right paper type is in the printer. If the paper is too thin or thick, it might cause a paper jam. Also, watch for paper that has been exposed to humidity.
	4. Check for dirty or cracked rollers. A temporary fix for dirty rubber rollers is to use isopropyl alcohol. A permanent fix would be to replace the roller.
	5. Check if the fusing assembly has overheated. Sometimes the printer just needs time to cool, or perhaps the printer is not in a well enough ventilated area. In uncommon cases the fuser might have to be replaced. Be sure to unplug the printer and let the printer sit for an hour or so before doing so due to the high temperatures of the fuser. The fusing assembly can usually be removed with a few screws.
	6. Finally, check the entire paper path. Duplexing printers (ones that print on both sides of the paper) will have more complicated and longer paper paths with more chances for paper to get jammed.
Blank paper	1. Empty toner cartridge. Install a new one.
	2. Toner cartridge was installed without the sealing tape removed.
	3. Transfer corona wire has failed. If the transfer corona wire fails, there will be no positive (opposite) voltage to pull the toner to the paper. Replace the wire.
Multiple pages are fed in at once	If the printer feeds in multiple pages, then you should check if the separation pad is getting enough traction; it might need to be cleaned.
	Also check if the printer is too thin; 20 lb and higher paper is usually recommended.
Error codes	If a specific error is shown on the printer's LCD, read it. It might tell you exactly what the error is and how to fix it, or at least what the error is. On some printers it displays an error number. Check your printer's documentation to find out what the error means.
Out of memory error or low memory message	If this happens, check if the user's computer is spooling documents. The setting with the least chance of this error is the Start Printing Immediately spool setting. You might also need to restart the Print Spooling service. If a user tries to print a large image, he might need to change settings in the application in which the image was made. In some cases, the printer's RAM might need to be upgraded. Whenever installing RAM to a printer, take all the same precautions you would when working on a PC.
Lines, smearing, toner not fused to paper	Black lines can be caused by a scratch in the laser printer drum or a dirty primary corona wire. Usually, the toner cartridge needs to be replaced. White lines could be caused by a dirty transfer corona wire; this can be cleaned or replaced. Wide white vertical lines can occur when something is stuck to the drum. Smearing can occur if the fusing assembly has failed; in this case you might also notice toner coming off of the paper easily.
	If it is an inkjet, one or more ink cartridges might need to be replaced, or the printer might need to be calibrated.

TABLE 14.1 **Continued**

Printer Issue	Possible Solution
Garbage printout or garbled characters	This can occur due to an incorrect driver. Some technicians like to try "close" drivers. This is not a good idea. Use the exact driver for the exact model of the printer that corresponds to the appropriate version of the operating system. A bad formatter board or printer interface can also be the cause of a garbage printout. These can usually be replaced easily by removing two screws and a cover.
Ghosted image	Ghosted images or blurry marks can be a sign that the drum has some kind of imperfection or is dirty. Especially if the image reappears at equal intervals. Replace the drum (or toner cartridge). Another possibility is that the fuser assembly has been damaged and needs to be replaced.
No connectivity	If there is no connectivity, check the following: ▶ Printer is plugged into an AC outlet and it is "online." ▶ Printer is securely connected to the local computer or to the network. ▶ The computer has the correct print driver installed. ▶ The printer is shared to the network. ▶ The printer has a properly configured IP address. (This can be checked on the LCD display of most networkable laser printers.) ▶ Remote computers have a proper connection over the network to the printer. ▶ The printer is set up as the default printer if necessary.
Access denied	If an Access Denied message appears on the screen while attempting to print, then the user doesn't have permission to use the printer. You (or the network administrator) will have to give the user account permissions for that particular printer. This message might also be displayed if a person attempts to install a printer without the proper administrative rights.
Backed up print queue	If your printer window shows several documents listed in the queue, but is not currently printing anything, then a document might have stalled and needs to be restarted. Also, the print spooler might need to be restarted within the Services console window or in the Command Prompt.
Color printouts are different color than the screen	The printout will always be *slightly* different than the screen. But if the difference is more noticeable, check the ink or toner cartridges and make sure none of the colors are empty. Verify that the printer is a PostScript capable printer that can do raster image processing (RIP). If this functionality is not built into the printer, then it might be available as a separate software solution.

In general, when working with printers, try to keep them clean and use printer maintenance kits. Like changing the oil in a car, printers need maintenance also. HP and other manufacturers offer maintenance kits that include items such as fusers, rollers, separation pads, and instructions on how to replace all these items. Manufacturers recommend that this maintenance be done every once in a while, for example every 200,000 pages printed. When you finish installing a maintenance kit, be sure to reset the maintenance count. You should also have a vacuum available if there is a toner spill. A can of compressed air can be helpful if you need to clean out toner from the inside of a laser printer; remember to do this outside. Vacuum up any left over residue.

When troubleshooting printers, don't forget to RTM! Read The Manual! Most printers come with one, and they often have a troubleshooting section toward the back. In some cases, the manual will be in PDF format on the disc that accompanied the printer. Regardless of whether a manual accompanied the printer or if it can't be found, the manufacturer will usually have the manual on its website in addition to a support system for its customers. Use it! And keep in mind that many products come with a warranty, or the customer might have purchased an extended warranty. I remember one time I was troubleshooting two color-laser printers. They were only two weeks old when they failed. When the manufacturer knew the error code that was flashing on the printer's display, it didn't want to hear anything else; it simply sent out a tech the next day because the device was under warranty. To sum up, let the manufacturer help you. If it doesn't cost the company anything, it can save you a lot of time and aggravation.

Cram Quiz

Answer these questions. The answers follow the last question. If you cannot answer these questions correctly, consider reading this section again until you can.

220-801 Questions

1. When connecting a laser printer's power cable, what type of device is not recommended?

   ○ **A.** Surge protector

   ○ **B.** Line conditioner

   ○ **C.** UPS

   ○ **D.** AC outlet

2. When finished installing a new printer and print drivers, what should you do? (Select all that apply.)

   ○ **A.** Calibrate the printer.

   ○ **B.** Install the print drivers.

   ○ **C.** Check for compatibility.

   ○ **D.** Print a test page.

3. Which is the faster option for spooling documents?

   ◯ **A.** Print directly to the printer.

   ◯ **B.** Start printing immediately.

   ◯ **C.** Start printing after the last page is spooled.

   ◯ **D.** Start printing after the separator page.

4. What command turns off the print spooler?

   ◯ **A.** `net disable print spooler`

   ◯ **B.** `net stop print spooler`

   ◯ **C.** `net restart spooler`

   ◯ **D.** `net stop spooler`

5. What is it known as when two printers are joined together so that they can work as a team?

   ◯ **A.** Printer pooling

   ◯ **B.** Printer spooling

   ◯ **C.** pscript.sep

   ◯ **D.** Printer joining

220-802 Questions

6. What window in Windows 7/Vista enables printer sharing?

   ◯ **A.** Network Connections

   ◯ **B.** Network and Sharing Center

   ◯ **C.** Network

   ◯ **D.** My Network Places

7. How can a paper jam be resolved? (Select all that apply.)

   ◯ **A.** Clear the paper path.

   ◯ **B.** Use the right type of paper.

   ◯ **C.** Check for damaged rollers.

   ◯ **D.** Check for a damaged primary corona wire.

8. What is a possible reason for having blank pages come out of a laser printer?

   ◯ **A.** Failed transfer corona wire

   ◯ **B.** Failed primary corona wire

   ◯ **C.** Failed fusing assembly

   ◯ **D.** Damaged roller

9. What is a possible reason for having black lines on printouts?

   ○ **A.** Scratch on the laser printer drum

   ○ **B.** Damaged roller

   ○ **C.** Damaged transfer corona wire

   ○ **D.** Scratch on the fusing assembly

10. Which of the following are usually included in a laser printer maintenance kit?
    (Select the two best answers.)

    ○ **A.** Rollers

    ○ **B.** Image drum

    ○ **C.** Toner

    ○ **D.** Duplexer

    ○ **E.** Fuser

11. On of your customers is connected to a standalone printer. The customer says
    there is an Out of Memory Error when printing large graphic files. What should
    you do?

    ○ **A.** Upgrade the hard drive on the computer.

    ○ **B.** Upgrade RAM on the printer.

    ○ **C.** Upgrade RAM on the computer.

    ○ **D.** Reinstall the printer drivers.

12. What should you do first when removing a paper jam?

    ○ **A.** Take the printer offline.

    ○ **B.** Clear the print queue.

    ○ **C.** Open all the doors of the printer.

    ○ **D.** Turn off the printer.

Cram Quiz Answers

220-801 Answers

1. **C.** An uninterruptible power supply (UPS) is not recommended for laser printers
   due to the high draw of the laser printer. When using a surge suppressor, the
   laser printer should be the only device connected to it.

2. **A** and **D.** After the printer is installed, meaning it has been connected, and the
   drivers have been installed, you should calibrate the printer (if necessary) and
   print a test page. Before starting the installation, you should check for compatibility with operating systems, applications, and so on.

3. **B.** Start Printing Immediately is the faster print option when spooling documents. Print Directly to the Printer doesn't use the spooling feature, and there is no Start Printing After the Separator Page.

4. **D.** The command **net stop spooler** stops or turns off the print spooler service.

5. **A.** Printer pooling is when two or more printers are combined to get print jobs out faster.

220-802 Answers

6. **B.** The Network and Sharing Center in Windows 7/Vista is where printer sharing is enabled.

7. **A, B,** and **C.** There are several possible reasons why a paper jam might occur. The paper could be stuck somewhere in the paper path, the paper could be too thick, or the rollers could be damaged.

8. **A.** If the transfer corona wire has failed, there is no way for the toner to be "attracted" to the paper, resulting in blank sheets coming out of the printer. In addition to the explanation listed, it is also possible for the toner cartridge to fail, causing blank pages to print. This would mean that blank pages could be caused by failures during the Developing and the Transferring stages of the laser printing process, with failures during the Developing stage being more common.

9. **A.** A scratch on the laser printer drum can account for black lines showing up on printouts. Another culprit can be a dirty primary corona wire.

10. **A** and **E.** Maintenance kits usually include things like paper pickup rollers, transfer rollers, and a fuser. The duplexer, image drum, and toner are parts of the printer and/or toner cartridges. Toner cartridges are not included in maintenance kits.

11. **B.** You should upgrade the RAM on the printer. Large graphic files need a lot of memory to work with both on the PC and the printer. But if the PC can send the file to the printer, then it has enough RAM and hard drive space. Printer drivers will not cause an Out of Memory Error to display on the printer.

12. **D.** Turn off the printer before you start working inside of the printer. You want to make sure it is off (and unplugged) before you put your hands inside of it. Taking it offline is not enough in this case.

CHAPTER 15

Networking

This chapter covers the following A+ exam topics:

▶ Types of Networks and Network Devices

▶ Cables, Connectors, and Tools

▶ TCP/IP

▶ SOHO Windows Networking

▶ Troubleshooting Networks

You can find a master list of A+ exam topics in the "Introduction."

This chapter covers CompTIA A+ 220-801 objectives 2.1 through 2.10 and 220-802 objectives 1.5, 1.6 and 4.5.

Virtually every business has one or more computer networks, and it seems that nowadays just about every home has a network as well. But what is a computer network? The simple answer: A computer network is two or more computers that communicate. For the more in-depth answer, read on!

We use networks so that computers can share files, access databases, collaborate on projects, connect to the Internet, and send e-mail. Important considerations in networking include the technologies used, devices, protocols, cabling; plus the installation, configuration, and troubleshooting of networks. Other things to think about are how the network is organized, what types of communications are necessary, in what way devices share information, how the network is secured, and what is the effect of the network on the budget. As you can see, so much is dependent on a well-designed, quick-and-efficient, and cost-effective network, making this an important chapter for the exam.

This is a monster chapter, so let's take it slow. You will definitely want to review the chapter when you finish. Let's begin by discussing the types of computer networks you should know for the exam and the devices that connect those networks together.

Types of Networks and Network Devices

Computer networks might inhabit one small area or larger areas; different terms such as LAN and WAN are used to describe these types of networks. To connect computers together in these networks, we use a variety of devices such as switches and routers. How the computers physically connect to each other is known as a topology. These three concepts make up the core of networking fundamentals.

Network Types

It's important to know how networks are classified. The two most common terms are local area network (LAN) and wide area network (WAN). But you should also know what a MAN and PAN are. Let's begin with LAN and WAN.

A LAN is a group of computers and other devices that are usually located in a small area: a house, a small office, or a single building. The computers all connect to one or more switches, and a router allows the computers access to the Internet.

A WAN is a group of one or more LANs over a large geographic area. Let's say a company had two LANs; one in New York, and one in Los Angeles. Connecting the two would result in a WAN. However, to do this, we would require the help of a telecommunications company. This company would create the high-speed connection required for the two LANs to communicate quickly. Each LAN would require a router to connect to each other.

There is a smaller version of a WAN known as a metropolitan area network (MAN) also known as a municipal area network. This is when a company has two offices in the same city and wants to make a high-speed connection between them. It's different from a WAN in that it is not a large geographic area, but it is similar to a WAN in that a telecommunications company is needed for the high-speed link.

On a slightly different note, a personal area network (or PAN) is a smaller computer network used for communication by smartphones, PDAs, and other small computing devices. Take this to the next level by adding wireless standards such as Bluetooth and you get a wireless PAN, or WPAN. These networks are ad-hoc, meaning that there is no single controlling device or server.

> **Exam Alert**
>
> Be able to define LAN, WAN, MAN, and PAN for the exam.

Network Devices

To allow communication between computers, we need to put some other devices in place. For example, hubs, switches, and access points connect computers on the LAN. Routers and firewalls enable connectivity to other networks and protect those connection points. There are ten types of devices you should know for the A+ exams; let's start with basic connectivity of computers on the LAN that use the Ethernet standard.

Hub

The hub is the original connecting device for computers on the LAN. It creates a simple shared physical plant that all computers use to send data. It's a basic device that has multiple ports, usually in intervals of four. Internally, the hub actually has only one trunk circuit that all the ports connect to. It regenerates and passes on the electrical signals initiated by computers. This device broadcasts data out to all computers. The computer that it is meant for accepts the data, the rest drop the information. Because of this broadcasting and sharing, this device allowed only two computers to communicate with each other at any given time. In the days of 10 Mbps and 100 Mbps networks, it was common to have a hub. But today in most instances, the hub has given way to the switch.

Switch

Ethernet Switching was developed in 1996 and quickly took hold as the preferred method of networking. A switch, like a hub, is a central connecting device that all computers connect to, and like a hub it regenerates the signal, but that's where the similarity ends. A switch takes the signal (frames of data) and sends it to the correct computer instead of broadcasting it out to every port. It does this by identifying the MAC address of each computer. This can effectively make every port an individual entity, and it increases data throughput exponentially. Switches employ a matrix of copper wiring instead of the standard trunk circuit. They are intelligent, and use this intelligence to pass information to the correct port. This means that each computer has its own bandwidth, for example 100 Mbps. In today's networks, the switch is king and is common in 100 Mbps, 1000 Mbps, and 10 Gbps networks. Hubs and switches both work within the Ethernet standard which is the most common networking standard used today; it was ratified by the IEEE and is documented in the 802.3 set of standards.

Wireless Access Point (WAP)

A wireless access point (WAP) enables data communications over the air if your computer is equipped with a wireless networking adapter. They transmit their data over radio waves either on the 2.4 GHz or 5 GHz frequencies. This brings mobility to a new level. Some WAPs also have a router built in, such as the D-Link router we refer to in this chapter. This enables wireless computers to not only communicate with each other but to access the Internet as well. Many of these devices also come equipped with a firewall. At this point they are referred to as multifunction network devices, SOHO routers, or simply routers. Although hubs and switches deal with wired networks, the WAP deals with wireless connections. It is also based on Ethernet but now we are talking about the IEEE 802.11 group of standards that define wireless LANs (WLANs). Wireless access points act as a central connecting point for Wi-Fi-equipped computers; like switches, the WAP identifies each computer by its MAC address.

Bridge

The bridge is a device that can either connect two LANs together or separate them into two sections. There are wired and wireless bridges that are more commonly used today to increase the size of networks.

Network Attached Storage (NAS)

A NAS is a device that contains multiple hard drives (often hot-swappable) that connects directly to the network. Data can be stored to and retrieved from these devices by way of mapped network drives, and of course exploring the network. They offer high-speed access with no operating system to slow things down. There are basic examples of NAS devices for home use that might have one or two drives and much more advanced examples for corporate use that have many hard drives and incorporate RAID functionality.

Modem

Now, let's move outside of the LAN and talk about Internet and WAN connectivity. The term modem is a combination of the words *mo*dulate and *dem*odulate. It is a device that allows a computer (or in rare cases multiple computers) access to the Internet by changing the digital signals of the computer to analog signals used by a typical land-based phone line. These are slow devices and are usually used only if no other Internet option is available. However, they might be used in server rooms as a point of remote administration as well.

Internet Appliance

The term Internet appliance refers to any device that enables easy connectivity to the Internet. Historically, that was usually its only function and was often implemented in the form of handheld devices. Nowadays, some people refer to tablets such as Apple's iPad as an Internet appliance; although the iPad is not limited to that singular purpose. On a side note, some technicians refer to Internet appliances as any device that allows connectivity to the Internet. We talk more about iPads and other similar Internet appliances in Chapter 17, "Mobile Devices."

Router

A router is used to connect two or more networks together to form an internetwork. They are used in LANs and WANs and on the Internet. This device routes data from one location to another, usually by way of IP address and IP network numbers. Routers are intelligent and even have their own operating systems. The router enables connections with individual high-speed interconnection points. A common example would be an all-in-one device, or multifunction network device that might be used in a home or small office. These devices route signals for all the computers on the LAN out to the Internet. Larger organizations use more advanced routers that can make connections to multiple various networks as well as the Internet.

Firewall

A firewall is any hardware appliance or software application that protects a computer from unwanted intrusion. In the networking world we are more concerned with hardware-based devices that protect an entire group of computers such as a LAN. When it comes to small offices and home offices firewall functionality is usually built into the router. In larger organizations it is a separate device. The firewall stops unwanted connections from the outside and can block basic networking attacks.

VoIP Phones

Voice over Internet Protocol (VoIP) is a collection of technologies, devices, and protocols that allow voice communication over IP-based networks. VoIP phones are the Internet telephony devices that a person would use to make conversations. These devices connect directly to the Ethernet network and communicate on the network just like a computer. All the words you speak are converted and encapsulated into packets that are sent across the network. It is a cheaper method of telephony, but there can be sound quality and latency issues if they are not configured properly.

Network Topologies

Topologies are the physical ways that computers are cabled together. The most common by far is the star topology, but you should also know bus, ring, mesh, and hybrid for the exam. They are often described graphically, as shown in Figure 15.1. Let's briefly discuss each of these now.

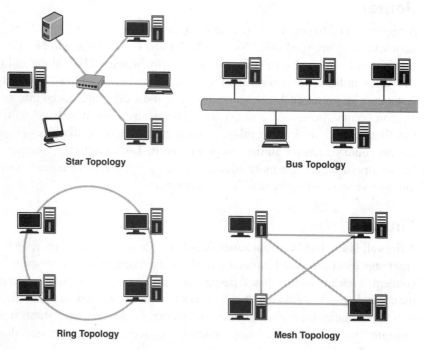

FIGURE 15.1   Four types of network topologies

Star

The star topology is the most common. When this topology became main-stream, it quickly did away with 90% of the bus and ring topologies around the world. As shown in Figure 15.1, it uses a central connecting device (such as a switch) to unite all of the computers on the LAN. The biggest benefit of the star topology is that if one computer fails, it doesn't affect the rest of the network.

Bus

You will rarely see this setup, and it's easy to understand why. Refer to Figure 15.1. Notice that all computers are connected to a backbone cable, not a central connecting device such as a switch. This means that if you want to add or remove computers from a bus network, you would have to take the whole network down first.

Ring

This is another uncommon type of topology with no central connecting device. You will notice that they took both ends of the bus and connected them together. So as the name implies, a ring of computers is formed. The physical ring, like the bus, suffers from the need to bring the whole network down before computers could be added. There are more advanced networks that rely and thrive on the ring concept, but these technologies are outside of the scope of the A+ exams.

Mesh

A completely different type of topology. Every device connects to every other device. Phew! That could be a lot of connections. Take a look at Figure 15.1 and you will see my point. This figure shows what is also known as a Full Mesh. The amount of network connections that each computer will need is the total number of computers in the network minus one. As you can guess, this is extremely rare, but special computing environments may use this. Another lesser version of this is the Partial Mesh. This is when only a few of the computers on the network have secondary network connections to other systems. You may see this with database replication. These computers would then be known as multihomed systems.

Hybrid

Hybrid topologies combine some of the characteristics of two different topologies. A couple common examples are star-bus and hierarchical star. In some cases, you may need to connect two star networks to each other. If this is the case, then the easiest way to do it is to connect the two central connecting devices to each other. Let's say that each star network has a switch at the center. By connecting the two switches, you are effectively creating a bus between the two. Therefore, it is known as a star-bus. Now take it to the next level. Use one powerful central switch as a "backbone," and connect several other switches to it, each with its own star topology. Now you have the hierarchical star. This is common in large corporate networks. An example of this is illustrated in Figure 15.2. There are three different groups of computers each connected to their own switch. All three switches are connected to a backbone switch, which will offer higher data transfer rates.

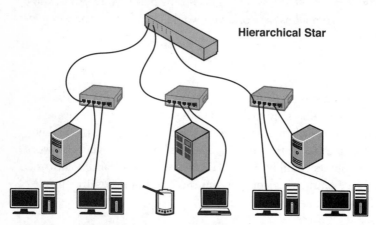

Hierarchical Star

FIGURE 15.2   **Hybrid example: hierarchical star**

> **ExamAlert**
>
> Know the 5 network topology types: star, bus, ring, mesh, and hybrid.

Cram Quiz

Answer these questions. The answers follow the last question. If you cannot answer these questions correctly, consider reading this section again until you can.

220-801 Questions

1. Which of the following is a group of computers located in a small area?
   - ○ **A.** LAN
   - ○ **B.** WAN
   - ○ **C.** PAN
   - ○ **D.** MAN

2. Which of the following are most often used to connect a group of computers in a LAN? (Select the two best answers.)
   - ○ **A.** Hub
   - ○ **B.** Switch
   - ○ **C.** Bridge
   - ○ **D.** WAP

3. What device contains multiple hard drives and is connected directly to the network?

   ○ **A.** Internet appliance
   ○ **B.** Router
   ○ **C.** NAS
   ○ **D.** Firewall

4. Which of the following allows voice communication over IP-based networks?

   ○ **A.** Firewall
   ○ **B.** Modem
   ○ **C.** NAS
   ○ **D.** VoIP

5. What network topology is the most common?

   ○ **A.** Ring
   ○ **B.** Star
   ○ **C.** Bus
   ○ **D.** Mesh

6. What network topology combines the characteristics of two other topologies?

   ○ **A.** Hybrid
   ○ **B.** Star
   ○ **C.** Bus
   ○ **D.** Mesh

7. Which of the following network devices moves frames of data between a source and destination based on their MAC addresses?

   ○ **A.** Hub
   ○ **B.** Switch
   ○ **C.** Router
   ○ **D.** Modem

Cram Quiz Answers

220-801 Answers

1. **A.** A local area network (LAN) is a group of computers such as a SOHO network located in a small area. A wide area network (WAN) is a group of one or more LANs spread over a larger geographic area. A personal area network (PAN) is a smaller computer network used by smartphones and other small computing devices. A metropolitan area network (MAN) is a group of LANs in a smaller geographic area of a city.

2. **B** and **D**. Computers in a LAN are connected together by a central connecting device; the most common of these are the switch and the wireless access point (WAP). Hubs are deprecated devices; the predecessor of the switch. A bridge is used to connect two LANs together or separate a single LAN into two sections.

3. **C**. Network attached storage (NAS) devices contain multiple hard drives and connect directly to the network. Internet appliances are small devices that enable quick and easy connectivity to the Internet. A router is used to connect two or more networks together. A Firewall is a hardware appliance or software that protects one or more computers from unwanted intrusion.

4. **D**. Voice over Internet Protocol (VoIP) is a technology that allows for voice communication over IP-based networks. A firewall is a device or software that protects computers from threats on the Internet. A modem is a device that allows a computer to connect to the Internet by way of a standard phone line. Network attached storage (NAS) is a device that serves data and connects directly to the network.

5. **B**. The star topology is the most common; it is when computers are wired to a central connecting device such as a switch. The ring is when computers are connected to a single cable in a circular fashion. A bus topology is when computers are connected to a single cable that has a starting and ending point. Mesh is when computers have multiple connections to each other.

6. **A**. The hybrid topology combines the characteristics of two other topologies; for example the star-bus or hierarchical star.

7. **B**. A switch sends frames of data between computers by identifying the systems by their MAC addresses.

Cables, Connectors, and Tools

Though wireless is becoming more and more popular, cables still provide huge amounts of data transfer over today's networks. In this section we'll discuss twisted-pair, fiber optic, and coaxial cable types, their varying characteristics, and connectors. Plus we'll briefly go over some of the cabling tools you should be aware of.

Cable Types and Connectors

Cable types are broken down into two categories: cables that use electricity and cables that use light. Twisted-pair and coaxial cables use copper wires as their transmission media and send electricity over those wires. Fiber optic on the other hand uses glass or plastic as the transmission media and sends light (photons) over those.

Twisted Pair

The most common type of cable used in today's networks is *twisted pair*. It is referred to as twisted pair because the copper wires inside of the cable are twisted together into pairs throughout the entire length of the cable. Regularly, admins use UTP cable, short for unshielded twisted pair. Today, the most frequently used twisted-pair types are *Category 5e* and *Category 6* (often abbreviated to just Cat 5e or Cat 6). Table 15.1 shows the various categories of twisted pair and the networks they are rated for.

TABLE 15.1 **UTP Categories and Speeds**

Category UTP	Rated for:
Category 3	10 Mbps networks
Category 5	100 Mbps networks
Category 5e	Rated for 100 Mbps and gigabit networks
Category 6	Rated for 100 Mbps and gigabit networks

Network data transfer rates (also known as speed or bandwidth) are normally measured in bits because networks usually transfer data serially, or one bit at a time. 100 Mbps is 100 megabits per second. 1 Gbps is equal to 1 gigabit per second (known as a gigabit network).

ExamAlert

Know what network speeds Cat 3, 5, 5e, and 6 are rated for.

Most wiring standards are based on the original BOGB standard, which specifies that wire pair colors go in this order: *Blue, Orange, Green, Brown*. The
568A and B standards are based on this. Generally speaking, the most common standard you see is the 568B standard. Any physical cabling equipment
used in the network must comply with this standard. This includes cables,
patch panels, jacks, and even connectors. The connector used with twisted-
pair networks is known colloquially as the RJ45 (more specifically the 8P8C
connector). RJ45 plugs connect to each end of the cable, and these connect to
RJ45 sockets within network adapters and on network switches.

> **ExamAlert**
>
> If a computer cannot connect to the network, check the network cable first. Make
> sure the RJ45 plug has a solid connection.

As you can see in Figure 15.3, RJ45 plugs look a lot like the plugs that connect your telephone (known as RJ11). However, the RJ45 plug is larger and
contains eight wires, whereas the RJ11 plug can hold only a maximum of six.

RJ45   RJ11

FIGURE 15.3   **RJ45 and RJ11 plugs**

A standard twisted-pair patch cable that you would use to connect a computer
to a switch or RJ45 jack is wired for 568B on each end. That makes it a
straight through cable. However, if you wanted to connect a computer directly
to another computer you would need a different cable: a *crossover cable*. This
type of cable is wired for 568B on one end and 568A on the other. You can
also use a crossover cable to connect one switch to another; though this is
usually not necessary nowadays as most switches will auto-sense the type of
cable you plug into them.

UTP has a few disadvantages; it can be run only 100 meters (328 feet) before signal attenuation, it's outer jacket is made of plastic, and it has no shielding, making it susceptible to electromagnetic interference (EMI) and vulnerable to unauthorized network access in the form of wire tapping.

Because the UTP cable jacket is made of PVCs (plastics) and can be harmful to humans if they catch on fire, most municipalities require that plenum-rated cable be installed in any area that cannot be reached by a sprinkler system. A plenum is an enclosed space used for airflow. For example, if cables are run above a drop ceiling, building code requires that they are plenum-rated: This means that the cable has a special Teflon coating or is a special low-smoke variant of twisted pair, reducing the amount of PVCs that are released into the air in the case of fire.

ExamAlert

To meet fire code, use plenum-rated cable above drop ceilings and anywhere else necessary.

Because UTP is susceptible to electromagnetic interference (EMI), a variant was developed known as STP or shielded twisted pair. This includes metal shielding over each pair of wires, reducing external EMI and the possibility of unauthorized network access. A couple of disadvantages of STP include higher cost of product and installation, and the fact that the shielding needs to be grounded to work effectively. Keep in mind that all patch panels, punch blocks, and wiring racks should be permanently grounded before use.

ExamAlert

STP cable is resistant to EMI.

Coaxial

Coaxial cable is another way to transfer data over a network. This cable has a single conductor surrounded by insulating material, which is then surrounded by a copper screen, and finally an outer plastic sheath. Some networking technologies still use coaxial cable; for example, cable Internet connections use coaxial cable (known as quad shield coaxial cable) with RG-6 connectors (previously RG-59). These screw on to the terminals of a cable modem or cable TV set-top box (STB). These connectors are known as F-connectors.

The older bus topology, coaxial-cabled LANs that used RG-58 BNC connectors are a thing of the past, and it is extremely unlikely that you will see a LAN using coaxial cable.

Fiber Optic

Fiber optic is fast; and when dealing with EMI, a better option than copper-based cables. Because fiber optic cables transmit data by way of light instead of electricity, they can send signals much faster and further than copper wires, and EMI doesn't even play into the equation. Plus, fiber optic cables are difficult to splice into, unlike copper-based cables. Due to these reasons, fiber optic cable is the most secure type of cable.

You might encounter single-mode and multimode fiber; for the most part single-mode fiber is used over longer distances, but both types are capable of supporting 1000 Mbps and 10 Gbps networks and can be run farther than twisted-pair cable. A couple types of connectors used with fiber include ST and SC, as shown in Figure 15.4. Another connector is LC, which looks quite similar to SC.

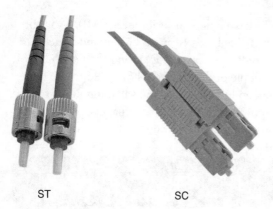

ST   SC

FIGURE 15.4   **ST and SC connectors**

Multimode cables have a larger core diameter than single-mode cables, either 50 or 62.5 microns (millionths of a meter). The smaller 50 micron version can handle three times the bandwidth and supports longer cable runs than the 62.5 micron version. It is the more commonly used fiber optic cable in server rooms and when making backbone connections between buildings in a campus. It transmits data approximately 600 meters. Single-core on the other hand is only 8 to 10 microns and is used for longer distance runs, perhaps from one city to the next, in the thousands of kilometers. At shorter distances, single-mode cable can go beyond 10 Gbps.

> **Exam Alert**
>
> Know the differences between multimode and single-mode for the exam.

Cabling Tools

If you plan on building a physical network, you will need to stock up on some key networking tools. These tools will aid you when running, terminating, and testing cable. For this short section, let's imagine a scenario where you are the network installer and are required to install a wired network for twelve computers.

To start, you should check with your local municipality for any rules and regulations for running networking cable. Some municipalities require a person to have an electrician's license. But most require only an exemption of some sort that anyone can apply for at the town or county seat. Due to the low-voltage nature of network wiring (for most applications), some municipalities have no rules regarding this. But in urban areas you will need to apply for a permit and have at least one inspection done when you are done with the installation. Permits and regulations aside, let's say that in this scenario you have been cleared to install 12 wired connections to computers (known as drops) and have diagrammed where the cables will be run and where they will terminate. All cables will come out of a wiring closet where you will terminate them to a small patch panel. On the other end, they will terminate at in-wall RJ45 jacks near each of the computers. Let's discuss each of the tools that you will use to complete this job.

- ▶ **Cable cutter:** The first tool you should have is a good, sharp cutting tool. You will need to make a clean cut on the end of the network cable; scissors will not do. Either cut pliers or other cable cutting tools will be necessary. Klein is an excellent manufacturer of these types of tools.

- ▶ **Wire stripper:** The second tool is a wire stripper. This tool is used to strip a portion of the plastic jacket off the cable exposing the individual wires. At this point you can separate the wires and get ready to terminate them.

- ▶ **Punch down tool:** The third tool is a punch down tool. This device punches the individual wires down into the 110 IDC clips of an RJ45 jack and the patch panel. This "punching down" of the wires is the actual termination.

- ▶ **Cable testers**: The last tool necessary for the job is a cable testing tool. There are a few options here:

> ▶ The best option is a proper network cable tester, also known as a continuity tester. This device will have a LAN testing unit that you can plug into a port on the patch panel and a terminator that you plug in to the other end of the cable in the corresponding RJ45 jack. This tool will test for continuity and will test each wire in the cable making sure every one is wired properly.

> ▶ Another option is the tone and probe kit (referred to in the CompTIA objectives as toner probe). This kit consists of two parts: a tone device, which connects to one end of the network cable and when turned on sends a tone along the length of the cable; and a probing device, also known as an inductive amplifier that can pick up the tone anywhere along the cable length and at the termination point. This tool is not as good as a proper network cable tester because it tests only one of the pairs of the wires. However, it is an excellent tool for finding individual phone lines and is more commonly used for that. You can also use a multimeter to do various tests of individual lines, but it is usually not necessary if you own the other tools mentioned.

At this point, the cables have been run, terminated on both ends, and tested. The only other thing you need is patch cables. The patch cables connect the various ports of the patch panel to a switch, and the RJ45 jacks to the computers.

> ▶ **RJ45 crimper:** Usually, you would buy patch cables for $2 or $3 each. However, you can make them. You would have to purchase cable, as well as RJ45 plugs. The plugs are attached to the cable ends with an RJ45 crimping tool. This tool can come in especially handy if you need to make a crossover patch cable. There are other types of crimpers for coaxial cable as well.

> ▶ **Patch tester:** Before connecting the patch cables, you should test them with a patch tester. This device has two RJ45 jacks; you plug each end of the patch cable into the tester, and press the button to make sure each wire on each connection makes a proper connection.

> ▶ **Loopback plug:** Another tool every PC tech should have in his kit is a loopback plug. This connects directly to the RJ45 port of a PC's network adapter. It simulates a network and tests if the network adapter and TCP/IP are functioning properly.

> ▶ **Time-domain reflectometer (TDR):** These measuring instruments can locate faults in a cable or discontinuities in a connector. They transmit a short pulse across the cable. If the cable is installed properly, no signal will be reflected back to the TDR, but if there are any impedance discontinuities, an error signal will be reflected back and displayed on the TDR.

That's about it for networking tools. For the A+ exam you should know the basics purposes of wire cutters, wire strippers, punch down tools, cable testing tools, and loopback plugs.

Cram Quiz

Answer these questions. The answers follow the last question. If you cannot answer these questions correctly, consider reading this section again until you can.

220-801 Questions

1. Which of the following would be suitable for 1000 Mbps networks? (Select all that apply.)
   - O **A.** Category 3
   - O **B.** Category 5
   - O **C.** Category 5e
   - O **D.** Category 6

2. Which type of cable would you use if you were concerned about EMI?
   - O **A.** Plenum-rated
   - O **B.** UTP
   - O **C.** STP
   - O **D.** Coaxial

3. Which type of cable can connect a computer to another computer directly?
   - O **A.** Straight-through
   - O **B.** Crossover
   - O **C.** Rolled
   - O **D.** 568B

4. Which of the following cables has a core diameter of 62.5 microns?
   - O **A.** Single-mode
   - O **B.** Category 6
   - O **C.** Multimode
   - O **D.** STP

5. Which connector would you use for cable Internet?

   ○ **A.** LC

   ○ **B.** F-connector

   ○ **C.** BNC

   ○ **D.** RJ45

6. Which tool would you use to test a network adapter not connected to the network?

   ○ **A.** Punch down tool

   ○ **B.** Cable tester

   ○ **C.** Loopback plug

   ○ **D.** Tone and probe

Cram Quiz Answers

220-801 Answers

1. **C** and **D.** Category 5e and Category 6 are suitable for 1000 Mbps networks. Category 3 is suitable for 10 Mbps networks only. Category 5 is suitable for 100 Mbps networks.

2. **C.** STP (shielded twisted pair) is the only cable listed here that can reduce electromagnetic interference. Plenum-rated cable is used where fire code requires it; it doesn't burn as fast, releasing less PVCs into the air.

3. **B.** A crossover cable is used to connect like devices: computer to computer or switch to switch. Straight-through cables (the more common patch cable) connect unlike devices, for example from a computer to a switch. Rolled cables were not mentioned yet, which allow a PC to communicate with the console port of a corporate router. 568B is the typical wiring standard you will see in twisted-pair cables. A crossover cable uses the 568B wiring standard on one end and 568A on the other end.

4. **C.** Multimode cable has a core diameter of either 50 or 62.5 microns. Single-mode is between 8 to 10 microns. Category 6 is twisted pair and uses between 22 and 24 gauge copper wire. STP is shielded twisted pair.

5. **B.** Cable Internet connections would use RG-6 coaxial cable (usually) with an F-connector on the end. LC is a type of fiber optic connector. BNC is an older connector type used by coaxial networks. RJ45 is the connector used on twisted-pair patch cables.

6. **C.** To test a network adapter without a network connection, you would use a loopback plug. This simulates a network connection. Punch down tools are used to punch individual wires to a patch panel. Cable testers such as continuity testers will test the entire length of a terminated cable. The tone and probe kit also tests a cable's length but only one pair of wires.

TCP/IP

You all have heard of TCP/IP. The most famous acronym in networking; it stands for Transmission Control Protocol/Internet Protocol. Within the name are the two most used protocols when computers send information to each other on an IP network. However, there are lots of other protocols and ports within, which we will speak to a little later in this section. The two versions of IP you need to know for the exam are IPv4 and the newer IPv6. Let's start with Internet Protocol version 4.

Configuring IPv4

Configuring IP works the same way in most versions of Windows. First we navigate to the Internet Protocol (TCP/IP) Properties window, which we refer to as the IP Properties dialog box.

▶ **In Windows 7/Vista:** Navigate to Start > Control Panel > Network and Internet > Network and Sharing Center. Select the Change Adapter Settings link (In Windows Vista: Manage My Network Connections link). Then right-click the Local Area Connection icon and select Properties. Finally, highlight Internet Protocol Version 4 and click the Properties button. (For speed, right-click the network icon in the Notification Area and select Open Network and Sharing Center.)

▶ **In Windows XP**: Navigate to Start > Control Panel > Network and Internet Connections. Select the Control Panel icon Network Connections. Then right-click the Local Area Connection icon and select Properties. Finally, highlight Internet Protocol and click the Properties button.

The first item to be configured is the IP address. The IP address is the unique assigned number of your computer on the network. IP addresses consist of four octets. Each octet's value can be between 0 and 255. Each number is separated by a dot. For example: 192.168.0.100. The binary equivalent of 0–255 would be 00000000 through 11111111. For example, 192 is equal to 11000000 in binary. Because each octet contains 8 bits, and there are four octets, the IP address collectively is a 32-bit number but is normally expressed in dotted-decimal notation.

There are two main types of addresses: dynamic and static. Dynamically assigned addresses are more common for a client computer; this is when the computer seeks out a DHCP server so that it can get its IP information automatically. In Figure 15.5, you note a radio button that says Obtain an IP Address Automatically. If you select this, the rest of the information becomes grayed out, and the computer attempts to get that IP information from a host such as a multifunction network device or DHCP server. This is common; in fact it's the default configuration for Windows. Static addresses are when we configure the IP information manually. Figure 15.5 shows an example of statically configured IP settings in the IP Properties dialog box. In the figure we configured the computer to use the address 192.168.0.100, but the IP address differs from machine to machine depending on several factors. Remember that the address should be unique for each computer on the network.

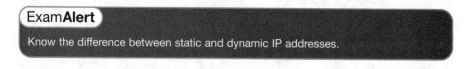

ExamAlert

Know the difference between static and dynamic IP addresses.

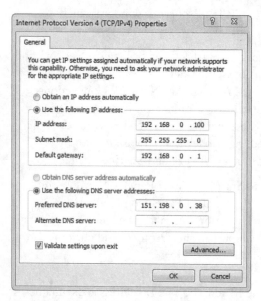

FIGURE 15.5 **IP Properties Dialog Box in Windows 7**

There is another possibility when it comes to IP addresses, and that is when the computer self-assigns an address. This is known as *automatic private IP addressing (APIPA)* and happens when a computer cannot contact a DHCP server to obtain an IP address. If APIPA self-assigns an address, it will be on the 169.254.0.0 network.

IP addresses are divided into two sections: the network portion, which is the number of the network the computer is on, and the host portion, which is the individual number of the computer. The subnet mask defines which portion of the IP address is the network number and which portion is the individual host number. In this case the subnet mask is 255.255.255.0. The 255s indicate the network portion of the IP address. So, 192.168.0 is the network this computer is a member of. The zeros (in this case there is only one of them) indicate the host number, so 100 is the individual number of this computer. Quite often the subnet mask will be configured automatically by Windows after you type in the IP address.

The gateway address is the IP address of the host that enables access to the Internet or to other networks. The IP address of the gateway should always be on the same network as the computer(s) connecting to it. In Figure 15.5 we know it is because the first three octets are 192.168.0. If a computer is not configured with a gateway address, it cannot connect to the Internet.

> ### Exam**Alert**
>
> To use the gateway, computers must be on the same network number as the gateway device.

The DNS server address is the IP address of the host that takes care of domain name translation to IP. When you use your browser to connect to a website, you might type something like www.davidlprowse.com. What you need to remember, however, is that computers actually communicate by IP address, not by name. So the DNS server takes care of translating the name davidlprowse.com to its corresponding IP address and forwarding that information back to your computer. When your computer knows the IP address of the website, it can go ahead and start a session with the website and transmit and receive files. Notice in Figure 15.5 that the DNS server address is on a completely different network than our computer. This is typical, in this case the DNS server is run by the Internet service provider (ISP) who provides me with my Internet connection. However, DNS servers can also be run internally by a company; this happens more often with larger companies.

You will also note a check box labeled Validate Settings Upon Exit. If you set up a static IP address on a computer you should select this. This way, Windows will check if the configuration works properly and will let you know if any basic errors arise. Who knows, the IP configuration might have an incorrect DNS server, gateway address, or IP network number.

If your IP Properties dialog box is set to Obtain an IP address automatically, you will see the Alternate Configuration tab. This allows you to have a secondary IP configuration. Let's say there was a scenario in which you used a laptop at work and got your IP address from a DHCP server, but you also go on the road. The alternate configuration would kick in automatically when you are away from the office and allow you access to the Internet or to virtual private networks, depending on how you configure it. The alternate configuration can be on a wholly different IP network than the main configuration.

IPv4 Classes

When working with classful IP addresses, the first number in the IP address dictates what class the address is part of. For example, suppose you use 192.168.0.100. In that case, the first number is 192, which means that the IP address is part of a Class C network.

Table 15.2 shows the various classes and their associated IP address ranges. Table 15.3 shows the IP classes and their associated default subnet masks, which as we mentioned, identify which portion of the IP address is the network portion and which is the host portion.

Take a look at Table 15.2 and try to get a feel for the different IP Classes available. You realize that this classification system was created to appease different organizations of different sizes. If you have a small network at home, it is simplest and most common to use Class C.

TABLE 15.2 **IP Classifications**

IP Class	Range	Number of Networks	Number of Hosts per Network	Who Uses It?
A	1–126	126	16,777,214	Large Corps, ISPs
B	128–191	16,384	65,534	Corps, Universities
C	192–223	2,097,152	254	Small offices/Home offices (SOHO)

> **Note**
>
> Class D (224-239) is used for multicast testing, and Class E (240-255) is reserved for future use.
>
> APIPA addresses on the 169.254 network are part of Class B.

You probably noticed that the number 127 was skipped. That is because this network number is reserved for loopback testing. Technically, it is part of the Class A range, but it cannot be configured as an IP address within the IP Properties dialog box. The built-in loopback address is 127.0.0.1.

You might have also noticed that there are only 254 possible hosts per network in Class C instead of 256. This is because you can never use the first or the last address in the range; the first is actually the network number and the last is the broadcast address.

The total hosts, for all classes combined, is 3,720,314,628. That's just under four billion—and we have pretty much used up all those addresses. This is one of the reasons for the inception of IPv6.

ExamAlert

Memorize the IP ranges for Class A, B and C

TABLE 15.3 **IP Class Ranges and Their Equivalent Binary Values and Subnet Masks**

IP Class	Binary Equivalent	Default Subnet Masks
A: 1-126	00000001—01111110	255.0.0.0 Net.node.node.node
B: 128-191	10000000—10111111	255.255.0.0 Net.net.node.node
C: 192-223	11000000—11011111	255.255.255.0 Net.net.net.node

Notice in Table 15.3 how the number 255 in a subnet mask coincides with the name *net*. Also, notice the 0 coincides with the name *node*. Net is the network portion of the IP address, whereas node is the host, or computer portion of the address.

ExamAlert

Memorize the default subnet masks for Class A, B and C.

It is also important to know the difference between private and public addresses. A private address is one that is not displayed directly to the Internet and is normally behind a firewall. Typically, these are addresses that a SOHO router would assign automatically to clients. A list of reserved private IP ranges is shown in Table 15.4. Public addresses are addresses that *are* displayed directly to the Internet; they are addresses that anyone could possibly connect to around the world. Most addresses, besides the private ones listed in Table 15.4, are considered public addresses.

TABLE 15.4 **Private IP Ranges (As Assigned by the IANA)**

IP Class	Assigned Range
A	10.0.0.0—10.255.255.255
B	172.16.0.0—172.31.255.255
C	192.168.0.0—192.168.255.255

ExamAlert

Memorize the private IP ranges for Class A, B, and C.

Note

Something else to note: Classful IP addresses used in Class A, B, and C are not quite as necessary anymore. In fact, many corporate networks use *classless* IP addressing. This means that any network number can use any subnet mask. (Breaking all the rules!) For example, one of my test networks uses the 10.254.254.0 network and the 255.255.255.0 subnet mask, making the network number 10.254.254, instead of just 10. How is this done? By changing the subnet mask to 255.255.255.0 instead of the default 255.0.0.0. (I guess this means my test network has no class. Ouch!) Seriously though, this method is known as Classless Inter-Domain Routing, or CIDR for short, and you will deal with this more if you decide to enter into the realm of Network+.

Configuring IPv6

IPv6 is the next generation of IP addressing. Used on the Internet and on many LANs and WANs, it is designed to meet the inadequacies of IPv4. One of the main reasons for the development of IPv6 was the rapidly approaching global shortage of IPv4 addresses. Where IPv4 (a 32-bit system) can have approximately 4 billion total theoretical addresses, IPv6 (128-bit) can have a total of 340 *undecillion* theoretical addresses; a far greater total. Various limitations of the system will drastically reduce that number, but the remaining result is still orders of magnitude above and beyond the IPv4 system. However, IPv6 is also known for security. IPsec is a fundamental piece of the IPv6 puzzle and if used properly can offer much more secure communications than IPv4. IPv6 also supports larger packet sizes known as jumbograms. Table 15.5 summarizes some of the differences between IPv4 and IPv6.

TABLE 15.5 **IPv4 Versus IPv6**

IPv4	IPv6
32-bit	128-bit
4 billion addresses	340 undecillion addresses
Less secure	More secure, IPsec is embedded
65,536 byte packet size max	4 billion bytes max

IPv6 addresses are 128-bit hexadecimal numbers that are divided into eight groups of four numbers each. The most commonly used type is the unicast address, which defines a single IP address on a single interface (such as a network adapter). Windows auto-configures a unicast address when IPv6 is installed. The address will either start with FE80, FE90, FEA0, or FEB0. (Collectively, this range is shown as FE80::/10.) Every Windows computer with IPv6 installed also receives a loopback address that is ::1. The IPv6 address ::1 is the equivalent to IPv4's loopback address of 127.0.0.1.

ExamAlert

Know the loopback addresses for IPv6 and IPv4.

There are three types of IPv6 addresses, as shown in Table 15.6.

TABLE 15.6 **IPv6 Address Types**

IPv6 Type	Address Range	Description
Unicast	Global Unicast, begins at 2000	▶ Address assigned to one interface ▶ Link-Local addresses begin at FE80::/10 ▶ Loopback is ::1
Anycast	Uses the Unicast structure	▶ Address assigned to a group of interfaces. ▶ Packets are delivered to the first interface only.
Multicast	FF00::/8	▶ Address assigned to a group of interfaces. ▶ Packets are delivered to all interfaces.

Here's an example of an IPv6 address:

```
2001:7120:0000:8001:0000:0000:0000:1F10
```

IPv6 addresses are broken down into three sections: the global routing prefix in this case 2001:7120:0000; a subnet that is 8001; and the individual interface ID, shown as 0000:0000:0000:1F10.

This is the full address, but you will more commonly see truncated addresses. There are two ways to truncate, or shorten, an IPv6 address. First is to remove leading zeroes. Any group of 4 zeroes can be truncated down to a single zero; basically zero is always zero, so the additional zeroes are not necessary. Also, one consecutive group of zeroes can be truncated as a double colon ::. In the example we have 12 consecutive zeroes that can be truncated all the way down to a double colon. (A double colon can be used only once in an address.) The end result of both of these abbreviations would be

```
2001:7120:0:8001::1F10
```

> **ExamAlert**
>
> Understand how IPv6 addresses can be truncated.

IPv6 addresses can be assigned statically as well; this can be done within the Internet Protocol Version 6 Properties dialog box, which can be accessed from Local Area Connection Properties; it is listed right next to IPv4.

TCP/IP Protocols and Their Ports

Network sessions on an IP network are normally either TCP or UDP. Let's briefly discuss these two.

Transmission Control Protocol (TCP) sessions are known as connection-oriented sessions. This means that every packet that is sent is checked for delivery. If the receiving computer doesn't receive a packet, it cannot assemble the message and will ask the sending computer to transmit the packet again. No one packet is left behind.

User Datagram Protocol (UDP) sessions are known as connectionless sessions. UDP is used in streaming media sessions. In these cases if a packet is dropped, it is not asked for again. Let's say you were listening to some streaming music and you heard a break in the song or a blip of some kind. That indicates some missing packets, but you wouldn't want those packets back because by the time you get them, you would be listening to a totally different part of the music stream!

It's expected to lose packets in UDP streams but not when making TCP connections. Both TCP and UDP utilize protocols and ports to make connections. Let's further discuss these protocols and ports.

For two computers to communicate, they must both use the same protocol. For an application to send or receive data, it must use a particular protocol designed for that application and open up a port on the network adapter to make a connection to another computer. For example, let's say you want to visit www.google.com. You would open up a browser and type in `http://www.google.com`. The protocol used is HTTP, short for Hypertext Transfer Protocol. That is the protocol that makes the connection to the web server: google.com. The HTTP protocol selects an unused port on your computer (known as an outbound port) to send and receive data to and from google.com. On the other end, google.com's web server has a specific port open at all times ready to accept sessions. In most cases the web server's port is 80, which corresponds to the HTTP protocol. This is known as an inbound port. Figure 15.6 illustrates this.

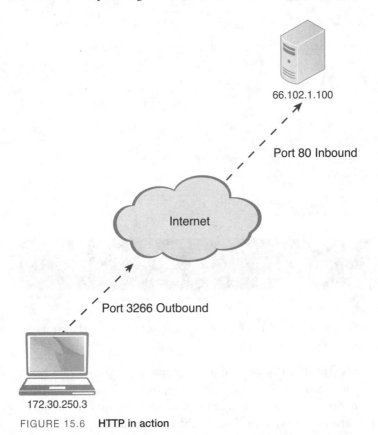

66.102.1.100

Port 80 Inbound

Internet

Port 3266 Outbound

172.30.250.3

FIGURE 15.6   **HTTP in action**

The local computer on the bottom-left part of Figure 15.6 has been given the IP address 172.30.250.3, a Class B private address. It uses port 3266 to go out to the Internet and start a session with google.com. For security purposes this is a dynamically assigned port and will be different every time you connect to another web server, but it will normally be somewhere in the thousands. The session is accepted by google.com's web server, using the public IP address 66.102.1.100, inbound port 80. Conversely, if you want to run your own web server at home and sell widgets and such, then that web server would need to have port 80 open to the public at all times. If it were ever closed, you would lose sales! People's computers that connected to your web server would use dynamically assigned ports.

There are 65536 ports in total, numbered between 0 and 65535, and almost as many protocols! Don't worry; you need to know only several for the exam, which are listed in Table 15.7.

TABLE 15.7 **Common Protocols and Their Ports**

Protocol	Port
FTP	21
SSH	22
TELNET	23
SMTP	25
DNS	53
HTTP	80
POP3	110
IMAP	143
HTTPS	443
RDP	3389

ExamAlert

Memorize the protocol port numbers in Table 15.7!

The ports mentioned in Table 15.7 are the inbound ports used by the computer that runs one of the following services:

▶ **FTP:** The File Transfer Protocol allows computers to transfer files back and forth. When you connect to a FTP server, that FTP server will have port 21 open. Some type of FTP client software is necessary to connect to the FTP server; this could be done in the command-line within the FTP shell or by using a GUI-based application like FileZilla.

▶ **SSH:** Secure Shell enables data to be exchanged between computers on a secured channel. This protocol offers a more secure replacement to FTP and TELNET. The Secure Shell server housing the data you want to access would have port 22 open. There are several other protocols that use SSH as a way of making a secure connection. One of these is Secure FTP (SFTP). Regular FTP can be insecure. SFTP combats this by providing file access over a reliable data stream, generated and protected by SSH.

▶ **TELNET:** Short for Telecommunication network, this provides remote access to other hosts within the CLI. It uses port 23 but is an insecure and somewhat deprecated protocol. However, because some companies still use it to access routers and other hosts, you might see a question about it on the exam.

▶ **SMTP:** Simple Mail Transfer Protocol sends e-mail. When you send e-mail from home, it goes to an SMTP server (which has inbound port 25 open) at your ISP and is then sent off to its destination. A good way to remember this is by using the mnemonic device Send Mail To People. It is worth noting that another port (587) can be used with SMTP in the case that an ISP or other agency blocks port 25.

▶ **DNS:** The Domain Name System is the group of servers on the Internet that translate domain names to IP addresses.

▶ **HTTP:** Hypertext Transfer Protocol transfers web pages and other web-based material from a web server to your web browser. It is normally done in a compressed format but not in a secured format. Web servers have port 80 open by default.

▶ **POP3:** Post Office Protocol Version 3 is used by e-mail clients to retrieve incoming e-mail from a mail server. The POP3 mail server uses port 110.

▶ **IMAP:** The Internet Message Access Protocol (IMAP) is an e-mail protocol that enables messages to remain on the e-mail server, so they can be retrieved from any location. IMAP also supports folders, so users can organize their messages as desired.

▶ **HTTPS:** Hypertext Transfer Protocol Secure sends and receives information like HTTP but includes the Transport Layer Security protocol (successor of the Secure Sockets Layer [SSL] protocol) to encrypt the information, most commonly when making purchases/payments online or when logging in to a confidential website. The HTTPS server has port 443 open.

▶ **RDP:** To facilitate connections to remote computers and allowing full remote control, Microsoft uses the Remote Desktop program, which is based off the Remote Desktop Protocol (RDP). This works in three ways. First, users can be given limited access to a remote computer's applications such as Word or Excel. Second, administrators can be given full access to a computer so that they can troubleshoot problems from another location. Third, another part of the program known as Remote Assistance allows users to invite a technician to come and view their desktop in the hopes that the technician can fix any encountered problems. These invitations can be made via e-mail or by Windows Messenger. The RDP port, 3389, is also used by Microsoft Terminal Services, which is the server-based companion of Remote Desktop.

There are some additional TCP/IP protocols you should know for the exam:

- **DHCP:** The Dynamic Host Configuration Protocol (DHCP) is used to automatically assign IP addresses to hosts. These hosts could be computers, printers, servers, routers, and so on. In most SOHO networks a router will use DHCP to assign IP addresses to the client computers. However, your ISP will also use DHCP to assign an IP address to you; usually your router gets this. The DHCP service makes life easier for the network administrator by automatically assigning IP addresses, subnet masks, gateway addresses, DNS servers, and so on, from a central location. If you get your address from a DHCP server, you are getting your address assigned dynamically, and it could change periodically. Computers that do obtain IP addresses from a DHCP server have the advantage of automatically getting new addressing when they are moved to a different network segment. However, some computers require a static address, one that is assigned by the network administrator manually. It is better in many situations for servers and printers to use static addresses, so you know exactly what the address is, and so it won't change.

- **SNMP:** Simple Network Management Protocol (SNMP) is used as the standard for managing and monitoring devices on your network. It manages routers, switches, and computers and is often incorporated in software known as a network management system or NMS. The NMS is the main software that controls everything SNMP-based; it is installed on a computer known as a manager. The devices to be monitored are known as managed devices. The NMS installs a small piece of software known as an agent that allows the NMS to monitor those managed devices.

- **SMB:** Server Message Blocks (SMB) provide access to shared items such as files and printers. They are actual packets that authenticate remote computers through what are known as interprocess communication mechanisms.

- **LDAP:** Lightweight Directory Access Protocol (LDAP) is used to access and maintain distributed directories of information such as the kind involved with Microsoft domains. Microsoft refers to this as directory services.

ExamAlert

I know there's a lot, but know your protocols and their functions for the exam! Write 'em down or make flash cards to commit them to memory.

Cram Quiz

Answer these questions. The answers follow the last question. If you cannot answer these questions correctly, consider reading this section again until you can.

220-801 Questions

1. Which protocol uses port 22?

   ○ **A.** FTP

   ○ **B.** TELNET

   ○ **C.** SSH

   ○ **D.** HTTP

2. Which of these addresses needs to be configured to enable a computer access to the Internet or to other networks?

   ○ **A.** Subnet mask

   ○ **B.** Gateway address

   ○ **C.** DNS address

   ○ **D.** MAC address

3. The IP address 128.0.0.1 would be part of what IPv4 class?

   ○ **A.** Class A

   ○ **B.** Class B

   ○ **C.** Class C

   ○ **D.** Class D

4. What technology assigns addresses on the 169.254.0.0 network number?

   ○ **A.** DHCP

   ○ **B.** Static IP

   ○ **C.** APIPA

   ○ **D.** Class B

5. What type of IPv6 address is commonly assigned to client computers?

   ○ **A.** Unicast

   ○ **B.** Anycast

   ○ **C.** Multicast

   ○ **D.** FF00

6. You want to test the local loopback IPv6 address. Which address would you use?

  ○ **A.** 127.0.0.1

  ○ **B.** ::1

  ○ **C.** FE80::/10

  ○ **D.** ::0

7. Which of these would be used for streaming media?

  ○ **A.** TCP

  ○ **B.** RDP

  ○ **C.** UDP

  ○ **D.** DHCP

8. Which port is used by the IMAP protocol?

  ○ **A.** 53

  ○ **B.** 80

  ○ **C.** 110

  ○ **D.** 143

9. Which protocol sends and receives information in an encrypted manner by default?

  ○ **A.** FTP

  ○ **B.** HTTP

  ○ **C.** HTTPS

  ○ **D.** POP3

10. Which IP address can be a gateway for a computer using the IP address 10.58.64.192 and a subnet mask of 255.255.255.0?

  ○ **A.** 10.58.64.255

  ○ **B.** 10.58.64.1

  ○ **C.** 10.58.64.0

  ○ **D.** 10.59.64.1

220-802 Questions

11. A user can receive e-mail but cannot send any. Which protocol is not configured properly?

  ○ **A.** POP3

  ○ **B.** FTP

  ○ **C.** SMTP

  ○ **D.** SNMP

Cram Quiz Answers

220-801 Answers

1. **C.** SSH (Secure Shell) uses port 22, FTP uses port 21, TELNET uses port 23, and HTTP uses port 80.

2. **B.** The gateway address must be configured to enable a computer access to the Internet through the gateway device. By default, the subnet mask defines the IP address's network and host portions. The DNS server takes care of name resolution, and the MAC address is the address that is burned into the network adapter; it is configured at the manufacturer.

3. **B.** The IP address 128.0.0.1 is part of the Class B range that encompasses 128–191. Class A is 1–126. Class C is 192–223. Class D is 224–239.

4. **C.** If you see an address with 169.254 as the first two octets, then it is Automatic Private IP Addressing (APIPA). The Dynamic Host Configuration Protocol (DHCP) assigns IP addresses automatically to clients but by default does not use the 169.254 network number. Static IP addresses are configured manually by the user in the IP Properties window. Class B is a range of IP networks from 128 through 191.

5. **A.** Unicast addresses beginning with FE80::/10 are commonly assigned to client computers automatically. Anycast and multicast addresses are assigned to a group of interfaces; the difference being that anycast packets are delivered to the first interface only, and multicast packets are delivered to all interfaces. FF00::/8 is the address range of multicast packets.

6. **B.** You would use the ::1 address. That is the local loopback address for IPv6. 127.0.0.1 is the local loopback for IPv4. FE80::/10 is the range of unicast auto-configured addresses. ::0 is not valid but looks similar to how multiple zeroes can be truncated with a double colon.

7. **C.** User Datagram Protocol (UDP) is used for streaming media. It is connectionless, whereas TCP is connection-oriented and not a good choice for streaming media. RDP is the Remote Desktop Protocol used to make connections to other computers. DHCP is the Dynamic Host Configuration Protocol used to assign IP addresses to clients automatically.

8. **D.** The Internet Message Access Protocol (IMAP) uses port 143. DNS uses port 53. HTTP uses port 80. POP3 uses port 110. Know those ports!

9. **C.** Hypertext Transfer Protocol Secure (HTTPS) sends information like HTTP but over a secure channel via SSL or TLS. The other three protocols do not encrypt the data by default.

10. **B.** The gateway address should be 10.58.64.1. This question got a bit trickier. This not a Class A network we are dealing with. It is a classless network; the network number is 10.58.64 because we are using the 255.255.255.0 subnet mask. So the gateway cannot be on the 10.59.64 network; the gateway needs to be on the same network number as the client IP addresses. We cannot use 255 or 0 as the last digit of the IP address because 255 is the broadcast, and 0 is the network number.

220-802 Answers

11. **C.** The Simple Mail Transfer Protocol (SMTP) is probably not configured properly. It deals with sending mail. POP3 receives mail. FTP sends files to remote computers. SNMP is used to manage networks.

SOHO Windows Networking

In this section we'll discuss what it takes to set up a small Windows network and connect it to the Internet. We'll assume that your Windows operating systems are all installed but not yet quite configured for networking. Before we can connect the Windows computers to the network and the Internet, we need to create a network first. We'll need a multifunction network device, which I will refer to as a router for simplicity. And the router must be compatible with the Internet service we want to use. So first, we'll talk about the types of Internet connections available. Then, we'll discuss the router and its various configurations. Finally, we'll configure and connect the computers' network adapters and Windows operating systems so that they can connect to the network and out to the Internet. Let's go!

Internet Services

There are a lot of different options for connecting to the Internet including fiber-based systems, DSL, cable Internet, the venerable dial-up, and more. The type of Internet connection dictates download speeds to the clients on a SOHO network.

Dial-Up

Strange as it might seem, dial-up Internet is still used by millions, and in some areas of the United States, it is the only Internet connectivity available. Dial-up connections are inexpensive but at the cost of slow data throughput and dropped connections. To connect to a dial-up service, a user needs four things: a working phone line (with RJ11 connection), an account with an ISP, a modem to dial up to the ISP's networks, and some type of software to control the dial-up connection, for example dial-up networking. The modem serves to modulate and demodulate signals that travel between the computer and the phone line. It sends and receives data in a serial fashion, meaning one bit at a time. It is now possible to purchase devices that enable multiple computers to share the dial-up modem. The modem can be an internal adapter card or an external device that connects to a serial port. The difference is that the internal card incorporates a universal asynchronous receiver transmitter (UART) that converts the serial information coming in from the phone line into parallel data to be sent to the processor. The external modem relies on the UART that is built into the serial port of the computer. Dial-up utilizes the plain old telephone service/public switched telephone network (POTS/PSTN). POTS is that simple landline that comes into a home allowing a person to make phone calls. PSTN is the entire set of hardware and technologies at a telephone company's central office that controls POTS connections. Be careful when connecting a phone line to a computer. Make sure that it is connected to a modem (RJ11) and not to the network card (RJ45). The phone company sends a strong voltage through the line, which can damage a network adapter.

ExamAlert

Know what POTS and PSTN are for the exam.

ISDN

Integrated Services Digital Network (ISDN) is a digital technology developed to combat the limitations of PSTN. Users can send data, talk on the phone, fax, all from one line. It is broken down into two types of services:

▶ **BRI: Basic Rate ISDN:** 128 Kbps. Two equal B channels at 64 Kbps each for data and one separate 16 Kbps D channel for timing.

▶ **PRI: Primary Rate ISDN:** 1.536 Mbps, runs on a T-1 circuit; 23 equal 64 Kbps B channels for data and one 64 Kbps D channel for timing.

ISDN is not used as often as cable Internet or fiber-optic services, but some companies still use ISDN for video conferencing or as a fault-tolerant secondary Internet access connection. Data commuters use this if DSL or cable is not available.

DSL

Digital subscriber line (DSL) builds on dial-up by providing full digital data transmissions over phone lines but at high speeds. DSL modems connect to the phone line and to the PC's network adapter or to a SOHO router enabling sharing among multiple computers. One of the benefits of DSL is that you can talk on the phone line and transmit data at the same time. There are several derivatives of DSL, for example:

▶ **ADSL (Asymmetrical Digital Subscriber Line):** ADSL can run on your home telephone line so that you can talk on the phone and access the Internet at the same time. It is usually not as fast as cable Internet.

▶ **SDSL (Symmetrical Digital Subscriber Line):** SDSL is installed (usually to companies) as a separate line and is more expensive. SDSL data transfer rates can be purchased at 384 K, 768 K, 1.1 M, and 1.5 M. The upload and download speed are the same, or symmetrical, unlike ADSL.

Cable Internet

Broadband cable, used for cable Internet and cable TV, offers higher speeds than DSL and can usually get up to an average of 5 Mbps to 15 Mbps. Like most Internet connectivity options, cable Internet is shared by the customer base. The more users that are on the Internet, the slower it becomes for everyone. A SOHO network can use a cable modem to connect to the Internet. An RG-6 cable is run into the office and connected to the cable modem by way of a screw-on F-connector. The cable modem also has an RJ45 connection for patching to the router.

> **ExamAlert**
>
> Understand how cable Internet connections are made.

Fiber Optic

Instead of using a copper connection to the home or business the way dial-up, DSL, or cable Internet do, some companies offer fiber optic connections direct to the SOHO network. Fiber optic cables can run at much higher data transfer rates than copper-based cables. One example where this is evident is Verizon FIOS, which can be used to bundle various services but especially offers much faster download speeds from 3 to 150 Mbps. Upload speeds are typically less, as they are in most Internet services, generally from 1 to 35 Mbps.

> **ExamAlert**
>
> Cable Internet and fiber optic Internet services are common in the United States and in many other countries.

WiMAX

The Worldwide Interoperability for Microwave Access (WiMAX) is a wireless technology that offers high-speed connections within the 4G cellular range but over much larger distances than a standard Wi-Fi access point could, on the average 50 kilometers. So, if your organization is within 50 km of an urban area, it might be able to connect it's LAN to the Internet at high speed, in a completely wireless fashion. There are individual WiMAX modems for laptops and PCs, and gateway devices for entire LANs. For an optimal connection, these gateways (or routers) will usually be placed on a window sill facing where the signal is coming from.

Satellite

Satellite connectivity uses a parabolic antenna (satellite dish) to connect via line of sight to a satellite; it is used in places in which standard landline Internet access is not available. The satellite is in geosynchronous orbit, at 22,000 miles (35,406 Km) above the Earth. This is the farthest distance of any Internet technology. The "dish" connects to coax cable that runs to a switching/channeling device for your computers. Today's satellite connections offer speeds close to traditional broadband access. One of the issues with satellite is electrical and natural interference. Another problem is latency. Due to the distance (44,000 miles total) of the data transfer, there can be a delay of .5 seconds to 5 seconds. That's the highest latency of any Internet technology. Latency goes hand-in-hand with distance.

Another technology similar to this is *line-of-sight* microwave links. These are often made between wireless towers (such as WiMAX) but can also be installed at a campus. Parabolic antennae are positioned on different buildings, so they can see each other and send information at high speed without the need for a cabled connection.

Cellular

Cellular has become more popular of late as a means to access the Internet from mobile devices. The term *cellular* has grown to encompass several different technologies such as GSM, CDMA, GPRS, EDGE, and more. Although it's not necessary to know these technologies for the exam, you might want to know 3G and 4G because they are all the rage right now. Cellular Internet connections are also referred to as wireless WAN or WWAN connections (as are WiMAX connections.) Use of cellular on a phone, tablet, or with a WAN card requires a subscription with a cellular provider.

3G (short for third-generation telecommunications) has been in use for several years. Many new phones and PDAs are equipped to connect to 3G networks. The main purpose is to enable these mobile devices to send data at higher speeds. However, these speeds vary depending on the vendor, the country you are in, and whether you move while you send data. For stationary transmissions, possible data rates range from 2 Mbps to 14 Mbps; for moving transmissions, data rates fall below 1 Mbps. Of course, network congestion also has a hand in 3G data rates. Manufacturers suggest that a user can expect 384 Kbps while stationary or walking and less than that in a moving car. There are millions of 3G users; 3G devices are available for laptops in the form of PC Cards and embedded within PDAs. 3G is made out to be the best thing since sliced bread by ISPs and telecommunications companies, but it is questionable whether it has actually lived up to expectations.

4G (short for fourth generation) is expected to completely replace current networks and create a much faster, more secure IP solution. This is where the real increases in data rates can be found; from 100 Mbps in a moving vehicle to 1 Gbps when stationary. One of the goals is to have a data rate of 100 Mbps between any two points in the world at any time. 4G devices are available for laptops, tablet computers, and smartphones the same way that 3G devices are.

Router Setup and Wireless

Okay! Now that we have Internet connectivity out of the way, let's talk about the setup and configuration of our SOHO router. These devices have been called a plethora of different names, from router, switch, firewall, access point, and multifunction network device. Again, for simplicity, we'll refer to this as a router. In this section, I refer to a D-Link DIR655 that has served me well and is one of the easier devices to understand.

SOHO Router Set Up

Most SOHO routers are set up to be plug-and-play, meaning that computers can be plugged in and they can communicate with each other and access the Internet. But a word of caution: You don't want to use the default settings that the manufacturer gives you; they are quite insecure. So the first thing we want to do is to log in to the router so that we can make some changes. (We'll assume that your computers are already cabled to the router.) To do this, open a browser window and type the IP address of the router. For our D-Link DIR655, the default address is 192.168.0.1, the login is admin, and there is no password. A web-based emulator of this router is available at http://support.dlink.com/emulators/dir655/. If for some reason this link does not work, or is changed, simply go to www.dlink.com, and search for the DIR-655 emulator, or use your favorite search engine.

The first thing we want to do is to update the firmware so that we have the latest options and security available. This can be done in the Tools\Firmware section. Always make sure the router's firmware is updated before proceeding to configure it.

Next we access the Manual Internet Connection Setup button toward the bottom of the default screen. From here we see that the router is set up by default to obtain its WAN IP address automatically from the ISP, but in some cases you need to use a static IP address, or perhaps configure a secure connection to the Internet with Point to Point Tunneling Protocol (PPTP) or Layer 2 Tunneling Protocol (L2TP). Figure 15.7 shows these options.

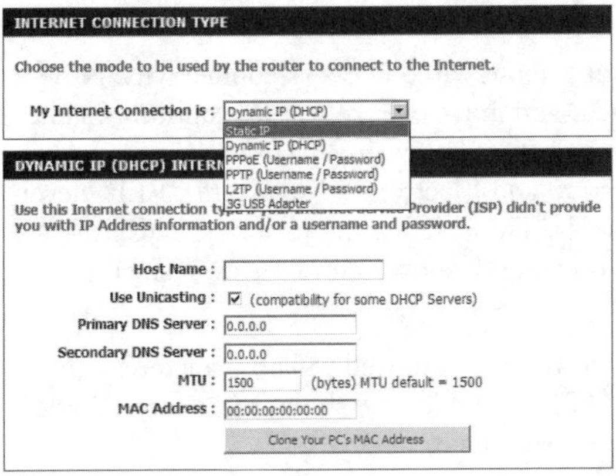

FIGURE 15.7   Internet Connection Type on a Common Router

If we selected any of the other options, we would have to input the correct information including IP address, username, and so forth. This information should be provided to you by the ISP you connect to.

Next we take a look at the network settings by clicking the link called Network Settings on the left side. As shown in Figure 15.8, this is where we can change the LAN IP address and subnet mask of the router and enable or disable the DHCP server. By default on a router such as this, the DHCP server is running and will automatically assign IP addresses to Windows clients as long as their IP Properties pages are set to Obtain an IP Address Automatically.

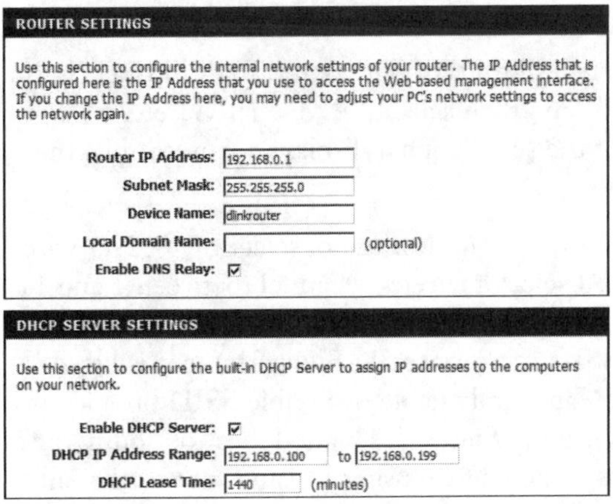

FIGURE 15.8   Network settings on a common router

802.11 Wireless

Up until now, we have been talking about wired network connectivity. Now I'd like to shift gears for a moment and move over to wireless options for the LAN. This type of wireless connectivity is known as Wi-Fi or wireless LAN (WLAN). The Institute of Electrical and Electronics Engineers (IEEE) developed the 802.11x series of protocols. These define the various speeds, frequencies, and protocols used to transmit data over radio waves in small geographic areas using unlicensed spectrums.

There are four different 802.11 derivatives you need to know for the exam: 802.11a, 802.11b, 802.11g, and 802.11n. Table 15.8 shows these technologies and the characteristics that differentiate them.

TABLE 15.8 **802.11x Standards**

802.11 Version	Maximum Data Rate	Frequency	Range Indoor	Range Outdoor
802.11a	54 Mbps	5 GHz	35 m/115 ft	120 m/390 ft
802.11b	11 Mbps	2.4 GHz	35 m/115 ft	140 m/460 ft
802.11g	54 Mbps	2.4 GHz	38 m/125 ft	140 m/460 ft
802.11n	600 Mbps	5 and/or 2.4 GHz	70 m/230 ft	250 m/820 ft

ExamAlert

Know the data rates, frequencies used, and ranges for each of the 802.11 versions!

Now let's take a look at the wireless settings of our router; to do this, click the Wireless Settings link on the left, and then select the Manual Wireless Network set up at the bottom of the screen. That displays a window like the one shown in Figure 15.9.

From here, we can enable or disable the wireless radio, select the 802.11 wireless technology of our choice, and select a wireless channel (between 1 and 11 usually). For noninterference with other wireless devices, choose channel 1, 6, or 11. We can also modify the SSID (or Service Set Identifier) that is listed in the figure as Wireless Network Name and enable or disable SSID broadcasts, which is listed in the figure as Visibility Status. It's a good idea to modify the SSID. Think about it; thousands of people are using D-Link routers that all default to the same SSID! Later, when all the computers using wireless are connected to the wireless network, we can disable the SSID to help prevent intruders. And finally, we can modify our encryptions settings for wireless. WPA2 utilizing AES is the most secure encryption that this router offers. We'll talk more about SOHO and wireless security in Chapter 16, "Security."

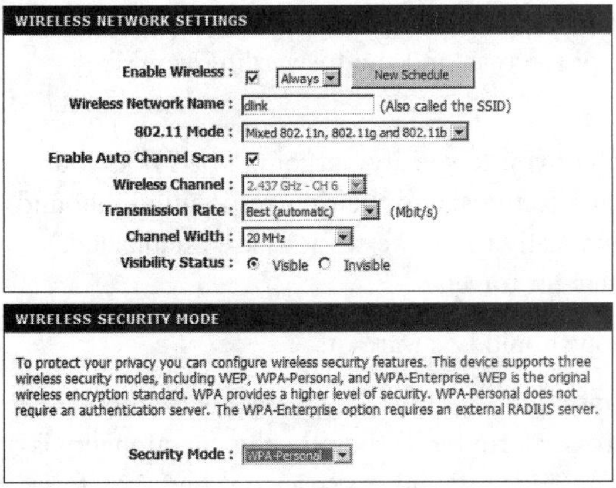

WIRELESS NETWORK SETTINGS

Enable Wireless :	☑ Always ▼ New Schedule
Wireless Network Name :	dlink (Also called the SSID)
802.11 Mode :	Mixed 802.11n, 802.11g and 802.11b ▼
Enable Auto Channel Scan :	☑
Wireless Channel :	2.437 GHz - CH 6 ▼
Transmission Rate :	Best (automatic) ▼ (Mbit/s)
Channel Width :	20 MHz ▼
Visibility Status :	● Visible ○ Invisible

WIRELESS SECURITY MODE

To protect your privacy you can configure wireless security features. This device supports three wireless security modes, including WEP, WPA-Personal, and WPA-Enterprise. WEP is the original wireless encryption standard. WPA provides a higher level of security. WPA-Personal does not require an authentication server. The WPA-Enterprise option requires an external RADIUS server.

Security Mode : WPA-Personal ▼

FIGURE 15.9 **Wireless networking settings**

More SOHO Router Tidbits

Most people are wireless crazy nowadays, but don't forget that these SOHO routers normally come with four wired LAN ports. Some people love wired connections, and this D-Link device is considered 10/100/1000BASE-T. That means that it can auto-negotiate connections at 10 Mbps, 100 Mbps, and 1000 Mbps (1 Gbps). The BASE applies to any speed, and it is short for baseband, meaning every computer on the network shares the same channel or frequency. The T is short for twisted pair. By default, unshielded twisted-pair cables can send data 100 meters before the electronic signal attenuates to such a point where it is useless.

These devices can usually do another two things concerning ports, but now we are talking about those virtual ports that we spoke of earlier in the chapter such as FTP port 21:

▶ **Port forwarding:** This forwards an external network port to an internal IP address and port. This enables you to have a web server, FTP server, and other servers, but you need to have only one port for each open on the WAN side of the router. It can be any port you like; of course, you would need to tell people which port they need to connect to if it is not a standard one.

The D-Link device we have been using takes this to a new level by enabling what it calls Virtual Servers, making the process a lot more user-friendly. So, for example, you might have an FTP server running internally on your LAN; its IP address and port might be 192.168.0.100:21 (notice how the colon separates the IP address from the port), but you would have users on the Internet connect to your router's WAN address, for example 65.43.18.1 and any port you want. The router takes care of the rest, and the forwarding won't be noticed by the typical user.

- ▶ **Port triggering:** This enables you to specify outgoing ports that your computer uses for special applications, and their corresponding inbound ports will be opened automatically when the sessions are established. This is helpful for things like bit torrents.

There are some other options you should be aware of:

- ▶ **NAT:** Network address translation (NAT) is the process of modifying IP addresses as information crosses a router. Generally, this functionality is built into a router. It hides an entire IP address space on the LAN, for example 192.168.0.1 through 192.168.0.255. Whenever an IP address on the LAN wants to communicate with the Internet, the IP is converted to the public IP of the router, for example 68.54.127.95, but it will be whatever IP address was assigned to the router by the ISP. This way, it looks like the router is the only device making the connection to remote computers on the Internet, providing safety for the computers on the LAN. It also allows a single IP to do the work for many IP addresses in the LAN.

- ▶ **DMZ:** A demilitarized zone (DMZ) is an area that is not quite on the Internet and not quite part of your LAN. It's a sort of middle ground that is for the most part protected by a firewall, but particular traffic will be let through. It's a good place for web servers, e-mail servers, and FTP servers because these are services required by users on the Internet. The beauty of this is that the users will not have access to your LAN—if it is configured correctly of course.

- ▶ **QoS:** Quality of service is a feature that attempts to prioritize streaming media, such as VoIP phone calls and audio or video playback, over other types of network traffic.

- ▶ **WPS: Wi-Fi Protected Setup:** This is a standard used by many router manufacturers to make connecting to a wireless network easier for the user. It usually consists of an 8 to 10 digit PIN and is located on the bottom of the router. It can also be viewed within the router's firmware. There have been several problems with WPS, and most manufacturers recommend that you disable it within the firmware.

Finally, when configuration is complete, we need to place our SOHO router. It is important to keep the device away from any electrical sources such as outlets, UPSes, microwaves, and any large amounts of metal to avoid interference (EMI). The basement is probably not the best place for a router due to the thick walls, copper pipes, and electrical panels causing interference. The device should be placed in the physical center of the office or the home for best reception. The more centralized the router is, the better the wireless access your computers will get. The antennas should be either at a 90-degree angle from each other or pointing toward where the computers are. And that pretty much wraps up the set up of our router. Let's move on to the Windows computers!

Windows Configurations

For this section we'll be focusing on Windows 7. For the exam you need to know how to configure network adapter settings, become a member of a network, make networking connections, and configure Internet Explorer settings. Let's begin with network card properties.

Network Card Properties

When configuring and analyzing the network adapter, we can use several status indicators; some are hardware-based and some are software-oriented.

> **Note**
>
> Technicians use several terms when referring to a network card: network adapter, network interface controller (NIC), Ethernet card, and so on. Be ready for different terminology on the exam and in the field. For this chapter I usually refer to it as network adapter because it won't always be in card format.

The first type of indicators are physical; they show up as LED lights on the network adapter itself. Different network adapters have different LED lights, but typically you have a connectivity LED and an activity LED. The connectivity LED tells you if you have a good connection to a router or switch by displaying a solid color, for example, solid green, which would mean connectivity at 100 Mbps or 1000 Mbps. However, if the connectivity LED is blinking, then you know there is an intermittent connection that should be troubleshot. The activity LED blinks when data is passing through the network adapter.

The second type of indicators are logical and show up in the operating system. These normally manifest themselves in the Notification Area (System Tray) and can be put there by Windows or by the manufacturer of the network adapter, depending on whether you let Windows install the card or if you used the additional software that came with the network adapter. However, you can add a shortcut to network adapters if you want and place them on the desktop or in the Quick Launch area. By default, Windows 7 uses the Network icon in the Notification Area exclusively.

Let's check out the status of a network connection. Right-click the Network icon in the Notification Area and select Open Network and Sharing Center. In the Network and Sharing Center window click the Change adapter settings link. This opens the Network Connections window. Double-click the Local Area Connection to see its status as shown in Figure 15.10. From here we can see what our "speed" is, how long we have been connected, and how many bytes have been sent and received. Also, if we click the Properties button, it brings us to the Local Area Connection properties window—a nice shortcut!

FIGURE 15.10 **Network adapter status**

How well your network adapter operates depends on a few different factors including bandwidth, latency, and what duplex setting it is configured for.

In computer networking, bandwidth refers to the maximum data throughput of the connection and is measured in bits per second (bps). In Figure 15.10 we see that our speed is 100 Mbps; this would also be known as bandwidth. To get this speed, every link in the networking chain must operate at 100 Mbps including the network adapter, cables, and central connecting devices such as SOHO router or switch. If any one of those links runs at less than 100 Mbps, the entire connection would be brought down to 10 Mbps. The same holds true for gigabit connections. Just because your network adapter can operate at 1 Gbps doesn't mean it will. The patch cable and router must also operate at this speed; otherwise it will be dropped down to 100 Mbps.

Latency is the time it takes for sent data packets to be received by a remote computer. An easy way to show this would be to *ping* another computer, for example open the Command Prompt and type ping davidlprowse.com; the ensuing replies should show a "time=" amount, probably around 100 ms. This tells us that the ping packet took a round-trip time of 100 milliseconds to get from your computer to the destination and back. Of course the faster the Internet connection, the less the latency.

There are two duplex settings that a network adapter can be set for: half-duplex and full-duplex. Half-duplex means that your network adapter can send or receive data but not at the same time; full-duplex means that the adapter can do both simultaneously, thus doubling the maximum data throughput. This can be configured by navigating to the Device Manager and then going to the properties of the network adapter. Finally, access the Advanced tab and the Link Speed & Duplex setting (or like name). This is normally set to auto-negotiation, but you can modify the speed or duplexing settings to take full advantage of your network. Of course, this depends on the type of device your network adapter connects to and how that device is configured. If your router is capable of 1000 Mbps in full duplex mode, by all means select this on the network adapter!

> **ExamAlert**
>
> Know the difference between half-duplex and full-duplex.

You might also decide to configure other settings such as Wake-on-LAN (WOL), Power over Ethernet (PoE), and quality of service (QoS), if your network adapter supports them. WOL is used so that the computer can be woken up by a remote computer when that remote system sends data to the network adapter. (This can be a special packet known as a magic packet.) This is great for small networks when you store data on one computer that is set to sleep after say 15 minutes. The data sent to the network adapter will wake up the computer allowing the remote user to get the data required. (I have a video about WOL on my website if you are interested.) PoE is when a device is supplied power by the Ethernet networking connection. The power travels along the network cable along with the data. You might not use this much on a computer, but this is common for VoIP phones. QoS as mentioned before attempts to prioritize streaming media and other types of data.

Workgroups Versus Domains

After you have configured your network adapter, you are ready to join a network. There are a few choices; in the business world it's either workgroup or domain. A home or home office that is inhabited by Windows 7 computers can be configured for HomeGroup, another type of workgroup.

Workgroups and domains are more logical groupings of computers. A workgroup (sometimes also referred to as peer-to-peer) is usually a small group of computers, often ten or less, which share the same network name. No one computer controls the network, and all systems are considered equal. One of the disadvantages is that a computer storing data can be accessed only by a maximum of 10 other systems simultaneously. A domain builds on this by having one or more computers that are in control of the network and enabling for more computers, more simultaneous access, and centralized administration. Domains also get a name and are sometimes also referred to as client/server networks.

You can select whether your computers will be part of a workgroup or a domain by opening the System Properties dialog box and selecting the Computer Name tab. (Or go to Run and type **SystemPropertiesComputerName**.) Then click the Change button. This displays the Computer Name/Domain Changes dialog box, as shown in Figure 15.11.

FIGURE 15.11   Computer Name/Domain Changes dialog box

From here you can join a workgroup (which is the default, by the way) or attempt to join a domain. Your SOHO network will probably not have a domain, but who knows. If you are anything like me, you might end up running multiple domains, which is entirely possible even in a small SOHO network. However, most SOHO networks in the field will not use domains; they are more commonly found in larger organizations. The domain is controlled by a Microsoft server known as a Domain Controller. To connect to the domain from a client computer, you would need to know the domain name (for example supernetwork.com) and the DNS server IP address for that domain. At this point, it gets beyond the scope of the A+ exams and into the realm of Microsoft certifications.

Windows can help you to select your computer's location and optimize the system for that location. To change the location, open the Network and Sharing Center, and click the link underneath where it says, View Your Active Networks. From here you can select whether the computer is part of a Home network, a Work network, or a public network. (This is also asked of you when you complete the Windows 7 installation.) The most common and default option is the Home network. When part of a Home network, you can create or join HomeGroups.

The HomeGroup element of Windows 7 offers SOHO users a quick-and-dirty way to accomplish networking. It is aimed at sharing files, multimedia, printers and so on. HomeGroups are automatically created on Windows 7 Home Premium, Professional, Ultimate, and Enterprise. Other versions of Windows 7 cannot create a HomeGroup, but they can join one.

To configure HomeGroup go to Start > Control Panel > HomeGroup. From here you can leave and join HomeGroups, view the password (an alpha-numeric code created by the OS automatically), and configure advanced settings, for example enabling/disabling network discovery, enabling/disabling file and printer sharing, media streaming, and file sharing encryption. Take a look at the options available to you. You will find the same settings listed in the Network and Sharing Center > Advanced Sharing Settings.

ExamAlert

Be able to define the differences between a HomeGroup, workgroup, and domain.

Sharing Resources and Making Network Connections

Before anyone can view the amazing things you have to offer on your computer, you need to *share* them. As mentioned previously, sharing needs to be turned on in the Network and Sharing Center or the HomeGroup Advanced Settings. Then it can be enabled for individual resources. For example, let's say we had a folder named "data" and we wanted to share the contents of that folder to other users and computers. We would need to locate the folder in Windows Explorer, right-click it, and either select Share with or select Properties and then click the Sharing tab. Figures 15.12 and 15.13 show both of these.

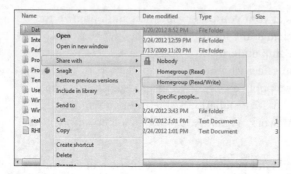

FIGURE 15.12   **Right-clicking a folder and selecting Share With**

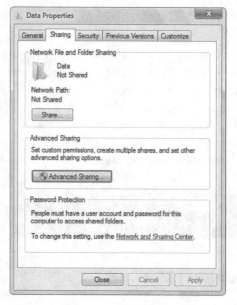

FIGURE 15.13   **The Sharing tab of the Data folder Properties windows**

In Figure 15.12, you can see that folders are locked by default and are shared with no one. However, you can opt to have other users in the HomeGroup read the data or be able to read and modify the data. Figure 15.13 shows that we can share here as well, plus we can enable Advanced Sharing and set custom permissions for users. Now, in some cases you might find that HomeGroup doesn't do exactly what you want. For example, when you share a folder, it might add to the network path in a way that doesn't allow third-party devices to connect. If that is the case, use the Advanced Sharing button within the Sharing tab of the folder's Properties sheet. That will eliminate any additions to the network path. And for whatever reason, in the future you might not want to be a member of a HomeGroup anymore. To exit the HomeGroup, open the HomeGroup window again, and select Leave. Then, you can also stop and disable the services HomeGroup Listener and HomeGroup Provider. Later, if the computer becomes a member of a domain, it can still access shared resources on other computers in the HomeGroup, but the computer will not be able to share its own resources to other systems.

> **Note**
>
> For more information about older sharing functionality in Windows Vista/XP, see the document at my website: http://www.davidlprowse.com/220-801.

Now, if you want to access shares on another computer, you can do it in a myriad of ways. First, if you are part of a HomeGroup, go to Windows Explorer, and click HomeGroup on the left window pane. Any shares on other computers should show up there. You can also browse the network through the Network component in Windows Explorer.

Another way to access shares is to map a network drive. This makes a permanent connection to a shared folder in Windows Explorer and assigns it a drive letter. To map a drive, open Windows Explorer, click Tools on the menu bar and Map Network Drive. These network drives are mapped according to the universal naming convention (UNC), which is \\computername\sharename. An example is shown in Figure 15.14. You'll note the computer name is Music-Box and the share name is Data.

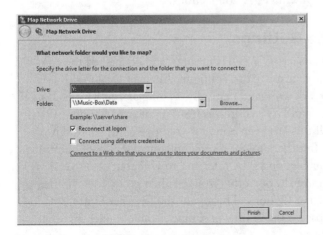

FIGURE 15.14 **Map Network Drive window**

Mapping network drives can also be done in the Command Prompt with the Net Use command. For example, to map the same drive as shown in Figure 15.14, the syntax would be `net use y: \\Music-Box\data`.

> ## ExamAlert
>
> Know how to map network drives in the GUI and in the Command Prompt.

Let's say you want to connect to your network, but you are at a remote location. Enter the VPN. Virtual private networks (VPNs) were developed so that telecommuters, salespeople, and others could connect to the office from a remote location. If set up properly, the remote logon connection is seamless and appears as if you are actually at the LAN in the office. You log on just as you would if you were at your desk at headquarters. VPNs give the user access to all the resources that they get when logging on locally. VPNs take advantage of the infrastructure of the Internet and fast connections such as cable, DSL, and so on. A VPN connection can be identified by an additional network connection in the Notification Area, as an additional network connection when using the ipconfig command, or as a pop-up window that comes up during the logon process, for example the kind used by Cisco VPN software. Connections to VPNs can be initiated by navigating to the Network and Sharing Center and selecting the Set Up a New Connection or Network link. From there you would opt for Connect to a Workplace and select VPN. You would need to know the IP address or name of the VPN server you are connecting to, as well as a username and password to get in. Alternate IP configurations are sometimes used with VPN connections.

Internet Explorer Settings

Ok. We've set up Internet service, a SOHO router, and connected the computers to networks; now we just need to configure Internet Explorer. By default the web browser will work automatically, as long as you have configured the correct gateway and DNS addresses. And if you are obtaining IP from a DHCP server, all this has been done for you. (Actually, you did it previously in this chapter!) But there might be a couple of special configurations you want to make. In this section I'll be referring to IE 8, but other versions will be similar. To configure IE, open the browser; then go to Tools on the menu bar, and click Internet Options. This opens the Internet Options dialog box. This has several tabs; for the exam you should be able to identify what each of these can do.

▶ **General:** This tab allows you to select the default home page, delete browsing history and cookies, and modify the appearance of the browser.

▶ **Security:** This tab creates and modifies levels of security zones. A zone could be the Internet, a company intranet (like the Internet but in-house), or a group of websites that you trust. Levels for the Internet include medium, medium-high (the default), and high. From here you can also enable/disable ActiveX, and various scripting (such as JavaScript) within websites by accessing the Custom level button.

▶ **Privacy:** Here you can configure the blocking level of cookies. Third-party cookies collect information about the user; many organizations will set this to a high blocking level, but it is set to Medium by default.

▶ **Content:** This section contains the parental controls and content advisor, secure certificate information that deals with encrypted connections to certain websites, and AutoComplete settings.

▶ **Connections:** This is the networking tab if one can be called that. From here you can set up new Internet connections and make dial-up and VPN connections. (Remember how I said there is always more than one way to do something in Windows?) If you click the LAN settings button, you can configure connection scripts and a proxy server as well. A proxy server is a computer that acts as a go-between for PCs and web servers on the Internet. It caches (stores) website information so that users can get web data quicker. It can also be used to cache FTP and secure information. By default this is not configured. Figure 15.15 shows IE configured to use a proxy server. As you can see, the IP address of the proxy server is 192.168.0.15 and uses port 80, just like a web server would.

▶ **Programs:** From here you can set IE as the default browser, in case another web browser took over as default. You can also work with browser add-ons such as extra toolbars and extensions. And you can set program and file associations from here.

▶ **Advanced:** This tab has lots of advanced settings such as options for the text size, which can be adjusted in IE by pressing and holding CTRL and moving the mouse wheel. You can also configure what type of security protocol will be used during secure sessions, for example Transport Layer Security (TLS) or Secure Sockets Layer (SSL). Plus, you can reset the IE configuration if you want.

Of course, IE isn't the only browser in town. Firefox and Chrome are also popular, among others. They all have similar settings but navigating to those settings will be slightly different. Don't ask me which is better; I use them all!

FIGURE 15.15 **Proxy server configuration in IE**

ExamAlert

Know where to go to configure a proxy server connection in IE.

Cram Quiz

Answer these questions. The answers follow the last question. If you cannot answer these questions correctly, consider reading this section again until you can.

220-801 Questions

1. Which Internet service makes use of PSTN?

   ○ **A.** Dial-up

   ○ **B.** ISDN

   ○ **C.** DSL

   ○ **D.** Cable Internet

2. Which Internet service is wireless and has a range of 50 kilometers?

   ○ **A.** Fiber optic

   ○ **B.** WiMAX

   ○ **C.** Satellite

   ○ **D.** Wi-Fi

3. Which 802.11 version has a maximum data rate of 54 Mbps and uses the 2.4 GHz frequency range?

- ○ **A.** 802.11a
- ○ **B.** 802.11b
- ○ **C.** 802.11g
- ○ **D.** 802.11n

4. Which of the following forwards an external network port to an internal IP address/port on a computer on the LAN?

- ○ **A.** Port triggering
- ○ **B.** Port forwarding
- ○ **C.** DMZ
- ○ **D.** WPS

5. Which of the following is described as the simultaneous sending and receiving of network data?

- ○ **A.** Half-duplex
- ○ **B.** Latency
- ○ **C.** PoE
- ○ **D.** Full-duplex

220-802 Questions

6. Which of the following requires a Windows-created password to gain access to?

- ○ **A.** Workgroup
- ○ **B.** Client/Server
- ○ **C.** HomeGroup
- ○ **D.** Domain

7. You want to connect to a share on \\server1\data-share. What should you use to accomplish this?

- ○ **A.** HomeGroup.
- ○ **B.** Right-click the folder and select Share with.
- ○ **C.** Ipconfig.
- ○ **D.** Net use.

8. Which tab of Internet Options would you go to if you wanted to configure a Proxy Server?

   ○ **A.** General

   ○ **B.** Security

   ○ **C.** Connections

   ○ **D.** Advanced

Cram Quiz Answers

220-801 Answers

1. **A.** Dial-up internet connections make use of the public switched telephone network (PSTN),and POTS phone lines. ISDN was developed to meet the limitations of PSTN. DSL provides faster data transmissions over phone lines (or separate data lines.) Cable Internet is a broadband service that offers higher speeds than DSL; it is provided by cable TV companies.

2. **B.** WiMAX is a wireless Internet service that has a maximum range of approximately 50 kilometers. Fiber optic is a type of cable. Satellite is wireless but it has a far greater range. Wi-Fi is wireless but it deals with the LAN and is usually limited to approximately 250 meters (800 feet) outdoors.

3. **C.** 802.11g uses the 2.4 GHz range and has a maximum rate of 54 Mbps. 802.11a also has a rate of 54 Mbps but uses the 5 GHz range. 802.11b is 11 Mbps. 802.11 is 600 Mbps max.

4. **B.** Port forwarding is used to forward external network ports to an internal IP and port. This is done so a person can host services such as FTP internally. Port triggering allows you to specify outgoing ports that a computer on the LAN uses for special applications. The DMZ is an area that is protected by the firewall but separate from the LAN. Servers are often placed here. WPS is Wi-Fi Protected Setup; it is used to make wireless network connections easier for the user by employing an 8 to 10 digit pin.

5. **D.** Full-duplex is when a network adapter (or other device) can send and receive information at the same time. Half-duplex is when only sending or receiving can be done at one time. Latency is the delay it takes for data to reach a computer from a remote location. PoE is Power over Ethernet, a technology that allows devices to receive data and power over an Ethernet network cable.

220-802 Answers

6. **C.** HomeGroup connections require an alphanumeric password that was created by Windows automatically. Joining or creating a workgroup does not require a password. Client/server networks such as Microsoft domains require a username and password, but these are created by the administrator of the network or selected by the user.

7. **D**. The net use command can connect to shares such as \\server1\data-share or any other share on the network. Of course, you could also do this by mapping a network drive in Windows Explorer. HomeGroup uses a more user-friendly approach to sharing and connecting to shares. Right clicking the folder and selecting Share with will share the folder but won't make a connection to the share. Ipconfig is used to find out the IP configuration of the network adapter in the Command Prompt.

8. **C**. You would go to the Connections tab, and select the LAN settings button to configure a proxy server connection. The general tab has more generalized settings such as the default home page. The Security tab deals with security zones, ActiveX controls, and scripting. The Advanced tab has many settings that can adjust the browser and secure it.

Troubleshooting Networks

Okay, now that we've shown some of the basics of networking, let's get into a little bit of network troubleshooting. To troubleshoot client connectivity properly, we need to know a little bit more about command-line interface (CLI) tools and be able to identify some of the common symptoms you will encounter when networking computers together.

Command-Line Interface Tools

There are many command-line tools that we can use in Windows to help us troubleshoot situations; in this section we delve into seven of them. I recommend that you try all the variations of these on your computer. To open the command-line interface (known as the Command Prompt in Windows), do one of the following:

▶ Click Start > All Programs > Accessories > Command Prompt. (If you need to run a command in elevated mode, right-click Command Prompt and select Run as Administrator.)

▶ Open the Run prompt (by pressing Windows +R) and type **cmd**.

Ipconfig

Internet protocol configuration or ipconfig displays current TCP/IP network configuration values. This is one of the first tools you should use when troubleshooting network connectivity. If you type **ipconfig** you get results similar to the following:

```
Windows IP Configuration

Ethernet adapter Local Area Connection:

Connection-specific DNS Suffix . :

Link-Local IPv6 Address. . . . . : fe80::404b:e781:b150:b91a%11

IPv4 Address. . . . . . . . . . . : 192.168.0.100

Subnet Mask . . . . . . . . . . . : 255.255.255.0

Default Gateway . . . . . . . . . : 192.168.0.1
```

Ipconfig combined with the /all switch shows more information including the DNS server address and the MAC address. The MAC address is the hexadecimal address that is burned into the ROM of the network adapter. This is a set of six hexadecimal numbers, for example, 00-03-FF-A0-55-16.

This command can offer a lot of information about a problem. For example, if a person cannot connect to any Internet resources, it could be because the gateway address is improperly configured. Remember that the gateway address must be on the same network number as the IP address of the client computer. If a user can't connect to any websites but they can connect to other computers on the LAN, it could be that the DNS server address is incorrectly configured. Ipconfig also tells you whether the client computer's IP address is obtained from a DHCP server or assigned via APIPA, and whether it is a private or public address.

Ipconfig can also be used to release and renew IP addresses. Sometimes this needs to be done if a computer's IP address is not working properly, and you want to obtain a new address from a DHCP server. To release the current IP address type **ipconfig/release**; to renew, type **ipconfig/renew**.

Finally, if you are having DNS issues, for example problems connecting to websites, you can erase the DNS cache by typing **ipconfig/flushdns**. Check out the various ipconfig switches by opening the Command Prompt and typing **ipconfig /?**. You should try this with every command in this section.

Ping

Ping tests whether another host is available over the network. It's the easy way to see if another host is "alive." Let's say your gateway's IP address was 192.168.0.1. To ping that computer, you would type **ping 192.168.0.1**, as an example and hopefully get the following output:

```
Pinging 192.168.0.1: with 32 bytes of data:
Reply from 192.168.0.1: bytes=32 time<1ms TTL=64
Reply from 192.168.0.1: bytes=32 time<1ms TTL=64
Reply from 192.168.0.1: bytes=32 time<1ms TTL=64
Reply from 192.168.0.1: bytes=32 time<1ms TTL=64
```

```
Ping statistics for 192.168.0.1:
Packets: Sent = 4, Received = 4, Lost = 0 (0% loss),
Approximate round trip times in milli-seconds:
Minimum = 0ms, Maximum = 0ms, Average = 0ms
```

The replies indicate that the host is alive and can be communicated with on the network. Any other message would indicate a problem, for example the Request Timed Out or Destination Host Unreachable messages would require further troubleshooting. Keep in mind that if it's the local computer that is configured incorrectly, you might not be able to ping anything! Also watch for the amount of time the ping took to reply back. A longer latency time could indicate network congestion.

You can also use ping to test whether a computer has TCP/IP installed properly, even if it isn't wired to the network! To do this use the **ping 127.0.0.1** command for IPv4 and **ping ::1** for IPv6. These IP addresses are known as loopback addresses, are used for testing, and are available on every host that has TCP/IP installed. They differ from the IP addresses we talked about previously (for example 192.168.0.100) in that they work internally. Loopback ping commands essentially enable you to ping yourself, meaning you can test the local computer's network connection without a valid IP configuration and without a physical connection to the network. Replies are simulated within the local computer; they prove if the network adapter and TCP/IP have been installed properly. However, it does not prove if TCP/IP has been *configured* properly for your particular network.

> **Note**
>
> You can also use the `ping loopback` and `ping localhost` commands; but for testing, pinging a number will give better results.

> **ExamAlert**
>
> Know how to ping the local loopback IPv4 and IPv6 addresses.

You can also modify the way that ping works with switches. There are several, but three you should know for the exam, -t, -n, and -l:

▶ **ping –t:** This pings the host until the command is stopped. Remember, a host is any device or computer with an IP address. An example of this would be `ping -t 192.168.0.1`; the switch can go before or after the IP address. You will keep getting replies (or timeouts) until you stop the command by pressing CTRL+C or by closing the Command Prompt. This is a great way to test cable connections. After running the command you can plug and unplug cables and watch the screen to see which cables or ports are live. You can also use it to monitor a connection over a period of time discerning if there are many packet drops or if the connection slows down at certain times.

▶ **ping –n:** This pings a host a specific amount of times. For example, the syntax `ping -n 20 192.168.0.1` would ping that host 20 times and then display the results. This can be a good baselining tool if you run it every day against a router or server and compare the results. (You would probably want to do a higher quantity than 20.)

▶ **ping –l:** This pings the host but you can specify the amount of bytes per packet to be sent. If you look at the previous ping results you can see that the default amount of bytes is 32, but this can be increased to simulate real data. For example, `ping -l 1500 192.168.0.1` would send four 1500 byte packets to the other host. This can also be beneficial when testing how a server, router, or other device react to larger packet sizes.

ExamAlert

Know how to use the –t, –n, and –l switches with ping.

These switches can be combined as well, for example:

`Ping -n 450 -l 1500 192.168.0.1` would send 450 pings, each 1500 bytes in size. To create a baseline you could do this at a specific time every month, store the results, and compare them to find possible deficiencies in performance of a server, router, and so on.

Tracert

Tracert, short for traceroute, builds on ping in that it send packets to destinations beyond the local computer's network. It pings each router along the way between you and the final destination. An example of tracert output follows:

```
Tracing route to davidlprowse.com [216.97.236.245] over a maximum of
30 hops:
```

```
1 6 ms 5 ms 5 ms bd11.eas-ubr16.atweas.pa.cable.rcn.net [10.21.80.1]
2 10 ms 9 ms 9 ms vl4.aggr1.phdl.pa.rcn.net [208.59.252.1]
```

The tracert would continue for a dozen or more lines and end in the following:

```
18 86 ms 86 ms 86 ms unused-240-180-214.ixpres.com [216.240.180.214]
19 98 ms 96 ms 97 ms lwdc.dbo2.gi9-4.host1.23680.americanis.net
[38.96.20.2]
20 97 ms 96 ms 96 ms zosma.lunarpages.com [216.97.236.245]
Trace complete.
```

Note that there are three pings per line item measured in milliseconds (ms). Also note that every line item contains a router name and IP address. It starts by sailing through the various routers in our ISP, RCN.net. It ends at a server named zosma.lunarpages.com that hosts www.davidlprowse.com (as of the writing of this book). If you saw any asterisks in the place of the millisecond amounts, you might question whether the router is functioning properly. If the tracert stops altogether before saying Trace Complete, you would want to check your network documentation to find out which router it stopped at, and/or make sure that the router is troubleshot by the appropriate personnel.

Tracert /d will not resolve IP addresses to hostnames. So instead of seeing zosma.lunarpages.com on the last line, you would see only the IP address 216.97.236.245. Running numerical versions of commands can be faster because there is no name resolution to get in the way. Connecting directly by IP will always be faster than connecting by name.

Netstat

Moving on to another concept, netstat shows the network statistics for the local computer. The default command displays sessions to remote computers. In the following example, I connected to www.google.com and ran the netstat command. Output follows:

```
Active Connections

TCP Music-Box:1395 8.15.228.165:http ESTABLISHED

TCP Music-Box:1396 he-in-f101.google.com:http ESTABLISHED
```

This output shows that there are two established TCP sessions (they're actually both to the same website) to google.com. In the local address column we see our computer called Music-Box and the outbound ports it uses to access the website, 1395 and 1396. In the foreign address column, we see an IP address and the protocol used (http) and in the second session, a hostname followed by the protocol (again http). The protocol used by google.com corresponds to port 80. This command can tell us a lot about our sessions; for example, if a session times out or if it closes completely. To see this information numerically, try using the –n switch. To see TCP *and* UDP sessions, use the –a switch. To see TCP and UDP in numeric format use the –an switch.

NBTSTAT

NBTSTAT displays network protocol statistics that use NetBIOS over TCP/IP connections. NBTSTAT can be used to show the services running on the local computer or a remote computer. It calls this the name table. For example, you could find out what services are running, what the computer's name is, and what network it is a part of by typing **nbtstat –A 192.168.0.100** (or whatever your local IP is.) The results would be similar to the following:

```
Computer1              <00>    Unique      Registered
Workgroup              <00>    Group       Registered
Computer1              <20>    Unique      Registered
```

The computer and network names are easy to see: Computer1 and Workgroup. But also notice that there are numbers in alligators such as <00> and <20>. These are the services mentioned previously. <00> is the workstation service, the service that allows your computer to redirect out to other systems to view shared resources. <20> is the server service that allows your computer to share resources with other systems.

The -a switch (lowercase a) shows the same name table but you invoke this information using the computer name instead of the IP address. Nbtstat has a variety of other switches that can display, purge, and reload name tables and sessions. Check out the other various switches by typing **nbtstat /?**.

Nslookup

Nslookup queries DNS servers to discover DNS details including the IP address of hosts. For example, if I want to find the IP address of davidlprowse.com, I would type **nslookup davidlprowse.com**. The resulting output should look something like this:

```
Non-authoritative answer:
Name: davidlprowse.com
Address: 216.97.236.245
```

So from the output, we now know the IP address that corresponds to the domain name davidlprowse.com. Nslookup means name server lookup and can aid in finding DNS servers and DNS records in a domain as well. If the command nslookup is typed by itself, it brings the user into the nslookup shell. From here several commands can be utilized; to find out more about these, type **?**. To exit the nslookup shell type **exit**, press Ctrl+C, or press Ctrl+Break.

Net

The net command is actually a collection of commands. In Chapter 14, "Printers," we used the net stop command to stop the print spooler. In networking, you might use the net view command to see what computers are currently available on the network or the net share command to share folders and for other users to view. For the exam, you should know the types of net commands that enable you to view or create mapped network drives. To view any currently mapped network drives, simply type **net use**. To create a mapped network drive, use the following syntax:

```
net use x: \\computername\sharename
```

X: is the drive letter, in this case X is a variable; you can use whatever drive letter you want if it's available. Computername is the name of the remote host you want to connect to, and sharename is the share that was created on that remote host.

There is a network share on another computer on my network called C$. The following syntax shows the command to connect to it and the resulting output:

```
net use f: \\Music-Box\c$
The command completed successfully.
```

In this example, we used F: as our drive letter; the computer we connected to is called Music-Box, and the share is C$ (the default hidden share). For more information on the net command, type **net /?**. For more information on the net use command, type **net use /?**.

Troubleshooting Common Symptoms

Network troubleshooting? Oh yes, it could be the best way to learn. First, I recommend reviewing the six-step troubleshooting process in Chapter 1, "Introduction to Troubleshooting." Second, for successful troubleshooting remember to check the simple and obvious first. Power connections, network connections, and so on are common culprits for network problems.

Let's discuss some symptoms you might encounter and how to troubleshoot the underlying problems.

▶ **No connectivity:** If a user complains of a problem connecting to the network and you verify that there is indeed a problem, check that patch cable first and verify there is a link light. Make sure the user's computer is actually connected to the network. If it appears to be a cable issue, use a cable tester to solve the problem. If not a cable problem, make sure the network adapter is enabled. If a laptop, and the user has wireless, check the Wi-Fi switch or button. Next, run an ipconfig/all and check the settings. Afterward, ping the local computer to see if TCP/IP works. If you haven't resolved the problem by now (and you probably will), access the Network and Sharing Center in Windows 7 and view the graphical connections to see if there is a red x anywhere denoting a problem. Use the network troubleshooter if necessary. You can also right-click the Network icon in the Notification Area and select Troubleshoot Problems (in Vista it is Diagnose and Repair). This brings up the Windows Network Diagnostics program; follow the steps for a possible resolution. Check for the latest drivers for the network adapter. You can also try rebooting the computer to find out from the user if any programs were recently installed or updated. Sometimes antivirus software or firewall updates can cause connectivity issues. Some switches and routers have the capability to enable/disable specific ports; make sure the port in question is enabled in the firmware. If a networkwide problem, power down the network equipment (SOHO routers, cable modems, and so on); then disconnect the network and power cables and wait 10 seconds. Finally, reboot the network equipment. If users cannot find the wireless network, they need to connect to using Windows or the wireless adapter's software; there are third-party Wi-Fi locator programs that can be downloaded for free. These will locate all wireless networks in the vicinity and display SSID, signal quality, distance, and channel used (as long as the wireless network adapter is functional). If an SSID does not show up in Windows or in third-party software, you should enter the SSID manually.

▶ **Limited and intermittent connectivity:** If the problem is limited connectivity, attempt some pings. First, ping the localhost to see if TCP/IP is functioning. If that works, ping the router or another system on the network. If that fails, then the user only has local connectivity. Run an ipconfig/all and check the rest of the IP settings. If pinging the router *did* work, try pinging a website by domain name. If that fails, then the DNS server address is probably not configured properly. Check it with an ipconfig/all and modify in the IP Properties dialog box if necessary. Run an ipconfig/release and /renew if you suspect an issue obtaining an address from a DHCP server. Intermittent connectivity could be caused by a faulty patch cable, wireless network adapter that is too far away from the WAP, or the router needs to be reset. In a larger environment, if a person can access some networks but not others, you might want to try a tracert to inaccessible networks to see where the problem lies. This type of network troubleshooting gets a bit more in depth, but the tracert program will basically show what router between you and the final destination has failed.

▶ **Slow transfer speeds:** The type of Internet connection is going to be the biggest contributor to this. If a person has dial-up and complains about slow transfer speeds, then it's time to upgrade! Even though dial-up can be tweaked for speed, it's simply easier to move up to DSL, cable, or fiber-based services. Slow transfer speeds could also be caused by the network equipment, patch cables, and network adapter. The newer and faster the equipment and cables, the better the data transfer rate. Of course, slow speeds could also be caused by network congestion. Run a netstat –a to see what types of connections the local computer has to the Internet currently. If you see dozens of connections, the computer might be compromised by malware or be part of a botnet. Or perhaps the user runs torrent software or just goes to a lot of websites for various reasons. Check the router as well. See what kind of traffic is passing through it. Update everything, clear all cache, power cycle all equipment, and you just might see an improvement.

▶ **Low RF signal:** A low radio frequency signal spells doom for wireless users. The first thing to check is the distance of the computer from the WAP. Know your 802.11 ranges, and make sure the computer is within the appropriate range. If the WAP uses 802.11n and the wireless adapter is 802.11g, consider upgrading to an 802.11n adapter. Update the software on the wireless adapter and WAP as well. Placement of the router is important; it should be in the middle of the organization and away from sources of EMI. Try different antenna placement on the router and the wireless adapter. Normally, the 90 degree angle is best, but a little tweaking can go a long way. Also, some routers can boost their wireless signal. Check for this setting in the firmware.

▶ **IP conflict:** An IP conflict message will pop up on the displays of both Windows computers that are causing the conflict. Usually, the first computer that used the IP address will continue to function, whereas the second computer will not be able to access the network. The second computer will have to be reconfigured to a different IP address and rebooted. Reboot the first computer for good measure. IP conflicts usually happen only when static IP addresses are being used. If this is the case, consider using DHCP for all client computers.

▶ **APIPA address:** If a computer is showing an APIPA address (such as 169.254.49.26) when you type ipconfig/all, it means that the computer is attempting to obtain an IP address from a DHCP server but is failing to do so. APIPA addresses always start with 169.254. APIPA is assigned internally, so the real problem could be that the computer is not getting connectivity to the network. Check everything from the first bullet point. Also, consider an ipconfig/release and /renew. Finally, if these do not work, check the DHCP server to make sure it is functional.

> **ExamAlert**
>
> Double-study your troubleshooting techniques!

Cram Quiz

Answer these questions. The answers follow the last question. If you cannot answer these questions correctly, consider reading this section again until you can.

220-802 Questions

1. Which of the following commands will display the MAC address of a computer?

   ○ **A.** Ping

   ○ **B.** Netstat

   ○ **C.** Ipconfig/all

   ○ **D.** Ipconfig/renew

2. Which command will ping continuously?

   ○ **A.** Ping /?

   ○ **B.** Ping –t

   ○ **C.** Ping –l

   ○ **D.** Ping –n

3. Which command will show the path of routers between your computer and a web server?

   ○ **A.** Ping

   ○ **B.** Ipconfig

   ○ **C.** Tracert

   ○ **D.** NBTSTAT

4. You need to map a network drive to a share named data1 on a computer named Jupiter-Server. You want to use the J: drive letter. What syntax should you use if you were to do this in the Command Prompt?

    ○ **A.** net use J: \\Jupiter-Server\data1

    ○ **B.** net use J \Jupiter-Server\data1

    ○ **C.** net use Jupiter-Server\J\data1

    ○ **D.** net use J: \Jupiter-Server\data1

5. A user complains that the computer is not connecting to the network. What should you check first?

    ○ **A.** Ipconfig/all

    ○ **B.** Ping the router

    ○ **C.** Patch cable

    ○ **D.** Network drivers

6. One computer loses connectivity. All connectors and settings appear to be correct. What tool should you use to fix the problem?

    ○ **A.** Multimeter

    ○ **B.** PSU tester

    ○ **C.** Loopback plug

    ○ **D.** Cable tester

7. One of your customers no longer has access to a frequently accessed website. You ping another computer and the router on the network successfully. What should you do next?

    ○ **A.** Check the IP configuration.

    ○ **B.** Ping the website.

    ○ **C.** Update the OS.

    ○ **D.** Update the AV software.

8. A user moves a laptop from one office to another. The patch cable and the network adapter do not appear to be working properly at the new office. The cable is plugged in correctly and tests okay when checked with a patch tester. What should you do first?

    ○ **A.** Check if the port on the switch is enabled.

    ○ **B.** Update the network adapter driver.

    ○ **C.** Replace the patch cable with a crossover cable.

    ○ **D.** Make sure the network adapter is compatible with the OS.

Cram Quiz Answers

220-802 Answers

1. **C.** Ipconfig/all will display the MAC address of a computer. Ping is used to test whether other computers are available on the network. Netstat displays all the network session to remote computers. Ipconfig/renew is used with /release to re-issue DHCP-obtained IP addresses.

2. **B.** Ping –t is a continuous ping. It can be stopped by pressing Ctrl+C. Ping /? will display the help file. Ping –l allows you to specify the amount of bytes per ping. Ping –n specifies the exact amount of pings to send.

3. **C.** Tracert is used to run a trace between the local system and a remote destination. It shows all routers along the way. Ping is used to test connectivity to another system directly. Ipconfig will display the Internet Protocol configuration of the local computer. Nbtstat shows the name table cache and services running on the system.

4. **A.** You should use this syntax: net use J: \\Jupiter-Server\Data1. All other answers are incorrect. The UNC is \\computername\sharename.

5. **C.** Check the super-obvious first. Make sure the computer has a physical cabled connection to the network. Then attempt things such as ipconfig, ping, and network driver updates.

6. **D.** Use a patch cable tester to check the patch cable and possibly a continuity tester to test longer network cable runs. Multimeters are great for testing wires inside the computer or AC outlets but not for network troubleshooting. A PSU tester tests power supplies. The loopback plug will verify if the local computer's network adapter is functional.

7. **B.** This is the concept of pinging outward. Start by pinging the localhost, then a computer, and the router on the network. Then ping a domain name or website. If you can ping the website but the browser cannot get through, the browser might have been compromised. If you cannot ping the website, then you should check the IP configuration; the DNS server address might be incorrectly configured. Updating the OS and AV software should be done right away if you guess that the browser has been compromised.

8. **A.** Some routers and switches can disable physical ports (a smart security measure). Check that first. Later you can check if the network adapter is compatible with the OS and update it if necessary. Do not replace the cable with a crossover; those are used to connect one computer to another.

CHAPTER 16

Security

This chapter covers the following A+ exam topics:

▶ Security Threats and Prevention

▶ Windows Security

▶ SOHO Security

You can find a master list of A+ exam topics in the "Introduction."

This chapter covers CompTIA A+ Objectives 220-802 1.8, 2.1 through 2.6, and 4.7.

Everyone should have some basic knowledge on security. Computers and computer networks are constantly at risk, and new risks are always rearing their ugly head.

This chapter concentrates on demonstrating how to secure an individual computer system as well as a basic SOHO network. But you must ask yourself some questions: What kind of computers and network devices am I trying to secure? What operating systems are in use, and what applications are loaded? How will the files be protected? What type of computer hardware is employed, and what BIOS is in place? What kind of networking hardware is being utilized? What kind of threats should I be prepared for? And how can I prevent security breaches, and troubleshoot security issues if they do occur? We'll answer all these questions in the hope that you end up with a secure computer and network.

Security Threats and Prevention

This section covers common security threats, prevention techniques, and physical and digital security methods. From the entrance to your building, to the most hidden confidential file, you should have a security focus to your mindset. Let's start with a most dangerous foe: malicious software.

Malicious Software

Malicious software, or *malware*, is software designed to infiltrate a computer system and possibly damage it without the user's knowledge or consent. Malware is a broad term used by computer professionals to include viruses, worms, Trojan horses, spyware, rootkits, adware, and other types of undesirable software.

Of course, we don't want malware to infect our computer system, but to defend against it we first need to define it and categorize it. Then we can put preventative measures into place. It's also important to locate and remove/quarantine malware from a computer system in the case that it does manifest itself. Table 16.1 summarizes the various malware threats you should know for the exam.

TABLE 16.1 **Malware Types**

Malware Threat	Definition	Example
Virus	Code that runs on a computer without the user's knowledge; it infects the computer when the code is accessed and executed.	Love Bug virus Ex: love-letter-for-you.txt.vbs
Worm	Similar to viruses except that it self-replicates whereas a virus does not.	Nimda Propagated through network shares and mass e-mailing
Trojan horse	Appears to perform desired functions but are actually performing malicious functions behind the scenes.	Remote access Trojan Ex: SubSeven malware application
Spyware	Malicious software either downloaded unwittingly from a website or installed along with some other third-party software.	Internet Optimizer (aka DyFuCA)
Rootkit	Software designed to gain administrator-level control over a computer system without being detected.	Boot loader rootkits Ex: Evil Maid Attack
Spam	The abuse of electronic messaging systems such as e-mail, broadcast media, and instant messaging.	Phishing identity theft e-mails Lottery scam e-mails

Preventing and Troubleshooting Malicious Software

Now that we know the types of malware, let's talk about how to stop them before they happen, and how to troubleshoot them if they do happen. If a system is affected by malware, it might be sluggish in its response time or display unwanted pop-ups and incorrect home pages; or applications (and maybe even the whole system) could lock up or shut down unexpectedly. Quite often, malware uses CPU and memory resources directly or behind the scenes, causing the system to run slower than usual. A technician should look for erratic behavior from the computer, as if it had a mind of its own! Let's go over how to prevent malware and how to troubleshoot it if it does occur.

Preventing and Troubleshooting Viruses

We can do several things to protect a computer system from viruses. First, every computer should have antivirus software running on it. McAfee, Norton, and Vipre are examples of manufacturers of AV software, but there are many others. Second, the AV software should be updated, which means that the software will require a current license; this is renewed yearly with most providers. When updating, be sure to update the AV engine *and* the definitions if you are doing it manually. Otherwise, set the AV software to automatically update at periodic intervals, for example, every day or every week. It's a good idea to schedule regular full scans of the system within the AV software.

As long as the definitions have been updated, antivirus systems will usually locate viruses along with worms and Trojans. However, these systems will usually not locate rootkit activity. Keep in mind that AV software is important but it is not a cure all.

Next, we want to make sure that the computer has the latest service packs and updates available. This goes for the operating system and applications such as Microsoft Office. Backdoors into operating systems and other applications are not uncommon, and the OS manufacturers often release fixes for these breaches of security. Windows offers the Windows Update program. This should be enabled, and you should either check for updates periodically, or set the system to check for updates automatically. It might be that your organization has rules governing how Windows update will function. If so, configure Automatic Updates according to your company's policy. You can check if your computer is up to date by going to Start > All Programs > Windows Update. In Windows 7/Vista you can check for updates directly within the Automatic Updates program. In Windows XP, it directs you to a website that prompts you to install a Windows Update component and then checks if the computer has the latest security (and other) patches.

It's also important to make sure that a firewall is available, enabled, and updated. A firewall closes all the inbound ports to your computer (or network) in an attempt to block intruders. The Windows Firewall is a built-in feature of Windows 7/Vista/XP, and you might also have a SOHO router with a built-in firewall. By using both, you have two layers of protection from viruses and other attacks. You can access the Windows Firewall by navigating to the Control Panel. Keep in mind that you might need to set exceptions for programs that need to access the Internet. This can be done by the program, or the port used by the protocol, and can be configured in the Exceptions tab, enabling specific applications to communicate through the firewall while keeping the rest of the ports closed.

Another good technique when trying to prevent viruses (and just about any malware) is to disable Autorun for CD, DVD, and Blu-ray drives. If you disable Autorun, a CD or DVD won't automatically start its Autorun application (if it has one), and any embedded malware won't have a chance to infect the system before you scan the media. To disable Autorun in Windows 7, complete the following steps:

Step 1. Click Start and in the search field type gpedit.msc. This opens the Local Group Policy Editor.

Step 2. Navigate to: Computer Configuration > Administrative Templates > Windows Components > AutoPlay Policies.

Step 3. Double-click the Turn Off Autoplay setting. This displays the Turn Off AutoPlay configuration window.

Step 4. Click the Enabled radio button and click OK. You are actually enabling the policy named Turn Off Autoplay.

> **Note**
>
> This turns off all AutoPlay and Autorun features. Use this sparingly on laptops that do presentations, as these computers might require AutoPlay.

Finally, educate users as to how viruses can infect a system. Instruct them on how to screen their e-mails and tell them not to open unknown attachments. Show them how to scan removable media before copying files to their computer, or set up the computer to scan removable media automatically. Sometimes user education works; sometimes it doesn't. One way to make user education more effective is to have a technical trainer educate your users, instead of doing it yourself. This can provide for a more engaging learning environment.

By using these methods, virus infection can be severely reduced. However, if a computer is infected by a virus, you want to know what to look for so that you can "cure" the computer.

Here are some typical symptoms of viruses:

- ▸ Computer runs slower than usual.

- ▸ Computer locks up frequently or stops responding altogether.

- ▸ Computer restarts on its own or crashes frequently.

- ▸ Disk drives and applications are not accessible or don't work properly.

- ▸ Windows Updates fail.

- ▸ Permission to specific files and folders is denied.

- ▸ Strange sounds occur.

- ▸ You receive unusual error messages or security alerts (which are most likely false).

- ▸ Display or print distortion occurs.

- ▸ New icons appear or old icons (and applications) disappear.

- ▸ There is a double extension on a file attached to an e-mail that was opened, for example: .txt.vbs or .txt.exe.

- ▸ Antivirus programs will not run, can't be installed, or can't be updated.

- ▸ Files disappear, have been renamed or corrupted; folders are created automatically.

If a system is infected, disconnect the network cable from the computer to stop the virus from spreading to any other systems on the network. Before making any changes to the computer, make sure that you back up critical data. If necessary, remove the hard drive and copy critical data to another system using an external connection.

ExamAlert

Know what to do first when troubleshooting a virus.

Now, the technician should attempt to identify the virus or viruses. To do this, perform a thorough scan of the system using the AV software's scan utility; if allowed by the software, run the scan in Safe Mode. (You might also need to disable System Restore before starting a scan.) Another option is to move the affected drive to a "clean machine," a computer that is used solely for the purpose of scanning for malware, which does not connect to the Internet. This can be done by slaving the affected drive to an IDE, SATA, or eSATA port of the other computer and running the AV software on the clean machine to scan that drive. PC repair shops have this kind of isolated clean machine.

Hopefully, the AV software will find and quarantine the virus on the system. In the case that the AV software's scan does not find the issue, or if the AV software has been infected and won't run, you can try using an online scanner such as Trend Micro's HouseCall: http://housecall.trendmicro.com/ or download Microsoft's Malicious Software Removal Tool:

http://www.microsoft.com/security/pc-security/malware-removal.aspx

If it is a new virus, you might have to download an individual antivirus definition. To make sure the definition is authentic, check the hash key. The key you saw on the website should match the hash key on your computer once downloaded.

If viruses are removed, but keep reappearing on the computer after reboot, consider reverting the computer to an older restore point.

In rare cases, you might need to delete individual files and remove Registry entries. This might be the only solution when a new virus has infected a system and there is no antivirus definition released. Instructions on how to remove viruses in this manner can be found on AV software manufacturers' websites.

When it comes to boot sector viruses, your AV software is still the best bet. The AV software might use a boot disk to accomplish scanning of the boot sector, or it might have boot shielding built in. Some BIOS programs have the capability to scan the boot sector of the hard drive at startup; this might need to be enabled in the BIOS setup first. Windows 7/Vista offers the `bootrec /fixmbr` command from within the System Recovery Options Command Prompt. Windows XP has the `FIXMBR` command available at the Recovery Console. Keep in mind that System Recovery Options and Recovery Console Command Prompts methods might not fix the problem; they might render the hard drive inoperable depending on the type of virus. It is best to use the AV software's various utilities that you have purchased for the system.

After viruses have been quarantined, go to Control Panel > Action Center in Windows 7 (Security Center in Vista) and make sure there are no security messages that need your attention. Check for any updates to Windows and the AV software, run a full scan of the system, and if everything checks out, create a new restore point. Then explain to the user what happened, and how the user can avoid viruses in the future.

> **Note**
>
> Many organizations use corporate-level, centrally managed antivirus solutions. These can push out updates to all the computers on the network at once.

Preventing and Troubleshooting Worms and Trojans

Worms and Trojans can be prevented and troubleshot in the same manner as viruses. There are scanners for Trojans as well, for example Microsoft's Malicious Software Removal Tool. In some cases, AV software scans for worms and Trojans in addition to viruses. Both of these tools can easily detect Trojans, regardless of whether it is the actual attacker's application or any .exe files that are part of the application and are used at the victim computer.

Preventing and Troubleshooting Spyware

Preventing spyware works in much the same manner as preventing viruses as far as updating the operating system and using a firewall. Also, because spyware has become much more common, antivirus companies have begun adding antispyware components to their software. Here are a few more things you can do to protect your computer in the hopes of preventing spyware:

▶ Download and install antispyware protection software. For example, Windows Defender, available at the following link: http://www. microsoft.com/download/en/details.aspx?id=17. Other options include Spyware Doctor with Antivirus, SpyBot S&D (free), or one of the antivirus programs previously mentioned if it includes spyware protection. Be sure to keep the antispyware software updated.

▶ Adjust Internet Explorer security settings. This can be done by clicking Tools on the menu bar, selecting Internet Options, and accessing the Security tab. From there, the security level can be increased, and trusted and restricted sites can be established. (It's a good thing.) Internet Explorer 7 and higher also have a phishing filter that you can turn on by going to Tools > Phishing Filter and clicking Turn on Automatic Website Checking. This attempts to filter out fraudulent online requests for usernames, passwords, and credit card information, which is also known as web-page spoofing. Higher security settings can also help to fend off session *hijacking*; that is, the act of taking control of a user session after obtaining or generating an authentication ID. Similar security settings are available on most of today's web browsers. Another attack similar to session hijacking is browser redirection. This is when a user's web browser is automatically redirected to one or more malicious websites. It can be done when a user inadvertently accesses a malicious website from a search, can be caused by a Trojan that modifies a computer's

DNS entries (ex. DNSChanger), or can be caused by spyware or a virus that configures a proxy server address within the browser and/or modifies the HOSTS.txt file. This can be avoided by increasing a browser's security settings, updating antivirus programs, and through user education. It can be fixed by scanning the system with antivirus software, removing the proxy server address from the browser's settings, and deleting and re-writing the HOSTS.txt file. More information about proxy server addresses is available in Chapter 15, "Networking." More information about browser and session hijacking can be found in Chapter 16, "Security."

▶ Uninstall unnecessary applications and turn off superfluous services (for example, Telnet and FTP if they are not used).

▶ Educate users on how to surf the web safely. User education is actually the number one method of preventing malware! Access only sites believed to be safe, and download only programs from reputable websites. Don't click OK or Agree to close a pop-up window; instead press Alt+F4 on the keyboard to close that window. Be wary of file-sharing websites and the content stored on those sites. Be careful of e-mails with links to downloadable software that could be malicious.

▶ Consider technologies that discourage spyware. For example, use a browser that is less susceptible to spyware. Consider running a browser within a virtual machine, or recommend tablet Internet appliances to users who use a computer to access the Internet only.

Here are some common symptoms of spyware:

▶ The web browser's default home page has been modified.

▶ A particular website comes up every time you perform a search.

▶ Excessive pop-up windows appear. Rogue antivirus applications seem to appear out of nowhere supposedly scanning the system.

▶ The network adapter's activity LED blinks frequently when the computer shouldn't be transmitting data.

▶ The firewall and antivirus programs turn off automatically.

▶ New programs, icons, and favorites appear.

▶ Odd problems occur within windows (slow system, applications behaving strangely, and such).

▶ The Java console appears randomly.

To troubleshoot and repair systems infected with spyware, first disconnect the system from the Internet. Then, try uninstalling the program from Control

Panel > Programs and Features in Windows 7/Vista, and Add/Remove Programs in Windows XP. Some of the less malicious spyware programs can be fully uninstalled without any residual damage. Be sure to reboot the computer afterward and verify that the spyware was actually uninstalled! Next, scan your system with the AV software to remove any viruses that might have infested the system, which might get in the way of a successful spyware removal. Again, do this in Safe Mode if the AV software offers that option.

Next, scan the computer with the antispyware software of your choice in an attempt to quarantine and remove the spyware. You can use other programs, such as HijackThis, in an attempt to remove malware, but be careful with these programs because you will probably need to modify the Registry. Remove only that which is part of the infection.

Finally, you need to make sure that the malware will not reemerge on your system. To do this, check your home page setting in your browser, verify that your host's file hasn't been hijacked (located in C:\WINDOWS\system32\ drivers\etc), and make sure that unwanted websites haven't been added to the Trusted Sites within the browser.

Preventing and Troubleshooting Rootkits

A successfully installed rootkit enables unauthorized users to gain access to a system acting as the root or administrator user. Rootkits are copied to a computer as a binary file; this binary file can be detected by signature-based and heuristic-based antivirus programs. However, after the rootkit is executed, it can be difficult to detect. This is because most rootkits are collections of programs working together that can make many modifications to the system. When subversion of the operating system takes place, the OS can't be trusted, and it is difficult to tell if your antivirus programs run properly, or if any of your other efforts have any effect. Although security software manufacturers are attempting to detect running rootkits, it is doubtful that they will be successful. The best way to identify a rootkit is to use removable media (USB flash drive or a special rescue CD-ROM) to boot the computer. This way, the operating system is not running, and therefore, the rootkit is not running, making it much easier to detect by the external media. One program that can be used to detect rootkits is Microsoft Sysinternals Rootkit Revealer:

http://technet.microsoft.com/en-us/sysinternals/bb897445.aspx

Unfortunately, because of the difficulty involved in removing a rootkit, sometimes the best way to combat rootkits is to reinstall all software. Generally, a PC technician upon detecting a rootkit will do just this because it usually takes less time than attempting to fix all the rootkit issues, plus it can verify that the rootkit has been removed completely.

Preventing and Troubleshooting Spam

The key is to block as much spam as possible, report those who do it, and train your users. Here are several ways that spam can be reduced:

▶ **Use a strong password:** E-mail accounts can be hijacked if they have weak passwords. This is especially common with web-based e-mail accounts such as Gmail or Yahoo Mail. After he gets access, the hijacker sends spam out to everyone on the user's contact list. Use a complex password and change it often to prevent e-mail hijacking.

▶ **Use a spam filter:** This can be purchased for the server-side as software or as an appliance. One example of an appliance is the Barracuda Networks Spam Firewall (www.barracudanetworks.com). Barracuda monitors spam activity and creates and updates whitelists and blacklists, all of which can be downloaded to the appliance automatically. On the client-side, you can configure Outlook and other mail programs to a higher level of security against spam; this is usually in the Junk E-mail Options area. Many popular antivirus suites have built-in spam filtering. Make sure it is enabled!

▶ **Use whitelists and blacklists:** Whitelists are lists of e-mail addresses or entire e-mail domains that are trusted, whereas blacklists are not trusted. These can be set up on e-mail servers, e-mail appliances, and within mail client programs such as Outlook.

▶ **Train your users:** Have them create and use a free e-mail address whenever they post to forums and newsgroups, and not to use their company e-mail for anything except company-related purposes. Make sure that they screen their e-mail carefully; this is also known as e-mail vetting. E-mail with attachments should be considered volatile unless the user knows exactly where it comes from. Train your users and customers never to make a purchase from an unsolicited e-mail.

Unauthorized Access

Unauthorized access is access to an organization's premises, computer resources and data without consent of the owner. It might include approaching the system, trespassing, communicating, storing and retrieving data, intercepting data, or any other methods that would interfere with a computer's normal work. Access to data must be controlled to ensure privacy. Improper administrative access would fall into this category as well.

Unauthorized access can be prevented through the use of authentication. Authentication is the verification of a person's identity. It is a preventative measure that can be broken down into four categories:

- ▶ Something the user knows, for example a password or PIN

- ▶ Something the user has, for example a smart card or other security token

- ▶ Something the user is, for example the biometric reading of a finger-print or retina scan

- ▶ Something the user does, for example a signature or speaking words

We'll talk about various methods of operating system authentication in the Windows Security section. For now, let's talk about some ways to enforce physical security.

Physical Locks

In addition to main entrances, you should always lock server rooms, wiring closets, labs, and other technical rooms when not in use. The concept of a lock and physical key that you need to carry around can't be denied. It should be documented who has the keys to server rooms and wiring closets. Locks should be changed out and rotated with other locks every so often. This keeps things dynamic and harder to guess at. Another type of lock is the cipher lock, which uses a punch code to unlock the door. These physical methods might be used by themselves or combined with an electronic system.

Special locks can also be installed for PCs and laptops. Some PC cases come with built-in locks. Configure the BIOS to log whether someone opened the case of the computer. This is logged as chassis intrusion.

Entry Systems

The most common electronic entry system is the cardkey system. These use proximity-based door access cards that you simply press against a transmitter next to the door handle. Although these are common, they are not the best option. But because they are inexpensive compared to other systems, you will see them quite often. Other electronic systems will use key cards that incorporate a photo ID (a worker's badge), or magnetic stripe, barcode, or a radio-frequency identification (RFID) chip. Each of these can contain information about the identity of the user. These don't have to be cards either; they can come in smaller form factors such as key fobs, which can be attached right to a user's keychain.

Moving on to the next level of security, let's talk briefly about the smart card. These are cards that have a nano-processor and can actually communicate with the authentication system. Examples of these include the Personal Identity Verification (PIV) card used by U.S. government employees and contractors, and the Common Access Card (CAC) used by DoD personnel. These cards identify the owner, authenticate them to areas of the building and to computers, and can digitally sign and encrypt files and e-mail with the RSA encryption algorithm. Due to the fact that these are physical items a user carries with them to gain access to specific systems, they are known as tokens. A token might also display a code that changes say every minute or so. If a person wants access to a particular system, such as accounting or other confidential area, the person would have to type the current code that is shown on the token into the computer. This is a powerful method of authentication but can be expensive as well.

Some organizations will design what is known as a mantrap; an area with two locking doors. A person might get past a first door by way of tailgating, but might have difficulty getting past the second door, especially if there is a guard in between the two doors. If the person doesn't have proper authentication, they will be stranded in the mantrap until authorities arrive.

Biometrics

Biometrics is the science of recognizing humans based on one or more physical characteristics. Biometrics is used as a form of authentication and access control. It is also used to identify persons that might be under surveillance.

Biometrics falls into the category of "something a person is." Examples of bodily characteristics that are measured include fingerprints, retinal patterns, iris patterns, and even bone structure. Biometric readers, for example fingerprint scanners, are becoming more common in door access systems and on laptops or as USB devices. Biometric information can also be combined with smart card technology. An example of a biometric door access system is Suprema, which has various levels of access systems including some that incorporate smart cards and biometrics, together forming a multifactor authentication system. One example of biometric hardware for a local computer is the Microsoft Fingerprint Scanner, which is USB-based.

Biometrics can be seen in many movies and TV shows. However, many biometric systems over the past decade have been easily compromised. It has only been of late that readily available biometric systems have started to live up to the hype. Thorough investigation and testing of a biometric system is necessary before purchase and installation. In addition, it should be used in a multifactor authentication scheme. The more factors the better, as long as your users can handle it. (You would be surprised what a little bit of training can do.) Voice recognition software has made great leaps and bounds since the turn of the millennium. A combination of biometrics, voice recognition, and pin access would make for an excellent three-factor authentication system. But as always, only if you can get it through budgeting!

Protecting Data Physically

Confidential documents should never be left sitting out in the open. They should either be properly filed in a locking cabinet or shredded and disposed of if they are no longer needed. Passwords should not be written down and definitely not left on a desk or taped to a monitor where they can be seen. Many organizations implement a clean desk policy that states each user must remove all papers from their desk before leaving for lunch, breaks, or at the end of the day. Anything that shows on the computer screen can be protected in a variety of ways. To protect data while the person is working you can install a privacy filter, which is a transparent cover for PC monitors and laptop displays. It reduces the cone of vision, usually to about 30 degrees, so that only the person in front of the screen can see the content. Many of these are also antiglare, helping to reduce eye stress of the user. Also, users should lock their computers whenever they leave their workstation. Windows can also be automatically set to lock after a certain amount of time, even if users forget to do so manually.

Social Engineering

Social engineering is the act of manipulating users into revealing confidential information or performing other actions detrimental to the user. Almost everyone gets e-mails nowadays from unknown entities making false claims or asking for personal information (or money!); this is one example of social engineering. Here are the social engineering techniques you should know for the exam.

Phishing

Phishing is the attempt at fraudulently obtaining private information. A phisher usually masquerades as someone else, perhaps another entity. Phishing is usually done by electronic communication/phone. Little information about the target is necessary. A phisher may target thousands of individuals without much concern as to their background. An example of phishing would be an e-mail that requests verification of private information. The e-mail will probably lead to a malicious website designed to lure people into a false sense of security to fraudulently obtain information. The website will often look like a legitimate website. A common phishing technique is to pose as a vendor (such as an online retailer or domain registrar) and send the target e-mail confirmations of orders that they supposedly placed.

A lot of different types of social engineering are often lumped into what is referred to as phishing, but actual phishing for private information is normally limited to e-mail and websites. To defend against this, a phishing filter or add-on should be installed and enabled on the web browser. Also, a person should be trained to realize that institutions will not call or e-mail requesting private information. If people are not sure, they should hang up the phone or simply delete the e-mail. A quick way to find out if an e-mail is phishing for information is to hover over a link (but don't click it!). You will see a URL domain name that is far different from the institution that the phisher is claiming to be, probably a URL located in a distant country.

Shoulder Surfing

Shoulder surfing is when a person uses direct observation to find out a target's password, PIN, or other such authentication information. The simple resolution for this is for the user to shield the screen, keypad, or other authentication requesting devices. A more aggressive approach is to courteously ask the assumed shoulder surfer to move along. Also, private information should never be left on a desk or out in the open. Computer's should be locked or logged off when the user is not in the immediate area. Shoulder surfing and the following two sections are examples of no-tech hacking.

Piggybacking/Tailgating

Piggybacking is when an unauthorized person tags along with an authorized person to gain entry to a restricted area—usually with the person's consent. Tailgating is essentially the same with one difference: It is usually without the authorized person's consent. Both of these can be defeated through the use of mantraps. A mantrap is a small space that can usually fit only one person. It has two sets of interlocking doors; the first set must be closed before the other will open, creating a sort of waiting room where people are identified (and cannot escape). Multifactor authentication is often used in conjunction with a mantrap, for example, using a proximity card and PIN at the first door, and biometric scan at the second. A mantrap is an example of a preventive security control. Turnstiles, double entry doors, and employing security guards are other less expensive (and less effective) solutions to the problem of piggybacking and tailgating and help address confidentiality in general.

Hard Drive Recycling and Disposal

Hard drives that contain an organization's data can also be a security threat. When a hard drive is removed from a computer, it either needs to be recycled or disposed of in a proper manner. Sanitizing the hard drive is a common way of removing data but not the only one. The way data is removed might vary depending on its proposed final destination. Proper data removal goes far beyond file deletion or the formatting of digital media. The problem with high-level formats done in the operating system, and low-level formats done by the BIOS, is the data remanence, or the residue, that is left behind, from which re-creation of files can

be accomplished with the use of various third-party software. Organizations typically employ one of three options when met with the prospect of data removal:

▶ **Clearing:** This is the removal of data with a certain amount of assurance that it cannot be reconstructed. The data is actually recoverable with special techniques. In this case, the media is recycled and used within the company again. The data wiping technique (also known as shredding) is used to clear data from media by overwriting new data to that media. In some cases, patterns of ones and zeros are written to the entire drive. Several software programs are available to accomplish this.

▶ **Purging:** Also known as sanitizing, this is again the removal of data, but this time, it's done in such a way so that it cannot be reconstructed by any known technique; in this case the media is released outside the company. Special bit-level erasure software (or other means) is employed to completely destroy all data on the media. This type of software will comply with the U.S. Department of Defense (DoD) 5220.22-M standard, which requires seven full passes of rewrites. It is also possible to degauss the disk, which will render the data unreadable but might also cause physical damage to the drive. Tools such as electromagnetic degaussers and permanent magnet degaussers can be used to permanently purge information from a disk.

▶ **Destruction:** This is when the storage media is physically destroyed through pulverizing, drilling holes through the platters, and so on. At this point, the media can be disposed of in accordance with municipal guidelines.

ExamAlert

Know the differences between clearing, purging, and destruction.

The type of data removal used will be dictated by the data stored on the drive. If there is no personally identifiable information, or other sensitive information, it might simply be cleared and released outside the company. But in many cases, organizations will specify purging of data if the drive is to leave the building. In cases where a drive previously contained confidential or top secret data, the drive will usually be destroyed.

Cram Quiz

Answer these questions. The answers follow the last question. If you cannot answer these questions correctly, consider reading this section again until you can.

220-802 Questions

1. Which of the following types of malware self-replicates?

   ○ **A.** Virus

   ○ **B.** Worm

   ○ **C.** Trojan

   ○ **D.** Rootkit

2. What type of malware is the abuse of electronic messaging systems?

   ○ **A.** Virus

   ○ **B.** Spyware

   ○ **C.** Spam

   ○ **D.** Worm

3. Which of the following are symptoms of viruses? (Select the three best answers.)

   ○ **A.** Computer runs slowly.

   ○ **B.** Computer locks up.

   ○ **C.** Excessive pop-up windows appear.

   ○ **D.** A strange website is displayed whenever a search is done.

   ○ **E.** Unusual error messages are displayed.

4. Which of the following is the science of recognizing humans based on physical characteristics?

   ○ **A.** Mantraps

   ○ **B.** Biometrics

   ○ **C.** Tailgating

   ○ **D.** Something a person is

5. A hard drive needs to be disposed of in a way so that no one can access the data. Which method should you use?

   ○ **A.** Phishing

   ○ **B.** Clearing

   ○ **C.** Shoulder Surfing

   ○ **D.** Destruction

6. Which of the following is the best mode to use when scanning for viruses?

   ○ **A.** Safe Mode

   ○ **B.** Last Known Good Configuration

   ○ **C.** Command Prompt only

   ○ **D.** Boot into Windows normally

7. Which of the following is one way to prevent spyware?
   - ○ **A.** Use firewall exceptions.
   - ○ **B.** Adjust Internet Explorer security settings.
   - ○ **C.** Adjust the Internet Explorer home page.
   - ○ **D.** Remove the spyware from Add/Remove Programs.

8. One of your customers tells you that a bank employee called and asked for the person's bank balance and telephone number. What is this an example of?
   - ○ **A.** Spam
   - ○ **B.** Virus
   - ○ **C.** Social Engineering
   - ○ **D.** Trojan

Cram Quiz Answers

220-802 Answers

1. **B.** A worm will self-replicate whereas a virus will not; otherwise, the two are very much the same. Trojans perform malicious functions behind the scenes and allow remote access to systems. Rootkits are designed to gain administrator (or root) level access to the computer.

2. **C.** Spam is the abuse of electronic messaging systems such as e-mail. Viruses and worms are code that run on a system, infecting its files. Spyware is malicious software downloaded from the Internet that spies on a user's web activities.

3. **A, B and E.** Some symptoms of viruses are: computer running slowly, computer locking up, and unusual errors. Excessive popups and strange websites displaying after searches are symptoms of spyware.

4. **B.** Biometrics is the science of recognizing humans based on physical characteristics. It falls into the category of "something a person is." Mantraps are areas of a building implemented to stop tailgating.

5. **D.** You should destroy the hard drive, sanitize it with special bit-level erasure software, or degauss it. Phishing is a type of social engineering where a person attempts to gain confidential information from unwitting users by e-mail. Clearing is the removal of data from a drive that is to be recycled and used again within the organization. Shoulder surfing is when a person attempts to find out passwords or other information by viewing another user's display without his or her knowledge.

6. **A.** Safe Mode should be used (if your AV software supports it) when scanning for viruses.

7. **B.** Adjust the Internet Explorer security settings so that security is at a higher level, and add trusted and restricted websites.

8. **C.** A bank employee will never ask for this information. This is someone masquerading as a bank employee and is a type of social engineering known as *phishing*. (More to the point, *vishing*, because it was done by phone.) Spam is the abuse of e-mail. A virus infects files on a computer. Trojans are used to gain access to the computer system usually through back doors.

Windows Security

Windows Security is all about authenticating users and protecting files. Proper usage of usernames and passwords, user accounts, permissions, encryption, and firewalls can lead to a secure Windows computer.

User Accounts

Users are what it's all about when it comes to Windows security. There are four types of user accounts you should know for the exam. First is the Administrator; this account has full (or near full) control of an operating system. It is usually the most powerful account in Windows and has access to everything. Then there is the Standard User account (also simply referred to as User); this is the normal account for a person on a network. The User has access to his own data (owns the data), but has access to no one else's, and cannot accomplish administrative tasks such as installing software without an administrative password. In older versions of Windows the Power User is somewhere in between the two; with the ability to do some administrative tasks such as installing software. However, the Power User account is listed only in Windows 7 for backward compatibility with older Windows operating systems. Finally, the Guest account has limited access to the system. A Guest cannot install software or hardware, cannot change settings or access any data, and cannot change the password.

You need to make sure that users' data is secured and that no one else can masquerade as a legitimate user. Windows user accounts can be secured through a combination of a strong username/password, user policies, and User Account Control.

Usernames and Passwords

The username/password combination is the most common type of authentication for gaining access to computers. The username is known to all parties involved and can be seen as plain text when typed. In some cases, the user has no control over what the username will be, or it will be the name or e-mail address of the user. However, the password is either set by the user or created automatically for the user. It is common knowledge that a strong password is important for protecting a user account, whether the account is with a bank, at work, or elsewhere. But what is a strong password? Many organizations define a *strong* password as a password with at least 8 characters, including at least one 1 uppercase letter, 1 number, and 1 special character. The *best* passwords have the same requirements but are 15 characters or more. Many password checker programs are on the web, for example Microsoft's password checker and The Password Meter. Table 16.2 shows a strong password and a "best" password.

TABLE 16.2 **Strong and Stronger Passwords**

Password	Strength of Password
|Ocrian7	Strong
This1sV#ryS3cure	Very strong or "best"

Notice the first password is using the | pipe symbol instead of the letter L. This is a special character that shares the \ backslash key on the keyboard. In the second password we have 16 characters, 3 capital letters, 2 numbers, and a partridge in a pear tree, um, I mean 1 special character ☺. Just checking if you are still with me! Of course a partridge wouldn't help your password security, but the other methods make for an extremely strong password that would take a super-computer a long time to crack.

ExamAlert

Understand what is required for a complex password.

Changing your password at regular intervals is important as well. The general rule of thumb is to change your password as often as you change your toothbrush. However, because this is a subjective concept (to put it nicely!), many organizations have policies concerning your password. It might need to meet certain requirements, or be changed at regular intervals, and so forth. Figure 16.1 shows an example of the default password policy on a Windows 7 Ultimate computer. This can be accessed by navigating to Start > All Programs > Administrative Tools > Local Security Policy. When in the Local Security Settings window, continue to Security Settings > Account Policies > Password Policy.

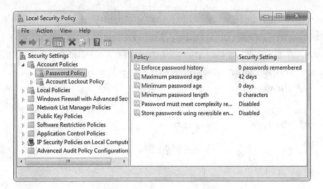

FIGURE 16.1   Default password policy in Windows 7

As you can see in the figure, there are several items that we can configure or could be configured by the network administrator centrally if the computer is part of a domain. The four important ones for the exam include:

▶ **Enforce password history:** When this is defined, users cannot use any of the passwords that are remembered in the history. If you set the history to 3, then the last three passwords cannot be used again when it is time to change the password.

▶ **Maximum and minimum password age:** This defines exactly how long a password can be used. The maximum is initially set to 42 days but does not affect the default Administrator account. To enforce effective password history, the minimum must be higher than zero.

▶ **Minimum password length:** This requires that the password must be at least the specified amount of characters. For a strong password policy, set this to between 8 and 14. (14 is the maximum in Windows 7.)

▶ **Passwords must meet complexity requirements:** This means that passwords must meet three of these four criteria: uppercase characters, lowercase characters, digits between 0 and 9, and nonalphabetic characters (special characters).

> **Note**
>
> For more information on password best practices, see the following link: http://technet.microsoft.com/en-us/library/cc784090.aspx

Now that we have a secure password, and a password policy in place, let's talk about securing the user accounts for Windows. There are a few things we can do to secure these:

1. **Rename and password protect the Administrator account:** It's nice that Windows has incorporated a separate administrator account: The problem is that by default the account has no password. To configure this account, navigate to Computer Management > System Tools > Local Users and Groups > Users and locate the Administrator account. By right-clicking the account, you see a drop-down menu in which you can rename it and/or give it a password. (Just remember the new username and password!) Now it's great to have this additional administrator account on the shelf just in case the primary account fails; however, Windows 7/Vista disables this account by default. (A down arrow indicates a disabled account, just as a down arrow in the Device Manger indicates a disabled device.) To enable it, right-click the account and select Properties. In the General tab, deselect the Account is disabled check box. Alternatively, open the command line and type `net user administrator /active:yes`.

> **Note**
>
> Alternatively, you can use the User Accounts applet in the Control Panel to accomplish these tasks for any account in 7/Vista, and for any account except Administrator in XP, but using Computer Management is recommended because it is more consistent and thorough.

2. **Verify that the Guest account (and other unnecessary accounts) are disabled:** This can be done by navigating again to Local Users and Groups > Users, and right-clicking the account in question, selecting Properties, and then selecting the check box named Account Is Disabled. (It is disabled by default in Windows 7.) It is also possible to delete accounts (aside from built-in accounts such as the Guest account); however, companies usually opt to have them disabled instead so that the company can retain information linking to the account.

3. **Set the Account lockout threshold:** If a user attempts to log on to a system and is unsuccessful, the user will be locked out of the system (after a specified number of attempts). The settings and thresholds for this can be configured in the Local Security Settings window. Navigate to Security Settings > Account Policies > Account Lockout Policy. From here you can set the threshold to a certain amount of invalid logons, set how long the user will be locked out, and set how long until the lockout counter is reset. If an account is locked out and you need to unlock it immediately, follow one of the options at the end of step 1.

ExamAlert

Know how to enable/disable accounts, reset passwords, and modify password policy for the exam!

Note

Lockouts due to forgotten passwords are common in organizations. Sometimes a user will have several passwords to gain access to various systems, making the problem worse. Several complex passwords can be confusing to users and cause many tech support calls requiring accounts be unlocked. To combat this, some organizations implement a technique known as *single sign-on*. This is when a user needs only one password to gain access to two or more systems.

It's important to note that when logging on to a Microsoft network, the logon process is secured by the Kerberos protocol, which is run by the Domain Controller. This adds a layer of protection for the username and password as they are being authenticated across the network.

Regardless of whether a user is part of a domain or not, if the user is going to take a break or go to lunch, the computer should be locked. This can be done by pressing Windows+L. When doing so, the operating system goes into a locked state, and the only way to unlock the computer is to enter the username and password of the person who locked the computer. The difference between this and logging out is that a locked computer keeps all the session's applications and files open, whereas logging out closes all applications and open files.

Aside from locking the computer manually, the user can opt to put the computer to sleep after a certain period of time, or enable a password-protected screensaver, both of which will force the user to logon when returning to the computer. Sleep settings can be accessed at Control Panel > Power Options (for more information on that, see Chapter 9, "Configuring Windows".) To password-protect the screen saver in Windows 7, go to Control Panel >

Personalization, and click the Screen Saver link on the bottom right side. Then, pick a screen saver, select the timeout, and check the On Resume, Display Logo Screen check box.

User Account Control (UAC)

User Account Control (UAC) is a security component of Windows 7/Vista that keeps every user (besides the actual Administrator account) in standard user mode instead of as an administrator with full administrative rights—even if they are a member of the administrators group. It is meant to prevent unauthorized access and avoid user error in the form of accidental changes. With UAC enabled users perform common tasks as non-administrators, and when necessary, as administrators, without having to switch users, log off, or use Run As.

UAC is partially based on the *principle of least privilege*. This principle says that a user should have access to only what is required. If a person needs to update Excel files and browse the Internet, that person should not be given administrative access. You might think of this as common sense, but it should not be taken lightly. When user accounts are created locally on a computer and especially on a domain, great care should be taken when assigning users to groups. Also, many programs when installed will ask who can use and make modifications to the program; quite often the default is All Users. Some technicians just click Next when hastily installing programs, without realizing that the user now has full control of the program; something you might not want. Just remember, keep users on a need-to-know basis; give them access only to what they specifically need, and no more.

Basically, UAC was created with two goals in mind: First, to eliminate unnecessary requests for excessive administrative-level access to Windows resources. And second, to reduce the risk of malicious software using the administrator's access control to infect operating system files. When a standard end user requires administrator privileges to perform certain tasks such as installing an application, a small pop-up UAC window appears notifying the user that an administrator credential is necessary. If the user has administrative rights and clicks Continue, the task will be carried out, but if he or she does not have sufficient rights (and can't provide an administrative password), the attempt fails. Note that these pop-up UAC windows do not appear if the person is logged on with the actual Administrator account.

In Windows 7, you can turn off UAC by going to Start > Control Panel > User Accounts and Family Safety. Then select User Accounts, and click the Change User Account Control settings link. Unlike Windows Vista, where you can only turn UAC on or off, Windows 7 displays a slider that enables you to select from four different settings:

▶ **Always Notify:** This will configure the OS to notify the user whenever software installations are started, or when any changes to Windows settings are attempted by the user.

▶ **Default: Notify Me Only When Programs Try to Make Changes to My Computer:** This configures the OS to notify the user if a program attempts to make a change, but not when the user attempts to make a change to settings.

▶ **Notify Me Only When Programs Try to Make Changes to My Computer (Do Not Dim My Desktop):** This is essentially the same as the last item, but the desktop is not dimmed when the notifications appear.

▶ **Never Notify:** This effectively turns UAC off, and UAC will not notify the user regardless of the program or user change.

So, UAC, by default, notifies a user before changes are made to a computer that requires administrator-level permission. In Windows Vista this can be turned off altogether only, whereas in Windows 7 it can be controlled with a little bit more definition. Of course, a user will need administrative rights to make changes to UAC settings.

> **ExamAlert**
>
> Be sure to know how to turn UAC on and off for the exam!

File Security

To start, files can be assigned four different attributes in Windows: Read-Only, Hidden, Compression, and Encryption. To access these, right-click any file and select Properties. On the General tab you will see the Read-Only check box; this makes it so no one can save modifications to the file; however a new file can be saved with the changes. The Hidden check box makes the file invisible to all users except the user who created the file. Admins can unhide files individually or for the entire system, as I will explain in a moment. If you were to click the Advanced button, you would also see Compression, which allows you to convert the file to a smaller size that takes up less space on the drive and Encryption, which scrambles the file content so only the user who created the file can read it. We'll discuss encryption later in this chapter.

> **Note**
>
> The Attrib command in the Command Prompt can modify the Read-Only, Archive, System, and Hidden attributes for files, and display the attributes for each file. This older command is still available in Windows 7 but is not used often. For more on this command see the document on my website: http://www.davidlprowse.com/220-801.

System files and folders are hidden from view by the OS to protect the system. In some cases you can simply click the link Show the Contents of This Folder, but to permanently configure the system to show hidden files and folders navigate to Windows Explorer > Tools menu, and click Folder Options. Then select the View tab and under Hidden Files and Folders select the Show Hidden Files > Folders > and Drives radio button. Note that in Windows 7/Vista, the menu bar can also be hidden; to view it press Alt+T on the keyboard. To configure the system to show protected system files, deselect the Hide Protected Operating System Files check box, located shortly after Show Hidden Files and Folders. This enables you to view files such as bootmgr, pagefile.sys and hiberfil.sys.

> **Exam Alert**
>
> To view files such as bootmgr, pagefile.sys, and hiberfil.sys, deselect the Hide Protected Operating System Files check box.

Administrative Shares

Folders and files need to be shared so that other users on the local computer and on the network can gain access to them. Windows operating systems use an Access Control Model for securable objects like folders. This model takes care of rights and permissions, usually through discretionary access control lists (DACL) that contain individual access control entries (ACEs). All the shared folders can be found by navigating to Computer Management > System Tools > Shared Folders > Shares as shown in Figure 16.2. You can see that I have shared a folder named Data.

Here we also see the hidden *administrative shares* that can be identified by the $ on the end of the share name. These shares cannot be seen by standard users when browsing to the computer over the network; they are meant for administrative use. Note that every volume (C: or F:, for example) has an administrative share. Although it is possible to remove these by editing the Registry, it is not recommended because it might cause other networking issues. You should be aware that only administrators should have access to these shares. Administrative shares can be created by simply adding a $ to the end of the share name when enabling the share. Administrative shares can be accessed only if the person knows the exact network path to the folder and has permissions to access it.

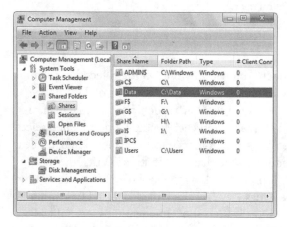

FIGURE 16.2   **Windows 7 Shares**

Permissions

Folders are shared by accessing the Sharing tab of the folder's Properties window. There are two levels of permissions: Share permissions and NTFS permissions.

▶ Share permissions can be accessed from the Sharing tab. By default the Everyone group has read-only access by default. The other two permissions available to us are Change and Full Control. Only administrators should have Full Control.

▶ NTFS permissions are accessed from the Security tab. Here we have six default levels of permissions from Read and Write to Full Control, as shown in Figure 16.3. NTFS permissions take precedence over share permissions. So for example, if a user was given Full Control access in the Share permissions and only Read in the NTFS permissions, the user would ultimately have only the Read permission.

ExamAlert

NTFS permissions are modified in the Security tab of the folder's Properties window.

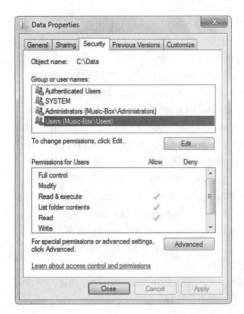

FIGURE 16.3   Security tab of a folder's Properties window

The weakest of the NTFS permissions is Read, and the strongest, of course, is Full Control. Administrators have Full Control by default. However, typical users have only Read, List Folder Contents, and Read & Execute by default. You also note that we have the option to Allow access or Deny access and that this can be done by the user or by their user group, thus the term user-level security. Generally, if you want users to have access to the folder, you would add them to the list and select Allow for the appropriate permission. If you don't want to allow them access, normally you simply wouldn't add them. But in some cases, an explicit Deny is necessary. This could be because the user is part of a larger group that already has access to a parent folder, but you don't want the specific user to have access to this particular subfolder.

Of course, permissions can get very in depth; for more information on NTFS file and folder permissions, see the following link:

http://technet.microsoft.com/en-us/library/bb727008.aspx

Permission Inheritance and Propagation

If you create a folder, the default action it takes is to inherit permissions from the parent folder. So any permissions that you set in the parent will be inherited by the subfolder. To view an example of this, locate any folder within an NTFS volume (besides the root folder), right-click it and select Properties, access the Security tab, and click the Advanced button; then click the Change

Permissions button (in Windows 7). Here you see an enabled check box named Include Inheritable Permissions from the Object's Parent toward the bottom of the window, as shown in Figure 16.4. (Names will be slightly different in other versions of Windows.) What this means is that any permissions added or removed in the parent folder will also be added or removed in the current folder. In addition, those permissions that are inherited cannot be modified in the current folder. To make modifications in this case, deselect the check box. When you do so, you have the option to copy the permissions from the parent to the current folder or remove them entirely. So by default, the parent is automatically propagating permissions to the subfolder, and the subfolder is inheriting its permissions from the parent. You can also propagate permission changes to subfolders that are not inheriting from the current folder. To do so, select the Replace All Child Object Permissions with Inheritable Permissions from this Object check box. (Again names will vary depending on the version of Windows.) This might all seem a bit confusing, and you will probably not be asked many questions on the subject. Just remember that folders automatically inherit from the parent unless you turn inheriting off—and you can propagate permission entries to subfolders at any time by selecting the Replace option.

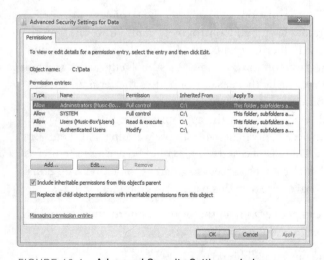

FIGURE 16.4 Advanced Security Settings window

Moving and Copying Folders and Files

This subject (and the previous one) is actually an advanced Microsoft Windows concept, so we'll try to keep this simple. Moving and copying folders have different results when it comes to permissions. Basically, it breaks down like this:

▶ If you *copy* a folder on the same or to a different volume, the folder inherits the permissions of the parent folder it was copied to (target directory).

▶ If you *move* a folder to a different location on the same volume, the folder retains its original permissions.

> **Note**
>
> Keep in mind that when you move data, the data isn't actually relocated; instead the pointer to the file or folder is modified.

Encryption

Encryption is the process of converting information, with the use of a cipher (algorithm), making it unreadable by other users unless they have the correct "key" to the information. Cryptography is the practice of hiding information. In a cryptosystem, information is protected by disguising it.

Encrypting File System (EFS)

There are a few different encryption technologies used in Windows. For example, whenever you log on to a Windows network, that authentication is secured with the Kerberos protocol. Another example is when you want to encrypt one or more files or folders. In this case Windows uses the Encrypting File System (EFS), a component of NTFS. Follow these steps to encrypt a file in Windows:

1. Locate the file, right-click it, and select Properties. This brings up the General tab within the file's Properties window.

2. At the bottom of the General tab, click the Advanced button. This brings up the Advanced Attributes window.

3. Check the box labeled Encrypt Contents to Secure Data.

4. Click OK for both windows. (When you do so, the system should ask whether you want to encrypt the parent folder and the file or just the file. It's recommended that the file's parent folder be encrypted as well.)

The file should now appear green within Windows Explorer. To unencrypt the file and return it to normal, simply deselect the check box.

> **Note**
>
> By the way, green is not the only filename color you might see. Black is the standard file color, blue indicates a compressed file, and red files can be accessed only by Windows.

If a file needs to be decrypted and the original user (owner of the key or certificate) isn't available, an EFS recovery agent will need to be used. In many cases, the default recovery agent is the built-in Administrator account. It is important to note a couple more items: One is that EFS isn't designed to protect data while it is transferred from one computer to another; the other is that it is not designed to encrypt an entire disk.

> **Note**
>
> File-sharing connections are also encrypted in Windows 7. You can modify this setting within the Network and Sharing Center > Advanced Sharing Settings, or in HomeGroup > Advanced Sharing Settings. 128-bit encryption is the recommended default.

BitLocker Encryption

To encrypt an entire disk, you need some kind of full disk encryption software. There are several currently available on the market; one developed by Microsoft is called BitLocker—available only on 7/Vista Ultimate and 7/Vista Enterprise. This software can encrypt the entire disk which, after complete, is transparent to the user. However, there are some requirements for this including

- ▶ A Trusted Platform Module (TPM): A chip residing on the motherboard that actually stores the encrypted keys.

or

- ▶ An external USB key to store the encrypted keys.

and

- ▶ A hard drive with two volumes, preferably created during the installation of Windows. One volume is for the operating system (most likely C:) that will be encrypted; the other is the active volume that remains unencrypted so that the computer can boot. If a second volume needs to be created, the BitLocker Drive Preparation Tool can be of assistance and can be downloaded from Windows Update.

ExamAlert

Know the components necessary for BitLocker.

BitLocker software is based on the Advanced Encryption Standard (AES) and uses a 128-bit key. Keep in mind that a drive encrypted with BitLocker usually suffers in performance compared to a nonencrypted drive and could have a lesser shelf life as well.

By default, BitLocker is used to encrypt the internal drive of a system. However, you can also encrypt USB drives and other removable devices by using BitLocker To Go. To read the content on other Windows XP and Vista computers, use the BitLocker To Go Reader:

http://www.microsoft.com/download/en/details.aspx?id=24303

Windows Firewall

The Windows Firewall is meant to protect client computers from malicious attacks and intrusions, but sometimes it can be the culprit when it comes to certain applications failing. You can access the firewall in Windows 7 by going to Start > Control Panel > Windows Firewall. When you turn on the firewall, the default setting is to shield all inbound ports (effectively closing them). This means that certain applications that need to communicate with a remote host might not work properly. Or if the client computer wanted to host some services such as FTP or a web server, the firewall would block them. That's where exceptions come in. You can still use the firewall, but you can specify applications that are exceptions to the rule. Figure 16.5 shows an example of exceptions. To create exceptions, click the Allow a Program or Feature Through Windows Firewall link.

Note

Older versions of Windows store the firewall settings within the Properties sheet of the network adapter.

In this example, we have two applications that are not blocked from incoming connections. Remote Assistance is not blocked at all, on the LAN or on the Internet. However, Remote Desktop is allowed only on the LAN (listed as Home/Work Private Network). So, as long as the firewall is enabled, this computer can make remote assistance calls to other users on the Internet. But, if a person wanted to connect to this system through Remote Desktop without an invitation, that person would have to be on the LAN. This way, we aren't sacrificing the entire security of the system. All other incoming connections will be blocked.

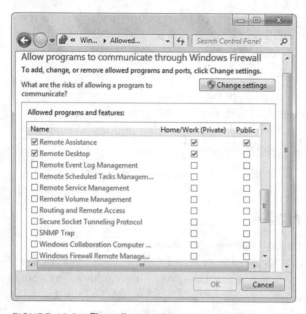

FIGURE 16.5   **Firewall exceptions**

We can get more in depth with the firewall settings. By clicking the Advanced Settings link, we can make use of the Windows Firewall with Advanced Security (also available in Administrative Tools and as a snap-in in the MMC).

If for some reason the firewall gives you errors when attempting to either update the firewall settings, add exceptions, or access the advanced settings, then make sure the Windows Firewall service is enabled and running.

Cram Quiz

Answer these questions. The answers follow the last question. If you cannot answer these questions correctly, consider reading this section again until you can.

220-802 Questions

1. Which of the following is the strongest password?

   ○ **A.** |ocrian#

   ○ **B.** Marqu1sD3S0d

   ○ **C.** This1sV#ryS3cure

   ○ **D.** Thisisverysecure

2. Which of these is a security component of Windows 7/Vista?

   ○ **A.** UAC

   ○ **B.** UPS

   ○ **C.** Gadgets

   ○ **D.** Control Panel

3. A customer complains that while away at lunch someone used his computer to send e-mails to other co-workers without his knowledge. What should you recommend?

   ○ **A.** Enable a screensaver.

   ○ **B.** Unplug the network cable before leaving for lunch.

   ○ **C.** Use the Windows lock feature.

   ○ **D.** Enable the out-of-office message in e-mail when leaving for lunch.

4. Which of the following best describes encryption?

   ○ **A.** Prevents unauthorized users from viewing or reading data

   ○ **B.** Prevents unauthorized users from deleting data

   ○ **C.** Prevents unauthorized users from posing as the original source sending data

   ○ **D.** Prevents unauthorized users from decompressing files

5. One of the users on your network is trying to access files shared on a remote computer. The file's share permissions allow the user full control. But, the NTFS permissions allow the user Read access. What will be the resulting access for the user?

   ○ **A.** Full Control

   ○ **B.** Modify

   ○ **C.** Read

   ○ **D.** Write

6. You are the administrator for your network. You set up an administrative share called Data$. What is necessary for another user to access this share? (Select the two best answers.)

   ○ **A.** The user must be part of a HomeGroup.

   ○ **B.** The user must have permissions to access the share.

   ○ **C.** The user must know the decryption key.

   ○ **D.** The user must know the exact network path to the share.

   ○ **E.** The user must enable File Sharing in the Network and Sharing Center.

Cram Quiz Answers

220-802 Answers

1. **C.** Answer C incorporates case-sensitive letters, numbers, and special characters and is 16-characters long.

2. **A.** User Account Control (UAC) adds a layer of security to Windows 7/Vista to protect against malware and user error, and conserve resources.

3. **C.** Tell the customer to lock the computer (Windows+L or from the Start menu) before leaving for lunch. As long as there is a strong password, other co-workers should not be able to access the system. Screensavers by themselves do not secure the system, but a person can enable the password-protected screensaver feature, however there is a delay before the screen saver turns on. Unplugging the network cable is not a legitimate answer, plus it can always be plugged back in. The out-of-office message will reply only to people e-mailing the user, it won't stop outgoing e-mails.

4. **A.** Encryption Prevents unauthorized users from viewing or reading data. Properly configured permissions prevents unauthorized users from deleting data or attempting to decompress files. A strong logon password will prevent unauthorized users from posing as the original source sending data.

5. **C.** The user will get only Read access. Remember that NTFS-level permissions take precedence over Share-level permissions.

6. **B** and **D.** The user needs to have permissions to the share, and must know the exact path to the network share because it is an administrative share. HomeGroup does not play into this scenario. Also, the question does not mention if the file is encrypted. The user doesn't need to enable sharing, the person is trying to *access* a share.

SOHO Security

In the previous chapter we discussed the set up of a small office/home office (SOHO) network. But without securing the network, we may as well just call up a hacker and ask them to invade the network. The core of the SOHO network is the multifunction network device. This device acts as a switch, router, firewall, and wireless access point. For the rest of this section we'll talk about how to secure this device, and refer to it simply as a router.

> **Note**
>
> As mentioned in the previous chapter you can access an emulator for the D-Link Dir-655 router at: http://support.dlink.com/emulators/dir655/. It's good to run through these configurations on your own router or an emulator of some sort.

Changing Default Passwords

The first thing we should do to secure the router is to change the password. Most routers come with a blank password. Connect to the router by opening up your favorite browser (your favorite should be the most secure one) and typing the IP address of the router, for example 192.168.0.1. That is the default IP address for D-Link routers. The log in username is admin, and the password is usually blank by default. Some routers allow you to change the username; if so, do it, just like you would for a Windows computer. But no matter what the router, you will definitely be able to change the password, and you should. Make it something complex based on the rules we discussed in the Windows Security section. Save the settings (which will log you out) and then log in with the new password to make sure it took effect.

> **ExamAlert**
>
> Remember to change the admin password first before anything else!

Some routers also have a user password. Change this as well but to a different password than the admin password.

Changing and Disabling the SSID

The Service Set Identifier (SSID) is used to name a wireless network. Default SSIDs are usually basic; for example, the D-Link SSID is usually just dlink. It is wise to change the name of the wireless network before enabling wireless on the router. Names that include uppercase and lowercase letters, and numbers will be less memorable to casual wireless passersby.

After all wireless clients are connected to the network, consider disabling the SSID. Though it is not a perfect solution, it will mask part of the SSID broadcast, making it impossible to see with normal wireless locating software. Take a look at Figure 16.6, you will see a new SSID name Saturn6Network, and that it is set to Invisible.

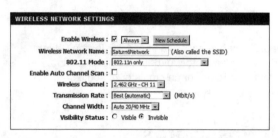

FIGURE 16.6   Renamed and Disabled SSID

When the SSID is disabled, wireless clients won't be able to scan for it. If you need to connect additional wireless clients, you will either have to enable the SSID broadcast or enter the wireless SSID manually when connecting. To connect manually, open the Network and Sharing Center and select the Connect to a network link. Then select Manually connect to a wireless network. (The wireless adapter must be installed with correct drivers to see this link.) You will have to type in the SSID, type of wireless, and security key to get in the network.

Configuring Wireless Encryption

Windows supports wireless networking protocols such as WPA2, and encryption methods such as AES to provide data confidentiality. Figure 16.7 displays a common secure wireless encryption technique on a D-Link router. Table 16.3 shows the characteristics of the various wireless protocols and encryption methods.

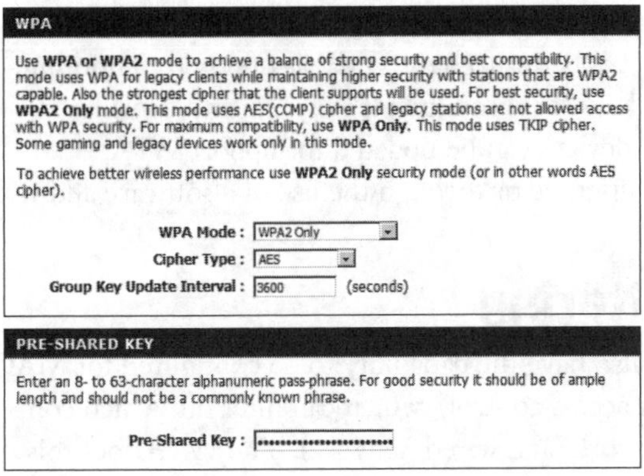

FIGURE 16.7   Wireless Network Settings on a Common Router

TABLE 16.3 **Wireless Encryption Methods**

Wireless Protocol	Description	Encryption Level
WEP	Wired Equivalent Privacy (Deprecated)	64-bit
WPA	Wi-Fi Protected Access	128-bit
WPA2	Version 2	256-bit
TKIP	Temporal Key Integrity Protocol Deprecated encryption protocol used with WEP or WPA	128-bit
CCMP	Counter Mode with Cipher Block Chaining Message Authentication Code Protocol Encryption protocol used with WPA2 Addresses the vulnerabilities of TKIP.	128-bit
AES	Advanced Encryption Standard Encryption protocol used with WPA/WPA2 Strongest encryption method in this table	128, 192, and 256-bit

In Figure 16.7 you can see the router is using WPA2 only and AES as the encryption protocol. It also has a 16-character key for accessing the wireless network. Aside from using external servers for authentication, this is the best method on this router, and similar routers as well. This is the best line of defense against war drivers—attackers who attempt to gain access to unprotected wireless networks. They drive around and use a laptop looking for wireless networks in range.

WEP is the weakest type of encryption; WPA is stronger, and WPA2 is the strongest of the three. However, it is better to have WEP as opposed to nothing. If this is the case, use encryption keys that are difficult to guess, and consider changing those keys often. Some devices can be updated to support WPA, whether it is through a firmware upgrade or through the use of a software add-on.

Enabling MAC Filtering

The wireless access point might also have the capability to be configured for MAC filtering (a basic form of network access control), which can filter out which computers can access the wireless network (and wired network). The WAP does this by consulting a list of MAC addresses that have been previously entered. Only the network adapters with those corresponding MAC addresses can connect; everyone else cannot join the wireless network. In some cases, a device might broadcast this MAC table. If this is the case, look for an update for the firmware of the access point, and attempt to fine-tune the broadcast range of the device so that it does not leak out to other organizations. Because MAC filtering and a disabled SSID can be easily circumvented using a network sniffer, it is important to also use strong encryption and possibly consider other types of network access control (such as 802.1X) and external authentication methods (such as RADIUS).

Disabling WPS

Wi-Fi Protected Setup was originally intended to make connecting to a wireless access point easier for the average user. However, anything that is made more simple is often less secure as well. Case in point, WPS is vulnerable to brute-force attacks, which can lead to intrusions on the network. Brute-force attacks are used to guess passwords and codes by trying combinations of letters, numbers, and symbols. The WPS code is usually 8 to 10 digits long, not quite that difficult to crack. So, your best bet is to disable WPS on the router to help secure the network. Figure 16.8 shows WPS as disabled. You can also see the basic 8-digit PIN code that is used.

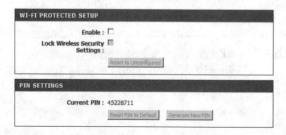

FIGURE 16.8 Disabled Wi-Fi Protected Setup on a common router

Assigning Static IP Addresses

A SOHO router can be set to limit the amount of dynamic addresses it hands out. If there are not enough to go around, you might find that certain hosts such as servers or printers lose connectivity when there are more client computers on the network. First, consider increasing the scope of addresses that the router is configured to hand out to clients. Second, try assigning static IP addresses to the servers and printers; essentially any hosts that share information or services. If more clients obtaining dynamic addresses are added in the future, the servers and printers will not be affected.

Disabling Physical Ports

Many routers come with the capability to disable the physical ports on the switch portion of the device. This is a wise precaution. If you disable unused physical ports, a rogue computer can be plugged into the router physically but won't have any hopes of accessing the network. This concept is a policy in most organizations. Unused router or switch ports are disabled so that a person can't connect a laptop to any old RJ45 jack on the premises.

> **ExamAlert**
>
> Know the various ways to secure a SOHO router.

Final Word on SOHO Routers

To round out this section, make sure that the router's firmware is up to date. Also, always make sure the built-in firewall is enabled. This firewall is going to be much more important than the Windows firewalls on the individual computers, though both are recommended. Most routers' firewalls are on by default, but you should always check. If you do any kind of port forwarding, port triggering, DMZ configurations, or remote connections of any kind, make sure the firewall is allowing traffic only through the specific port or ports you require and that everything else is blocked. Check for updates every month or so, and while you are at it, change the administrator password for good measure.

Cram Quiz

Answer these questions. The answers follow the last question. If you cannot answer these questions correctly, consider reading this section again until you can.

220-802 Questions

1. Which of the following describes an attempt to guess a password by using a combination of letters and numbers?

   ○ **A.** Brute force

   ○ **B.** Social Engineering

   ○ **C.** WPS

   ○ **D.** War driving

2. Which of the following will help to secure a SOHO router? (Select the three best answers.)

   ○ **A.** Change default passwords.

   ○ **B.** Enable SSID.

   ○ **C.** Enable MAC filtering.

   ○ **D.** Enable WPS.

   ○ **E.** Enable WPA2.

3. Which is the strongest form of wireless encryption?

   ○ **A.** WPA

   ○ **B.** WEP

   ○ **C.** AES

   ○ **D.** TKIP

4. You want to prevent rogue employees from connecting a laptop to the SOHO router and accessing the network. How can you accomplish this? (Select the two best answers.)

   ○ **A.** Enable MAC filtering.

   ○ **B.** Create a DMZ.

   ○ **C.** Configure a complex SSID.

   ○ **D.** Disable physical ports.

Cram Quiz Answers

220-802 Answers

1. **A.** Brute force attacks use a combination of letters, numbers, and symbols to guess passwords, PINs, and passcodes. Social engineering is the attempt to manipulate people into giving confidential information. WPS stands for Wi-Fi Protected Setup; this uses a code that attackers might try to crack with a brute force attack. War driving is the act of attempting to intrude on wireless networks with a laptop from within a vehicle.

2. **A, C**, and **E.** Changing default passwords, enabling MAC filtering, and enabling WPA2 can all increase the security of a SOHO router. However, enabling the SSID makes it visible. And enabling WPS makes it easier to connect to but has security implications.

3. **C.** Advanced Encryption Standard (AES) is the strongest form of wireless encryption (given the listed answers.) WPA is a wireless encryption protocol that is not bad, but WPA2 is recommended. WEP and TKIP are deprecated, have been compromised, and should be avoided.

4. **A** and **D.** By enabling MAC filtering, you can create a list of MAC addresses that the SOHO router will accept. Any other computers with different MAC addresses will not be allowed access to the network. This works for wired and wireless connections. You can also disable physical ports on the router; this blocks any physical signal from being sent to those unused ports. A DMZ is used to host servers and acts as a separate area between the LAN and the Internet. A complex SSID is great but won't matter to a person connecting a laptop physically to the router because the SSID affects only wireless access.

CHAPTER 17

Mobile Devices

This chapter covers the following A+ exam topics:

▶ Mobile Hardware and Operating Systems

▶ Mobile Networking and Synchronization

▶ Mobile Security

You can find a master list of A+ exam topics in the "Introduction."

This chapter covers CompTIA A+ 220-802 objectives 3.1 through 3.5.

Mobile devices have simply exploded on to the mainstream scene. Especially since 2010, the amount of mobile devices in use has been growing exponentially. Now, it seems that everywhere you look there is someone tapping away on a tablet computer, smartphone, or other mobile device. As of 2012, half a million Android and Apple devices are activated daily—and that number is increasing! Because of this CompTIA has added an entire mobile devices section to the A+ 220-802 exam. As an A+ technician you need to know the basic hardware of these devices, the differences between the two main mobile operating systems, how to network and synchronize the devices, and how to secure them.

In this chapter we'll pay the most attention to Apple devices and Android-based devices, but we'll also briefly discuss some of the other players in the market. For this edition of the book I will refer to an Apple iPad2 tablet computer and an Android HTC Evo smartphone. I do this so that you can see some important configurations on the two most-used platforms in the mobile device market. So enough talk...let's get mobile!

Mobile Hardware and Operating Systems

Mobile devices are computers, smaller and lighter than desktops and laptops, but computers nonetheless. There are similarities and differences in hardware between the two. You will find there are new players on the software side, and these too have similarities and differences compared to PCs and laptops. But remember that at their core, mobile devices are still computers, and many of the principles and rules that you have learned earlier in this book regarding hardware and software still apply.

Mobile Hardware Examples

A common device as of the writing of this book is the Apple iPad2. It is known as a tablet computer and is manufactured by Foxconn, who also constructs the iPhone, Kindle, Playstation 3, and Xbox 360. Table 17.1 gives a list of the hardware the iPad2 uses.

TABLE 17.1 **Apple iPad2 Hardware**

Hardware Component	Description
1 GHz ARM CPU	▶ 32-bit Advanced RISC Machine Processor ▶ Designed for simplicity and low-power
512 MB DDR2 RAM	▶ Similar DDR standard to what PCs use ▶ Smaller form factor
16 GB Flash Memory	▶ Similar to solid-state flash memory in a USB flash drive ▶ Used for permanent storage instead of an SATA or IDE hard drive
Multitouch touchscreen	▶ Capacitive touchscreen that responds to fingers and stylus devices
Lithium-ion polymer battery	▶ Similar to lithium-ion batteries in laptops ▶ Can be made into any shape ▶ Lasts for 10 hours on a full charge

Exam Alert

Memorize the basic types of hardware used by a tablet computer.

As you can see from the table, the basic components of CPU, RAM, and so on are the same as desktop/laptop computers. But the *types* of components are different. The whole concept of this hardware configuration is based on portability and ease of use. Therefore, tablet computers will be less powerful than desktop computers and laptops; but, the hardware is matched to the type of applications the device will be used for.

Similar tablets (but with different software) include the Motorola Xoom, Samsung Galaxy, and Asus Transformer. These will often be less proprietary than an Apple device; for example, they might use Micro-USB ports for charging and synchronization of data, whereas the Apple iPad2 has a proprietary charging port. You might also see different names for the touch interface of a device. For example, the company HTC developed a user interface called TouchFLO for its smartphones that enabled the user to drag the screen up, left, or right. This has been replaced by HTC Sense, which is a multitouch-enabled touch screen similar to the Apple multitouch technology. As of 2012, most new smartphones and tablets feature multitouch touch screens.

Hardware Differences Between Tablets and Laptops

One of the big distinctions between tablets and laptops is the lack of field serviceable parts. Another difference is that tablets and other similar devices are usually not upgradeable. Some mobile devices, such as smartphones, can have upgraded memory cards and/or batteries, but that's about it, and these are usually not serviceable in the field because it is difficult to protect yourself from ESD when working on these devices. (But that doesn't mean it isn't done.) Many organizations recommend you bring the device back to the lab for upgrades or parts swaps. Other devices such as the iPad2 are not user-serviceable whatsoever; and any attempt at doing so voids the warranty. If repair, upgrade, or replacement is necessary, most organizations utilize the warranties built in to these products, instead of trying to do the work in-house.

ExamAlert

Know the basic differences between tablets and laptops.

A laptop is actually just a smaller, portable version of a desktop computer. Like the desktop computer, it contains a similar processor, similar DDR RAM, and a hard drive that could possibly be solid-state, but regardless will most likely be plugged into an SATA port. It also has a keyboard, and a touchpad similar to a mouse. All this hardware is designed to make the best use of operating systems that you would normally find on a desktop computer. Tablets on the other hand use ARM-based processors and use nonvolatile flash memory hard-wired to the system instead of a magnetic or solid-state hard drive. So, as you can imagine, the tablet has a loss of performance when compared to a laptop. In addition, the tablet utilizes an on-screen keyboard and doesn't require any type of mouse due to the touchscreen capability. All this hardware is designed to run mobile device software such as Android or iOS.

Mobile Operating Systems

Currently, mobile device software comes in one of two forms: open-source, which is effectively free to download and modify; and closed-source, otherwise known as *vendor-specific*, which cannot be modified without express permission and licensing. There are benefits and drawbacks to each type of system. Because you will see both in the field, you should know each one equally. Let's go over these two systems.

Open-Source: Android

Android is an example of open source software. It is a Linux-based operating system used mostly on smartphones and tablet computers and is developed by the Open Handset Alliance, a group directed by Google. Google releases the Android OS code as open-source, allowing developers to modify it, and freely create applications for it. Google also commissioned the Android Open-Source Project (AOSP); its mission is to maintain and further develop Android. You'll know when you are dealing with the Android open-source OS and related applications when you see the little robot caricature, usually in green.

Android OS versions are dubbed with names such as Cupcake, Gingerbread, and the two latest: Honeycomb (version 3) and Ice Cream Sandwich (version 4). To find out the version you are currently running, start at the Home screen; this is the main screen that boots up by default. Then tap the Menu button, and then tap Settings. (Settings is used often in this chapter as a starting point, so remember how to get there!) Scroll to the bottom and tap the About Phone (or just About) option. Then tap Software Information or similar option. This displays the version of Android. Figure 17.1 shows a smartphone using Android version 2.3.3 (Gingerbread)

Say a company wanted to create a custom version of the Android OS for a handheld computer that it was developing. According to the license, the company would be allowed to do this and customize the OS to its specific hardware. Some companies opt to use Android for this purpose, whereas others use Windows CE or Windows Mobile (for a fee), both designed for handheld computers.

FIGURE 17.1   Typical smartphone using Android version 2.3.3

Closed-Source: iOS

Apple's iOS is an example of closed-source software. It is found on iPhones and iPads as well. It is based off Mac OS X (used on Mac desktops and laptops) and is Unix-based.

To find out the version of iOS you are running go to the Home screen, and then tap Settings. Tap General and then tap About. You see the Version number. For example, Figure 17.2 shows an iPad2 running Version 5.0 (9A334). 9A334 is the build number; this was the public release of version 5.0.

Unlike Android, iOS is not open-source, and is not available for download to developers. Only Apple hardware uses this operating system. This is an example of vendor-specific software. However, if a developer wants to create an application for iOS, they can download the iOS software development kit (SDK). Apple license fees are required when a developer is ready to go live with the application.

> ExamAlert
>
> Understand the difference between open-source and closed-source.

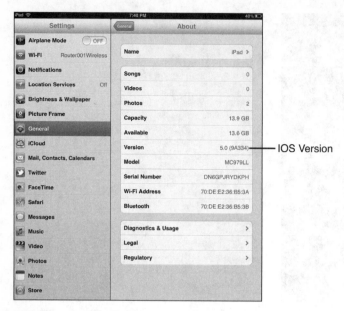

FIGURE 17.2   iPad2 using version 5.0 of iOS

Obtaining Applications

Mobile devices are nothing without applications. To this end, both Android and iOS have application sources where you can download free and paid applications (also known as *apps*).

Android users download applications from the Android Market (also accessible through Google Play.) This can be done directly from the mobile device. Or if a mobile device is connected via USB to a computer, the user can browse apps on the Google Play website while working on the computer and download directly from the site to the phone, passing through the computer.

iOS users download applications from the App Store. This was originally an update to the iTunes store, but on newer iOS mobile devices, it is now a separate icon on the Home screen. Apps can also be downloaded from a Mac or from a PC through the iTunes application.

ExamAlert

Know where to obtain applications for Apple and Android devices.

Regardless of the OS, users would search for the name of the application they want, download it, start the installation process, agree to a license, and then finally make use of the app.

Some applications don't work unless a person was to hack the OS and gain "superuser" privileges. In the Android world this is known as *rooting* the phone or other mobile device. In the iOS world it is *jailbreaking*. Note that performing either of these could be a breach of the user license agreement. It can also be dangerous. These types of hacks often require a person to wipe out the device completely, and install a special application that may or may not be trustworthy. Many phones are rendered useless or are compromised when attempting this procedure. Applications that have anything to do with rooting or jailbreaking should generally be avoided.

Screen Configurations

Mobile device displays rotate by default if the user turns the device, allowing the screen to be viewed vertically or horizontally. This aids when looking at pictures, movies, or viewing websites. But in some cases, a user might want to lock the rotation of the device so that it stays as either vertical or horizontal, without moving. On an Android device this can be done by accessing Settings, then tapping Display, and then deselecting Auto-rotate screen. On an iOS device (version 4 or 5) this can be done by double-tapping the Home button (which brings up the multitasking bar on the bottom) and then swiping the bar all the way to the right. Finally, a circular arrow is shown to the far left; tap this, and rotation will be locked. Some iPads (such as the iPad2) also have a side switch that can be configured to enable/disable rotation lock; this feature can be turned on in Settings > General > Use side switch to: Lock Rotation.

Screen orientation is a simple concept to understand and use. But it can be more complicated when it comes to applications. For example, Apple mobile devices make use of the *Accelerometer*: a combination of hardware and software that measure velocity; they detect rotation, shaking of the device and so on. It's the accelerometer that enables a mobile device to automatically adjust from portrait (vertical) to landscape (horizontal) mode using the three axes: the X-axis (left to right), the Y-axis (up and down), and the Z-axis (back to front). These are manipulated by developers for applications and games so that the program can recognize particular movements of the device and translate them to specific application functions. Newer Apple devices include a *gyroscope*, which adds the measurements of pitch, roll, and yaw, just like in the concept of flight dynamics. You won't need a pilot's license to use an iPad, but this additional measurement of movement has a great impact on the development of newer applications and especially games. Of course, if the accelerometers or gyroscope of the mobile device fail and a reset of the device doesn't fix the problem, it must be repaired at an authorized service center.

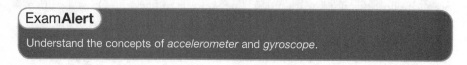

ExamAlert

Understand the concepts of *accelerometer* and *gyroscope*.

Android devices have a screen calibration utility called G-Sensor calibration. It is found in Settings > Display. To make sure that the three axes are calibrated properly, this program is run while the mobile device is laid on a flat surface. You can tell if the surface is level by the horizontal and vertical leveling bubbles on the display. Then press the Calibrate button to reset the G-sensor, as shown in Figure 17.3.

FIGURE 17.3   **G-Sensor calibration on a typical smartphone**

Other mobile devices' calibration programs show a crosshair or similar image in the center of the screen. You need to tap with a stylus as close to the center of the display as possible. If a stylus is not available, use the pointed end of a pen cap.

ExamAlert

Know how to calibrate the screen of an Android device.

A reset can also fix problems with calibration (as well as other types of problems). There are two types of resets: soft and hard. A soft reset is usually performed simply by powering the device off and then powering it back on again. This can fix temporary problems quickly and easily. It is similar to rebooting a PC. However, more advanced problems require a hard reset. Warning! A hard reset may remove all data and applications and return the device to its original factory state. Do not perform a hard reset without backing up the contents of the memory card in the mobile device, and any additional settings you require. You can find more information on resets in the section titled "Mobile Security."

Today's Apple devices do not offer a calibration utility. Sometimes, issues that appear to be calibration problems are actually something else with an easy fix. For example, cheaper screen protectors can bubble and otherwise cause problems when tapping on the screen. Removing the protector and installing a new one properly can fix this problem. When installing a screen protector, use a long, flat surface to squeeze all the bubbles out; there are shims that can be purchased for just this purpose. Use a decent screen protector such as Ghost Armor or something similar. Good quality screen protectors will not only protect the display, but they will also reduce glare, smudging, and fingerprints, without reducing sensitivity. Dirty screens can also be a culprit when a user is having difficulty tapping on icons or smaller items. Clean the display with a lint-free cloth. If the screen is very dirty, mix 50% isopropyl alcohol and 50% water, apply conservatively to the cloth, and then clean the display with the cloth. Make sure all traces of liquid are removed when you are done. If none of these steps work, the device needs to be brought in to an authorized service center for repair.

GPS and Geotracking

The Global Positioning System (GPS), developed by the U.S. DoD is a worldwide system of satellites that provide location information for anything with a GPS receiver. Any mobile device with a GPS receiver can use this system to identify its location and utilize mapping programs and any other applications that rely on GPS. Some mobile devices do not have a GPS receiver, and instead use cell tower triangulation, or Location Services that uses crowd-sourced Wi-Fi locations to determine the approximate location of the device.

To enable/disable GPS on an Android-based device go to Settings > Location, and select Use GPS satellites. To enable/disable GPS on an Apple device such as an iPad, go to Settings > Location Services.

> **Exam Alert**
>
> Memorize how to enable GPS for Android and Apple devices.

Geotracking is the practice of tracking and recording the location of a mobile device over time. This location tracking is done by Apple and Google as well as other organizations and governments. Privacy issues aside, this practice *is* being done, so if a user doesn't want their location known, simply disable the GPS setting.

> **Exam Alert**
>
> Understand the definition of geotracking for the exam.

Cram Quiz

Answer these questions. The answers follow the last question. If you cannot answer these questions correctly, consider reading this section again until you can.

220-802 Questions

1. A user is having difficulty tapping on icons. What should you do to help the user? (Select the two best answers.)

   ○ **A.** Clean the display.

   ○ **B.** Tap the Home button.

   ○ **C.** Install a screen protector.

   ○ **D.** Initiate a soft reset.

   ○ **E.** Initiate a hard reset.

2. Which of the following can aid a mobile user in finding the nearest coffee shop? (Select the best answer.)

   ○ **A.** Geotracking

   ○ **B.** iOS

   ○ **C.** GPS

   ○ **D.** GSM

3. A user wants to stop his tablet from shifting horizontally when he turns it. Which of the following should you enable?

   ○ **A.** Lock Rotation

   ○ **B.** Accelerometer

   ○ **C.** Gyroscope

   ○ **D.** Screen Calibration

4. What kind of display would an iPad2 use?

   ○ **A.** CRT

   ○ **B.** Multitouch

   ○ **C.** Tap screen

   ○ **D.** Singletouch

5. What are two common operating systems used by mobile devices? (Select the two best answers.)

   ○ **A.** Blueberry OS

   ○ **B.** iOS

   ○ **C.** Google OS

   ○ **D.** Android OS

6. What type of CPU do mobile devices use?

   ○ **A.** Core i7

   ○ **B.** Phenom II

   ○ **C.** ARM

   ○ **D.** Pentium

7. Which OS is considered to be closed-source?

   ○ **A.** Android OS

   ○ **B.** Bluetooth

   ○ **C.** Linux

   ○ **D.** iOS

8. What are a couple of differences between a tablet computer and a laptop? (Select the two best answers.)

   ○ **A.** Tablets have little or no field serviceable parts.

   ○ **B.** Tablets are upgradeable.

   ○ **C.** Laptops don't use touch screens.

   ○ **D.** Tablets use flash memory as the hard drive.

   ○ **E.** Tablets use RAM.

Cram Quiz Answers

220-802 Answers

1. **A and D.** A dirty display can cause issues when trying to manipulate a multi-touch screen. By cleaning it, the user might find that is it easier to use. A soft reset (turning the device off and on) can sometimes fix the problem as well. Tapping the Home button simply brings the person to the Home screen. Screen protectors are a good idea, but if installed incorrectly, they could actually be the reason that a user has issues tapping icons. After the screen is cleaned, a decent quality screen protector should be installed. Hard resets often initiate a complete wipe of the system. Use this only as a last resort.

2. **C.** GPS is used to locate the mobile user. From that information, one of several programs can locate that all-important nearest coffee shop. Geotracking is the practice of tracking and recording the location of a mobile device. However, geo-tracking is done by organizations, whereas GPS is something installed to the mobile device. iOS is the operating system used by Apple mobile devices. GSM is a cellular standard.

3. **A.** Enable Lock Rotation on Apple devices. On Android devices disable Auto-rotate. The Accelerometer is a term used by Apple to describe the hardware/software that controls the three axes of movement. The Gyroscope is another term used by Apple to describe the device that measures the additional three movements (pitch, roll, and yaw) of newer Apple devices. Screen calibration is used to reset the device that measures the three axes.

4. **B.** iPad2 devices use multitouch screens, which allow more than one contact point. Cathode ray tube (CRT) is an older technology monitor used by desktop computers. You would "tap" the screen, but it is known as a touchscreen. Singletouch screens are an older technology; you won't see much of that in the field.

5. **B and D.** Two common operating systems used by mobile devices are iOS and Android OS. *Black*berry OS is the OS used on Blackberry devices. Android is effectively controlled by Google. There is a Google Chrome OS designed to work with web applications that is also open-source.

6. **C.** Most commonly, mobile devices use ARM (Advanced RISC Machine) CPUs. Core i7, Phenom II and the older Pentium are used by desktop and laptop computers.

7. **D.** The Apple iOS is a closed-source vendor specific operating system. Android is a type of Linux that is open-source. Bluetooth is a wireless standard, not an operating system.

8. **A and D.** Unlike laptops, tablets are not field-serviceable. They use flash memory instead of an SATA hard drive. Tablets are for the most part not upgradeable. Some laptops do come with touchscreens. Both tablets and laptops use RAM.

Mobile Networking and Synchronization

Now that we've discussed mobile hardware and software, let's go ahead and harness their power through networking and synchronization.

From cellular GSM connections to Wi-Fi and Bluetooth, a mobile device can create connections to computers and networks, download e-mail, and work with headsets and remote printers.

Synchronization is the matching up of files, e-mail, and other types of data between one computer and another. We use synchronization to bring files in line with each other and to force devices to coordinate their data. When dealing with synchronization, a mobile device can connect to a PC via USB (the most common), RS-232 serial connections (less common), Wi-Fi, and Bluetooth.

GSM Cellular Connectivity

Cellular phones use the Global System for Mobile Communications (GSM) to make voice calls, and GSM or the general packet radio service (GPRS) to send data at 2G speeds through the cellular network. Extensions of these standards, 3GPP and EDGE are used to attain 3G speeds. 4G speeds can be attained only if a mobile device complies with the International Mobile Telecommunications Advanced (IMT-Advanced) requirements, has a 4G antenna, and is in range of a 4G transmitter, which as of the writing of this book, are only common in urban areas.

Most devices cannot shut off the cellular antenna by itself (unless shutting down the whole device.) However, every device manufactured now is required to have an "airplane mode," which turns off any wireless antenna in the device including GSM, Wi-Fi, GPS, and Bluetooth. On a typical Android device, this can be done by going to Settings > Wireless & Networks > and check marking Airplane Mode. You will find that some airlines don't consider this to be acceptable and will still ask you to turn off your device, either for the duration of the flight or at least during takeoff and landing. Android devices can also access Airplane Mode by pressing and holding the power button. To enable airplane mode on an Apple tablet you would go to Settings > Airplane Mode.

ExamAlert

Know how to configure airplane mode for Android and Apple devices.

Wi-Fi Network Connectivity

Using a cellular connection can be slow when transmitting data (unless you happen to get a 4G signal). That's why all mobile devices are equipped with an embedded wireless antenna to connect to wireless LANs. This WLAN antenna (often referred to as a Wi-Fi antenna) can allow access to 802.11a, b, g, and n networks. The wireless configuration works similar to a wireless connection on a PC or laptop. See Chapter 15, "Networking," for a detailed description of connecting to wireless networks.

In general, the mobile device must first search for wireless networks before connecting. On a typical Android smartphone, this can be done in the following steps:

1. Go to Settings > Wireless & Networks > Wi-Fi Settings.

2. From there, most devices usually scan for wireless networks automatically, or you could tap Add Wi-Fi Network to add one manually.

3. If adding a network manually, enter the SSID of the wireless access point in the Add Wi-Fi Network window, as shown in Figure 17.4.

FIGURE 17.4   Android OS Prompting for the user to enter an SSID

4. Enter the passcode for the network. If the code is correct, then the wireless adapter in the mobile device gets an IP address allowing it to communicate with the network. If a wireless network uses WPA2, and the mobile device isn't compatible, you should search for an update to the operating system to make it WPA2-compliant.

Follow these steps to access wireless networks on an iPad or similar device:

1. Go to Settings > Wi-Fi.

2. The device usually scans for networks automatically. To connect to a network manually, tap Other.

3. If adding a network manually, type the SSID of the network in the Name field.

4. Type the passcode for the network. If adding the network manually, you can select the type of security, for example WPA2, as shown in Figure 17.5.

FIGURE 17.5   iOS Prompting for the user to enter an SSID for a WPA2-secured network

ExamAlert

Understand how to configure Wi-Fi connections for Android and Apple devices.

Almost all types of devices display the universal wireless icon when connected to a wireless network, as shown in Figure 17.6. This icon not only let's you know when you are connected, but also how strong the connection is. The more curved lines you see, the better the connection.

FIGURE 17.6   Universal wireless symbol

Some mobile devices can also perform *Wi-Fi tethering*. This is when the mobile device shares its Internet connection with other Wi-Fi capable devices. For example, if one user had a smartphone that could access the Internet through 3G or GPRS networks, then it could be configured to become a portable Wi-Fi hotspot for other mobile devices that are Wi-Fi capable but have no cellular or GPRS option. Another option in Android is *USB tethering*. When an Android phone is connected to a desktop computer via USB, the desktop (Windows or MAC) can share the phone's mobile network.

A lot of devices can also be configured for *Internet pass-through* as well. This means that the phone or other device connects to a PC via USB and accesses the Internet using the PC's Internet connection.

> **Exam Alert**
>
> Know the terms Wi-Fi tethering, USB tethering, and Internet pass-through.

Wi-Fi Troubleshooting

When troubleshooting mobile device wireless connections, always make sure of the following basic wireless troubleshooting techniques:

▶ Device is within range.

▶ The correct SSID was entered (if manually connecting).

▶ The device supports the encryption protocol of the wireless network.

▶ Wi-Fi tethering or Internet pass-through is not conflicting with the wireless connection.

If you still have trouble, here are a few more methods that can help to connect, or reconnect to a wireless network:

▶ Power cycle the mobile device.

▶ Power cycle Wi-Fi.

▶ Remove or "forget" the particular wireless network and then attempt to connect to it again.

▶ Access the advanced settings and check if there is a proxy configuration, if a static IP is used, or if there is a Wi-Fi sleep policy. Any of these could possibly cause a conflict. You might also try renewing the lease of an IP address, if the device is obtaining one from a DHCP server (which it most likely will be.) Some devices also have an option for Best Wi-Fi Performance, which uses more power but might help when connecting to distant WAPs. Advanced settings can be found on an Android device by going to Settings >

Wireless and Networks > Wi-Fi Settings; then tap the Menu button and select Advanced. This is shown in Figure 17.7. On an Apple iPad advanced settings can be located at Settings > Wi-Fi; then tap on the arrow of an individual wireless network. This is shown in Figure 17.8.

FIGURE 17.7   Advanced wireless settings in Android

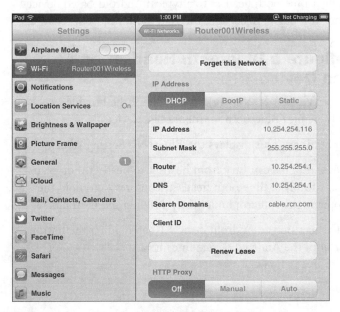

FIGURE 17.8   Advanced wireless settings in iOS

One of these methods usually works when troubleshooting a wireless connection but if all else fails; a hard reset can bring the device back to factory settings. (Always back up all data and settings before performing a hard reset.) And if the mobile device still can't connect to any of several known good wireless networks, bring the device to an authorized service center.

> **ExamAlert**
>
> Know your Wi-Fi troubleshooting techniques for the exam!

Bluetooth Configuration

Bluetooth is a wireless standard for transmitting data over short distances. It is commonly implemented in the form of a headset or printer connection by mobile users. It is also used to create wireless personal area networks (WPANs) consisting of multiple Bluetooth-enabled mobile devices.

By default, Bluetooth is usually disabled on Android devices but is enabled on devices such as iPads. To connect a Bluetooth device to a mobile device, Bluetooth first needs to be enabled. Then the Bluetooth device needs to be synchronized to the mobile device. This is known as *pairing* or *linking*. It sometimes requires a pin code. When synchronized, the device needs to be connected. Finally, the Bluetooth connection should be tested. Following are the steps involved in connecting a Bluetooth headset to a typical Android-based device and to an iPad. Before you begin, make sure the Bluetooth headset is charged.

Steps to Configure a Bluetooth Headset on an Android-based Device

1. Go to Settings > Wireless & Networks > and check the box for Bluetooth. This enables Bluetooth on the mobile device.

2. Tap Bluetooth Settings. This displays the Bluetooth Setting screen.

3. Prepare the headset. This can vary from headset to headset. For example, on a typical Motorola Bluetooth headset, you press and hold the button while opening the microphone. Keep holding the button.

4. Tap Scan for Devices on the Android device. Keep holding the button on the headset until the Android device finds it.

5. On the Android device, under the Bluetooth device tap Pair with This Device. Most Android devices pair the Bluetooth headset to the mobile device and then complete the connection automatically, allowing full use of the device.

6. Enter a pin code if necessary. Many devices come with a default pin of 0000.

When finished, the screen on the Android device will look similar to Figure 17.9. Note the Bluetooth icon at the top of the screen. This icon tells you if Bluetooth is running on the device. It will remain even if you disconnect the Bluetooth device. For this headset device we would test it simply by making a phone call. To disconnect it, simply tap the device on the screen and tap OK. It will remain paired but nonfunctional until a connection is made again.

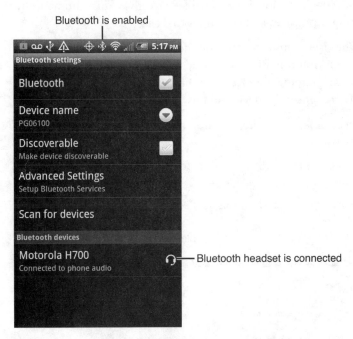

FIGURE 17.9   Installed Bluetooth device on an Android phone

Mobile devices can also connect to other Bluetooth-enabled devices (forming a PAN), or to a computer equipped with a Bluetooth dongle. To do this, you must set the mobile device to discoverable (which generally lasts for only 2 minutes). In the same fashion that the headset was discovered by the mobile device in the previous procedure, so can a mobile device be discovered by a computer or other mobile device. When connecting a mobile device to another mobile device or PC, it can be identified by its name. For example, the mobile device in Figure 17.9 is listed as PG06100. You can modify this name if you want. It is authenticated by a pin code chosen at the PC or other mobile device. We would test these types of connections by sending data or by initiating communications.

Steps to Configure a Bluetooth Headset on an iOS-based Device

This exercise refers to an iPad2.

1. Go to Settings > General > and tap Bluetooth. This displays the Bluetooth screen.

2. Tap Bluetooth to enable it (if it isn't enabled already). This automatically starts searching for devices and continues to do so.

3. Prepare the headset. This can vary from headset to headset. For example, on a typical Motorola Bluetooth headset, you press and hold the button while opening the mic. Keep holding the button. The iPad2 will automatically recognize the device and list it as discoverable.

4. Tap the device name, and it should automatically connect, as shown in Figure 17.10.

5. Enter a pin code if necessary.

To remove the device, click it, and on the next screen click Forget.

FIGURE 17.10 Installed Bluetooth device on an iPad2

Bluetooth devices can be connected to only one mobile device at a time. If you need to switch the Bluetooth device from one mobile device to another, be sure to disconnect it or "forget" it from the current connection before making a new one.

> **ExamAlert**
>
> Know how to configure Bluetooth devices on Android and Apple devices.

Bluetooth Troubleshooting

If you have trouble pairing a Bluetooth device, and connecting or reconnecting to Bluetooth devices or PANs, try some of the following methods:

- ▶ Make sure the phone or other mobile device is Bluetooth-capable.

- ▶ Verify that your devices are fully charged, especially Bluetooth headsets.

- ▶ Check if you are within range. For example Class 2 Bluetooth devices have a range of 10 meters.

- ▶ Try restarting the mobile device and attempt to reconnect.

- ▶ Check for conflicting Wi-Fi frequencies. Consider changing the channel used by the Wi-Fi network.

- ▶ Try using a known good Bluetooth device with the mobile device to make sure that the mobile device's Bluetooth is functional.

- ▶ Remove or "forget" the particular Bluetooth device; then turn off Bluetooth in general, restart the mobile device, and attempt to reconnect.

> **ExamAlert**
>
> Know your Bluetooth troubleshooting techniques for the exam!

E-Mail Configurations

Though there are many other types of communication available to mobile users, e-mail still accounts for an important percentage. You should know how to configure a mobile device for web-based e-mail services such as Gmail, Yahoo, and so on. You should also know how to configure POP3, IMAP, and connections to Microsoft Exchange Servers.

Web-Based E-Mail for Mobile Devices

Mobile devices can access web-based e-mail through a browser, but this is not necessary nowadays due to the "app." For example, Android devices come with a Gmail application built in, allowing a user to access Gmail directly without having to use the browser. Apple iOS devices allow connectivity to Gmail, Yahoo, and a host of other e-mail providers as well.

Connecting to these services is simple and works in a similar fashion as when working on a desktop or laptop computer. Choose the type of provider you use, enter a username (the e-mail address) and password (on Apple devices an Apple ID is also required), and the user will have access to web-based e-mail.

When troubleshooting issues with e-mail, make sure that the username and password are typed correctly. Using onscreen keyboards often leads to mistyped passwords. Also make sure that the mobile device is currently connected to the Internet.

POP3, IMAP, and Exchange

If you need to connect your mobile device to a specific organization's e-mail system, it gets a little bit more complicated. You need to know the server that you want to connect to, the port you need to use, and whether security is employed.

Here's a step-by step process on how to connect a typical Android smartphone to a POP3 account.

1. Go to Home and tap the menu button. Then select All apps.

2. Scroll down until you see the Mail app, and tap it. (This might also be listed as E-mail.)

3. Select whether you want POP3, IMAP, or Exchange. (For this exercise select POP3.)

4. Type the e-mail address and the password of the account and tap Next.

5. Configure the incoming settings. Change the username if desired to something different than the e-mail address. Then type the POP3 server name. By default it will be the domain name portion of the e-mail address, which is usually correct. If security is used select SSL or TLS. This information should be supplied by the network administrator. Type the port number. For POP3 this is 110 by default. If port numbers are different, they will also be supplied to you by the network administrator. Then tap Next.

6. Configure the outgoing settings. Type the SMTP server. Organizations will often use the same server name as the POP3 server. However, small office and home users might have to use their ISP's SMTP server. If security is used, select SSL or TLS. Type the port number for SMTP, which is 25. (Again, this is a default.) Then tap Next.

7. Configure account options. From here you can tell the mobile device how often to check for mail and whether to notify you when it arrives. Tap Next. At this point, new e-mail should start downloading.

8. Finally, you can give the account an easier name for you to remember it by. Tap Done.

Adding an e-mail account to an iOS-based device works essentially the same, but the navigation will be slightly different. For example, to add an e-mail account to an iPad2, go to Home > Settings > Mail, Contact, Calendars > Add Account > Other > Add Mail Account. Then type the information in the same manner you would in the previous steps.

ExamAlert

Know how to add e-mail accounts in Android and iOS.

Now, if you instead have to connect an IMAP account, you have to type the IMAP server (for downloading mail) which uses port 143 by default, and the outgoing SMTP server (for sending mail). If you connect to a Microsoft Exchange mail server, that server name often takes care of both downloading and uploading of e-mail. You might need to know the domain that the Exchange server is a member of. Secure e-mail sessions require the use of SSL or TLS on port 443. Check with the network administrator to find out which protocol to use. POP3 also has a secure derivative known as APOP, a challenge/response protocol which uses a hashing function to prevent replay attacks during an e-mail session. This protocol can be chosen from the Android platform, and is also used by Mozilla Thunderbird, Windows Live Mail and Apple Mail.

Configuring e-mail accounts for other devices, such as the Blackberry, works in a similar fashion to other smartphones. However, you also have the option to connect to a Blackberry Enterprise Server, which is similar to Microsoft Exchange. These Blackberry servers are at the core of "pushed" e-mail, which Blackberry pioneered for users to get their e-mail immediately when it reaches the mail server.

Troubleshooting E-mail Connections

If you have trouble connecting an e-mail account, try some of the following methods:

▶ Make sure the mobile device has Internet access. If connecting through the cellular network, make sure there is a decent reception.

▶ Verify that the username, password, and server names are typed correctly. Remember that the username is often the e-mail address itself.

▶ Check the port numbers. By default POP3 is 110, SMTP is 25, and IMAP is 143. However, network administrators might decide to use nondefault port numbers!

> **Note**
>
> There is a newer SMTP mail submission port, 587, that can be used by e-mail clients. Due to security concerns with port 25, you will likely see more of port 587 in the future.

▶ Double-check whether security is required in the form of SSL or TLS. For nonstandard port numbers and security configurations, check with your network administrator.

> **ExamAlert**
>
> Double-check all e-mail settings such as username, password, server name, and port number.

Synchronizing an Android Device to a PC

If you connect an Android-based mobile device to a PC via USB, Windows will most likely recognize it, and you will have a few options display on the Android screen, as shown in Figure 17.11.

The first option is Charge Only. Aside from charging the Android device by connecting it to an AC outlet, a PC's USB port can charge it. (Though it will probably take longer to charge.) This first option is the default, so if you need to charge a device only, you won't have to change this setting. We'll skip the second option for now and come back to it later. The third option is Disk Drive. If you want to display the contents of the mobile device's memory card within Windows you have to select this. Then, the device shows up as a

Removable Disk in Windows Explorer. From there, data can be copied back and forth between the PC and the mobile device as you usually would within Windows. Older Android devices required you to tap "mount" to have the phone show as a Removable Disk.

FIGURE 17.11   **PC Connection Options on Android**

ExamAlert

Know how to connect a mobile device to a PC and read its data.

You will also note USB tethering on the list. This allows you to share the mobile device's cellular network with the PC. The last item on the list is Internet Pass-through, which as mentioned previously allows you to use the PC's Internet connection on the mobile device.

Now, none of these so far allow you to synchronize information from the mobile device to the PC. Only the second option HTC Sync allows this synchronization, but with a caveat: The PC must have the appropriate synchronization software installed. Keep in mind that this software (and connection name) will be different depending on the manufacturer of the device. This example shows an HTC Evo smartphone.

Most synchronization software requires the PC have Windows XP or higher, 1 GB of RAM or more, USB 2.0 ports minimum, and 300 MB of free space on the hard drive. Syncing software is freely downloadable from the manufacturer's website.

HTC Sync for example can synchronize music, pictures, the calendar, bookmarks and more. This synchronization can be initiated from the mobile device or from the program on the PC. Documents, music, pictures and video will be synchronized by default to the Windows Libraries of the same names.

If you use the mobile device's built-in contacts and e-mail programs, the information within those programs will be transferred to the PC's corresponding programs. For example the Calendar and Contacts will be synchronized with Microsoft Outlook. However, for this mobile device, Gmail or Exchange contacts information will not be synchronized, nor will any other third-party data besides data that originates from, or is destined for, a Microsoft application.

However, not everyone uses synchronization software. Some people exclusively use Gmail on the Android platform. Google automatically synchronizes mail, contacts, and the Calendar so that you can view the information on the mobile device or on the PC (when connected to the Gmail website). However, because the data is stored on a Google server, security can be compromised. If you choose to do this, you should use an extremely strong password, change it every month or so, and use a secure browser when connecting to Gmail from your PC. The same people who use Gmail usually transfer data by simply mounting the mobile device as a disk drive in Windows. This effectively renders the synchronization software unnecessary for those people.

Third-party tools (such as Mark/Space) are available if a person wants to synchronize an Android device with a PC or MAC via Bluetooth or Wi-Fi. Standard Microsoft ActiveSync is not used to synchronize data between Android and Windows. However, Exchange ActiveSync can be used to synchronize e-mail, contacts, and calendars between an Android 2.0 mobile device and higher with an Exchange Server.

ExamAlert

Know the various ways to synchronize data between an Android and a PC.

Synchronizing an iPad2 to a PC

Before getting into synchronizing, let's talk about charging. The best way to charge an iPad is by plugging the AC adapter into an outlet. If the iPad is connected to a desktop computer via USB and is turned on, it will not charge.

However, if it is connected by USB and it is sleeping or off, it will slowly charge. If the computer is not equipped with a high-power USB port, this could take a long time. Regardless, Apple recommends plugging these devices into the AC outlet to charge.

If you plug an iPad into a PC via USB, Windows should automatically recognize it and install the driver for it. At that point you can move files between the PC and the iPad's memory card. The iPad shows up in Windows Explorer as Apple iPad directly inside of Computer.

To synchronize data such as contacts, calendars, and so on, PC users need to use iTunes for Windows. From iTunes a user would select Sync Contacts or Sync Calendars, for example. This information can be synchronized to Microsoft Outlook 2003 or higher, Windows Address Book (in Windows XP), and Windows Contacts (in Windows 7/Vista). Mac users benefit from the simplicity of synchronization across all Apple products. They can use iTunes or can use the iCloud to store, backup, and synchronize information across all Apple devices. This can be done by USB or via Wi-Fi if the various Apple devices are on the same wireless network. Calendar items can also be synced from the iPad itself by going to Settings > Mail, Contacts, Calendars. Then scroll down and select Sync, as shown in Figure 17.12.

FIGURE 17.12   Apple iPad2 synchronization example

(Exam**Alert**)

Know the various ways to synchronize data between an Apple mobile device and a PC or Mac.

Synchronizing Other Devices

The two operating systems the CompTIA objectives are concerned with are Android and iOS. However, these are not the only players on the field! Let's mention a few other devices.

First of all, the Blackberry deserves some mention. For the longest time, this was the standard device a business person would use. It has lost some momentum, but you still see plenty of them in the field. Blackberry offers Desktop Software. Separate versions for PC and Mac are available at this link:

http://us.blackberry.com/apps-software/desktop/

The software works in a similar fashion to other synchronization software for Android or iOS.

And let's not forget about Microsoft mobile operating systems. Windows CE and Windows Mobile are commonly found in the transportation, medical, and surveying fields, as well as other niche markets that require rugged, waterproof devices. These devices synchronize to the PC by way of Microsoft ActiveSync (for Windows XP or earlier) and the Windows Mobile Device Center (Windows Vista or newer.) The Windows Mobile Device Center is available at this link:

http://www.microsoft.com/download/en/details.aspx?id=14

These programs can synchronize data between the mobile device and the PC via USB or Bluetooth connections. Microsoft does not allow synchronization over Wi-Fi as it is deemed a security issue.

Cram Quiz

Answer these questions. The answers follow the last question. If you cannot answer these questions correctly, consider reading this section again until you can.

220-802 Questions

1. Which of the following are valid Wi-Fi troubleshooting methods? (Select the two best answers.)

   ○ **A.** Power cycle the device.
   ○ **B.** Restart Bluetooth.
   ○ **C.** Use a static IP.
   ○ **D.** Make sure the device is within range.
   ○ **E.** Rename the SSID.

2. Which of the following connections requires a username, password, and SMTP server? (Select the two best answers.)

  ○ **A.** Bluetooth connection

  ○ **B.** Wi-Fi connection

  ○ **C.** POP3 connection

  ○ **D.** Exchange connection

  ○ **E.** IMAP connection

3. What is the most common connection method when synchronizing data from a mobile device to a PC?

  ○ **A.** Wi-Fi

  ○ **B.** Bluetooth

  ○ **C.** USB

  ○ **D.** FireWire

4. When configuring a Wi-Fi connection what step occurs after successfully entering the SSID?

  ○ **A.** Select POP3.

  ○ **B.** Check if the device is within range of the WAP.

  ○ **C.** Enter a passcode for the network.

  ○ **D.** Scan for networks.

5. Which technology would you use if you want to connect a headset to your mobile phone?

  ○ **A.** Bluetooth

  ○ **B.** GSM

  ○ **C.** Wi-Fi

  ○ **D.** Exchange

6. Which of the following allows other mobile devices to share your mobile device's Internet connection?

  ○ **A.** Internet pass-through

  ○ **B.** Locator application

  ○ **C.** IMAP

  ○ **D.** Wi-Fi tethering

7. What would a user need to synchronize contacts from an iPad to a PC?

  ○ **A.** Android Synchronization Application

  ○ **B.** Google Play

  ○ **C.** iTunes

  ○ **D.** ActiveSync

Cram Quiz Answers

220-802 Answers

1. **A** and **D**. Valid Wi-Fi troubleshooting methods include power cycling the device and making sure that the mobile device is within range of the wireless access point. Bluetooth could possibly cause a conflict with Wi-Fi. If you suspect this, Bluetooth should simply be turned off. Static IP addresses are one thing you can check for when troubleshooting. Normally, the mobile device should obtain an IP address from a DHCP server. Renaming the SSID of the access point could cause problems for all clients trying to connect. However, you should make sure that the correct SSID was typed (if the connection were made manually.)

2. **C** and **E**. POP3 and IMAP e-mail connections require an incoming mail server (either POP3 or IMAP), and an outgoing mail server (SMTP.) Bluetooth and Wi-Fi connections do not require a username or SMTP server. Exchange connections require a username and password, but no SMTP server. The Exchange server acts as the incoming and outgoing mail server.

3. **C**. USB is the most common connection method used when synchronizing data from a mobile device to a PC. Though Wi-Fi and Bluetooth are also possible, they are less common. Few mobile devices have FireWire connections.

4. **C**. After you enter the SSID (if it's correct) you would enter the passcode for the network. POP3 has to do with configuring an e-mail account. If you have already entered the SSID, then you should be within range of the wireless access point (WAP). Scanning for networks is the first thing you do when setting up a Wi-Fi connection.

5. **A**. The Bluetooth standard is used to connect a headset and other similar devices over short range to a mobile device. GSM is used to make voice calls over cellular networks. Wi-Fi is used to connect mobile devices to the Internet. Exchange is a Microsoft E-mail server; some mobile devices have the capability to connect to e-mail accounts stored on an Exchange server.

6. **D**. Wi-Fi tethering allows a mobile device to share its Internet connection with other Wi-Fi capable devices. Internet pass-through is when the mobile device connects to a PC to share the PC's Internet connection. Locator applications are used to find lost or stolen mobile devices through GPS. IMAP is another e-mail protocol similar to POP3.

7. **C**. PC users need iTunes to synchronize contacts and other data from an iPad to a PC. There are many Android sync programs, but they do not work on Apple devices. Google Play is a place to get applications and other items. ActiveSync is the older Microsoft sync program used to synchronize Windows CE and Mobile to PCs.

Mobile Security

Mobile devices need to be secure just like any other computing devices. But due to their transportable nature, some of the security techniques will be a bit different. I recommend that you prepare for the possibility of a stolen, lost, damaged, or compromised device. The following methods can help you to recover from these problems and also aid you in preventing them from happening.

Stolen and Lost Devices

Because mobile devices are expensive and could contain confidential data, they become a target for thieves. Plus, they are small and easy to conceal, making them easier to steal. But there are some things you can do to protect your data and attempt to get the mobile device back.

The first thing a user should do when receiving a mobile device is to set a *passcode*, which is a set of numbers. This is one of several types of *screenlocks*. Locking the device makes it inaccessible to everyone except experienced hackers. The screen lock can be a pattern that is drawn on the display, a PIN (passcode), or a password. A strong password will usually be the strongest form of screenlock.

This can be accessed on an Android device by going to Settings > Security. This screen on a typical Android smartphone is shown in Figure 17.13.

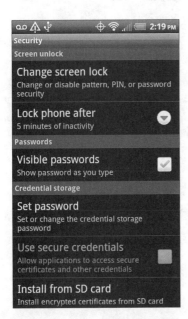

FIGURE 17.13   Android security screen

You can also select how long the phone will wait after inactivity to lock. Generally this is set to 3 or 5 minutes or so, but in a confidential environment you might set this to Immediate.

The next option on the Security screen is Visible Passwords. If check marked, this shows the current letter of the password being typed by the user. This type of setting is vulnerable to shoulder surfers (people looking over your shoulder to find out your password) and should be deselected. When deselected, only asterisks (*) are shown when the user types a password.

ExamAlert

Know how to configure a screenlock in Android and how to disable visible passwords.

Passcode locking can be accessed on an iPad device by going to Settings > General > and tapping Passcode Lock. This displays the Passcode Lock screen. Tap Turn Passcode On to set a passcode, as shown in Figure 17.14. Be sure that the Auto-Lock on the previous screen is set to an amount of minutes. If it is set to Never, the device never sleeps, negating the security of the passcode, and using valuable battery power. The default setting is 2 minutes. You'll also note in Figure 17.14 that Simple Passcode is enabled. This allows 4-digit numeric passcodes only. As this is probably not going to be secure enough for an organization, you should turn the Simple Passcode option off; that will allow alphanumeric passwords to be entered.

FIGURE 17.14   **iPad2 passcode lock screen**

> **Exam Alert**
>
> Know how to configure a passcode in iOS.

Aside from the default timeout, devices can also be locked by pressing the power button quickly. If configured, the passcode must be supplied whenever a mobile device comes out of a sleep or lock state and whenever it is first booted.

If a person fails to enter the correct passcode after a certain amount of attempts, the device locks temporarily and the person has to wait a certain amount of time before attempting the passcode again. For example, by default on the Android this is 5 attempts; if they all fail the user has to wait 30 seconds. If the person fails to enter the correct passcode again, the timeout increases on most devices. After a certain amount of attempts, the device either needs to be connected to the computer it was last synced to, or has to be restored to factory condition with a hard reset (which can wipe the data.)

> **Exam Alert**
>
> Understand the consequences of entering an incorrect passcode too many times.

Some devices (such as the iPhone) have a setting where the device will be erased after a certain amount of incorrect password attempts (10 in the case of the iPhone). There are also third-party apps available for download for most mobile devices that can wipe the data after x number of attempts. Some apps configure the device to automatically take a picture after 3 failed attempts and e-mail the picture to the owner.

There's an app for virtually everything. For example, say the device was lost or stolen. If the user had previously installed a locator application, such as Where's my Droid, Lookout Mobile Security, or Find iPhone, and the GPS/Location Services was enabled on the device, then the user would track where the device is. At that point, the organization would decide whether to get the police involved.

> **Exam Alert**
>
> Know what locator applications are.

Now, even if you track your mobile device and find it, it might be too late. A hacker can get past passcodes and other screen locks. It's just a matter of time before the hacker has access to the data. So, an organization with confidential information should consider a remote wipe program. As long as the mobile device still has access to the Internet, the remote wipe program can be initiated from a desktop computer, which will delete all the contents of the remote mobile device. Examples of software that can accomplish this include: Google Sync, Google Apps Device Policy, Apple's Data Protection, and third-party apps such as Mobile Defense. In some cases, such as Apple's Data Protection, the command that starts the remote wipe must be issued from an Exchange server or Mobile Device Management server.

> **ExamAlert**
>
> Know the remote wipe programs available for mobile devices.

You should also have a backup plan in place as well so that data on the mobile device is backed up to a secure location at regular intervals. This way, if the data needs to be wiped, you are secure in the fact that most of the data can be recovered. The type of remote wipe program, backup program, and policies regarding how these are implemented will vary from one organization to the next. Be sure to read up on your organization's policies to see exactly what is allowed from a mobile security standpoint.

Compromised and Damaged Devices

Theft and loss aren't the only risks a mobile device faces. We should protect against the chance that a mobile device is damaged, or if the device's security is compromised.

Many organizations implement backup and remote backup policies. iOS devices can be backed up to a PC via USB connection and by using iTunes. Also, they can be backed up remotely to the iCloud. In addition, there are other third-party apps for remote backup such as iDrive and Mozy. Information can even be restored to newer, upgraded iOS devices. Android (as of the writing of this book) doesn't allow a complete backup without rooting the phone (which I don't recommend.) However, almost all the data and settings can be backed up in a collection of ways. First, the Android Cloud backup can be used to backup e-mail, contacts, and other information. However, if you use Gmail, then e-mail, contacts, and calendars are backed up (and synchronized) to Google servers. If a mobile device is lost, the information can be quickly accessed from a desktop computer or other mobile device. Unlike Apple, Android applications can be backed up, as long as they are not copy-protected, with an app such as

Astro. Android settings can be backed up and restored from Settings > Privacy. If you choose not to use the Android cloud to backup files, or the synchronization program that came with the device, then there are plenty of third-party apps (such as iDrive, Mozy, HandyBackup, and so on) that can be used to back-up via USB to a PC, or to backup to the cloud.

One way to protect mobile devices from compromise is to patch or update the operating system. By default, you will be notified automatically about available updates on Android and iOS-based devices. However, you should know where to go to manually update these devices as well. For Android go to Settings > System Updates > Software Update (or similar path). From here tap Check Now. If you have a connection to the Internet, you will receive any information concerning system updates; an example is shown in Figure 17.15.

FIGURE 17.15   **Android system update available**

ExamAlert

Know how to check for, and perform, Android OS updates.

As you can see in the figure, the system update has an important new security feature that should be installed right away (which I will do when I finish writing this sentence!) Security patches are a large percentage of system updates because there are a lot of attackers around the world that want to compromise the Android operating system. But let's be real—attackers will go for any OS if it catches their fancy, be it Android, iOS or even Windows!

Updates for iOS can be located at Settings > General > Software Update. As shown in Figure 17.16, this iOS needs to be updated from 5.0 to 5.1 and should be done as soon as possible to patch up any security flaws, and make the best use of the system.

FIGURE 17.16   iOS system update available

Updates are great, but they are not created to specifically battle viruses and other malware. So, just like there is antivirus software for PCs, there is also AV software for mobile devices. These are third-party applications that need to be paid for, downloaded, and installed to the mobile device. Some common examples for Android include McAfee's Virusscan Mobile, AVG, Lookout, Dr. Web, and NetQin.

iOS works a bit differently. iOS is a tightly controlled operating system. One of the benefits of being a closed-source OS is that it can be more difficult to write viruses for, making it somewhat more difficult to compromise. But there is no OS that can't be compromised. For the longest time there was no antivirus software for iOS. That is until 2011 when a type of jailbreaking software called jailbreakme used a simple PDF to move insecure code to the root of the device causing a jailbreak.

iOS *jailbreaking* is the process of removing the limitations that Apple imposes on its devices that run iOS. This enables users to gain root access to the system and allows the download of previously unavailable applications and software not authorized by Apple.

> **ExamAlert**
>
> Understand the term jailbreaking for the exam.

Jailbreakme is used to gain root level access and take control of the device without the user's consent. Finally, Apple consented to the first antivirus software for iOS, Intego's VirusBarrier, a paid download through the App Store. Any AV software for Android or iOS should be checked regularly for updates.

For large organizations that have many mobile devices, a *Mobile Device Management (MDM)* suite can be implemented. McAfee, and many other companies from AirWatch to LANDesk Mobility Manager to Sybase, have Mobile Device Management software suites that can take care of pushing updates and configuring hundreds of mobile devices from a central location. Decent quality MDM software will secure, monitor, manage, and support multiple different types of mobile devices across the enterprise.

Stopping Applications

Applications that are opened on a mobile device will continue to run in the background unless they are specifically turned off within the app or within the OS.

To turn off apps (or services) that are running on an Android-based system, go to Settings > Applications > Running Services. That displays all the currently running services and applications, as shown in Figure 17.17.

You can see in the figure that there are several apps and services running including the droid VNC server, Calendar, and a GPS program. To see all the services and apps, just scroll down. As with PCs, mobile device apps use RAM. The bottom of the figure shows that 194 MB of RAM is currently being used, and 139 MB of RAM is free. The more RAM that is used by the mobile device, the worse it will perform: it will slow it down, and eat up battery power. So, to close an app, you would simply tap it and tap Stop. You can also stop services or processes in this manner (for example HTC DM in the figure), but this might require a Force Stop. If you are not absolutely sure what the service is, do not initiate a Force Stop, as it can possibly cause system instability.

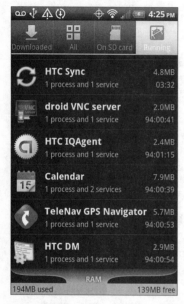

FIGURE 17.17   Services and apps running on an Android

To force quit an app on an iOS-based device, press and hold the Sleep/Wake button for a few seconds until a red slider appears. Then press and hold the home button until the app quits.

ExamAlert

Understand how to stop apps on Android and Apple devices.

There are third-party apps that can close down all of the apps in one shot if you need to save time. These include Task Manager, TasKiller, and AppControl.

If an application is causing the device to lock up and you can't stop the app, a soft reset or a hard reset will be necessary.

Initiating Resets

A soft reset is done by simply powering off the mobile device and powering it back on. This resets the drivers and the OS. So, soft resets are similar to shutting down a PC and powering it back up. Some technicians will also call this a power cycle. The soft reset can help when certain applications are not functioning properly, or if network connectivity is failing. If a smartphone is still locked up when it is restarted, try pulling the battery, replacing it, and restarting the phone again. In fact, for Blackberry devices, soft resets *require* a battery pull.

iOS-based devices can do a variety of more advanced software resets beyond a simple power-cycle, such as Reset All Settings, Erase All Content, Reset Networking settings, and so on. These are available by tapping Settings > General > Reset.

Hard resets should be initiated only when things have gone terribly wrong. For example, if hardware or software has been compromised, or has failed, and a soft reset does not fix the problem. You want to make sure that all data is backed up before performing a hard reset, as some hard resets will reset the mobile device back to the original factory condition.

> **ExamAlert**
>
> Warning!! All data will be wiped when a hard reset is initiated on an Android device!

Hard resets vary from one device to the next. For example, most Android-based systems such as the HTC smartphone mentioned previously use the following steps:

1. Turn the power off. If the device is locked (frozen), pull the battery out and reinsert it.

2. Hold the Volume Down button, and press and release the Power button.

3. This displays a menu that allows for Fastbook, Recovery, Clear Storage, and Simlock. Select Clear Storage by pressing the Volume Down button.

4. Press and release the Power button.

5. Confirm by pressing Volume Up for Yes or Volume Down for No.

At this point, the device will be reset and you will have to restore data and settings from backup.

> **ExamAlert**
>
> Know how to perform soft and hard resets on Android devices.

Unlike many other mobile devices, hard resets on iOS-based devices do not delete data. They instead stop all apps, and reset the OS and drivers. This can be accomplished with the following steps:

1. Make sure that the device has at least 20 percent battery life remaining. (This process could take some time, and you don't want the battery to discharge completely in the middle of it.)

2. Press the Sleep/Wake and Home buttons simultaneously for 10 seconds or until the Apple logo appears. (Ignore the red slider).

3. When the logo appears, the hard reset has been initiated. It may take several minutes to complete.

To fully reset an iOS-based device such as the iPad2 to factory condition, you need to go to Settings > General > Reset > Erase all Content and Settings. Another way to do this is to connect the iOS device to a computer via USB and open iTunes on the computer. Then, select the iPad2 option, Summary, and click Restore. Regardless of the method you choose, next, initiate a hard reset to complete the procedure.

> **ExamAlert**
>
> Remember how to reset settings and erase all content on iOS devices.

As you have seen with Android and Apple, the types of resets vary from one device to the next, so be sure to go to the manufacturer's website to find out exactly what the various resets do for your mobile device, and how you can perform them.

Cram Quiz

Answer these questions. The answers follow the last question. If you cannot answer these questions correctly, consider reading this section again until you can.

220-802 Questions

1. You want to prevent a person from accessing your phone while you step away from your desk. What should you do?

   ○ **A.** Implement remote backup.

   ○ **B.** Set up a remote wipe program.

   ○ **C.** Configure a screen lock.

   ○ **D.** Install a locator application.

2. What does the iOS Simple Passcode allow a person to enter?

   ○ **A.** 4-letter code

   ○ **B.** 6-number PIN

   ○ **C.** 4-digit passcode

   ○ **D.** Alpha-numeric passcode

3. What do third-party apps such as Find iPhone rely on?

   ○ **A.** Passcode

   ○ **B.** Google Apps Device Policy

   ○ **C.** Bluetooth

   ○ **D.** GPS

4. Which of the following can be described as removing limitations on iOS?

   ○ **A.** Rooting

   ○ **B.** Jailbreaking

   ○ **C.** Geotracking

   ○ **D.** AV software

5. An application won't close on an Android smartphone. You've tried to Force Stop it to no avail. What should you do?

   ○ **A.** Hard reset the device.

   ○ **B.** Stop the service in Running Services.

   ○ **C.** Soft reset the device.

   ○ **D.** Bring the device to an authorized service center.

6. Your organization is concerned about a scenario where a mobile device with confidential data is stolen. What should you recommend first? (Select the best answer.)

   ○ **A.** Remote backup application

   ○ **B.** Remote wipe program

   ○ **C.** Passcode locks

   ○ **D.** Locator application

7. You are concerned with the possibility of jailbreaks on your organization's iPhones, and viruses on the Android-based devices. What should you implement?

   ○ **A.** AV software

   ○ **B.** Firewall

   ○ **C.** Mobile Device Management

   ○ **D.** Device reset

Cram Quiz Answers

220-802 Answers

1. **C.** You should configure a screen lock: either a pattern drawn on the screen, a PIN, or a password. Remote backup, remote wipe, and locator applications will not prevent a person from accessing the phone.

2. **C.** The iOS Simple Passcode allows only a 4-digit numeric passcode. To enter alpha-numeric passwords, you need to disable Simple Passcode.

3. **D.** Third-party locator apps such as Find iPhone and Where's my Droid rely on GPS to locate the device. Passcodes are used to prevent unauthorized users from accessing the mobile device. Google Apps Device Policy can initiate a remote wipe on a mobile device. Bluetooth is used so the mobile device can communicate with other devices over short range.

4. **B.** Jailbreaking is the process of removing the limitations of an iOS-based device so that the user gets superuser abilities. Rooting is a similar technique used on Android mobile devices. Geotracking is the practice of tracking a device over time. AV software is antivirus software, used to combat malware.

5. **C.** If you've already tried to stop the application within Running Services, attempt a soft reset. Pull the battery if the application is frozen. Hard resets on Android devices should be used only as a last resort as they will return the device to factory condition—wiping all the data. The question said that the application won't close, not a service, though you could try finding an underlying service that might be the culprit. But try resetting the device before doing this or bringing it to an authorized service center.

6. **B.** The remote wipe application is the most important one listed. This will prevent a thief from accessing the data on the device. Afterward, you might recommend a backup program (in case the data needs to be wiped), as well as passcode locks and a locator application.

7. **A.** You should implement antivirus (AV) software. This can protect against viruses and other malware as well as jailbreaks on Apple devices. As of the writing of this book, firewalls for mobile devices are not common, but that could change in the future. Mobile Device Management (MDM) is software that runs at a central computer enabling a user to configure and monitor multiple mobile devices. Device resets are used to restart the mobile device, or to reset it to factor condition depending on the type of reset, and the manufacturer of the device.

CHAPTER 18

Safety, Procedures, and Professionalism

This chapter covers the following A+ exam topics:

► Safety

► Procedures and Environmental Controls

► Professionalism and Communication Skills

You can find a master list of A+ exam topics in the "Introduction."

This chapter covers CompTIA A+ 220-801 objectives 5.1 through 5.4.

Now we come to the crux of it all. Everything you have learned so far could be for naught if you do not make use of the crucial information in this chapter.

Safety should always be on your mind. Protect yourself; and protect your computer. Electrical safety, physical safety, and fire prevention are the keys to a happy and healthy career. And by using *electrostatic discharge (ESD)* prevention methods, you protect your computer's components and keep it safe as well.

Pay attention to the environment, and use your wisdom to control it when possible. Try to eliminate interference from electrical and radio devices. Understand what *material safety data sheets (MSDSs)* are, how to access them, and what to do when a particular material gives you trouble.

Finally, mind your customer service skills. You might be a super-tech, but without people skills, your job market will be limited. By being professional and utilizing good communication skills, you increase the chances to receive a good customer reaction. Also, these skills help you to get to the heart of the issue and can help to make you more efficient, saving time as you repair computer problems. Throughout the rest of the book, you learned how to repair the computer. Now put those abilities together with a professional demeanor and good communication skills, and there should be no lack of new customers in the future.

Safety

Safety first! Remember to put safety on the top of your priority list when dealing with computers, power, networking, and anything else in IT. Let's talk about some of the things to watch out for when working on computers, how to keep yourself and the computer safe, and how to be environmentally conscious.

Electrical Safety

Electricity is a great energy that should be treated as such. Before working on any computer component, turn off the power and disconnect the device from the AC outlet. If a device such as a power supply or video monitor has a label that says, No Serviceable Components Inside, take the manufacturer's word for it and send the component to the proper repair facility, or simply replace the component. The message on the device is intended to keep a person out, usually because the internal components might hold an electrical charge.

Be sure to use your multimeter and power supply tester properly. If you do not know how to use these, refer to Chapter 5, "Power," or escalate the issue to another person in your company. If you find issues with AC outlets, or other AC equipment, refer this to your manager or building supervisor. Do not try to fix these issues. If you find an issue like this in a customer's home, tell them about the problem and recommend that they have the AC outlet repaired before going any further.

Do not open power supplies. As far as the A+ exam is concerned, if a power supply goes bad, replace it, even if you think it is just the fan and would be an easy repair. It is known as a *field replaceable unit (FRU)* for a reason. Although it is possible to repair power supplies, it should be done only by trained technicians. Remember that the power supply holds a charge; this alone should be enough to keep you away from the internals of the power supply. But in addition to that, the amount of time it would take a person to repair a power supply would cost more to a company than just buying a new one and installing it.

It is recommended that you do not open CRT monitors; these also carry a lethal charge. Instead, refer these monitors to a company that specializes in monitor repair. If you need to dispose of CRTs, there are some monitor repair companies that will buy them, or simply accept them without charge. Otherwise, they need to be recycled in compliance with municipal ordinance.

LCD monitors can also be dangerous. I can't actually tell you *not* to work on them, especially because laptops integrate them. Regardless, it is again recommended that the failed monitor (or laptop) be sent to the proper repair organization, or to the manufacturer if the device is within warranty. However, if a technician does decide to work on the LCD, one thing to be careful of are capacitors; these are normally near the LCD power supply and hold a charge. Also, make sure that the device is turned off and unplugged, and if it is a laptop, that the battery has been removed. One of the items that can fail on an LCD monitor is the backlight inverter. The inverter is usually mounted on a circuit board, and if it fails, either a fuse needs to be replaced or the entire inverter board. The inverter is a high-voltage device; try not to touch it, and be especially sure not to touch it if the LCD device is on. A lot of this is common sense, but it is worthwhile to always be sure—like measuring twice before you cut.

> **Exam Alert**
>
> Do not touch an LCD's inverter if the device is on!

Another device that you need to make sure you turn off and unplug is the laser printer. Extremely dangerous high voltages are inside a laser printer. On a related note, watch out for the fuser if the printer were recently used; the fuser runs hot!

Finally, it is important to match the power requirement of your computer equipment with the surge protector, or uninterruptible power supply (UPS), that it connects to. Verify that the amount of watts your computer's power supply requires is not greater than the amount of power your surge protector can provide; the same goes for the watts (or volt-amps) that the UPS can provide. In addition, be sure that you do not overload the circuit that you connect to. For more information regarding electricity used by your computer, see Chapter 5. For additional information about electrical safety, see the electrical safety and health topics at the Occupational Safety & Health Administration (OSHA) website: http://www.osha.gov/SLTC/electrical/index.html.

Electrical Fire Safety

Let's talk a little about electrical fire safety. The safest measures are preventative ones. Buildings should be outfitted with smoke detectors and fire extinguishers. The proper type of fire extinguisher for an electrical fire is a Class C extinguisher. For example, CO_2-based BC fire extinguishers are common and relatively safe to humans, but they can cause damage to computers. If equipment needs to be protected more, then an ABC Halotron extinguisher should be used. Server rooms and data centers will often be protected by a larger special hazard protection system that uses the FM-200 clean agent system. This clean agent won't cause damage to servers and other expensive equipment.

If you see an electrical fire, use the proper extinguisher to attempt to put it out. If the fire is too big for you to handle, then the number one thing to do is dial 911. Then evacuate the building. Afterward, you can notify building management, your supervisor, or other facilities people.

Hopefully you will never come near a live electrical wire. But if you do, you want to attempt to shut off the source. Do not attempt to do this with your bare hands, and make sure that your feet are dry and that you are not standing in any water. Use a wooden stick, board, or rope. If this is not possible, you need to contact your supervisor or building management so that they can shut down power at another junction. If you find an apparently unconscious person underneath a live wire, do not touch the person! Again, attempt to move the live wire with a wooden stick or similar object. Never use anything metal, and do not touch anything metal while you are doing it. After moving the wire, call 911 and contact your superiors immediately. While waiting, attempt to administer first aid to the person.

ESD

Electrostatic discharge (ESD) occurs when two objects of different voltages come into contact with each other. The human body is always gathering static electricity, more than enough to damage a computer component, for example, that $500 video card you just purchased! ESD is a silent killer. If you were to touch a component without proper protection, the static electricity could discharge from you to the component, most likely damaging it, but with no discernable signs of damage. Worse yet, it is possible to discharge a small amount of voltage to the device and damage it to the point at which it works intermittently, making it tough to troubleshoot. It takes only 30 volts or so to damage a component. On a dry winter day, you could gather as much as 20,000 volts when walking across a carpeted area! You can equalize the electrical potentials in several ways, allowing you to protect components from ESD, including the following:

> ▶ **Use an antistatic wrist strap:** The more common kind is inexpensive and takes only a moment to put on and connect to the chassis of the computer. (The chassis is an unpainted portion of the frame inside the case.) By doing so you constantly discharge to the case's metal frame instead of to the components that you handle. Of course, the chassis of the computer can absorb only so much ESD, so consider another earth-bonding point to connect to or try to implement as many other antistatic methods as possible. Most wrist straps come equipped with a resistor (often 1 megaohm) that protects the user from shock hazards when working with low-voltage components.

More advanced types of wrist straps are meant to connect to an actual *ground*; a ground strip or the ground plug of a special dedicated AC outlet. These are used in more-sophisticated repair labs. Do *not* attempt to connect the alligator clip of a basic wrist strap (purchased at an office store) to the ground plug of an outlet in your home.

▶ **Touch the chassis of the computer:** Do this before handling any components to further discharge yourself. This is also a good habit to get into if an antistatic strap is not available.

▶ **Use antistatic bags:** Adapter cards, motherboards, and the like are normally shipped in antistatic bags; hold on to them! When installing or removing components, keep them either inside or on top of the bag until you are ready to work with them.

Note

Remember to keep the computer unplugged—Disconnect the power or hit the kill switch on the back of the computer (if there is one) before working on the system. You might not know if the AC outlet is wired properly. Regardless, by simply disconnecting the power, you eliminate any chance of a shock.

ExamAlert

Remember the three main ways to avoid ESD: antistatic strap, touch the computer case, and use antistatic bags.

▶ **Handle components properly**: If you are sitting at your desk without any ESD protection, there is no reason to be handling components, so don't. Handle components only when you are fully protected. When you do handle components, try to hold them at the edge. For example, when installing RAM, hold the module at the sides. This will inhibit any direct handling of the chips, contacts, and other circuitry. Adapter cards should either be held by the metal plate (bracket), or by the edge of the fiberglass board, but never the contacts.

▶ **Use an antistatic mat:** Place the computer on top of the antistatic mat and connect the alligator clip of the mat to the computer's chassis in the same manner that you did with the wrist strap. (Some people stand on the mat and connect its alligator clip to the computer, which is also an option.)

- ▶ **Use antistatic wipes:** Use products, such as Endust, to clean the outside of monitors, computer cases, and keyboards; they apply a certain amount of ESD protection.

- ▶ **Use antistatic sprays:** These can be sprayed on clothing or on the floor or table in which a technician works.

A few less direct ways to reduce ESD follow:

- ▶ **Keep your feet stationary:** When working on the computer and touching components, keep your feet stationary to reduce friction.

- ▶ **Work in a noncarpeted area:** Carpeting creates additional friction that leads to ESD. Some computer labs have special tiling with antistatic properties, but if you work for a company that doesn't have a proper lab or repair room, consider using an uncarpeted warehouse space or uncarpeted cafeteria. If you work at home, consider uncarpeted areas such as the kitchen, basement, or garage.

- ▶ **Raise the humidity:** By increasing the humidity to 50 percent (if possible), you decrease the chance of friction and ultimately decrease the chance of ESD. Did you ever notice that electrostatic discharges happen more readily during the winter? This is because of the lower humidity during that season.

- ▶ **Remove jewelry, and wear protective clothing:** Remove any jewelry before working on a computer. You don't want this to come into contact with any components. Consider wearing clothes that are tighter fitting so that there is no chance of anything contacting the computer components. In some labs you might see technicians wearing antistatic nylon jumpsuits. For the average person, rubber-soled shoes can also help to prevent ESD.

- ▶ **Keep away from devices that use electricity:** Try to steer clear of mechanized tools such as battery operated screw guns. Watch out for vacuums as well. Keep anything that is AC powered far away from the computer. Keep battery operated devices away as well unless it's your trusty multimeter.

- ▶ **Don't use a vacuum cleaner:** Vacuum cleaners can be a deadly source of ESD. When cleaning those dust-bunnies out of the computer, do it outside, and consider using compressed air or other specialized cleaning kits. Use Stabilant-22a or a similar cleaner to enhance any contacts' connectivity when you finish.

Remember ESD needs to happen only once, and that $500 video card you try to install is toast!

Physical Safety

Physical safety considerations include the following:

▶ Securing cables

▶ Using caution with heavy items

▶ Not touching hot components

▶ Considering workplace ergonomics

Cables can be a trip hazard. Employ proper cable management by routing cables away from high-traffic areas and keep computer cables stowed away and tie-wrapped. Network cables should have been installed permanently within the walls and ceiling, but sometimes you might find a rogue cable. If you discover a cable lying on the floor, or hanging from the ceiling, alert your network administrator or your manager. Do not attempt to reroute the network cable. You don't know what data is transferred on the cable. Because network cabling is monitored by municipalities the same way other electrical work is done, only qualified, trained technicians should take care of the network wiring.

Lifting heavy items incorrectly can cause many types of injuries. As a general rule, if an item is heavier than one quarter of your body weight, you should ask someone else to help. When lifting items, stand close to the item, squat down to the item by bending the knees, grasp the item firmly, keep the back straight, and slowly lift with the legs, not the back. Be sure not to twist the body, and keep the item close to the body. This helps to prevent back injuries. When moving items, it is best to have them stored at waist level so that minimal lifting is necessary. OSHA has plenty of guidelines and recommendations for physical safety at the workplace. Their website is http://www.osha.gov/.

Be careful when handling components that might be hot. The best method is to wait when dealing with hot items such as a laser printer's fuser, a burned out power supply, or a CPU or hard drive that needs to be replaced. To be safe, before replacing items, wait 15 minutes for them to cool. Servers and networking equipment can get quite hot as well, even if they are stored in a climate controlled room. Take great care when working with these devices. Also, be careful with items that hold a charge. For the A+ certification, know that if a device has the possibility of holding a charge, you should not open it. This includes power supplies and CRT monitors. These types of electronics can be recycled in most municipalities. Programs might include curb-side pickup, drop-off centers, or recycling events. Usually these are free. There are also many donation programs for equipment that still functions.

You probably won't get any questions on the exam about this, but ergonomics are important when operating the computer. Ergonomics can affect the long-term health of the computer operator. It is important to keep the wrists and hands in-line with the forearms and to use proper typing technique. Keep the elbows close to the body and supported if possible. The lower back should be supported as well, and your head and neck should be straight and in-line with your back; the shoulders should be relaxed. Keep the top of the monitor at or just below eye level. Take breaks at least every 2 hours to avoid muscle cramps and eyestrain. To further reduce eyestrain, increase the refresh rate of the monitor if possible. For more information on ergonomics, see OSHA's information on computer work-stations at http://www.osha.gov/SLTC/etools/computerworkstations/index.html.

Cram Quiz

Answer these questions. The answers follow the last question. If you cannot answer these questions correctly, consider reading this section again until you can.

220-801 Questions

1. If a power supply fails, what should you do?
   - A. Replace it.
   - B. Repair it.
   - C. Use a different computer.
   - D. Switch it to a different voltage setting.

2. Which of the following are ways to avoid ESD? (Select three.)
   - A. Use an antistatic wrist strap.
   - B. Use a vacuum cleaner.
   - C. Use an antistatic mat.
   - D. Touch the chassis of the computer.

3. You walk into the server room and see a person lying on the floor with a live electrical wire draped over. What should you do first?
   - A. Run out and call 911.
   - B. Grab the wire and fling it off the person.
   - C. Grab the person and drag them out from under the wire.
   - D. Grab a piece of wood and use it to move the wire off the person.

Cram Quiz Answers

220-801 Answers

1. **A.** Replace the power supply. It can be dangerous to try to repair it and is not cost-effective to the company.

2. **A, C,** and **D.** Antistatic wrist straps, mats, and touching the chassis of the computer are all ways to stop ESD. Vacuum cleaners can cause damage to components.

3. **D.** The first thing you should do is get a wooden stick, rope, or something similar (every server room should have one), and use it to CAREFULLY move the wire off of the person. In reality, the first thing you should do is to breathe, and not make any rash decisions because in the heat of the moment, you might think a bit less clearly than you are right now. Anyways, after the wire is removed, you should call 911 and then attempt to offer first aid to the victim. DO NOT ever touch a live wire or anything that the live wire is coming into contact with.

Procedures and Environmental Controls

Environmental factors vary from one organization to the next. For the exam you need to know how and why to control temperature and humidity, what an MSDS is and how to use it, and how to deal with dust and debris when it comes to computers. You should also have a basic understanding of some of the procedures that a typical organization puts into practice.

Temperature, Humidity, and Air

You should be aware of the temperature and humidity measurements in your building. You should also be thinking about airborne particles and proper ventilation. Collectively, OSHA refers to this as "air treatment"; the removal of air contaminants and/or the control of room temperature and humidity. Though there is no specific government policy regarding this, there are recommendations including a temperature range of 68 to 76 degrees Fahrenheit (20 to 24 degrees Celsius), and a humidity range of between 20% and 60%. Remember, the higher the humidity, the less chance of ESD, but it might get a bit uncomfortable for your co-workers; they might not want to work in a rainforest, so a compromise will have to be sought. If your organization uses air handlers to heat, cool, and move the air, it will be somewhat difficult to keep the humidity much past 25% or 30%. That brings us to ventilation. An organization should employ the use of local exhaust (to remove contaminants generated by the organization's processes), and the introduction of an adequate supply of fresh outdoor air through natural or mechanical ventilation.

For air treatment, organizations should make use of filtration devices, electronic cleaners, and possibly chemical treatments activated with charcoal or other sorbents (materials used to absorb unwanted gases.) Most filtration systems make use of charcoal and HEPA filters. These filters should be replaced at regular intervals. Air ducts and dampers should be cleaned regularly. And ductwork insulation should be inspected now and again. If there still is a considerable amount of airborne particles, portable air filtration enclosures can be purchased that also use charcoal and HEPA filters, or possibly utilize ultraviolet light to eliminate particles. These are commonly found in PC repair facilities due to the amount of dust and dirt sitting in PCs that are waiting for repair. Some organizations even foot the bill for masks or even respirators for their employees. Many PC workbenches will be equipped with a compressed air system and vacuum system. This way, the PC tech can blow out the dust and dirt from a computer, and vacuum it up at the same time. Otherwise, it is usually best to take the computer outside, unless it is windy.

EMI and RFI

Electromagnetic interference (EMI) is an unwanted disturbance that affects electrical circuits. Network interference could be caused by EMI, for example, if an unshielded network cable were inadvertently draped over a fluorescent light above the drop ceiling. The light's EMI could cause data loss on that cable. Keep network cables away from lights, junction boxes, and any other AC electrical sources. Anything with magnets (speakers, CRTs, and UPSes) should be kept away from the computer, and cables should be routed away from these devices. It's possible that lightning can cause EMI line noise to occur within the power cable. A good surge protector or line-conditioning device should deflect this.

Radio frequency interference (RFI) is closely related to EMI. For the A+ exam, some things to consider include cordless phone and microwave usage. Because these devices can also inhabit the 2.4 GHz frequency range used by 802.11b, g, and n networks, they can interfere with the network signal. Be sure that all devices are on different channels (1, 6, and 11 are the nonoverlapping ones) and that the microwave is not physically near any wireless devices.

Cables can act as antennas for radiated energy and should be shielded if possible.

MSDS and Disposal

Products that use chemicals require material safety data sheets (MSDSs). These are documents that give information about particular substances, for example the ink in inkjet cartridges. Information in the MSDS includes:

▶ Proper treatment if the substance is ingested or comes into contact with the skin.

▶ How to deal with spills and other hazards.

▶ How to dispose of the substance.

▶ How to store the substance.

It's easy to find MSDSs; most companies have them online. You can search for them at the manufacturer's website or with a search engine. For example, the following link has all the Hewlett Packard MSDSs: http://www.hp.com/hpinfo/globalcitizenship/environment/products/msds-specs.html. Click any category and then a specific product to see its MSDS. An MSDS identifies the chemical substance, possible hazards, fire-fighting measures, handling and storage, and so on. Make sure you have Adobe Acrobat Reader installed because most MSDSs are in PDF format.

It's important to know what to do in the case that someone is adversely affected by a product that has chemicals. A person might have skin irritation due to coming into contact with toner particles, or a cleaner that was used on a keyboard or mouse. As a technician, your job is to find out how to help the person. If you do not have direct access to the MSDS, you should contact your facilities department or building management. Perhaps the cleaning crew uses a particular cleaning agent that you are not familiar with, and only the facilities department has been given the MSDS for this. It's better to review all MSDS documents and be proactive, but in this case, you probably won't have access to the document. Collaborate with the facilities department to get the person that was affected the proper first aid, and if necessary, take the person to the emergency room. Finally, remove the affected device if it is a keyboard or mouse, and so on. Replace it with a similar device until you can get the original device cleaned properly.

ExamAlert

Know that an MSDS contains information about chemical substances and hazards.

Generally, substances that contain chemicals should be stored in a cool, dry place, away from sunlight. "Cool" means the lower end of the OSHA guideline, approximately 68 degrees F (20 degrees C). Often, this will be in a storage closet away from the general work area and outside of the air filtration system. This also allows the items to be stored in a less humid area.

Recycling and proper disposal are also important. Batteries should not be thrown away with normal trash because they contain chemicals. First, you should check your local municipal or EPA guidelines for proper disposal of batteries, and in some cases, you will find that there are drop-off areas for these, either at the town municipal center, or sometimes at office and computer supply stores. This applies to alkaline, lithium (for example CR2032), lithium-ion, and NiCd batteries.

ExamAlert

Check your local municipal and EPA guidelines for disposal of batteries and other equipment.

Ink and toner cartridges can usually be sent back to the manufacturer, or quite often office supply stores and printer repair outfits will take them for later recycling. Some municipalities have a method for recycling electrical devices in general.

Incident Response and Documentation

How you follow up on an incident is a good measure of your ability to an organization. Incident response is the set of procedures that any investigator follows when examining a technology incident. How you first respond, how you document the situation, and your ability to establish a chain of custody are all important to your investigating skills.

First Response

When you first respond to an incident, your first task will be to identify exactly what happened. You must first recognize if this is a simple problem that needs to be troubleshot, or if it is an incident that needs to be escalated. For example, if you encounter a person who has prohibited content on a computer, this can be considered an incident, and you will be expected to escalate the issue to your supervisor, reporting on exactly what you have found. Copyrighted information, malware, inappropriate content, and stolen information could all be considered prohibited. So before you do anything, you should report what you have found to the proper channels, and then make sure that the data and affected devices are preserved. This often means making a backup of the computer's image. However, this will depend on your organization's policies. You might be told to leave everything as is and wait for a computer forensics expert, or a security analyst; it will depend on the scenario. The idea here is that the scene will be preserved for that other person so that he can collect evidence.

Documentation

You want to document everything that you find and anything that happens after that. If your organization doesn't have any other methodology, write it down! When you leave the scene, you will be required to divulge all information to your supervisor. If you fixed the problem and no other specialists were required, the documentation process will continue through to the completion of the task and beyond when you monitor the system. You should also document any processes, procedures, and user training that might be necessary for the future.

Chain of Custody

If you are required to preserve evidence, one way to do this is to set up a chain of custody. This is the chronological documentation or paper trail of evidence. It should be initiated at the start of any investigation. It documents who had custody of the evidence all the way up to litigation (if necessary). It also verifies that the evidence has not been modified or tampered with.

As a PC tech, you will usually not get too involved with investigations. But you should know the basic concepts of first response, documentation, and chain of custody for the exam, and in the case that you find yourself in a situation where you have found prohibited content or illegal activities.

Cram Quiz

Answer these questions. The answers follow the last question. If you cannot answer these questions correctly, consider reading this section again until you can.

220-801 Questions

1. What document can aid you if a chemical spill occurs?

   ○ **A.** MSKB

   ○ **B.** MSDS

   ○ **C.** MCSE

   ○ **D.** DSS

2. A co-worker complains that after the cleaning crew has come through, the keyboard irritates his hands and leaves some green residue. What should you do?

   ○ **A.** Call the fire department.

   ○ **B.** Contact the facilities department.

   ○ **C.** Contact the manufacturer of the keyboard.

   ○ **D.** Call OSHA and complain.

3. You find illegal materials on a customer's computer. Your boss commands you to preserve computer evidence until he gets to the scene. What is your boss asking you to begin?

   ○ **A.** Documentation

   ○ **B.** Chain of custody

   ○ **C.** First response

   ○ **D.** EMI prevention

Cram Quiz Answers

220-801 Answers

1. **B.** The material safety data sheet (MSDS) defines exactly what a chemical is, what the potential hazards are, and how to deal with them.

2. **B.** Contact the facilities department to see if they have the MSDS for the cleaner. You and/or the facilities department should then treat the irritation according to the MSDS. If this does not work, and the problem gets worse, bring the co-worker to the emergency room. Remove the keyboard from the work environment.

3. **B.** Your boss is asking you to begin the process of a chain of custody: the chronological paper trail of evidence. It is a form of documentation, but a specific one. You were the first responder. These cases will be rare, but you should understand the terminology and what to do if you find illegal materials.

Professionalism and Communication Skills

For the A+ exams, professionalism and communication consists of ten categories:

- **Punctuality:** Be on time! If a customer has to wait, he might become difficult before you even begin. If you are running late, contact the customer, apologize, and let him know that you will be late.

- **Listen to the customer:** Don't interrupt the customer, even if you think you know what the problem is before she has fully explained the situation. Be respectful and allow her to complete her explanation. Her tale just might give you clues as to what the *real* problem is. Listen carefully but be assertive when eliciting answers.

- **Clarify the problem:** Ask open-ended questions to the customer to further identify what the issue is, and narrow the scope of the problem. After you think you understand what the problem is, you should always clarify by repeating the problem back to the customer. Restate the issue to verify everyone understands the problem.

- **Be positive:** Try to maintain a positive attitude, even if the customer thinks the situation is hopeless, or if the customer is frustrated. Sometimes problems that appear to be the worst have the easiest solutions! And there is *always* a solution. It's just a matter of finding it.

- **Speak clearly:** Use proper language, and speak slowly and clearly so the customer can fully understand what you tell them. Avoid computer jargon and acronyms (for example WPA or TCP/IP). By using computer jargon, the customer might think that you are insecure and cannot clearly explain things. Stay away from the techno-babble. The customer expects you to know these things technically but to explain them in a simple manner.

- **Set and meet expectations:** When you have a clear idea of what the customer's trouble is, set a timeline; offer a reasonable assessment of how long it will take to fix the issue and what will be involved. Stay in contact with the customer giving him updates at certain intervals—every half hour for smaller jobs and perhaps two or three times a day for larger jobs. If applicable, offer different repair or replacement options as the job progresses. At first you might inform a customer that it appears a power supply needs to be changed. Later you might find that an optical drive also needs to be replaced. Keep the customer up to date and offer options. Whatever the service, be clear as to the policies of your company and provide the proper documentation about the services you will be performing. After you finish the job, follow up with the customer to verify that the computer runs smoothly and that he is satisfied.

▶ **Avoid distractions:** Cell phone calls should be screened and left to go to voicemail unless it is an emergency. The same goes for e-mails that arrive on your smartphone/PDA and text messages on the phone. If other customers call, explain to them that you are with a customer and will call them back shortly, or have your manager or co-worker take care of them if they are available. Avoid talking to co-workers when dealing with customers. The customer wants to feel valued and wants to get her problem fixed in a timely manner. Try to avoid personal interruptions in general.

▶ **Do not look at or touch confidential information:** Ask the customer to move the confidential items to another area where you cannot see them. Do not look at or touch the confidential materials. This could include bank statements, accounting information, legal documents, and other top secret company information.

▶ **Do the right thing:** If a customer asks you to do something that you think is inappropriate, be sure to verify exactly what it is the customer wants you to do. Then take appropriate action. For example, if a customer asks you to install company software on the person's personal laptop, you should verify that the installation is allowed under the company's licensing agreements. If so, no harm done. If not, you will have to politely refuse the customer. This type of customer behavior, while rare, should be reported to your manager.

▶ **Deal with customers professionally:** Understand that customers can come from all walks of life. By being patient, understanding, and respectful, you show customers that you are a professional and serious about fixing their computer problems. Never argue with customers or take a defensive or offensive stance. This is another one of those times in which I like to think of Mr. Spock. Approach customers' computer problems and complaints from a scientific point of view. Try not to make light of a customer's computer issues, no matter how simple they might seem, and avoid being judgmental of any possible user error. Never ask things such as "What did you do?" or "Who was working on this?" because these questions can come across as accusations. Ask computer-oriented open-ended questions when eliciting answers from the customers, for example, "What is wrong with the computer?" or "What can you tell me about this computer?" Stick with the senses; questions such as "What type of strange behavior did you *see* from the computer?" keeps customers more relaxed and can help you to narrow down the cause of the problem. Again, if a customer doesn't come across clearly, restate what you believe to be the issue, or repeat your question so that you can verify understanding and so both of you will be on the same page.

Cram Quiz

Answer these questions. The answers follow the last question. If you cannot answer these questions correctly, consider reading this section again until you can.

220-801 Questions

1. How will speaking with a lot of jargon make a technician sound?

   ○ **A.** Competent
   ○ **B.** Insecure
   ○ **C.** Smart
   ○ **D.** Powerful

2. A customer experiences a server crash. When you arrive, the manager is upset about this problem. What do you need to remember in this scenario?

   ○ **A.** Stay calm and do the job as efficiently as possible.
   ○ **B.** Imagine the customer in his underwear.
   ○ **C.** Avoid the customer and get the job done quickly.
   ○ **D.** Refer the customer to your supervisor.

3. Which of the following are good ideas when dealing with customers? (Select two.)

   ○ **A.** Speak clearly.
   ○ **B.** Ignore them.
   ○ **C.** Avoid distractions.
   ○ **D.** Explain to them what they did wrong.

4. You are a field technician working at a customer's site. One of the workers asks you to load a copy of an organization's purchased software on a personal laptop. What should you do first?

   ○ **A.** Verify that the installation is allowed under the company's licensing agreement.
   ○ **B.** Act as though you are distracted and ignore the user.
   ○ **C.** Leave the premises and inform the police.
   ○ **D.** Tell the worker that installing unlicensed software is illegal.
   ○ **E.** Notify the worker's manager of a security breach.

Cram Quiz Answers

220-801 Answers

1. **B.** Too much computer jargon can make an end user think that you do not have the qualifications needed and are masking it with techno-babble.

2. **A.** There isn't much you can do when a customer is upset except stay calm and fix the problem!

3. **A** and **C** are correct. Speak clearly so that customers understand you, and avoid distractions so that the customers know they have your complete attention.

4. **A.** You should first check if the company allows installations of paid software on personal computers or laptops. If it is allowed, go ahead and do the installation. If not, then you should refuse, and notify *your* manager of the occurrence.

CHAPTER 19
Taking the Real Exams

This chapter provides the following tools and information to help you be successful when preparing for and taking the CompTIA A+ 220-801 and 220-802 exams:

- ▶ Getting Ready and the Exam Preparation Checklist
- ▶ Tips for Taking the Real Exam
- ▶ Beyond the CompTIA A+ Certification

Getting Ready and the Exam Preparation Checklist

The CompTIA A+ certification exams can be taken by anyone; there are no prerequisites although CompTIA recommends one year of prior lab or field experience working with computers. For more information on CompTIA and the A+ exam, go to

http://www.comptia.org

Also visit my A+ page: www.davidlprowse.com/220-801 for information, additions, and updated errata.

To acquire your A+ certification, you need to pass two exams: 220-801, and 220-802, each of which is 90 questions. Although it is possible, I don't recommend taking both exams on the same day but instead spacing them a week or so apart. These exams are administered by Pearson Vue (www.vue.com). You need to register with Pearson Vue to take the exam.

You must be fully prepared for the exam, so I created a checklist that you can use to make sure you have covered all the bases. The checklist is shown in Table 19.1. Go through the checklist twice, once for each exam. For each exam place a check in the status column as each item is completed. Do this first with the 220-801 exam and then again with the 220-802 exam. I highly recommend completing each step in order and taking the 220-801 exam first. Historically, my readers and students have benefited greatly from this type of checklist.

TABLE 19.1 **Exam Preparation Checklist**

Step	Item	Details	220-801 Status	220-802 Status
1.	Review Exam Alerts.	The little gray boxes with Exam Alerts are interspersed throughout the book. Review these and make sure you understand every one.		
2.	Review Cram Quizzes.	Cram Quizzes are categorized by exam. You can review them in the text or on the disc. On the first run-through of this checklist, start with the 220-801 questions. On the second run-through, use the 220-802 questions.		
3.	Complete the Practice Exam in the book.	Directly after this chapter are two practice exams, one for 220-801 and 220-802. They are also available on the disc. Your goal should be to get at least 80% correct on each exam on the first try. (100% would be preferable!)		

TABLE 19.1 **Continued**

Step	Item	Details	220-801 Status	220-802 Status
		If you score under 80%, go back and study more! Also, consider getting my book: *A+ Exam Cram Practice Questions*, 5th edition. It comes with 700 questions and in-depth explanations.		
4.	Create your own cheat sheet.	Although there is a Cram Sheet in the beginning of this book, you should also create your own. See Table 19.2 for an example. The act of writing down important details helps to commit them to memory. Keep in mind that you will not be allowed to take this or the Cram Sheet into the actual testing room.		
5.	Register for the exam.	Do not register until you have completed the previous steps; you shouldn't register until you are fully prepared. When you are ready, schedule the exam to commence within a couple days so that you won't forget what you learned! Registration can be done online. Register at Pearson Vue: www.vue.com. It accepts payment by major credit cards for the exam fee. (You need to create an account to sign up for exams.)		
6.	Study the Cram Sheet and cheat sheet.	The Cram Sheet is a fold out in the beginning of this book. It is also on the disc. Study from this and your cheat sheet during the last 24 hours before the exam. (If your exam is delayed for any reason, go back to step 2 and retake the cram quizzes and practice exams until once again the test day is 24 hours off.)		
7.	Take the exam!	Check mark each exam to the right as you pass them. Good luck!		

Table 19.2 gives a partial example of a cheat sheet that you can create to aid in your studies. Fill in the appropriate information in the right column. For example, the first step of the six-step troubleshooting process is "Identify the problem."

TABLE 19.2 **Example Cheat Sheet**

Concept	Fill in the Appropriate Information Here
The six-step troubleshooting process	1. 2. 3. 4. 5. 6.
The motherboard form factors you should know	
The three types of DDR and their data transfer rates	
The EP printing process	
Six types of expansion buses and their maximum data transfer rates	
Windows 7/ Vista startup files	
Windows XP startup files	
Etc.*	

*Continue Table 19.2 in this fashion on paper. The key is to write down various technologies, processes, step-by-steps, and so on to commit them to memory.

Tips for Taking the Real Exam

Some of you will be new to exams. This section is for you. For other readers who have taken exams before, feel free to skip this section or use it as a review.

The exam is conducted on a computer and is multiple choice. You have the option to skip questions. If you do so, be sure to "mark" them before moving on. There is a small check box that you can select to mark them. Feel free to mark any other questions that you have answered but are not completely sure about. When you get to the end of the exam, there will be an item review section, which shows you any questions that you did not answer and any that you marked.

The following list includes tips and tricks that I have learned over the years. I've taken at least 20 certification exams in the past decade, and the following points have served me well.

General Practices for Taking Exams

▶ **Pick a good time for the exam:** It would appear that the least amount of people are at test centers on Monday and Friday mornings. Consider scheduling during these times. Otherwise, schedule a time that works well for you, when you don't have to worry about anything else. Keep in mind that Saturdays can be busy. Oh, and don't schedule the exam until you are ready. I understand that sometimes deadlines have to be set, but in general, don't register for the exam until you feel confident you can pass. Things come up in life that can sometimes get in the way of your study time. Keep in mind that most exams can be canceled as long as you give 24 hours' notice. (Check that time frame when registering to be sure.)

▶ **Don't over-study the day before the exam:** Some people like to study hard the day before; some don't. My recommendations are to study off the Cram Sheet and your own cheat sheets, but in general, don't overdo it. It's not a good idea to go into overload the day before the exam.

▶ **Get a good night's rest:** A good night's sleep (7 to 9 hours) before the day of the exam is probably the best way to get your mind ready for an exam.

▶ **Eat a decent breakfast:** Eating is good! Breakfast is number two when it comes to getting your mind ready for an exam, especially if it is a morning exam. Just watch out for the coffee and tea. Too much caffeine for a person who is not used to it can be detrimental to the thinking process.

▶ **Show up early:** The testing agency recommends that you show up 30 minutes prior to your scheduled exam time. This is important; give yourself plenty of time, and make sure you know where you are going. You don't want to have to worry about getting lost or being late. Stress and fear are the mind killers. Work on reducing any types of stress the day of and the day before the exam. By the way, you do need extra time because when you get to the testing center, you need to show ID, sign forms, get your personal belongings situated, and be escorted to your seat. Have two forms of ID (signed) ready for the administrator of the test center. Turn your cell phone or smartphone off when you get to the test center; they'll check that, too.

▶ **Bring ear plugs:** You never know when you will get a loud testing center, or worse yet, a loud test taker next to you. Ear plugs help to block out any unwanted noise that might show up. Just be ready to show your ear plugs to the test administrator.

▶ **Brainstorm before starting the exam:** Write down as much as you can remember from the Cram and cheat sheets before starting the exam. The testing center is obligated to give you *something* to write on; make use of it! By getting all the memorization out of your head and on "paper" first, it clears the brain somewhat so that it can tackle the questions. I put paper in quotation marks because it might not be paper; it could be a mini dry erase board or something similar.

▶ **Take small breaks while taking the exam:** Exams can be brutal. You have to answer 100 questions while staring at a screen for an hour. Sometimes these screens are old and have seen better days; these older flickering monitors can cause a strain on your eyes. I recommend small breaks and breathing techniques. For example, after going through every 25 questions or so, close your eyes, and slowly take a few deep breaths, holding each one for 5 seconds, and releasing each one slowly. Think about nothing while doing so. Remove the test from your mind during these breaks. It takes only 1/2 a minute but can help to get your brain refocused. It's almost a Zen type of thing; but for me, when I have applied this technique properly I have gotten a few perfect scores. It's amazing how the mindset can make or break you.

▶ **Be Confident:** You have studied hard, gone through the practice exams, created your cheat sheet—done everything you can to prep. These things alone should build confidence. But actually, you just have to be confident for no reason whatsoever. Think of it this way: You are great... I am great... (to quote Dr. Daystrom.) But truly, there is no disputing this! That's the mentality you must have. You are not being pretentious about this if you think it to yourself. Acting that way to others…well that's another matter. So build that inner confidence and your mindset should be complete.

Smart Methods for Difficult Questions

▶ **Use the process of elimination:** If you are not sure about an answer, first eliminate any answers that are definitely *incorrect*. You might be surprised how often this works. This is one of the reasons why it is recommended that you not only know the correct answers to the practice exam questions, but also know *why* the wrong answers are wrong. The testing center should give you something to write on; use it by writing down the letters of the answers that are incorrect to keep track. Even if you aren't sure about the correct answer, if you can logically eliminate anything that is incorrect, then the answer will become apparent. To sum it up, the character Sherlock Holmes said it best: "When you have eliminated the impossible, whatever remains, however improbable, must be the truth." There's more to it of course, but from a scientific standpoint, this method can be invaluable.

▶ **Be logical in the face of adversity:** The most difficult questions are when two answers appear to be correct, even though the test question requires you to select only one answer. Real exams do not rely on "trick" questions. Sometimes you need to slow down, think logically, and compare the two possible correct answers. Also, you must imagine the scenario that the question is a part of. Think through step by step what is happening in the scenario. Write out as much as you can. The more you can visualize the scenario, the better you can figure out which of the two answers is the best one.

▶ **Use your gut instinct:** Sometimes a person taking a test just doesn't know the answer; it happens to everyone. If you have read through the question and all the answers and used the process of elimination, sometimes this is all you have left. In some scenarios, you might read a question and instinctively know the answer, even if you can't explain why. Tap into this ability. Some test takers write down their gut instinct answer before delving into the question and then compare their thoughtful answer with their gut instinct answer.

▶ **Don't let one question beat you!** Don't let yourself get stuck on one question. Skip it and return to it later. When you spend too much time on one question, the brain gets sluggish. The thing is with these exams is that you either know it or you don't. And don't worry too much about it; chances are you are not going to get a perfect score. Remember that the goal is only to pass the exams; how many answers you get right after that is irrelevant. If you have gone through this book thoroughly, you should be well prepared, and you should have plenty of time to go through all the exam questions with time to spare to return to the ones you skipped and marked.

▶ **If all else fails, guess:** Remember that the exams might not be perfect. A question might seem confusing or appear not to make sense. Leave questions like this until the end, and when you have gone through all the other techniques mentioned, make an educated, logical guess. Try to imagine what the test is after, and why it would be bringing up this topic, vague or strange as it might appear.

Wrapping up the Exam

▶ **Review all your answers:** If you finish early, use the time allotted to you to review the answers. Chances are you will have time left over at the end, so use it wisely! Make sure that everything you have marked has a proper answer that makes sense to you. But try not to over think! Give it your best shot and be confident in your answers. You don't want to second guess yourself!

Beyond the CompTIA A+ Certification

CompTIA started a new policy on January 1, 2011. A person who passes the A+ exams will be certified for 3 years. To maintain the certification beyond that time, you must enroll in the CompTIA Continuing Education Program. This program has an annual fee and requires that you obtain Continuing Education Units (CEUs) that count toward the recertification. For more information on this policy see the following link:

http://certification.comptia.org/getCertified/stayCertified.aspx

After you pass the exams, consider thinking about your technical future. Not only is it important to keep up with new technology and keep your technical skills sharp, but technical growth is important as well.

Usually, companies wait at least 6 months before implementing new operating systems and other applications on any large scale, but you will have to deal with it sooner or later, most likely sooner. Microsoft is always releasing new products. Consider getting access to the latest Microsoft software and operating systems, and practice installing, upgrading, configuring, and troubleshooting them. And Microsoft isn't the only player in town; you should also keep up to date with OS X, Linux, iOS, and Android. Consider becoming proficient in these other operating systems.

To keep on top of the various computer technologies, think about subscribing to technology websites, RSS feeds, and periodicals, and read them on a regular basis. After all, a technician's skills need to be constantly honed and kept up to date. Feel free to contact me for specific website recommendations.

Information Technology (IT) people need to keep learning to foster good growth in the field. Consider taking other certification exams after you complete the A+. The CompTIA A+ certification acts as a springboard to other certifications. For example, the CompTIA Network+ is designed to identify a technician's knowledge of network operating systems, equipment, and networking technologies. The CompTIA Security+ takes this to another level, evaluating the technician's knowledge of how to secure networks, and computers and their applications. Now that you know exactly how to go about passing a certification exam, consider more certifications to bolster your resume.

The best advice I can give is to do what you love. From an IT-perspective, I usually break it down by technology, as opposed to by the vendor or certification. For example, you might want to learn more about e-mail systems, or securing internetworks, or you might prefer to work on databases. Whatever the field, learn as much as you can about that field and all its vendors to stay ahead.

Final Note: I wish you the best of luck on your exams and in your IT career endeavors. Please let me know when you pass your exams. I would love to hear from you! Also, remember that I am available to answer any of your questions about this book via my website: http://www.davidlprowse.com.

Sincerely,

David L. Prowse

Practice Exam 1

CompTIA A+ 220-801

The 100 multiple-choice questions provided here help you to determine how prepared you are for the actual exam and which topics you need to review further. Write down your answers on a separate sheet of paper so that you can take this exam again if necessary. Compare your answers against the answer key that follows this exam.

1. How can you reduce the chance of ESD? (Select the two best answers.)
   - ○ A. Use an antistatic wrist strap.
   - ○ B. Raise the temperature in the room.
   - ○ C. Touch an unpainted portion of the computer case.
   - ○ D. Lower the humidity.
   - ○ E. Plug the computer into an AC outlet.

2. Which of the following disperses heat but requires no moving parts?
   - ○ A. Heat sink
   - ○ B. CPU fan
   - ○ C. Case fan
   - ○ D. Liquid cooling system

3. Why should VoIP not be used with satellite Internet?
   - ○ A. Bandwidth limitations
   - ○ B. Difficult to install
   - ○ C. Latency
   - ○ D. Cost

4. A customer wants to control several computers with a single set of input devices. What solution should you provide for them?
   - ○ A. Barcode reader
   - ○ B. Smartcard reader
   - ○ C. Ethernet switch
   - ○ D. KVM

5. Which the following would best be used for high-end graphics cards?
   - ○ A. PCIe
   - ○ B. PCI
   - ○ C. AGP
   - ○ D. ISA

6. Which of the following materials should a computer never be placed on?
   - ○ A. Wood
   - ○ B. Carpet
   - ○ C. Plastic
   - ○ D. Tile

7. Of the following default ports, which one is used by the TELNET protocol?

   ○ **A.** 23

   ○ **B.** 25

   ○ **C.** 80

   ○ **D.** 110

8. Which of the following is the latest type of memory for a computer?

   ○ **A.** RAMBUS

   ○ **B.** DRAM

   ○ **C.** DDR

   ○ **D.** SDRAM

9. Which of the following can be potential sources of EMI? (Select the two best answers.)

   ○ **A.** Flat-panel televisions

   ○ **B.** AC power lines

   ○ **C.** Cordless phones

   ○ **D.** Electric motors

   ○ **E.** Faraday cage

10. Which type of cable needs to be fire resistant?

    ○ **A.** STP

    ○ **B.** Coaxial

    ○ **C.** Plenum

    ○ **D.** UTP

11. Which wireless standard has the shortest indoor range?

    ○ **A.** 802.11a

    ○ **B.** 802.11b

    ○ **C.** 802.11g

    ○ **D.** 801.11n

12. Which of the following types of storage media can hold the most data?

    ○ **A.** Blu-ray

    ○ **B.** DLT

    ○ **C.** DVD-ROM

    ○ **D.** SD card

13. Which type of Internet connection provides typical downstream networking speeds of 5 to 12 Mbps utilizing phone lines?

    ○ **A.** ADSL

    ○ **B.** VPN

    ○ **C.** Bluetooth

    ○ **D.** 802.3u

14. Which of the following is a common power rating for a desktop PC that runs office applications?

    ○ **A.** 12 volts

    ○ **B.** 400 watts

    ○ **C.** 120 volts

    ○ **D.** 900 watts

15. You have a PCIe card that you need to install. The card's documentation says that it requires a x4 slot. The computer you are installing to has only x1 and x16 slots. What should you do?

    ○ **A.** Install the card to the x1 slot and get normal performance.

    ○ **B.** Install the card to the x16 slot and get four times the performance.

    ○ **C.** Install the card to the x1 slot and get half the performance.

    ○ **D.** Install the card to the x16 slot and get normal performance.

16. Your boss asks you to replace his laptop's 500 GB hard drive with a new 640 GB hard drive. What interface would you most likely use?

    ○ **A.** PATA

    ○ **B.** SATA

    ○ **C.** IDE

    ○ **D.** SCSI

17. Which type of printer requires special paper to operate?

    ○ **A.** Laser

    ○ **B.** Impact

    ○ **C.** Thermal

    ○ **D.** Inkjet

18. What is the recommended maximum cable length for USB 2.0?

    ○ **A.** 15 meters

    ○ **B.** 10 meters

    ○ **C.** 7 meters

    ○ **D.** 5 meters

19. What should be used when installing or upgrading a CPU to ensure that heat will be dissipated efficiently through the heat sink?

- ○ **A.** Thermal compound
- ○ **B.** Power supply
- ○ **C.** Case fan
- ○ **D.** Fire extinguisher

20. How should you attempt to demonstrate professionalism when dealing with a customer? (Select the three best answers.)

- ○ **A.** Avoid distractions.
- ○ **B.** Retain a chain of custody.
- ○ **C.** Avoid being judgmental.
- ○ **D.** Leave documentation to the customer.
- ○ **E.** Meet expectations that the customer sets for you.

21. What type of card would you use to record off-air television programs?

- ○ **A.** Wireless card
- ○ **B.** Video capture card
- ○ **C.** POST card
- ○ **D.** PCIe video card

22. What is the maximum data transfer rate of IEEE 1394a?

- ○ **A.** 400 Mbps
- ○ **B.** 480 Mbps
- ○ **C.** 800 Mbps
- ○ **D.** 1600 Mbps

23. Which of the following IP addresses is private?

- ○ **A.** 8.58.12.192
- ○ **B.** 173.169.254.1
- ○ **C.** 192.168.58.11
- ○ **D.** 11.23.185.57

24. Which type of memory module has 240 pins?

- ○ **A.** SODIMM DDR3
- ○ **B.** DDR
- ○ **C.** SODIMM DDR2
- ○ **D.** DDR2

25. Which type of RAID stripes data across three or more disks along with parity?

   ○ **A.** RAID 0

   ○ **B.** RAID 1

   ○ **C.** RAID 5

   ○ **D.** RAID 10

26. What is the greatest number of primary partitions on a single physical hard drive?

   ○ **A.** 1

   ○ **B.** 2

   ○ **C.** 3

   ○ **D.** 4

27. Which of the following types of PCs would need a powerful CPU, high-end video card, and as much RAM as possible?

   ○ **A.** Home theater PC

   ○ **B.** CAD workstation

   ○ **C.** Virtualization workstation

   ○ **D.** Thin client

28. You are tasked with upgrading the RAM in a customer's laptop. What type of memory should you select?

   ○ **A.** SODIMM

   ○ **B.** DDR3

   ○ **C.** RIMM

   ○ **D.** SDRAM

29. Which of the following is the correct data connector for an internal SATA hard drive?

   ○ **A.** 7-pin

   ○ **B.** 15-pin

   ○ **C.** 34-pin

   ○ **D.** 40-pin

30. A frustrated customer calls you about a PC that is not functioning properly. What should you ask the user?

   ○ **A.** "What were you doing when the computer crashed?"

   ○ **B.** "Don't use that computer until it's fixed."

   ○ **C.** "What was the last thing that occurred before the computer stopped functioning properly?"

   ○ **D.** "What was the last thing you did before the computer stopped functioning properly?"

31. Which type of RAM is used to solve memory errors?

   ◯ **A.** ECC

   ◯ **B.** Parity

   ◯ **C.** Non-parity

   ◯ **D.** Non-ECC

32. What does Hyper-Threading do?

   ◯ **A.** It works only on PCs with more than one core.

   ◯ **B.** It enables two independent CPUs to work on the same task simultaneously.

   ◯ **C.** It enables the computer operating system to work on multiple tasks simultaneously.

   ◯ **D.** It allows a processor to work with two independent computer instructions at once.

33. Which printing technology uses multilayer carbonless copy paper?

   ◯ **A.** Dot matrix

   ◯ **B.** Print spooling

   ◯ **C.** Inkjet

   ◯ **D.** Thermal

34. Which one of the following DDR modules is a DDR3 module?

   ◯ **A.** PC1600

   ◯ **B.** PC2700

   ◯ **C.** PC5300

   ◯ **D.** PC8500

35. In the electrophotographic printing process, which one of the following printers uses a charged corona wire?

   ◯ **A.** Laser

   ◯ **B.** Thermal

   ◯ **C.** Impact

   ◯ **D.** Inkjet

36. Which sockets could be used by a Core i5 CPU?

   ◯ **A.** 1155

   ◯ **B.** 775

   ◯ **C.** Socket M

   ◯ **D.** 1366

   ◯ **E.** 1156

37. What is the most secure type of wireless communication?

   ○ **A.** WPA2

   ○ **B.** WPA

   ○ **C.** WEP

   ○ **D.** SSID

38. Which networking technology has the highest potential throughput?

   ○ **A.** Cable

   ○ **B.** Satellite

   ○ **C.** Fiber

   ○ **D.** DSL

39. Which of the following CPU types is manufactured by AMD?

   ○ **A.** Pentium

   ○ **B.** Celeron

   ○ **C.** Core i7

   ○ **D.** Phenom

40. You are attempting to set up a laptop that will display through a projector. Nothing is appearing on the projector screen. What should you press to enable viewing on the projector screen?

   ○ **A.** Power button

   ○ **B.** Control+ESC

   ○ **C.** Function keys

   ○ **D.** ALT+Insert

41. Which of the following types of RAM can transfer 12,800 MB/s?

   ○ **A.** DDR3-1600

   ○ **B.** DDR3-1333

   ○ **C.** DDR2-1066

   ○ **D.** DDR2-800

42. What command would you use to verify the IP address of a gateway on a local computer?

   ○ **A.** PING

   ○ **B.** IPCONFIG

   ○ **C.** NET USE

   ○ **D.** NETSTAT

43. Which chip is responsible for maintaining the data flow between a SATA hard drive and the processor?

- ○ **A.** BIOS
- ○ **B.** Northbridge
- ○ **C.** FSB
- ○ **D.** Southbridge

44. Which video resolution type should you use to attain a resolution of 1600x1050?

- ○ **A.** WSXGA+
- ○ **B.** UXGA
- ○ **C.** SXGA
- ○ **D.** SVGA

45. Which one of the following types of printers allows for the lowest cost per page?

- ○ **A.** Dot matrix
- ○ **B.** Inkjet
- ○ **C.** Laser
- ○ **D.** Thermal

46. What is an example of EMI?

- ○ **A.** Degraded network performance due to network cables and AC power cables in close proximity
- ○ **B.** Degraded network performance due to too many Bluetooth devices being used in close proximity
- ○ **C.** Degraded network performance due to smartphone usage in close proximity
- ○ **D.** Degraded network performance due to poorly punched down network cables

47. You need to retrieve e-mail on a laptop using Microsoft Outlook. Which protocol should you use to retrieve the e-mail?

- ○ **A.** SMTP
- ○ **B.** FTP
- ○ **C.** POP3
- ○ **D.** PING

48. You are required by a customer to configure energy-saving measures on a laptop for when it switches to battery power. What utility should you configure?

    ○ **A.** MSCONFIG

    ○ **B.** DXDIAG

    ○ **C.** BIOS

    ○ **D.** ACPI

49. Which of the following are digital, audio only formats? (Select the two best answers.)

    ○ **A.** WMA

    ○ **B.** AVI

    ○ **C.** WPA

    ○ **D.** AAC

    ○ **E.** MOV

50. Which of the following would you install into an AGP slot on a motherboard?

    ○ **A.** Memory

    ○ **B.** Video card

    ○ **C.** CPU

    ○ **D.** Soundcard

51. You want to add a network printer in Windows 7. Which of the following ports is the best solution?

    ○ **A.** TCP/IP

    ○ **B.** LPT1

    ○ · **C.** USB

    ○ **D.** COM1

52. Which connector is most used with POTS lines?

    ○ **A.** RJ45

    ○ **B.** RJ11

    ○ **C.** BNC

    ○ **D.** SC

53. You need to test a newly installed printer from Windows. Where is the location of the Print Test Page button?

    ○ **A.** In the Print Spooler service

    ○ **B.** In Administrative Tools

    ○ **C.** On the General tab of the printer's Properties page

    ○ **D.** On the Ports tab

54. You are required to perform preventative maintenance on a laser printer. What should be replaced? (Select the three best answers.)

- ○ **A.** Toner
- ○ **B.** Fuser
- ○ **C.** Pickup rollers
- ○ **D.** Paper
- ○ **E.** Paper trays
- ○ **F.** Transfer bar

55. What is the purpose of a power inverter?

- ○ **A.** Backup source of power
- ○ **B.** Converts AC to DC
- ○ **C.** Provides regulated AC voltage
- ○ **D.** Protects against surges

56. Which of the following is affected the least by EMI?

- ○ **A.** Twisted pair
- ○ **B.** Coaxial
- ○ **C.** STP
- ○ **D.** Fiber

57. What is the most common form factor used by HTPCs?

- ○ **A.** AT
- ○ **B.** ATX
- ○ **C.** microATX
- ○ **D.** Pico-ITX

58. Which of the following does *not* have to do with virtualization?

- ○ **A.** VMware
- ○ **B.** Hypervisor
- ○ **C.** Virtual PC
- ○ **D.** CAD/CAM

59. One of the computers in your warehouse often requires the replacement of power supplies, CPUs, and optical drives. What tool can help to prevent these types of hardware faults?

- ○ **A.** Compressed air
- ○ **B.** Antistatic wrist straps
- ○ **C.** Rescue disk
- ○ **D.** Multimeter

60. Which solution would provide the best cooling to the CPU?

- ○ **A.** Heat sink
- ○ **B.** Liquid cooling
- ○ **C.** CPU fan
- ○ **D.** Case fan

61. Which of the following best describes a quad-core processor?

- ○ **A.** PC with four unique processors
- ○ **B.** CPU with four cache memory locations
- ○ **C.** PC with two dual-core CPUs
- ○ **D.** CPU package with four CPU cores

62. A customer has asked you to set up a network printer that will be connected to a print server. The customer would like the default configuration set to duplex printing for all users. Which of following will allow you to configure this?

- ○ **A.** Configure the settings through the printer's web interface.
- ○ **B.** Configure the settings from the users' printer properties.
- ○ **C.** Configure the settings through the computer's Control Panel.
- ○ **D.** Configure the printer from the users' page setup menu.

63. You are required to install an operating system to a remote PC without the use of any physical media such as CD-ROMs. What should you use to complete the task?

- ○ **A.** TELNET
- ○ **B.** FTP
- ○ **C.** PXE
- ○ **D.** NET USE

64. Which of these is a feature of a docking station?

- ○ **A.** Provides built-in power surge protection
- ○ **B.** Provides additional connectivity
- ○ **C.** Expands the laptop memory
- ○ **D.** Provides a second monitor

65. What type of adapter card is used to connect external hard disk drives?

- ○ **A.** eSATA
- ○ **B.** PCIe x16
- ○ **C.** PATA
- ○ **D.** Network

66. Which of the following is a valid IPv6 address?

    ○ **A.** FE08::279B::91A1/122

    ○ **B.** 9031:8611::5468/64

    ○ **C.** ABC0::0011/130

    ○ **D.** FE0G:8B1D::0001/64

67. Which of the following optical media has the largest storage space?

    ○ **A.** Hard drive

    ○ **B.** DVD-ROM

    ○ **C.** Blu-Ray

    ○ **D.** DVD-18

68. Which one of the following is a valid APIPA address?

    ○ **A.** 192.168.1.1

    ○ **B.** 10.1.1.1

    ○ **C.** 172.16.1.1

    ○ **D.** 169.254.1.1

69. You've just set up 10 computers in a small LAN. They're all the same make and model that will remotely turn on using Wake-on-LAN (WOL). Eight computers wake up as they are supposed to, but two systems do not wake correctly. What is the most likely problem with the two systems?

    ○ **A.** The network adapter settings in Windows are incorrect.

    ○ **B.** WOL is not enabled in the BIOS.

    ○ **C.** The two computers do not support WOL functionality.

    ○ **D.** The two computers' gateway IP address is configured incorrectly.

70. One of your customers tells you of some trouble accessing the company wireless network with a laptop. The person could access the network yesterday before they went on the road with a laptop. What is most likely cause of the problem?

    ○ **A.** The laptop battery needs to be recharged.

    ○ **B.** The wireless network is down.

    ○ **C.** The laptop's wireless antenna is disconnected.

    ○ **D.** The laptop's wireless switch is off.

71. Which wireless standards operate at a maximum of 54 Mbps? (Select the two best answers.)

   ○ **A.** 802.11a

   ○ **B.** 802.11b

   ○ **C.** 802.11g

   ○ **D.** 802.11n

   ○ **E.** 802.11x

72. Which of the following storage media types has no moving parts?

   ○ **A.** Tape drive

   ○ **B.** PATA magnetic hard drive

   ○ **C.** DVD-ROM

   ○ **D.** Flash

73. Why do CRT monitors have a degauss feature?

   ○ **A.** To reset the monitor to factory default settings

   ○ **B.** To automatically adjust the display settings for optimal performance

   ○ **C.** To increase video monitor brightness

   ○ **D.** To remove magnetic fields

74. What is the data transfer rate of USB 3.0?

   ○ **A.** 480 Kbps

   ○ **B.** 12 Mbps

   ○ **C.** 480 Mbps

   ○ **D.** 5.0 Gbps

75. Based on the following information, which address is most likely the DNS server?

```
Fe80::403b:e791:b151:b92a%11(Preferred)
192.168.1.115(Preferred)
255.255.255.0
192.168.1.1
151.198.0.38
```

   ○ **A.** 192.168.1.115

   ○ **B.** 255.255.255.0

   ○ **C.** 192.168.1.1

   ○ **D.** 151.198.0.38

76. Which of the following ports is commonly used for RS-232 connections?

- ○ **A.** USB
- ○ **B.** DB-9
- ○ **C.** Parallel
- ○ **D.** SCSI

77. What is the best way for a technician to prevent ESD when installing RAM?

- ○ **A.** Wear a grounded wristband.
- ○ **B.** Touch grounded metal before making contact with components.
- ○ **C.** Make sure the AC plug has a ground post.
- ○ **D.** Wear rubber-soled shoes.

78. One of the users in your organization complains that their fingers are sticky, green, and a bit irritated after using a mouse. You find out that the mouse was cleaned but with an unknown solution. Where can you go to find out information about what solution was used on the mouse?

- ○ **A.** Procedures manual
- ○ **B.** Fire department
- ○ **C.** Facilities department of the organization
- ○ **D.** MSDS

79. Which of the following protocols does not depend on an acknowledgment of receipt from the sender?

- ○ **A.** HTTP
- ○ **B.** UDP
- ○ **C.** TCP
- ○ **D.** IP

80. Which of the following ports is used by default by RDP?

- ○ **A.** 53
- ○ **B.** 1723
- ○ **C.** 3389
- ○ **D.** 8080

81. Which of these connector types are typically used on LCD displays? (Select the two best answers.)

- ○ **A.** DVI
- ○ **B.** XGA
- ○ **C.** HDMI
- ○ **D.** USB
- ○ **E.** VGA

82. Which of the following is the fastest cache in a computer?

- ○ **A.** L1
- ○ **B.** L2
- ○ **C.** L3
- ○ **D.** L4

83. You just arrived at a user's desk and are about to start troubleshooting a problem. The user's desk is covered with papers, and you can see that some of these papers are probably confidential in nature. What should you do first?

- ○ **A.** Work around the papers and resolve the problem.
- ○ **B.** Refuse to work until the user has cleared the desk.
- ○ **C.** Put the confidential papers in a neat pile.
- ○ **D.** Ask the user to clear the desk of confidential papers.

84. What type of printer uses a fuser to print documents?

- ○ **A.** Inkjet
- ○ **B.** Dot matrix
- ○ **C.** Laser
- ○ **D.** Thermal

85. Of the following, which is a limitation of terrestrial microwave broadband connections?

- ○ **A.** They require line of sight.
- ○ **B.** They cannot be used in remote locations.
- ○ **C.** It is a receive-only transmission.
- ○ **D.** The speed is less than dial-up.

86. Which one of the following commands can obtain an IP address from a DHCP server?

- ○ **A.** PING –t
- ○ **B.** NSLOOKUP
- ○ **C.** IPCONFIG /RENEW
- ○ **D.** MSCONFIG

87. Which of the following is the fastest expansion bus on a laptop?

- ○ **A.** PCMCIA
- ○ **B.** PC Card Type III
- ○ **C.** Infrared
- ○ **D.** ExpressCard

88. You need to transfer data from a laptop's older IDE drive to a new SATA drive. What pin configurations would you need on the adapter that will be connected between both drives?

- ○ **A.** 40-pin and 15-pin
- ○ **B.** 44-pin and 7-pin
- ○ **C.** 40-pin and 7-pin
- ○ **D.** 44-pin and 15-pin

89. Which of the following can increase the efficiency in which programs execute?

- ○ **A.** Defrag
- ○ **B.** Disk Cleanup
- ○ **C.** Task Manager
- ○ **D.** Task Scheduler

90. What is the recommended method to clean a laptop's screen?

- ○ **A.** Paper towel and water
- ○ **B.** Dry lint-free cloth
- ○ **C.** Water with mild detergent
- ○ **D.** Rubbing alcohol and a tissue

91. One of your technicians is on a service call and is dealing with a furious customer who has been shouting loudly. The technician tries but cannot calm the customer down. What should the technician do next?

- ○ **A.** Let the customer continue to shout; sooner or later the customer will get tired and calm down.
- ○ **B.** Call the supervisor and complain.
- ○ **C.** Leave the customer site, and document the incident.
- ○ **D.** Shout back at the customer and remain in control of the situation.

92. What tools would you use to test an AC outlet? (Select the two best answers.)

- ○ **A.** Multimeter
- ○ **B.** Tweezers
- ○ **C.** PSU tester
- ○ **D.** Receptacle tester
- ○ **E.** POST tester

93. You have been tasked with running a network extension to the warehouse that is 50 meters (164 feet) away. The proposed path will take the network extension near several fluorescent light fixtures and a large electric motor. What type of cable would be best for this environment?

   ○ **A.** Unshielded twisted-pair

   ○ **B.** Coaxial

   ○ **C.** Fiber-optic

   ○ **D.** Shielded twisted-pair

94. What protocol uses port 443?

   ○ **A.** SMTP

   ○ **B.** FTP

   ○ **C.** RDP

   ○ **D.** HTTPS

95. What happens in the writing stage of the laser printing process?

   ○ **A.** A rubber blade removes excess toner from the drum.

   ○ **B.** A negative charge is applied to the drum by the primary corona wire.

   ○ **C.** The laser is activated and exposes the drum.

   ○ **D.** The surface of the drum is applied with negatively charged toner.

   ○ **E.** The toner is transferred to paper as the drum rolls over it.

96. You are working on a server that has several hard drives connected to a SCSI card. The card does not appear to be functioning at top efficiency. You determine that the card requires an update to its embedded code. What is this referred to as? (Select the best answer.)

   ○ **A.** Operating system

   ○ **B.** Driver files

   ○ **C.** Firmware

   ○ **D.** Shareware

97. Which of the following memory types can fit in a 168-pin DIMM slot?

   ○ **A.** SDRAM

   ○ **B.** DDR

   ○ **C.** DDR2

   ○ **D.** SODIMM

98. In which of the following is a CR 2032 CMOS battery usually found?

    ○ **A.** Portable printers

    ○ **B.** Smartphones

    ○ **C.** Bluetooth mice

    ○ **D.** Desktops

99. What kind of adapter card can use a RJ45 connector?

    ○ **A.** Sound

    ○ **B.** NIC

    ○ **C.** Video

    ○ **D.** Dial-up modem

100. What should you not plug a laser printer into?

    ○ **A.** UPS

    ○ **B.** Power strip

    ○ **C.** Surge suppressor

    ○ **D.** Line conditioner

Answers at a Glance

1. A and C	35. A	69. B
2. A	36. A and E	70. D
3. C	37. A	71. A and C
4. D	38. C	72. D
5. A	39. D	73. D
6. B	40. C	74. D
7. A	41. A	75. D
8. C	42. B	76. B
9. B and D	43. D	77. A
10. C	44. A	78. C
11. A	45. C	79. B
12. B	46. A	80. C
13. A	47. C	81. A and E
14. B	48. D	82. A
15. D	49. A and D	83. D
16. B	50. B	84. C
17. C	51. A	85. A
18. D	52. B	86. C
19. A	53. C	87. D
20. A, C, and E	54. B, C, and F	88. B
21. B	55. B	89. A
22. A	56. D	90. B
23. C	57. C	91. C
24. D	58. D	92. A and D
25. C	59. A	93. C
26. D	60. B	94. D
27. B	61. D	95. C
28. A	62. A	96. C
29. A	63. C	97. A
30. C	64. B	98. D
31. A	65. A	99. B
32. D	66. B	100. A
33. A	67. C	
34. D	68. D	

Answers with Explanations

1. Answer **A** and **C** are correct. The best answers are to use an antistatic wrist strap and to touch an unpainted portion of the computer case. The alligator clip of the wrist strap should be connected to an unpainted portion of the computer case. Other things that can help reduce electro-static discharge (ESD) include using an antistatic mat, raising the humidity, working in a noncarpeted area, wearing rubber-soled shoes, and using antistatic spray. Going beyond this, you might see antistatic wrist straps that connect to specific earth grounding points used in computer labs. As to the incorrect answers: The temperature will not have an effect on ESD, and lowering the humidity will make ESD more likely. It is not necessary to keep the computer plugged into an AC outlet. You should not plug the computer into an AC outlet because you might not know if the outlet is wired properly, and a surge could be dangerous. The two most important points to remember are to use an antistatic strap, and touch an unpainted portion of the case. See the section titled "Safety" in Chapter 18, "Safety, Procedures, and Professionalism," for more information.

2. Answer **A** is correct. A heat sink disperses heat away from the CPU, but it requires no moving parts. It is a passive cooling device requiring no power. CPU fans and case fans have moving parts and require power; they are therefore considered active cooling devices. A liquid cooling system utilizes a pump, hoses, and coolant that is moved through the system. See the section titled "Installing and Troubleshooting CPUs" in Chapter 3, "The CPU," for more information.

3. Answer **C** is correct. The number one problem with satellite Internet is latency. Because the signal must travel to a satellite in orbit around the Earth, there can be an unacceptable delay (between .5 and 5 seconds) that makes VoIP difficult to use properly. Essentially, anything you or the other caller say could overlap due to the latency, making conversation quite problematical. Satellite Internet usually has enough bandwidth to support VoIP; although, some connections are limited to a 28.8 Kbps upload through a phone line. It is not difficult to install (on the end user's side at least), plus the cost can be comparable to some other Internet services. The main issue is the distance that the signal must travel and the latency that ensues. See the section titled "SOHO Windows Networking" in Chapter 15, "Networking," for more information.

4. Answer **D** is correct. KVM stands for Keyboard, Video, and Mouse. A KVM is a switch that enables the connection of one keyboard, monitor, and mouse. However, the KVM has connections for several computers, which can be selected by pressing a button on the KVM. A barcode reader is a scanning device that can read and interpret information from barcodes and send that information to the computer. A smartcard reader is a device that reads smart identification cards when they are swiped and sends that information to an authenticating system. A different type of switch, the Ethernet switch, is a common LAN device that enables the connectivity of multiple computers for the purpose of networking. See the section titled "Input/Output Devices and Peripherals" in Chapter 13, "Peripherals and Custom Computing," for more information.

5. Answer **A** is correct. PCIe (Peripheral Component Interconnect Express or PCI Express) would be the best solution for a high-end graphics card. This is

because it has the highest data transfer rate of all the listed answers. Generally, a computer has one PCIe slot, and that slot is meant to be used for a video card. PCI was the standard for a long time but has given way to faster slots as far as video cards goes. You may still use other devices, such as network adapters or sound cards, in a standard PCI slot. After PCI, AGP (Accelerated Graphics Port) was the previous video card standard until PCIe replaced it. ISA (Industry-Standard Architecture) is an older expansion bus that you will not commonly see, unless you work with a PC from the '80s or '90s. By far PCIe is the most common for video cards. See the section titled "The Video Subsystem" in Chapter 12, "Video and Audio," for more information.

6. Answer **B** is correct. Computers should never be placed on carpet. Carpets gather static electricity and can cause ESD, ultimately damaging devices in the computer, so carpets should be avoided. Wood, plastic, and tile do not gather static electricity, so they are safe to work on, as long as you still employ antistatic measures. See the section titled "Safety" in Chapter 18, "Safety, Procedures, and Professionalism," for more information.

7. Answer **A** is correct. TELNET uses port 23 by default. It is a deprecated protocol that should be avoided and disabled if it is found to be running on a computer. Newer computer operating systems remove TELNET altogether, but you should still know it for the exam and the field. Port 25 is used by SMTP (Simple Mail Transfer Protocol). Port 80 is used by HTTP (Hypertext Transfer Protocol). Port 110 is used by POP3 (Post Office Protocol version 3). See the section titled "TCP/IP" in Chapter 15, "Networking," for more information.

8. Answer **C** is correct. DDR is the latest type of memory for a personal computer. DDR stands for Double Data Rate and is a derivative of SDRAM (Synchronous Dynamic RAM). It's rare to find Rambus nowadays because DDR is the most common. DRAM stands for dynamic random access memory. The rest of the memory types listed in the answers are types of DRAM. Usually, if you install a stick of memory (SIMM or DIMM) it will be DRAM. See the section titled "RAM Basics and Types of RAM" in Chapter 4, "RAM," for more information.

9. Answers **B** and **D** are correct. AC power lines and electric motors can be potential sources of electromagnetic interference (EMI). They can cause various computer and networking equipment to malfunction if they are in close proximity to each other. Flat-panel televisions, as opposed to CRTs, are not large sources of EMI; they generally do not affect the usage of computers. Cordless phones also do not affect computers. Like flat-panel televisions they use a small amount of electricity and therefore emit a small amount of EMI. However, cordless phones can be a source of radio frequency interference (RFI). A Faraday cage is a shielded enclosure that is generally meant to keep static, radio transmissions, and interference, outside of a working area. See the section titled "Procedures and Environmental Controls" in Chapter 18, "Safety, Procedures and Professionalism," for more information.

10. Answer **C** is correct. Plenum cable is required to be fire resistant; it should not emit toxic fumes if it is exposed to high temperatures. Regular unshielded twisted-pair cable is covered with a PVC jacket. When this burns it creates a toxic smoke. Plenum cable combats this by using a covering (Teflon or other similar material) that is more fire resistant. A plenum is any airway where fire can

spread. Municipal code requires fire resistant cable in a plenum. STP (shielded twisted-pair) cable uses an aluminum shield that surrounds the individual wires; however, this is inside the PVC jacket, making it just as susceptible to fire as UTP. Coaxial cable also has a PVC jacket. See the section titled "Cables, Connectors, and Tools" in Chapter 15, "Networking," for more information.

11. Answer **A** and **B** are both correct. This is because 802.11a and 802.11b are very similar when it comes to indoor range. 802.11g is not far behind. For the exam, remember that 802.11n has close to double the range of 802.11a, b, and g.. See the section titled "SOHO Windows Networking" in Chapter 15, "Networking," for more information.

12. Answer **B** is correct. The Digital Linear Tape can hold more data than any of the other answers. With storage capacities that approach a terabyte, it can hold much more than the other solutions. Common DLT capacities include 160 GB, 300 GB, and 800 GB. Blu-ray discs typically hold up to 50 GB. DVD-ROM discs can hold between 4.7 and 17 GB of data. Common SD card capacities are 32, 64, and 128 GB. See the section titled "Magnetic Storage Media" in Chapter 6, "Storage Devices," for more information.

13. Answer **A** is correct. Asymmetric Digital Subscriber Line (ADSL) is a type of Internet connection that offers downstream networking speeds of 1.5, 5, 8, 12, and 24 Mbps. Upstream rates will be slower, as implied by the name asymmetric. ADSL uses a phone line to send data. VPN stands for virtual private network, which enables users to connect to the main office from a remote location in a secure fashion. The speed of the VPN connection will be based on the type of Internet connection. Bluetooth is not a type of Internet connection; instead it is a short distance wireless technology that enables devices such as mobile phones and headsets to be used together. 802.3u is a type of Ethernet that enables local area networking at 100 Mbps. See the section titled "SOHO Windows Networking" in Chapter 15, "Networking," for more information.

14. Answer **B** is correct. 400 watts is a common power rating for a standard desktop PC. This is enough to power all the devices a typical office user might need. Power ratings are measured in watts. There are 900-watt power supplies, but something that powerful would be necessary only for a custom PC or advanced workstation. Volts measure electric potential, not power ratings. 12 volts is one of the DC voltages that the power supply sends to the motherboard and through SATA and Molex connections. 120 volts is the standard voltage of an AC outlet in the United States and in many other countries. The power supply converts this AC power to DC power that the motherboard, CPU, and other devices can utilize. See the section titled "Power Supplies" in Chapter 5, "Power," for more information.

15. Answer **D** is correct. The card should be installed to the x16 slot, not the x1 slot. When this is done, it will get normal performance as if it were connected to a x4 slot. It will *not* get four times the performance. A PCIe x4 card will not fit in a x1 slot, the slot is too small. But conversely, most PCIe cards can be installed to a higher level slot. It's important to plan well; if you think you might be using a x4 card in the future, attempt to get a motherboard that has a x4 slot. Most motherboards have only one PCIe x16 slot, and it is usually used by the video card,

which could limit your options in a scenario such as this one. See the section titled "Motherboard Components and Form Factors" in Chapter 2, "Motherboards," for more information.

16. Answer **B** is correct. You would most likely use a Serial ATA (SATA) interface. First, because it is the most common type of interface in today's laptops. Second, it is more likely to find a 640 GB SATA hard drive than a 640 GB Parallel ATA (PATA) hard drive. IDE stands for Integrated Device Electronics. PATA and IDE are synonymous in this scenario. SCSI stands for Small Computer System Interface. SCSI drives are more common on specialized PCs and are rare inside laptops. See the section titled "Magnetic Storage Media" in Chapter 6, "Storage Devices," for more information.

17. Answer **C** is correct. The thermal printer requires special paper to operate. The specially coated paper is heated by a thermal printhead to create images and text. Laser, inkjet, and impact printers do not require special paper to operate. Though impact printers have perforated edges used to help feed the paper, it is still the same type of paper that laser and inkjet printers use. See the section titled "Printer Types and Technologies" in Chapter 14, "Printers," for more information.

18. Answer **D** is correct. The recommended maximum cable length for USB 2.0 devices is 5 meters (16 feet). USB 1.1 has a limitation of 3 meters for devices running at low speed (1.5 Mbps) whereas USB 1.1 at full speed (12 Mbps) and USB 2.0 is 5 meters. As of the writing of this book, USB 3 length is not specified, but cables are generally no longer than 3 meters (10 feet) in length. See the section titled "Input/Output Devices and Peripherals" in Chapter 13, "Peripherals and Custom Computing," for more information.

19. Answer **A** is correct. Thermal compound helps to disperse heat through a CPU's heat sink. When upgrading a CPU, thermal compound should be applied to the bottom of the heat sink. This seals any microscopic fractures in the heat sink and allows for efficient transference of heat from the CPU through the heat sink. The power supply and case fans will exhaust heat out of the case, which ultimately helps to keep the CPU's temperature down, but the important part of this question is, "when upgrading a CPU." A fire extinguisher should not be used with the internals of a computer, unless of course that computer is on fire. See the section titled "Installing and Troubleshooting CPUs" in Chapter 3, "The CPU," for more information.

20. Answers **A**, **C**, and **E** are correct. Professionalism comes in many forms. When dealing with a customer, you should avoid distractions, avoid being judgmental, and meet expectations that are set. Also, avoid arguing, talking to co-workers, and personal interruptions. Be positive, and listen to the customer. It is important to retain a chain of custody, but this has to do with tracking evidence and has less to do with professionalism. Documentation is important as well and should be developed by you the technician, not left to the customer. See the section titled "Professionalism and Communication Skills" in Chapter 18, "Safety, Procedures, and Professionalism," for more information.

21. Answer **B** is correct. The proper tool to use for recording off-air television programs is a video capture card. These video capture cards usually have a coaxial F connector for a connection to cable TV, or a video device. Wireless cards are

network adapters that enable a computer to connect to a wireless network. POST (power-on self test) cards are used to diagnose problems with a PC. PCIe video cards are the most common type of video card; however, they probably will not have video capturing capability, or the port necessary to do so. In HTPCs, video capture cards/TV tuners are often used in addition to a PCIe video card. See the section titled "The Video Subsystem" in Chapter 12, "Video & Audio," for more information.

22. Answer **A** is correct. The maximum data transfer rate of IEEE 1394a is 400 Mbps. IEEE 1394a is essentially an improved version of FireWire 400. 480 Mbps is the data rate of USB 2.0; 800 Mbps is the speed of FireWire 800/IEEE 1394b; and 1600 Mbps is the speed of FireWire S1600. See the section titled "Input/Output Devices and Peripherals" in Chapter 13, "Peripherals and Custom Computing," for more information.

23. Answer **C** is correct. The only address listed that is private is 192.168.58.11. This is part of the private range of Class C addresses that encompasses 192.168.x.x. Another common example of a private class C address would be 192.168.1.1, often used by SOHO routers. The address 8.58.12.192 is Class A and is public. Class A private IPs would start with the number 10. The address 173.169.254.1 is a Class B address. The private range for Class B is 172.16.x.x–172.31.x.x. The address 11.23.185.57 is another Class A public address. Addresses that *start* with 169.254 are private Class B addresses applied by APIPA on Windows clients. See the section titled "TCP/IP" in Chapter 15, "Networking," for more information.

24. Answer **D** is correct. DDR2 (and DDR3) used in a personal computer has 240 pins, but remember that DDR2 and DDR3 are not compatible with each other. The original DDR standard has 184 pins. Don't confuse DDR used in a PC with SODIMM DDR used in a laptop. SODIMM DDR3 has 204 pins, not 240. SODIMM DDR2 has 200 pins. Be sure to know the differences between laptop and PC memory, and remember to use the version of DDR that will be compatible with the motherboard. See the section titled "RAM Basics and Types of RAM" in Chapter 4, "RAM," for more information.

25. Answer **C** is correct. RAID 5 stripes data and parity across three or more disks. It is a fault tolerant method of data storage known as striping w/parity. RAID 0 stripes data only and can be used with two or more disks. Because it does not use parity, it is not fault tolerant. RAID 1 (mirroring) uses two disks only and writes an exact copy of all data to each disk; it is a fault tolerant method. RAID 10 (or RAID 1+0) is a stripe of mirrors. It is two sets of mirrors that are striped, but without parity. This would require a minimum of four disks. See the section titled "Files, File Systems, and Disks" in Chapter 9, "Configuring Windows," for more information.

26. Answer **D** is correct. A single physical hard drive can have four primary partitions maximum. If you decide to incorporate an extended partition, you could do so but will be limited to three primary partitions. Extended partitions can have many logical drives, allowing you to add more drive letters to your hard drive scheme. See the section titled "Files, File Systems, and Disks" in Chapter 9, "Configuring Windows," for more information.

27. Answer **B** is correct. A computer-aided design (CAD) workstation runs powerful software that must render complicated three dimensional graphics. Because of this, it should have a powerful CPU, high-end video card, and as much RAM as possible. Home theater PCs don't necessarily need any of the three items in the question but often have a surround sound audio card, a video card with HDMI output, a TV tuner/video capture card, and a small form factor such as micro-ATX. A virtualization workstation must have as much RAM as possible, and as many CPU cores as possible, but a high-end video card is usually not necessary. A thin client is used for basic applications and therefore doesn't need any of the three. Another type of computer that could benefit from all three requirements would be a gaming PC. See the section titled "Custom PC Configurations" in Chapter 13, "Peripherals and Custom Computing," for more information.

28. Answer **A** is correct. The majority of laptops use SODIMM memory. DDR3, RIMMS, and the older SDRAM are examples of memory used in a PC. Though SODIMMs are types of DDR, you must make the distinction. DDR3 would be memory used in a PC, and *SODIMM* DDR3 is memory used in a laptop. They are different sizes and have a different amount of pins: 240 for DDR3 and 204 for SODIMM DDR3. See the section titled "Installing, Configuring and Troubleshooting Internal Laptop Components," in Chapter 7, "Laptops," for more information.

29. Answer **A** is correct. SATA hard drives use a 7-pin data connector. For power they use a 15-pin connector. 34-pin ribbon cables are used to transfer data to a floppy drive. 40-pin ribbon cables are used to transfer data to an IDE drive. See the section titled "Magnetic Storage Media" in Chapter 6, "Storage Devices," for more information.

30. Answer **C** is correct. You should ask what the last thing was that occurred before the computer stopped functioning properly. Try not to ask the person what he did directly. That implies that the user is to blame. Instead, ask what the person witnessed. Never blame the user or insinuate blame. Telling the person not to use the computer will not solve the problem, and it will not help the customer's frustration. Approach conversations with customers from a methodical stand-point and try to be objective, calm, and understanding. See the section titled "Professionalism and Communication Skills" in Chapter 18, "Safety, Procedures, and Professionalism," for more information.

31. Answer **A** is correct. Error Correction Code (ECC) memory can detect *and* correct errors. Non-ECC (more common) does not detect or correct errors. Parity memory is used for error detection but not error correction. Most RAM today is non-ECC and non-parity; although, it does exist in special scenarios. See the section titled "RAM Basics and Types of RAM" in Chapter 4, "RAM," for more information.

32. Answer **D** is correct. Intel's Hyper-Threading enables a processor to work with two independent computer instructions at once. This technology can work on single-core CPUs as well as multicore CPUs. Dual core technology enables two CPUs to work on the same task simultaneously. When an operating system works on multiple tasks simultaneously, it is known simply as multitasking. See the section titled "CPU 101" in Chapter 3, "The CPU," for more information.

33. Answer **A** is correct. Dot matrix printers can use multilayer carbonless copy paper. This is because the printhead of a dot matrix printer can physically strike through multiple pieces of paper. Nowadays there are also carbonless multipart forms for laser printers as well. Print spooling is when documents are queued on a hard drive while waiting to be sent to a printer. Inkjet and thermal printers do not use multilayer copy paper normally. See the section titled "Printer Types and Technologies" in Chapter 14, "Printers," for more information.

34. Answer **D** is correct. PC8500 (or more accurately PC3-8500) is the only one listed that can possibly be DDR3. It is also known as DDR3-1066 and can transfer 8,533 MB/s. PC8500 could also be PC2-8500, a type of DDR2 that also transmits 8,533 MB/s; however the question was asking for a type of DDR3, not DDR2. PC5300 (also known as PC2-5300) is DDR2. PC2700 and PC1600 are from the original DDR standard. See the section titled "RAM Basics and Types of RAM" in Chapter 4, "RAM," for more information.

35. Answer **A** is correct. The laser printer uses a charged corona wire in the electrophotographic printing process. In the conditioning stage, a negative charge is applied to the primary corona wire. In the transferring stage a second corona wire is applied a positive charge. The laser printer is the only printer listed that uses a corona wire. Impact printers use force to transfer ink onto paper usually by utilizing a printhead. Inkjet printers store ink in a cartridge and propel the ink onto the paper. Thermal printers produce text and images by heating specially coated thermal paper. See the section titled "Printer Types and Technologies" in Chapter 14, "Printers," for more information.

36. Answers **A** and **E** are correct. Core i5 CPUs could possibly use the LGA 1155 or LGA 1156 socket. The 1155 is meant to be the replacement for the 1156. (Even though it is one pin less.) Both are meant to support Core i3, i5, and i7 CPUs. The LGA 775 socket supports Pentium 4 through Core 2 CPUs. Socket M supports Core Solo and Duo CPUs. The LGA 1366 was designed specifically for the Core i7 CPU. See the section titled "CPU 101" in Chapter 3, "The CPU," for more information.

37. Answer **A** is correct. Wi-Fi Protected Access version 2 (WPA2) is the most secure of the wireless encryption protocols listed. If you have a choice between WPA2, WPA, and WEP, select WPA2. Avoid the Wireless Equivalent Privacy (WEP) protocol as it is outdated. An SSID is a Secure Set Identifier, which is the name of the wireless network. To aid in securing the network, your first and best solution will be WPA2 encryption, but you could also disable the SSID so that the wireless network cannot be seen through normal methods. See the section titled "SOHO Security" in Chapter 16, "Security," for more information.

38. Answer **C** is correct. By far, fiber optic networking technology has the highest potential throughput. Thought of in terms of Internet services, fiber will easily outperform cable, DSL, and satellite connections. Fiber optic cable has the capability to easily transmit data at many gigabits per second. The other technologies are currently based primarily on copper cabling, which cannot realize the speeds of fiber optic cabling. See the section titled "SOHO Windows Networking" in Chapter 15, Networking," for more information.

39. Answer **D** is correct. Of the listed answers, the only CPU manufactured by AMD is the Phenom. The Phenom is offered in dual-core, triple-core, quad-core, and the Phenom II hex-core (6 cores). Pentium, Celeron, and Core i7 are all Intel CPUs, with the Core i7 being the latest of the three and providing competition for the AMD Phenom II. See the section titled "CPU 101" in Chapter 3, "The CPU," for more information.

40. Answer **C** is correct. One of the function keys will usually facilitate viewing the laptop display on an external monitor or projector. Pressing the Power button simply turns the laptop on and off. Control+ESC opens the Start menu in Windows. ALT+Insert opens the Insert menu in Microsoft Word. These two combo keys can also do a variety of other things in various systems but will not be used to enable an external monitor. See the section titled "Installing, Configuring, and Troubleshooting Visible Laptop Components" in Chapter 7, "Laptops," for more information.

41. Answer **A** is correct. DDR3-1600, also known as PC3-12800, can transfer 12,800 MB/s (12.8 GB/s.) Of the answers listed, it can do the most transfers per second, 1.6 billion in total. Two of the answers were DDR2, and two of the answers were DDR3. DDR2-800 has a transfer rate of 6,400 MB/s. DDR2-1066 has a transfer rate of 8,533 MB/s. DDR3-1333 has a transfer rate of 10,667 MB/s. See the section titled "RAM Basics and Types of RAM" in Chapter 4, "RAM," for more information.

42. Answer **B** is correct. IPCONFIG is the command you should use on a local computer to find out the IP address of a gateway device. When you run an IPCONFIG, the basic information that comes up includes the IP address of the local system, its subnet mask, and the default gateway. PING is used to test connectivity to other computers on the network. NET USE enables the mapping of network drives within the command prompt. NETSTAT shows all current network connections from the local computer to remote computers. See the section titled "Troubleshooting Networks" in Chapter 15, "Networking," for more information.

43. Answer **D** is correct. The southbridge is the chip responsible for maintaining the data flow between a SATA hard drive and the processor. Other devices that connect to the southbridge include USB, PATA drives, sound cards, floppy drives, and other secondary devices. The southbridge connects to the northbridge, which ultimately connects to the processor. The northbridge controls data flow from the processor to RAM and PCIe x16 devices. Collectively, the southbridge and the northbridge make up the chipset. The BIOS is the chip that checks all devices within the computer upon boot. FSB stands for front side bus; it connects the northbridge, or MCH, to the processor; though this has been abandoned by newer designs. (On newer Intel designs, the southbridge is simply known as the chipset.) See the section titled "Motherboard Components and Form Factors" in Chapter 2, "Motherboards," for more information.

44. Answer **A** is correct. Widescreen Super eXtended Graphics Array Plus (WSXGA+) is the resolution type you should select if you want to configure a resolution of 1600x1050. Make sure that the video card and monitor you decide on can support WSXGA+. Ultra eXtended Graphics Array (UXGA) has a maximum resolution of 1600x1200; a 4:3 screen ratio as opposed to the widescreen 16:10 ratio of WSXGA+. Super eXtended Graphics Array (SXGA) has a maximum resolution of

1280x1024. Super Video Graphics Array (SVGA) is an older standard that supports only a maximum of 800x600. See the section titled "The Video Subsystem" in Chapter 12, "Video and Audio," for more information.

45. Answer **C** is correct. The laser printer has the lowest cost per page of the four listed answers. Laser printers and their corresponding toner cartridges are designed to be long-lasting, and print many pages before needing maintenance or replacement. The dot matrix printer requires special perforated paper and needs to have the printing ribbon changed more often than a toner cartridge. The inkjet printer ink cartridges do not last nearly as long as the laser printer's toner cartridge, plus inkjet printers are not known for their durability. Thermal printers can be expensive and require more costly, specially coated paper. See the section titled "Printer Types and Technologies" in Chapter 14, "Printers," for more information.

46. Answer **A** is correct. One example of EMI is when degraded network performance occurs due to networking cables and AC power cables in close proximity to each other. The electromagnetic interference from the AC power cables could leak over to the network cables and cause data transmission failures. There are several ways to protect against this including running networking cables within shielded conduit; running the AC power cables within shielded conduit; using shielded twisted-pair (STP) networking cables; using BX-encased AC power cables; or using a combination of any of those. Networking cables should be kept away from any electrical connections, all electrical cables, and electronic devices. Bluetooth devices are meant to be used in close proximity to each other, especially class II and class III devices; they do not use enough electricity to create EMI within the network. The same holds true for smartphones. Poorly punched down network cables could cause intermittent data transmission issues and degraded network performance, but the cause of the degraded network performance in that case is the improper punch downs themselves, not EMI. See the section titled "Procedures and Environmental Controls" in Chapter 18, "Safety, Procedures, and Professionalism," for more information.

47. Answer **C** is correct. Post Office Protocol version 3 (POP3) is used within Microsoft Outlook to retrieve e-mail. It is the most common e-mail retrieving protocol. It is also possible to use IMAP for the retrieval of e-mail, and HTTP if you have a web-based e-mail service. The Simple Mail Transfer Protocol (SMTP) is used to send mail. The File Transfer Protocol (FTP) is used to send and receive files to and from a remote computer. PING is a command-line function used to test whether another computer on the network can be communicated with. See the section titled "TCP/IP" in Chapter 15, "Networking," for more information.

48. Answer **D** is correct. To configure energy-saving measures on a laptop, you should configure the Advanced Configuration and Power Interface (ACPI). Most of today's operating systems are ACPI-compliant, so you can configure energy-saving measures, and battery power options, from directly within the operating system. The older Advanced Power Management (APM) system required you to access the BIOS directly. MSCONFIG is a Windows utility that is used to enable and disable programs and services, and modify the way the system boots. DXDIAG is a Windows utility that enables you to analyze and configure your video card and other video devices. See the section titled "The BIOS" in Chapter 2, "Motherboards," for more information.

49. Answers **A** and **D** are correct. Of the listed answers, only Windows Media Audio (WMA) and Advanced Audio Coding (AAC) are digital, audio-only formats. WMA is used primarily by Microsoft, whereas AAC is used mostly by Apple. Another example of a digital, audio-only format is the MP3, which is used more openly by various operating systems and programs. Audio Video Interleaved (AVI) as the name implies can contain video and audio. The same is true for .MOV, part of the QuickTime File Format. WPA stands for Wi-Fi Protected Access and deals with wireless networking encryption. See the section titled "The Audio Subsystem" in Chapter 12, "Video and Audio," for more information.

50. Answer **B** is correct. The Accelerated Graphics Port (AGP) slot on a motherboard is used for video cards only. However, it is more common to see video cards installed into a PCI Express (PCIe) slot; it is the successor to AGP. Memory is usually installed into DDR slots. The CPU is installed into a socket, not a slot (except for older processors such as the PII and PIII). Sound cards are generally installed into PCI or PCIe x1 slots. See the section titled "The Video Subsystem" in Chapter 12, "Video and Audio," for more information.

51. Answer **A** is correct. If you want to add a network printer in Windows 7, you should create a TCP/IP port connection. This is done in Devices and Printers by right-clicking the printer, selecting Printer Properties, selecting the Ports tab, and clicking Add Port. From there you select Standard TCP/IP Port. The TCP/IP port enables computers to connect to remote printers on the network that have an IP address. All the other answers are ports on a local computer that would allow connectivity only to the local computer. LPT1 is an older 25-pin parallel port used for printers. USB enables localized printers and could possibly enable printers on a network via a print server w/USB port. But in an organization, and even in SOHO, networking the best solution is the TCP/IP solution. COM1 is not normally used with printers, but instead for devices such as dial-up modems. See the section titled "Installing, Configuring, and Troubleshooting Printers" in Chapter 14, "Printers," for more information.

52. Answer **B** is correct. RJ11 connections are most commonly used with POTS lines. The RJ11 is the telephone jack in the wall that you would plug a phone into. POTS stands for Plain Old Telephone System; this refers to the standard Public Switched Telephone Network (PSTN), the technology that requires an analog "landline," a technology slowly becoming more and more obsolete. The POTS line uses a cable that consists of two twisted pairs of copper wires. RJ45 refers to the jacks and plugs used in twisted-pair networking connections; networking cables have four twisted pairs of copper wires. BNC is the type of connector used in older coaxial thinnet networks; it uses a single copper core. SC is a type of fiber optic cable connector; the cable has glass or plastic fibers within it. See the section titled "Cables, Connectors, and Tools" in Chapter 15, "Networking," for more information.

53. Answer **C** is correct. The Print Test Page button is located on the General tab of any printer's Properties page. It is easily accessible simply by right-clicking the printer and selecting Properties. Always print a test page after you install a printer to make sure it is printing properly! The Print Spooler service is used on a computer to queue multiple documents for sending to the printer; in the Services section of Computer Management, it can be started and stopped and enabled or disabled. Administrative Tools gives access to such consoles as the Computer

Management window and Print Management. The Ports tab is where you would make the logical port connection for the printer. See the section titled "Installing, Configuring, and Troubleshooting Printers" in Chapter 14, "Printers," for more information.

54. Answers **B**, **C**, and **F** are correct. The fuser, pickup rollers, and transfer bar should be replaced. These are normally contained within a printer maintenance kit. Many printers warn you when the fuser and possibly the transfer bar are just about ready to be replaced. When you get a warning like this, you should install the maintenance kit right away. Toner and paper are consumables that need to be replaced more often; they are not part of a maintenance kit. They are usually not the responsibility of the technician, but the department where the printer is located. The paper trays will rarely fail and are not part of a maintenance kit. But they should be checked to make sure they are in working order when mainte-nance is required on the printer. See the section titled "Installing, Configuring, and Troubleshooting Printers" in Chapter 14, "Printers," for more information.

55. Answer **B** is correct. A power inverter is used to convert alternating current (AC) power to direct current (DC) power. Of the many examples, devices that use an inverter include UPSs, air conditioning units, and switched power supplies in PCs. The PC power supply actually makes use of a transformer (which essentially steps down power), a rectifier, and an inverter, working together to convert AC to DC. An example of a backup source of power would be a UPS or a gas generator. A device that provides regulated AC voltage would be a line conditioner (or UPS). A device that protects against surges would be—you guessed it: a surge protector (or surge suppressor); although UPSs can protect against surges as well. See the section titled "Power Supplies" in Chapter 5, "Power," for more information.

56. Answer **D** is correct. Of the listed answers, fiber optic cable is the least affected by EMI and RFI. This is because fiber optic cable does not use copper as its transmission medium, instead it uses glass/plastic. Fiber optic cable makes use of light as opposed to electricity. Because twisted pair, coaxial, and shielded twisted pair (STP) all use copper, and thus electricity, they always have the poten-tial to be more greatly affected by EMI and RFI. STP is shielded, which does help, but it is still not as resistant as fiber optic cable. See the section titled "Cables, Connectors, and Tools" in Chapter 15, "Networking," for more information.

57. Answer **C** is correct. The most common form factor used by home theater PCs (HTPCs) is microATX; though you will also see Mini-ITX and occasionally ATX. HTPCs are usually built with a horizontal case similar to a desktop case. These cases usually don't have enough space for the 12 x 9.6 inch (305 x 244 mm) full ATX form factor motherboard and instead use microATX motherboards, which are 9.6 x 9.6 inches (244 x 244 mm.) AT is an older standard that has been com-pletely phased out by ATX and its derivatives. Nano, Pico, and Mobile-ITX boards are used by smaller computing platforms and smartphones. See the sec-tion titled "Motherboard Components and Form Factors" in Chapter 2, "Motherboards," for more information.

58. Answer **D** is correct. The only answer that does not have anything to do with vir-tualization is CAD/CAM, short for computer-aided design/computer-aided manu-facturing. CAD/CAM computers must run on their own individual physical plat-form because they require so many resources. All the other answers deal with

virtualization: the creation of a virtual hardware platform, an OS, a storage platform, or a network resource. VMware and Virtual PC are commercial virtualization applications that allow you to run virtual operating systems within your OS, or directly within a bare metal hypervisor. The hypervisor is the manager that houses guest operating systems within virtualization software. It can be Type I (bare-metal), which runs directly on top of the PCs hardware; or Type II (hosted), which runs within the current OS. See the section titled "Custom PC Configurations" in Chapter 13, "Peripherals and Custom Computing," for more information.

59. Answer **A** is correct. Compressed air, if used periodically inside the computer, can help to prevent the hardware faults that occur. Most likely, the warehouse is not the cleanest, and the computer is sucking in dirt 24 hours a day. If you take the computer outside, remove the cover, and carefully blow out the dust bunnies with compressed air, you might increase the life expectancy of the hardware components. Other ways to help prevent this problem are to install a filter in front of the computer where air is drawn into the system, and to enable hibernation of the computer during off hours. During this time, the computer does not draw any air into the case, limiting the intake of dust, dirt, and other pollutants. Antistatic wrist straps are necessary when installing devices, and if they are not used, devices could become damaged, but the frequency of the issues in the question points to environmental conditions, and not ESD. A rescue disk is used to repair an OS when a catastrophic stop error or other similar error occurs. It rebuilds the OS so that it can function again. Because in this scenario the problem is hardware-related, a rescue disk does not help the situation. See the section titled "Procedures and Environmental Controls" in Chapter 18, "Safety, Procedures, and Professionalism," for more information.

60. Answer **B** is correct. Liquid cooling would provide the most, or best, cooling to the CPU. However, it might not be the most efficient, or cost-effective. Most PCs need only a CPU fan and possibly an additional case fan. Due to the complexity, need for maintenance, and possibility of failure of liquid cooling systems, and because they are not always needed, you see them far less often than simple CPU heat sink/fan combinations. They are common in gaming systems though, and sometimes in other custom computing solutions. The heat sink by itself is not a robust enough solution; it should be combined with a CPU fan. The case fan by itself is definitely not enough but is a welcome and inexpensive addition to just about any PC. See the section titled "CPU 101" in Chapter 3, "The CPU," for more information.

61. Answer **D** is correct. The best description for a quad-core processor is a single CPU package with four CPU cores. Two Intel examples of quad-core CPUs are the Core i5 Lynnfield model and Core 2 Quad. The AMD Phenom and Phenom II each have quad-core versions as well. In any of these examples, each core has its own Level 1 cache, but Level 2 and 3 caches are shared by the entire CPU. Because of this the answer "A CPU with four cache memory locations" is partially correct but not the best answer. A PC with four unique processors is probably some kind of server or power workstation; this would require four separate sockets and a CPU for each one. You rarely see a PC with this, or with two dual-core CPUs; instead, you would probably see a PC with a single quad-core CPU. See the section titled "CPU 101" in Chapter 3, "The CPU," for more information.

62. Answer **A** is correct. You should configure the settings through the printer's web interface. The printer should either come with software that can be installed, or it can be accessed directly through a web browser. Either way, you would not use the operating system's printer properties window. After you access the web interface, you can configure whatever type of printing the users might need including duplex printing. This question has little to do with the users, the user's computers, or Windows. You might need to configure the print server as well. See the section titled "Installing, Configuring, and Troubleshooting Printers" in Chapter 14, "Printers," for more information.

63. Answer **C** is correct. You should use the Preboot Execution Environment (PXE) to boot the computer from the network and locate a server and an image on the network to install from. Of course, the network adapter must be PXE-compatible. This is one way of installing Windows or other operating systems over the network. TELNET is a deprecated protocol used to remotely control other systems from the command line. FTP is a protocol that enables the transfer of files between remote computers. NET USE is the command you would use to map a network drive. See the section titled "The BIOS" in Chapter 2, "Motherboards," for more information.

64. Answer **B** is correct. A docking station provides additional connectivity for a laptop such as external keyboards, mice, monitors, and networking connections, just to name a few. A docking station generally does not provide built-in surge suppression. Laptop memory can be added only by opening the laptop or accessing a hatch on the bottom of the laptop. The docking station does not provide a second monitor, but it usually provides the connectivity for that second monitor. See the section titled "Installing, Configuring, and Troubleshooting Visible Laptop Components" in Chapter 7, "Laptops," for more information.

65. Answer **A** is correct. External SATA (eSATA) adapter cards are used to connect external hard disk drives to a computer. PCIe is an expansion bus; most PCIe x16 cards are video cards. PATA (IDE) drives are normally inside the computer. Network adapter cards are used to connect the computer to the network. See the section titled "Magnetic Storage Media" in Chapter 6, "Storage," for more information.

66. Answer **B** is correct. 9031:8611::5468/64 is the only valid IPv6 address listed. The /64 tells you it uses stateless address autoconfiguration (SLAAC). FE08::279B::91A1/122 is incorrect because there are two double colons; IPv6 addresses can have only one double colon within the address. Also, the /122 subnet is incorrect. Common subnets include /64, /56, and /48. ABC0::0011/130 is incorrect because of the subnet /130. FE0G:8B1D::0001/64 is incorrect because there is a G in the number, hexadecimal numbers are 0–9 and A–F only. See the section titled "TCP/IP" in Chapter 15, "Networking," for more information.

67. Answer **C** is correct. Blu-ray has the largest storage space of any optical media listed. Generally, a Blu-ray disc can hold 50 GB. The hard drive is magnetic storage media, not optical storage media. A standard DVD-ROM holds 4.7 GB of data, whereas the largest capacity DVD, DVD-18, can hold 17 GB of data. See the section titled "Optical Storage Media" in Chapter 6, "Storage Devices," for more information.

68. Answer **D** is correct. The only valid APIPA address is 169.254.1.1. Whenever you see an IP address that starts with 169.254, you know it's being applied automatically by Windows through Automatic Private IP Addressing (APIPA). 169.254 is the only network that APIPA utilizes. 192.168.1.1 is a Class C private address; 10.1.1.1 is a Class A private address; and 172.16.1.1 is a Class B private address. See the section titled "TCP/IP" in Chapter 15, "Networking," for more information.

69. Answer **B** is correct. The most likely cause of this problem is that WOL is not enabled in the BIOS. Because it is the BIOS, the setting needs to be configured individually on each computer. Keep in mind that the computers' BIOS and network adapter must support WOL, but in this scenario all the computers are the same make and model, so they should all have the same functionality. They just need to all be configured the same way. Network adapter settings in Windows could possibly be the culprit for waking issues, for example, when you deal with magic packets, but WOL functionality usually resides in the BIOS. Even if the computers had an incorrectly configured gateway IP address, they should still be woken up by other computers on the LAN. However, they will have problems accessing the Internet or other networks outside of the LAN. See the section titled "The BIOS" in Chapter 2, "Motherboards," for more information.

70. Answer **D** is correct. The most likely cause is that the laptop's wireless switch is off. It's common for a user to turn off wireless connectivity when the person leaves the office because it is more secure and saves power. This switch (or button) is usually located directly above the keyboard and is often accompanied by a LED indicator. If the battery needs to be recharged, the laptop should still work normally as long as it is plugged into an AC outlet; if not, then the system would not boot. It is unlikely that the wireless network would be down, but if you find that the laptop wireless switch is on, and everything appears to be configured properly, you might want to check the wireless network itself, especially if other people have trouble accessing it. The laptop's wireless antenna is usually embedded within a card inside the laptop and cannot easily be disconnected. In some cases the laptop may use an external wireless adapter, which might be wholly disconnected, or the actual antenna can become unscrewed, but again this is rare. See the section titled "SOHO Windows Networking" in Chapter 15, "Network," for more information.

71. Answers **A** and **C** are correct. The IEEE wireless standard 802.11a and 802.11g operate at a maximum of 54 Mbps but on different frequencies. 802.11b has a maximum of 11 Mbps; 802.11n has a maximum of approximately 600 Mbps; and 802.11x is not an IEEE wireless standard. Because "x" is often used to represent a variable, the IEEE skipped that letter, and all the 802.11 standards are collectively referred to by some technicians as 802.11x. See the section titled "SOHO Windows Networking" in Chapter 15, "Network," for more information.

72. Answer **D** is correct. Flash memory and flash drives are the only type of storage media listed that have no moving parts. Tape drives mechanically turn the tape to get to the desired location. PATA magnetic hard drives rotate a platter to locate data. DVD-ROM discs spin within the DVD drive. See the section titled "Solid-State Storage Media" in Chapter 6, "Storage Devices," for more information.

73. Answer **D** is correct. The degauss feature within a CRT monitor's on-screen display (OSD) menu has the purpose to remove stray magnetic fields. Most monitors have a reset option within the OSD that can restore the monitor to its factory default settings, but this does not degauss the monitor. Some monitors have different preset modes that can be selected from the OSD, such as normal and optimal. The OSD also has options to increase or decrease monitor brightness. See the section titled "The Video Subsystem" in Chapter 12, "Video and Audio," for more information.

74. Answer **D** is correct. The default data rate of USB 3.0 is 5.0 Gbps (625 MB/s). USB 1.1 is 12 Mbps. USB 2.0 is 480 Mbps (60 MB/s). See the section titled "Input/Output Devices and Peripherals" in Chapter 13, "Peripherals and Custom Computing," for more information.

75. Answer **D** is correct. The information in the scenario was generated with the IPCONFIG/ALL command. The DNS address is most likely `151.198.0.38`. `Fe80::403b:e791:b151:b92a%11(Preferred)` is the link-local IPv6 address. `192.168.1.115(Preferred)` is the IPv4 address of the computer. `255.255.255.0` is the subnet mask. `192.168.1.1` is the gateway address. The DNS server IP address does not have to be on the same network as the IP address of the local computer. However, by default the gateway IP address will be on the same network as the local computer. In this case, the network number is 192.168.1.0. Analyze the different lines of information within your own computer by running the IPCONFIG/ALL command. See the section titled "TCP/IP" in Chapter 15, "Networking," for more information.

76. Answer **B** is correct. RS-232 connections commonly use the serial 9-pin DB-9 port (which is more accurately referred to as a DE-9 port.) This port is uncommon on today's PCs, but there are many organizations that still utilize devices that require an RS-232 connection to be programmed and tested; so there is a good chance that you will still see this port in action in the field. USB is a common replacement for devices that previously used RS-232 connections and PS/2 connections, but it utilizes a quite different 4-pin port. Parallel connections (for example LPT1) are rarer than RS-232 connections and were historically used mainly with printers. SCSI connections are still in use today, but there are several different types of SCSI ports. RS-232 and USB connections are both serial in data transfer (one bit at a time) whereas LPT1 and most SCSI connections send data in parallel (8 bits at a time or multiples of 8). See the section titled "Input/Output Devices and Peripherals" in Chapter 13, "Peripherals and Custom Computing," for more information.

77. Answer **A** is correct. The best way for a person to prevent ESD while working on any components inside the computer is to wear an antistatic wristband that connects to an unpainted portion of the computer chassis or other earth ground. The second best way is to touch grounded metal before coming into contact with any devices. The unpainted chassis of the computer case is a good option. Other good ways to decrease the chance of ESD include wearing rubber-soled shoes, working in a noncarpeted area, and raising the humidity. The AC plug should not come into this conversation. Keep the computer unplugged and stay away from any AC power. Of course, when you finish working on the computer and go to plug it in, you should make sure the AC outlet has a ground post; consider testing the outlet with a receptacle tester or multimeter. See the section titled "Safety" in Chapter 18, "Safety, Procedures, and Professionalism," for more information.

78. Answer **C** is correct. Your organization will often have a Facilities department that takes care of cleaning and maintenance. It should know what types of cleaners are used throughout the building. For smaller companies, you would check with the cleaning crew that was hired. The user should be given medical attention if necessary, and the mouse should be swapped out, and the affected mouse should be held for further analysis. After you find out from the Facilities department what solution was used, either you or it should consult the material safety data sheet (MSDS) to find out the best way to treat any symptoms that might have occurred from using the mouse. A procedures manual might have this information, but it might not, especially considering that procedure manuals often have only the information that that department requires. The fire department is not necessary at this juncture because this is not an emergency. Also, it is not the best place to go to find out what kind of solution was used. See the section titled "Procedures and Environmental Controls" in Chapter 18, "Safety, Procedures, and Professionalism," for more information.

79. Answer **B** is correct. The User Datagram Protocol (UDP) is a connectionless protocol. Unlike the Transmission Control Protocol (TCP) it does not need acknowledgment for each packet sent. It is used especially in the streaming of media. In this scenario, by the time an acknowledgment (ACK) receipt got back to the sender, it would be too late to re-send the packet because many other packets have already been streamed. UDP streaming sessions expect a percentage of bounced, dropped, and otherwise undeliverable packets as part of the technology. HTTP stands for Hypertext Transfer Protocol, used to display website information within a browser program. IP is the Internet Protocol, the second half of TCP/IP that deals primarily with IP addresses and packets. See the section titled "TCP/IP" in Chapter 15, "Networking," for more information.

80. Answer **C** is correct. The Remote Desktop Protocol (RDP) is a Microsoft program that enables a person to remotely control another system; it uses port 3389 by default. Port 53 is used by the Domain Naming System (DNS). Port 1723 is used by the Point-to-Point Tunneling Protocol (PPTP). Port 8080 is an alternative for HTTP, instead of the standard port 80. See the section titled "TCP/IP" in Chapter 15, "Networking," for more information.

81. Answers **A** and **E** are correct. The Digital Visual Interface (DVI) and Video Graphics Array (VGA) are the common connectors on LCD displays. The XGA standard is designed to work on a VGA connector. HDMI can be found on some higher-end monitors, but currently it is not as common as DVI. USB is used for other external devices; though there are some USB to video adapters. Most video monitors come with a DVI and VGA port. See the section titled "The Video Subsystem" in Chapter 12, "Video and Audio," for more information.

82. Answer **A** is correct. L1 cache is the fastest in a computer. It is embedded directly within the core of the processor. L2 and L3 cache are slower because they are on-die, which means that they inhabit the surface of the CPU. Because of the distance, L2 and L3 are slower than L1. L4 cache is rare, but it can be found on some workstations such as ones that use Xeon processors. Some technicians refer to L4 cache as main memory, but this isn't quite accurate. Regardless, L1 cache is the fastest memory of the four. See the section titled "CPU 101" in Chapter 3, "The CPU," for more information.

83. Answer **D** is correct. You should ask the user to clear the desk of confidential papers before you begin troubleshooting. This will dispel any possible notion of you seeing or touching any of the confidential papers—not to say that you would! Working around the papers is not good enough because it may be breaking some rules and policies that the organization might have regarding the secrecy of documents. You want to ask the user nicely and respectfully to clear the desk. Only after doing so is there the possibility of refusing to work until the desk has been cleared, and even then only if company policy dictates that you should do so. You don't want to put the confidential papers in a neat pile because you should not be handling the papers in any way, or even looking at the papers. Confidentiality is important in any organization, and given some policies and procedures of some organizations, you could be reprimanded or possibly lose your job for handling or viewing confidential documents. See the section titled "Professionalism and Communication Skills" in Chapter 18, "Safety, Procedures and Professionalism," for more information.

84. Answer **C** is correct. The laser printer uses a fuser to print documents. The fuser heats the toner on the paper up to 400°F to make it permanent and stick to the paper. Afterward, the toner is pressurized to the paper via pressure rollers and exits the printer through the exit rollers. Inkjet printers use a cartridge of ink that is sprayed on the paper; it dries on its own. Dot matrix printers use a ribbon and a printhead that forces the ribbon's ink onto the paper. Thermal printers heat specially coated paper to apply images and text. See the section titled "Printer Types and Technologies" in Chapter 14, "Printers" for more information.

85. Answer **A** is correct. Terrestrial microwave broadband connections require line of sight to communicate. Say a business owns two buildings across the street from each other and want to connect the buildings' networks without involving a telecommunications company and any wires. They could put parabolic antennae (similar to satellite dishes) on each building, and as long as they are facing each other, the two buildings' networks can communicate. They can be used in remote locations, but it will most likely be rare; however, this is not a limitation of the technology. Microwave broadband connections can transmit or receive information. The speed will be far greater than dial-up, but less than fiber-optic connections, and some cable Internet connections. See the section titled "SOHO Windows Networking" in Chapter 15, "Networking," for more information.

86. Answer **C** is correct. IPCONFIG /RENEW is used on a Windows OS to obtain an IP address from a DHCP server. IPCONFIG /RELEASE can be used to temporarily remove the IP address from the Windows OS. The two are often used to troubleshoot a client attempting to get an IP address from a DHCP server. PING –t tests whether another computer on the network is alive; the –t switch means that the ping is continuous and doesn't end until you press CTRL+C. NSLOOKUP can find the name servers including DNS servers and can tell you the IP addresses of corresponding domain names among other things. MSCONFIG is the Microsoft System Configuration tool that enables you to change boot settings and enable/disable applications at startup. See the section titled "Troubleshooting Networks" in Chapter 15, "Networking," for more information.

87. Answer **D** is correct. Of the listed answers, the fastest expansion bus on a laptop is ExpressCard. ExpressCard can make use of PCI Express mode, which

sends information at 2.5 Gbps (250 MB/s). Compare this to a PC Card Type III running in CardBus mode at 133 MB/s. PCMCIA is the organization that develops the standards for PC Card technology; though the two terms are often used interchangeably. Infrared is far slower than ExpressCard. See the section titled "Installing Configuring and Troubleshooting Visible Laptop Components" in Chapter 7, "Laptops," for more information.

88. Answer **B** is correct. If you transfer data between an older laptop IDE drive and a newer laptop SATA drive, you need an adapter that is 44-pin IDE on one end and 7-pin SATA on the other. Remember that laptops' hard drives have a slightly different connector than the standard PC IDE drive. A PC's IDE drive will be 40-pin. SATA power connectors are 15-pin, but the data connector is 7-pin. This does not take into account all power requirements for both drives. Usually an adapter kit will be used for this type of data transfer. See the section titled "Installing Configuring and Troubleshooting Internal Laptop Components" in Chapter 7, "Laptops," for more information.

89. Answer **A** is correct. The Disk Defragmenter in Windows can take fragmented sections of a hard drive and rearrange them in a contiguous fashion, allowing programs to execute faster, and allowing the hard drive to work more efficiently. Disk Cleanup removes temporary files. Task Manager enables you to stop processes and applications and view the performance of the computer. Task Scheduler enables you to run particular programs at specific times. See the section titled "Files, File Systems, and Disks" in Chapter 9, "Configuring Windows," for more information.

90. Answer **B** is correct. The best way to clean a laptop's screen is to use a dry lint-free cloth. Simply wipe off the dust on the screen as this will usually be the only thing to remove from the screen. If the screen becomes seriously dirty to the point where it can't be read, and a dry lint-free cloth doesn't help, then use a mixture of 50% rubbing alcohol and 50% water. Apply the mixture to a lint-free cloth, and clean the display, trying to stay away from the edges if possible. Paper towels and tissues are not recommended because they disintegrate and leave residue on the screen. Do not use detergents on displays because they will damage them over time; the only place to use detergent on a computer is on the external case. See the section titled "Safety" in Chapter 18, "Safety, Procedures, and Professionalism," for more information.

91. Answer **C** is correct. The technician should leave the customer site and document the incident. In rare cases, there is no way to calm the customer down. If the customer has been shouting for a while and the technician cannot calm the customer down, it's pointless to stay and wait. However, you don't want to call your supervisor and complain about it while you're at the customer's location; this will probably serve to infuriate the customer further. Never shout back at the customer; this is not a battle for power, and never take it personally. Be sure to document the incident in depth after leaving the customer's location. Definitely let your supervisor know what has happened—without complaining. See the section titled "Professionalism and Communications Skills" in Chapter 18, "Safety, Procedures, and Professionalism," for more information.

92. Answers **A** and **D** are correct. To test an AC outlet, you should use either a receptacle tester or a multimeter. Plastic tweezers are an excellent tool to use if

you drop a screw within a computer; however, never stick tweezers in an AC outlet. A PSU tester is used to test power supplies. POST card testers are used to test computers that will not boot properly, or have nothing on the display when they boot. See the section titled "Troubleshooting Examples and PC Tools" in Chapter 1, "Introduction to Troubleshooting," for more information.

93. Answer **C** is correct. Fiber optic cable would be the best for this environment. This is not because of the distance that fiber-optic cable can be run (the other three options can be run farther than 50 meters); it is because of the EMI that will be emitted by the fluorescent light fixtures and electric motor. Fiber optic cable is the best choice when attempting to resist the EMI, even better than shielded twisted-pair cable (STP.) See the section titled "Cables, Connectors, and Tools" in Chapter 15, "Networking," for more information.

94. Answer **D** is correct. Hypertext Transfer Protocol Secure (HTTPS) uses port 443 by default. An example of this is when you open your web browser and log in to your bank. SMTP, which stands for Simple Mail Transfer Protocol, uses port 25 by default. FTP, which stands for File Transfer Protocol, uses port 21 by default. RDP, which stands for Remote Desktop Protocol, uses port 3389 by default. See the section titled "TCP/IP" in Chapter 15, "Networking," for more information.

95. Answer **C** is correct. During the writing stage of the laser printing process, the laser is activated, and it exposes the drum as the drum spins. This dissipates the negative charge toward the center of the drum, and the written areas of the drum will have a lesser negative charge. This is also known as the exposing stage. A rubber blade removes excess toner from the drum during the cleaning stage. A negative charge is applied to the drum by the primary corona wire during the conditioning stage, which is also known as the charging stage. The surface of the drum is applied with negatively charged toner during the developing stage. The toner is transferred to paper as the drum rolls over it during the transferring stage. Though not listed in the answers, finally, the toner is fused to the paper and pressurized during the fusing stage, and the paper exits the printer. See the section titled "Printer Types and Technologies" in Chapter 14, "Printers," for more information.

96. Answer **C** is correct. An update to a card's embedded code is known as a firmware update. Firmware is somewhere between hardware and software. It is not an OS, and it is not driver files that are loaded within an OS. More accurately, it is code that has been written that will be installed to a ROM chip in an adapter card, or in a motherboard. SCSI cards, just like motherboards, have their own BIOS. It can be accessed when the system first boots. Shareware is free software that can be downloaded from the Internet and shared with other users without any licensing or payment required. Although firmware is usually free as well, it is for specific devices, whereas the term shareware applies to software, such as applications and games, which can be downloaded and used by anyone. See the section titled "Magnetic Storage Media" in Chapter 6, "Storage Devices," for more information.

97. Answer **A** is correct. The older original SDRAM is 168-pin. DDR is 184-pin. DDR2 is 240-pin. SODIMMs do not fit in a DIMM slot; they must be installed into a laptop's SODIMM slot and have 200 pins. See the section titled "RAM Basics and Types of RAM" in Chapter 4, "RAM," for more information.

98. Answer **D** is correct. The CR 2032 CMOS battery is most often found in desktop computers. It is the battery backup for the stored CMOS settings that are originally defined or configured by the BIOS. Portable printers use a more powerful battery, possibly rechargeable. Smartphones and Bluetooth mice use rechargeable batteries. The CR 2032 battery is not rechargeable. See the section titled "The BIOS" in Chapter 2, "Motherboards," for more information.

99. Answer **B** is correct. The RJ45 connector is commonly found on network adapters, otherwise known as network interface cards (NIC). Soundcards have 1/8-inch TRS connectors, and possibly optical and gaming connectors. Video cards have DVI, VGA, and HDMI connectors. Dial-up modems have RJ11 connectors. See the section titled "Cables, Connectors, and Tools" in Chapter 15, "Networking," for more information.

100. Answer **A** is correct. Because of how a UPS changes the electricity flow, it can cause damage to a laser printer. Laser printers draw too much current, which can cause issues with any other devices connected to the same power device. Make sure your power strip or surge suppressor can supply enough power to your laser printer. Do not plug any other devices into the power strip or surge suppressor. The same holds true for a line conditioner, which is probably the best device to use for a laser printer. See the section titled "Printer Types and Technologies" in Chapter 14, "Printers," for more information.

Practice Exam 2

CompTIA A+ 220-802

The 100 multiple-choice questions provided here help you to determine how prepared you are for the actual exam and which topics you need to review further. Write down your answers on a separate sheet of paper so that you can take this exam again if necessary. Compare your answers against the answer key that follows this exam.

1. You are helping a customer with an Internet connectivity problem. The customer tells you that the computer cannot connect to a favorite website. After quickly analyzing the computer, you note that it cannot connect to *any* websites. What should you do next?

   ○ **A.** Identify the problem.

   ○ **B.** Establish a theory of probable cause.

   ○ **C.** Test your theory to determine cause.

   ○ **D.** Establish a plan of action.

2. You need to automatically check for performance issues in Windows 7. Which tool is the best option?

   ○ **A.** Device Manager in the Control Panel

   ○ **B.** Troubleshooting item in the Control Panel

   ○ **C.** Task Manager

   ○ **D.** Upgrade Advisor

3. Which of the following is used by BitLocker to provide an encryption key and to protect data? (Select the best answer.)

   ○ **A.** TPM

   ○ **B.** CMOS

   ○ **C.** IRQ

   ○ **D.** AGP

4. You want to verify that the local computer's network card is functioning properly. Which IP address should you use?

   ○ **A.** 10.0.0.1

   ○ **B.** 255.255.255.0

   ○ **C.** 127.0.0.1

   ○ **D.** 192.168.0.1

5. How would you secure a smartphone and its data? (Select the two best answers.)

   ○ **A.** Passcode lock

   ○ **B.** Bluetooth

   ○ **C.** SSID

   ○ **D.** GPS tracking

   ○ **E.** Remote wipe

6. Your customer has a computer (called comp112) that has been infected by a worm. The worm has propagated to at least 30 other computers on the network. What should you do first before attempting to remove the worm from the computer named comp112?

   ○ **A.** Log the user off the system.

   ○ **B.** Boot the system in Safe Mode.

   ○ **C.** Run a full virus scan.

   ○ **D.** Disconnect the network cable from the computer.

7. Which command should you use to find out the integrity of a hard drive?

   ○ **A.** CHKDSK

   ○ **B.** FDISK

   ○ **C.** FORMAT

   ○ **D.** IPCONFIG

8. Your boss asks you to find a list of routers along a given path through multiple networks. What command can help you?

   ○ **A.** PING

   ○ **B.** IPCONFIG

   ○ **C.** TRACERT

   ○ **D.** NSLOOKUP

9. Your customer's laptop's LCD is being scratched by the keyboard when the lid is closed. What would prevent this from happening?

   ○ **A.** Replace the rubber bumpers.

   ○ **B.** Replace the LCD hinges.

   ○ **C.** Replace the LCD panel.

   ○ **D.** Replace the keyboard.

10. You have determined that the USB controller is malfunctioning. What should you do first to troubleshoot this problem?

   ○ **A.** Replace the USB controller.

   ○ **B.** Test the voltage of the USB controller using a multimeter.

   ○ **C.** Use the System Information utility.

   ○ **D.** Use the Windows Device Manager.

11. You have been asked by a customer to add a second optical drive, to be refer-
enced as M: on a computer running Windows 7. What is the best place to
accomplish this?

   ○ **A.** Disk Management

   ○ **B.** Administrative Tools

   ○ **C.** Device Manager

   ○ **D.** Event Viewer

12. A user attempts to print a large image but only half the graphic prints out. What
is the most likely reason for this?

   ○ **A.** The printer doesn't support the job's language.

   ○ **B.** The printer needs more memory.

   ○ **C.** The print driver needs to be updated.

   ○ **D.** The network connection is faulty.

13. Which of the following printer failures is described as a condition in which the
internal feed mechanism stopped working temporarily?

   ○ **A.** No connectivity

   ○ **B.** Corrupt driver

   ○ **C.** Paper jam

   ○ **D.** Power cycle

14. Which command would you use to delete an empty directory?

   ○ **A.** EDIT

   ○ **B.** RD

   ○ **C.** FORMAT

   ○ **D.** DIR

15. One of your co-workers is attempting to access a file on a share located on a
remote computer. The file's share permissions are set to allow the user full control; however, the NTFS permissions allow the user to have read access. What
will be the user's resulting access level for the file?

   ○ **A.** Read

   ○ **B.** Write

   ○ **C.** Modify

   ○ **D.** Full Control

16. You are upgrading a computer from Windows Vista to Windows 7. What is the best tool to use to move a user's documents and file settings?

    ○ **A.** System Restore

    ○ **B.** Easy Transfer

    ○ **C.** XCOPY

    ○ **D.** Backup and Restore

17. You work at a PC bench and receive a laptop that has a dim display. You confirm that it is a hardware issue. Which part should be replaced first?

    ○ **A.** LCD panel

    ○ **B.** Video adapter

    ○ **C.** Display harness

    ○ **D.** LCD inverter

18. A customer reports to you that he can no longer open any .tiff files. What is the most likely cause?

    ○ **A.** The .tiff files are corrupted.

    ○ **B.** File associations have been removed.

    ○ **C.** There is no photo-editing program available.

    ○ **D.** File extension is not a commonly used type.

19. Which of the following answers can be the cause of a blue screen error?

    ○ **A.** Rogue DHCP server

    ○ **B.** Incorrect router configuration

    ○ **C.** Bad driver

    ○ **D.** Incompatible USB device

20. A customer cannot access some Internet websites but can connect to resources inside the LAN. You can use the PING command to test the user's connectivity. What command should you run next to troubleshoot this issue?

    ○ **A.** NET USE

    ○ **B.** NETSTAT -r

    ○ **C.** NBTSTAT -R

    ○ **D.** IPCONFIG/FLUSHDNS

21. You just finished upgrading a video card in a PC. When you reboot the system, nothing displays on the screen. What is the most likely cause?

   ○ **A.** The onboard video of the motherboard is still enabled in the BIOS.

   ○ **B.** New video cards require new monitors because their resolutions do not match.

   ○ **C.** The new video card must be enabled by a dipswitch on the mother- board.

   ○ **D.** The new video card must be installed within the OS first.

22. A program is no longer responding. Where would a technician go to end the program?

   ○ **A.** Computer Management

   ○ **B.** Task Manager

   ○ **C.** Registry

   ○ **D.** Services console

23. You are setting up a SOHO wireless network. Which of the following provides the best security?

   ○ **A.** Disable SSID broadcasting and configure WEP

   ○ **B.** MAC address filtering

   ○ **C.** IP address filtering

   ○ **D.** Enable SSID and configure WPA2

24. After replacing a motherboard in a PC, the system overheats and fails to boot. What is the most likely cause?

   ○ **A.** The GPU is not compatible with the CPU.

   ○ **B.** The new motherboard's firmware is out of date.

   ○ **C.** Thermal paste was not applied between the heat sink and the CPU.

   ○ **D.** The case fan failed.

25. Which of the following is a common e-mail service that people use on their smartphone?

   ○ **A.** POP3

   ○ **B.** Outlook

   ○ **C.** HTTP

   ○ **D.** GMAIL

26. A technician is attempting to backup 5 GB of data to an external hard drive that has been formatted as FAT32; however the backup keeps failing. What is the best way to solve the problem?

   ○ **A.** Reformat the drive as NTFS.

   ○ **B.** Replace the drive.

   ○ **C.** Back up the data to a USB drive.

   ○ **D.** Back up to CD-ROM.

27. A laptop you are troubleshooting will not display any video through the laptop's screen or through external monitors. What should you replace?

   ○ **A.** Inverter

   ○ **B.** Video card

   ○ **C.** LCD

   ○ **D.** Drivers

28. Which of the following utilities enables a Windows 7 user to edit a file offline, and then automatically update the changes when the user returns back to the office?

   ○ **A.** Sync Center

   ○ **B.** Windows Aero

   ○ **C.** Windows Defender

   ○ **D.** HomeGroup

29. A customer's laser printer is printing a blank streak along one edge of each page, but is otherwise printing normally. What is the most likely reason?

   ○ **A.** The paper is too thick.

   ○ **B.** The toner cartridge is low.

   ○ **C.** The fuser is damaged.

   ○ **D.** The printer needs to be rebooted.

30. Which of the following tools can illuminate a network card's LED light when connected?

   ○ **A.** POST card

   ○ **B.** Loopback plug

   ○ **C.** PSU tester

   ○ **D.** Multimeter

31. One of your organization's technicians reconfigures the BIOS boot order on a PC and sees that the system time is incorrect. The technician resets the clock to the correct time but sees that a couple days later, the system time is wrong again. What is the most likely cause?

   ○ **A.** The motherboard is not seated properly.

   ○ **B.** The time zone settings are incorrect in the OS.

   ○ **C.** The CMOS battery has failed.

   ○ **D.** The power supply is not providing the correct voltage.

32. Which Windows 7/Vista files replaced NTLDR?

   ○ **A.** bootmgr.exe, bootsect.dos, io.sys

   ○ **B.** io.sys, win.exe, bootmgr.exe

   ○ **C.** ntdetect.exe, ntoskrnl.exe, io.sys

   ○ **D.** bootmgr.exe, winload.exe, and winresume.exe

33. You reboot a customer's computer and see a pop-up message that says one or more services failed to start. Which of the following can give you more information?

   ○ **A.** System event logs

   ○ **B.** Task Manager

   ○ **C.** Application event logs

   ○ **D.** Security log

34. Which of the following would extend the wireless network range and allow out-of-range users to share an Internet connection?

   ○ **A.** Implement a wireless access point for the out of range users.

   ○ **B.** Enable network sharing on the users' computers that are within range

   ○ **C.** Upgrade the out-of-range users' SSID searching software.

   ○ **D.** Create a new VLAN for the out of range users.

35. What can the command ping –t do?

   ○ **A.** Continuous ping of an IP address until the target responds

   ○ **B.** Continuous ping of an IP address until it's canceled

   ○ **C.** Continuous ping of an IP address until the count reaches 20

   ○ **D.** Continuous ping of an IP address where each packet is equal to 1000 bytes

36. You are installing a 32-bit program on a 64-bit version of Windows 7. Where does the program get installed to?

   ○ **A.** C:\

   ○ **B.** C:\Program Files

   ○ **C.** C:\Windows

   ○ **D.** C:\Program Files (x86)

37. Which of the following paths is the default directory for user profiles in Windows 7?

    ○ **A.** C:\Program Files

    ○ **B.** C:\Users

    ○ **C.** C:\Users and Settings\

    ○ **D.** C:\Document and Settings\

38. You are working on a computer that is giving a non-system disk error. Which of the following is most likely the cause?

    ○ **A.** There is a disk in the floppy drive.

    ○ **B.** The registry has become corrupted.

    ○ **C.** The incorrect driver was loaded.

    ○ **D.** The RAM is not seated properly.

39. One of the tape drives in the server room is reporting errors. What should you do first to maintenance the tape drive?

    ○ **A.** Use the included cleaning tape for the drive.

    ○ **B.** Uninstall the backup software and reinstall it.

    ○ **C.** Install a new IDE cable.

    ○ **D.** Replace the tape with a new one.

40. Your co-worker is having trouble tapping icons on his smartphone. What should you check first?

    ○ **A.** Screen orientation

    ○ **B.** Geotracking

    ○ **C.** Global positioning

    ○ **D.** Screen calibration

41. At one of your customer's locations, two users share the same Windows 7 computer. The first user creates a document intended to be used by both users and then logs off the computer. The second user logs on and types the name of the document in the Start menu but the document cannot be found. What is the problem?

    ○ **A.** The document is locked.

    ○ **B.** The document is set to hidden.

    ○ **C.** The document is owned by the first user.

    ○ **D.** The document is encrypted.

42. You receive a message in Windows XP that warns you of a memory-read error. What should you do to fix this?

    ○ **A.** Reseat or replace RAM modules.

    ○ **B.** Change the memory settings in the BIOS.

    ○ **C.** Replace the hard drive.

    ○ **D.** Remove any USB flash drives.

43. Which component is usually removed to access a laptop's motherboard and other internal components?

    ○ **A.** Display

    ○ **B.** Bezel

    ○ **C.** Keyboard

    ○ **D.** Battery

44. A user tells you that her Windows 7 laptop does not display a picture when it is connected to a projector. However, there is a picture on the laptop's screen. What is the most likely cause?

    ○ **A.** Windows 7 does not support multiple displays on laptops.

    ○ **B.** The Windows 7 video driver is missing.

    ○ **C.** The presentation resolution is too big.

    ○ **D.** The laptop external display setting has been turned off.

45. A co-worker attempts to run an old program on his Windows 7 computer. The program briefly opens, but then it closes immediately. What can you do to enable the program to run correctly?

    ○ **A.** Run the program in Windows Compatibility mode.

    ○ **B.** Run the program from the Command Prompt.

    ○ **C.** Run the program inside a virtual machine.

    ○ **D.** Run the program from another computer.

46. What color do EFS files display in by default?

    ○ **A.** Blue

    ○ **B.** Black

    ○ **C.** Green

    ○ **D.** Red

47. You want to create a spanned volume over two hard drives that are separate from the system volume of a Windows 7 workstation. What tool can help you determine if the hard drives can support spanned volumes?

- ○ **A.** Disk Management
- ○ **B.** Task Manager
- ○ **C.** Device Manager
- ○ **D.** System Information

48. What is another name for a mirrored set?

- ○ **A.** RAID 0
- ○ **B.** RAID 1
- ○ **C.** RAID 5
- ○ **D.** RAID 6

49. What would you replace in a laser printer if you see ghosted images?

- ○ **A.** Fuser
- ○ **B.** Cartridge
- ○ **C.** Drum
- ○ **D.** Printhead

50. Of the following ways to manipulate a file, which can retain the file's NTFS permissions?

- ○ **A.** Moving the file to another NTFS volume
- ○ **B.** Copying the file to another FAT32 volume
- ○ **C.** Moving the file to a new location on the same volume
- ○ **D.** Copying the file to a new location on the same volume

51. A customer's computer states that USB 3.0 devices are running at USB 2.0 speed. There is no kind of external USB hub. You test the devices on your computer, and they run at USB 3.0 speed. What should you do to provide USB 3.0 functionality for the customer?

- ○ **A.** Replace USB 2.0 cables with USB 3.0 cables.
- ○ **B.** Install a USB 3.0 firmware update to the motherboard.
- ○ **C.** Install an external USB 3.0 hub.
- ○ **D.** Upgrade the customer to IEEE 1394a.

52. A user can no longer print from their computer to the default printer. You can print a test page from the printer, and the printer's queue shows that the job is ready to print. What should you do to resolve the situation?

    ○ **A.** Delete the job and resubmit it.

    ○ **B.** Reinstall the print drivers.

    ○ **C.** Reset the printer.

    ○ **D.** Restart the printer spooler service.

53. You just installed a new computer for a customer who complains that there is an odor near the power supply when it is turned on. What should you do?

    ○ **A.** Replace the power supply.

    ○ **B.** Unplug the computer and contact the manufacturer.

    ○ **C.** Use compressed air to flush the odor from the power supply.

    ○ **D.** Run the computer for 48 hours and disregard if the odor goes away.

54. You just installed front panel USB ports that are not functioning properly. However, the ports on the back of the computer work fine. What should you do first?

    ○ **A.** Check the USB rear panel pinouts to verify that the ports are wired as per manufacturer instructions.

    ○ **B.** Check the Device Manager for any alerts or question marks over USB-related devices.

    ○ **C.** Test the voltage output of each USB port with a multimeter.

    ○ **D.** Make sure that any USB devices are not drawing too much power from the ports.

55. Which of the following programs are commonly found on a smartphone? (Select the three best answers.)

    ○ **A.** E-mail programs

    ○ **B.** Microsoft Word

    ○ **C.** Visual Basic

    ○ **D.** Contacts programs

    ○ **E.** Texting programs

56. Which of the following could be defined as standing behind a person at a desk attempting to view confidential information?

    ○ **A.** Root Kit

    ○ **B.** Phishing

    ○ **C.** Shoulder Surfing

    ○ **D.** Tailgating

57. A customer reports to you that he cannot access the company FTP site. He says that he is using the IP address given to him: 86200.43.118. What is most likely the problem?

- ○ **A.** Port 21 is blocked.
- ○ **B.** This is an invalid IP address.
- ○ **C.** The FTP site is down.
- ○ **D.** The FTP program is not working.

58. You just installed a second SATA hard drive into a Windows 7 computer. The computer boots normally, but you cannot locate the second drive in Windows Explorer. What is the problem? (Select the two best answers.)

- ○ **A.** The hard drive was formatted as FAT32.
- ○ **B.** The hard drive must be partitioned.
- ○ **C.** The hard drive was formatted as NTFS.
- ○ **D.** The hard drive must be assigned a drive letter.
- ○ **E.** The hard drive is not compatible with Windows 7.

59. You configured a customer's router to automatically assign only 5 IP addresses in an attempt to make the network more secure. Now you notice that the wireless printer is intermittently losing connections when there are multiple users on the wireless network. What is the best solution?

- ○ **A.** Increase the wireless router IP lease times.
- ○ **B.** Install another access point.
- ○ **C.** Configure the printer to use a static IP address.
- ○ **D.** Configure the printer for DHCP.

60. What kinds of data would people commonly synchronize from their mobile device to their PC? (Select the three best answers.)

- ○ **A.** Call history
- ○ **B.** Contacts
- ○ **C.** Music
- ○ **D.** E-mail
- ○ **E.** GPS tracking

61. A co-worker suspects that the AC voltage supplied to a PC power supply is flawed. What tool should be used to confirm this suspicion?

- ○ **A.** Oscilloscope
- ○ **B.** Cable tester
- ○ **C.** Multimeter
- ○ **D.** PSU tester

62. Your boss wants to transfer data to an external hard drive capable of data transfer rates as high as 600 Mbps. Which of the following has the fastest transfer
rate?

   ○ A. USB 1.1

   ○ B. Cable Internet

   ○ C. USB 2.0

   ○ D. IEEE 1394b

63. Which versions of Windows offer offline files and folders? (Select the two best
answers.)

   ○ A. Windows XP Home

   ○ B. Windows 7 Ultimate

   ○ C. Windows Vista Home Premium 64-bit

   ○ D. Windows XP Professional

   ○ E. Windows 7 Home Premium

64. You want to utilize the NET command to tell you how many Server Message
Blocks (SMB) were received by the workstation service. Which NET command
should you use?

   ○ A. View

   ○ B. Statistics

   ○ C. Stop

   ○ D. Use

65. You boot Windows 7 and see the error message One or More Services Failed to
Start. What methods can you use to view the status of services on the computer? (Select the two best answers.)

   ○ A. Right-click Computer, and select Manage from the menu.

   ○ B. Click Start > Control Panel > System.

   ○ C. Click Start > Control Panel > Administrative Tools.

   ○ D. Right-click the Desktop, and select Personalize from the menu.

   ○ E. Right-click Computer, and select Properties from the menu.

66. What is a difference between a domain and a workgroup?

   ○ A. A workgroup has a domain controller.

   ○ B. A domain is meant for 10 computers or less.

   ○ C. A workgroup has 20 or more computers.

   ○ D. A domain is controlled by a server.

67. How can you ensure that all external traffic to your website is directed through a firewall to the right computer?

- ○ **A.** Configure port forwarding.
- ○ **B.** List in the exceptions the IP address of the local website.
- ○ **C.** Configure NAT.
- ○ **D.** Configure all interior traffic appropriately.

68. Which command is the best option for verifying that the protected system files in Windows 7 are correct?

- ○ **A.** DISKPART
- ○ **B.** SFC
- ○ **C.** SCANDISK
- ○ **D.** FIXMBR

69. Which of the following is stored in the first sector of the hard drive?

- ○ **A.** Boot sector
- ○ **B.** Operating system
- ○ **C.** Master boot record
- ○ **D.** Master file table

70. One of your customers tells you that her laptop LCD keeps getting darker the more she uses it even though she maximized the brightness using the function keys. What is the best solution?

- ○ **A.** Check and replace the video memory.
- ○ **B.** Check and replace the backlight.
- ○ **C.** Replace the LCD.
- ○ **D.** Replace the inverter.

71. You turn on a computer, and a blue screen appears with an error code. Where should you go to find out what this error code means?

- ○ **A.** Third-party website
- ○ **B.** OS manufacturer's website
- ○ **C.** Hardware manufacturer's website
- ○ **D.** Installation manual

72. What command repairs the bootmgr.exe file in Windows 7?

   ○ **A.** bootrec /fixboot

   ○ **B.** bootrec /fixmbr

   ○ **C.** bootrec /rebuildbcd

   ○ **D.** boot\bcd

73. Which of the following allows you to make phone calls and transfer data from your smartphone without the need for additional programs?

   ○ **A.** Wi-Fi

   ○ **B.** Bluetooth

   ○ **C.** Cable Internet

   ○ **D.** GSM

74. A customer complains that they can only view their tablet vertically, and that it won't display horizontally. What is the problem?

   ○ **A.** Screen calibration

   ○ **B.** Screen orientation

   ○ **C.** Geotracking

   ○ **D.** The touchscreen needs to be replaced

75. A co-worker tells you that his Windows 7 computer is making noise constantly. You look at the computer and note that the hard drive activity light is frequently on. You also note that there is plenty of free space on the drive's only partition. Of the following, which best explains why the drive light is continuously active?

   ○ **A.** Page file issue

   ○ **B.** Too many documents on the partition

   ○ **C.** Drive needs a new SATA connector

   ○ **D.** Fragmented hard drive

76. All the printouts from a printer are displaying a random mix of letters, numbers, symbols, and in general, gibberish. What is the most likely cause of this problem?

   ○ **A.** There is an incorrect print driver.

   ○ **B.** The toner cartridge needs to be replaced.

   ○ **C.** The print spooler needs to be restarted.

   ○ **D.** The print drum needs to be replaced.

77. You are working on a PC that runs fine for close to an hour but then shuts down automatically. Which should you check first?

    ○ **A.** Hard disk drive

    ○ **B.** Power supply voltages

    ○ **C.** CPU fan

    ○ **D.** Optical drive

78. A user tells you that her computer worked fine until today when she heard a popping noise. Then, the computer shut down and couldn't be restarted. What should you check first?

    ○ **A.** Power supply

    ○ **B.** CPU

    ○ **C.** Hard disk drive

    ○ **D.** AC outlet

79. Which tool would you use if you wanted to do a Startup Repair in Windows 7?

    ○ **A.** Safe Mode

    ○ **B.** Recovery Console

    ○ **C.** WinRE

    ○ **D.** System Image Recovery

80. Which command would you use to display the contents of C:\Windows\System32\?

    ○ **A.** NET

    ○ **B.** CD

    ○ **C.** System Information Tool

    ○ **D.** DIR

81. Instead of incurring the expense of new computers, a customer of yours is trying to keep its Windows XP systems. The customer asks you to install 250 GB drives to each system. You do so, but a few of the systems recognize only 137 GB during usage. What is the problem?

    ○ **A.** Some of the hard drives are defective and need to be returned.

    ○ **B.** Windows XP does not support hard drives larger than 137 GB.

    ○ **C.** Service Pack 1 has not been installed.

    ○ **D.** The hard drive jumpers are not set properly.

82. A user tells you that his PC is making a strange noise. What is the most likely cause?

    ○ **A.** The CPU needs to be reseated.

    ○ **B.** A network cable is vibrating against the system case.

    ○ **C.** The thermal grease dried out and needs to be re-applied.

    ○ **D.** An internal wire is improperly routed and is hitting the CPU fan.

83. You just finished removing malware from a customer's computer located in a small office, but the Internet browser cannot access any websites. What should you do first?

    ○ **A.** Reset the router.

    ○ **B.** Remove the browser proxy settings.

    ○ **C.** Reboot the computer.

    ○ **D.** Install the latest service pack.

84. Which type of malware self-replicates?

    ○ **A.** Virus

    ○ **B.** Worm

    ○ **C.** Trojan

    ○ **D.** Spyware

85. You are installing a wireless access point. What should you do first?

    ○ **A.** Disable DHCP.

    ○ **B.** Enable MAC filtering.

    ○ **C.** Change the default password.

    ○ **D.** Download and install the latest firmware.

86. You need to find out which Windows OS is running on a computer. Which command should you use?

    ○ **A.** SET

    ○ **B.** VER

    ○ **C.** Device Manager

    ○ **D.** CMD

87. Which version of Windows 7 includes BitLocker encryption?

    ○ **A.** Starter

    ○ **B.** Home Premium

    ○ **C.** Professional

    ○ **D.** Ultimate

88. One of your customers tries to log in to a bookmarked site but instead of seeing the website expected, the user is prompted for a Social Security number, mother's maiden name, and date of birth. What most likely occurred?

   O **A.** The browser was hijacked.

   O **B.** The customer's identity was stolen.

   O **C.** The website the user accessed has updated their security policies.

   O **D.** The user typed the wrong URL.

89. A two-year-old inkjet printer just started printing faded and smeared pages. What is the best solution for this?

   O **A.** Reseat the print cartridges.

   O **B.** Use a lint-free cloth to clean the print heads.

   O **C.** Use compressed air on the print cartridges.

   O **D.** Run the printer's cleaning routine.

90. A user tells you that the monitor resolution was changed and now the user does not see a display. What should you do first?

   O **A.** Go into the Display Properties.

   O **B.** Reseat the video card.

   O **C.** Boot into Safe Mode.

   O **D.** Reset the monitor.

91. You install a Windows 7 computer for a customer. They already have three Windows XP computers on a network. The new Windows 7 computer can ping the Windows XP computers, but the Windows XP computers cannot ping the Windows 7 computer. What is the reason for this?

   O **A.** The firewall is on.

   O **B.** The network cable is unplugged.

   O **C.** The operating systems are not compatible.

   O **D.** Windows updates need to be installed.

92. You attempt to play audio from your Bluetooth-enabled smartphone to your Bluetooth-enabled Windows 7 computer, but you find that the phone cannot detect the computer. What will you do to solve this problem?

   O **A.** Install mobile phone synchronization software on the computer.

   O **B.** Place the phone in Bluetooth discovery mode.

   O **C.** Add the phone to a PAN.

   O **D.** Place the computer in Bluetooth discovery mode.

93. A user tells you that after he upgraded a computer from Windows XP to Windows Vista, the Run option is no longer in the Start menu. What is the most likely reason for this?

   ○ **A.** Vista replaced the Run option with the PowerShell.

   ○ **B.** The registry is corrupt.

   ○ **C.** The user must be an administrator to see the Run option.

   ○ **D.** The run command is not displayed by default on the Start menu.

94. Which of the following utilities is the fastest way to view the network adapter statistics?

   ○ **A.** Task Manager

   ○ **B.** System Information

   ○ **C.** Performance Monitor

   ○ **D.** Command Prompt

95. What is the best way to ensure that only certain computers can access your wireless network?

   ○ **A.** Disable the SSID.

   ○ **B.** Enable MAC filtering.

   ○ **C.** Change the SSID.

   ○ **D.** Change the default password.

96. A customer wants to store their Windows 7 documents on a different drive than the default C drive location. How can this be accomplished?

   ○ **A.** Add a documents folder location in the folder's properties.

   ○ **B.** Add a program files folder location in the folder's properties.

   ○ **C.** Add a Windows files folder location in the folder's properties.

   ○ **D.** Add a system files folder location in the folder's properties.

97. What state must a Windows 7 partition be in to allow the OS to boot?

   ○ **A.** Primary

   ○ **B.** Healthy

   ○ **C.** Active

   ○ **D.** Logical

98. You are working as a technician for a data mining organization. You just moved files from one folder to another, but now you cannot open them. What should you do to regain access to the files?

- ○ **A.** Perform the file transfer again.
- ○ **B.** Take ownership of the files.
- ○ **C.** In Folder Options, select Show hidden files and folders.
- ○ **D.** Reboot the system, and the files will be accessible.

99. You are troubleshooting a Windows 7 computer that has you perplexed. Apparently, the computer has been showing strange behavior since the user of the system was given administrative privileges a month ago. What is the easiest way for you to return the computer to its last known good state of functionality?

- ○ **A.** When the system boots, press F8 and select Last Known Good Configuration.
- ○ **B.** Boot into Safe Mode and revoke the administrative rights.
- ○ **C.** Re-image the computer.
- ○ **D.** Perform a System Restore to the day before the user was given administrative rights.

100. Which of the following is part of the second step of the CompTIA A+ troubleshooting process: Establish a theory of probable cause?

- ○ **A.** Question the user.
- ○ **B.** Question the obvious.
- ○ **C.** Test the theory to determine cause.
- ○ **D.** Establish a plan of action.

Answers at a Glance

1. B	35. B	69. C
2. B	36. D	70. B
3. A	37. B	71. B
4. C	38. A	72. A
5. A and E	39. A	73. D
6. D	40. D	74. B
7. A	41. C	75. D
8. C	42. A	76. A
9. A	43. C	77. C
10. D	44. D	78. A
11. A	45. A	79. C
12. B	46. C	80. D
13. C	47. A	81. C
14. B	48. B	82. D
15. A	49. C	83. B
16. B	50. C	84. B
17. D	51. B	85. C
18. B	52. D	86. B
19. C	53. D	87. D
20. D	54. B	88. A
21. A	55. A, D, and E	89. D
22. B	56. C	90. C
23. D	57. B	91. A
24. C	58. B and D	92. D
25. D	59. C	93. D
26. A	60. B, C, and D	94. A
27. B	61. C	95. B
28. A	62. D	96. A
29. C	63. B and D	97. C
30. B	64. B	98. B
31. C	65. A and C	99. D
32. D	66. D	100. B
33. A	67. A	
34. A	68. B	

Answers with Explanations

1. Answer **B** is correct. In this scenario you have already identified the problem: The computer cannot connect to any websites. So, the next thing you should do according to the CompTIA A+ six-step troubleshooting process is to: Establish a theory of probably cause. For example, maybe your theory is that the network cable is not plugged into the computer, or perhaps the computer is not obtaining an IP address. Pick one theory (the most likely in the situation) and move to step 3: Test the theory to determine the cause. If you were to look behind the computer and see that the network patch cable was unplugged (and there is no possibility of wireless), well then the theory has tested positive, and you can move to step 4: Establish a plan of action to resolve the problem. In this case, it's easy: Plug in the cable! Afterward, you would verify full system functionality (step 5) by testing whether the web browser can access websites. Finally, in the last step, document the problem, the solution, and any additional details such as advice you gave to the customer. When working on computers, apply the six-step troubleshooting methodology to your thinking process as much as possible!

   See the section "The Six-Step A+ Troubleshooting Process" in Chapter 1, "Introduction to Troubleshooting," for more information.

2. Answer **B** is correct. The Troubleshooting item in the Control Panel of Windows 7 can automatically check for performance issues. You can check for issues with hardware, networking, applications, and security. You must set the Control Panel to either small or large icons because the Troubleshooting item is not shown in Category view. The Device Manager is where you go to reconfigure devices, change device settings, and install/update drivers. The Task Manager gives some information about the performance of the computer, but there is no automatic check for performance issues. The Upgrade Advisor (for Windows 7) is a downloadable tool that can tell you whether an older OS can be upgraded to Windows 7. See the section "Windows Tools and Errors" in Chapter 11, "Troubleshooting Windows," for more information.

3. Answer **A** is correct. A Trusted Platform Module (TPM) is used by BitLocker to provide an encryption key and to protect data. This module is normally located on the motherboard in the form of a chip. You can also use a USB drive to store the encryption key if the computer does not have a TPM chip. CMOS stands for complementary metal-oxide semiconductor, the chip that retains the time and date, and other settings for the BIOS. An IRQ is an Interrupt ReQuest; the number that identifies a device to the CPU. AGP stands for Accelerated Graphics Port, a video-only expansion bus that has been mostly replaced by PCI Express. See the section "Windows Security" in Chapter 16, "Security," for more information.

4. Answer **C** is correct. You should ping the local loopback address of the computer. The best way to do this would be to type `ping 127.0.0.1` in the Command Prompt. However, you could also type `ping localhost`, or `ping loopback`.

This can tell you if the network card (and TCP/IP) is working properly for the local computer. If IPv6 is installed and working properly, `ping localhost` and `ping loopback` return the result: `Reply from ::1`. Afterward, if the computer is cabled to the network, you could attempt to ping the default gateway, whatever that address might be. 10.0.0.1 and 192.168.0.1 are possible IP addresses for hosts and are common for default gateways, but in this scenario you don't know if these addresses are being used, or if a default gateway even exists. Also, neither of them are the local loopback address. Most of the time, addresses ending in .1 will be reserved for routers, servers, and so on, not client computers. For example, D-Link historically has used 192.168.0.1 as the default IP address for its routers. 255.255.255.0 is a default Class C subnet mask and not an IP address. You would not ping that address. See the section "TCP/IP" in Chapter 15, "Networking," for more information.

5. Answers **A** and **E** are correct. Passcode locks and remote wipe are effective ways to secure a smartphone and its data. The passcode (usually a 4-to-8-digit number) stops the average person from accessing the phone unless he knows the code. Remote wipe allows the owner to remove any and all confidential data on the phone from a remote location if the phone is stolen. Both of these are good ways to secure a smartphone. You might also consider encryption and document passwords. Secure Set Identifier (SSID) names are given to wireless access points and are effectively the name of the wireless network. GPS tracking might seem like a good way to secure the phone. But it doesn't actually secure the phone or the data; it secures only the possibility of retrieving the phone if it is lost or stolen. Bluetooth is a wireless standard in which devices are used to communicate with the smartphone, such as headsets. Bluetooth is not secure out-of-the-box, and the owner should make use of a secure pairing passcode instead of the default 0000 code. See the section "Mobile Security" in Chapter 17, "Mobile Devices," for more information.

6. Answer **D** is correct. Before you do anything else, disconnect the network cable from the computer, in this case comp112. This can help to isolate the problem. You might also decide to disconnect the network cables from any other systems that were infected by this worm. Sometimes, it is easier to do this at the server room. After the network cable is disconnected, the computer should be shut down (which will log off the user anyway) and rebooted into Safe Mode. Then, the worm should be isolated and quarantined. Finally, a full virus scan should be run. This of course is just a quick example; you probably need to do more to resolve this problem on all computers concerned. See the section "Security Threats and Prevention" in Chapter 16, "Security" for more information.

7. Answer **A** is correct. CHKDSK is the best tool listed to determine the integrity of a hard drive. It can also check the disk surface for errors such as bad sectors and can repair some errors. Another good answer would be the System File Checker (SFC) tool, which can repair errors that CHKDSK cannot. FDISK is a DOS-based command that allows you to partition a hard drive from the command-line; it is not used in newer versions of Windows. FORMAT is the command used to write a file system to a partition, logical drive, or volume of a hard drive. IPCONFIG is used to find out the TCP/IP configuration of a network adapter. See the section titled "Command-Line Tools" in Chapter 11, "Troubleshooting Windows," for more information.

8. Answer **C** is correct. The trace route (TRACERT) program displays a list of routers along a path that starts at the local computer and ends at the requested destination. For example, `tracert davidlprowse.com` would show all network routers between the computer initiating the trace and the final destination: the web server that hosts the davidlprowse.com website. PING tells you if another computer on the network is accessible. IPCONFIG shows the TCP/IP configuration for your computer's network adapters. NSLOOKUP gives information about a name server and can resolve domain names to IP address. See the section titled "Troubleshooting Networks" in Chapter 15, "Networking," for more information.

9. Answer **A** is correct. You should replace the rubber bumpers. These can wear down over time or might become unstuck from the laptop. These bumpers create a space between the keyboard and the LCD; without them, the LCD can get scratched by the keyboard. If the laptop opens and closes okay, then there is no reason to replace the hinges, because they won't change how the screen is touching the keyboard. The LCD panel is only scratched; it hasn't failed as of yet, so it doesn't need to be replaced. The keyboard is most likely not the cause of the problem. There is the uncommon possibility that the keyboard is not mounted properly; a quick sideways glance at the laptop keyboard surface can tell you right away. You would have to remove the laptop bezel and reconnect the keyboard properly if this is the case. However, it is more likely that the rubber bumpers fell off or became worn down. See the section titled "Installing, Configuring, and Troubleshooting Visible Laptop Components" in Chapter 7, "Laptops," for more information.

10. Answer **D** is correct. If the USB controller is malfunctioning, the first thing you should do is analyze the problem with the Device Manager. This displays one of a variety of symbols over the USB controller if there is an issue. You can also take the code of the error and cross reference that on the Microsoft Help and Support website support.microsoft.com for more information. Until you know why the USB controller is malfunctioning, you should not replace it. It could be that it is simply disabled or a setting needs to be changed; these changes can be made within the Device Manager. If you find you cannot fix the problem in software, you might move on to testing the voltage with a multimeter, but this will usually not be necessary. The System Information utility shows information about devices but not as much as the Device Manager, plus you can't make configuration changes in the System Information utility. See the section titled "Windows Tools and Errors" in Chapter 11, "Troubleshooting Windows," for more information.

11. Answer **A** is correct. After you physically install the drive, it needs to be configured as M: within the Disk Management tool. Disk Management is where you go to create partitions, assign drive letters, work with volumes, format drives, and so on. Administrative Tools is an entire set of tools that includes the Computer Management console, another location that offers the Disk Management tool. This answer is incorrect because it is not the actual tool needed, but an indirect way to access it. The Device Manager is used to analyze and configure devices. The Event Viewer is used to analyze the log files concerning the OS, applications, and security. See the section titled "Files, File Systems, and Disks" in Chapter 9, "Configuring Windows," for more information.

12. Answer **B** is correct. If the printer is printing only half of an image, it probably needs a memory upgrade. Larger print jobs require more memory. Most laser printers can be upgraded to 2x or 4x the stock amount of RAM. The standard "language" for printers is Printer Command Language (PCL), and most printers will be compatible with this protocol. If the driver is incorrect, the document will either not print at all or will print as gibberish. If the network connection is faulty, the print job would fail altogether. See the section titled "Installing, Configuring, and Troubleshooting Printers" in Chapter 14, "Printers," for more information.

13. Answer **C** is correct. A failure that occurs due to the internal feed mechanism stopping is known as a paper jam. For example, an HP LaserJet might show an error code 13.1 on the display, which means that there is a paper jam at the paper feed area. You would want to verify that the paper trays are loaded and adjusted properly. A No Connectivity message would mean that the printer is not currently connected to the network. A corrupt driver loaded on a workstation would cause any print job from that computer to either fail or print nonsense. A Power Cycle message means that the self-diagnostic program has encountered a problem and is telling you to shut down the printer and turn it back on. This will reset the printer, which can fix many of the issues that can occur. See the section titled "Installing, Configuring, and Troubleshooting Printers" in Chapter 14, "Printers," for more information.

14. Answer **B** is correct. The command used to delete an empty directory in a Windows Command Prompt is RD. RD stands for remove directory. CD is change directory, and MD is make directory. Know your old DOS commands! The EDIT command is used to make changes to text files within the Command Prompt, for example if you were to edit a batch file. FORMAT writes a new file system to a partition, while overwriting any file information located there. DIR is the directory command; it enables you to see the contents of a particular folder. See the section titled "Files, File Systems, and Disks" in Chapter 9, "Configuring Windows," for more information.

15. Answer **A** is correct. The user will have only read access to the file. Remember that NTFS permissions take precedence over share permissions, even if the share-level permissions offer a higher level of access. It is possible for the user to get write, modify, or full control access, but only if the NTFS permissions are configured to allow the user to do so. See the section titled "Windows Security" in Chapter 16, "Security," for more information.

16. Answer **B** is correct. The easiest tool for moving a user's documents and settings is the Easy Transfer tool. Windows Easy Transfer can be installed on 32-bit and 64-bit versions of Windows 7, Vista, and XP. System Restore doesn't back-up files; it restores the system to an earlier configuration. XCOPY is a command-line tool used to copy entire directory structures. It has been deprecated in favor of Robocopy, but neither of these tools is as easy to use as Easy Transfer. Backup and Restore is meant more for keeping a backup of your data in the event of a disaster, whereas Easy Transfer is meant for when a user is moving from one PC to another, or perhaps is upgrading from one OS to another. See the section titled "System Tools and Utilities" in Chapter 9, "Configuring Windows," for more information.

17. Answer **D** is correct. If you see a dim laptop display that cannot be brightened through the use of a button or knob near the keyboard, then the LCD inverter might need to be replaced. The inverter supplies the power to the backlight of the display. If it fails, you should still dimly see the displayed OS; using a flashlight can aid in this. To fix this, you would need to disassemble the LCD and then replace the inverter, which is simply a small circuit board. If the video adapter fails, you won't see anything on the screen, even dimly. This is rarer, and the video adapter is usually integrated into the motherboard. The inverter is often connected to the display harness of the LCD. See the section titled "Installing, Configuring, and Troubleshooting Internal Laptop Components" in Chapter 7, "Laptops," for more information.

18. Answer **B** is correct. If users were able to open .tiff files but can no longer do so, then the most likely cause is that the file associations for .tiff (and possibly .tif) have been removed. Programs such as Photoshop, Fireworks, and SnagIt can save and open files with the .tiff and/or .tif extension. When a program such as Photoshop is installed, a file association between that program and .tiff files is automatically created. This can be removed on purpose in the OS, by associating the file type with another program, or inadvertently by installing another program. When the person goes to open the file, a message should display asking to open the file automatically, or select a program to use to open it. Chances are that multiple .tiff files will not have been corrupted at the same time. If it were one file, that would be a different story, but that the user cannot open *any* .tiff files should be an indicator of an application issue. If the person were able to open the files previously, then there should still be a photo-editing program such as Photoshop loaded on the computer. .tiff and .tif are common lossless file formats for storing images. See the section titled "Files, File Systems, and Disks" in Chapter 9, "Configuring Windows," for more information.

19. Answer **C** is correct. Bad drivers can be the cause of a stop error or blue screen error (also known as a BSOD), for example, if cdrom.sys, the basic CD-ROM system driver file, were to fail during bootup. The CPU and RAM can also cause these errors to occur. The blue screen error affects only the local computer; it is not a networkwide problem that could be associated with a rogue DHCP server or incorrect router configuration. An incompatible USB device should not cause a blue screen error, nor should that device's driver. Also, the whole idea of USB is that devices you connect to it are automatically recognized and are generally all compatible. However, the USB driver could be a culprit though less common. See the section titled "Windows Tools and Errors" in Chapter 11, "Troubleshooting Windows," for more information.

20. Answer **D** is correct. You should run an IPCONFIG/FLUSHDNS. This remove entries from the local computer's DNS cache that has the domain name to IP address mappings. If customers can access *some* websites, you know they have connectivity to the Internet; however, it could be that the DNS cache is corrupted, or that the HOSTS file has been compromised, causing certain websites to become inaccessible. NET USE enables you to map network drives in the command-line. NETSTAT –r displays the local computer's routing table. NBTSTAT –R (note the capital "R") purges and reloads the *remote* cache name table. See the section titled "Troubleshooting Networks" in Chapter 15, "Networking," for more information.

21. Answer **A** is correct. If you upgrade a video card and nothing displays on the screen, then the onboard video of the motherboard might still be enabled in the BIOS. This can cause a conflict until it is turned off. New video cards do not necessarily require a new monitor unless the current monitor does not use the same video standard or connector; the resolution of each usually does not play into this scenario. Dipswitches are far less common on motherboards nowadays; the video card need only be installed and given power to function. The video card should display to the monitor when first installed, but it won't have full functionality until the driver is installed. See the section titled "The Video Subsystem" in Chapter 12, "Video and Audio," for more information.

22. Answer **B** is correct. If a program is nonresponsive, it can be shut down from the Task Manager either as an application, or as a process if it happens to be causing the computer to falter. Computer Management is a console window that contains the Event Viewer, Device Manager, and Disk Management among other tools. The registry stores all the settings for the computer; this is where you would go to make modifications that can't be done elsewhere in the OS. The Services console window (also part of Computer Management) is where you can start, stop, pause, enable, and disable services such as the Print Spooler or the DNS Client. See the section titled "System Tools and Utilities" in Chapter 9, "Configuring Windows," for more information.

23. Answer **D** is correct. Of the answers, the *best* security in a SOHO wireless network is to enable SSID and to configure WPA2. Yes, disabling SSID is a common security technique employed by security professionals, but having SSID enabled with WPA2 is far more secure than disabling the SSID with WEP configured. WEP is deprecated, and WPA2 is much more secure. In essence, the number one thing you should be concerned with for wireless security is strong encryption—everything else is secondary including disabling the SSID, MAC address filtering, and IP address filtering—if your SOHO device is even capable of that. See the section titled "SOHO Security" in Chapter 16, "Security," for more information.

24. Answer **C** is correct. If a motherboard were just replaced and the system overheats when booted, then there's a good chance that thermal paste was not applied to the CPU. When you install a new motherboard, the CPU must be removed from the old board and installed to the new one, or a new CPU needs to be installed. Either way, the heat sink must come off. Whenever a heat sink is connected (or reconnected) to a CPU, thermal compound (also known as thermal paste) should be applied; otherwise overheating can easily occur. The GPU is the video card's processor; it's not quite possible for this to be incompatible with the CPU. It is possible for the video card to be incompatible with the expansion bus slots on the new motherboard, though. Even if the new motherboard's firmware has not been updated, the system should not overheat. If the case fan fails, the computer should not overheat. The CPU will still have its own fan, and the power supply will still be exhausting hot air. See the section titled "Installing and Troubleshooting CPUs" in Chapter 3, "The CPU," for more information.

25. Answer **D** is correct. Gmail is a common e-mail service provided by Google that people can use on their smartphone. HTTP is the Hypertext Transfer Protocol and is not a service. Users might utilize Gmail on their computer as well as within a web browser, but that uses the protocol HTTPS because those sessions should be secure. POP3 is a protocol used by applications such as Microsoft

Outlook to download e-mail. Outlook normally runs on a computer and not on a smartphone. See the section titled "Mobile Networking and Synchronization" in Chapter 17, "Mobile Devices," for more information.

26. Answer **A** is correct. If the backup keeps failing, you should look at the file system used on both drives. If the drive where the data is backed up to uses FAT32, and there is currently no data on that drive, it should be reformatted as NTFS. NTFS is the superior choice for a variety of reasons, plus it is more common than FAT32. Always try to reformat the drive before you incur the cost of a replacement. From the scenario, you don't know the original type of backup drive. It might already be a USB drive, but who knows? Many USB flash drives are preformatted as FAT32. Regardless of all this, before trying another drive, try reformatting to NTFS first. A CD-ROM does not have enough storage space for the amount of data you need to backup. Plus, optical media is good for long-term backups that won't be used often. But if the technician in the scenario is trying to back up to hard disk, then it can be assumed that the data will be needed more often, and requires a faster solution such as SATA, or at least USB, either of which should be formatted as NTFS. See the section titled "Files, File Systems, and Disks" in Chapter 9, "Configuring Windows," for more information.

27. Answer **B** is correct. If the laptop can't display on the LCD or on an external monitor, that tells you that the video card is most likely faulty. The laptop would need to be opened to replace this. In some cases, it is integrated to the motherboard, requiring an entire motherboard replacement. If the inverter fails you would still see a dim display (which can be aided by using a flashlight) and the external monitor should work fine. If the LCD fails, you would not see anything on the display, but the external monitor again would function fine. Incorrect drivers can give a variety of problems such as unattainable maximum resolutions, or a garbled screen. However, the display should show *something* in that case, and should work fine in Safe Mode, where new drivers could be installed. See the section titled "Installing, Configuring, and Troubleshooting Internal Laptop Components" in Chapter 7, "Laptops," for more information.

28. Answer **A** is correct. The Sync Center is a feature of Windows that enables you to keep information synchronized between your computer and network servers. You can still access the files and modify them even if you don't have physical access to the server; in this case they are modified "offline" and are synchronized automatically when you return to the network. Some mobile devices are also compatible with Sync Center. The Sync Center can be configured within the Control Panel. Windows Aero is the premium visual experience included in some versions of Windows Vista and Windows 7. Windows Defender is the free Microsoft antimalware program. HomeGroup is meant to quickly and easily share printers and media between Windows 7 computers in a home network. See the section titled "System Tools and Utilities" in Chapter 9, "Configuring Windows," for more information.

29. Answer **C** is correct. If you see a blank streak along one edge of each page, but the rest of the print job is normal, then the fuser could be damaged. You need to shut down the printer and wait for 10 to 15 minutes while the fuser cools before replacing it. While replacing it, consider installing the entire maintenance kit for the printer. Some printers' displays let you know when the fuser needs to be replaced. If the paper is too thick it can most likely cause a paper jam at the entrance or exit rollers; if it is extremely thick and it happens to make it past the entrance rollers, it

probably won't even get past the fuser. If the toner cartridge is low, the entire page of information will be lighter. Rebooting this printer will not fix the fuser, but the printer should be rebooted several times after the fuser is installed to make sure it works properly. Some error messages on printers require a reboot only, but this issue is too serious, and the printer needs to be taken offline, shut down, and properly repaired. See the section titled "Installing, Configuring, and Troubleshooting Printers" in Chapter 14, "Printers," for more information.

30. Answer **B** is correct. The loopback plug is used to test a network card. It acts as a pseudo-network for the network card and tests whether the card is functional; if so, the LED lights up on the card. A POST card is plugged into a motherboard and is used to analyze PC booting issues. A PSU tester is used to test a power supply. The multimeter has a variety of testing purposes such as testing individual wires in a computer and testing AC outlets. See the section titled "Cables, Connectors, and Tools" in Chapter 15, "Networking," for more information.

31. Answer **C** is correct. If the technician reset the time in the BIOS and it fails a few days later, this most likely means that the CMOS battery has failed. The CMOS battery is in charge of keeping the time and date. When it fails, it often changes to Jan 1, 2000, and in many cases this will affect the OS time as well. Changing the OS time will not fix the problem because every time the system is rebooted, the BIOS will feed the false time to the OS. The battery, usually a CR 2032 lithium battery needs to be replaced; they only have a shelf life of 5 to 10 years or so. Even if the computer's operating system has its time synchronized to a time server, the battery should still be replaced because it maintains many other settings for the BIOS. If the motherboard were not seated properly, it could possibly fail, and the system would not boot. As long as the power supply can connect to the motherboard, it should provide the correct voltage; the battery typically needs 3 volts. However, if the power supply doesn't provide enough *wattage*, then the system might intermittently shut down or have problems booting. See the section titled "The BIOS" in Chapter 2, "Motherboards," for more information.

32. Answer **D** is correct. NTLDR is the boot file for Windows XP, 2000, and NT operating systems. It was replaced in Windows Vista (and continuing on through Windows 7) with bootmgr.exe, winload.exe, and winresume.exe. Bootsect.dos is used with NTLDR if an older dual-boot system is required such as Windows NT and Windows 98. Io.sys is the MS-DOS core file that contains device drivers and the initialization program; it works along with msdos.sys as the main OS files for DOS. Win.exe is the executable that runs older versions of Windows on top of DOS. Ntdetect.*exe* is a known Trojan, watch out for it; ntdetect.*com* on the other hand is a component of Windows NT systems that detects basic hardware at startup. Ntoskrnl.exe was originally the main core file for Windows NT systems but it is still used through Windows 7. See the section titled "Files, File Systems, and Disks" in Chapter 9, "Configuring Windows," for more information.

33. Answer **A** is correct. If you get a message that says One or More Services Failed to Start, then you should follow-up on this and look for more information within the System log in the Event Viewer. The Application log contains information, warnings, and errors pertaining to programs built into the OS as well as third-party applications. The Security log shows information regarding file access, permissions, logins, and so forth. The Task Manager gives you performance information about the computer and shows what processes and applications are

681

Answers with Explanations

running. See the section titled "Windows Tools and Errors" in Chapter 11, "Troubleshooting Windows," for more information.

34. Answer **A** is correct. To extend the wireless network range, and allow out of range users to share an Internet connection, you would add a wireless access point for the out of range users. The wireless access point will ultimately connect to the organization's router which will allow the out of range users the ability to share the Internet connection. By adding wireless access points at various locations of the building, you can increase the wireless network range. Network sharing allows users to share folders and files with other users, but only if those computers are on the network; however, network sharing does not increase the range of a wireless network, nor can it help out-of-range users to connect. The capability for a user's computer to scan for a wireless access point's SSID is more based on the strength and location of the wireless access point and the strength of the computer's wireless network adapter, and based little on the software. So, this is not the best answer, but wireless adapters should be updated to the latest software. VLAN stands for virtual local area network, which is a group of computers that communicate in the same fashion regardless of their physical location; computers can be grouped via port or protocol. See the section titled "SOHO Windows Networking" in Chapter 15, "Networking," for more information.

35. Answer **B** is correct. A ping –t is a continuous ping. An example of this would be `ping -t 192.168.1.1`. The command continually pings the remote host until you manually stop it; for example, utilizing the key stroke CTRL+C. The target will respond only if it is live on the network. A ping that reaches a count of 20 would use the –n parameter, for example `ping -n 20 192.168.1.1`. A ping that has packets equal to a certain amount of bytes uses the – l parameter; for example, a ping where each packet is 1,000 bytes instead of the default 32 would be `ping -l 1000 192.168.1.1`. See the section titled "Troubleshooting Networks" in Chapter 15, "Networking," for more information.

36. Answer **D** is correct. The program would be installed to C:\Program Files (x86). This is the default folder for 32-bit programs when installed to a 64-bit version of Windows. 64-bit programs are installed to the C:\Program Files folder. The operating system is installed to C:\Windows. Finally, C:\ is the root of the hard drive. A few system files are placed in the root, but otherwise the OS and applications are installed to folders within the root. x86 is the general term applied to 32-bit computers, whereas x86-64, or simply x64, is the term applied to 64-bit computers. See the section titled "Installing and Upgrading to Windows 7" in Chapter 8, "Installing and Upgrading Windows," for more information.

37. Answer **B** is correct. The default directory for user profiles in Windows 7 is C:\Users. Previously in Windows XP, user profiles were stored solely in C:\Documents and Settings. That folder still exists in Windows Vista and Windows 7 but is redirected to the \Users folder, and Documents and Settings is locked out. This redirection is known as a *Junction*, where the information appears to reside in two separate locations. The folder you will be working with in the GUI will be \Users, so that is the best answer here. Also, remember that the answers show C:\ in the path. This could be different depending on where the OS was installed to. C:\Program Files is where applications are installed to. There is no \Users and Settings folder. See the section titled "Files, File Systems, and Disks" in Chapter 9, "Configuring Windows," for more information.

38. Answer **A** is correct. A Non-System Disk error tells you that the computer cannot boot properly and that the boot media is the culprit. A common cause of this is a disk in the floppy drive. Floppy drives are definitely older technology, but you may still see them in the field; however, another example of this would be a non-bootable CD-ROM or DVD-ROM in an optical drive. If the floppy drive or the optical drive is set to first in the BIOS boot order, and the drive contains a non-bootable disc, then you will get this error. The same holds true if you have a hard drive without an OS. Check the drives for nonbootable disks, and check the BIOS boot sequence; normally the hard drive should be first, which is also a security precaution. If the registry becomes corrupted, the system could have trouble booting, but the message will be different. An example of a corrupted registry error message is Windows Could Not Start Because the Following File Is Missing or Corrupt: \WINDOWS\SYSTEM32\CONFIG\SYSTEM. This is a dire message that requires more troubleshooting than in the current scenario. The answer The Incorrect Driver Was Loaded is a vague answer; it is possible that an incorrect SCSI driver was loaded, and the system won't boot, but you won't necessarily get the same error. Other drivers won't be the cause of this problem. If the RAM is not seated properly, the system will simply not boot, or you will get a different error message from the BIOS. See the section titled "Magnetic Storage Media" in Chapter 6, "Storage Devices," for more information.

39. Answer **A** is correct. If the tape drive reports errors, the first thing you should do is use the included cleaning tape. You must remove the current tape and insert the cleaning tape; then run through the cleaning process. Finally, replace the original tape to see if it works without the tape drive reporting errors. If there is a problem with the backup software, the backup software usually displays an error, not the tape drive. It is more likely that the tape drive needs a simple cleaning than the backup software needing to be reinstalled. It's more common for a tape drive to use a SCSI cable as opposed to an IDE cable. You don't just want to replace the tape because that tape may have information that you need. Try cleaning the drive first, and if the tape has failed, make sure you back up the original data to a new tape. See the section titled "Magnetic Storage Media" in Chapter 6, "Storage Devices," for more information.

40. Answer **D** is correct. If a user has trouble tapping icons on a smartphone, tablet, or other touch-oriented device, you should check the screen calibration tool. This tool calibrates the screen properly when you place the device down on a flat surface with its face up. The calibration could have been put off center due to a user's settings, new programs, an update to the OS, and so on. Screen orientation is the way that the screen is displayed to the user: for example horizontal or vertical, depending on how the device is held. Geotracking is the identification of users from their location; the geotracking information might be used to aid in searching and for marketing purposes. Global positioning refers to locating users by their device. It is used by GPS and other applications that require an actual location of the users. See the section titled "Mobile Hardware and Operating Systems" in Chapter 17, "Mobile Devices," for more information.

41. Answer **C** is correct. The problem in this scenario is that the document is owned by the first user. By default, files created under one user account cannot be seen by another user account. For the second user to see the file, the user needs to become an owner or needs to be given permissions to the file. In this scenario the user never locked, hid, or encrypted the document in any way; this is simply a default security precaution that is built into Windows. See the section titled "Windows Security" in Chapter 16, "Security," for more information.

42. Answer **A** is correct. Windows XP might give memory read errors when RAM cannot be read from properly. If it is definitely a RAM error and not an OS issue; the best thing to try is to reseat and/or replace the RAM. While you're there you can try using compressed air on the RAM and the RAM slots to remove any dust that has accumulated over time. Other similar errors in Windows such as The Memory Could Not Be Read could be an issue with the OS reading from the hard drive and may require an update of the service pack. Generally, if the BIOS memory settings are not correct, the system will not boot and will give memory errors during POST. Because this is an issue related directly to RAM, you do not want to replace the hard drive. Most likely, a USB flash drive will not give a memory error; regardless, simply removing the USB flash drive will not fix the problem. See the section titled "Installing and Troubleshooting DRAM" in Chapter 4, "RAM," for more information.

43. Answer **C** is correct. The keyboard is the component usually removed to access a laptop's motherboard and other internal components. The bezel is not a component of the laptop; it is usually a piece of plastic, but a bezel might need to be removed to get access to the keyboard. However, removing the bezel does not give access to any internal components. A separate bezel usually must be removed to get at the display, and although you may need to remove the display to get at a few components such as the inverter, it is not as common to remove the display as it is to remove the keyboard. Generally, the battery is on the bottom of the laptop, and is part of the frame; removing it gives no access to internal components. See the section titled "Installing, Configuring, and Troubleshooting Internal Laptop Components" in Chapter 7, "Laptops," for more information.

44. Answer **D** is correct. If you can see the display on the main laptop screen, but not on a projector, then the laptop external display setting has most likely been turned off. Most laptops come with a toggle button (or alternative display switch) that enables you to switch between the laptop screen, external display, or both. Windows 7 definitely supports multiple displays on PCs *and* laptops. This is known as Multiple Monitor and DualView. Even if the video driver were missing (which is unlikely on a Windows 7 laptop) the laptop would still display video at a basic resolution on the laptop screen and a projector. By default, presentations are usually at a 640x480 resolution; this is done on purpose so that the presentation can be displayed by just about any system or projector. See the section titled "Installing, Configuring, and Troubleshooting Visible Laptop Components" in Chapter 7, "Laptops," for more information.

45. Answer **A** is correct. Older programs might not be compatible with Windows 7. To make them compatible you would use Windows Compatibility mode by running the Program Compatibility Wizard from within Control Panel > Programs in Windows 7. It doesn't matter if you run the older program in the GUI or in the Command Prompt; it will fail either way. A virtual machine might work, but there are several factors involved, including the need to run an older OS within the virtual machine. Regardless, this is a time-consuming solution, whereas Windows Compatibility mode can be set up much faster. Your co-worker will not want to run the program from another computer; this is not a valid solution. See the sec-

tion titled "System Tools and Utilities" in Chapter 9, "Configuring Windows," for more information.

46. Answer **C** is correct. The Encrypting File System (EFS) is the Windows built-in file encryption standard. EFS filenames display in green by default. This means that the individual file has been encrypted from within the properties page in Windows. This is done so that other users cannot read the file. Compressed files show up in blue. Color assignments for encrypted and compressed files can be removed in Windows by accessing Folder Options > View tab. Regular files are shown in black. Red files are ones that can be accessed only by Windows. See the section titled "Windows Security" in Chapter 16, "Security," for more information.

47. Answer **A** is correct. The Disk Management tool can determine if hard drives support spanned volumes. A spanned volume in Windows 7 is a volume that extends across 2 or more dynamic disks (up to 32) but not including the startup disk. In this case, you should most likely create a spanned volume because the requirements have been met. The Disk Management tool (located in Computer Management) is where you can initialize disks, create and format partitions and volumes, and assign drive letters. The Task Manager shows the performance of a computer's CPU and RAM and displays the programs/processes currently running. Device Manager is used to configure devices, update drivers, and view device settings. The System Information tool is similar to the Device Manager, but you cannot make changes; this tool also shows information about the software environment. See the section titled "Files, File Systems, and Disks" in Chapter 9, "Configuring Windows," for more information.

48. Answer **B** is correct. RAID 1 is another name for a mirrored set. In a RAID 1 array, two hard drives are mirrored, meaning that an exact copy of the all data is written to each drive. If one fails, there is no down time because the other takes over immediately. This means that it is fault tolerant. RAID 0 is known as striping; the data is striped among two or more disks for speed; it is not fault tolerant. RAID 5 is striping with parity, a fault tolerant method that stripes data and parity information across three or more disks. RAID 6 is similar to RAID 5 but adds a parity block, plus it requires four disks minimum. Both RAID 5 and RAID 6 are fault tolerant. See the section titled "Files, File Systems, and Disks" in Chapter 9, "Configuring Windows," for more information.

49. Answer **C** is correct. Ghosted images often mean that the print drum of a laser printer needs to be replaced. Perhaps the drum cannot hold a charge any longer, causing an ineffective joining of toner to the drum, and ultimately leading to ghosted images. If the fuser fails you might see a blank line on the edge of each printed paper, or perhaps the toner will not dry properly. If the toner cartridge fails, you would either see blank printed pages, or perhaps lines and smearing. Printheads are found in inkjet and impact printers, but not laser printers. See the section titled "Installing, Configuring, and Troubleshooting Printers" in Chapter 14, "Printers," for more information.

50. Answer **C** is correct. Basically, the only way a file can retain its NTFS permissions is if the file is *moved* to a new location on the *same* volume. Moving it to any other volume and copying it anywhere can create new NTFS permissions for that newly moved or copied file. These permissions are taken by default from the parent folder. See the section titled "Windows Security" in Chapter 16, "Security," for more information.

51. Answer **B** is correct. In this scenario you should install the USB 3.0 firmware update to the motherboard. If the motherboard supports USB 3.0, you might need to flash the BIOS to accomplish this. Motherboard firmware updates can fix several different USB issues, yet another reason to always check for new flash updates. If the device and cable work at USB 3.0 speed (5 Gbps) on your computer, then no cables should have to be replaced. Try to fix the problem with an update before incurring the expense of an external USB hub; extra expenses are often not necessary. Your goal here is to take what the customers have and make it work to their expectations. New devices such as external USB hubs or IEEE 1394a devices take time to order and install, and might not be within the budget. Plus, IEEE 1394a transfers less data (400 Mbps). See the section titled "Input/Output Devices and Peripherals" in Chapter 13, "Peripherals and Custom Computing," for more information.

52. Answer **D** is correct. If the user could print to the printer previously, and the job is just sitting in the print queue, you should most likely restart the printer spooler service at the user's computer. This can be done in the GUI of Windows within Computer Management > Services and Applications > Services, or by typing `net stop spooler` and `net start spooler` in the Command Prompt. Deleting the job and resubmitting it will probably have the same effect, and you will have to restart the spooler anyway. Printer drivers are not the cause of a stalled print job. Resetting the physical printer will not help; the job will still be sitting in the user computer's print queue. See the section titled "Installing, Configuring, and Troubleshooting Printers" in Chapter 14, "Printers," for more information.

53. Answer **D** is correct. Power supplies have a burn-in period in which certain oils and residue will burn off while the power supply is on. This period is generally 24 to 48 hours. If the odor goes away within 48 hours, disregard the odor as normal; explain this to the customer as well. It is premature to replace the power supply because the current one works fine and hasn't completed its burn-in period yet. Contacting the manufacturer would simply elicit the same response: The power supply will smell slightly during the burn-in period. Usually, you do not want to use compressed air on a power supply, especially as the power supply gets older, it would just serve to push dust and dirt further into the power supply. However, if people want to use some kind of air freshener to mask the odor, just ask that they don't spray it into or near the power supply—or the entire computer for that matter! See the section titled "Power Supplies" in Chapter 5, "Power," for more information.

54. Answer **B** is correct. You should check the Device Manager for any alerts or question marks over USB-related devices. This can tell you if there are any problems with USB devices or USB ports. There's no point to check the rear panel pinouts because those function properly. It's the new front panel USB ports that you are concerned with. Regardless, if the USB ports are part of the motherboard, which they most likely are, they should in all likelihood be wired correctly. You could test the voltage output of each USB port; for example, if you want to compare the front and rear ports, but this should be done after checking the Device Manager. Most of the time, USB devices should not draw too much power from a USB port; the ports and the devices should be manufactured according to the same USB specifications. See the section titled "Input/Output Devices and Peripherals" in Chapter 13, "Peripherals and Custom Computing," for more information.

55. Answers **A**, **D**, and **E** are correct. Common applications found on a smartphone include e-mail programs, contacts programs, and texting programs. Though Microsoft Office could become more of a reality for smartphones in the future, as of the writing of this book, it is less likely to find Microsoft Word or Microsoft Visual Basic installed on them. These programs are more likely to be found on a PC, which shows one of the main distinctions between mobile devices and PCs. See the section titled "Mobile Hardware and Operating Systems" in Chapter 17, "Mobile Devices," for more information.

56. Answer **C** is correct. Shoulder surfing is when a person attempts to find confidential information by standing behind a user at a desk and looking over their shoulder. A rootkit is a type of malicious software installed by an attacker with administrative access; it hides the existence of certain processes or programs. Phishing is when a person attempts to get confidential information from an unsuspecting target by way of e-mail. Tailgating is when an unauthorized person attempts to enter a secure area by following an authorized person into that area. See the section titled "Security Threats and Prevention" in Chapter 16, "Security," for more information.

57. Answer **B** is correct. The most likely answer is that the IP address is invalid. If what the customer is telling you is what he is actually typing in, then it is an invalid IP address. 86200.43.118 is missing a dot, and the IP address should actually be 86.200.43.118. This is more likely than the other three answers. Though the FTP program could be configured improperly, it is more likely that user error is the culprit here. A company's servers will rarely go down (hopefully), and the FTP server would usually not block port 21 because that is the default FTP port, and blocking it would block *all* traffic to the FTP server! See the section titled "TCP/IP" in Chapter 15, "Networking," for more information.

58. Answers **B** and **D** are correct. When you install a second hard drive into a Windows computer, you will not automatically see it in Windows Explorer or Computer. That is because it first needs to be initialized, then partitioned, then formatted, and assigned a drive letter. A new SATA hard drive will not be partitioned or preformatted when you purchase it. It is best partitioned with NTFS. Almost every SATA drive will be compatible with Windows 7. See the section titled "Files, File Systems and Disks" in Chapter 9, "Configuring Windows," for more information.

59. Answer **C** is correct. If the wireless printer is losing connections when there are multiple users on the network, then it is probably because there aren't enough automatically assigned IP addresses to go around. You should configure the printer to use a static IP address, instead of receiving one dynamically from the router. This address will be permanent and should fix the problem. Often, companies insist that printers (as well as routers, switches, and servers) always get a static address to avoid problems of this sort. Increasing the IP lease times might work; it might not. When multiple users attempt to get on the wireless network, someone is going to lose out; it might be a person at a laptop, or it might be the printer or other device, so this is not a permanent solution. Another access point might increase your wireless coverage, but it will do nothing for your IP issue. The whole problem here was that the printer *was* configured for DHCP; it was obtaining its IP address automatically from the DHCP server within the router. By changing it to static, it doesn't have to compete for the five dynamically assigned IPs. See the section titled "Troubleshooting Networks" in Chapter 15, "Networking," for more information.

60. Answers **B**, **C**, and **D** are correct. Some of the data types that a person would commonly synchronize from their mobile device to their PC include contacts, music, and e-mail, as well as programs, pictures, and videos. Call history will usually not be synchronized because the PC will probably not have a compatible phone application installed. GPS tracking is usually not necessary on a PC either because PCs are fairly stationary. Data and programs can be synchronized from the mobile device to the PC by connecting them with a USB cable and utilizing the corresponding synchronization program that comes with, or can be downloaded for, the mobile device. See the section titled "Mobile Networking and Synchronization" in Chapter 17, "Mobile Devices," for more information.

61. Answer **C** is correct. If a person suspects that the AC voltage coming from an outlet is flawed in some way, the outlet should be tested with a multimeter. This tool can tell you the exact voltage that is supplied and can tell you if the outlet is wired correctly (which can also be found out by using a receptacle tester.) The multimeter can verify suspicions of dirty power, over- and under-voltage. It is a portable device that is easy to use in these scenarios. An oscilloscope on the other hand is far less portable and is used more commonly at a PC repair bench to test electronics. The answer "cable tester" is rather vague; what kind of cable tester are we referring to? A network cable tester? An electrical cable tester? It's unknown. Regardless, you wouldn't want any kind of cable tester in this scenario; the multimeter is the best answer. By the way: Vague answers are usually not correct answers! A PSU tester is a power supply unit tester. But the problem isn't the power supply; it's the AC power being fed to the power supply, so the PSU doesn't need to be tested. If it did need to be tested, a multimeter could also be used if a PSU tester is not available. See the section titled "Understanding and Testing Power" in Chapter 5, "Power," for more information.

62. Answer **D** is correct. The fastest transfer rate goes to IEEE 1394b. USB 1.1 sends information at 12 Mbps. USB 2.0 sends at 480 Mbps. IEEE 1394b sends data at 800 Mbps, which meets the requirements of the scenario. Cable Internet usually has a maximum capped speed of 20 Mbps, possibly less. Plus, you wouldn't connect an external hard drive to your cable Internet connection. It requires either USB, IEEE 1394, eSATA, or SCSI. See the section titled "Input/Output Devices and Peripherals" in Chapter 13, "Peripherals and Custom Computing," for more information.

63. Answers **B** and **D** are correct. Offline files and folders can be used in Windows 7 Professional and Ultimate, Windows Vista Business and Ultimate, and Windows XP Professional. Other versions such as Starter, Home, and Home Premium don't offer this functionality, regardless of whether they are 32 bit or 64 bit. See the sections titled "Installing and Upgrading to Windows 7" and "Installing and Upgrading to Windows XP" in Chapter 8, "Installing and Upgrading Windows," for more information.

64. Answer **B** is correct. The NET statistics command (more accurately, the net statistics workstation command) shows bytes received, SMBs sent and received, network errors, and lots more. In Windows 7, typing the net group

command elicits a response that says the command can be used only on a domain controller; it is used to make modifications to groups of users. `Net view` shows the other computers on the local area network. `Net stop` is used to stop a service such as the print spooler. See the section titled "Troubleshooting Networks" in Chapter 15, "Networking," for more information.

65. Answers **A** and **C** are correct. To see the status of services, you need to access Computer Management > Services and Applications > Services. Computer Management can be accessed either by right-clicking Computer and selecting Manage, or by accessing Administrative Tools from the Start menu. You can also access the Run prompt and type `services.msc` to be brought directly to the Services window. System shows the system properties such as type of operating system, Windows activation, and advanced settings. Right-clicking the desktop and selecting Personalize allows you to change the display themes. Right-clicking Computer and selecting Properties also brings you to the System window; it is an alternative way instead of using the Control Panel. See the section titled "System Tools and Utilities" in Chapter 9, "Configuring Windows," for more information.

66. Answer **D** is correct. One of the differences between a domain and a workgroup is that a domain is controlled by a server. This server is known as a domain controller. Windows Server 2008, 2003, or 2000 is necessary to have a domain controller. Workgroups do not have domain controllers; they are peer-to-peer (P2P) networks, with no controlling server. Domains are meant for larger networks— hundreds, even thousands, of computers. Workgroups are usually smaller than domains, less than 20 computers. In a workgroup a maximum of only 10 computers can access a particular resource at the same time. If you require more computers to access any resource at the same time, then you need a domain. See the section titled "System Tools and Utilities" in Chapter 9, "Configuring Windows," for more information.

67. Answer **A** is correct. In this scenario, your organization is running a web server on the LAN. Your job is to make sure that all clients outside your network on the Internet that are attempting to access the web server can do so. You must configure port forwarding for this to work. The HTTP requests, and/or whatever port the clients use to access the web server (perhaps 80, but not necessarily), should be forwarded to the IP address and port of the web server on your network. Exceptions are meant to allow certain computers access in or out of the firewall, but this would give the external clients too much access. You want to streamline this so that the external traffic is all directed to your web server, and port forwarding is the best way to do this. NAT stands for Network Address Translation and is used to match up the private IP address numbers of your internal computers to the external public IPs they attempt to connect to; it protects the private IP identity of the internal computers. However, it's actually not the interior traffic you are concerned with. Instead, you are concerned with the external traffic trying to get in to your network and visit your web server, and the web server *only*. See the section titled "SOHO Windows Networking" in Chapter 15, "Networking," for more information.

68. Answer **B** is correct. System File Checker (SFC) is the best option in this scenario. It checks, and if necessary, fixes system files in Windows 7 and earlier versions of Windows. DISKPART is the command-line partitioning tool, the counterpart of the

GUI version, Disk Management. SCANDISK is an older command-line tool used in previous versions of Windows. In Windows 7 the closest option would be CHKD-SK. FIXMBR is a tool used in Windows XP to rewrite a faulty Master Boot Record (MBR). See the section titled "Command-Line Tools" in Chapter 11, "Troubleshooting Windows," for more information.

69. Answer **C** is correct. The master boot record (MBR) is stored in the first sector of the hard drive. It is 512 bytes of data that is also considered to *be* the first sector, not just reside within it. In general, the first sector of a hard drive is referred to as a boot sector. There are two main types of boot sectors. For a hard drive that houses an operating system, the boot sector is known as the MBR sector. On the other hand, for hard drives that do not contain an operating system, the boot sector is known a volume boot record (VBR). The first sector of a hard drive does not house the operating system; given the size of today's operating systems, that would be difficult to say the least! The master file table (MFT) stores metadata information about every file and folder for a given NTFS volume. The MFT information is stored in the beginning of the volume just after the boot sector. Often, a copy is also stored in the middle of the disk. See the section titled "Files, File Systems, and Disks" in Chapter 9, "Configuring Windows," for more information.

70. Answer **B** is correct. If the LCD keeps getting darker even though the brightness is maximized, then the backlight probably needs to be replaced. LCD backlights work only for so many hours; you need to disassemble the LCD portion of the laptop to check if it is indeed the source of the problem and replace it if necessary. This is the best solution listed. However, you should always try the function keys just to make sure before going ahead and opening the laptop. Video memory does not affect the brightness; it affects the maximum resolution, colors, and frame rate that the LCD can display. For the LCD to be replaced, it would either have to be cracked or otherwise damaged, or not display anything at all. For the latter, you can connect an external monitor to make sure it is indeed the LCD that failed. In the case of inverter failure, the LCD would still show a faint display if you look carefully. Know how to troubleshoot for various failures including backlight, LCD, and inverter! See the section titled "Installing, Configuring, and Troubleshooting Internal Laptop Components" in Chapter 7, "Laptops," for more information.

71. Answer **B** is correct. A blue screen, or BSOD, is an error screen produced by Windows, so you should access the OS manufacturer's website: in this case Microsoft. Accessing third-party websites is not generally recommended and should be used only as a last resort because you never know exactly what kind of information you will get from those websites. The error code and the blue screen are not directly produced by the hardware, so you would not go to the hardware manufacturer's website. Installation manuals for operating systems usually do not go into this type of troubleshooting depth. However, manufacturers such as Microsoft have multiple websites that you can visit to figure out the problem such as Help and Support and the TechNet. In many cases you can even get support from them. See the section titled "Windows Tools and Errors" in Chapter 11, "Troubleshooting Windows," for more information.

72. Answer **A** is correct. bootrec /fixboot is one of the methods you can try to repair bootmgr.exe in Windows 7. Bootrec /fixmbr rewrites the master boot record in 7. Bootrec /rebuildbcd attempts to rebuild the boot configuration store, and boot\bcd is where the boot configuration store is located. See the section titled "Repair Environments and Boot Errors" in Chapter 11, "Troubleshooting Windows," for more information.

73. Answer **D** is correct. Global System for Mobile Communications (GSM) is the default for making phone calls and transferring data via the Internet on a smart-phone. As long as the phone has a signal, it can do both simultaneously. Wi-Fi is usually a better, faster option for transferring data; however, phone calls through Wi-Fi would require additional software (such as Skype) or additional hardware. Bluetooth is primarily used to connect peripherals to the phone such as head-sets or mobile printers. It *can* be "configured" to connect to the Internet through a PC or in other ways, but it cannot make voice calls. You might indirectly use cable Internet from your smartphone via a wireless network, which allows you to transfer data, but it does not allow voice calls without additional software/hard-ware. Be sure to know the various ways a mobile device can connect to the Internet and make voice calls for the exam. See the section titled "Mobile Networking and Synchronization" in Chapter 17, "Mobile Devices," for more information.

74. Answer **B** is correct. If the screen can be viewed only in the vertical position, and doesn't automatically shift to horizontal when the tablet is rotated, then the screen orientation needs to be reconfigured. This can be done within the main display menu of most devices. It may prompt you to place the tablet on a flat surface so that the gyroscope can be reconfigured. Screen calibration deals with how and where icons are tapped on the screen. Some devices configure the screen calibration and the orientation in one step. Geotracking is the identifica-tion of users from their location. Try reconfiguring the device's screen orientation before even considering a costly and time-consuming touchscreen replacement. See the section titled "Mobile Hardware and Operating Systems" in Chapter 17, "Mobile Devices," for more information.

75. Answer **D** is correct. If the hard drive is constantly accessed (and as a result makes a good deal of noise), and the activity light is frequently on, these are good signs that the drive is fragmented. You need to run the Windows Disk Defragmenter, located in Start > All Programs > Accessories > System Tools. This can analyze the disk and tell you if the partition is indeed fragmented and continues with the defragmentation if you authorize it. The page file deals with information transferred between RAM and the hard drive. Page file issues often hang Windows; the page file usually fails altogether if there is a problem. In the scenario, you noted that there is plenty of free space on the hard drive's parti-tion, so there can't be too many documents. However, if there was a full drive, it could become more difficult to defragment. The Windows Disk Defragmenter program requires 15% free space to work. If you have less than this, you must run a defrag –f in the command line. SATA connectors rarely fail, and if they do, then the hard drive would become inaccessible. In this case, if this were the only drive in the computer, the system would not boot to the operating system. See the section titled "Maintaining Hard Disks" in Chapter 10, "Maintaining Windows," for more information.

76. Answer **A** is correct. Strange cryptic printouts or printouts with gibberish usually mean that the print driver is incorrect. Remember that you need to use the *exact* printer driver for the printer model—close doesn't cut it! To avoid this garbage printout, download the correct printer driver from the manufacturer's website. If the toner cartridge needs to be replaced, the text and images would look mostly normal, but might be lighter, or have certain areas missing. The print spooler needs to be restarted when jobs are stuck in the queue and won't print. The print drum might need to be replaced if you encounter a ghosted image. See the section titled "Installing, Configuring, and Troubleshooting Printers" in Chapter 14, "Printers," for more information.

77. Answer **C** is correct. Unexpected shutdowns that occur after the computer has been running for some time could be hardware- or software-based; if hardware, the CPU fan is probably the perpetrator. If the CPU fan fails, or is not connected or otherwise properly installed, the CPU will overheat. Most computer systems' BIOS monitors the temperature and shuts down the system if it hits a certain threshold; often this is accompanied by a system beep. If the problem is software-related, the troubleshooting will go further; the cause could be malware or a stop error, for example. However, that is not the basis of this question. The hard disk drives and optical drives will not cause the PC to simply shut down in a fatal manner. However, the power supply could be delivering faulty power. It is less likely to cause a shutdown, but the power supply voltages could be checked after you first check the CPU fan. See the section titled "Installing and Troubleshooting CPUs" in Chapter 3, "The CPU," for more information.

78. Answer **A** is correct. Popping noises are usually associated with the power supply. If the transformer (or other component) in the power supply fails, it could cause a popping sound accompanied by a burning smell. This causes the computer to shut down, and it cannot be rebooted because power can not be converted properly from AC to DC. The power supply would have to be tested with a PSU tester and most likely replaced. Though the CPU can cause the system to stop working if it overheats, it cannot cause a popping sound. Also, you could restart the computer in that case after it has cooled down, and the system would run for a short while. The hard disk drive should not cause a permanent shut down of the system. The power supply could have been affected by the AC outlet. After replacing the power supply, and before plugging the computer back in, you should test the AC outlet with a receptacle tester and/or multimeter, and if necessary have a licensed electrician check the circuit. See the section titled "Power Supplies" in Chapter 5, "Power," for more information.

79. Answer **C** is correct. Startup Repair is part of WinRE (short for Windows Recovery Environment, also known as System Recovery Options). It starts automatically if Windows detects a startup problem but can be accessed through WinRE by booting to the OS installation disc, or to a special WinRE partition on the hard drive. Other options in WinRe include System Restore, System Image Recovery, and the Command Prompt. The Recovery Console is the predecessor to the WinRE Command Prompt; it is used in Windows XP/2000. See the section titled "Repair Environments and Boot Errors" in Chapter 11, "Troubleshooting Windows," for more information.

80. Answer **D** is correct. The DIR command shows the contents of a folder or directory within the command line. For example, if you were within the System32 folder, you could just type `DIR` to display its contents. If you were in any other folder, you would type `DIR C:\Windows\System32`. But be prepared to use the /p switch because there will be a lot of results! The NET command has many uses, for example: `net stop spooler`, to stop the print spooler; `net use`, to map network drives, and so on. CD stands for change directory. Within the command line it enables you to move from one directory to any other directory in the tree. The System Information Tool displays details about hardware resources, components, and the software environment. See the section titled "Files, File Systems and Disks" in Chapter 9, "Configuring Windows," for more information.

81. Answer **C** is correct. By default, Windows XP recognizes only 137 GB as a maximum. However, Service Pack 1 (SP1) uses 48-bit Logical Block Addressing (LBA) that enables XP to see larger drives. Apparently in this scenario, not all Windows XP computers were updated to the latest service pack. It is important that all computers on a network be updated to the latest service pack so that they can take full advantage of hardware and software, as well as networking and security features, and so that they are all compatible with each other. The hard drives are most likely not defective; plus, it is rare that you will get multiple defective hard drives in a single batch. SATA hard drives do not use jumpers. IDE drives still use jumpers, but only to configure master and slave options; they have no bearing on the storage space that can be recognized by Windows XP. See the section titled "Updating Windows" in Chapter 10, "Maintaining Windows," for more information.

82. Answer **D** is correct. Strange noises from inside the computer can usually be attributed to a loose wire hitting a fan, often the CPU fan. Open the PC and reroute cables and wires away from the CPU fan, and any other fans. If the CPU needed to be reseated, the users would probably have a worse problem on their hands, such as the system won't boot properly. Network cables usually don't rest against the system case, but it is possible. Reroute network cables as well so that they are away from the system case, are stationary, and don't pose a trip hazard. If the thermal compound dries out (which might happen in dry environments) it could cause the CPU to overheat and cause a system shutdown but shouldn't make any noise. See the section titled "Installing and Troubleshooting CPUs" in Chapter 3, "The CPU," for more information.

83. Answer **B** is correct. You should remove any proxy settings that were placed there by the malware. This is done by malicious individuals so that the computer's browser becomes hijacked and is redirected to the website(s) of the attacker's choice. Legitimate proxy servers are used by larger companies, but usually not in small offices. So if you see a proxy setting in the browser of a small office, it is probably not justifiable. Resetting the router will not fix the problem because the issue is relegated to the local computer. Rebooting the computer will have no effect because the setting is saved in the OS. Installing the latest service pack is always a good idea if the computer is not up to date but will not help in this situation because SP updates do not rewrite browser settings. See the section titled "Security Threats and Prevention" in Chapter 16, "Security," for more information.

84. Answer **B** is correct. A worm self-replicates. In most other ways it is similar to a virus. Both infect systems' files and are often transferred to a computer by e-mail or by removable media. A Trojan allows an attacker higher privileges than the owner and often is used to remotely control a computer without the user's consent. Spyware collects information about users without their consent when the users unwittingly download it through their browser. See the section titled "Security Threats and Prevention" in Chapter 16, "Security," for more information.

85. Answer **C** is correct. Most wireless access points and routers have blank passwords, so you should change the password to something secure before you do anything else. Next, you should download the latest firmware. On some devices you might need to reset the password again after a firmware update. Usually, you want to use DHCP, but if you want to disable it for security purposes, you would do that next. Finally, enable MAC filtering so that only the computers you want can connect. Of course, those are not the only security precautions you can take; for more see the section titled "SOHO Security" in Chapter 16, "Security," for more information.

86. Answer **B** is correct. The VER command shows the version of Windows. However, it might be more cryptic than accessing the System window in the GUI. For example, the VER command when typed in a Windows 7 SP0 Command Prompt can result in the following: Microsoft Windows [Version 6.1.7600]. 6.1 is the actual version of Windows 7, whereas 7600 is the build number! The better option is to use the System window. Or you could use the systeminfo command in the Command Prompt, which gets a bit more in depth for this explanation—more on this in Chapter 11. The SET command shows, and allows you to modify, all the variables in the computer; for example, where the temp folders are located. The Device Manager is not a command; it is an application where you can configure hardware. CMD (cmd.exe) is the Command Prompt executable. See the section titled "Command-Line Tools" in Chapter 11, "Troubleshooting Windows," for more information.

87. Answer **D** is correct. BitLocker is included only in Windows 7 Ultimate and Enterprise editions, and Windows Vista Ultimate and Enterprise editions. Windows 7 Starter, Home Premium, and Professional, as well as Windows Vista Home Basic, Home Premium, and Business do not offer BitLocker. Neither does any version of Windows XP; though it and Vista can use the BitLocker To Go Reader download. See the section titled "Installing and Upgrading to Windows 7" in Chapter 8, "Installing and Upgrading Windows," for more information

88. Answer **A** is correct. If the user gets prompted for confidential information instead of seeing the website he expected, then the browser was probably hijacked. You should temporarily install another browser program for the user until you can fully scan the system and remove any trace of hijacking and other forms of malware. You could also suggest virtual browsers to the user as another solution. The person's identity has not been stolen—yet. But if he types the asked for confidential information, it probably will be. Train your users never to give this information if possible, and tell them to realize that most companies will not ask for this type of information on their websites. If a website updates its security policies, the most that should happen is that you will get a pop-up notice about this. The user couldn't have typed the wrong URL because he connected to the website through a bookmark. See the section titled "Security Threats and Prevention" in Chapter 16, "Security," for more information.

89. Answer: **D** is correct. The best solution is to run the printer's cleaning routine. Many newer inkjet printers have this; it might be run through software, or it might be run by pressing a sequence of buttons on the printer. If this doesn't work, a mixture of isopropyl alcohol and water can be conservatively applied to the bottom of the print cartridges to clean them. If neither of these methods work, then you should check if perhaps the print head is malfunctioning. Finally, new cartridges and/or a new print head would be the last course of action. A lint-free cloth is good to use on a display but is not a good idea here because the cloth will be ruined. Reseating the cartridges cannot fix the problem, and using compressed air will probably get ink all over the place. See the section titled "Installing, Configuring, and Troubleshooting Printers" in Chapter 14, "Printers," for more information.

90. Answer **C** is correct. The first thing you should do is reboot the system, press F8, and access Safe Mode because this will start the system with a basic set of drivers and a lower resolution. It could be that someone set the resolution too high, and the monitor cannot support it. This can be changed in Safe Mode or in the option: Enable Low-Resolution Video (640x480). If a display is not showing up on the monitor, then getting into the Display Properties is going to be a tough task. But you *do* want to access the video properties once in Safe Mode and lower that resolution to a level the monitor can support. If there were no video, even when booting into Safe Mode, then perhaps you would have to reseat the video card. In general, try to keep away from opening the computer unless absolutely necessary. Resetting the monitor from the OSD menu reconfigures the monitor settings back to the factory default but does not help if the resolution in the OS was changed to a level higher than the monitor supports. In these cases, when the monitor is not getting any usable signal, the LED light will probably be amber. See the section titled "The Video Subsystem" in Chapter 12, "Video and Audio," for more information.

91. Answer **A** is correct. The Windows 7 computer probably has the firewall on; this is the default setting. This allows the Windows 7 computer to make contact with other systems but stops other computers from making inbound connections to it. If the network cable were unplugged, neither the Windows 7 system nor the Windows XP connections could connect to each other. The operating systems can coexist on the network, but remember to update all systems to their latest service packs for best compatibility. See the section titled "Windows Security" in Chapter 16, "Security," for more information.

92. Answer **D** is correct. If the phone's Bluetooth application can't detect the computer, it probably means that the computer's Bluetooth device is not set to discoverable. The phone doesn't need to be set to discoverable unless you decide to use another Bluetooth device that relies on the phone, such as a Bluetooth headset. Mobile synchronization software allows you to move data back and forth between the computer and the smartphone but won't allow you to play music. A PAN is a personal area network used to connect multiple personal devices such as phones, tablets, PDAs, and so on. Bluetooth-enabled devices would be part of a wireless PAN, otherwise known as a piconet. See the section titled "Mobile Networking and Synchronization" in Chapter 17, "Mobile Devices," for more information.

93. Answer **D** is correct. In Windows Vista and Windows 7, the Run command is not shown by default on the Start menu. It can be accessed by pressing the Windows+R keys. It can be permanently added to the Start menu by right-clicking the Taskbar and selecting Properties and enabling it. The Windows PowerShell is a more powerful version of the Command Prompt designed for systems administrators. If the registry were corrupt, you would probably get a message to that effect upon bootup of the computer. However, it is possible to remove components of Windows such as the Run command from within the registry, but that doesn't necessarily make the registry corrupt—perhaps the user who made the modification is corrupt, but not the registry in this case! You do not need to be an administrator to see or use the Run prompt. For all users, it is not displayed by default. See the section titled "Windows User Interfaces" in Chapter 9, "Configuring Windows," for more information.

94. Answer **A** is correct. The Task Manager is the fastest way to view network adapter statistics; it has a Networking tab designed to give a quick real-time snapshot of the performance of the network adapter. System Information gives a lot of information and some statistics of the network adapter in a static fashion. Performance Monitor can give real-time statistics of the network adapter, but it would need to be configured to do so. The Command Prompt can give all kinds of statistics about the network adapter, but not in real-time, and any one command would probably take longer to run compared to simply opening the Task Manager and clicking the Networking tab. See the section titled "System Tools and Utilities" in Chapter 9, "Configuring Windows," for more information.

95. Answer **B** is correct. The best way (of the listed answers) to ensure that only certain computers can access your wireless network would be to enable MAC filtering. In a "deny all except..." scenario, if the computer does not have one of the MAC addresses on the list, it will be denied access to the wireless network. Disabling and/or changing the SSID is a basic security measure, but computers can still connect to the wireless network manually as long as the person knows the name of the SSID. Changing the default password is important, but it governs only who has access to the firmware of the wireless access point, not who can connect to the wireless network. See the section titled "SOHO Security" in Chapter 16, "Security," for more information.

96. Answer **A** is correct. A folder such as Documents in Windows 7 can be redirected to another location on a different partition or drive by right-clicking the Documents library and selecting Properties. From here you would add the new documents folder location. Afterward, any time the Documents library is clicked, it automatically redirects to the new folder. Program files, Windows files, and System files are expected to be in a certain location and are not redirected in this manner. See the section titled "Files, File Systems, and Disks" in Chapter 9, "Configuring Windows," for more information.

97. Answer **C** is correct. For an OS to boot from a partition, that partition must be marked as active, which means that the computer can use the loader on that partition. A partition can be marked active within Disk Management. The system partition is automatically marked as active when an OS installation is complete. Primary refers to a type of partition on a hard drive—a "first" partition so to speak. You must have one of these before creating other types of partitions.

Healthy means that the partition is formatted and ready to be used. Logical refers to logical drives—the divisions of an extended partition in which each get their own drive letter. See the section titled "Files, File Systems, and Disks" in Chapter 9, "Configuring Windows," for more information.

98. Answer **B** is correct. In this case you need to take ownership of the files. If you were moving files on a server, chances are that the folder you moved them to won't allow you access. Aside from taking ownership, you may also need permissions to open the files, if the files were moved to another partition or drive. Performing the transfer again simply provides the same result. The files are not hidden, you still can see them, just not access them. Rebooting the system does not fix the problem. Be sure to know where you are moving files to before you do so! See the section titled "Windows Security" in Chapter 16, "Security," for more information.

99. Answer **D** is correct. The easiest way to get the computer to the last-known good state is to restore it to the day before the user was given the administrative rights because this is when the problematic behavior first began. Of course, there might not be a restore point on that day. So you would simply backtrack from that point in time until you find one. Pressing F8 and selecting Last Known Good Configuration cannot work because that option brings only the system back to the last successful login. Because the person has been logging on for a month, this cannot work. Revoking the user's administrative rights is not a viable option; the user needs to do her job. Plus it can't be done from Safe Mode. Re-imaging the computer might fix the problem, but at what cost! Data would have to be backed up, and a lot of time would be spent in the process. See the section titled "Windows Tools and Errors" in Chapter 11, "Troubleshooting Windows," for more information.

100. Answer **B** is correct. Question the obvious is a part of the second step of the CompTIA A+ troubleshooting process. In full, the second step is "Establish a theory of probable cause (Question the obvious)." Questioning the user is part of the first step, which is identifying the problem. Testing the theory to determine cause is the third step of the troubleshooting process. Establishing a plan of action is the fourth step. Be sure to know the CompTIA A+ six-step troubleshooting process and apply it during the 220-802 exam! See the section titled "The Six-Step A+ Troubleshooting Process" in Chapter 1, "Introduction to Troubleshooting," for more information.

Index

Numbers

A

U

W

To receive you 10% off Exam Voucher,
register your product at:
www.pearsonitcertification.com/register
and follow the instructions.